CADENCE BOOKS GRAPHIC NOVEL

ADOLF™
The Half-Aryan

CADENCE BOOKS GRAPHIC NOVEL

ADOLF ™
The Half-Aryan

STORY & ART BY
OSAMU TEZUKA

STORY & ART BY
OSAMU TEZUKA

Translation / Yuji Oniki
Touch-Up Art & Lettering / Viz Graphics
Cover Design / Viz Graphics
Editor / Annette Roman

Senior Editor / Trish Ledoux
Managing Editor / Satoru Fujii
Executive Editor / Seiji Horibuchi
Publisher / Keizo Inoue

Originally published as *Adolf ni Tsugu* by Bungei Shunju, Inc. in Japan in 1985.

Printed in Canada

Published by Cadence Books, Inc.
P.O. Box 77010 • San Francisco, CA 94107

ISBN 1-56931-107-2

10 9 8 7 6 5 4 3 2 1
First printing, May 1996

❖

Osamu Tezuka's *ADOLF* Series:
A Tale of the Twentieth Century
An Exile in Japan
The Half-Aryan
Days of Infamy
1945 and All That Remains

CONTENTS

INTRODUCTION

TEZUKA'S MODERNISM

By Matt Thorn

Osamu Tezuka is often characterized by casual commentators and critics as a "Humanist." "Humanism" is of course a vague term, meaning different things to different people in different contexts. In its most common usage—the one perhaps intended in reference to Tezuka—it simply indicates a concern with human beings, specifically with injustice, inequity, and tragedy in the broadest sense. To be sure, Tezuka was concerned with all those things.

In its technical usage, however, Humanism usually refers to a philosophy born in the European Renaissance, in which Homo sapiens is seen as being at the center of and superior to the rest of nature. This Humanism emphasizes free will: the ability of humans to determine their own fates and to work towards their own perfection. Humanist philosophy set itself against a Medieval philosophy in which human fate was entirely in the hands of God.

If this is Humanism, it is difficult to categorize Tezuka as a Humanist. In fact, more attentive commentators and critics have made just this point. Tezuka biographer Tetsuo Sakurai describes what he sees as a deep mistrust of Humanism in Tezuka's work. A common motif in Tezuka's science fiction work is human cruelty towards other sentient beings, such as sentient robots, aliens, newly evolved life forms, or sentient animals. The point of such stories is not to criticize a lack of respect for other sentient life forms (since we know of none such an argument would be entirely hypothetical), but rather to criticize a human tendency to be contemptuous and fearful of difference—a contempt and fear that has historically led to rationalizations of xenophobia, racism, exploitation, slavery, and even, as we see in *Adolf*, genocide. This message can be seen even in Tezuka's most commercially successful work, *Mighty Atom* (better known to speakers of English as Astro Boy). Although *Mighty Atom* may seem at first glance to embody the Modern era's optimistic enthusiasm for Science, a closer reading reveals a complex critique of human arrogance and bigotry.

This perspective, too, is very much a product of the Modern era, for if Modernism was enthusiastic about Science and other manifestations of Progress, it was also deeply ambivalent about those same developments. It is for this reason that I see Tezuka not as a Humanist, but rather as a Modernist. Many of the great thinkers and commentators of the Modern era, like Tezuka, recognized that while that era was characterized by an unprecedented movement to build a more rational, "better" society, it was at the same time characterized by unprecedented exploitation and "rationally" organized violence and destruction on a mass scale. This perspective can be seen again and again throughout Tezuka's vast body of work, created over more than four decades.

Tezuka was particularly suspicious of ideology and its capacity to separate people from one another and eventually lead to war. "If we pursue the true character of 'righteousness'," Tezuka once said, "we come face-to-face with a kind of egoism of the State." Tezuka had experienced such "state egoism" firsthand when the leaders of his own nation, claiming to be "champions of justice," waged an expansionist war in the name of "liberating" Asia from European imperialism. His own experience of the terrible consequences of war had a profound—perhaps even definitive—influence on the perspective he brought to his work.

Knowing this about Tezuka helps explain aspects of his style that may seem puzzling to many non-Japanese. Even Tezuka's most serious works—and *Adolf* is certainly the most serious of them all—are peppered with slapstick humor and gags that may at first seem grossly inappropriate to the material. In *Adolf*, for example, Tezuka casts as the cold-blooded Gestapo officer one of his stock characters, Acetylene Lampe, who, in addition to having an absurd name, occasionally appears with a lit candle sticking out of the back of his head. It is this seemingly ridiculous character to whom Tezuka assigns the task of carrying out the grimly ironic "final solution" that concludes the World War II segment of *Adolf*.

It may be that Tezuka chose this approach as a conscious rejection of what is known in literature as the "suspension of disbelief." That is, whereas most creators of fiction strive to make their readers forget that what they are reading is a fabrication representing the point of view of one person, Tezuka strove to do just the reverse. But it may also be that Tezuka may simply have seen humor—"low-brow" humor, at that—as an essential element of the comic medium. Whatever the reason, this approach continues to be popular among Japanese comic artists today, though it is jarring to many Western readers, for whom the suspension of disbelief is the *sine qua non* of "serious" fiction.

But in spite of the gags, there can be no doubt that throughout his career Tezuka was very much concerned with the most daunting issues of human existence, and that he often addressed these issues through parables. The story of the two Adolfs is such a parable, and one Tezuka has told before in different contexts. One volume of *Phoenix* (the sweeping epic Tezuka himself considered his life's work), titled *Turbulent Times*, is set in twelfth-century Japan and is based loosely on two historical figures, Yoshitsune and Benkei. Like the two Adolfs, Tezuka's Yoshitsune and Benta (Tezuka's name for Benkei) are childhood friends who are drawn apart as adults by conflicting loyalties and identities, until finally there remains nothing but hatred and anger between them and they essentially murder each other. The longer story of Yoshitsune and Benta is preceded by a short parallel story of a monkey and a dog, childhood friends who are fated to kill each other as leaders of their respective packs. Tezuka weaves this story into a vastly larger tale of Terran evolution, in which living creatures develop an instinct to form clans or tribes headed by strong leaders in order to ensure the survival of their line. Tezuka suggests it is the existence of such hierarchical "tribes" that separates living beings from one another, as tribes wage war against each other and members of tribes struggle for dominance within those tribes. For Tezuka, of course, "tribe" does not simply refer to lineage-based clans, but to any group that defines itself in contrast to other groups on the basis of ancestry, race, language, region, religion, ideology, caste, etc.

It is sometimes said that Post-Modernity (this non-era that is defined only by what it is not) is distinguished from Modernity by its lack of earnestness. Faith in Progress has been lost so utterly that we have moved even beyond cynicism, and accept as given that life can be either a beach or a bitch, or more likely both, and then we die. In this sense we have returned to an almost Medieval world view, in which fate is seen as entirely outside our hands. But whereas the Medieval Europeans entrusted themselves to God, we have no such anchor in the Post-Modern era. The Modernists were not anchored to God either, but they were always earnest. Even as they critiqued Progress and Civilization, they held on to a belief, inherited in modified form from the Humanists and Enlightenment philosophers who preceded them, that humanity *could* improve its lot, and this is no doubt why so many were drawn to ideologies: Marxism, Democracy, Capitalism, Anarchism...National Socialism.

Though Tezuka rejected ideology and was deeply suspicious of movements that claimed to offer a panacea for humanity's woes, he shared the earnestness of his fellow Modernists, and over the course of his career outlined a vision for a better (if not ideal) world. Biographer Sakurai nicely sums up the basics of Tezuka's vision as follows: (1) a critique of the tendency to exclude that which is different (that is, discrimination), (2) a deep suspicion of faith in absolutes (that is, ideology), (3) a conception of existence as cycles of destruction and rebirth, and (4) an ecological view of the interdependence of all living things. Tezuka himself expressed it in even simpler terms: "What I try to say through my work is simple. My message is as follows: 'Love all creatures! Love everything that has life!'" Simple, perhaps, but powerful. There are thousands, if not tens of thousands, of men and women who can testify to having been affected in some way by the manga of Osamu Tezuka, and I suppose I would have to count myself among them. (I've met two physicians and heard of others who were inspired to go into medicine by Tezuka's *Black Jack*.)

It is a shame that Tezuka's work has gone largely unrecognized in most of the world outside East Asia, but perhaps it is only now, in this era of supposed Post-Modernity, that the rest of the world is finally prepared to appreciate the message of this most Modern of artists.

Matt Thorn is earning a Ph.D. in anthropology at Columbia University; his dissertation is on Japanese shôjo *manga. His translations for Viz Comics include* A, A' [A, A Prime], Sanctuary, Nausicaä of the Valley of Wind, Horobi, 2001 Nights, Mermaid Forest, *and* Mermaid's Scar.

and [illegible] outlined [illegible] vision for a [illegible] of the [illegible] field [illegible] the essence of [illegible] as follows: (1) a [illegible] or tendency to [illegible] that which is different that is, discrimination; (2) a [illegible] absolute, that is, ideology; [illegible] necessary [illegible] view of the interdependence of all living things [illegible] What I try to say through my work is simple [illegible] as follows: Love all creatures! Love everything that has life [illegible] power! There are those [illegible] not [illegible] of [illegible] men and women who [illegible] medic[illegible] by the [illegible] of [illegible] and have [illegible] myself among them [illegible] into medicine [illegible]

I [illegible] believe that [illegible] work has [illegible] most of the world [illegible] only now in this [illegible] of the world is finally [illegible] the [illegible] Modern [illegible]

[illegible]

CHAPTER ONE

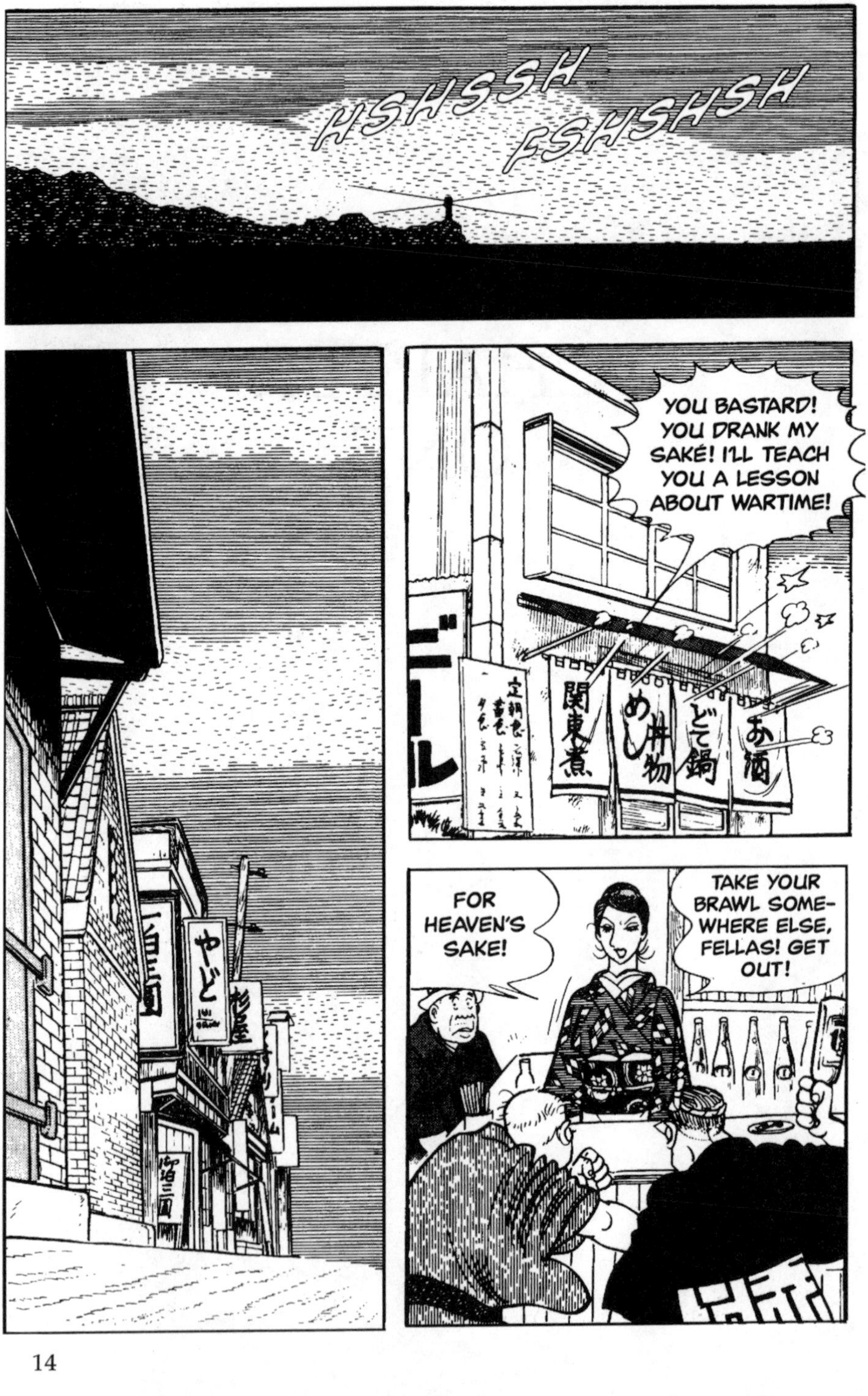
HSHSSSH
FSHSHSH
やど
YOU BASTARD! YOU DRANK MY SAKÉ! I'LL TEACH YOU A LESSON ABOUT WARTIME!
関東煮
めし
丼物
どて鍋
お酒
FOR HEAVEN'S SAKE!
TAKE YOUR BRAWL SOME-WHERE ELSE, FELLAS! GET OUT!

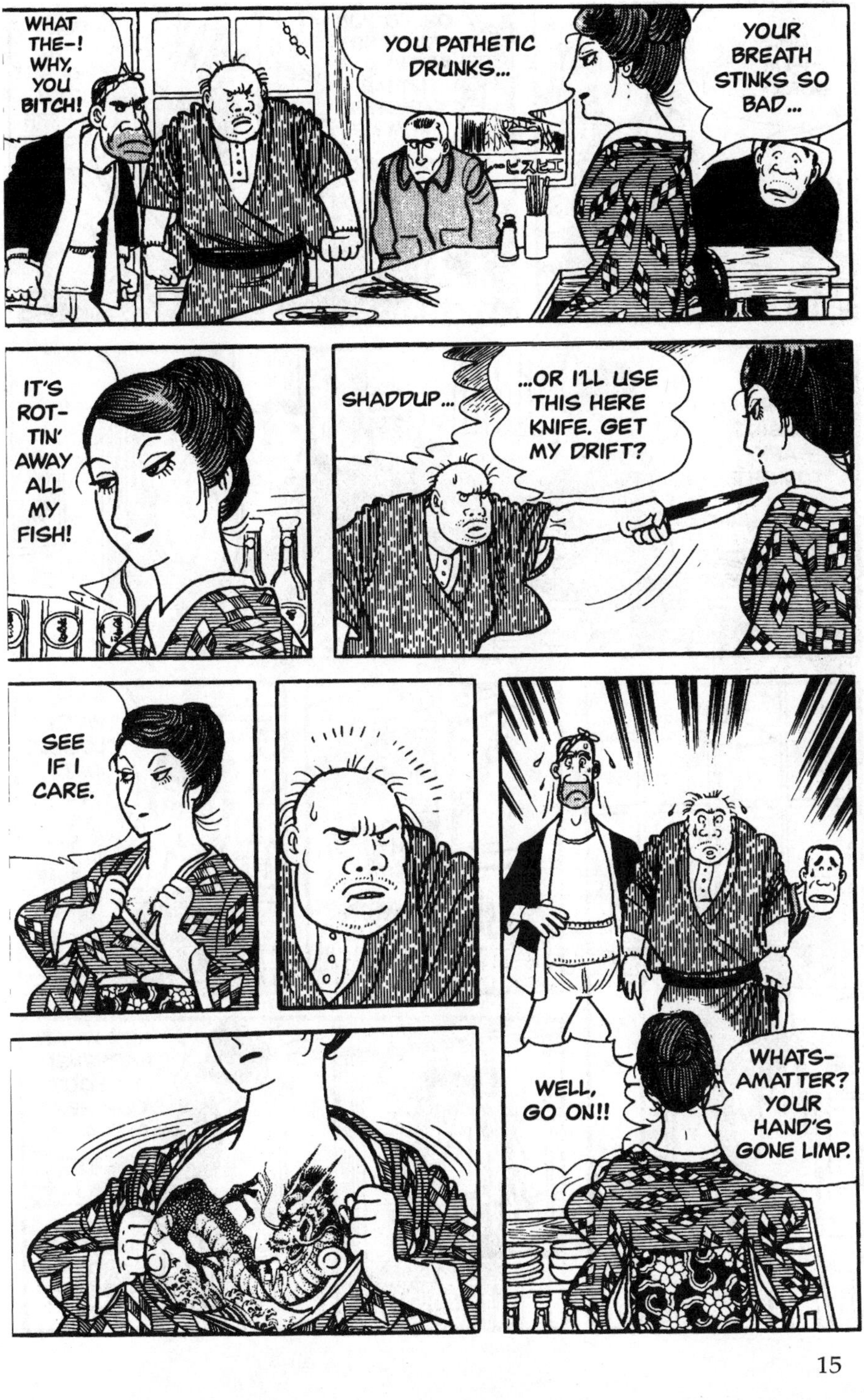
WHAT THE-! WHY, YOU BITCH!
YOU PATHETIC DRUNKS...
YOUR BREATH STINKS SO BAD...
IT'S ROT-TIN' AWAY ALL MY FISH!
SHADDUP...
...OR I'LL USE THIS HERE KNIFE. GET MY DRIFT?
SEE IF I CARE.
WELL, GO ON!!
WHATS-AMATTER? YOUR HAND'S GONE LIMP.

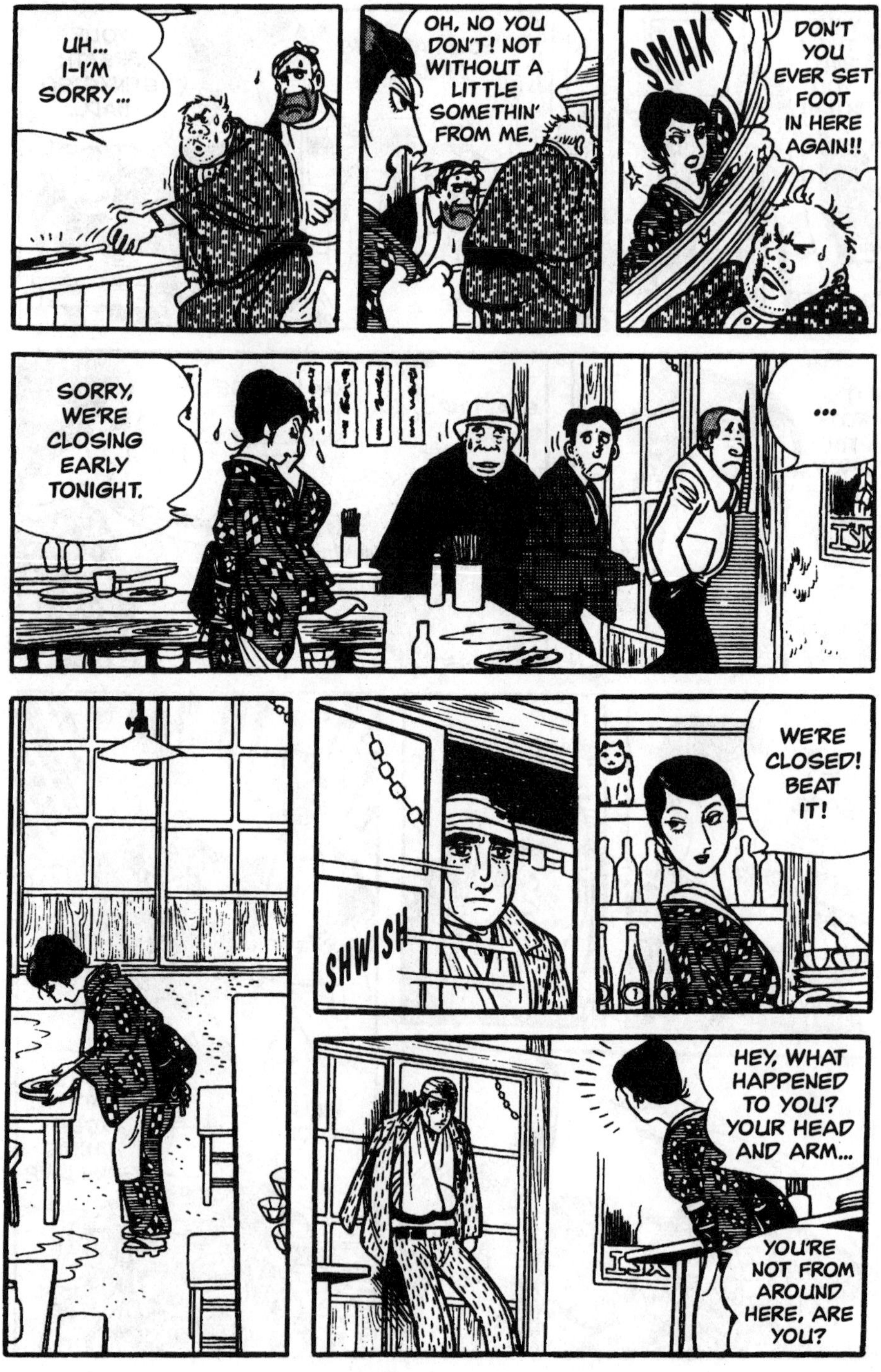
UH... I-I'M SORRY...
OH, NO YOU DON'T! NOT WITHOUT A LITTLE SOMETHIN' FROM ME.
SMAK
DON'T YOU EVER SET FOOT IN HERE AGAIN!!
SORRY, WE'RE CLOSING EARLY TONIGHT.
...
SHWISH
WE'RE CLOSED! BEAT IT!
HEY, WHAT HAPPENED TO YOU? YOUR HEAD AND ARM...
YOU'RE NOT FROM AROUND HERE, ARE YOU?

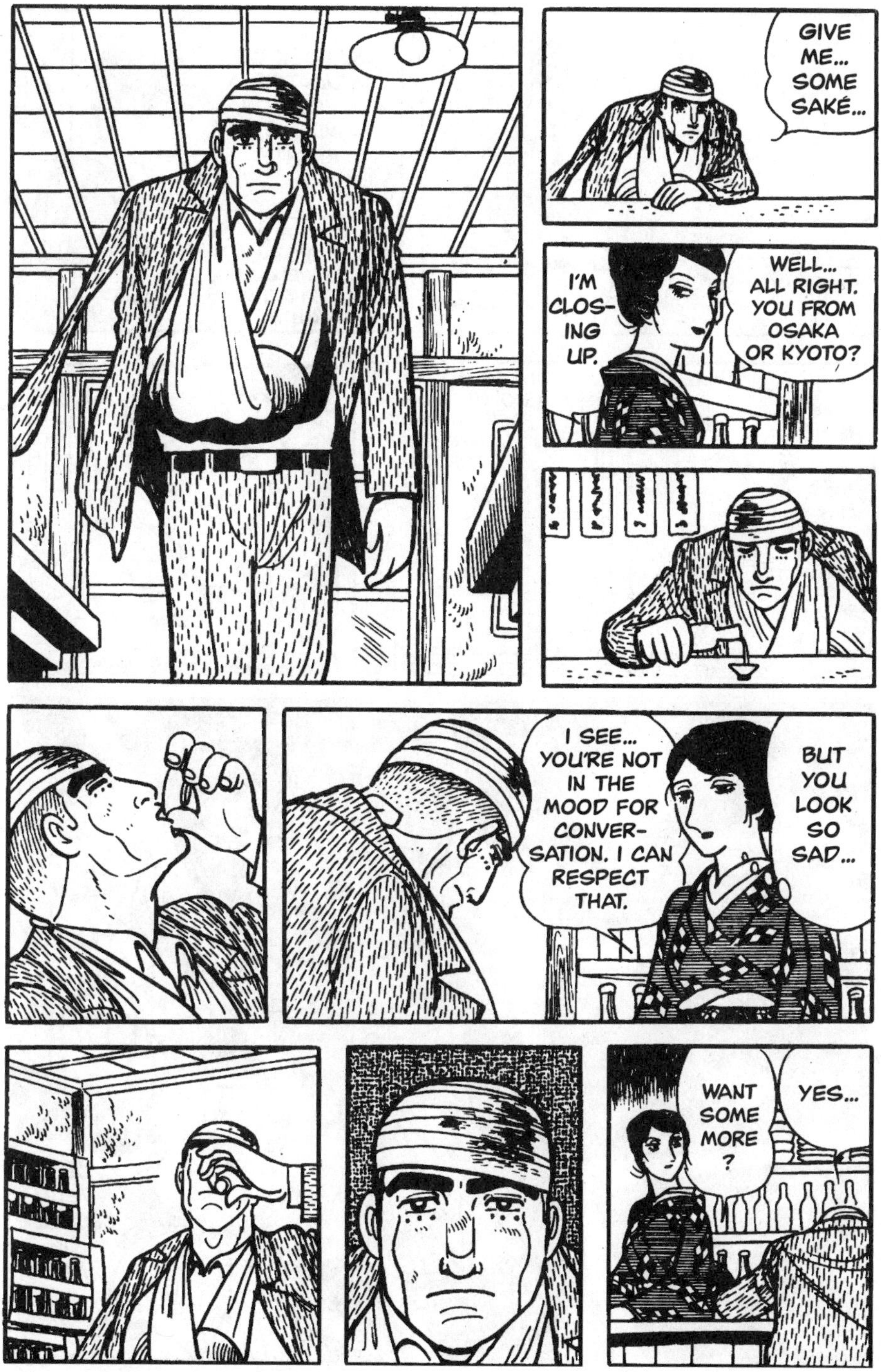
GIVE ME... SOME SAKÉ...
I'M CLOS-ING UP.
WELL... ALL RIGHT. YOU FROM OSAKA OR KYOTO?
I SEE... YOU'RE NOT IN THE MOOD FOR CONVER-SATION. I CAN RESPECT THAT.
BUT YOU LOOK SO SAD...
WANT SOME MORE ?
YES...

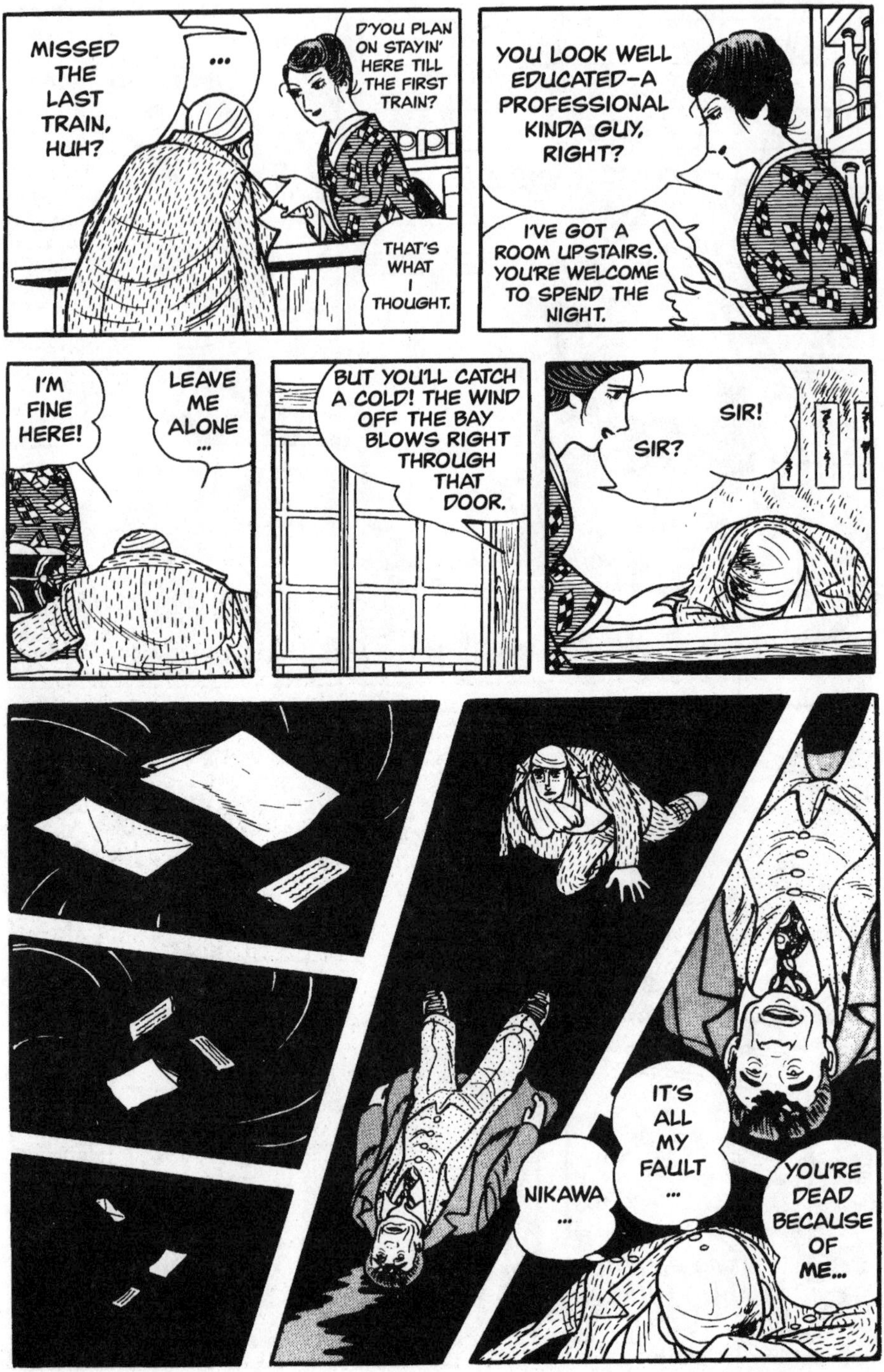
MISSED THE LAST TRAIN, HUH?
...
D'YOU PLAN ON STAYIN' HERE TILL THE FIRST TRAIN?
THAT'S WHAT I THOUGHT.
YOU LOOK WELL EDUCATED—A PROFESSIONAL KINDA GUY, RIGHT?
I'VE GOT A ROOM UPSTAIRS. YOU'RE WELCOME TO SPEND THE NIGHT.
I'M FINE HERE!
LEAVE ME ALONE ...
BUT YOU'LL CATCH A COLD! THE WIND OFF THE BAY BLOWS RIGHT THROUGH THAT DOOR.
SIR?
SIR!
NIKAWA ...
IT'S ALL MY FAULT ...
YOU'RE DEAD BECAUSE OF ME...

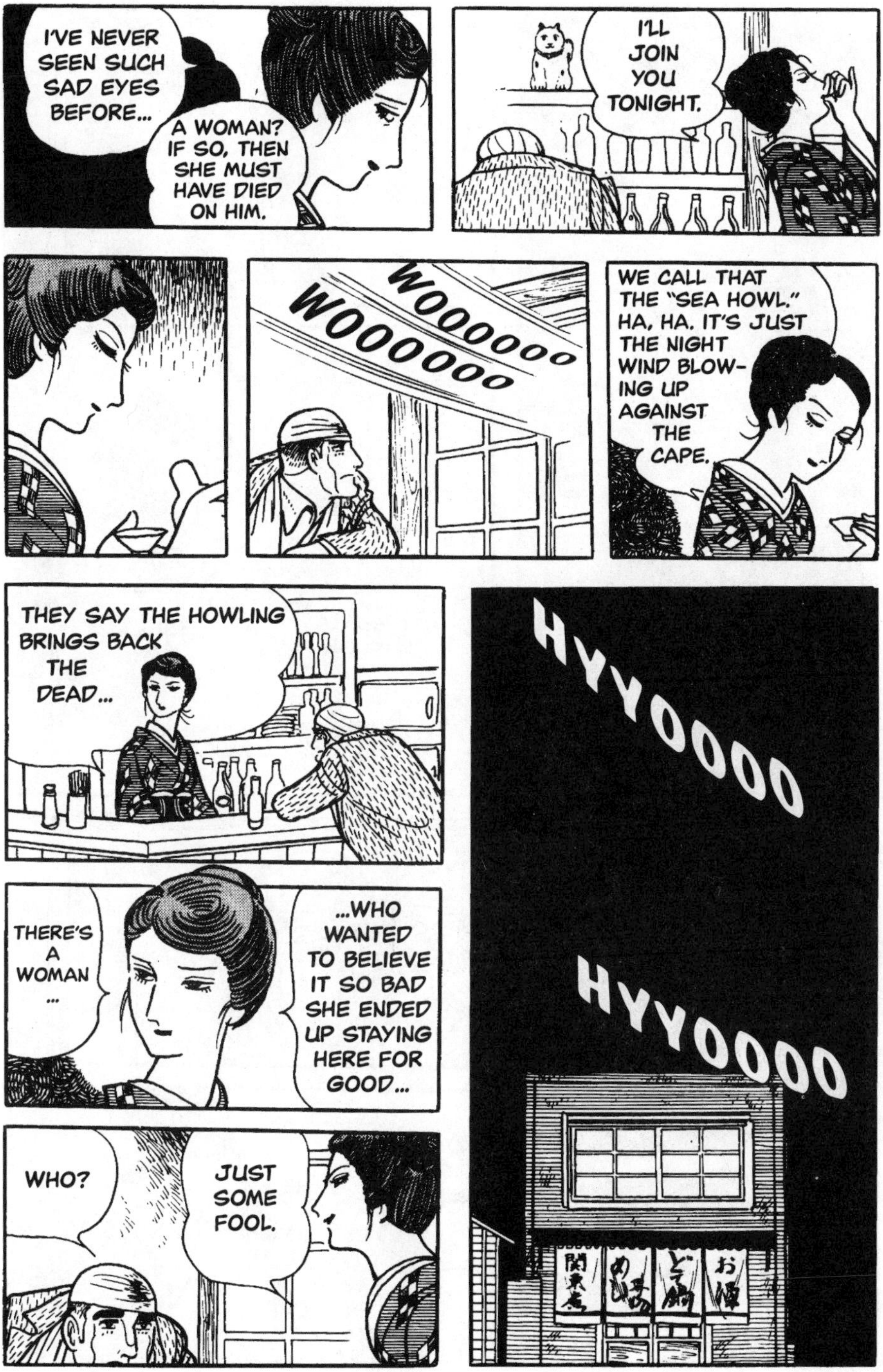
I'VE NEVER SEEN SUCH SAD EYES BEFORE...
A WOMAN? IF SO, THEN SHE MUST HAVE DIED ON HIM.
I'LL JOIN YOU TONIGHT.
WOOOOOOO
WOOOOOOO
WE CALL THAT THE "SEA HOWL." HA, HA. IT'S JUST THE NIGHT WIND BLOWING UP AGAINST THE CAPE.
THEY SAY THE HOWLING BRINGS BACK THE DEAD...
THERE'S A WOMAN ...
...WHO WANTED TO BELIEVE IT SO BAD SHE ENDED UP STAYING HERE FOR GOOD...
WHO?
JUST SOME FOOL.
HYYOOOO
HYYOOOO

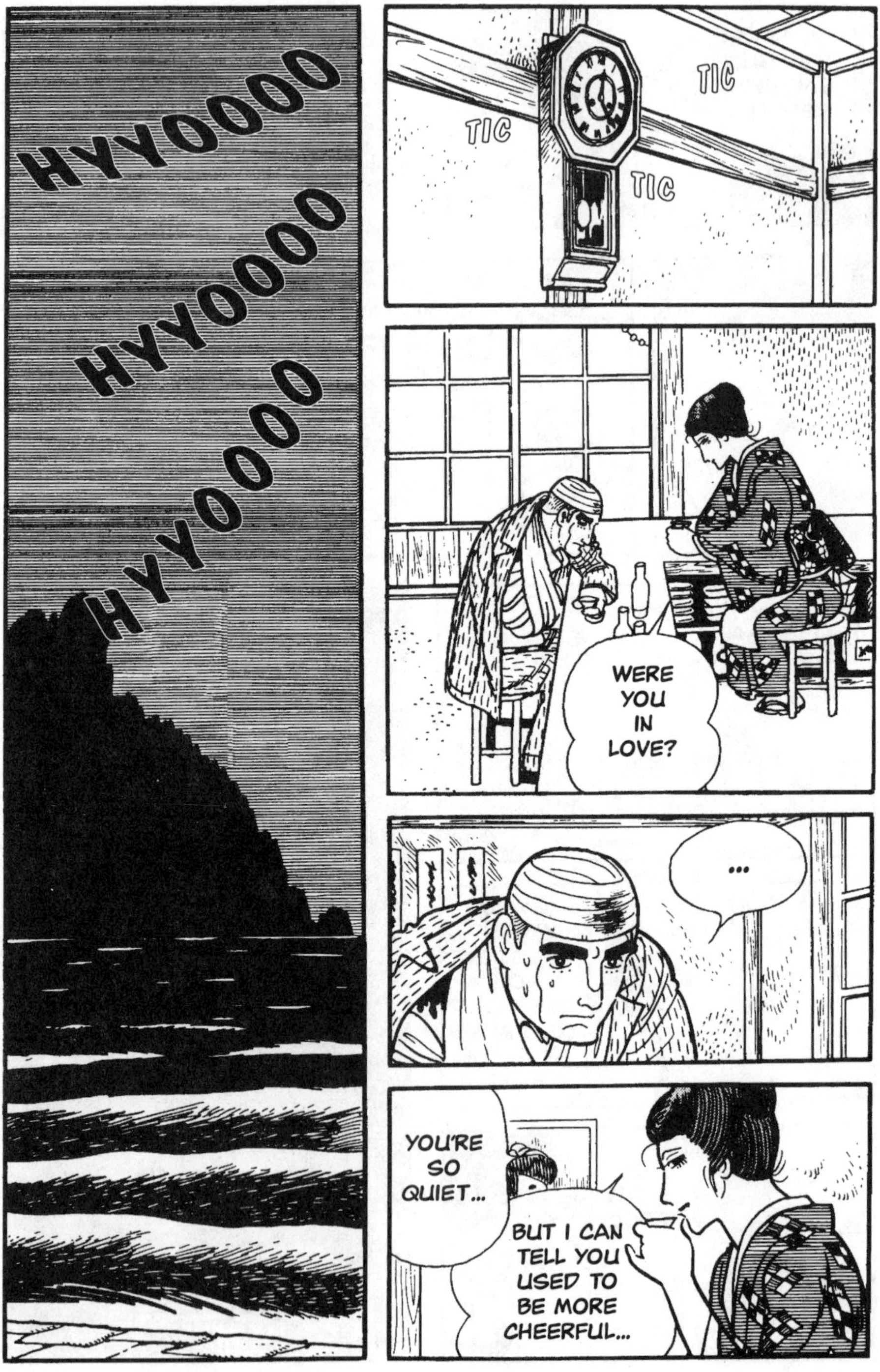
HYYOOOOO
HYYOOOOO
HYYOOOOO
TIC
TIC
TIC
WERE YOU IN LOVE?
...
YOU'RE SO QUIET...
BUT I CAN TELL YOU USED TO BE MORE CHEERFUL...

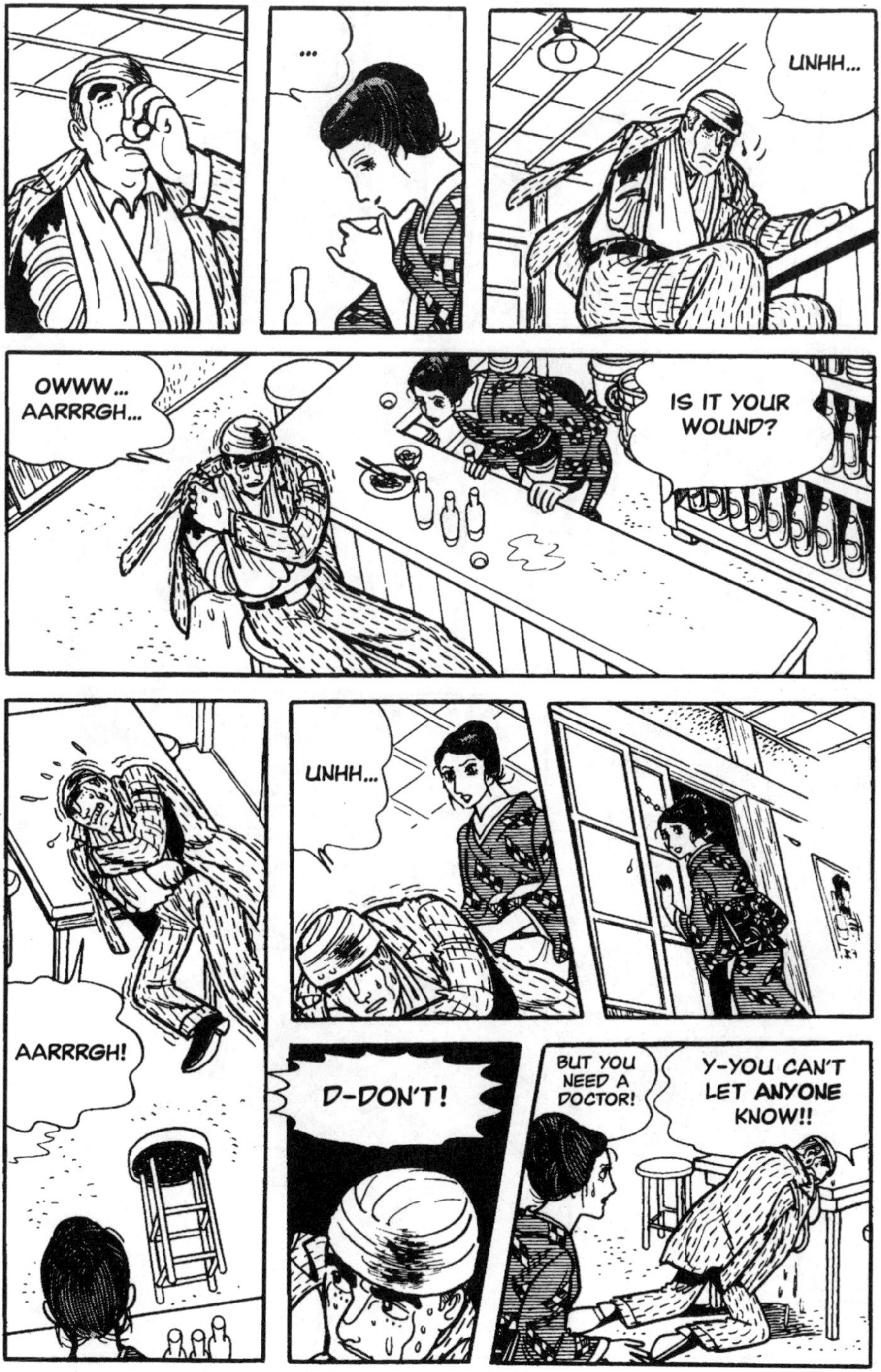
...
UNHH...
OWWW... AARRRGH...
IS IT YOUR WOUND?
AARRRGH!
UNHH...
D-DON'T!
BUT YOU NEED A DOCTOR!
Y-YOU CAN'T LET ANYONE KNOW!!

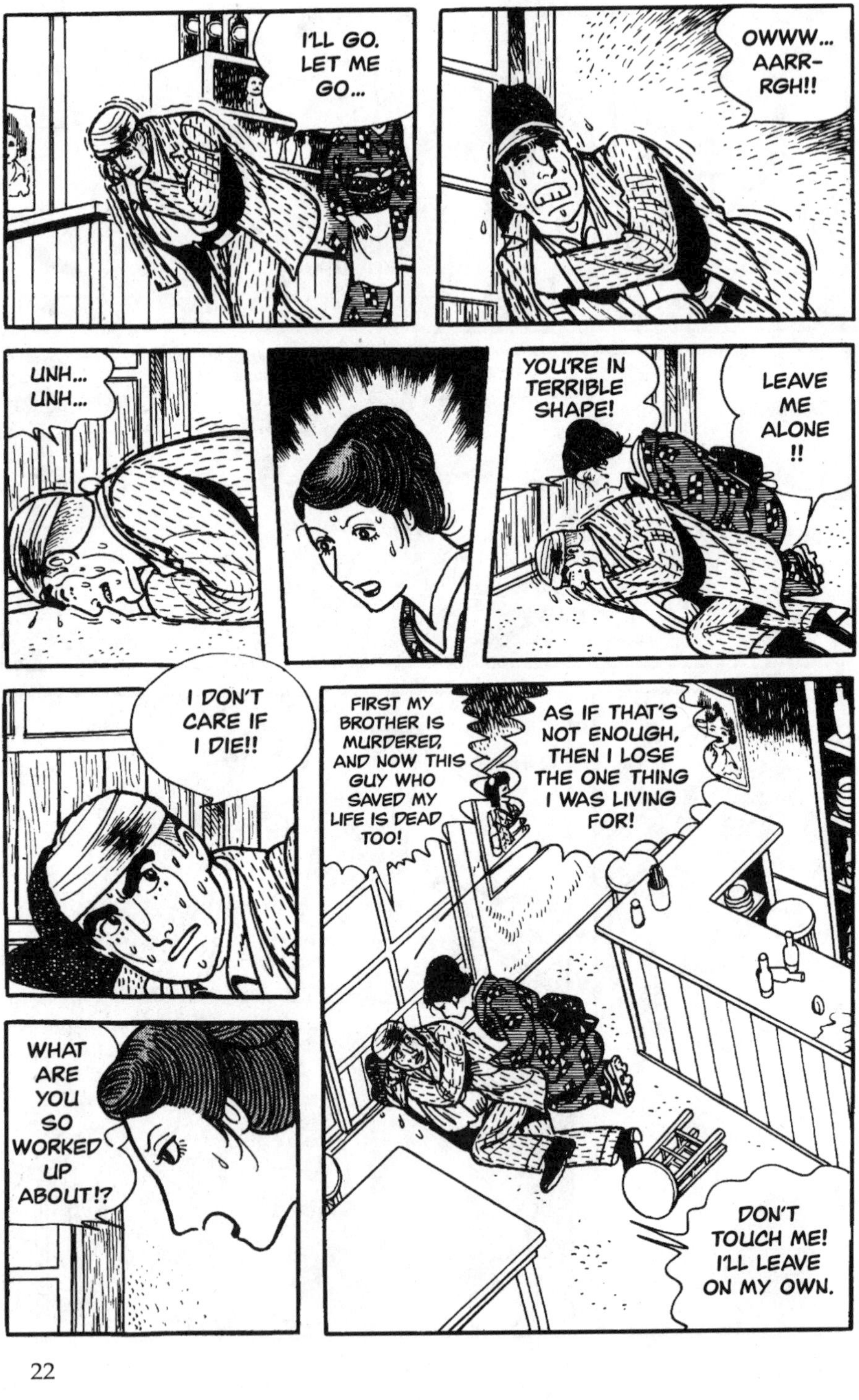
I'LL GO. LET ME GO...
OWWW... AARR-RGH!!
UNH... UNH...
YOU'RE IN TERRIBLE SHAPE!
LEAVE ME ALONE !!
I DON'T CARE IF I DIE!!
FIRST MY BROTHER IS MURDERED, AND NOW THIS GUY WHO SAVED MY LIFE IS DEAD TOO!
AS IF THAT'S NOT ENOUGH, THEN I LOSE THE ONE THING I WAS LIVING FOR!
DON'T TOUCH ME! I'LL LEAVE ON MY OWN.
WHAT ARE YOU SO WORKED UP ABOUT!?

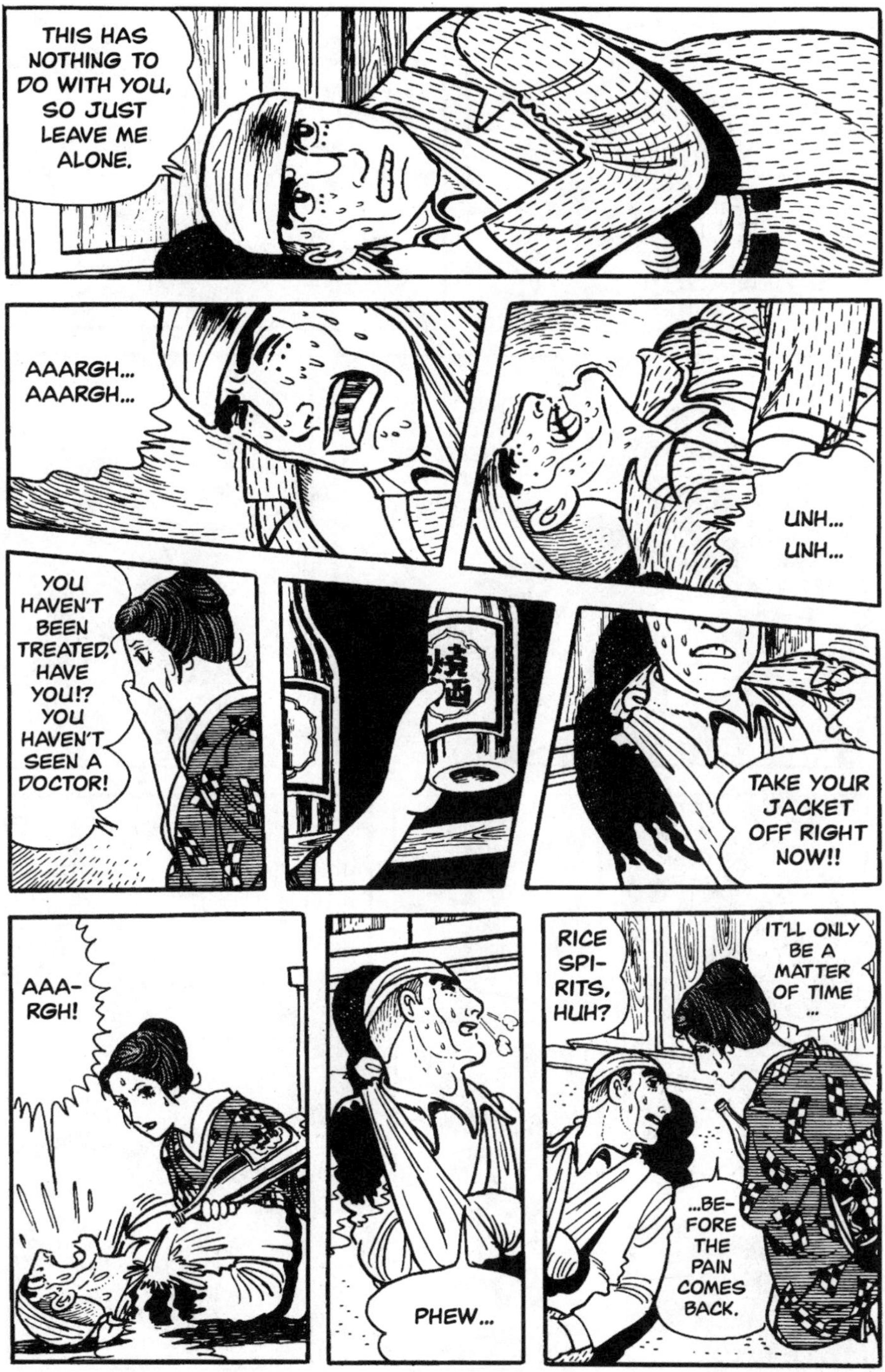
THIS HAS NOTHING TO DO WITH YOU, SO JUST LEAVE ME ALONE.
AAARGH... AAARGH...
UNH... UNH...
YOU HAVEN'T BEEN TREATED, HAVE YOU!? YOU HAVEN'T SEEN A DOCTOR!
TAKE YOUR JACKET OFF RIGHT NOW!!
AAA-RGH!
PHEW...
RICE SPI-RITS, HUH?
IT'LL ONLY BE A MATTER OF TIME ...
...BE-FORE THE PAIN COMES BACK.

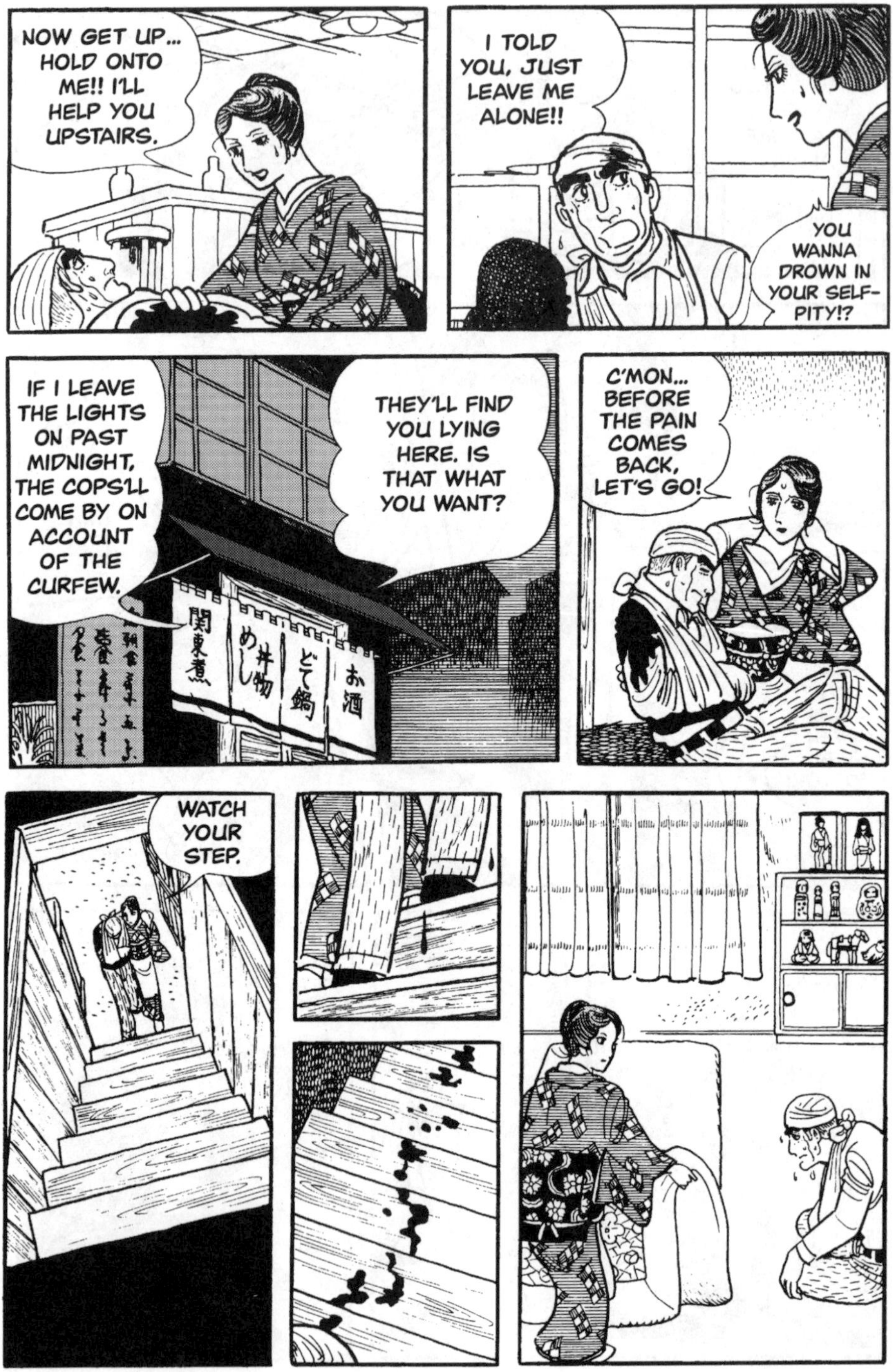
NOW GET UP... HOLD ONTO ME!! I'LL HELP YOU UPSTAIRS.
I TOLD YOU, JUST LEAVE ME ALONE!!
YOU WANNA DROWN IN YOUR SELF-PITY!?
IF I LEAVE THE LIGHTS ON PAST MIDNIGHT, THE COPS'LL COME BY ON ACCOUNT OF THE CURFEW.
THEY'LL FIND YOU LYING HERE. IS THAT WHAT YOU WANT?
お酒
どて鍋
丼物
めし
関東煮
C'MON... BEFORE THE PAIN COMES BACK, LET'S GO!
WATCH YOUR STEP.

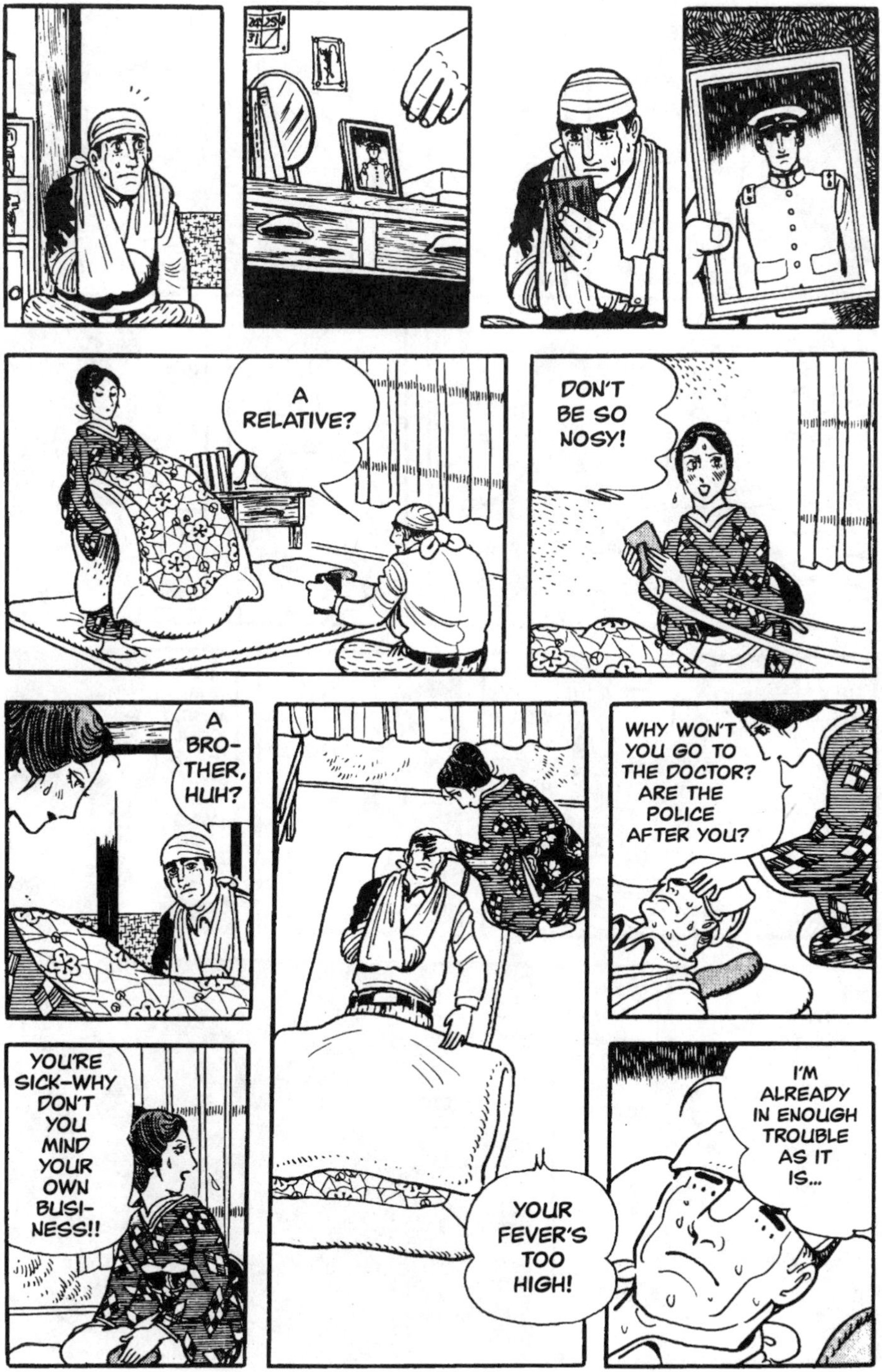
A RELATIVE?
DON'T BE SO NOSY!
A BROTHER, HUH?
WHY WON'T YOU GO TO THE DOCTOR? ARE THE POLICE AFTER YOU?
YOU'RE SICK–WHY DON'T YOU MIND YOUR OWN BUSINESS!!
YOUR FEVER'S TOO HIGH!
I'M ALREADY IN ENOUGH TROUBLE AS IT IS...

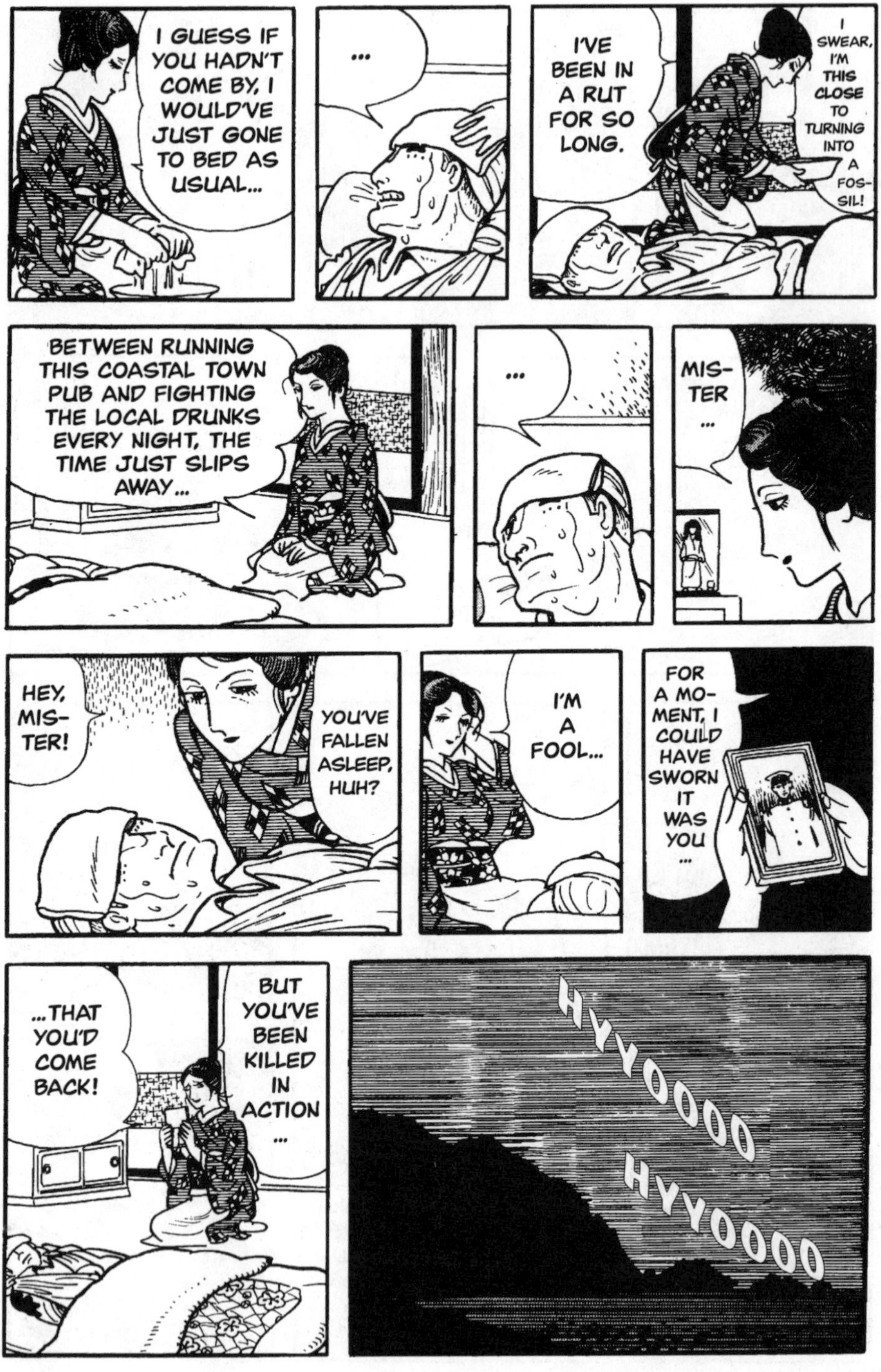
I GUESS IF YOU HADN'T COME BY, I WOULD'VE JUST GONE TO BED AS USUAL...
...
I'VE BEEN IN A RUT FOR SO LONG.
I SWEAR, I'M THIS CLOSE TO TURNING INTO A FOS-SIL!
BETWEEN RUNNING THIS COASTAL TOWN PUB AND FIGHTING THE LOCAL DRUNKS EVERY NIGHT, THE TIME JUST SLIPS AWAY...
...
MIS-TER ...
HEY, MIS-TER!
YOU'VE FALLEN ASLEEP, HUH?
I'M A FOOL...
FOR A MO-MENT, I COULD HAVE SWORN IT WAS YOU ...
...THAT YOU'D COME BACK!
BUT YOU'VE BEEN KILLED IN ACTION ...
HYYOOOO
HYYOOOO

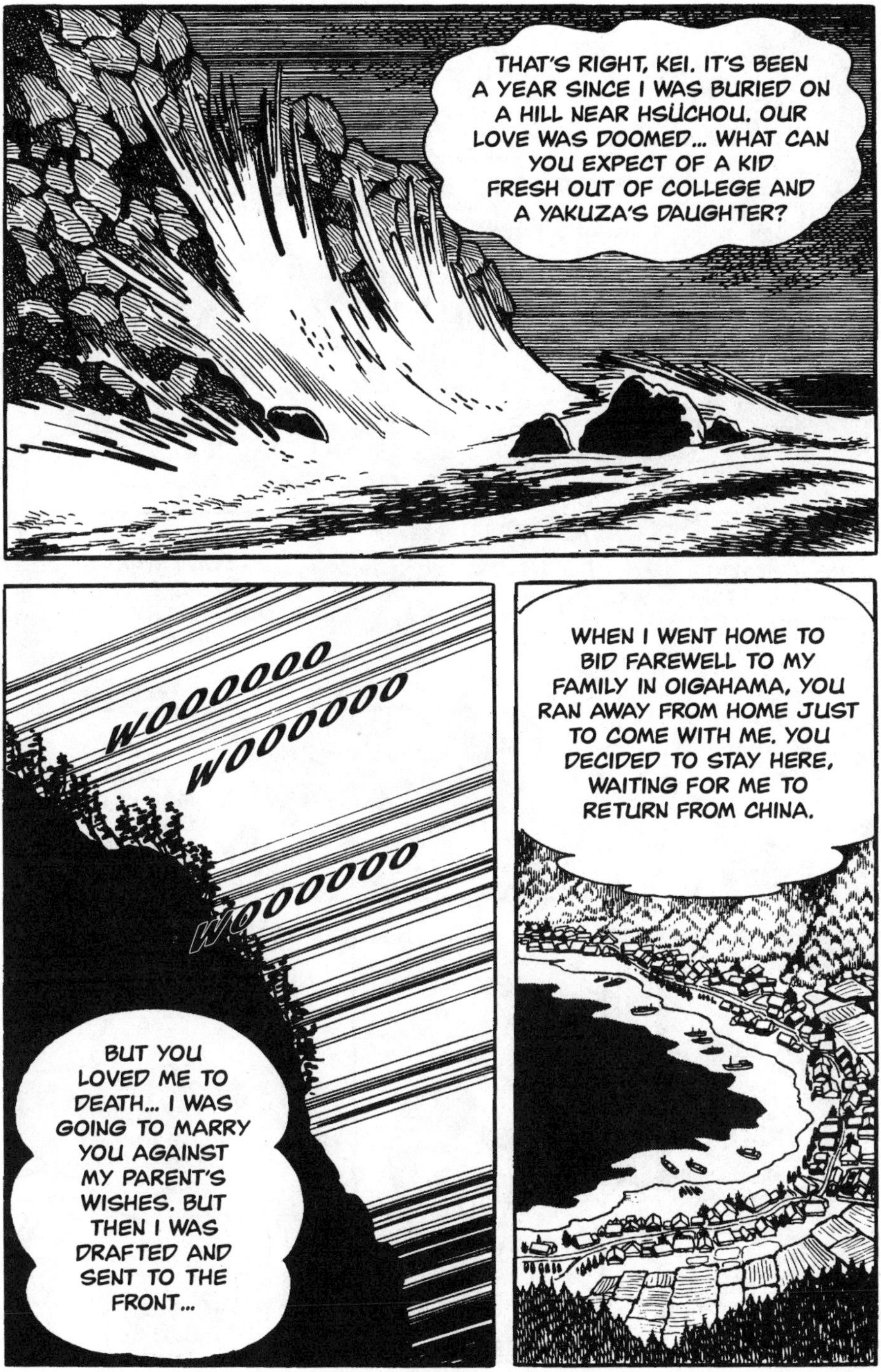
THAT'S RIGHT, KEI. IT'S BEEN A YEAR SINCE I WAS BURIED ON A HILL NEAR HSÜCHOU. OUR LOVE WAS DOOMED... WHAT CAN YOU EXPECT OF A KID FRESH OUT OF COLLEGE AND A YAKUZA'S DAUGHTER?
WOOOOOO
WOOOOOOO
WOOOOOOO
BUT YOU LOVED ME TO DEATH... I WAS GOING TO MARRY YOU AGAINST MY PARENT'S WISHES. BUT THEN I WAS DRAFTED AND SENT TO THE FRONT...
WHEN I WENT HOME TO BID FAREWELL TO MY FAMILY IN OIGAHAMA, YOU RAN AWAY FROM HOME JUST TO COME WITH ME. YOU DECIDED TO STAY HERE, WAITING FOR ME TO RETURN FROM CHINA.

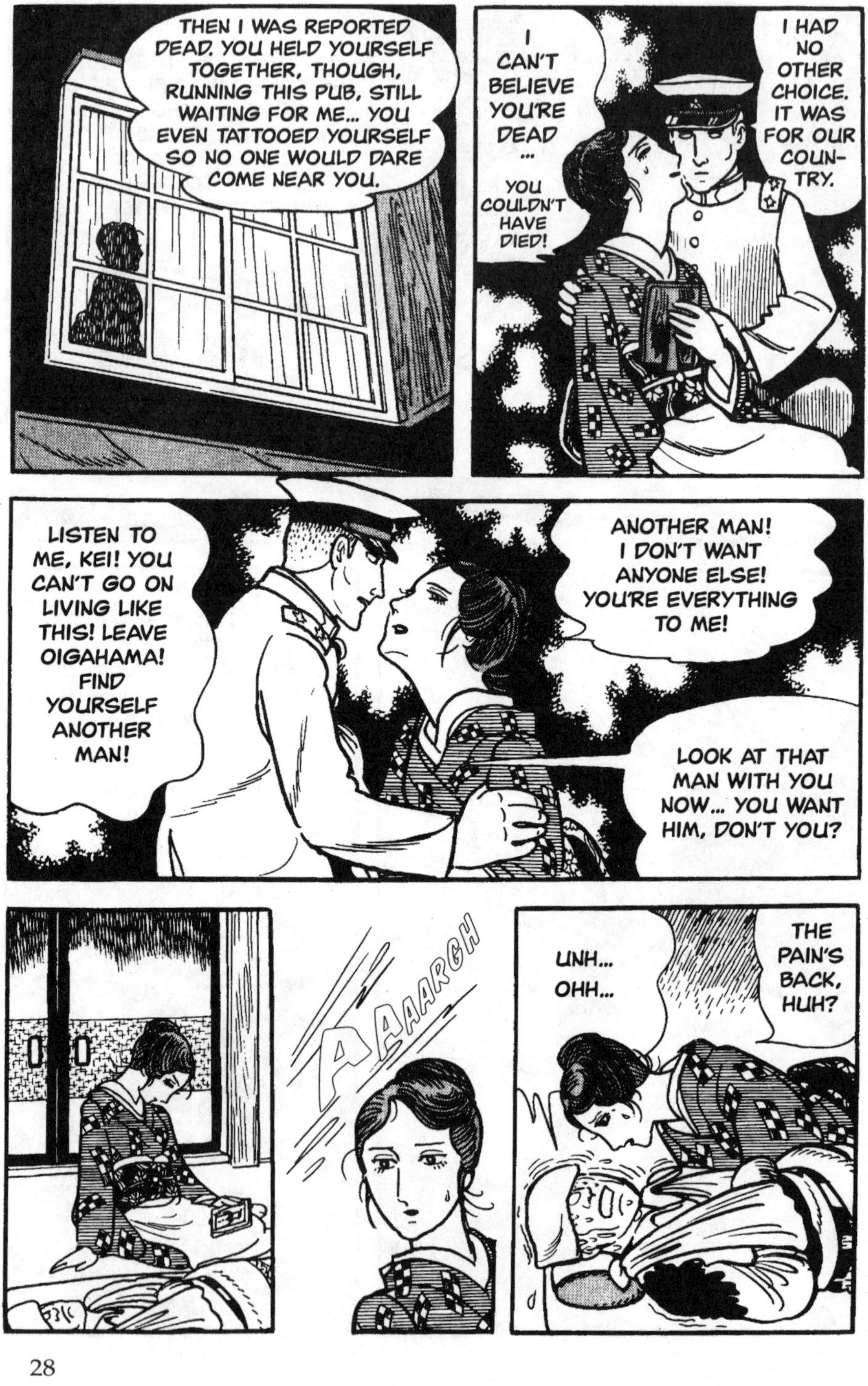
THEN I WAS REPORTED DEAD. YOU HELD YOURSELF TOGETHER, THOUGH, RUNNING THIS PUB, STILL WAITING FOR ME... YOU EVEN TATTOOED YOURSELF SO NO ONE WOULD DARE COME NEAR YOU.
I CAN'T BELIEVE YOU'RE DEAD ... YOU COULDN'T HAVE DIED!
I HAD NO OTHER CHOICE. IT WAS FOR OUR COUNTRY.
LISTEN TO ME, KEI! YOU CAN'T GO ON LIVING LIKE THIS! LEAVE OIGAHAMA! FIND YOURSELF ANOTHER MAN!
ANOTHER MAN! I DON'T WANT ANYONE ELSE! YOU'RE EVERYTHING TO ME!
LOOK AT THAT MAN WITH YOU NOW... YOU WANT HIM, DON'T YOU?
AAAARGH
UNH... OHH...
THE PAIN'S BACK, HUH?

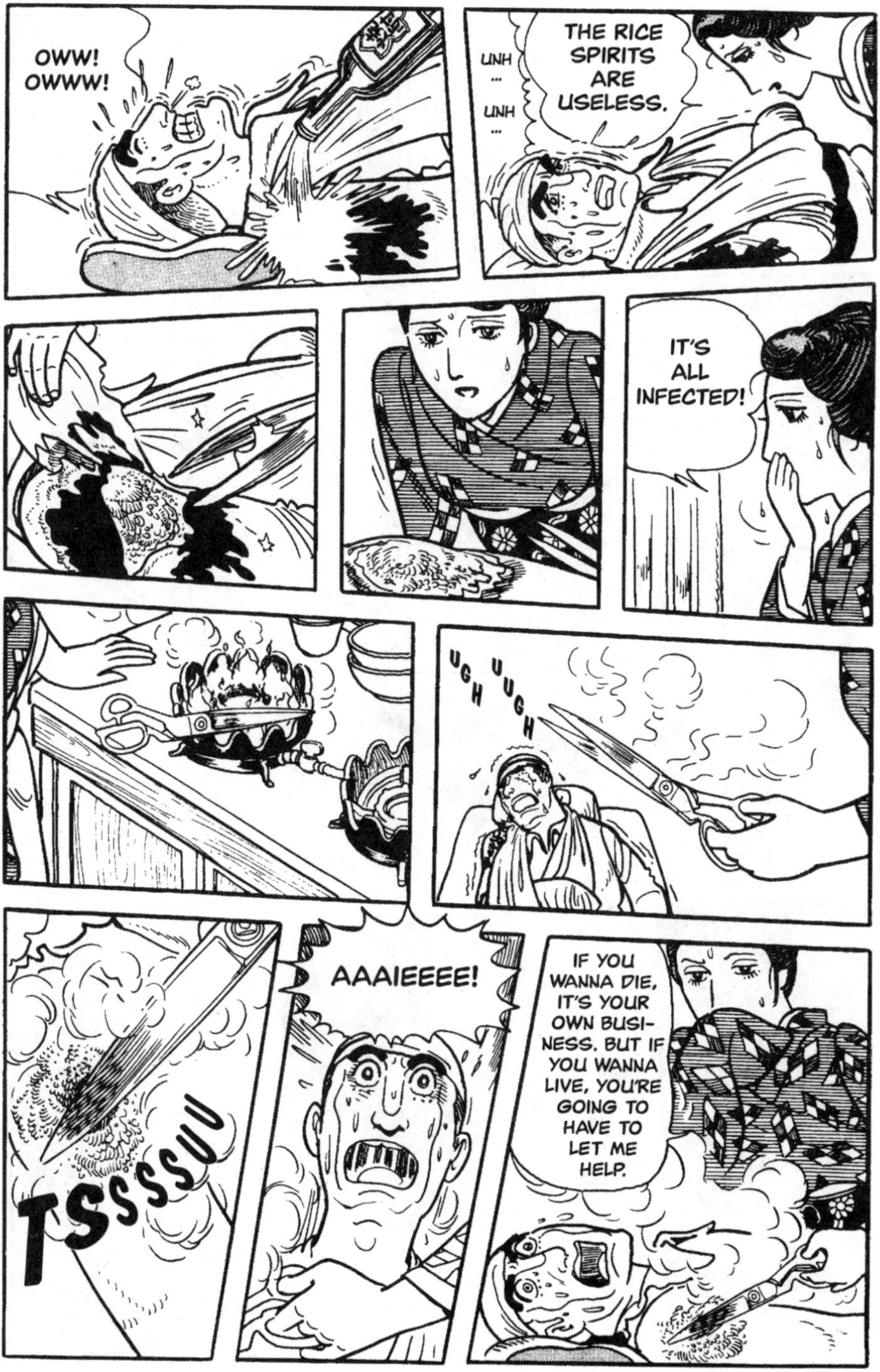
OWW! OWWW!
UNH ... UNH ...
THE RICE SPIRITS ARE USELESS.
IT'S ALL INFECTED!
UGH UUGH
TSSSSUU
AAAIEEEE!
IF YOU WANNA DIE, IT'S YOUR OWN BUSINESS. BUT IF YOU WANNA LIVE, YOU'RE GOING TO HAVE TO LET ME HELP.

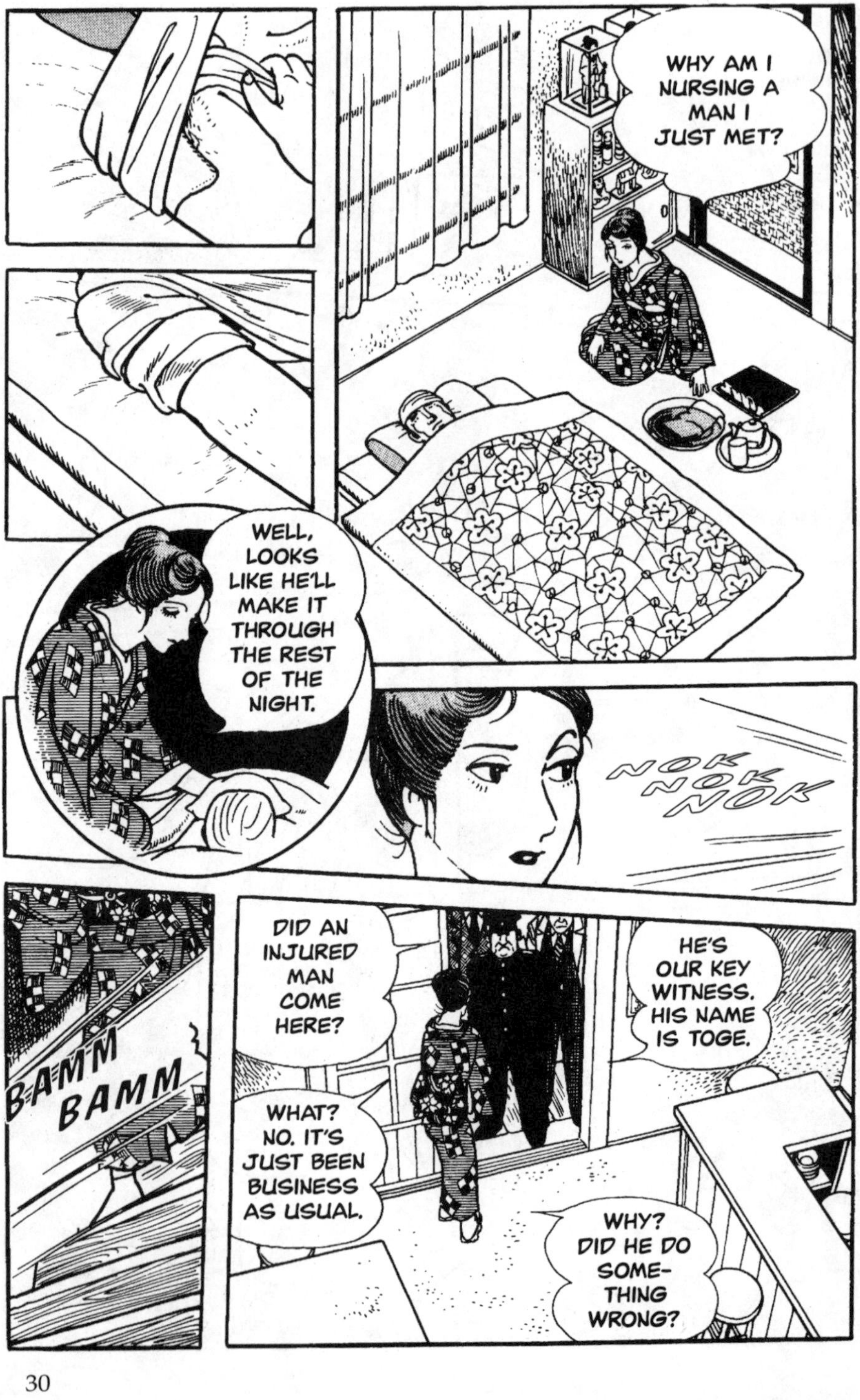
WHY AM I NURSING A MAN I JUST MET?
WELL, LOOKS LIKE HE'LL MAKE IT THROUGH THE REST OF THE NIGHT.
NOK NOK NOK
BAMM BAMM
DID AN INJURED MAN COME HERE?
WHAT? NO. IT'S JUST BEEN BUSINESS AS USUAL.
HE'S OUR KEY WITNESS. HIS NAME IS TOGE.
WHY? DID HE DO SOME-THING WRONG?

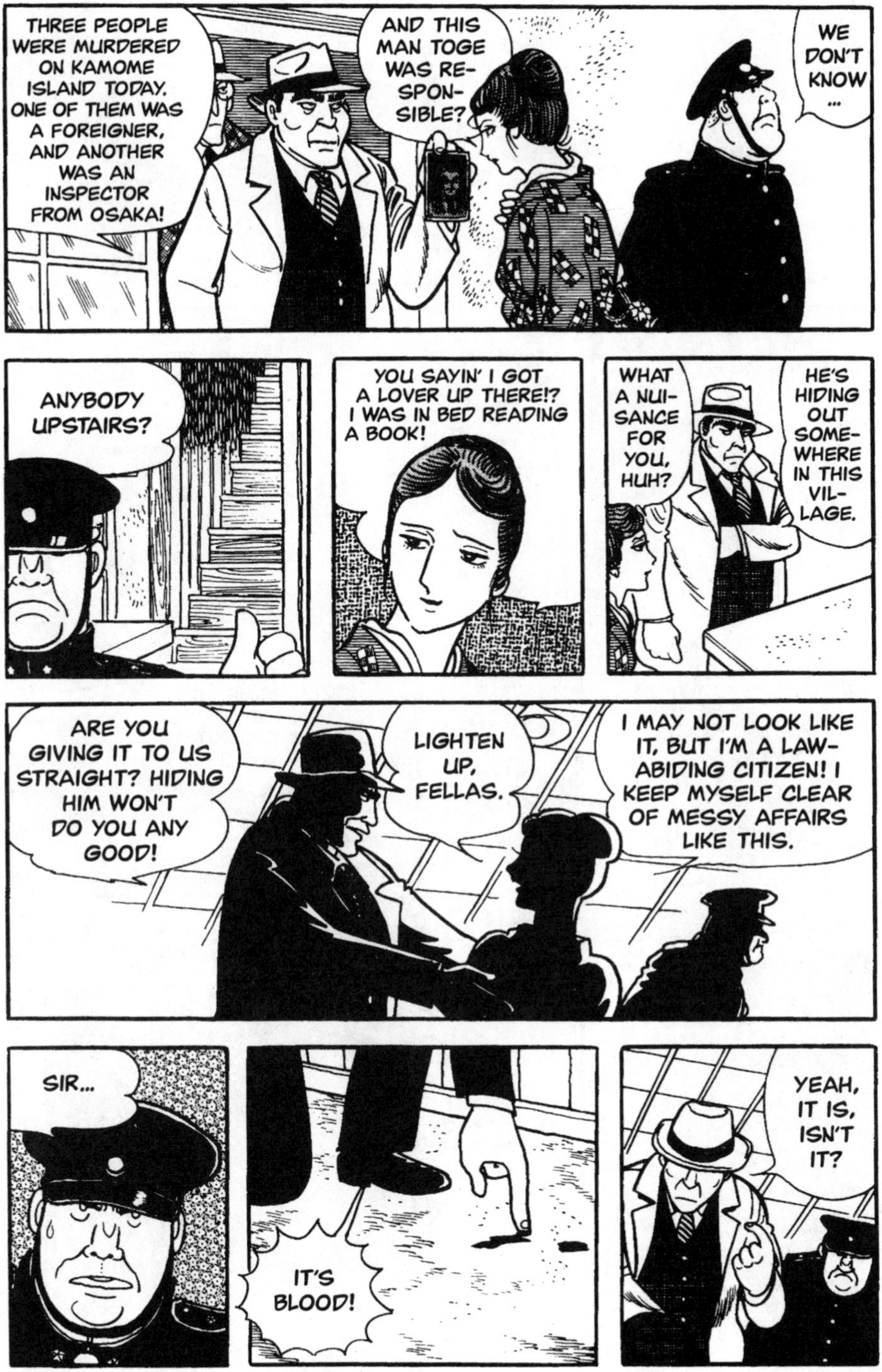
THREE PEOPLE WERE MURDERED ON KAMOME ISLAND TODAY. ONE OF THEM WAS A FOREIGNER, AND ANOTHER WAS AN INSPECTOR FROM OSAKA!
AND THIS MAN TOGE WAS RESPONSIBLE?
WE DON'T KNOW ...
ANYBODY UPSTAIRS?
YOU SAYIN' I GOT A LOVER UP THERE!? I WAS IN BED READING A BOOK!
WHAT A NUISANCE FOR YOU, HUH?
HE'S HIDING OUT SOMEWHERE IN THIS VILLAGE.
ARE YOU GIVING IT TO US STRAIGHT? HIDING HIM WON'T DO YOU ANY GOOD!
LIGHTEN UP, FELLAS.
I MAY NOT LOOK LIKE IT, BUT I'M A LAW-ABIDING CITIZEN! I KEEP MYSELF CLEAR OF MESSY AFFAIRS LIKE THIS.
SIR...
IT'S BLOOD!
YEAH, IT IS, ISN'T IT?

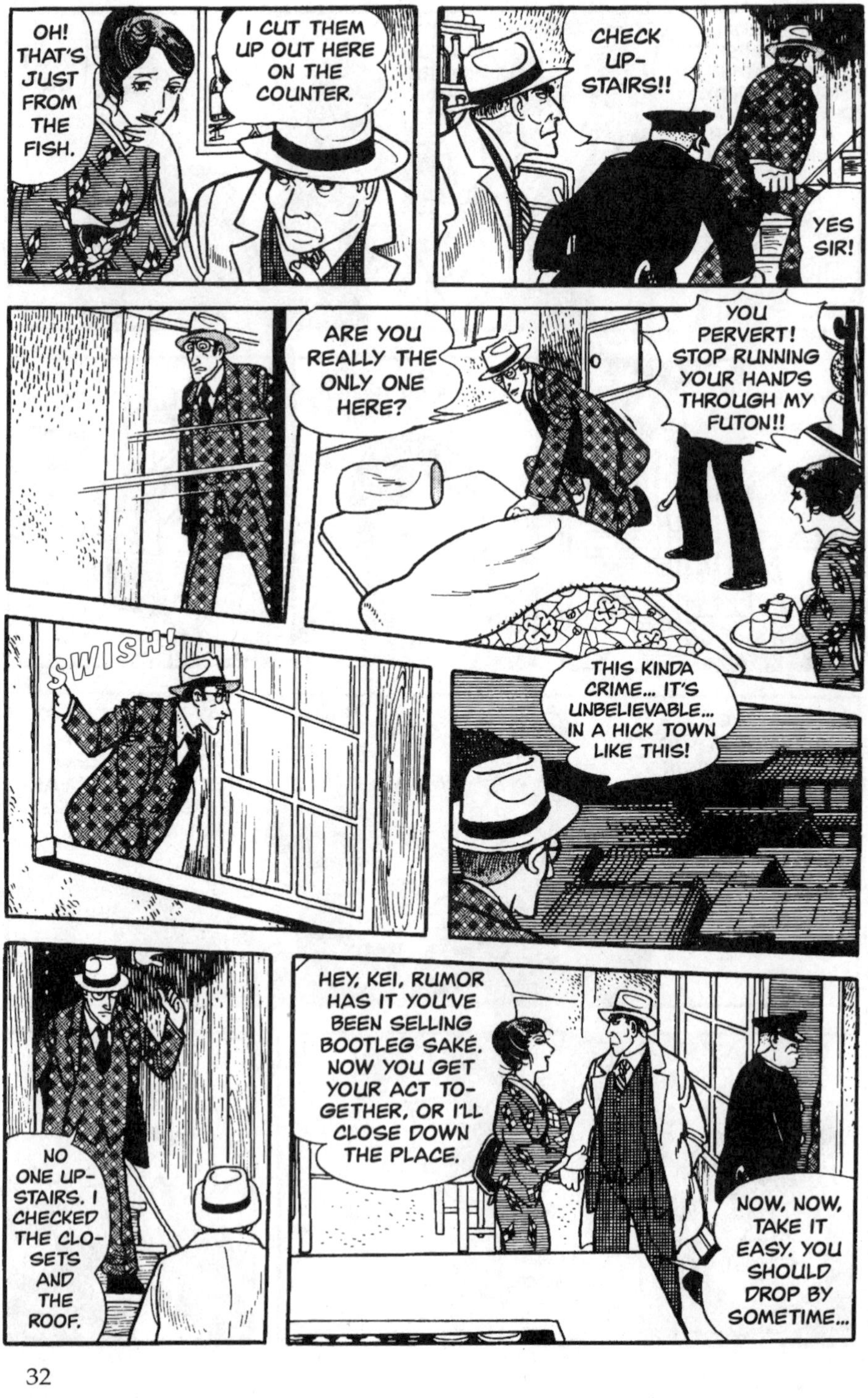
OH! THAT'S JUST FROM THE FISH.
I CUT THEM UP OUT HERE ON THE COUNTER.
CHECK UP-STAIRS!!
YES SIR!
ARE YOU REALLY THE ONLY ONE HERE?
YOU PERVERT! STOP RUNNING YOUR HANDS THROUGH MY FUTON!!
SWISH!
THIS KINDA CRIME... IT'S UNBELIEVABLE... IN A HICK TOWN LIKE THIS!
NO ONE UP-STAIRS. I CHECKED THE CLO-SETS AND THE ROOF.
HEY, KEI, RUMOR HAS IT YOU'VE BEEN SELLING BOOTLEG SAKÉ. NOW YOU GET YOUR ACT TO-GETHER, OR I'LL CLOSE DOWN THE PLACE.
NOW, NOW, TAKE IT EASY. YOU SHOULD DROP BY SOMETIME...

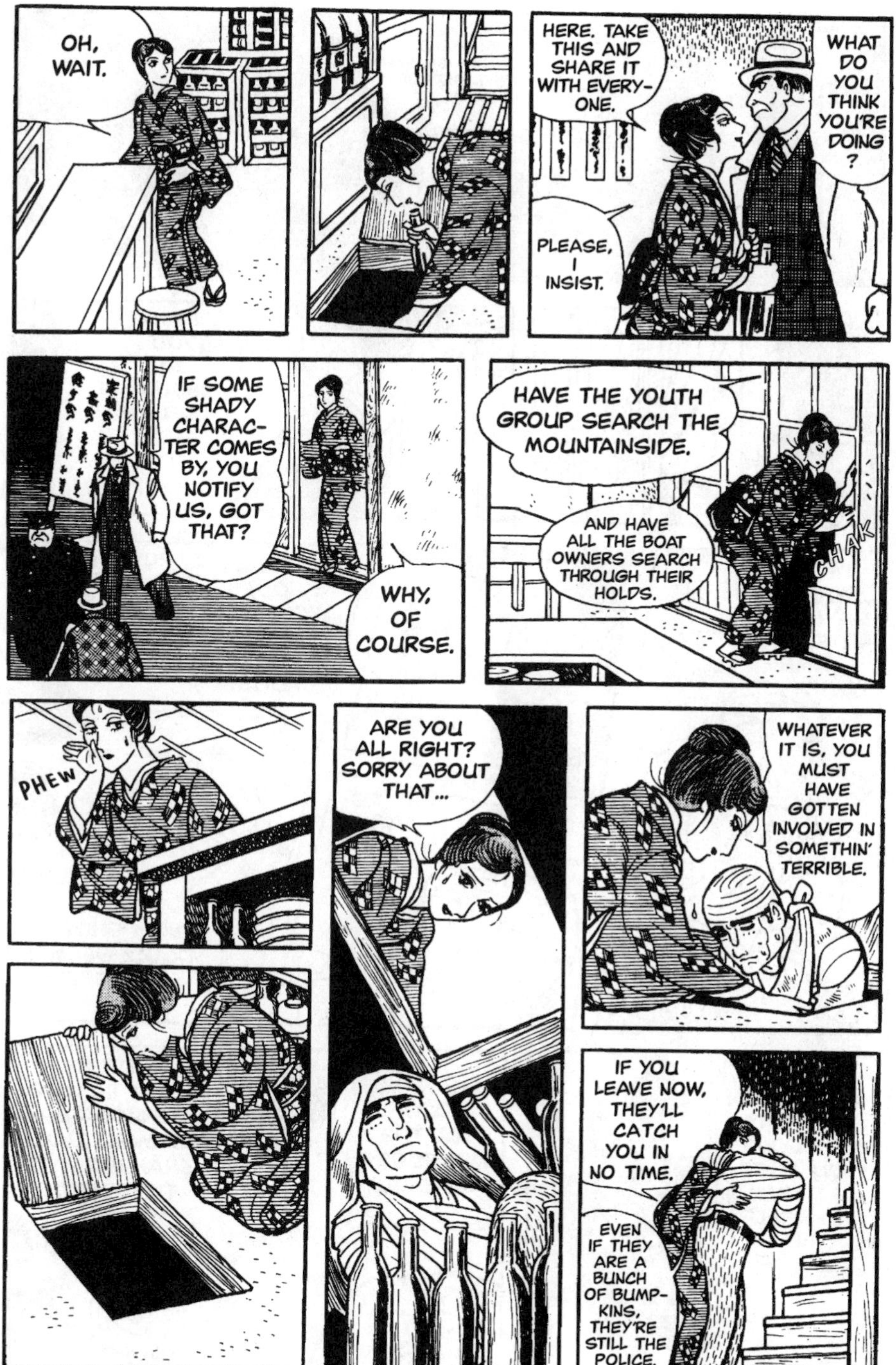
OH, WAIT.
HERE. TAKE THIS AND SHARE IT WITH EVERY-ONE.
WHAT DO YOU THINK YOU'RE DOING?
PLEASE, I INSIST.
IF SOME SHADY CHARAC-TER COMES BY, YOU NOTIFY US, GOT THAT?
WHY, OF COURSE.
HAVE THE YOUTH GROUP SEARCH THE MOUNTAINSIDE.
AND HAVE ALL THE BOAT OWNERS SEARCH THROUGH THEIR HOLDS.
CHAK
PHEW
ARE YOU ALL RIGHT? SORRY ABOUT THAT...
WHATEVER IT IS, YOU MUST HAVE GOTTEN INVOLVED IN SOMETHIN' TERRIBLE.
IF YOU LEAVE NOW, THEY'LL CATCH YOU IN NO TIME.
EVEN IF THEY ARE A BUNCH OF BUMP-KINS, THEY'RE STILL THE POLICE.

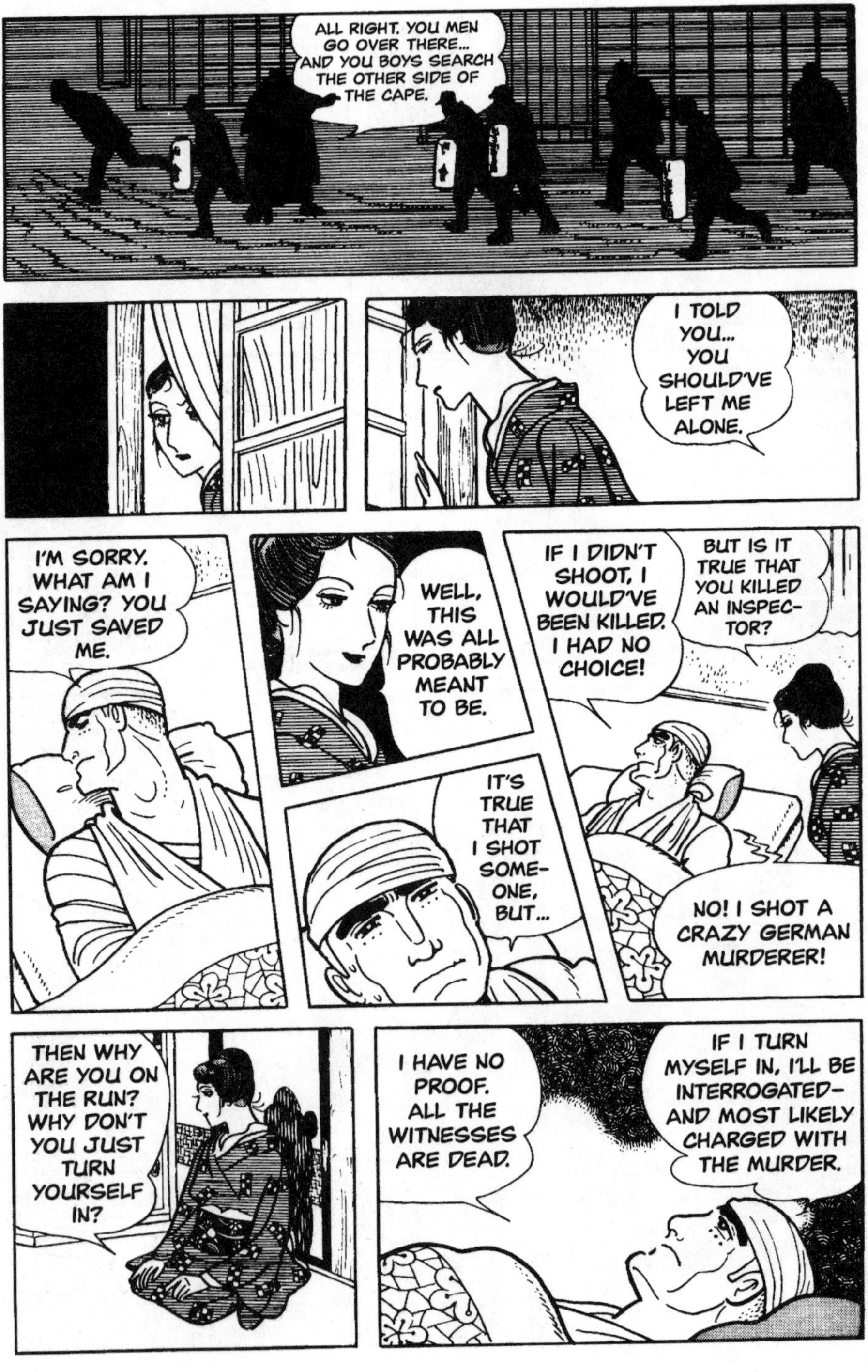
ALL RIGHT. YOU MEN GO OVER THERE... AND YOU BOYS SEARCH THE OTHER SIDE OF THE CAPE.
I TOLD YOU... YOU SHOULD'VE LEFT ME ALONE.
I'M SORRY. WHAT AM I SAYING? YOU JUST SAVED ME.
WELL, THIS WAS ALL PROBABLY MEANT TO BE.
IT'S TRUE THAT I SHOT SOME-ONE, BUT...
IF I DIDN'T SHOOT, I WOULD'VE BEEN KILLED. I HAD NO CHOICE!
BUT IS IT TRUE THAT YOU KILLED AN INSPEC-TOR?
NO! I SHOT A CRAZY GERMAN MURDERER!
THEN WHY ARE YOU ON THE RUN? WHY DON'T YOU JUST TURN YOURSELF IN?
I HAVE NO PROOF. ALL THE WITNESSES ARE DEAD.
IF I TURN MYSELF IN, I'LL BE INTERROGATED– AND MOST LIKELY CHARGED WITH THE MURDER.

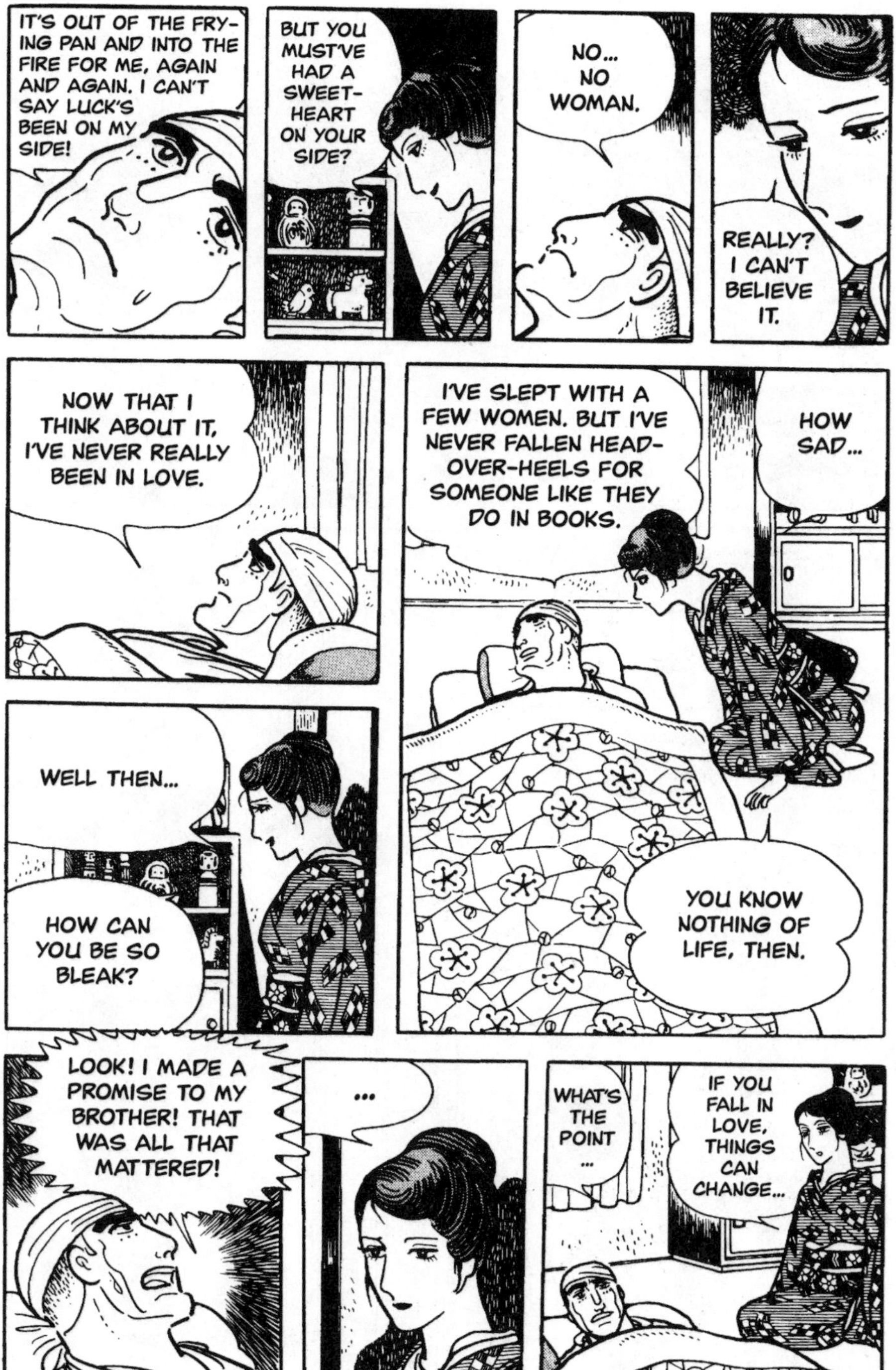
IT'S OUT OF THE FRYING PAN AND INTO THE FIRE FOR ME, AGAIN AND AGAIN. I CAN'T SAY LUCK'S BEEN ON MY SIDE!
BUT YOU MUST'VE HAD A SWEETHEART ON YOUR SIDE?
NO... NO WOMAN.
REALLY? I CAN'T BELIEVE IT.
NOW THAT I THINK ABOUT IT, I'VE NEVER REALLY BEEN IN LOVE.
WELL THEN...
HOW CAN YOU BE SO BLEAK?
I'VE SLEPT WITH A FEW WOMEN. BUT I'VE NEVER FALLEN HEAD-OVER-HEELS FOR SOMEONE LIKE THEY DO IN BOOKS.
HOW SAD...
YOU KNOW NOTHING OF LIFE, THEN.
LOOK! I MADE A PROMISE TO MY BROTHER! THAT WAS ALL THAT MATTERED!
...
WHAT'S THE POINT ...
IF YOU FALL IN LOVE, THINGS CAN CHANGE...

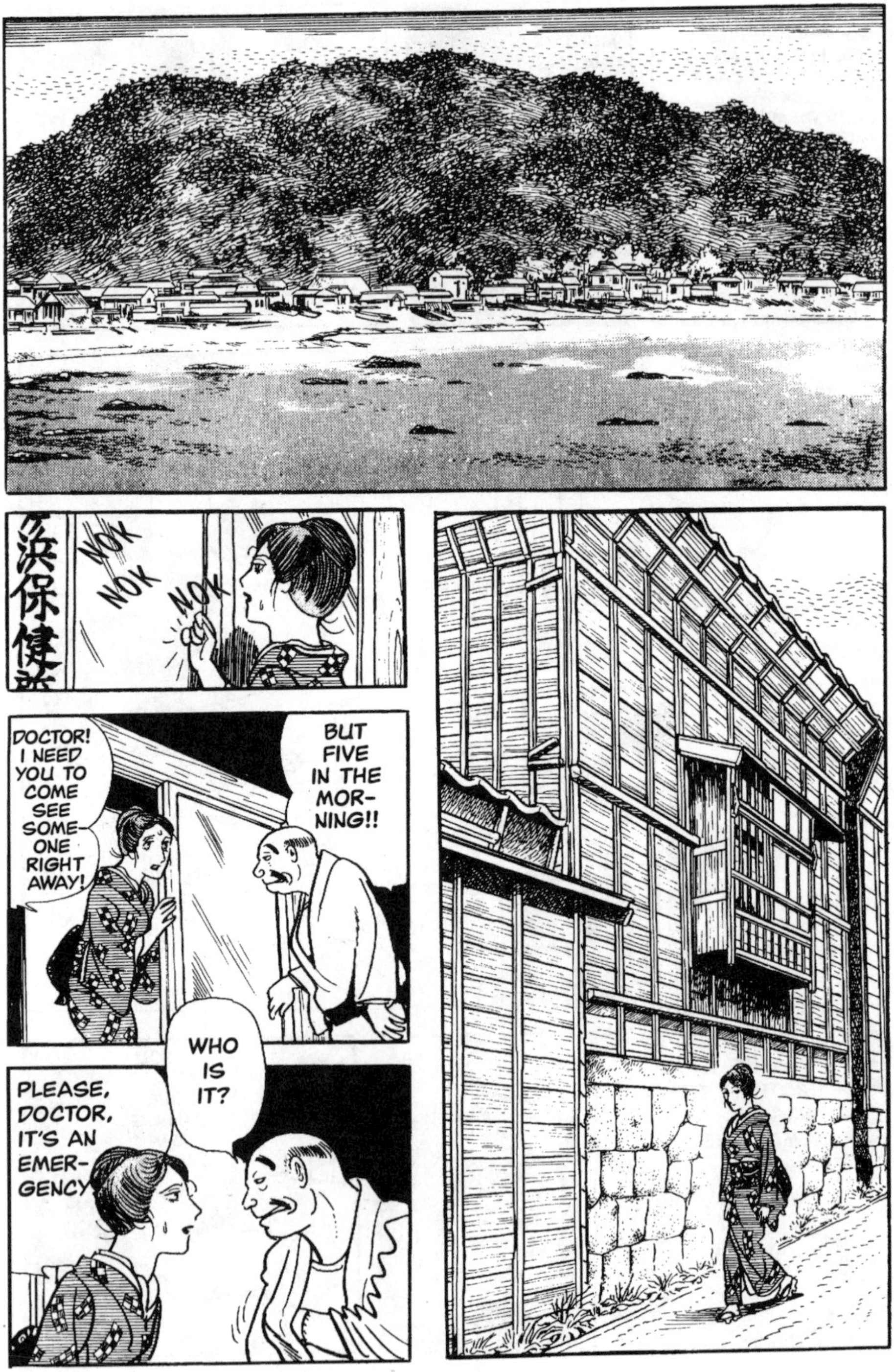
浜保健所
NOK
NOK
NOK
DOCTOR! I NEED YOU TO COME SEE SOME-ONE RIGHT AWAY!
BUT FIVE IN THE MOR-NING!!
WHO IS IT?
PLEASE, DOCTOR, IT'S AN EMER-GENCY

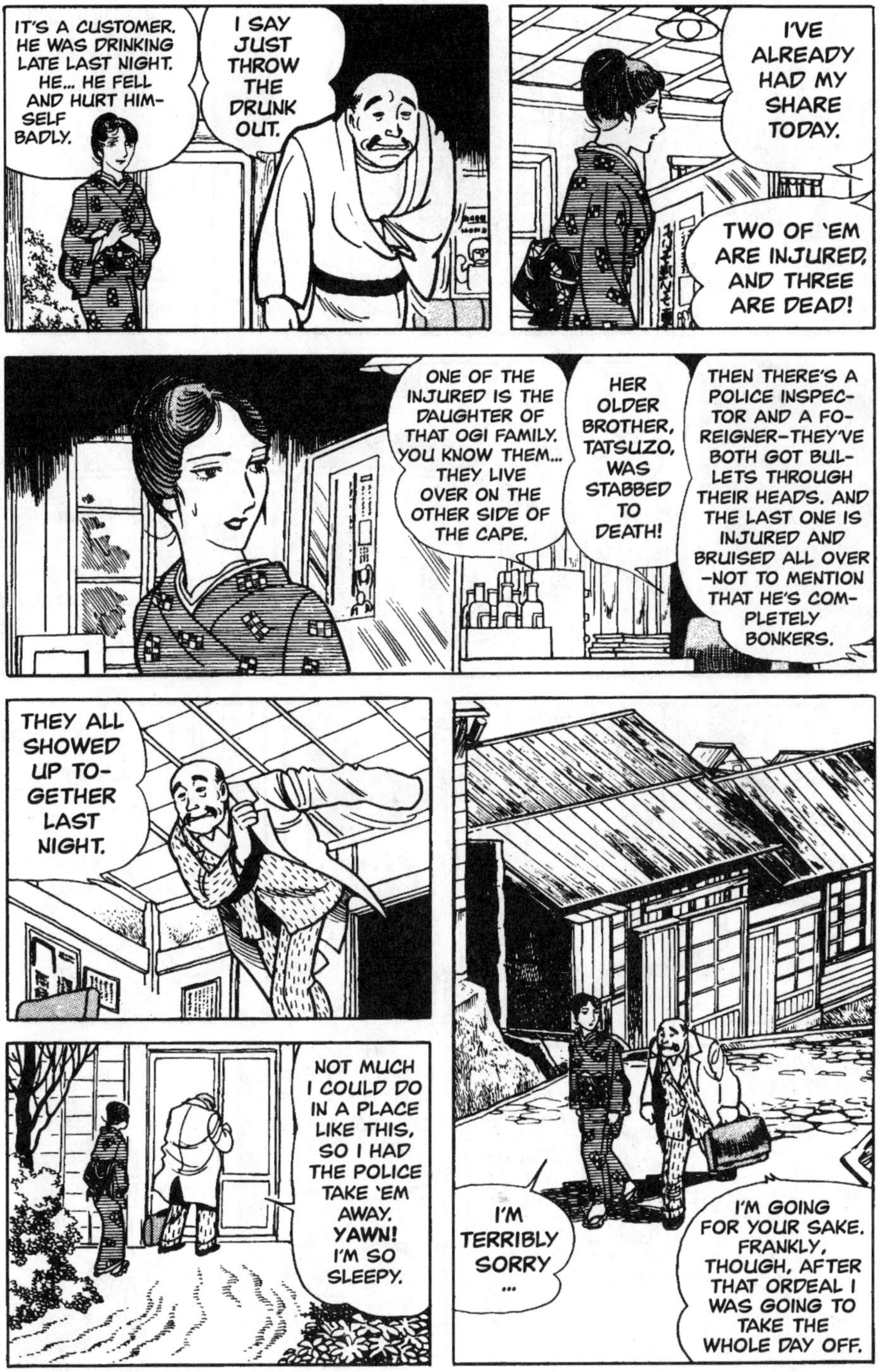
IT'S A CUSTOMER. HE WAS DRINKING LATE LAST NIGHT. HE... HE FELL AND HURT HIM-SELF BADLY.
I SAY JUST THROW THE DRUNK OUT.
I'VE ALREADY HAD MY SHARE TODAY.
TWO OF 'EM ARE INJURED, AND THREE ARE DEAD!
ONE OF THE INJURED IS THE DAUGHTER OF THAT OGI FAMILY. YOU KNOW THEM... THEY LIVE OVER ON THE OTHER SIDE OF THE CAPE.
HER OLDER BROTHER, TATSUZO, WAS STABBED TO DEATH!
THEN THERE'S A POLICE INSPEC-TOR AND A FO-REIGNER–THEY'VE BOTH GOT BUL-LETS THROUGH THEIR HEADS. AND THE LAST ONE IS INJURED AND BRUISED ALL OVER –NOT TO MENTION THAT HE'S COM-PLETELY BONKERS.
THEY ALL SHOWED UP TO-GETHER LAST NIGHT.
NOT MUCH I COULD DO IN A PLACE LIKE THIS, SO I HAD THE POLICE TAKE 'EM AWAY. YAWN! I'M SO SLEEPY.
I'M TERRIBLY SORRY ...
I'M GOING FOR YOUR SAKE. FRANKLY, THOUGH, AFTER THAT ORDEAL I WAS GOING TO TAKE THE WHOLE DAY OFF.

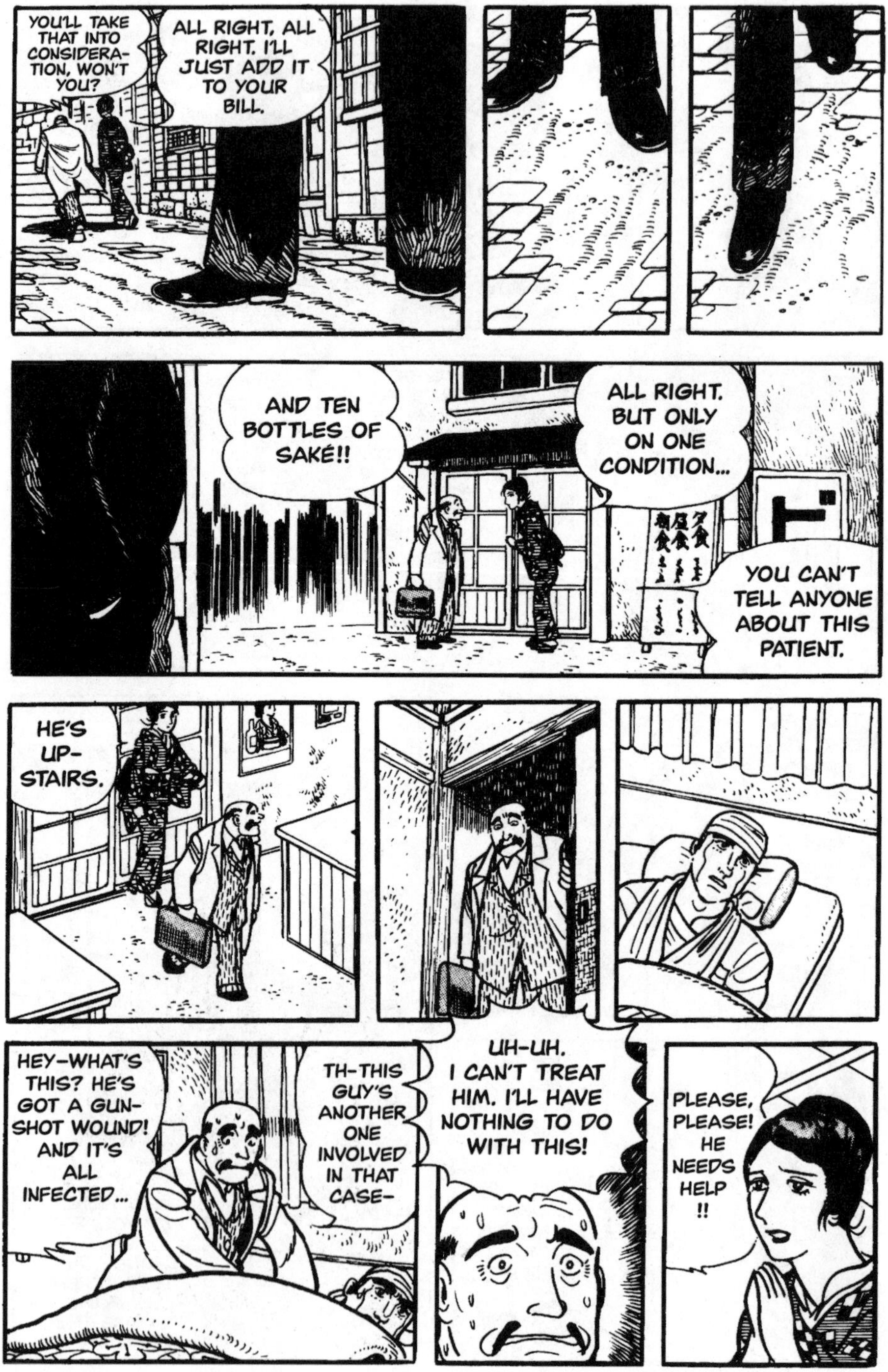
YOU'LL TAKE THAT INTO CONSIDERATION, WON'T YOU?
ALL RIGHT, ALL RIGHT. I'LL JUST ADD IT TO YOUR BILL.
AND TEN BOTTLES OF SAKÉ!!
ALL RIGHT. BUT ONLY ON ONE CONDITION...
YOU CAN'T TELL ANYONE ABOUT THIS PATIENT.
HE'S UP-STAIRS.
HEY–WHAT'S THIS? HE'S GOT A GUN-SHOT WOUND! AND IT'S ALL INFECTED...
TH-THIS GUY'S ANOTHER ONE INVOLVED IN THAT CASE–
UH-UH. I CAN'T TREAT HIM. I'LL HAVE NOTHING TO DO WITH THIS!
PLEASE, PLEASE! HE NEEDS HELP !!

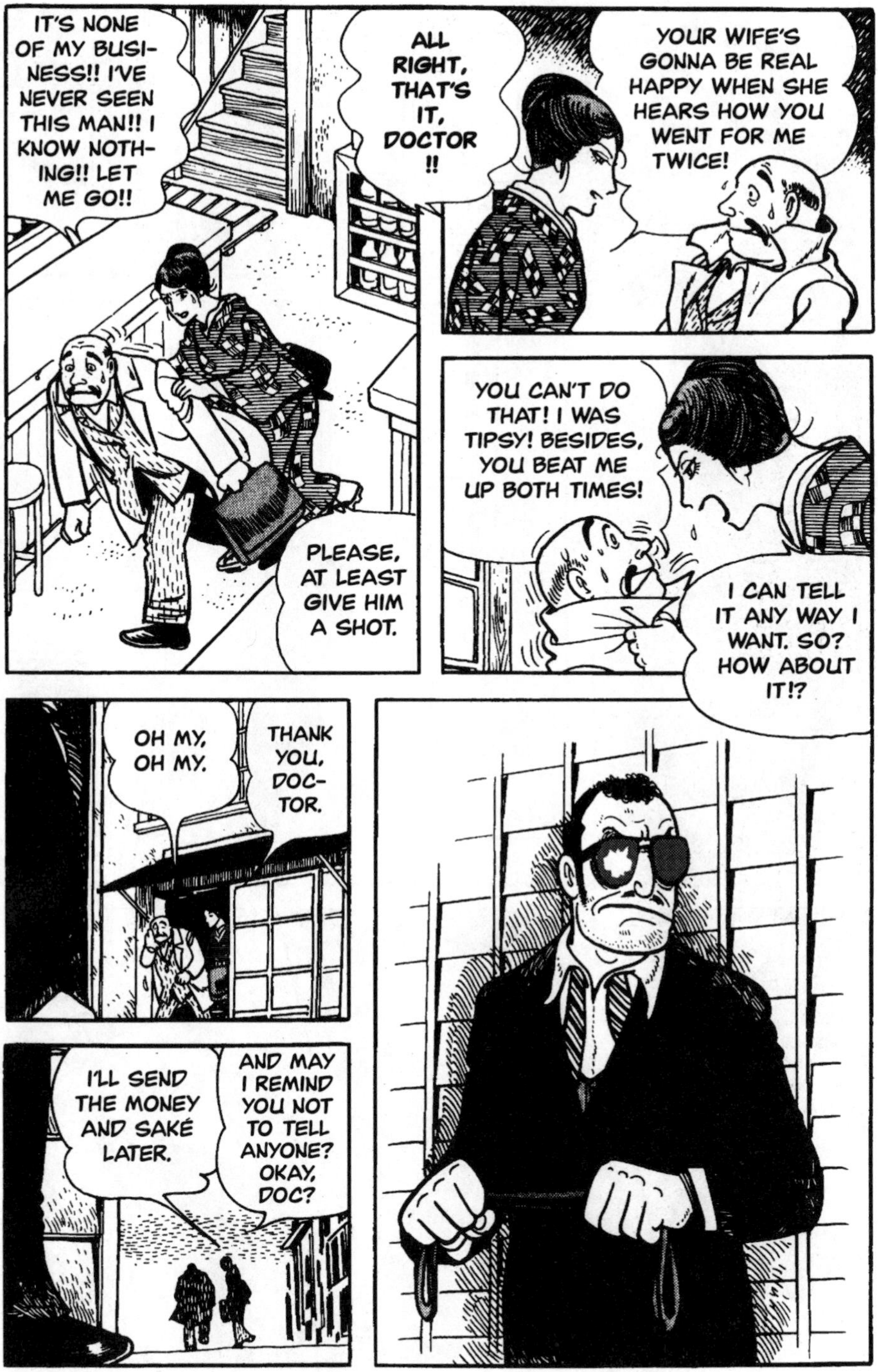
IT'S NONE OF MY BUSINESS!! I'VE NEVER SEEN THIS MAN!! I KNOW NOTHING!! LET ME GO!!
ALL RIGHT, THAT'S IT, DOCTOR!!
PLEASE, AT LEAST GIVE HIM A SHOT.
YOUR WIFE'S GONNA BE REAL HAPPY WHEN SHE HEARS HOW YOU WENT FOR ME TWICE!
YOU CAN'T DO THAT! I WAS TIPSY! BESIDES, YOU BEAT ME UP BOTH TIMES!
I CAN TELL IT ANY WAY I WANT. SO? HOW ABOUT IT!?
OH MY, OH MY.
THANK YOU, DOCTOR.
I'LL SEND THE MONEY AND SAKÉ LATER.
AND MAY I REMIND YOU NOT TO TELL ANYONE? OKAY, DOC?

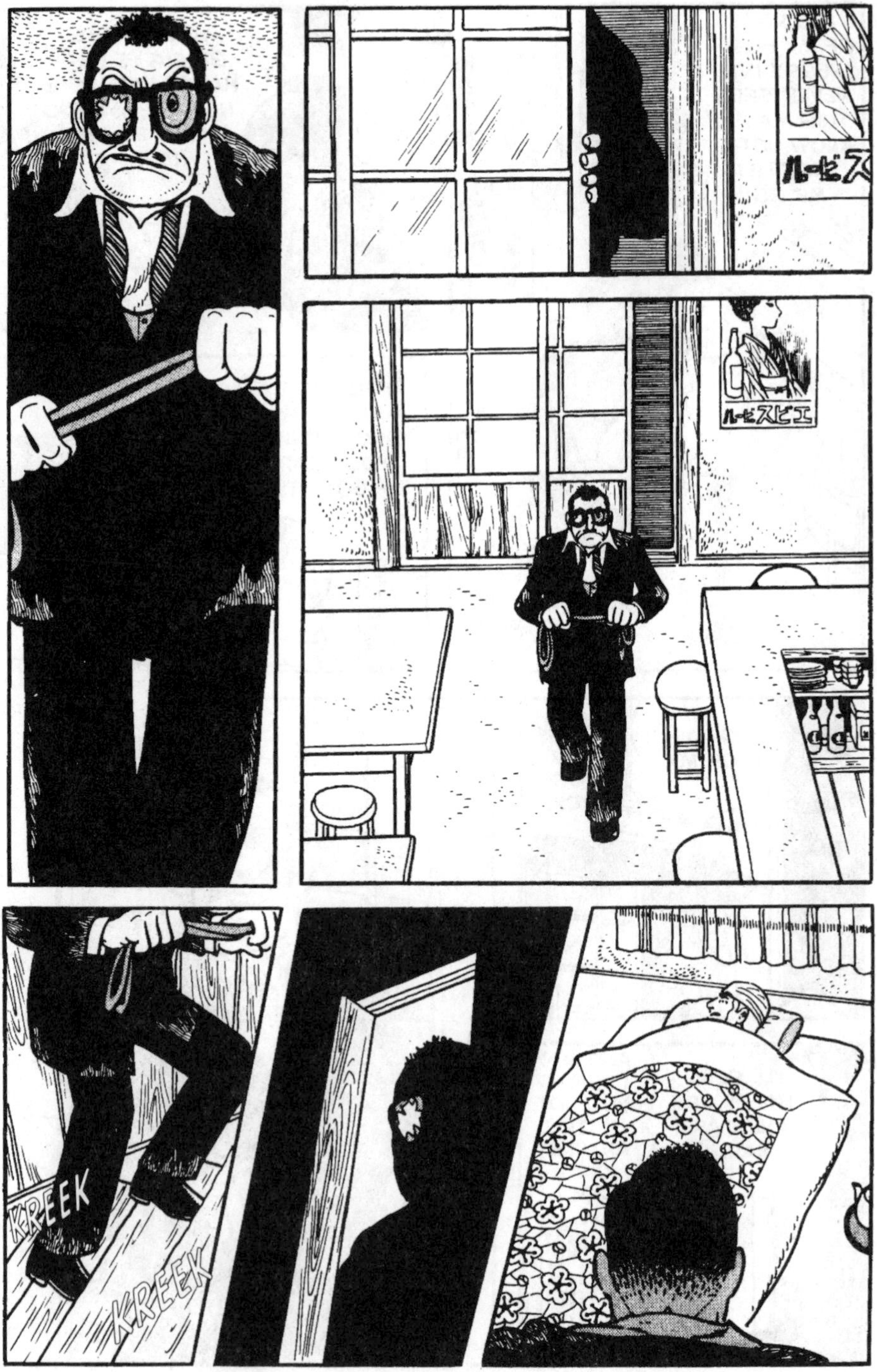
ルービスビエ
KREEK
KREEK

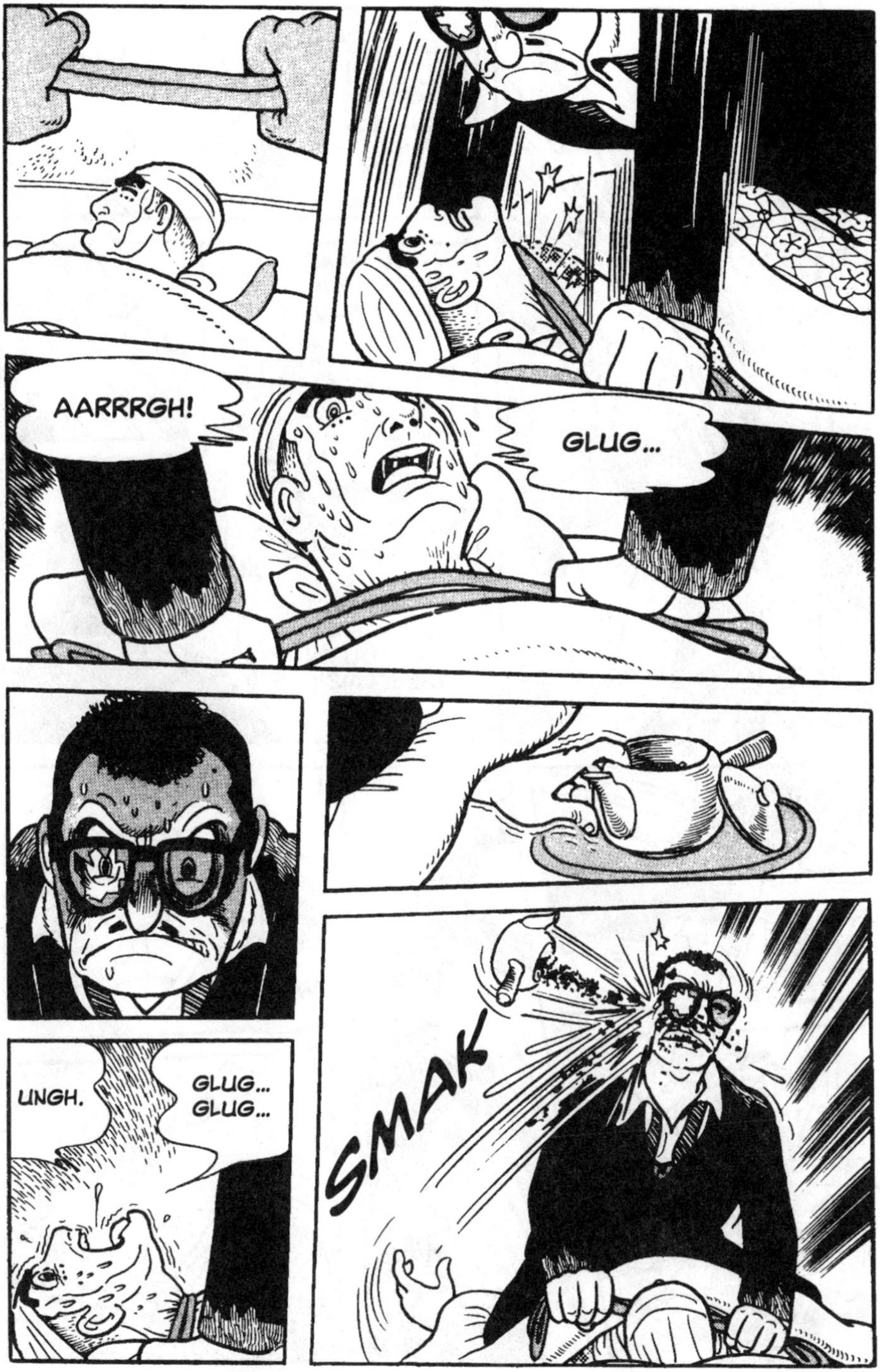
AARRRGH!
GLUG...
UNGH.
GLUG... GLUG...
SMAK

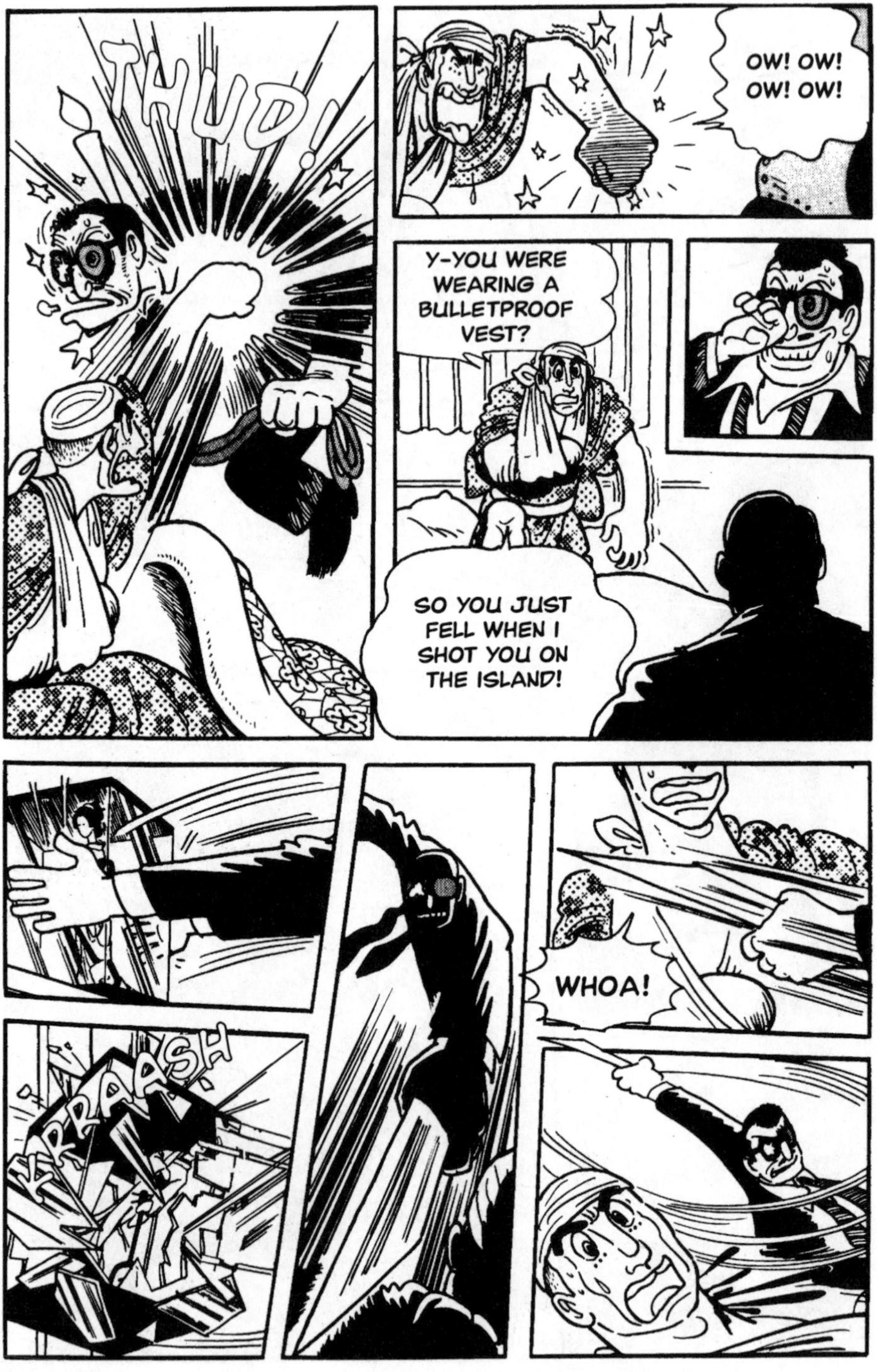
THUD!
OW! OW! OW! OW!
Y-YOU WERE WEARING A BULLETPROOF VEST?
SO YOU JUST FELL WHEN I SHOT YOU ON THE ISLAND!
KRRAASH
WHOA!

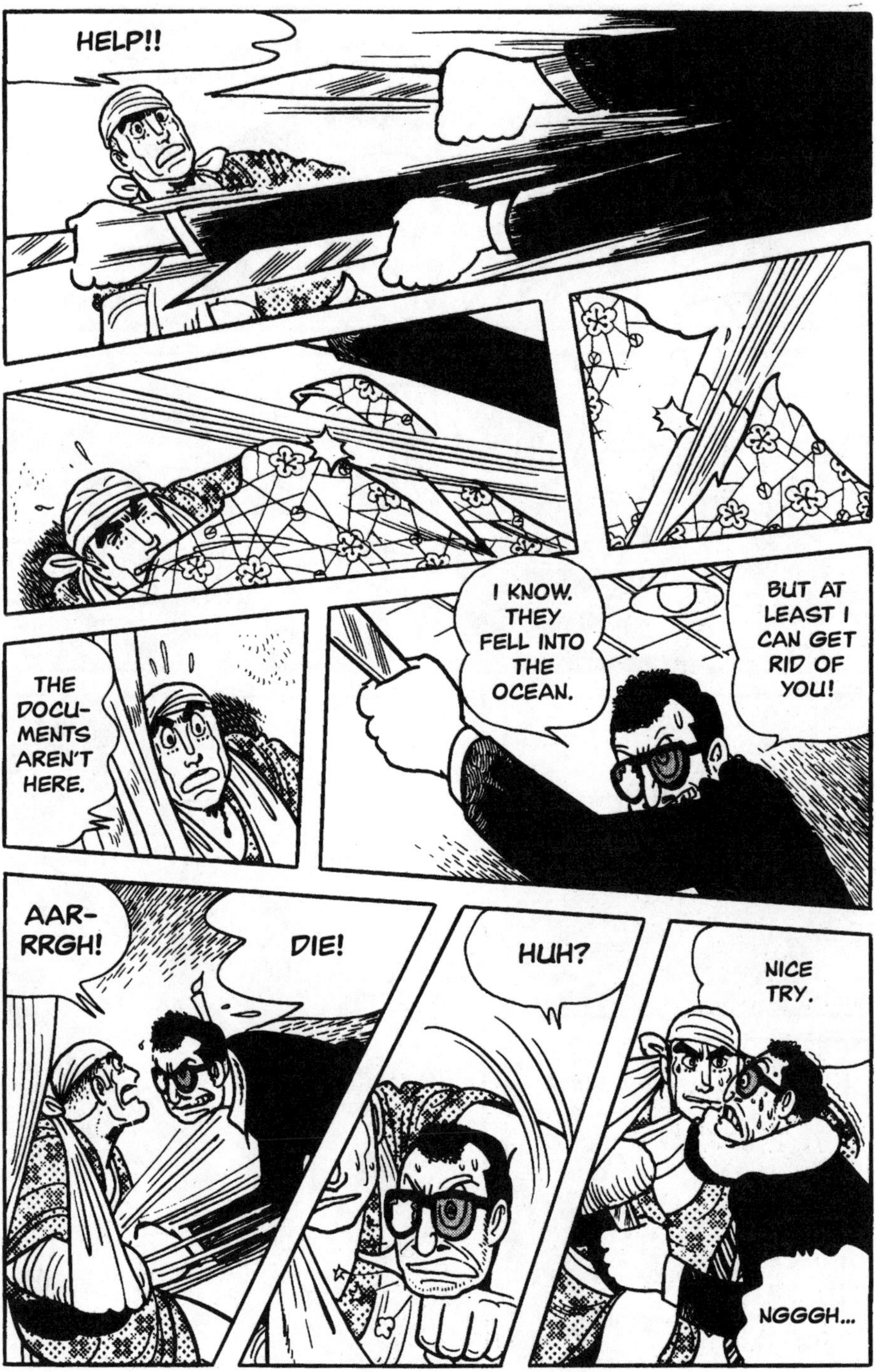
HELP!!
THE DOCU-MENTS AREN'T HERE.
I KNOW. THEY FELL INTO THE OCEAN.
BUT AT LEAST I CAN GET RID OF YOU!
AAR-RRGH!
DIE!
HUH?
NICE TRY.
NGGGH...

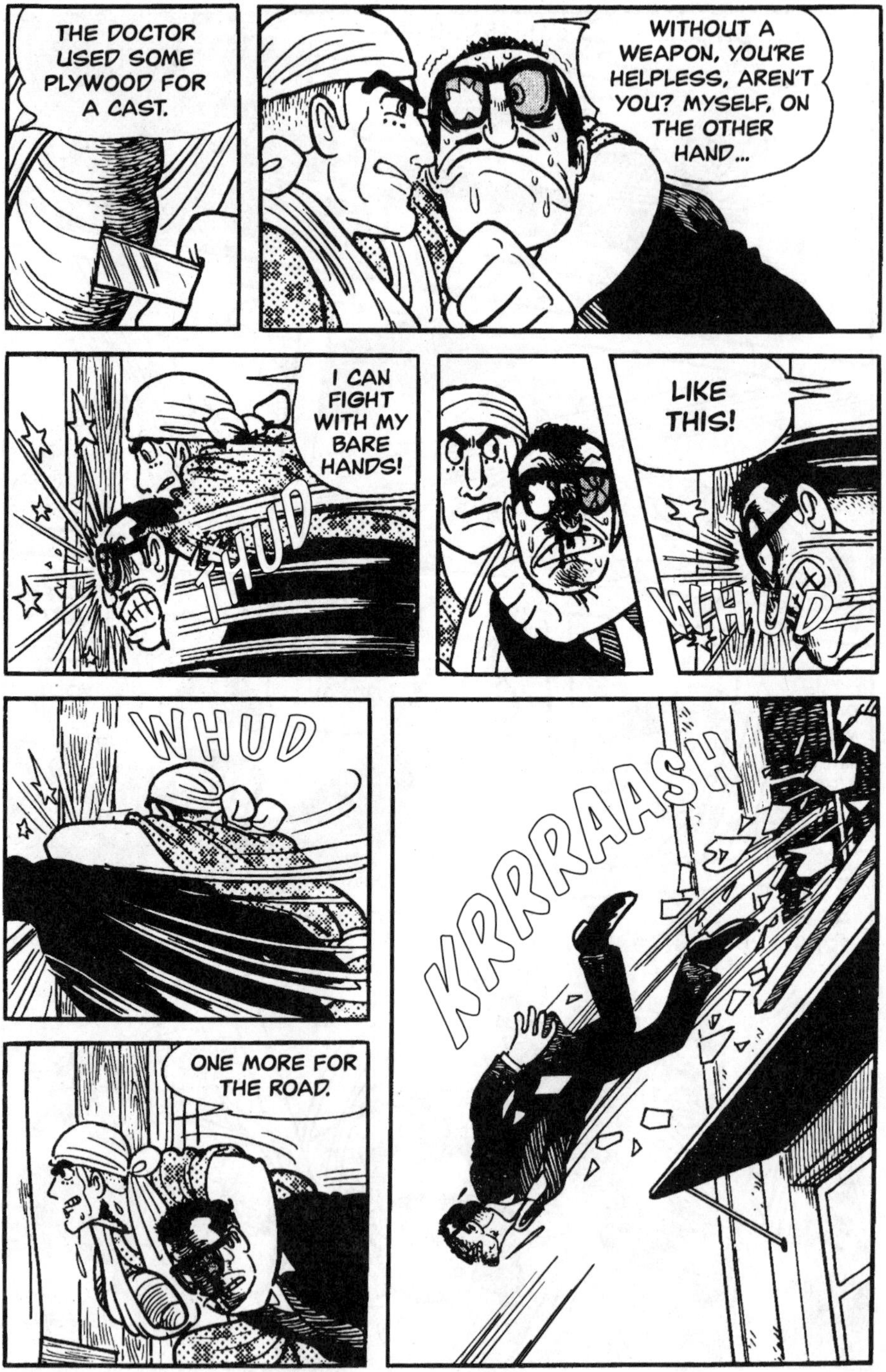
THE DOCTOR USED SOME PLYWOOD FOR A CAST.
WITHOUT A WEAPON, YOU'RE HELPLESS, AREN'T YOU? MYSELF, ON THE OTHER HAND...
I CAN FIGHT WITH MY BARE HANDS!
THUD
LIKE THIS!
WHUD
WHUD
ONE MORE FOR THE ROAD.
KRRRAASH

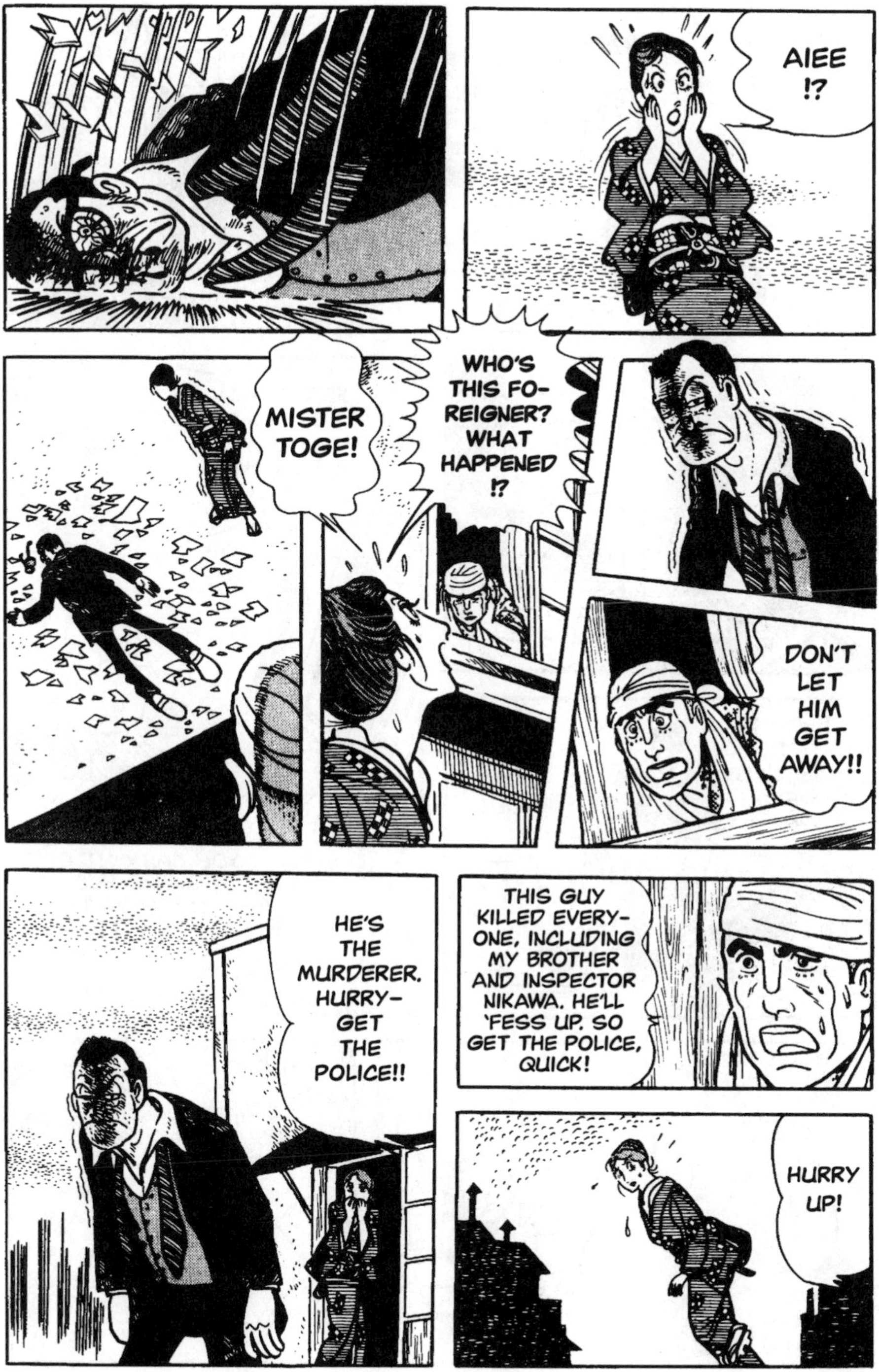
AIEE !?
MISTER TOGE!
WHO'S THIS FO-REIGNER? WHAT HAPPENED !?
DON'T LET HIM GET AWAY!!
HE'S THE MURDERER. HURRY-GET THE POLICE!!
THIS GUY KILLED EVERY-ONE, INCLUDING MY BROTHER AND INSPECTOR NIKAWA. HE'LL 'FESS UP. SO GET THE POLICE, QUICK!
HURRY UP!

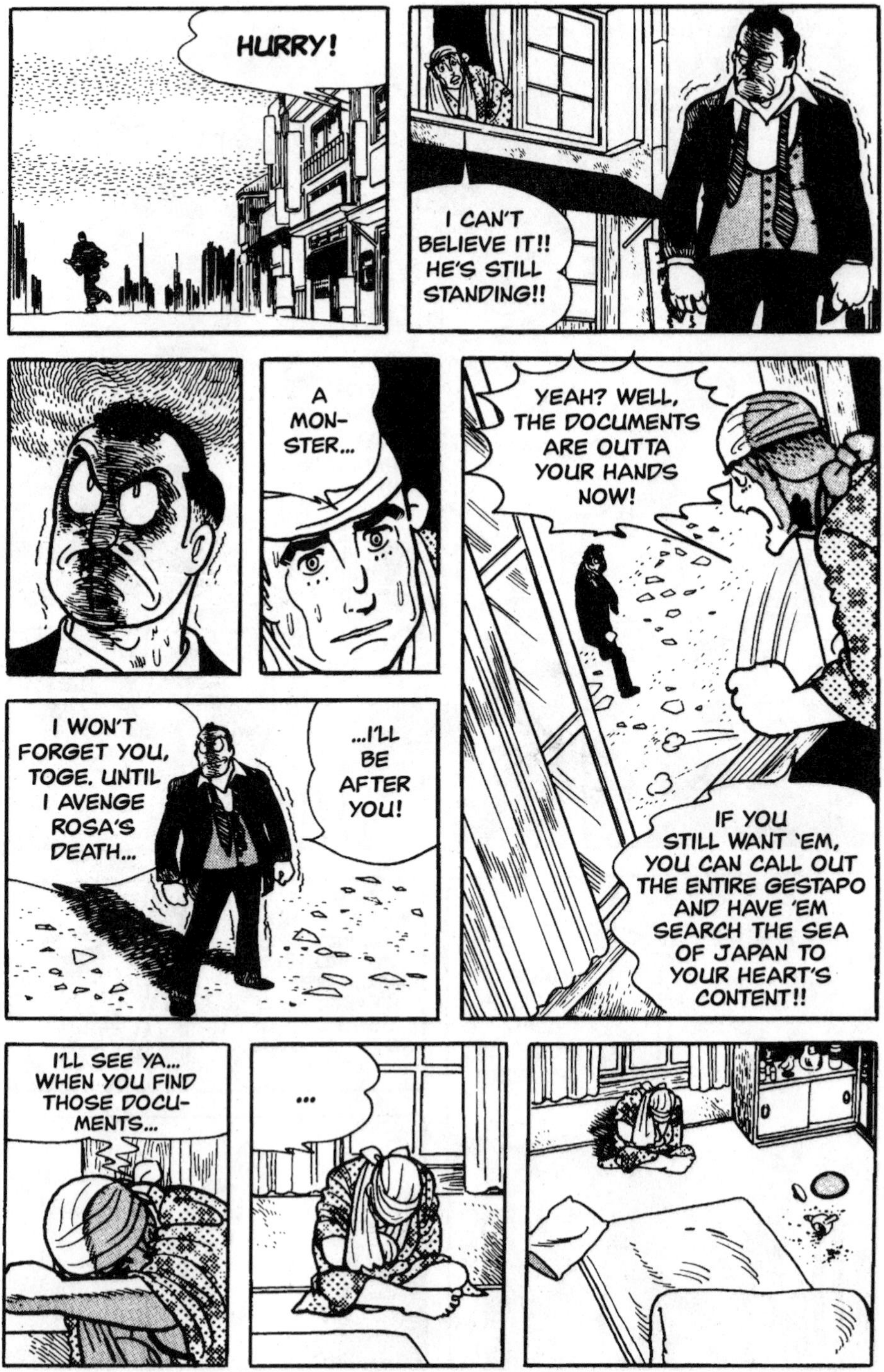
HURRY!
I CAN'T BELIEVE IT!! HE'S STILL STANDING!!
A MON-STER...
I WON'T FORGET YOU, TOGE. UNTIL I AVENGE ROSA'S DEATH...
...I'LL BE AFTER YOU!
YEAH? WELL, THE DOCUMENTS ARE OUTTA YOUR HANDS NOW!
IF YOU STILL WANT 'EM, YOU CAN CALL OUT THE ENTIRE GESTAPO AND HAVE 'EM SEARCH THE SEA OF JAPAN TO YOUR HEART'S CONTENT!!
I'LL SEE YA... WHEN YOU FIND THOSE DOCU-MENTS...
...

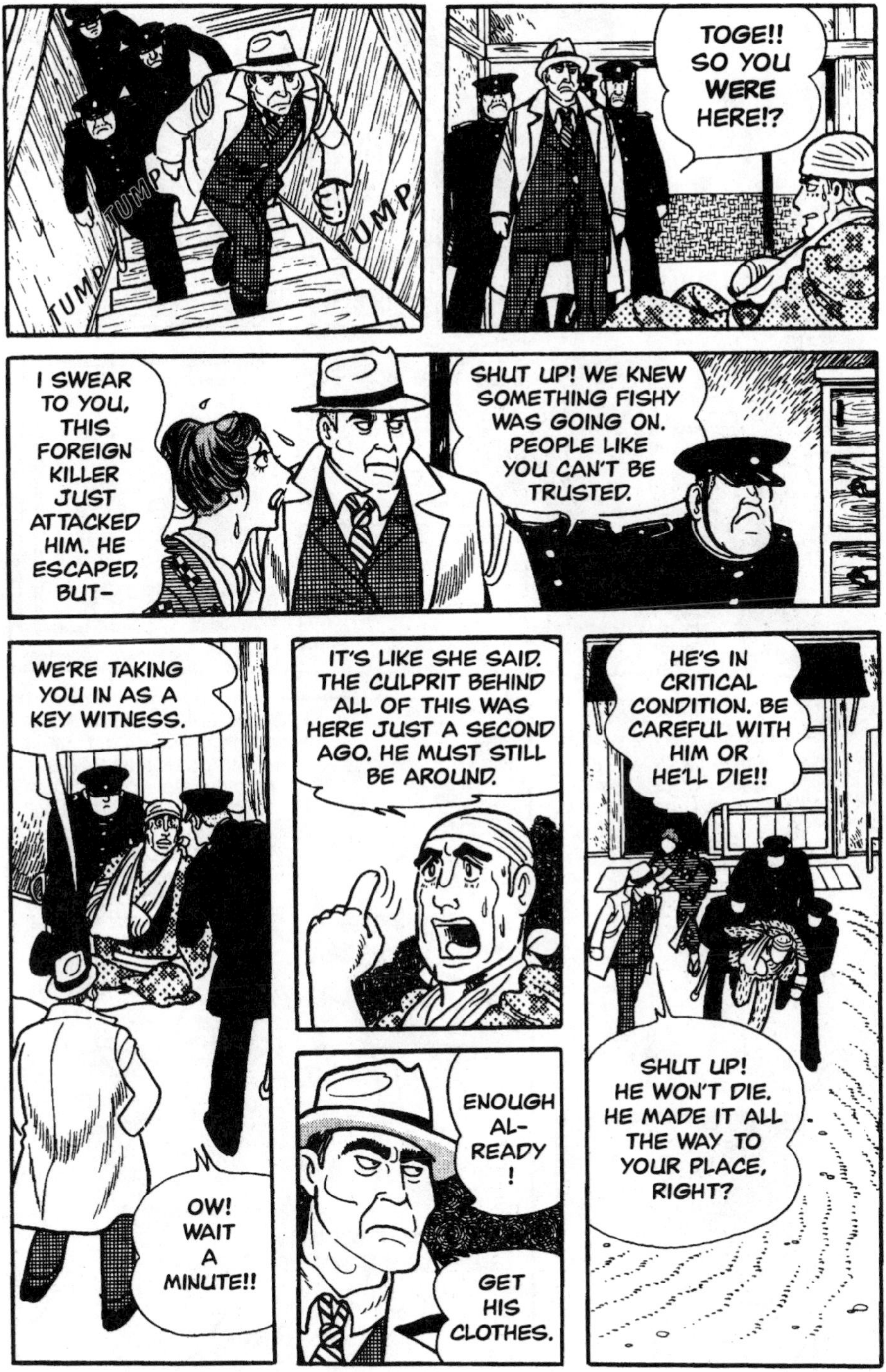
TUMP
TUMP
TUMP
TUMP
TOGE!! SO YOU WERE HERE!?
I SWEAR TO YOU, THIS FOREIGN KILLER JUST ATTACKED HIM. HE ESCAPED, BUT-
SHUT UP! WE KNEW SOMETHING FISHY WAS GOING ON. PEOPLE LIKE YOU CAN'T BE TRUSTED.
WE'RE TAKING YOU IN AS A KEY WITNESS.
OW! WAIT A MINUTE!!
IT'S LIKE SHE SAID. THE CULPRIT BEHIND ALL OF THIS WAS HERE JUST A SECOND AGO. HE MUST STILL BE AROUND.
ENOUGH AL-READY!
GET HIS CLOTHES.
HE'S IN CRITICAL CONDITION. BE CAREFUL WITH HIM OR HE'LL DIE!!
SHUT UP! HE WON'T DIE. HE MADE IT ALL THE WAY TO YOUR PLACE, RIGHT?

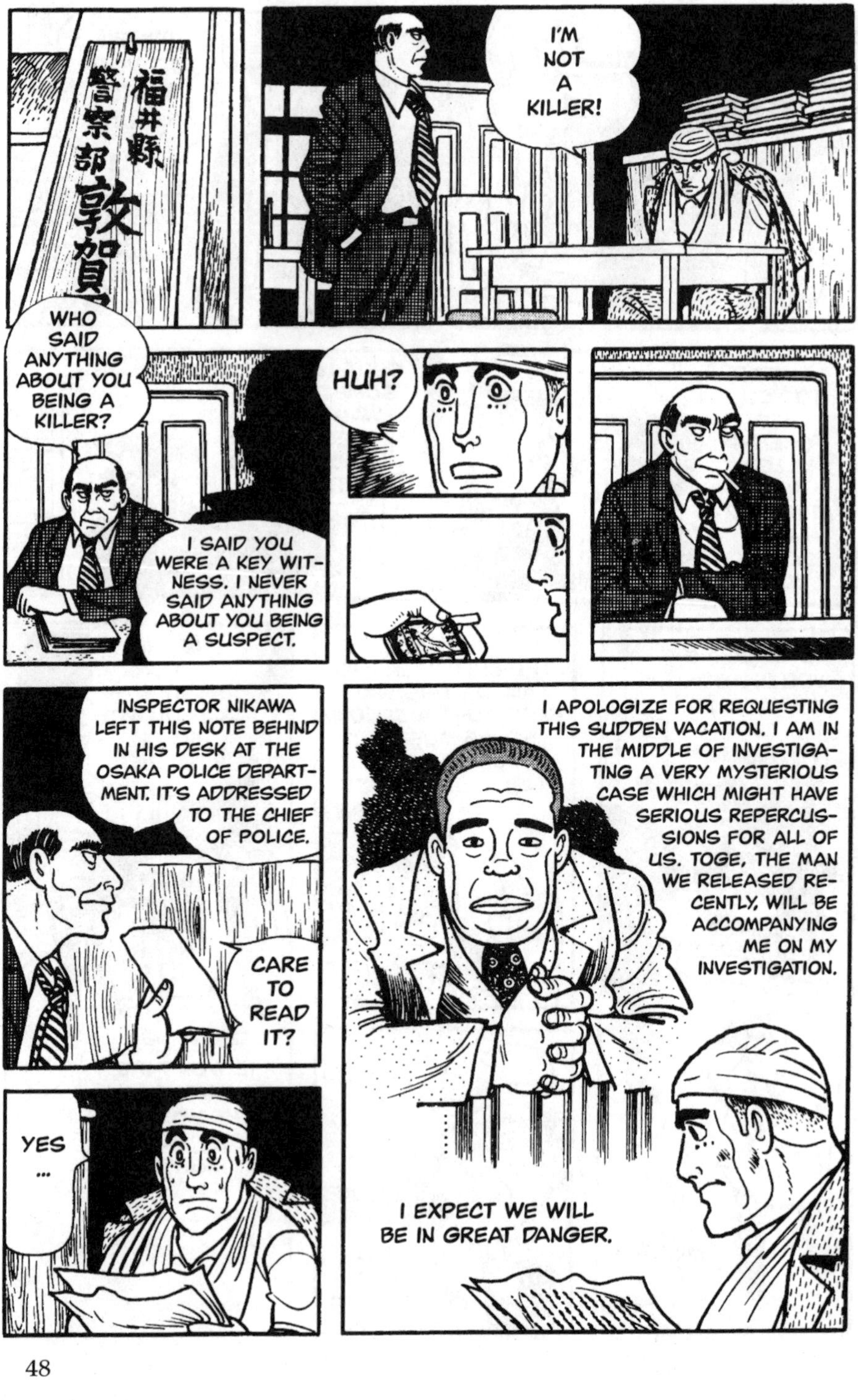
福井縣
警察部
敦賀
I'M NOT A KILLER!
WHO SAID ANYTHING ABOUT YOU BEING A KILLER?
I SAID YOU WERE A KEY WITNESS. I NEVER SAID ANYTHING ABOUT YOU BEING A SUSPECT.
HUH?
INSPECTOR NIKAWA LEFT THIS NOTE BEHIND IN HIS DESK AT THE OSAKA POLICE DEPARTMENT. IT'S ADDRESSED TO THE CHIEF OF POLICE.
CARE TO READ IT?
YES ...
I APOLOGIZE FOR REQUESTING THIS SUDDEN VACATION. I AM IN THE MIDDLE OF INVESTIGATING A VERY MYSTERIOUS CASE WHICH MIGHT HAVE SERIOUS REPERCUSSIONS FOR ALL OF US. TOGE, THE MAN WE RELEASED RECENTLY, WILL BE ACCOMPANYING ME ON MY INVESTIGATION.
I EXPECT WE WILL BE IN GREAT DANGER.

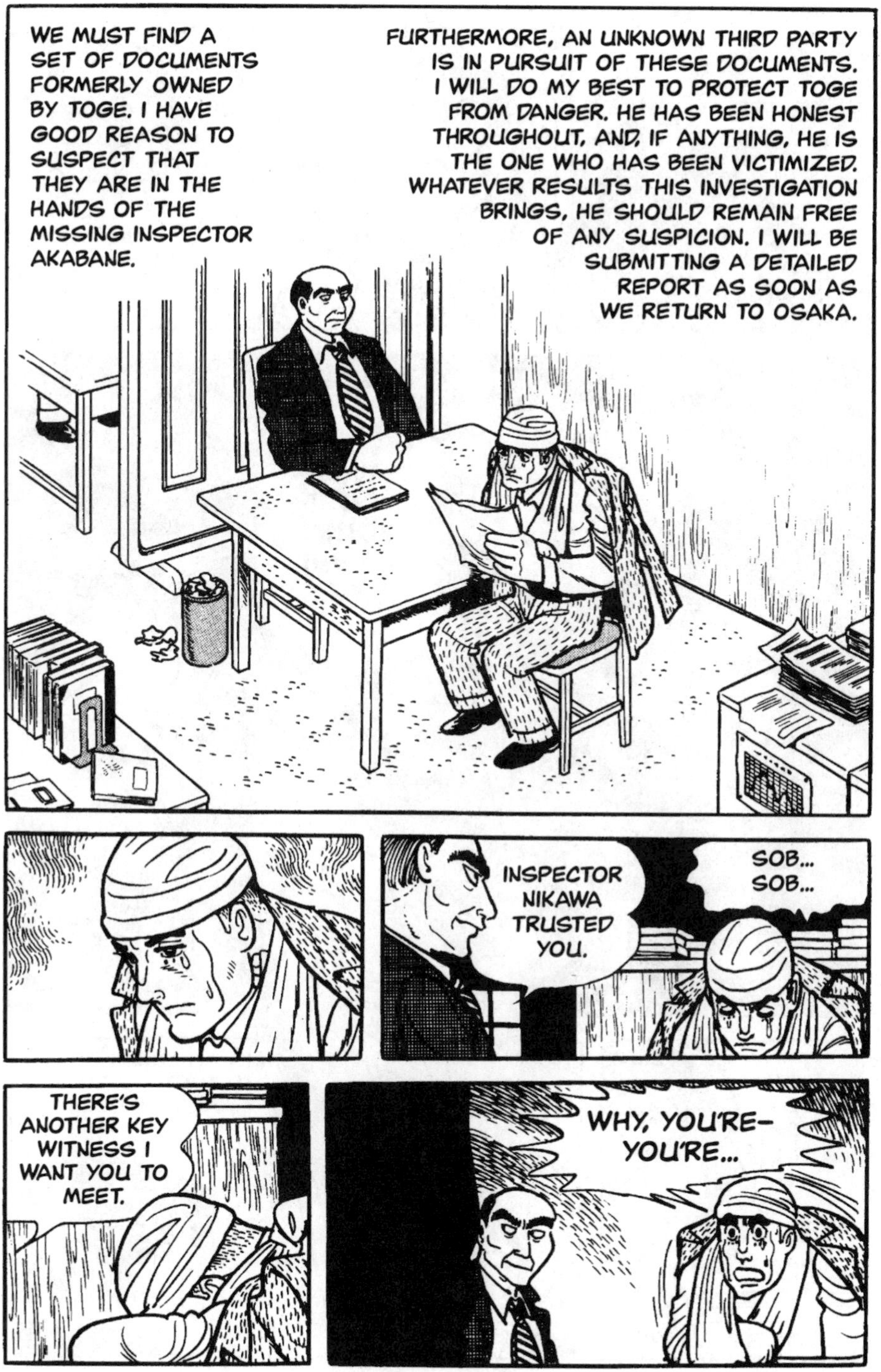
WE MUST FIND A SET OF DOCUMENTS FORMERLY OWNED BY TOGE. I HAVE GOOD REASON TO SUSPECT THAT THEY ARE IN THE HANDS OF THE MISSING INSPECTOR AKABANE.
FURTHERMORE, AN UNKNOWN THIRD PARTY IS IN PURSUIT OF THESE DOCUMENTS. I WILL DO MY BEST TO PROTECT TOGE FROM DANGER. HE HAS BEEN HONEST THROUGHOUT, AND, IF ANYTHING, HE IS THE ONE WHO HAS BEEN VICTIMIZED. WHATEVER RESULTS THIS INVESTIGATION BRINGS, HE SHOULD REMAIN FREE OF ANY SUSPICION. I WILL BE SUBMITTING A DETAILED REPORT AS SOON AS WE RETURN TO OSAKA.
INSPECTOR NIKAWA TRUSTED YOU.
SOB... SOB...
THERE'S ANOTHER KEY WITNESS I WANT YOU TO MEET.
WHY, YOU'RE- YOU'RE...

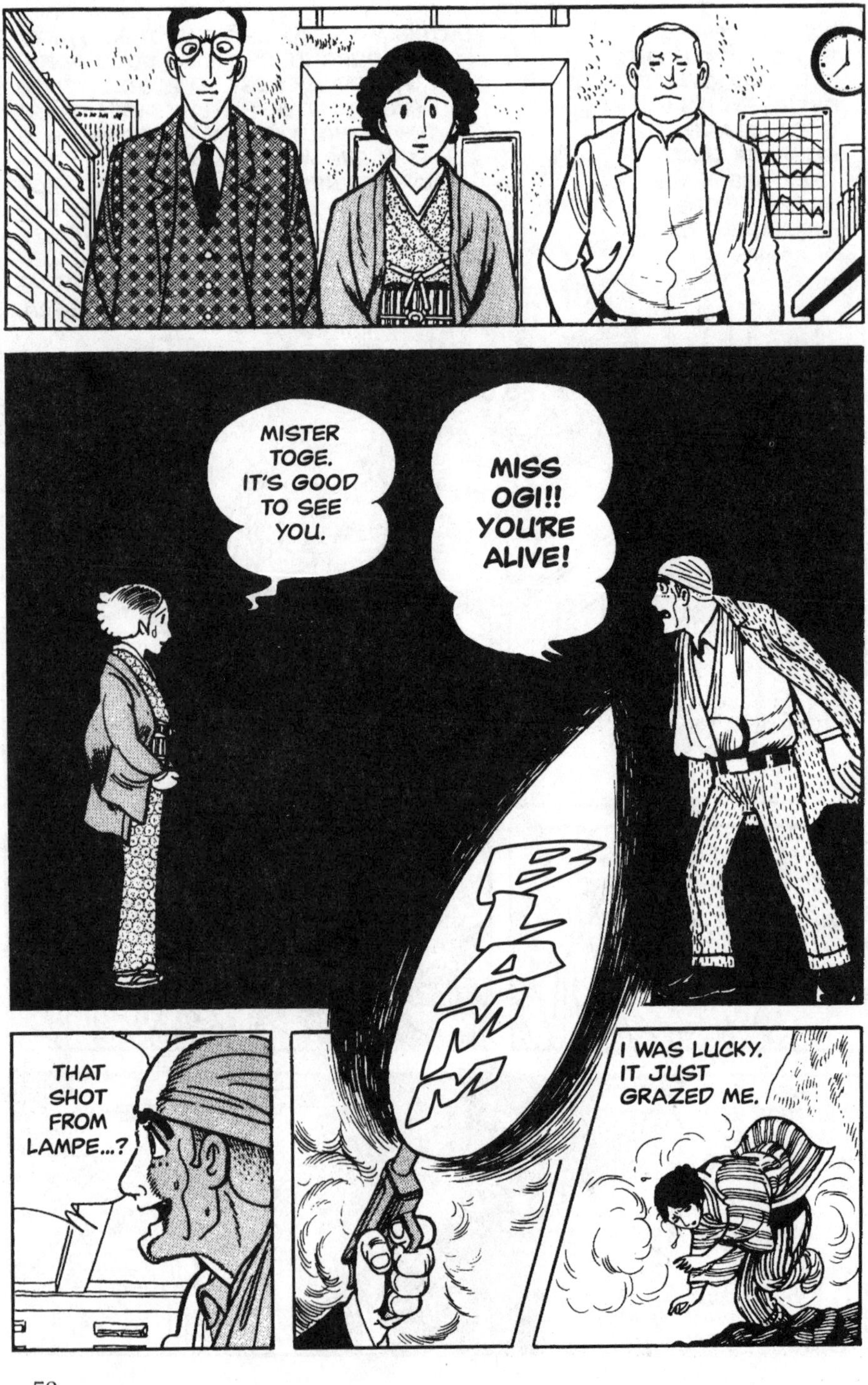
MISTER TOGE. IT'S GOOD TO SEE YOU.
MISS OGI!! YOU'RE ALIVE!
BLAMM
THAT SHOT FROM LAMPE...?
I WAS LUCKY. IT JUST GRAZED ME.

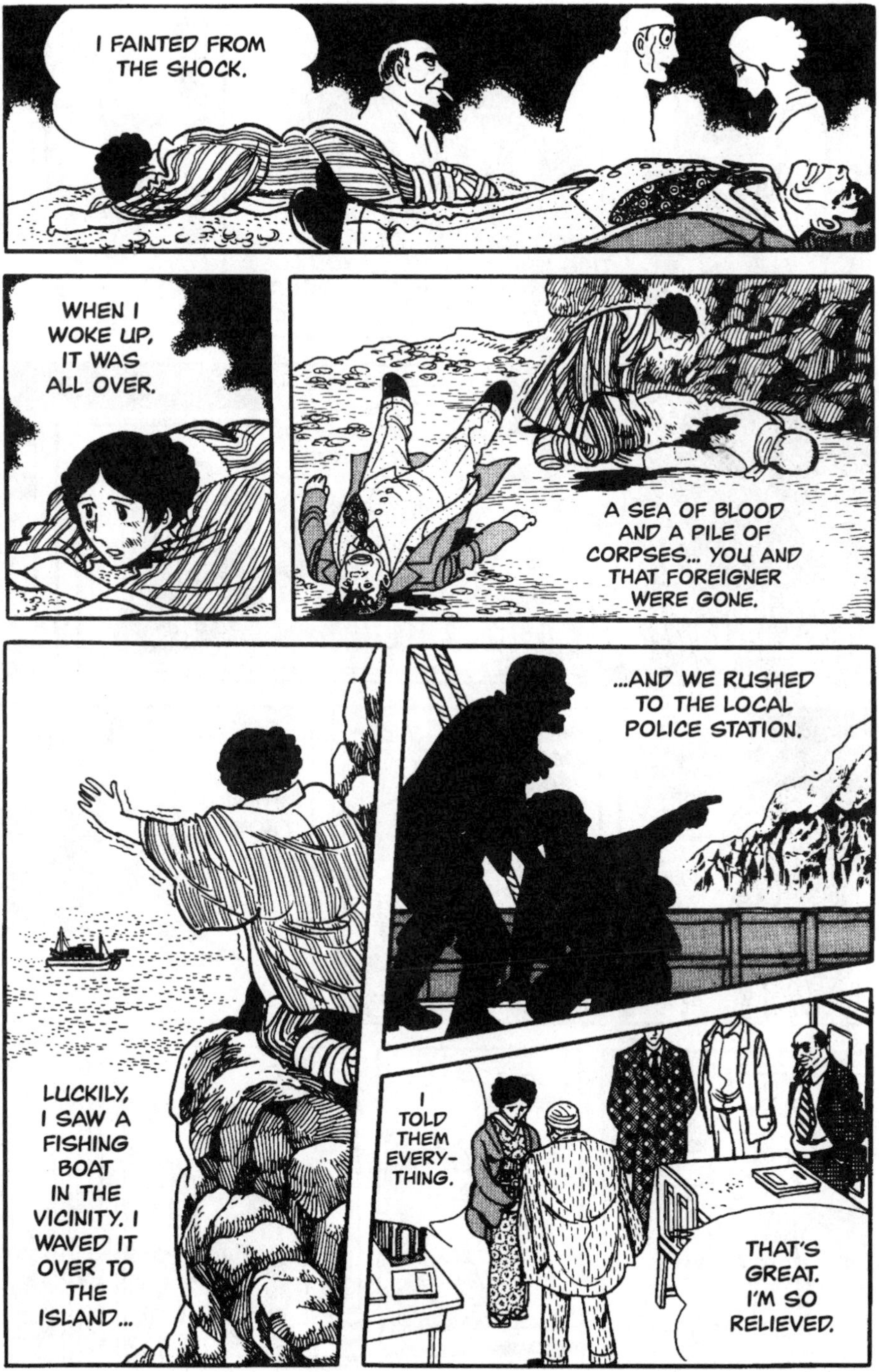
I FAINTED FROM THE SHOCK.
WHEN I WOKE UP, IT WAS ALL OVER.
A SEA OF BLOOD AND A PILE OF CORPSES... YOU AND THAT FOREIGNER WERE GONE.
LUCKILY, I SAW A FISHING BOAT IN THE VICINITY. I WAVED IT OVER TO THE ISLAND...
...AND WE RUSHED TO THE LOCAL POLICE STATION.
I TOLD THEM EVERY-THING.
THAT'S GREAT. I'M SO RELIEVED.

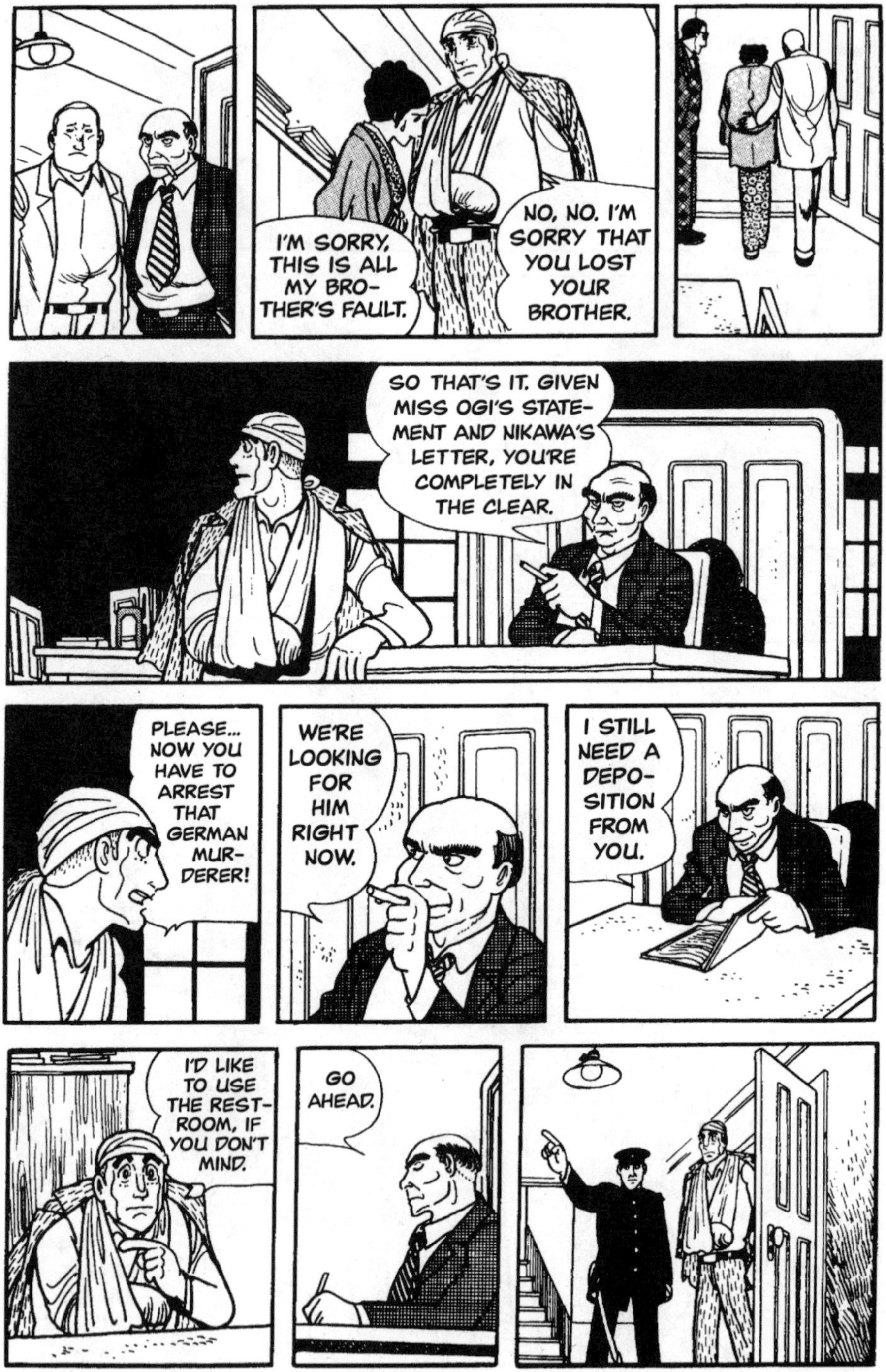
I'M SORRY, THIS IS ALL MY BROTHER'S FAULT.
NO, NO. I'M SORRY THAT YOU LOST YOUR BROTHER.
SO THAT'S IT. GIVEN MISS OGI'S STATEMENT AND NIKAWA'S LETTER, YOU'RE COMPLETELY IN THE CLEAR.
PLEASE... NOW YOU HAVE TO ARREST THAT GERMAN MURDERER!
WE'RE LOOKING FOR HIM RIGHT NOW.
I STILL NEED A DEPOSITION FROM YOU.
I'D LIKE TO USE THE RESTROOM, IF YOU DON'T MIND.
GO AHEAD.

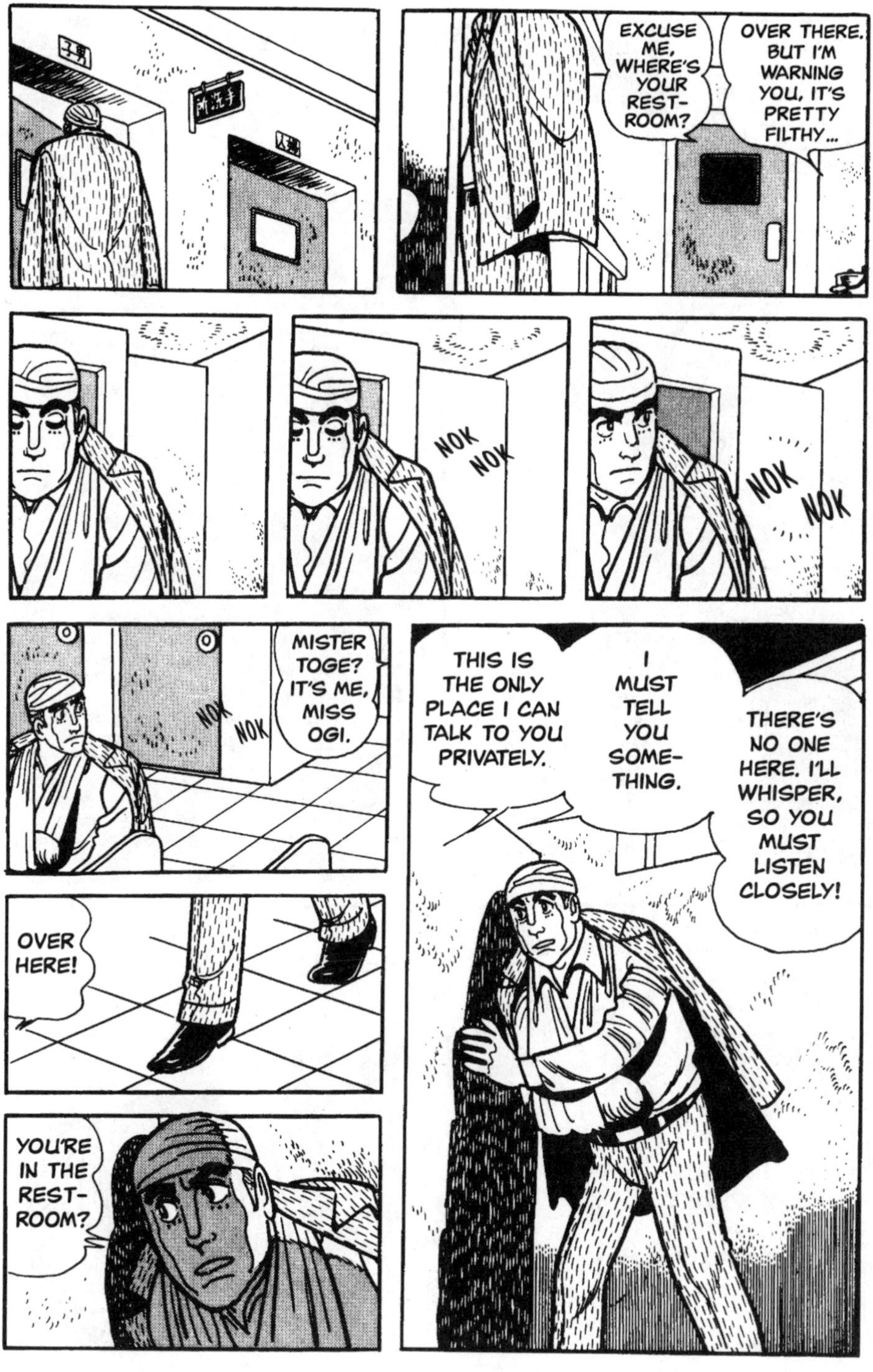
EXCUSE ME, WHERE'S YOUR REST-ROOM?
OVER THERE. BUT I'M WARNING YOU, IT'S PRETTY FILTHY...
NOK NOK
NOK NOK
NOK NOK
MISTER TOGE? IT'S ME, MISS OGI.
OVER HERE!
YOU'RE IN THE REST-ROOM?
THIS IS THE ONLY PLACE I CAN TALK TO YOU PRIVATELY.
I MUST TELL YOU SOME-THING.
THERE'S NO ONE HERE. I'LL WHISPER, SO YOU MUST LISTEN CLOSELY!

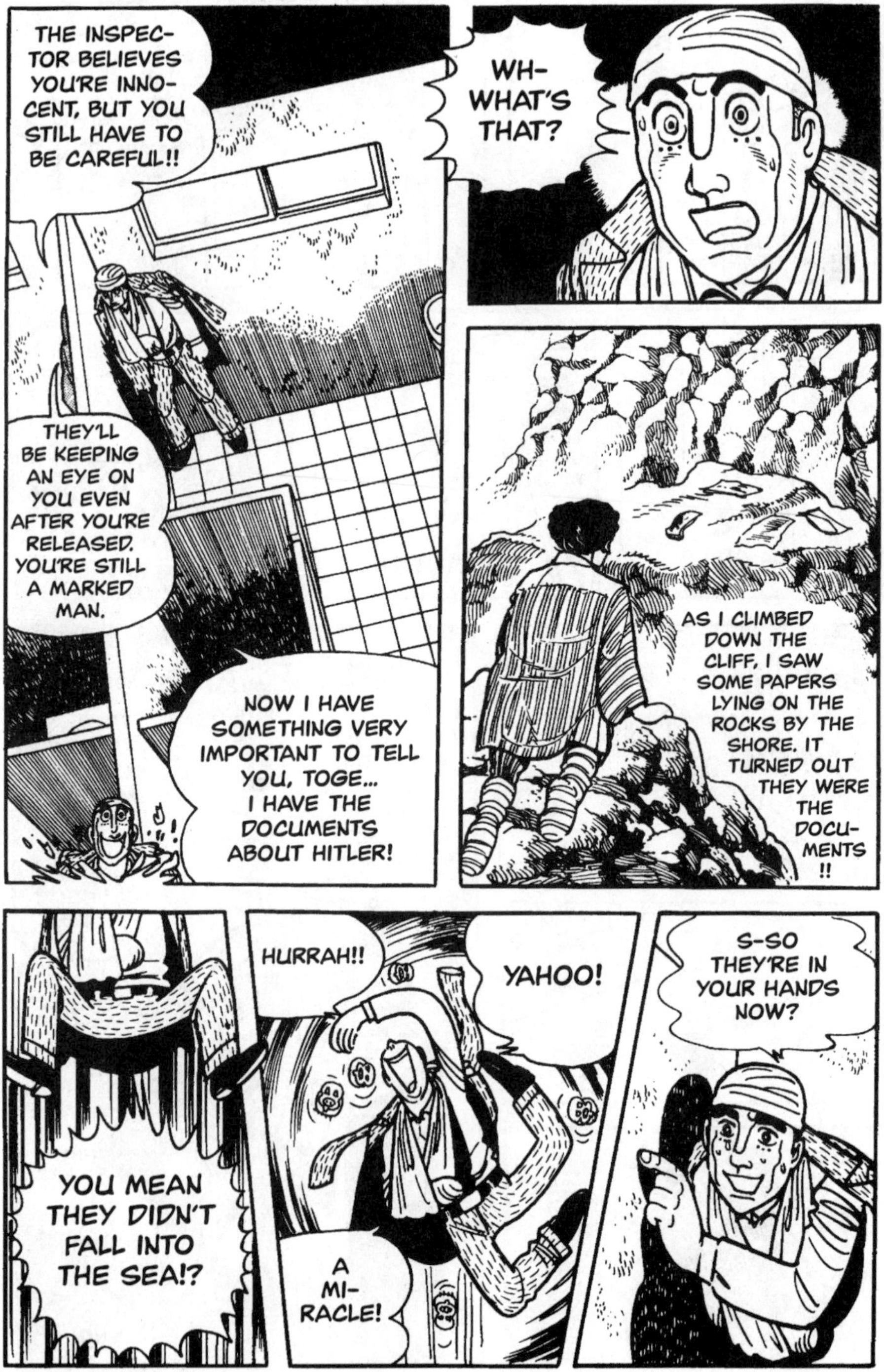
THE INSPECTOR BELIEVES YOU'RE INNOCENT, BUT YOU STILL HAVE TO BE CAREFUL!!
THEY'LL BE KEEPING AN EYE ON YOU EVEN AFTER YOU'RE RELEASED. YOU'RE STILL A MARKED MAN.
NOW I HAVE SOMETHING VERY IMPORTANT TO TELL YOU, TOGE... I HAVE THE DOCUMENTS ABOUT HITLER!
WH-WHAT'S THAT?
AS I CLIMBED DOWN THE CLIFF, I SAW SOME PAPERS LYING ON THE ROCKS BY THE SHORE. IT TURNED OUT THEY WERE THE DOCUMENTS!!
YOU MEAN THEY DIDN'T FALL INTO THE SEA!?
HURRAH!!
YAHOO!
A MIRACLE!
S-SO THEY'RE IN YOUR HANDS NOW?

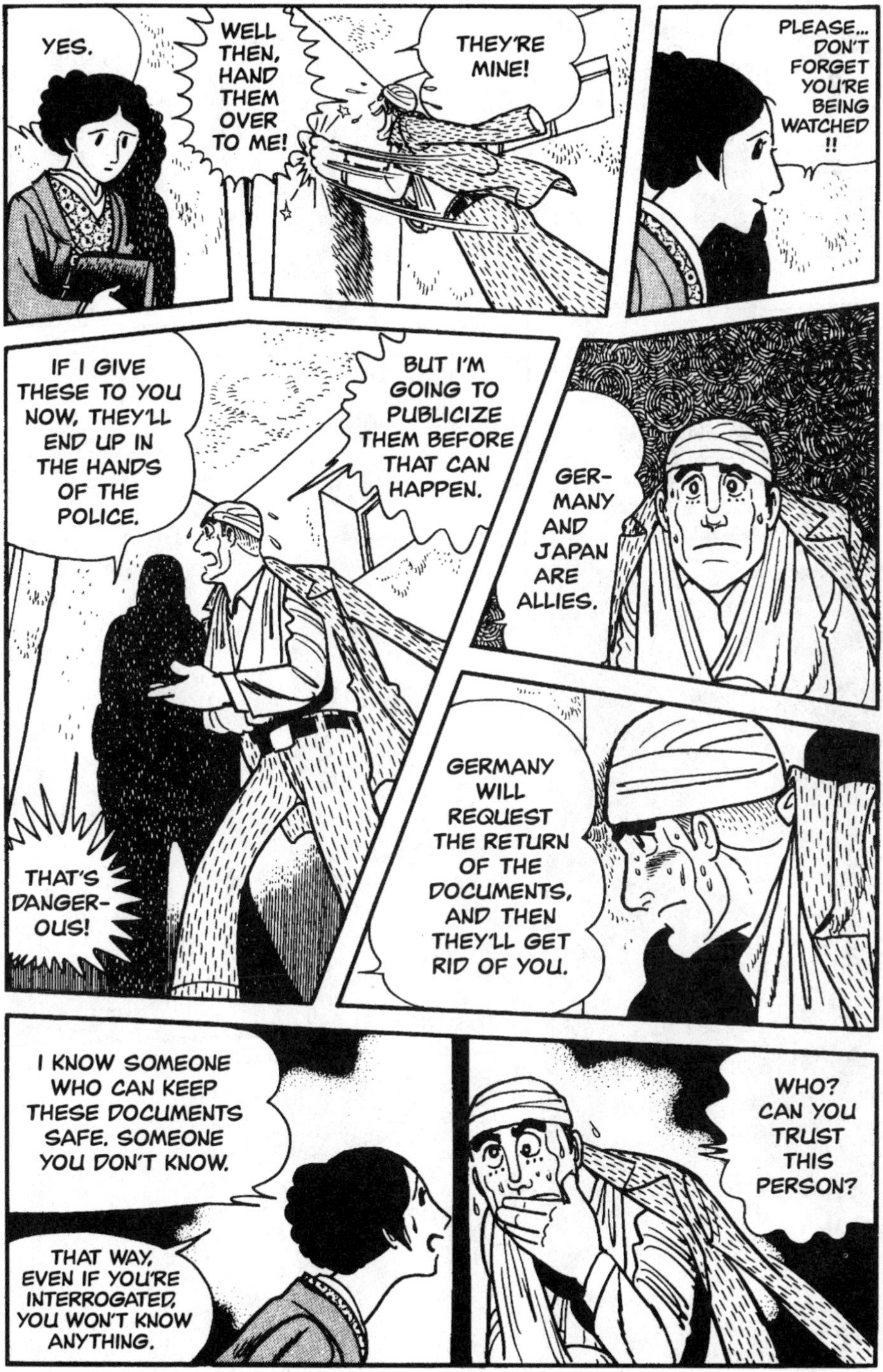
YES.
WELL THEN, HAND THEM OVER TO ME!
THEY'RE MINE!
PLEASE... DON'T FORGET YOU'RE BEING WATCHED !!
IF I GIVE THESE TO YOU NOW, THEY'LL END UP IN THE HANDS OF THE POLICE.
BUT I'M GOING TO PUBLICIZE THEM BEFORE THAT CAN HAPPEN.
THAT'S DANGER-OUS!
GER-MANY AND JAPAN ARE ALLIES.
GERMANY WILL REQUEST THE RETURN OF THE DOCUMENTS, AND THEN THEY'LL GET RID OF YOU.
I KNOW SOMEONE WHO CAN KEEP THESE DOCUMENTS SAFE. SOMEONE YOU DON'T KNOW.
THAT WAY, EVEN IF YOU'RE INTERROGATED, YOU WON'T KNOW ANYTHING.
WHO? CAN YOU TRUST THIS PERSON?

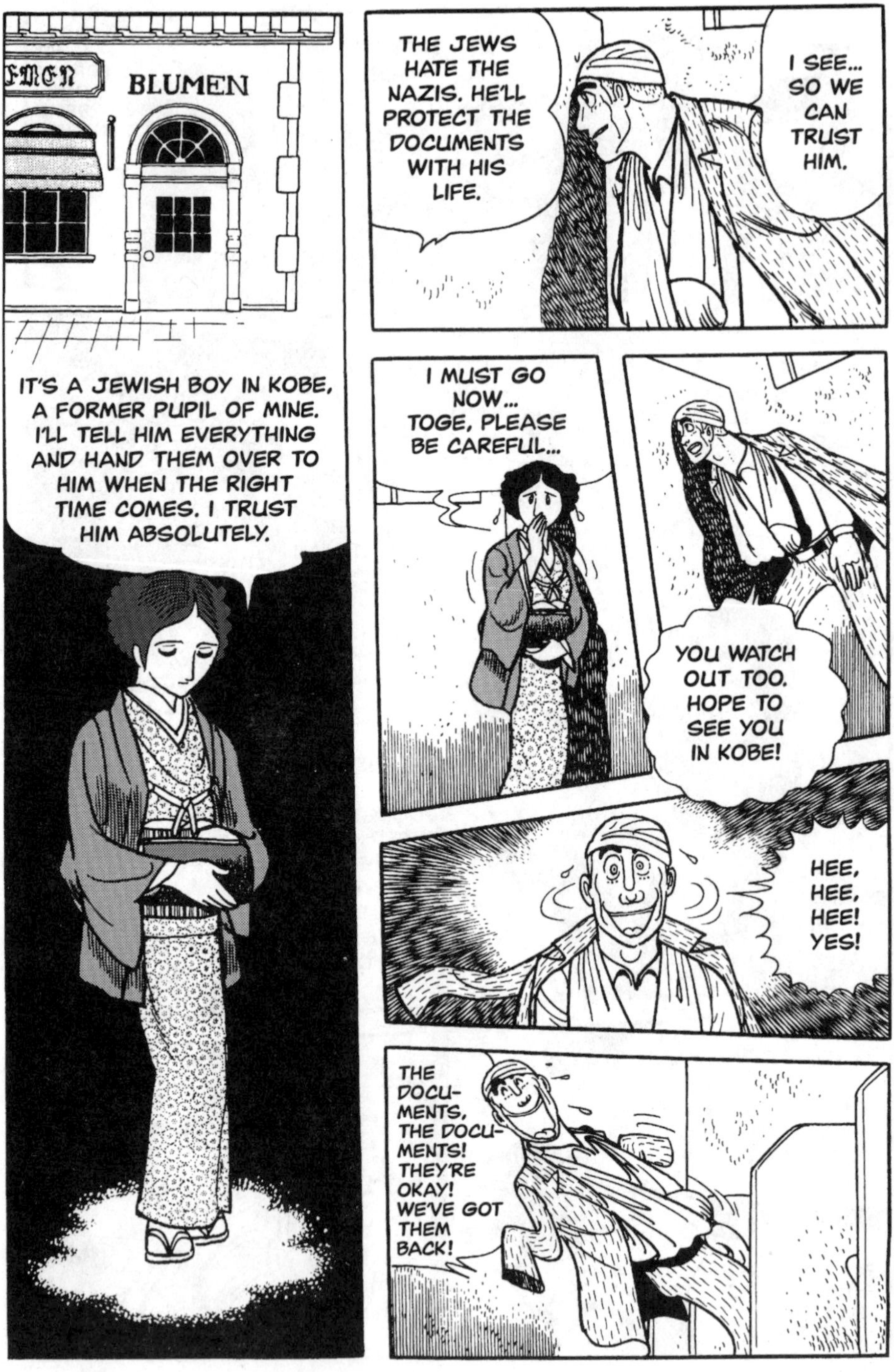
BLUMEN
IT'S A JEWISH BOY IN KOBE, A FORMER PUPIL OF MINE. I'LL TELL HIM EVERYTHING AND HAND THEM OVER TO HIM WHEN THE RIGHT TIME COMES. I TRUST HIM ABSOLUTELY.
THE JEWS HATE THE NAZIS. HE'LL PROTECT THE DOCUMENTS WITH HIS LIFE.
I SEE... SO WE CAN TRUST HIM.
I MUST GO NOW... TOGE, PLEASE BE CAREFUL...
YOU WATCH OUT TOO. HOPE TO SEE YOU IN KOBE!
HEE, HEE, HEE! YES!
THE DOCU-MENTS, THE DOCU-MENTS! THEY'RE OKAY! WE'VE GOT THEM BACK!

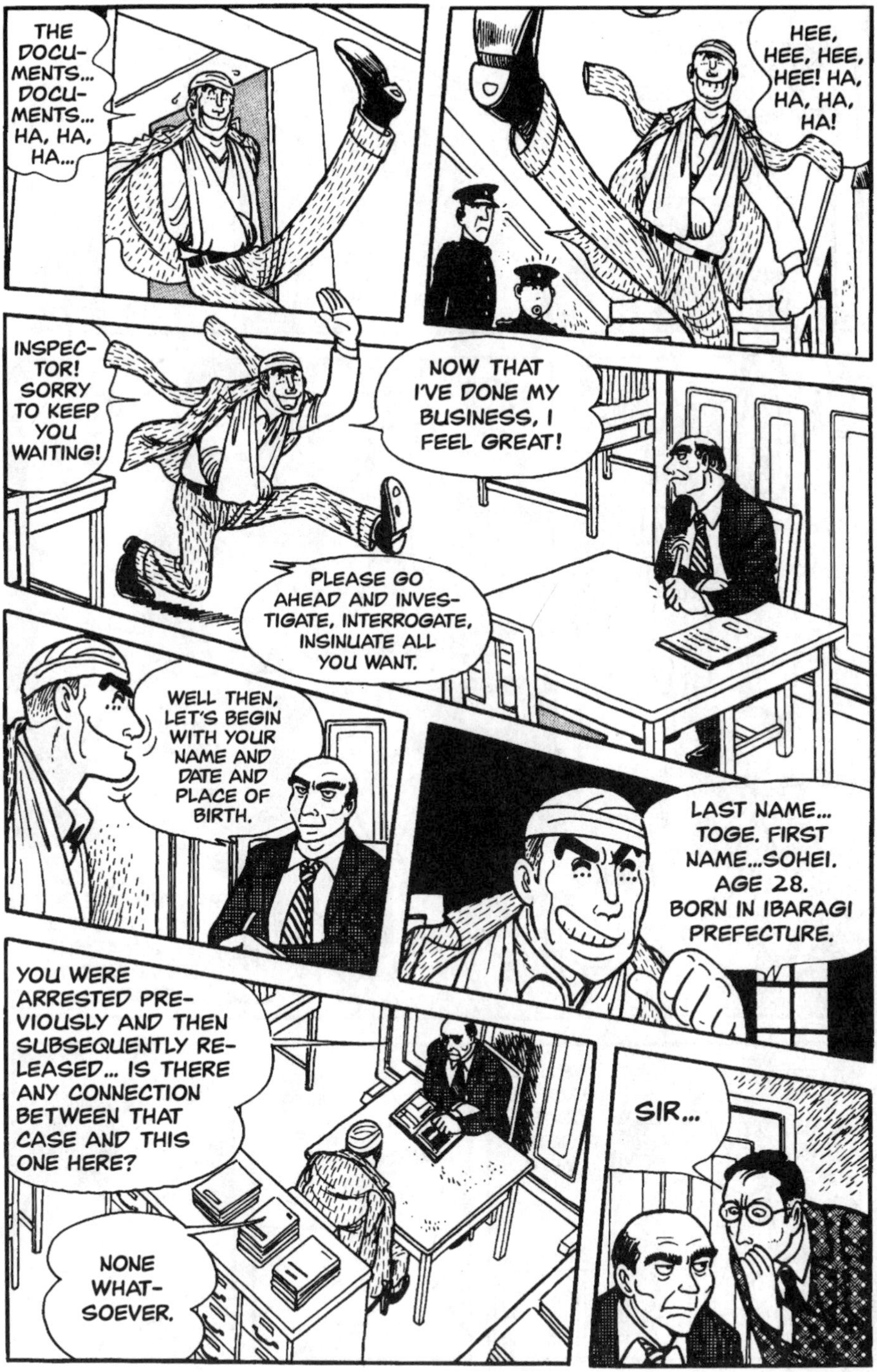
THE DOCUMENTS... DOCUMENTS... HA, HA, HA...
HEE, HEE, HEE, HEE! HA, HA, HA, HA!
INSPECTOR! SORRY TO KEEP YOU WAITING!
NOW THAT I'VE DONE MY BUSINESS, I FEEL GREAT!
PLEASE GO AHEAD AND INVESTIGATE, INTERROGATE, INSINUATE ALL YOU WANT.
WELL THEN, LET'S BEGIN WITH YOUR NAME AND DATE AND PLACE OF BIRTH.
LAST NAME... TOGE. FIRST NAME...SOHEI. AGE 28. BORN IN IBARAGI PREFECTURE.
YOU WERE ARRESTED PREVIOUSLY AND THEN SUBSEQUENTLY RELEASED... IS THERE ANY CONNECTION BETWEEN THAT CASE AND THIS ONE HERE?
NONE WHATSOEVER.
SIR...

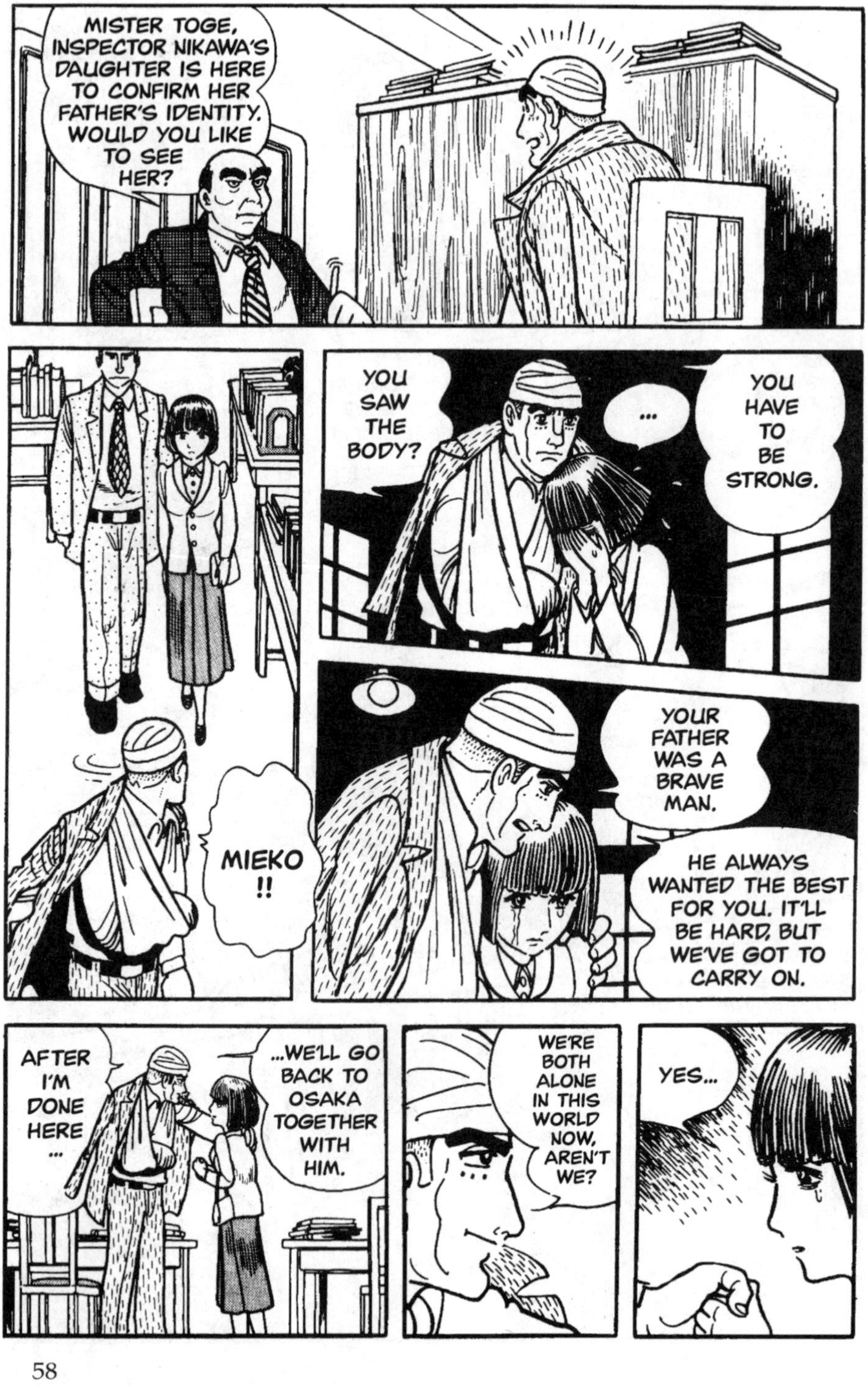
MISTER TOGE, INSPECTOR NIKAWA'S DAUGHTER IS HERE TO CONFIRM HER FATHER'S IDENTITY. WOULD YOU LIKE TO SEE HER?
MIEKO !!
YOU SAW THE BODY?
...
YOU HAVE TO BE STRONG.
YOUR FATHER WAS A BRAVE MAN.
HE ALWAYS WANTED THE BEST FOR YOU. IT'LL BE HARD, BUT WE'VE GOT TO CARRY ON.
AFTER I'M DONE HERE ...
...WE'LL GO BACK TO OSAKA TOGETHER WITH HIM.
WE'RE BOTH ALONE IN THIS WORLD NOW, AREN'T WE?
YES...

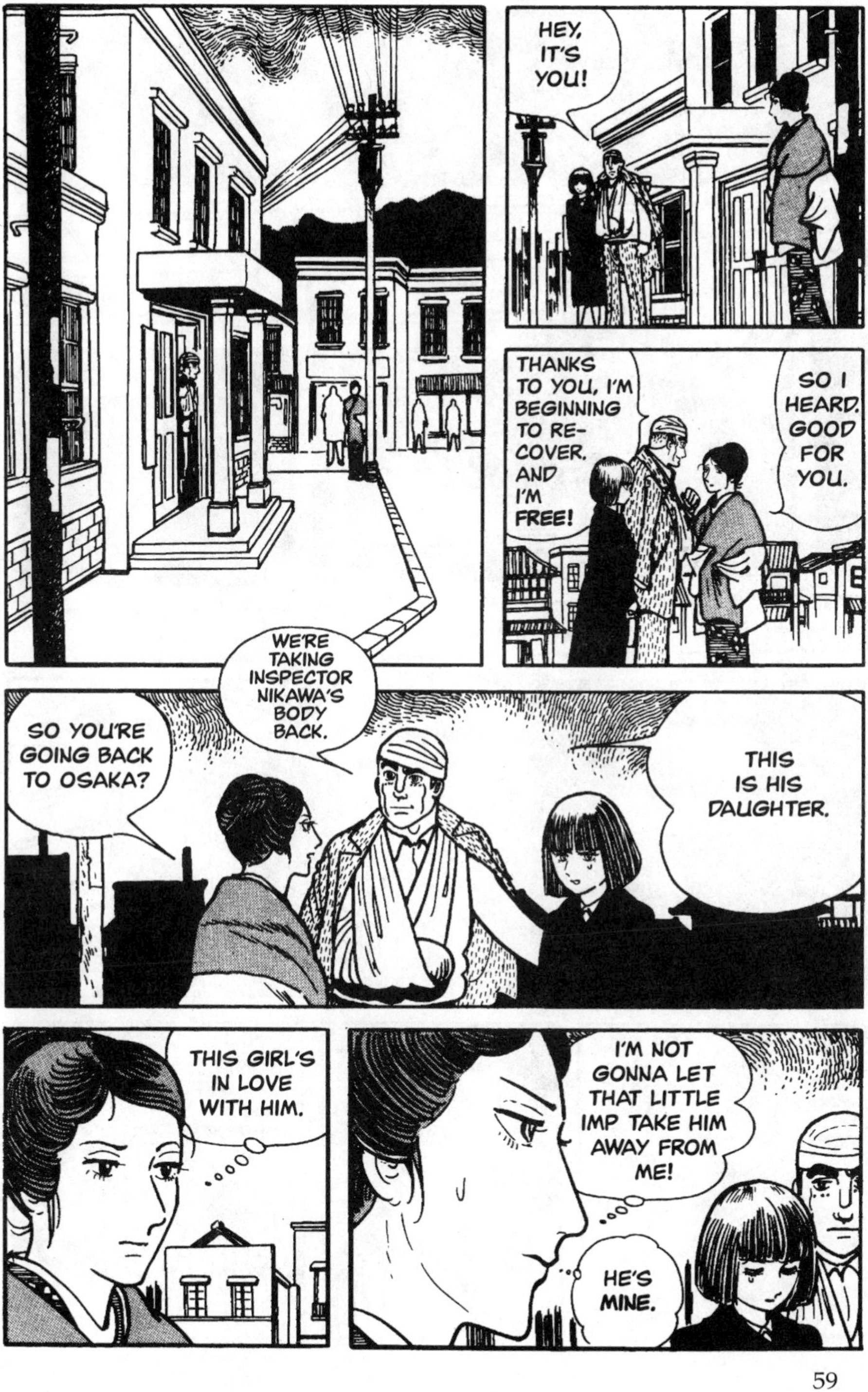
HEY, IT'S YOU!
THANKS TO YOU, I'M BEGINNING TO RE-COVER. AND I'M FREE!
SO I HEARD. GOOD FOR YOU.
SO YOU'RE GOING BACK TO OSAKA?
WE'RE TAKING INSPECTOR NIKAWA'S BODY BACK.
THIS IS HIS DAUGHTER.
THIS GIRL'S IN LOVE WITH HIM.
I'M NOT GONNA LET THAT LITTLE IMP TAKE HIM AWAY FROM ME!
HE'S MINE.

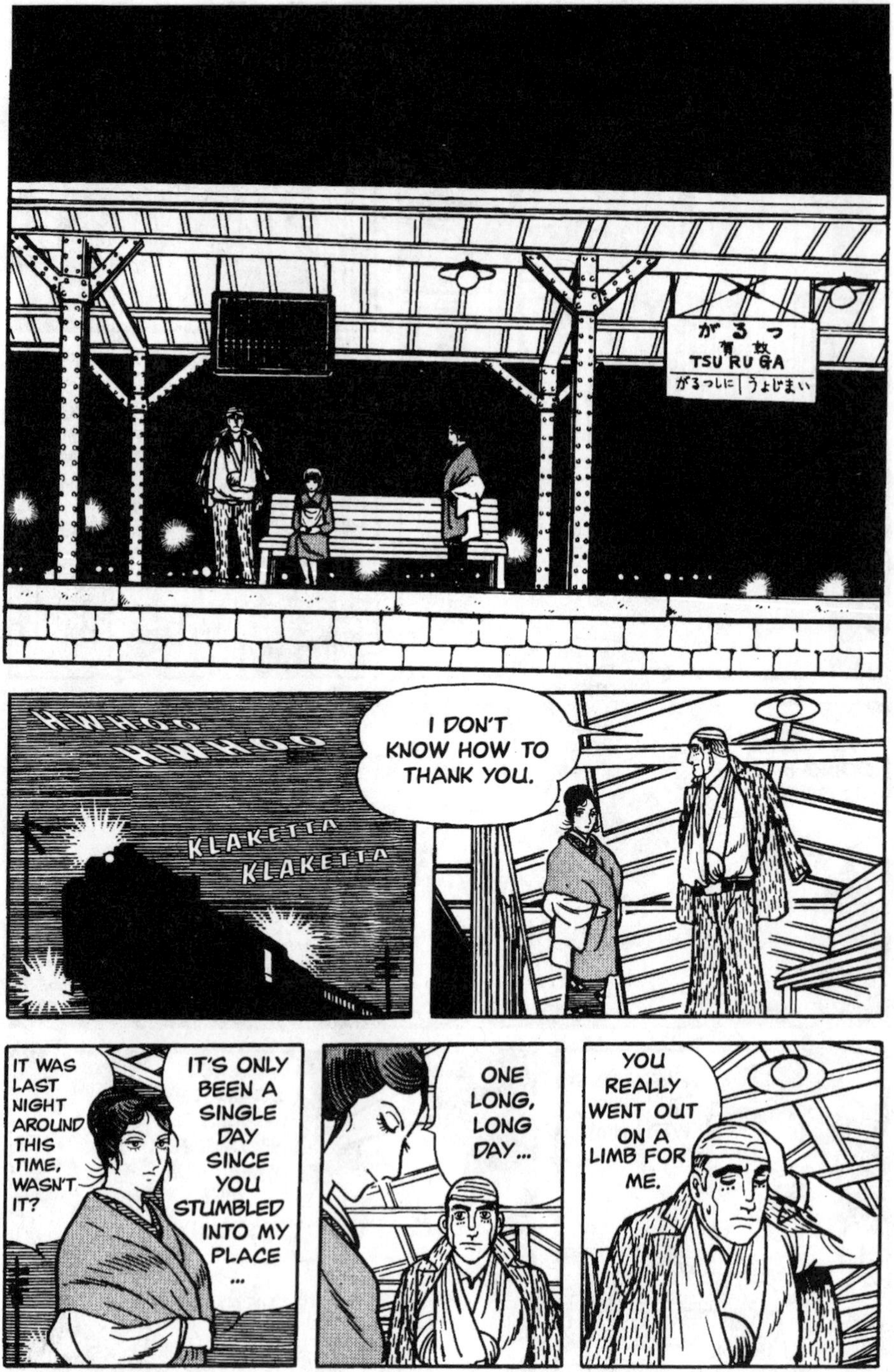
がるつ
賀敦
TSU RU GA
がるつしに | うょじまい
HWHOO HWHOO
KLAKETTA KLAKETTA
I DON'T KNOW HOW TO THANK YOU.
IT WAS LAST NIGHT AROUND THIS TIME, WASN'T IT?
IT'S ONLY BEEN A SINGLE DAY SINCE YOU STUMBLED INTO MY PLACE ...
ONE LONG, LONG DAY...
YOU REALLY WENT OUT ON A LIMB FOR ME.

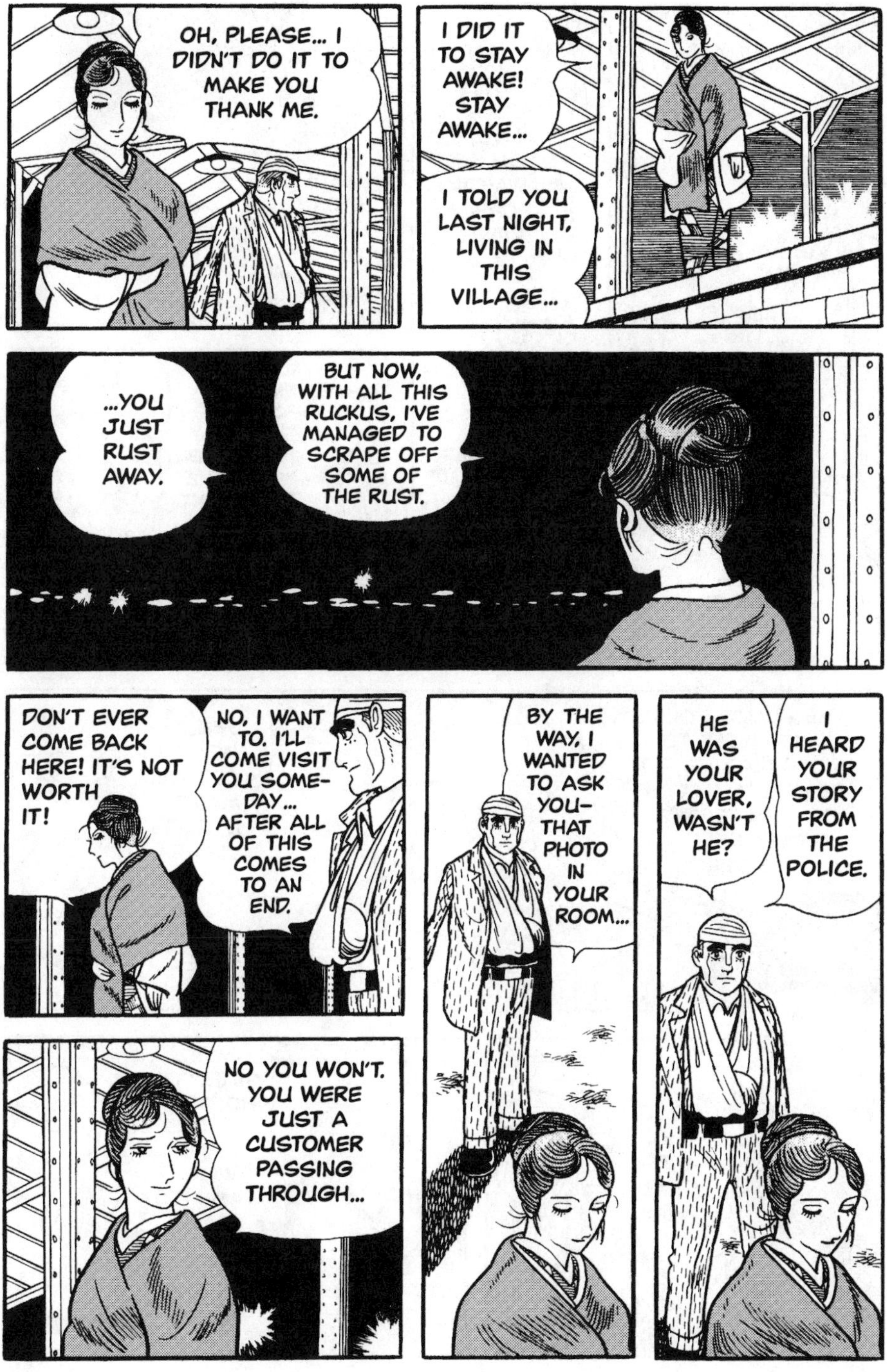
OH, PLEASE... I DIDN'T DO IT TO MAKE YOU THANK ME.
I DID IT TO STAY AWAKE! STAY AWAKE...
I TOLD YOU LAST NIGHT, LIVING IN THIS VILLAGE...
...YOU JUST RUST AWAY.
BUT NOW, WITH ALL THIS RUCKUS, I'VE MANAGED TO SCRAPE OFF SOME OF THE RUST.
DON'T EVER COME BACK HERE! IT'S NOT WORTH IT!
NO, I WANT TO. I'LL COME VISIT YOU SOME-DAY... AFTER ALL OF THIS COMES TO AN END.
NO YOU WON'T. YOU WERE JUST A CUSTOMER PASSING THROUGH...
BY THE WAY, I WANTED TO ASK YOU– THAT PHOTO IN YOUR ROOM...
HE WAS YOUR LOVER, WASN'T HE?
I HEARD YOUR STORY FROM THE POLICE.

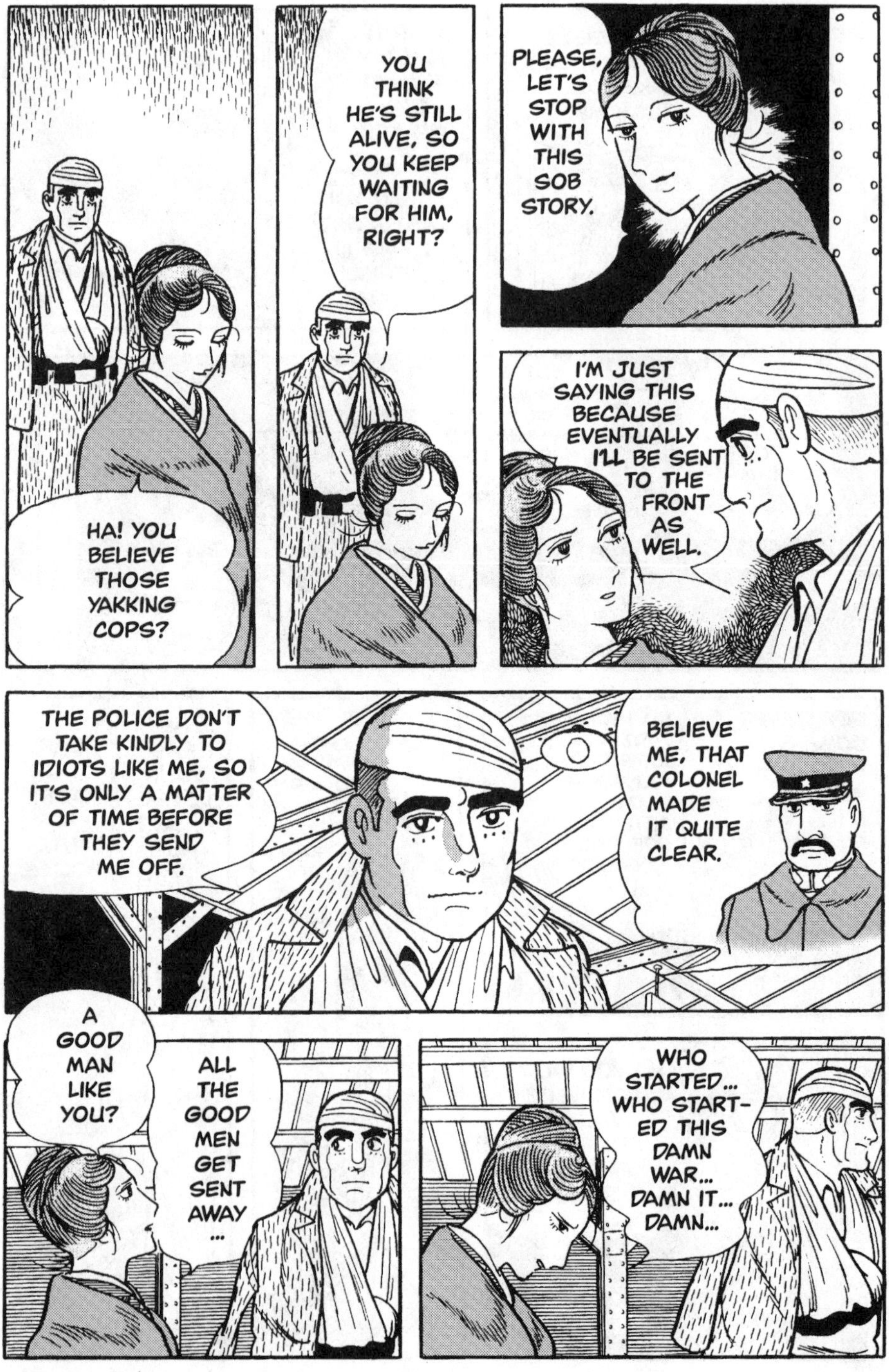
HA! YOU BELIEVE THOSE YAKKING COPS?
YOU THINK HE'S STILL ALIVE, SO YOU KEEP WAITING FOR HIM, RIGHT?
PLEASE, LET'S STOP WITH THIS SOB STORY.
I'M JUST SAYING THIS BECAUSE EVENTUALLY I'LL BE SENT TO THE FRONT AS WELL.
THE POLICE DON'T TAKE KINDLY TO IDIOTS LIKE ME, SO IT'S ONLY A MATTER OF TIME BEFORE THEY SEND ME OFF.
BELIEVE ME, THAT COLONEL MADE IT QUITE CLEAR.
A GOOD MAN LIKE YOU?
ALL THE GOOD MEN GET SENT AWAY ...
WHO STARTED... WHO START-ED THIS DAMN WAR... DAMN IT... DAMN...

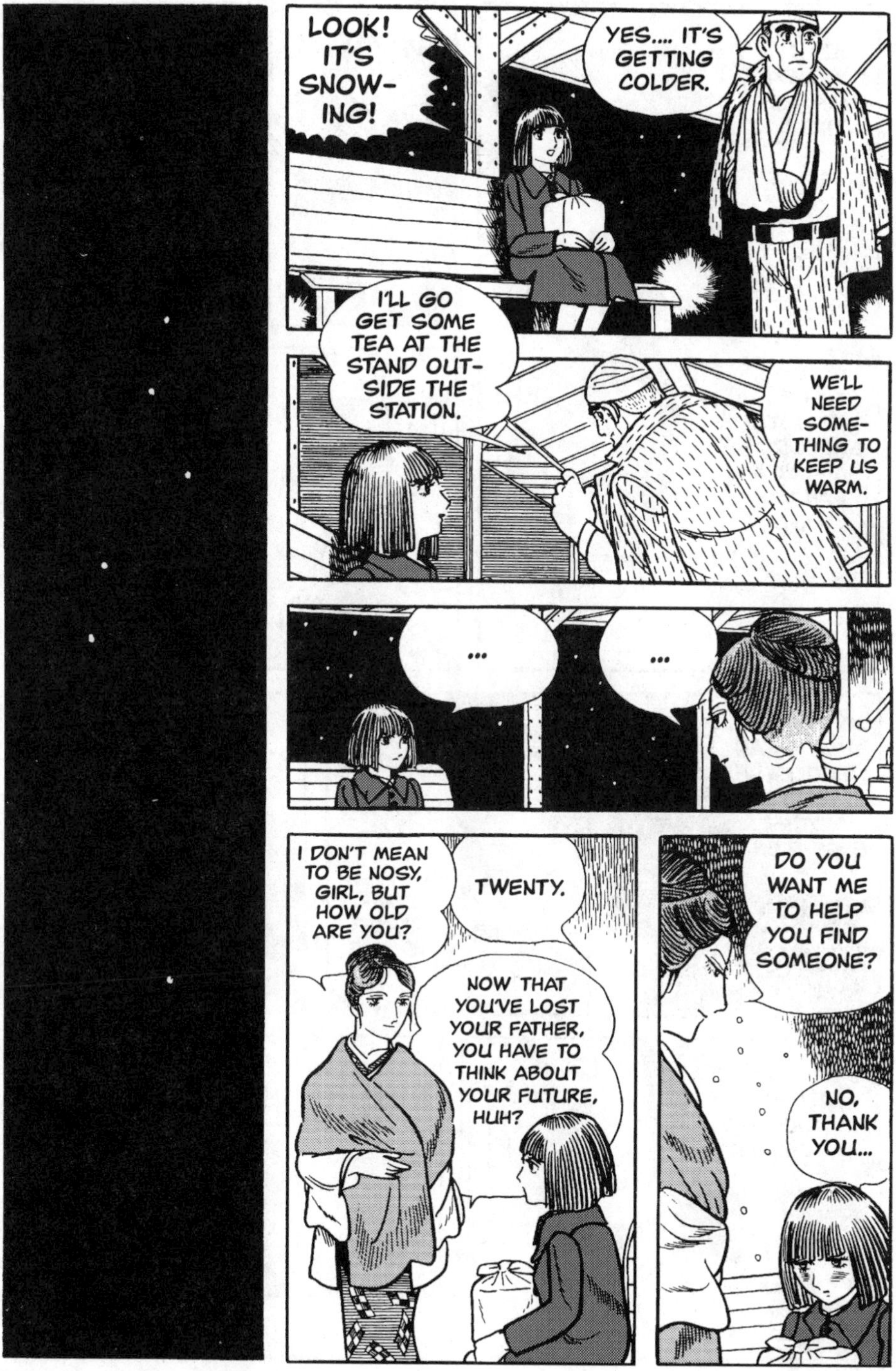
LOOK! IT'S SNOWING!
YES.... IT'S GETTING COLDER.
I'LL GO GET SOME TEA AT THE STAND OUTSIDE THE STATION.
WE'LL NEED SOMETHING TO KEEP US WARM.
...
...
I DON'T MEAN TO BE NOSY, GIRL, BUT HOW OLD ARE YOU?
TWENTY.
NOW THAT YOU'VE LOST YOUR FATHER, YOU HAVE TO THINK ABOUT YOUR FUTURE, HUH?
DO YOU WANT ME TO HELP YOU FIND SOMEONE?
NO, THANK YOU...

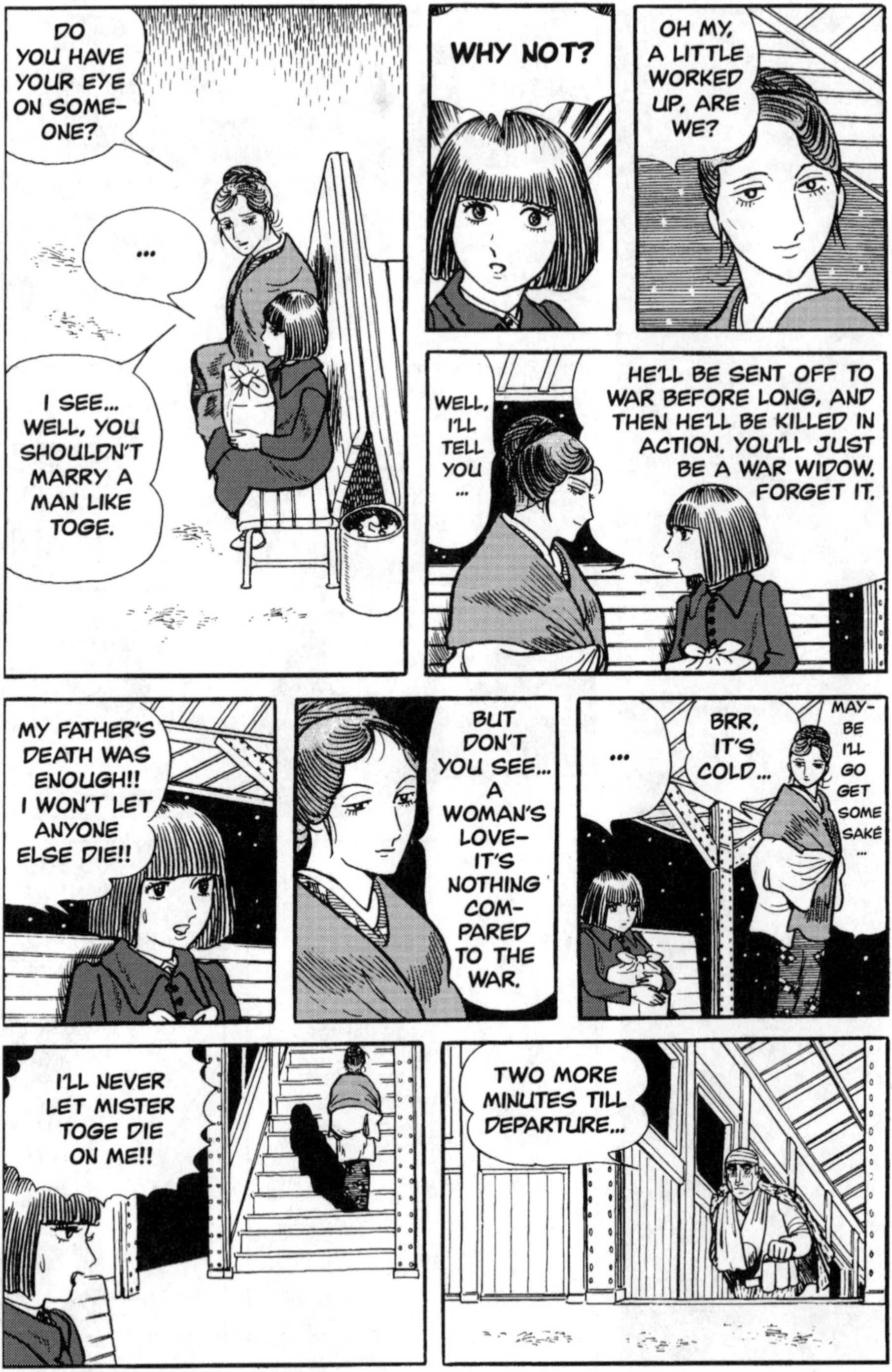
DO YOU HAVE YOUR EYE ON SOME-ONE?
...
I SEE... WELL, YOU SHOULDN'T MARRY A MAN LIKE TOGE.
WHY NOT?
OH MY, A LITTLE WORKED UP, ARE WE?
WELL, I'LL TELL YOU ...
HE'LL BE SENT OFF TO WAR BEFORE LONG, AND THEN HE'LL BE KILLED IN ACTION. YOU'LL JUST BE A WAR WIDOW. FORGET IT.
MY FATHER'S DEATH WAS ENOUGH!! I WON'T LET ANYONE ELSE DIE!!
BUT DON'T YOU SEE... A WOMAN'S LOVE– IT'S NOTHING COM-PARED TO THE WAR.
...
BRR, IT'S COLD...
MAY-BE I'LL GO GET SOME SAKÉ ...
I'LL NEVER LET MISTER TOGE DIE ON ME!!
TWO MORE MINUTES TILL DEPARTURE...

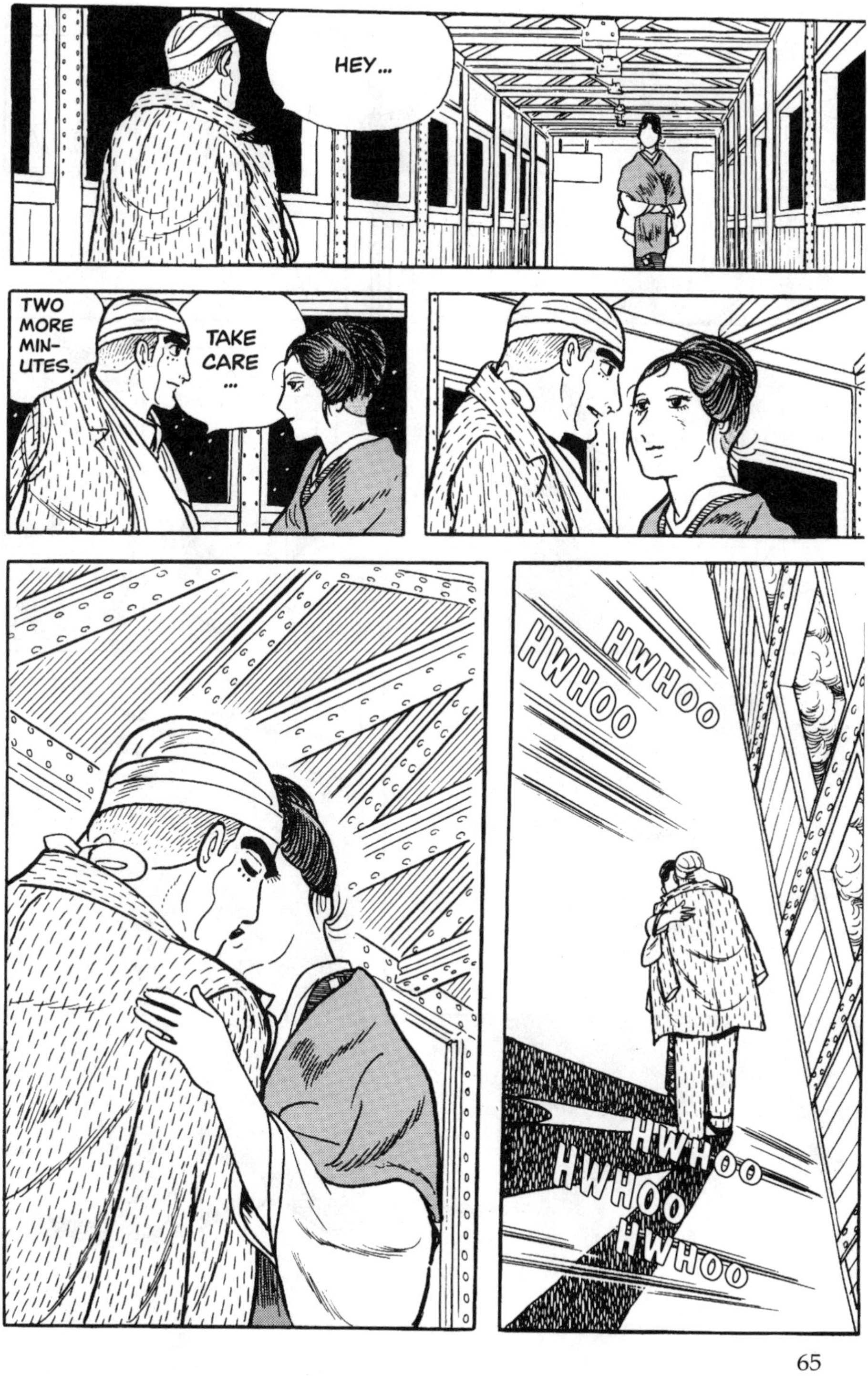
HEY...
TWO MORE MIN-UTES.
TAKE CARE ...
HWHOO
HWHOO
HWHOO
HWHOO
HWHOO

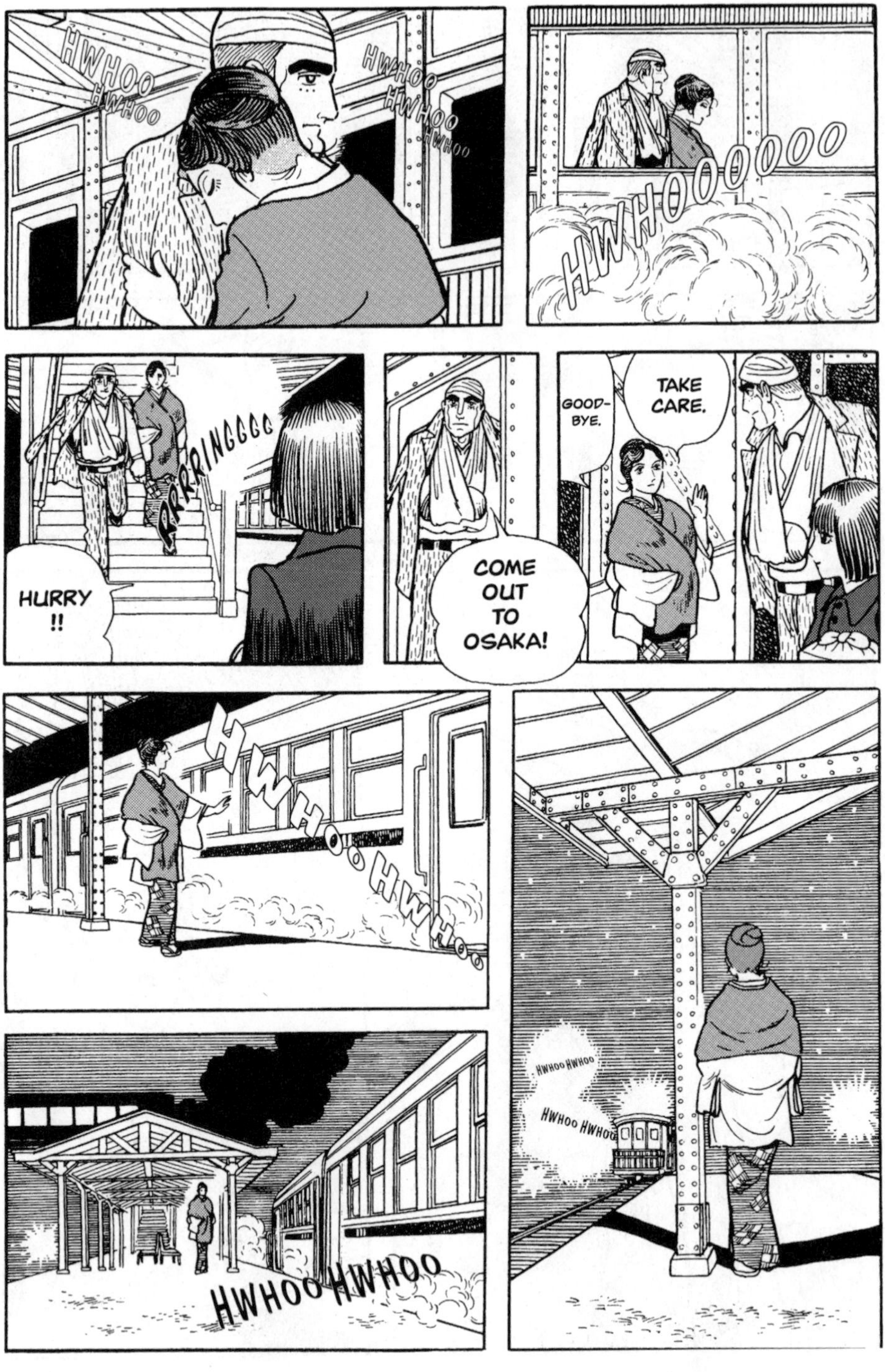
HWHOO
HWHOO
HWHOO
HWHOO
HWHOO
HWHOOOOOOO
PRRRINGGGG
HURRY !!
COME OUT TO OSAKA!
GOOD-BYE.
TAKE CARE.
HWHOO HWHOO
HWHOO HWHOO
HWHOO HWHOO
HWHOO HWHOO

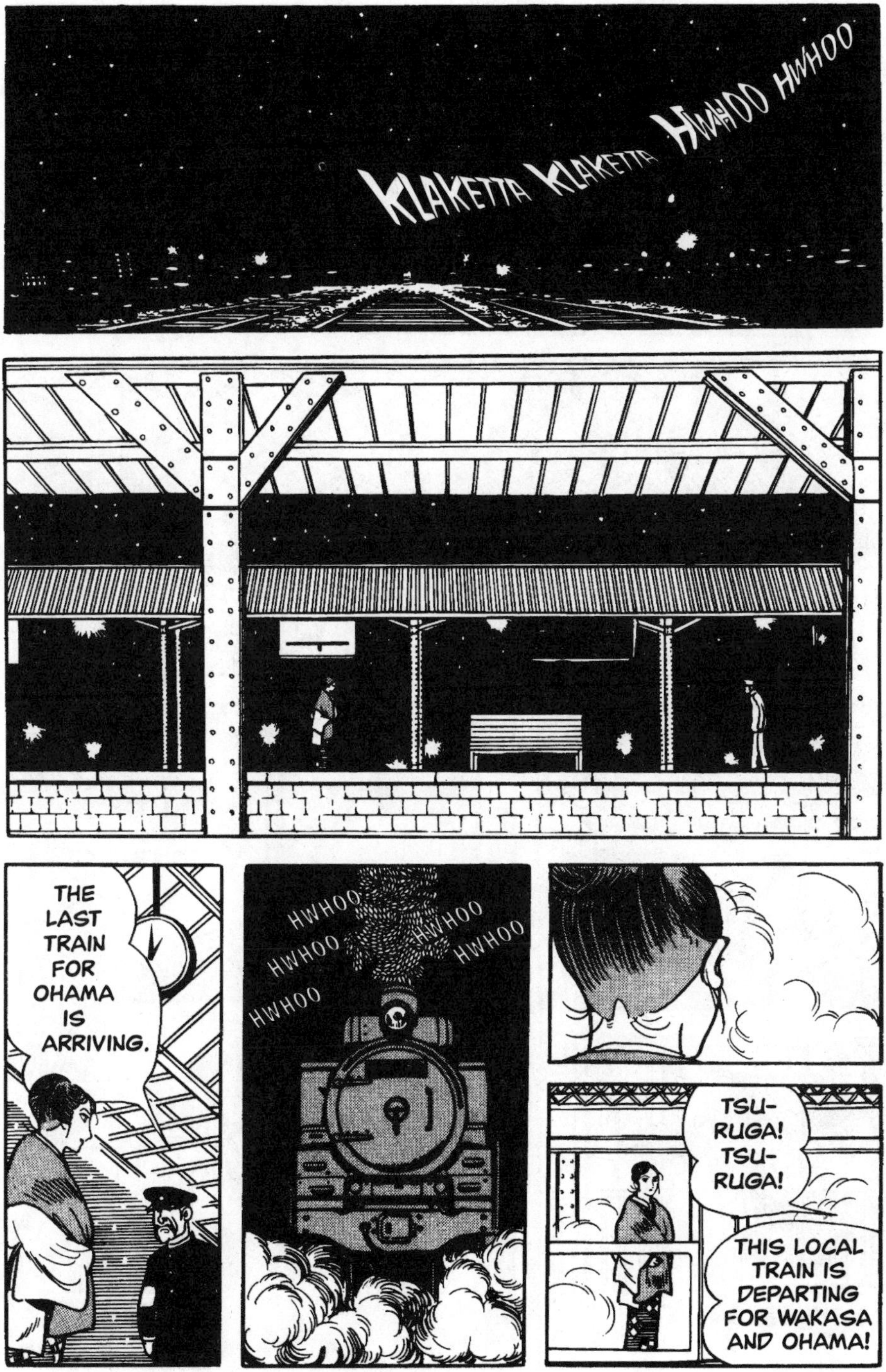
KLAKETTA KLAKETTA HWHOO HWHOO
THE LAST TRAIN FOR OHAMA IS ARRIVING.
HWHOO HWHOO HWHOO HWHOO HWHOO
TSU-RUGA! TSU-RUGA!
THIS LOCAL TRAIN IS DEPARTING FOR WAKASA AND OHAMA!

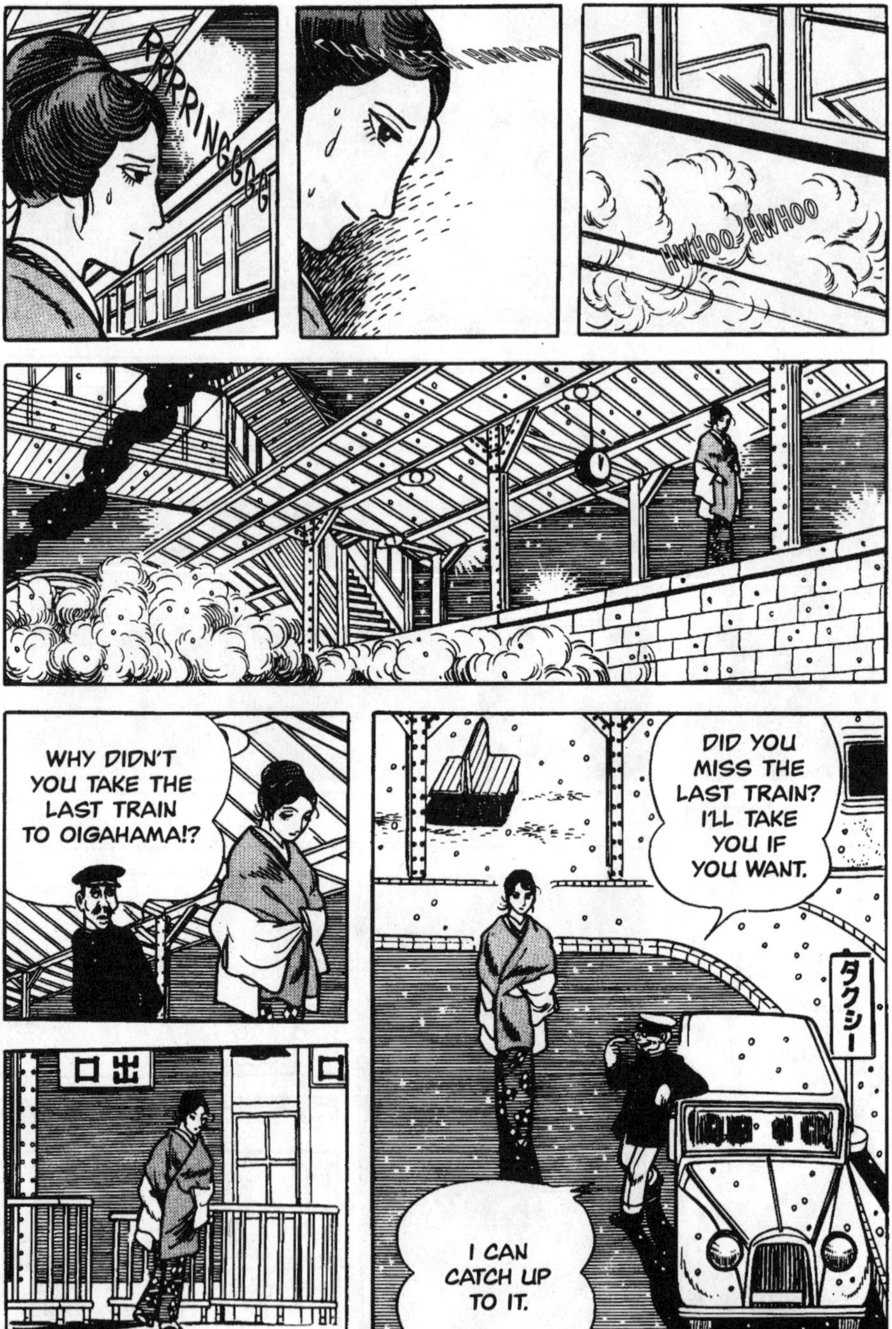

RRRRINGGGG
HWHOO HWHOO
WHY DIDN'T YOU TAKE THE LAST TRAIN TO OIGAHAMA!?
口出
DID YOU MISS THE LAST TRAIN? I'LL TAKE YOU IF YOU WANT.
タクシー
I CAN CATCH UP TO IT.

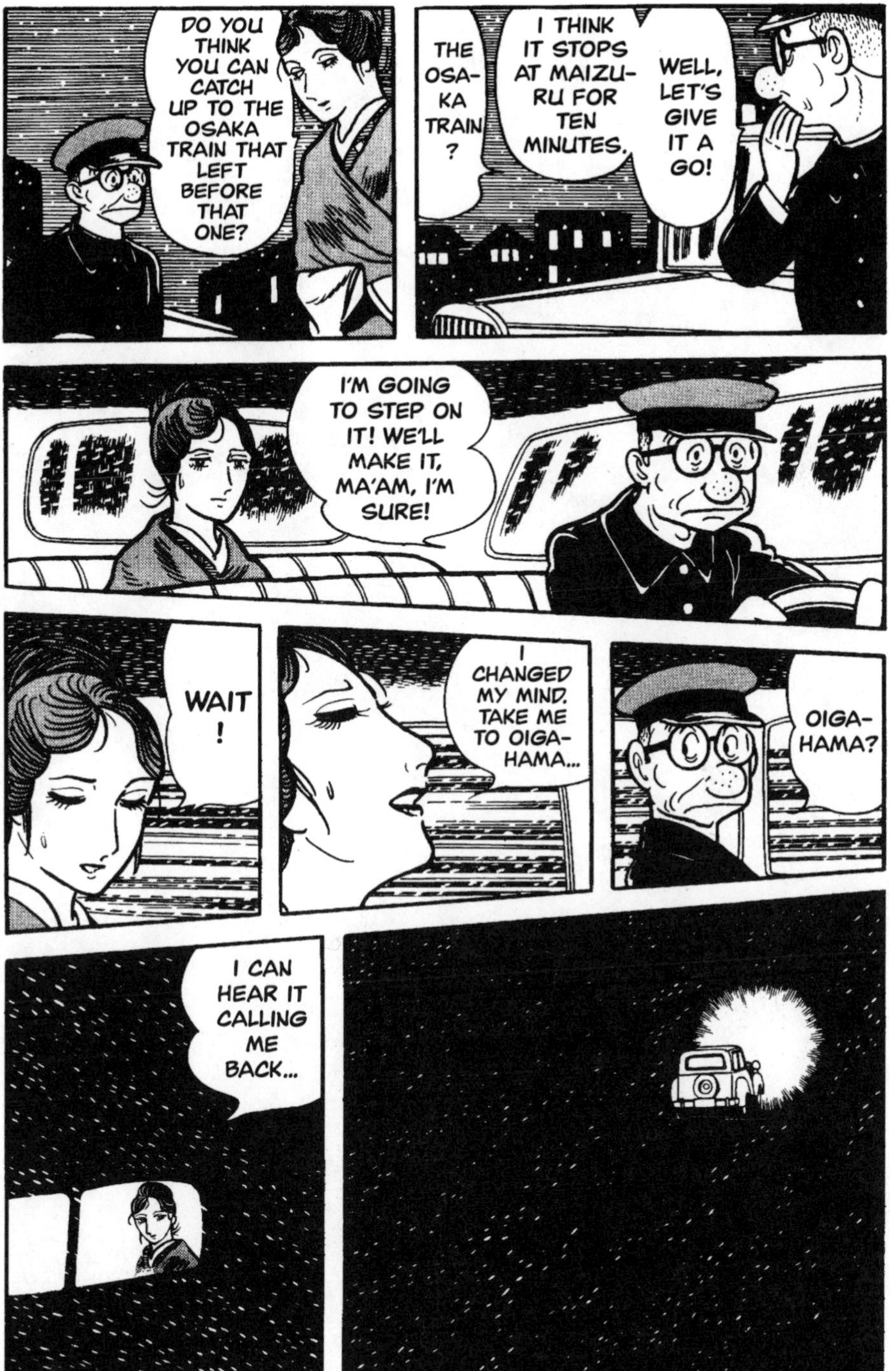
DO YOU THINK YOU CAN CATCH UP TO THE OSAKA TRAIN THAT LEFT BEFORE THAT ONE?
THE OSAKA TRAIN?
I THINK IT STOPS AT MAIZURU FOR TEN MINUTES.
WELL, LET'S GIVE IT A GO!
I'M GOING TO STEP ON IT! WE'LL MAKE IT, MA'AM, I'M SURE!
WAIT!
I CHANGED MY MIND. TAKE ME TO OIGAHAMA...
OIGAHAMA?
I CAN HEAR IT CALLING ME BACK...

CHAPTER TWO

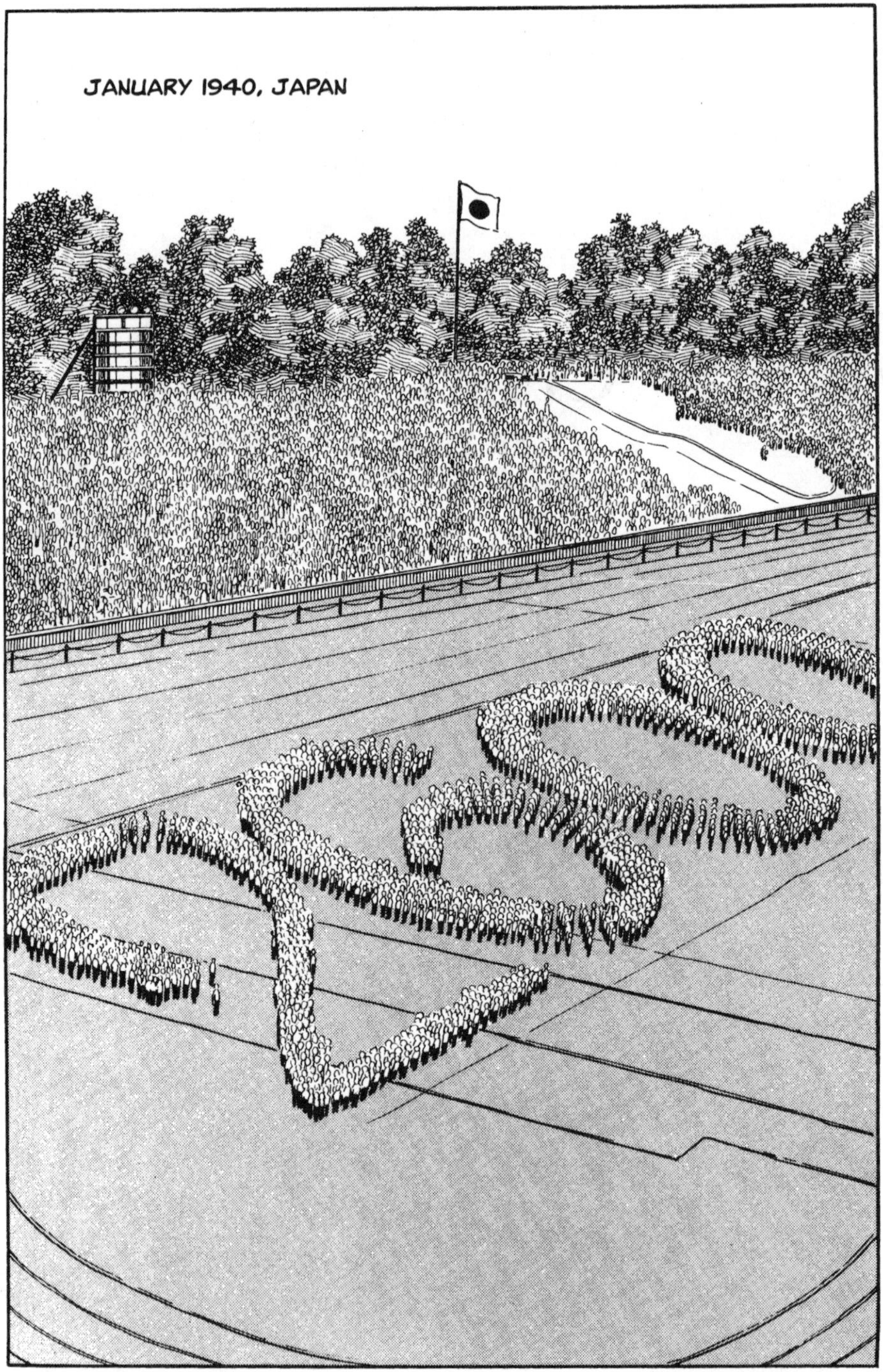
JANUARY 1940, JAPAN

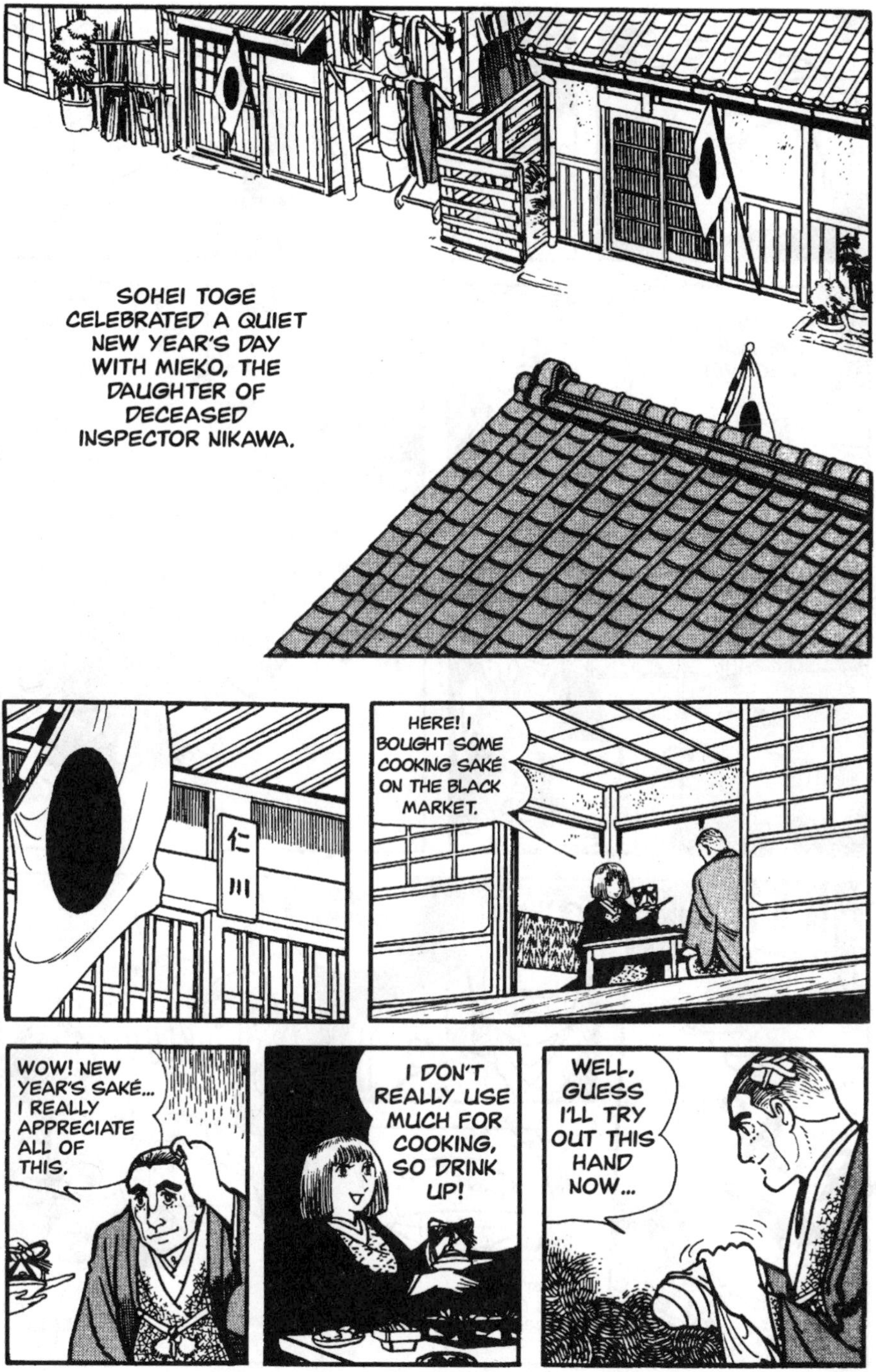
SOHEI TOGE CELEBRATED A QUIET NEW YEAR'S DAY WITH MIEKO, THE DAUGHTER OF DECEASED INSPECTOR NIKAWA.
仁川
HERE! I BOUGHT SOME COOKING SAKÉ ON THE BLACK MARKET.
WOW! NEW YEAR'S SAKÉ... I REALLY APPRECIATE ALL OF THIS.
I DON'T REALLY USE MUCH FOR COOKING, SO DRINK UP!
WELL, GUESS I'LL TRY OUT THIS HAND NOW...

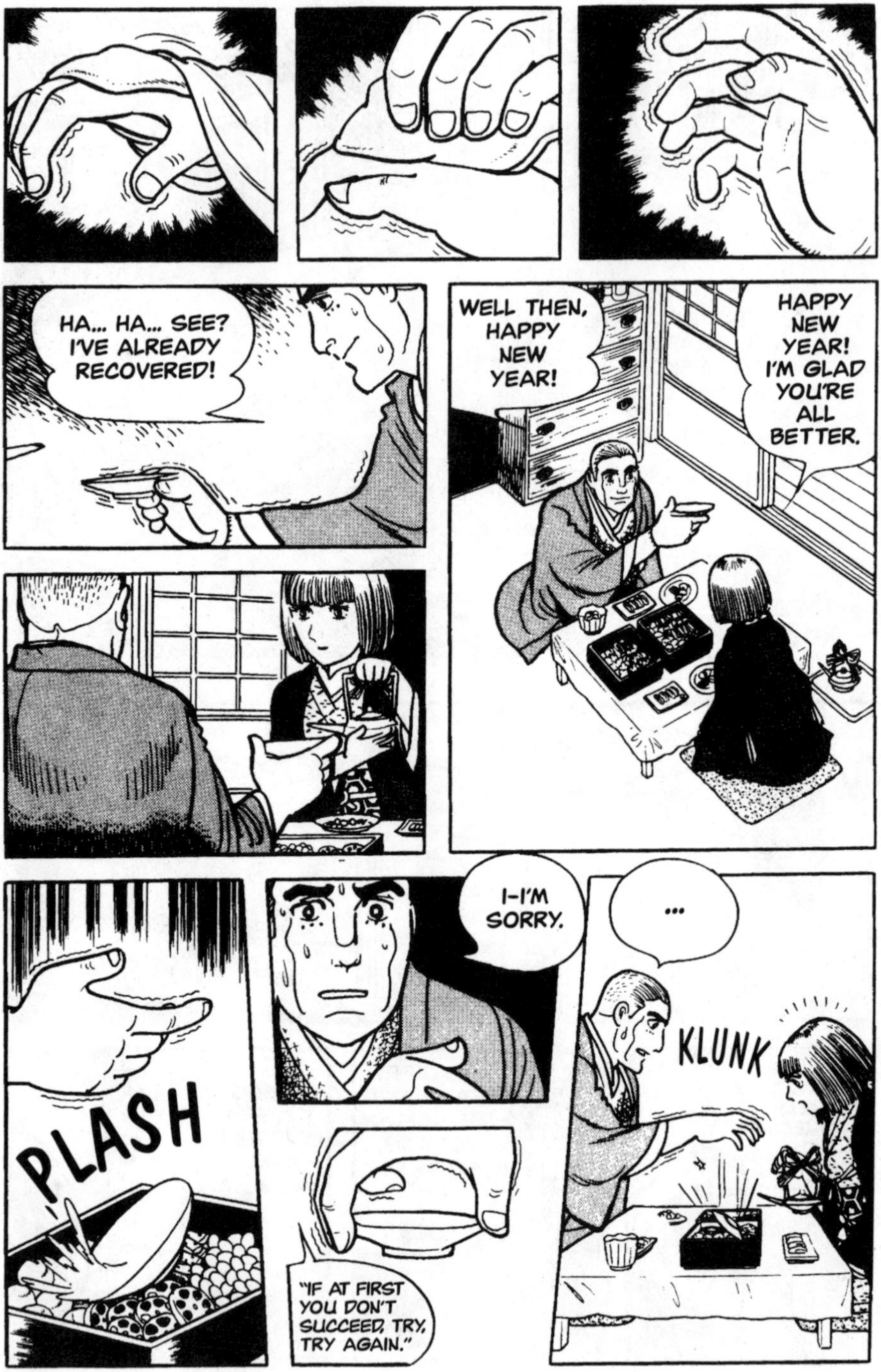
HA... HA... SEE? I'VE ALREADY RECOVERED!
WELL THEN, HAPPY NEW YEAR!
HAPPY NEW YEAR! I'M GLAD YOU'RE ALL BETTER.
PLASH
I-I'M SORRY.
"IF AT FIRST YOU DON'T SUCCEED, TRY, TRY AGAIN."
...
KLUNK

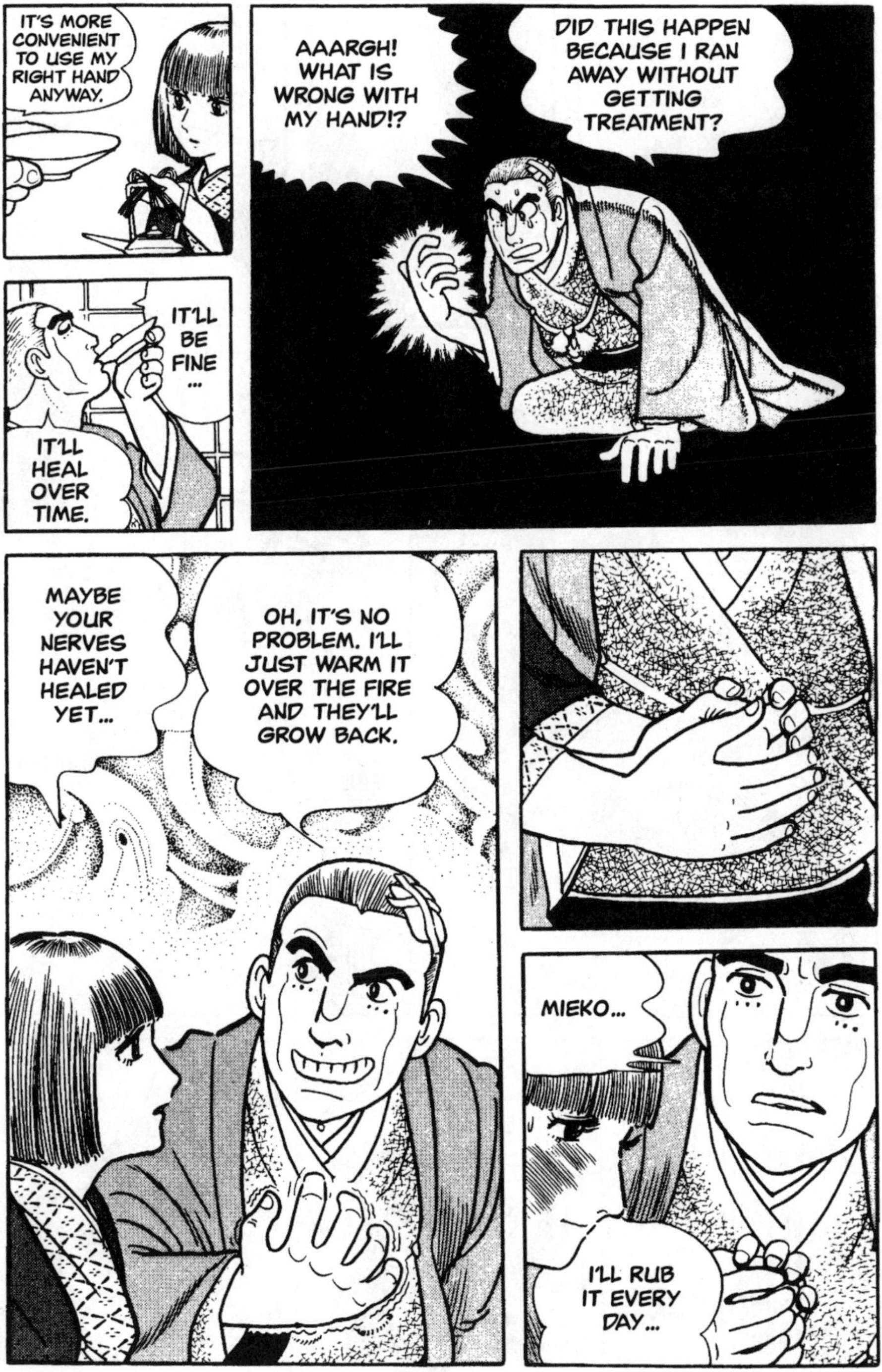
IT'S MORE CONVENIENT TO USE MY RIGHT HAND ANYWAY.
IT'LL BE FINE ...
IT'LL HEAL OVER TIME.
AAARGH! WHAT IS WRONG WITH MY HAND!?
DID THIS HAPPEN BECAUSE I RAN AWAY WITHOUT GETTING TREATMENT?
MAYBE YOUR NERVES HAVEN'T HEALED YET...
OH, IT'S NO PROBLEM. I'LL JUST WARM IT OVER THE FIRE AND THEY'LL GROW BACK.
MIEKO...
I'LL RUB IT EVERY DAY...

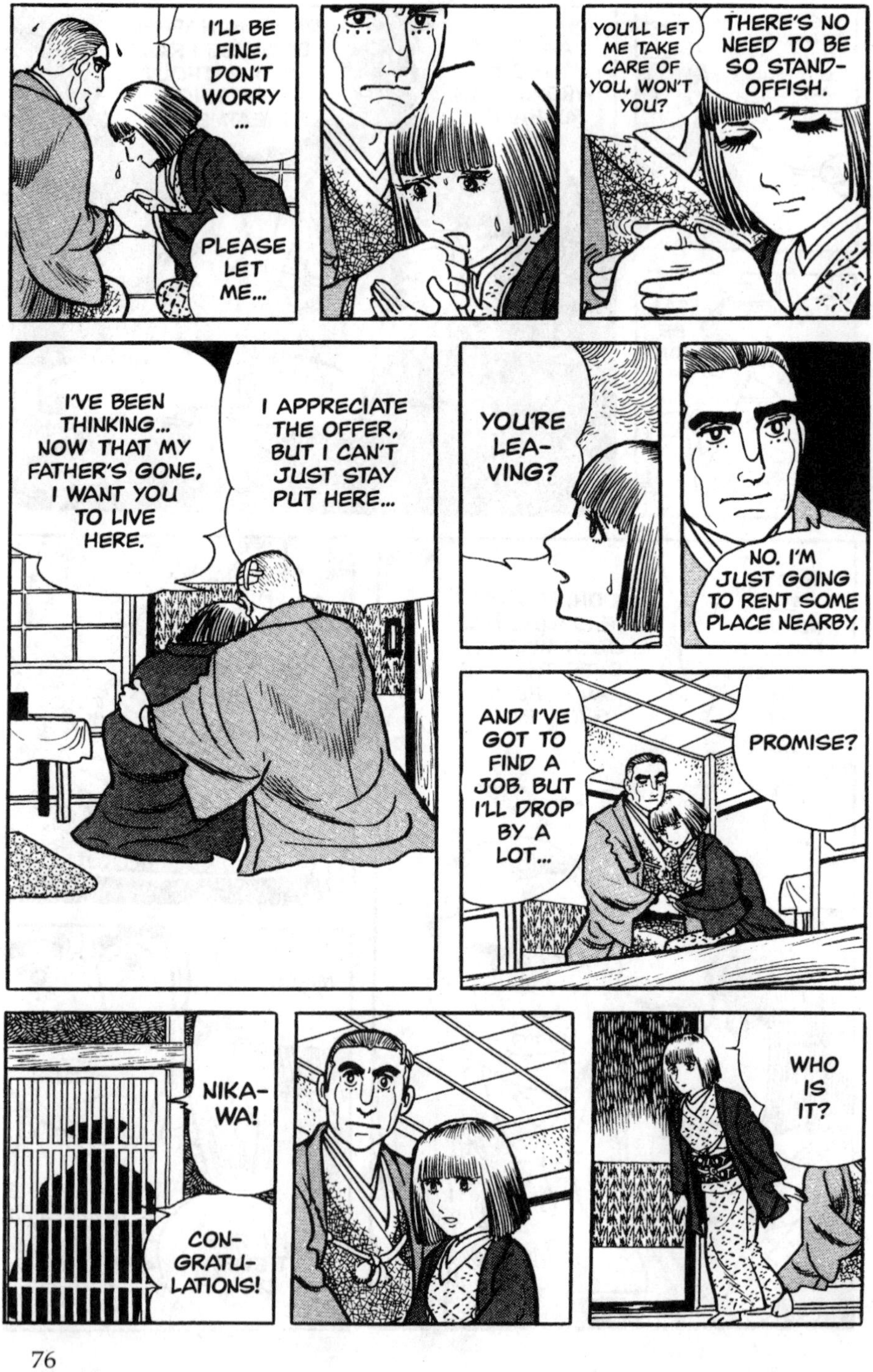
I'LL BE FINE, DON'T WORRY ...
PLEASE LET ME...
YOU'LL LET ME TAKE CARE OF YOU, WON'T YOU?
THERE'S NO NEED TO BE SO STAND-OFFISH.
I'VE BEEN THINKING... NOW THAT MY FATHER'S GONE, I WANT YOU TO LIVE HERE.
I APPRECIATE THE OFFER, BUT I CAN'T JUST STAY PUT HERE...
YOU'RE LEA-VING?
NO. I'M JUST GOING TO RENT SOME PLACE NEARBY.
AND I'VE GOT TO FIND A JOB. BUT I'LL DROP BY A LOT...
PROMISE?
NIKA-WA!
CON-GRATU-LATIONS!
WHO IS IT?

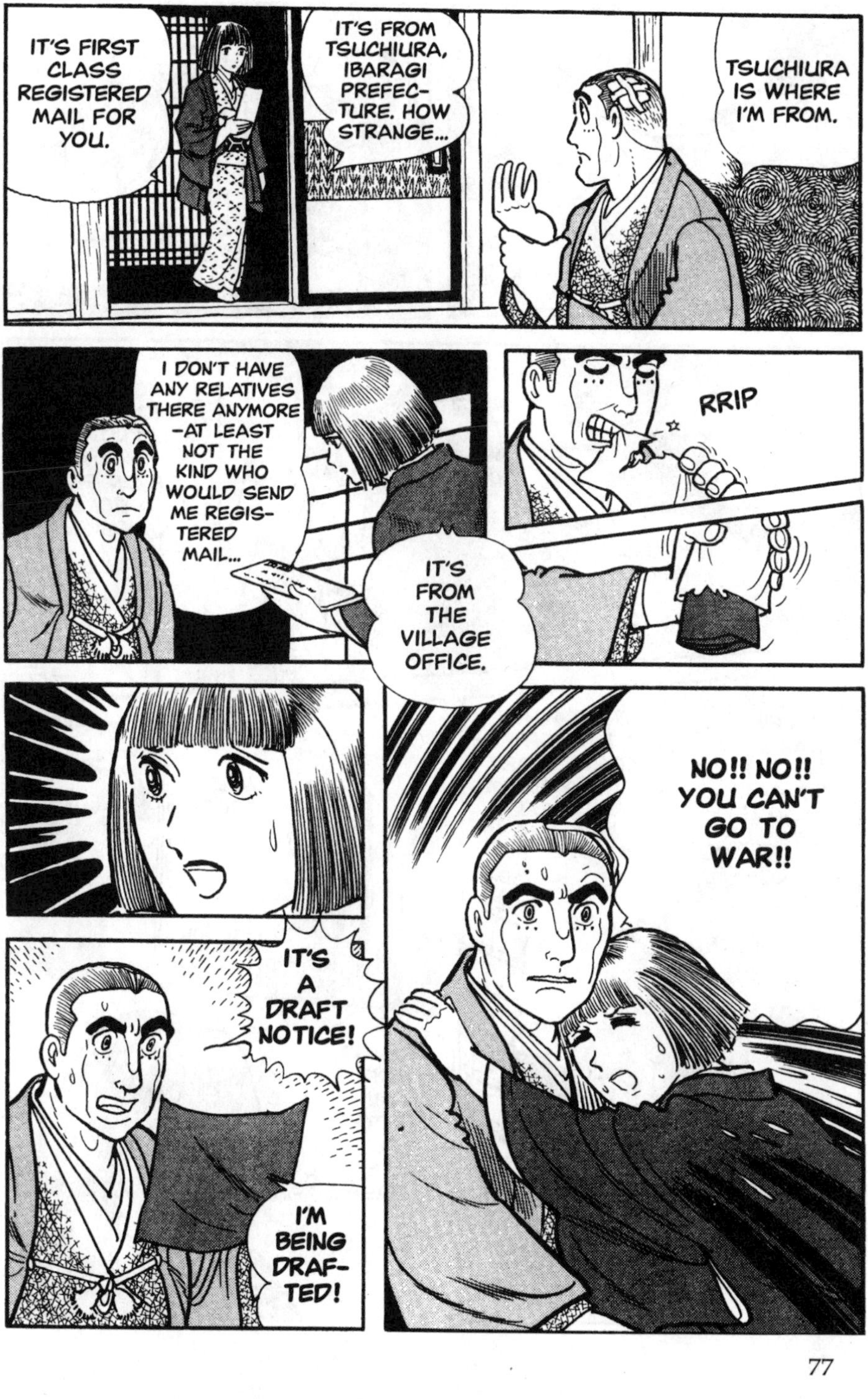
IT'S FIRST CLASS REGISTERED MAIL FOR YOU.
IT'S FROM TSUCHIURA, IBARAGI PREFECTURE. HOW STRANGE...
TSUCHIURA IS WHERE I'M FROM.
I DON'T HAVE ANY RELATIVES THERE ANYMORE —AT LEAST NOT THE KIND WHO WOULD SEND ME REGISTERED MAIL...
RRIP
IT'S FROM THE VILLAGE OFFICE.
IT'S A DRAFT NOTICE!
I'M BEING DRAFTED!
NO!! NO!! YOU CAN'T GO TO WAR!!

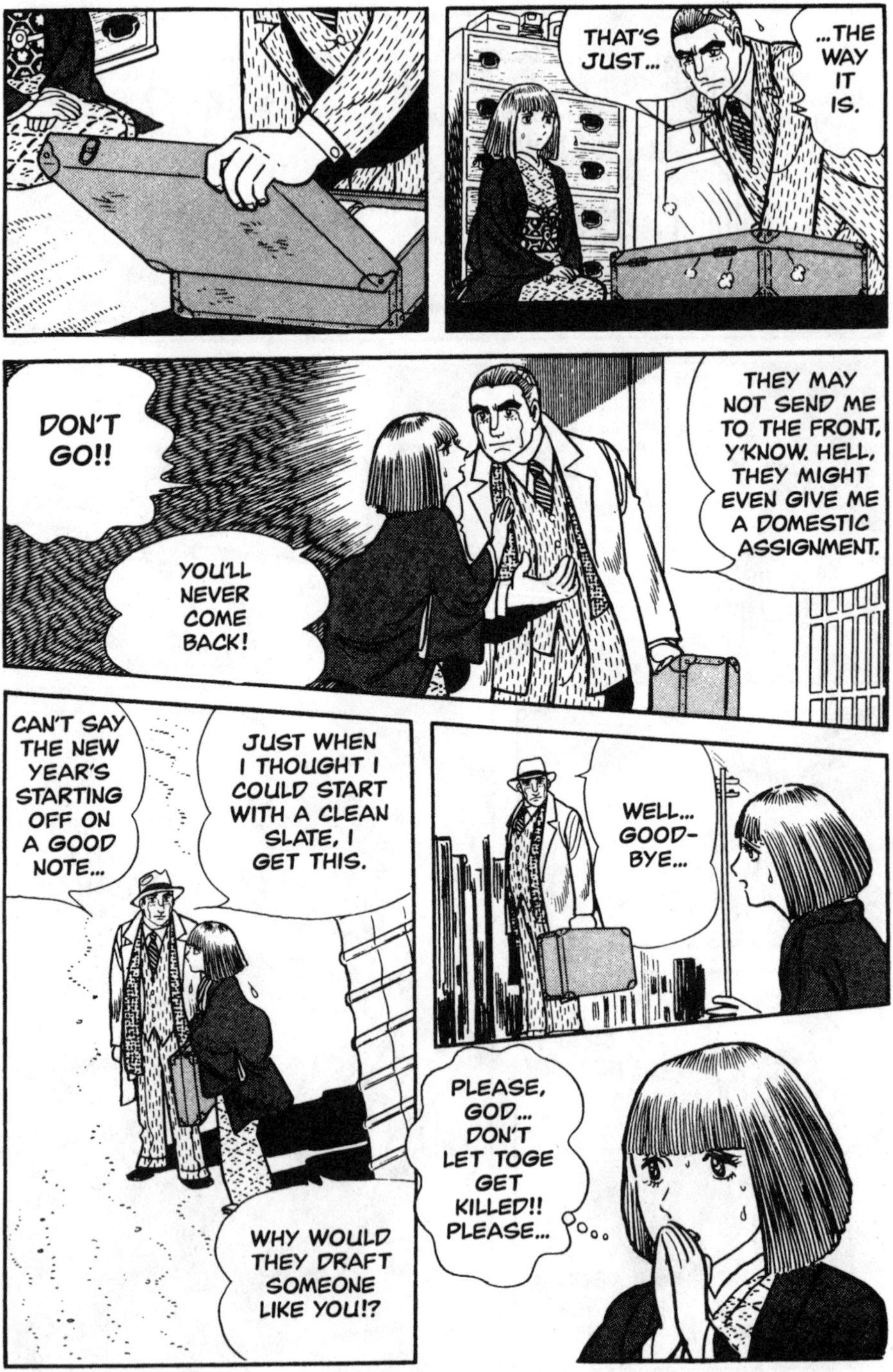
THAT'S JUST...
...THE WAY IT IS.
DON'T GO!!
YOU'LL NEVER COME BACK!
THEY MAY NOT SEND ME TO THE FRONT, Y'KNOW. HELL, THEY MIGHT EVEN GIVE ME A DOMESTIC ASSIGNMENT.
CAN'T SAY THE NEW YEAR'S STARTING OFF ON A GOOD NOTE...
JUST WHEN I THOUGHT I COULD START WITH A CLEAN SLATE, I GET THIS.
WHY WOULD THEY DRAFT SOMEONE LIKE YOU!?
WELL... GOOD-BYE...
PLEASE, GOD... DON'T LET TOGE GET KILLED!! PLEASE...

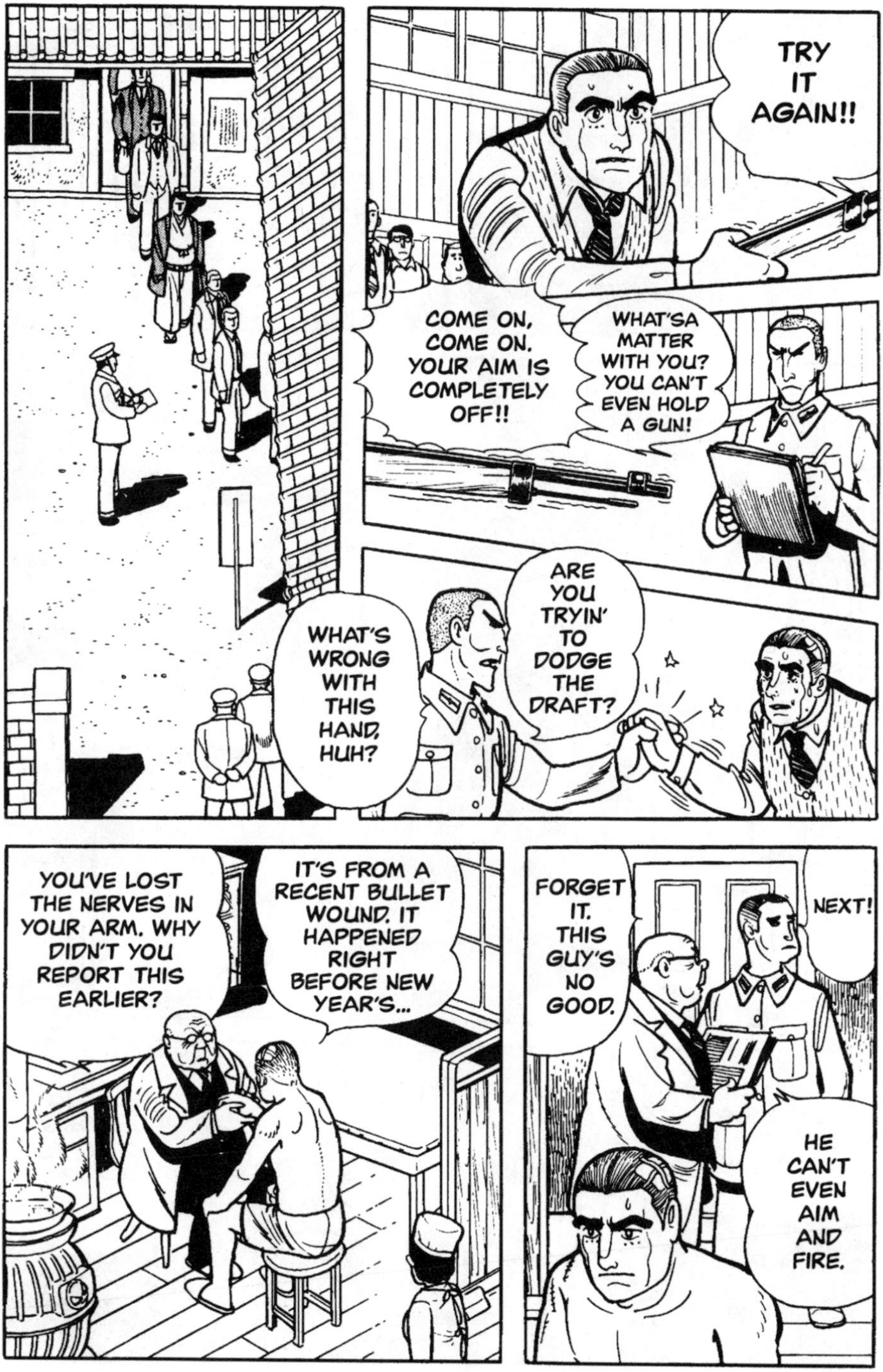
TRY IT AGAIN!!
COME ON, COME ON. YOUR AIM IS COMPLETELY OFF!!
WHAT'SA MATTER WITH YOU? YOU CAN'T EVEN HOLD A GUN!
WHAT'S WRONG WITH THIS HAND, HUH?
ARE YOU TRYIN' TO DODGE THE DRAFT?
YOU'VE LOST THE NERVES IN YOUR ARM. WHY DIDN'T YOU REPORT THIS EARLIER?
IT'S FROM A RECENT BULLET WOUND. IT HAPPENED RIGHT BEFORE NEW YEAR'S...
FORGET IT. THIS GUY'S NO GOOD.
NEXT!
HE CAN'T EVEN AIM AND FIRE.

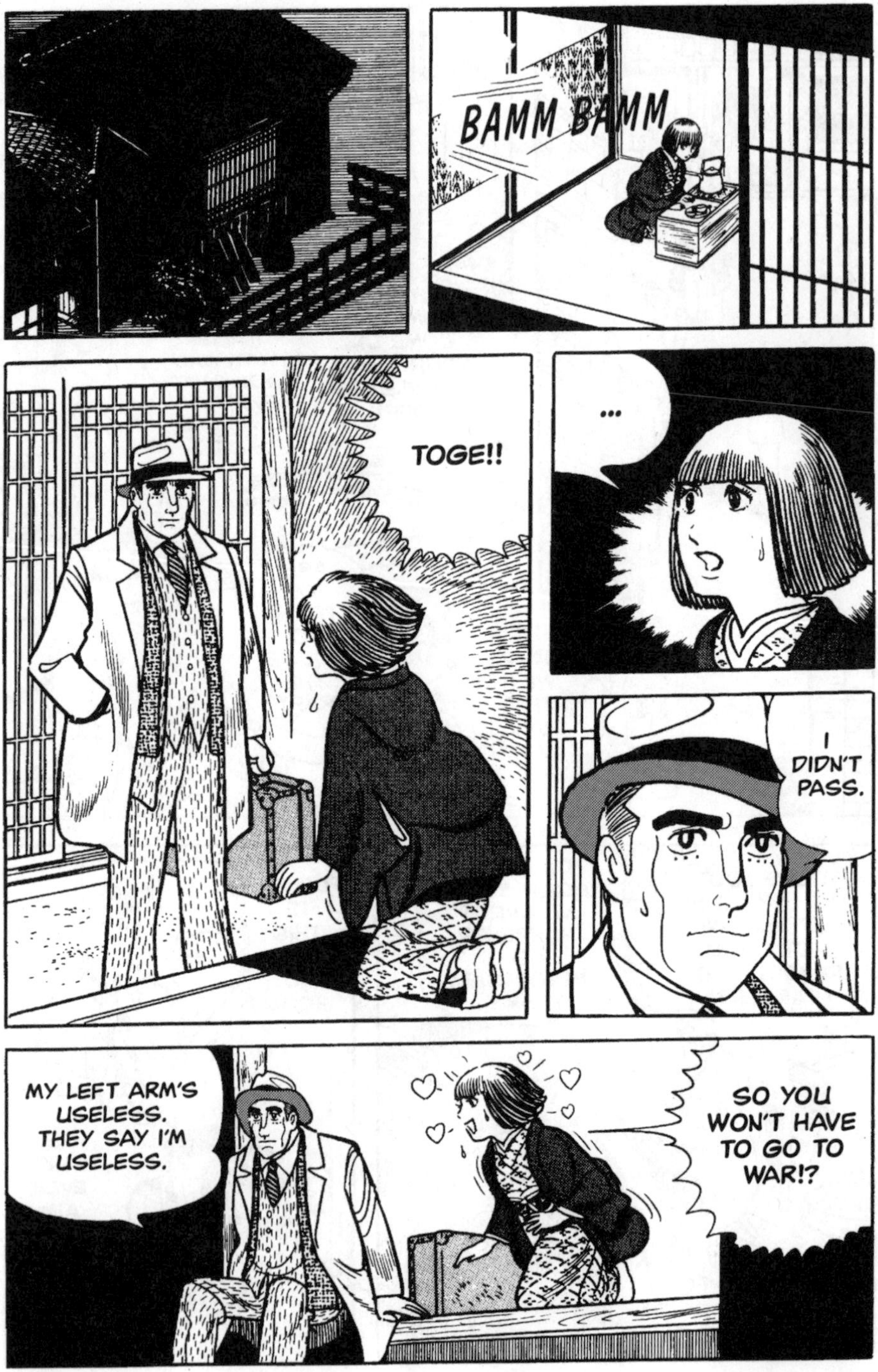
BAMM BAMM
TOGE!!
...
I DIDN'T PASS.
MY LEFT ARM'S USELESS. THEY SAY I'M USELESS.
SO YOU WON'T HAVE TO GO TO WAR!?

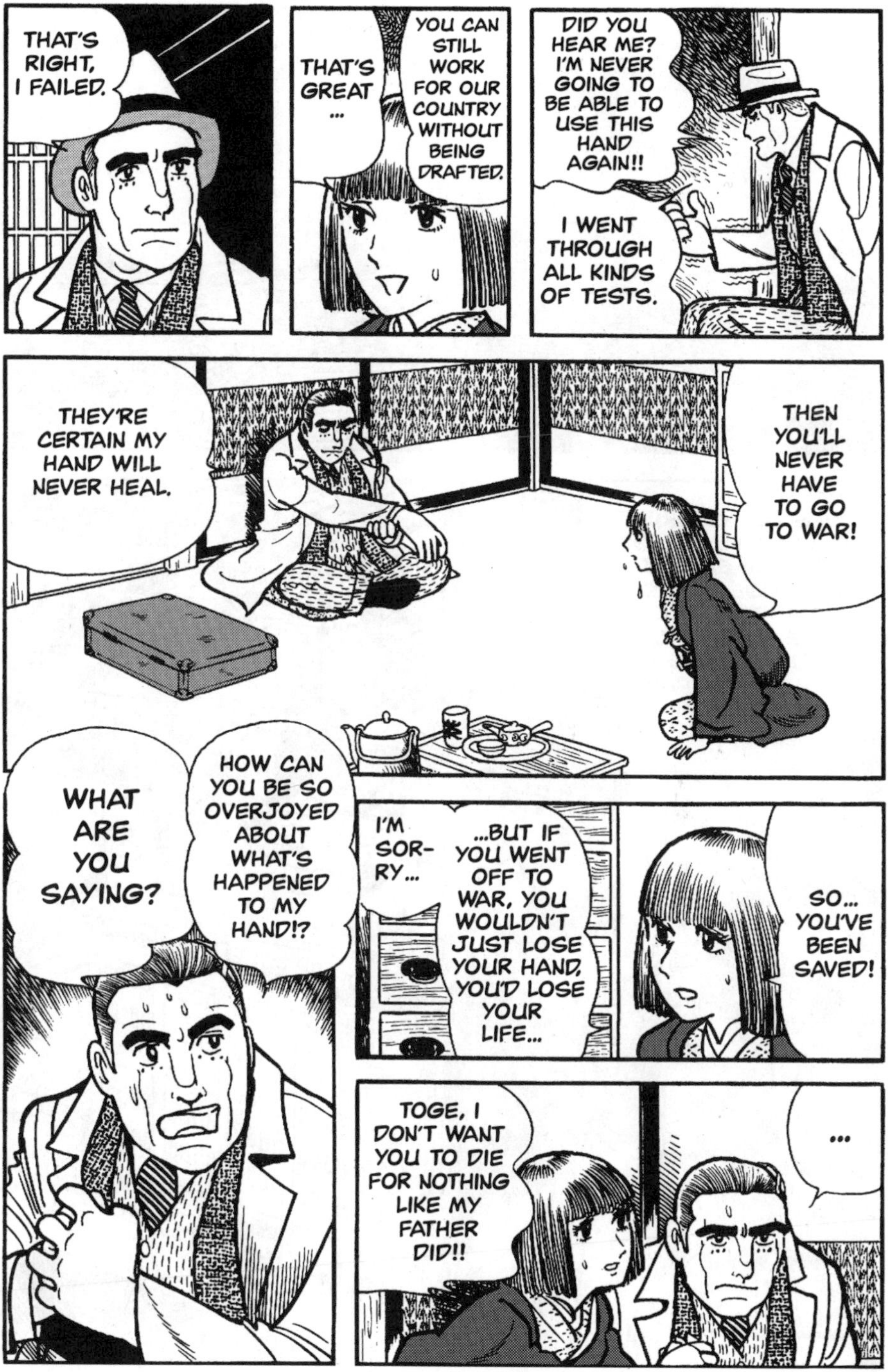
THAT'S RIGHT, I FAILED.
THAT'S GREAT ...
YOU CAN STILL WORK FOR OUR COUNTRY WITHOUT BEING DRAFTED.
DID YOU HEAR ME? I'M NEVER GOING TO BE ABLE TO USE THIS HAND AGAIN!!
I WENT THROUGH ALL KINDS OF TESTS.
THEY'RE CERTAIN MY HAND WILL NEVER HEAL.
THEN YOU'LL NEVER HAVE TO GO TO WAR!
WHAT ARE YOU SAYING?
HOW CAN YOU BE SO OVERJOYED ABOUT WHAT'S HAPPENED TO MY HAND!?
I'M SOR-RY...
...BUT IF YOU WENT OFF TO WAR, YOU WOULDN'T JUST LOSE YOUR HAND, YOU'D LOSE YOUR LIFE...
SO... YOU'VE BEEN SAVED!
TOGE, I DON'T WANT YOU TO DIE FOR NOTHING LIKE MY FATHER DID!!
...

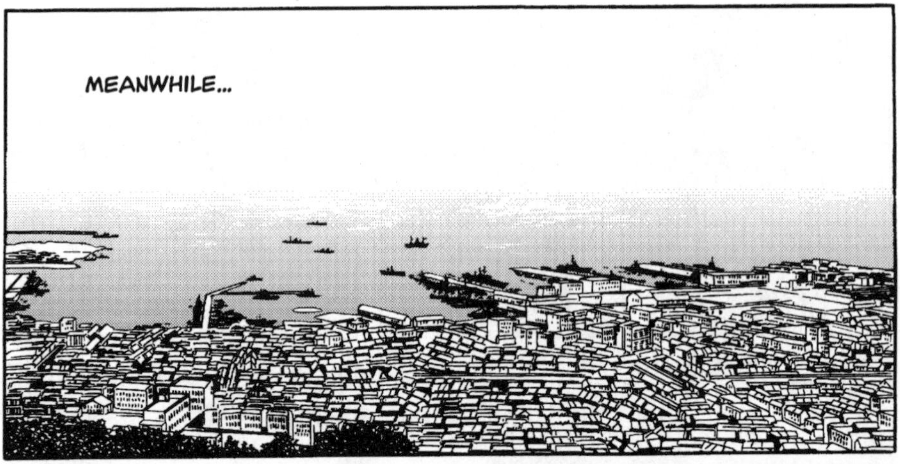
MEANWHILE...

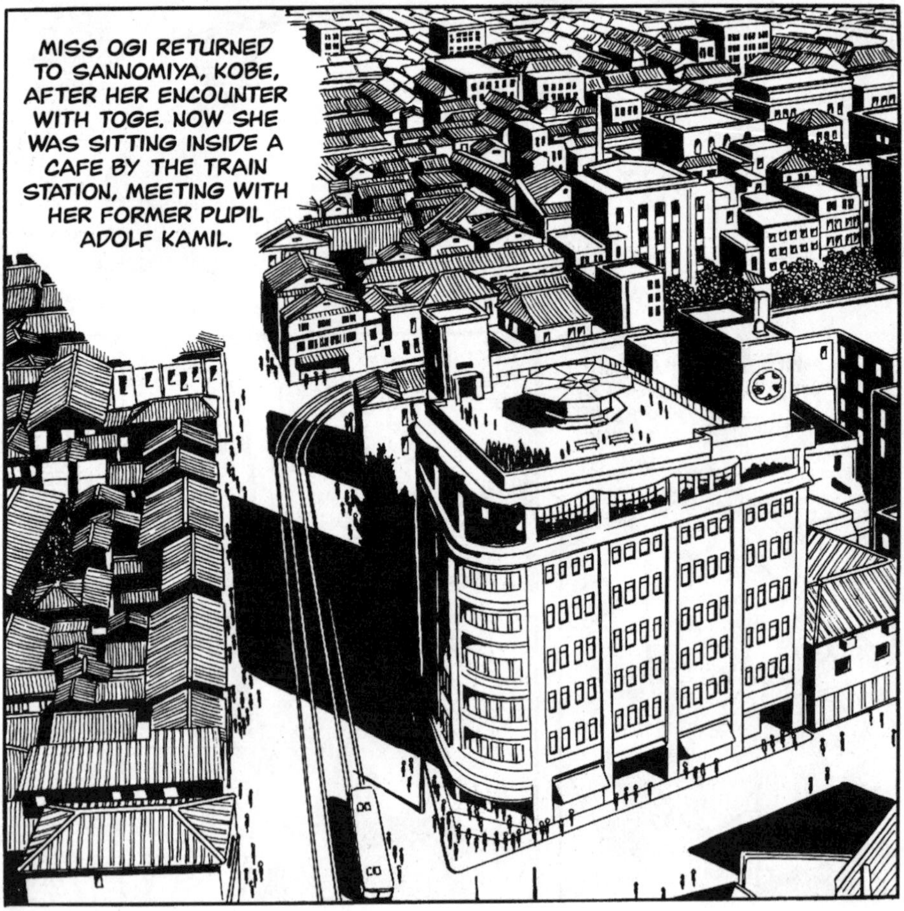
MISS OGI RETURNED TO SANNOMIYA, KOBE, AFTER HER ENCOUNTER WITH TOGE. NOW SHE WAS SITTING INSIDE A CAFE BY THE TRAIN STATION, MEETING WITH HER FORMER PUPIL ADOLF KAMIL.

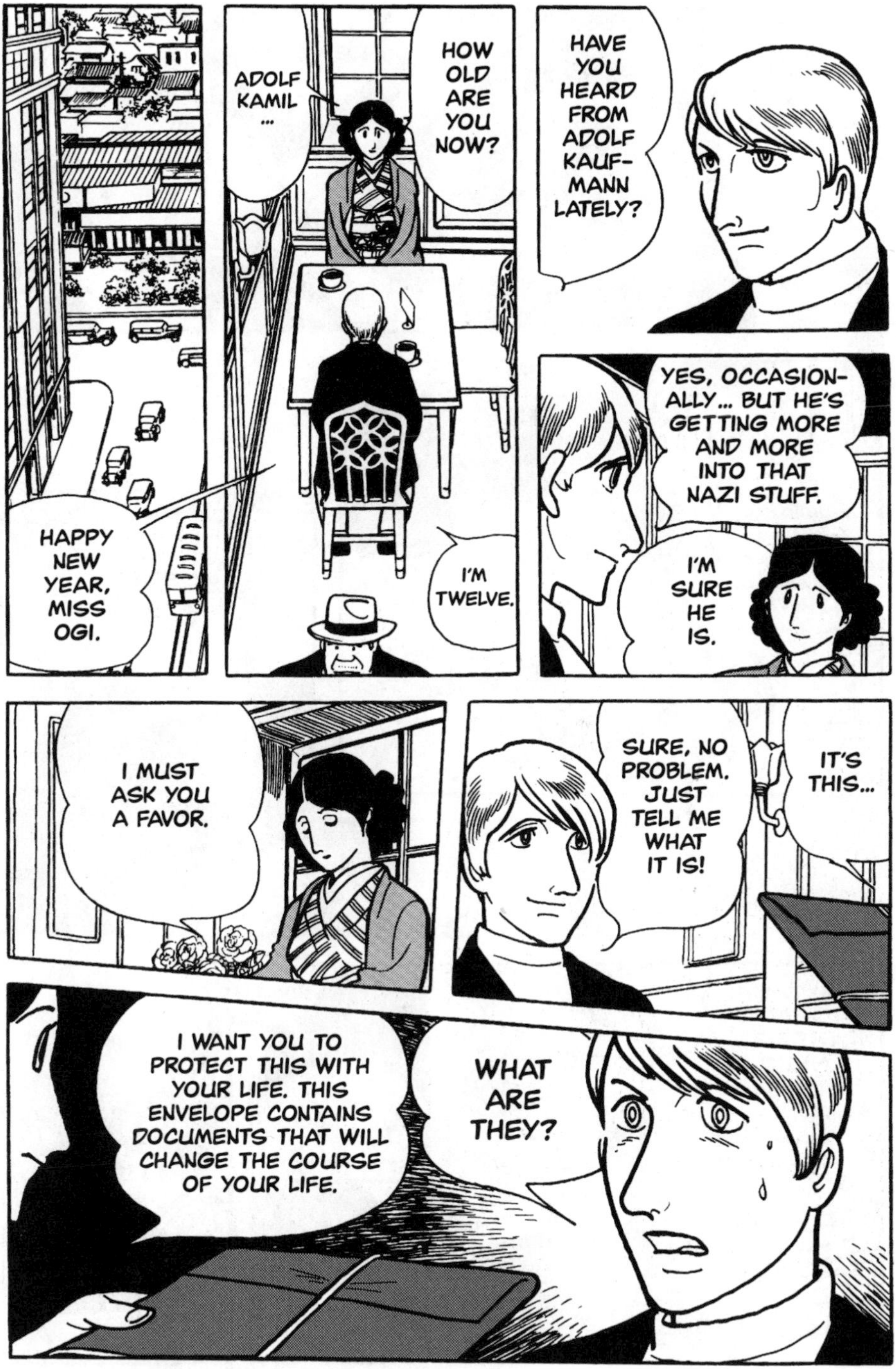
HAPPY NEW YEAR, MISS OGI.
ADOLF KAMIL ...
HOW OLD ARE YOU NOW?
I'M TWELVE.
HAVE YOU HEARD FROM ADOLF KAUF-MANN LATELY?
YES, OCCASION-ALLY... BUT HE'S GETTING MORE AND MORE INTO THAT NAZI STUFF.
I'M SURE HE IS.
I MUST ASK YOU A FAVOR.
SURE, NO PROBLEM. JUST TELL ME WHAT IT IS!
IT'S THIS...
I WANT YOU TO PROTECT THIS WITH YOUR LIFE. THIS ENVELOPE CONTAINS DOCUMENTS THAT WILL CHANGE THE COURSE OF YOUR LIFE.
WHAT ARE THEY?

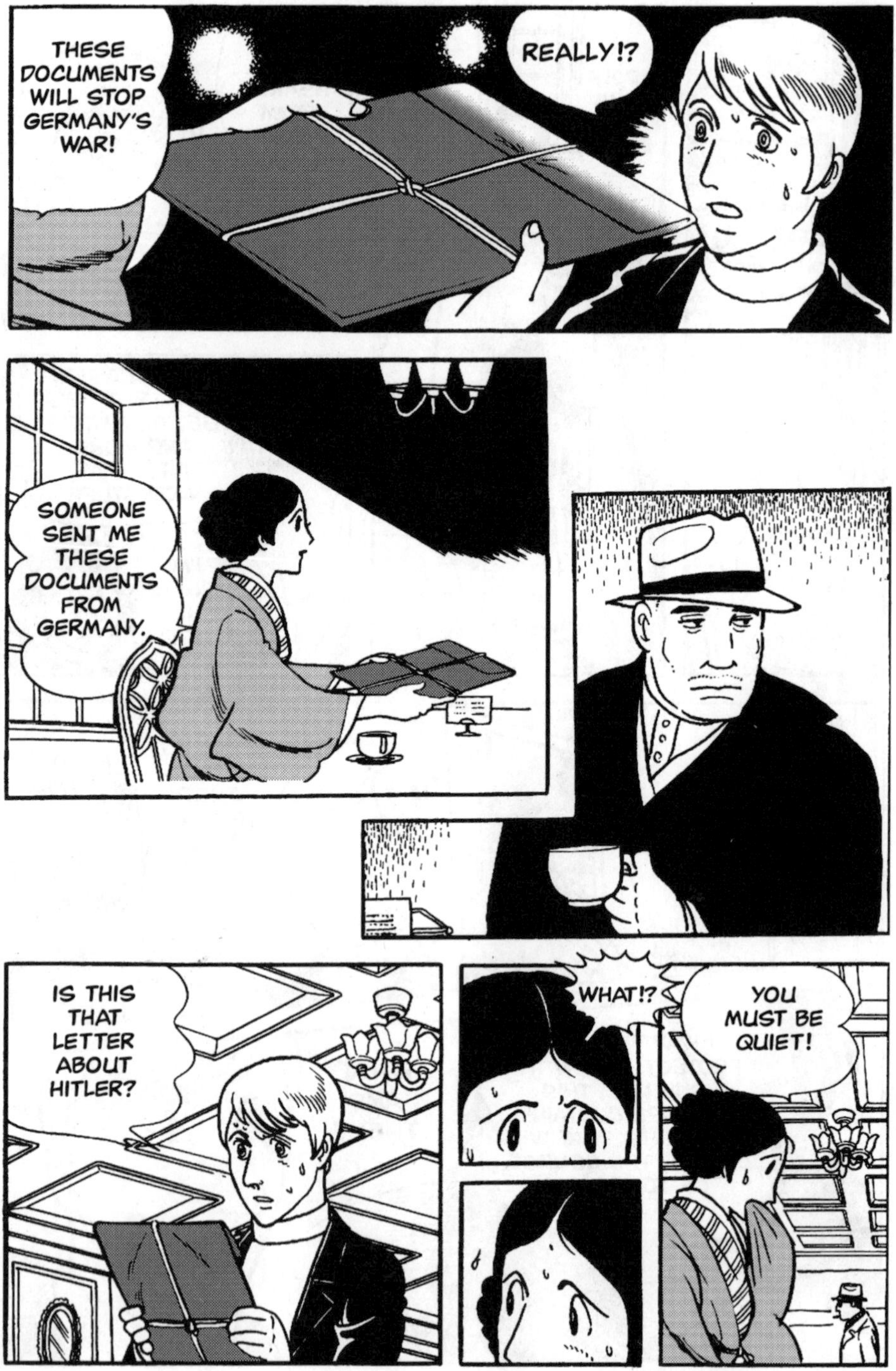
THESE DOCUMENTS WILL STOP GERMANY'S WAR!
REALLY!?
SOMEONE SENT ME THESE DOCUMENTS FROM GERMANY.
IS THIS THAT LETTER ABOUT HITLER?
WHAT!?
YOU MUST BE QUIET!

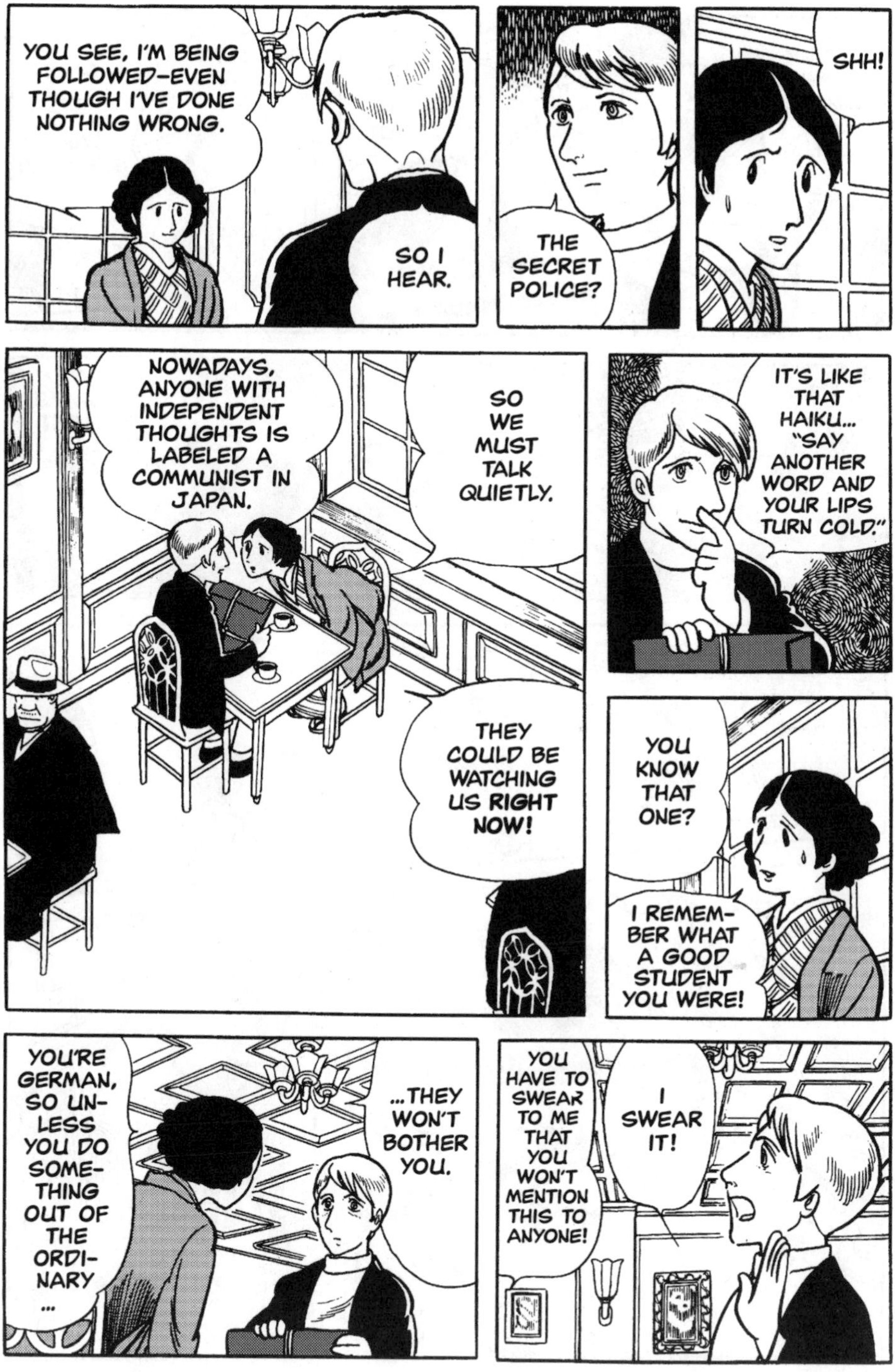
YOU SEE, I'M BEING FOLLOWED—EVEN THOUGH I'VE DONE NOTHING WRONG.
SO I HEAR.
THE SECRET POLICE?
SHH!
NOWADAYS, ANYONE WITH INDEPENDENT THOUGHTS IS LABELED A COMMUNIST IN JAPAN.
SO WE MUST TALK QUIETLY.
THEY COULD BE WATCHING US RIGHT NOW!
IT'S LIKE THAT HAIKU... "SAY ANOTHER WORD AND YOUR LIPS TURN COLD."
YOU KNOW THAT ONE?
I REMEMBER WHAT A GOOD STUDENT YOU WERE!
YOU'RE GERMAN, SO UNLESS YOU DO SOMETHING OUT OF THE ORDINARY...
...THEY WON'T BOTHER YOU.
YOU HAVE TO SWEAR TO ME THAT YOU WON'T MENTION THIS TO ANYONE!
I SWEAR IT!

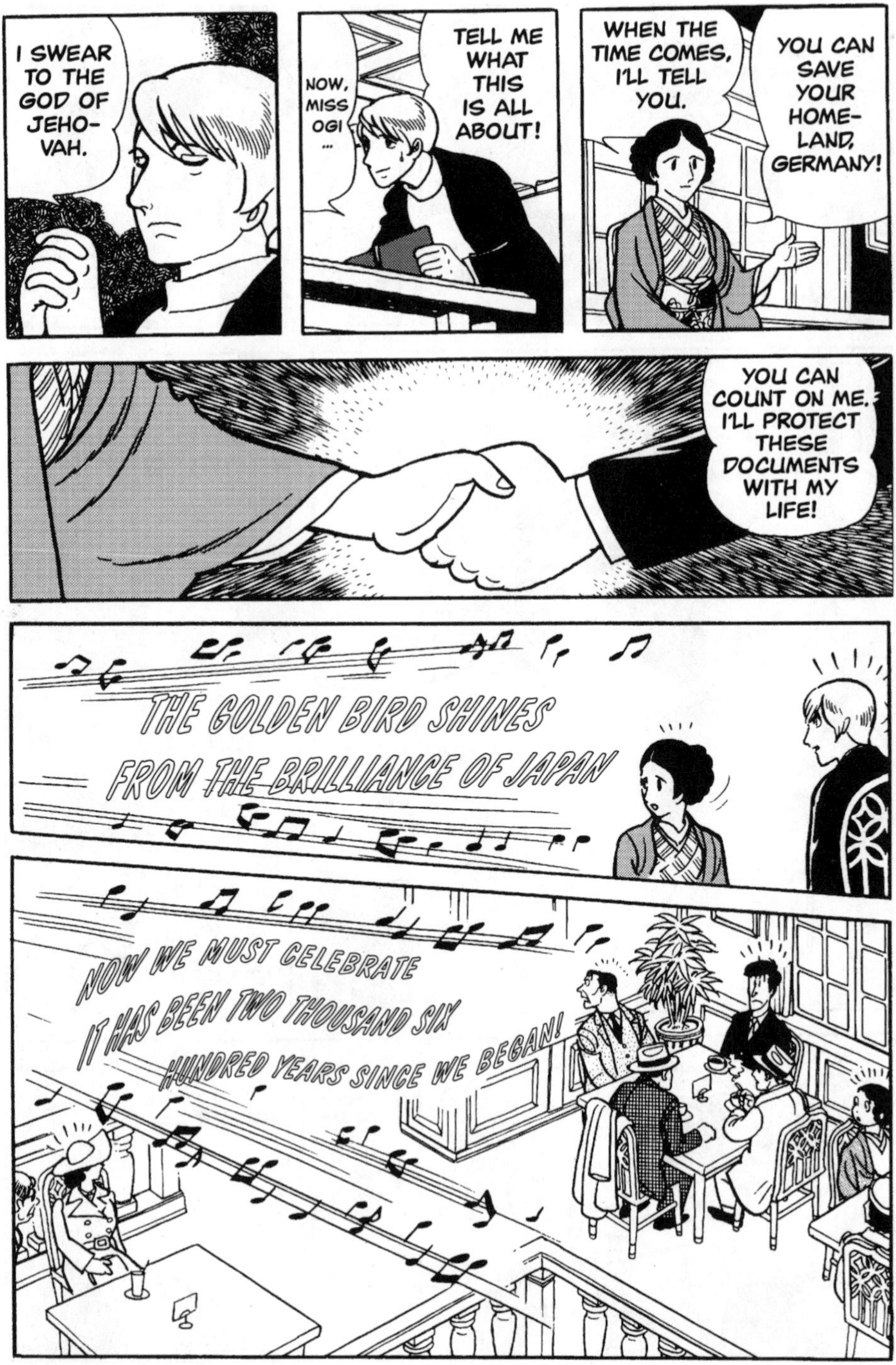
I SWEAR TO THE GOD OF JEHOVAH.
NOW, MISS OGI ...
TELL ME WHAT THIS IS ALL ABOUT!
WHEN THE TIME COMES, I'LL TELL YOU.
YOU CAN SAVE YOUR HOMELAND, GERMANY!
YOU CAN COUNT ON ME. I'LL PROTECT THESE DOCUMENTS WITH MY LIFE!
THE GOLDEN BIRD SHINES FROM THE BRILLIANCE OF JAPAN
NOW WE MUST CELEBRATE IT HAS BEEN TWO THOUSAND SIX HUNDRED YEARS SINCE WE BEGAN!

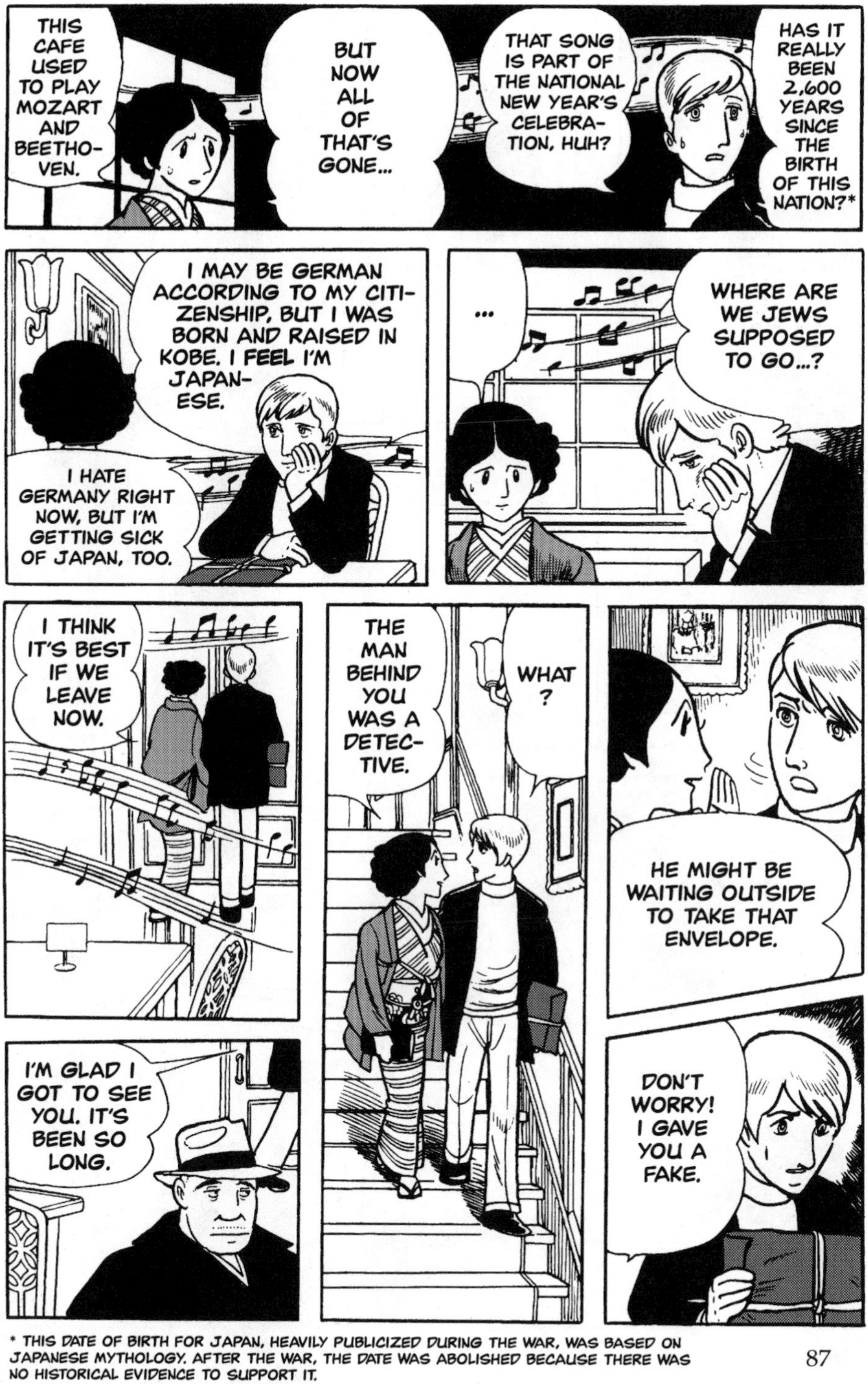
THIS CAFE USED TO PLAY MOZART AND BEETHO- VEN.
BUT NOW ALL OF THAT'S GONE...
THAT SONG IS PART OF THE NATIONAL NEW YEAR'S CELEBRA- TION, HUH?
HAS IT REALLY BEEN 2,600 YEARS SINCE THE BIRTH OF THIS NATION?*
I MAY BE GERMAN ACCORDING TO MY CITI- ZENSHIP, BUT I WAS BORN AND RAISED IN KOBE. I FEEL I'M JAPAN- ESE.
I HATE GERMANY RIGHT NOW, BUT I'M GETTING SICK OF JAPAN, TOO.
...
WHERE ARE WE JEWS SUPPOSED TO GO...?
I THINK IT'S BEST IF WE LEAVE NOW.
I'M GLAD I GOT TO SEE YOU. IT'S BEEN SO LONG.
THE MAN BEHIND YOU WAS A DETEC- TIVE.
WHAT ?
HE MIGHT BE WAITING OUTSIDE TO TAKE THAT ENVELOPE.
DON'T WORRY! I GAVE YOU A FAKE.

* THIS DATE OF BIRTH FOR JAPAN, HEAVILY PUBLICIZED DURING THE WAR, WAS BASED ON JAPANESE MYTHOLOGY. AFTER THE WAR, THE DATE WAS ABOLISHED BECAUSE THERE WAS NO HISTORICAL EVIDENCE TO SUPPORT IT.

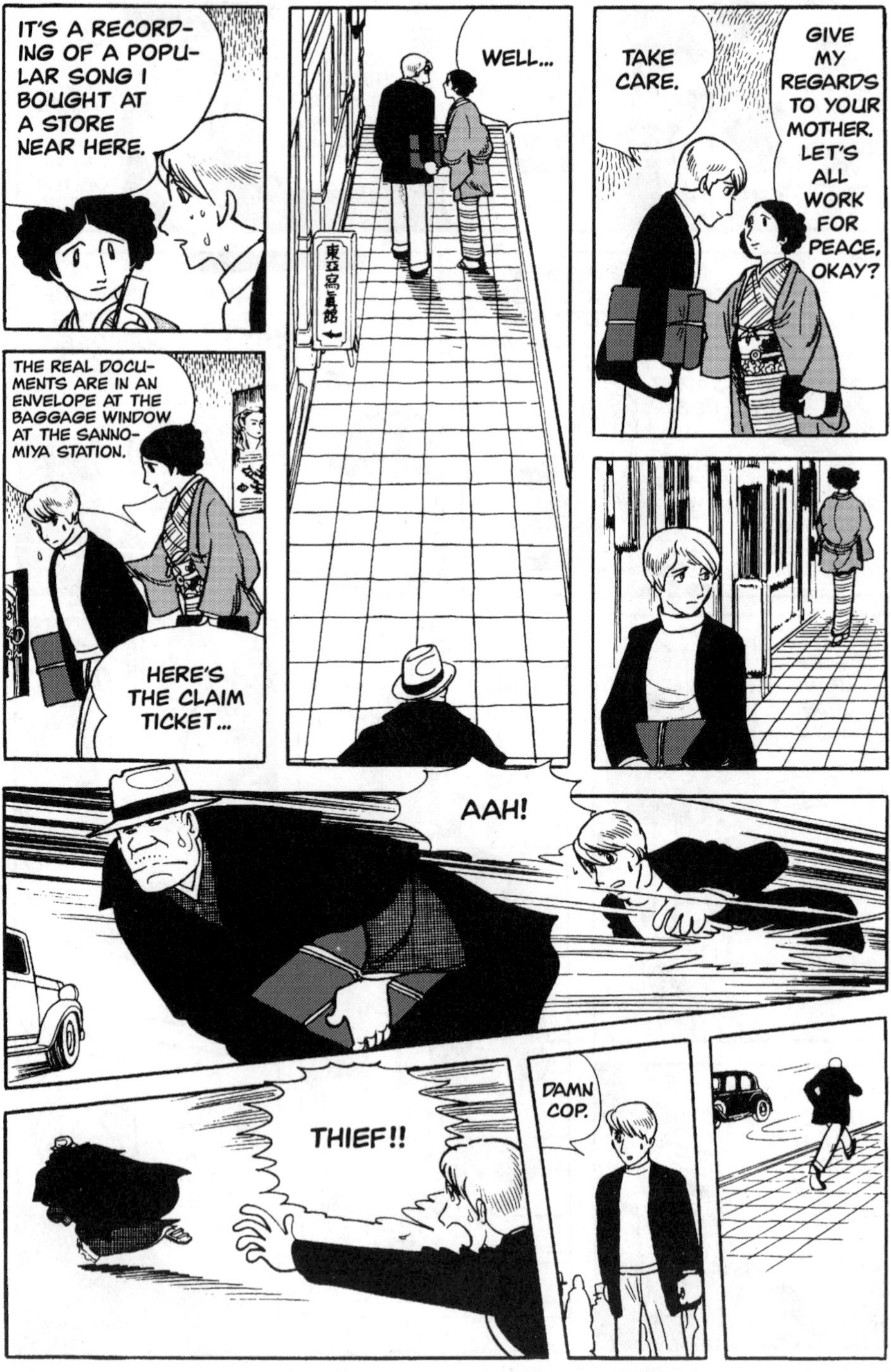
IT'S A RECORDING OF A POPULAR SONG I BOUGHT AT A STORE NEAR HERE.
THE REAL DOCUMENTS ARE IN AN ENVELOPE AT THE BAGGAGE WINDOW AT THE SANNOMIYA STATION.
HERE'S THE CLAIM TICKET...
WELL...
TAKE CARE.
GIVE MY REGARDS TO YOUR MOTHER. LET'S ALL WORK FOR PEACE, OKAY?
AAH!
THIEF!!
DAMN COP.

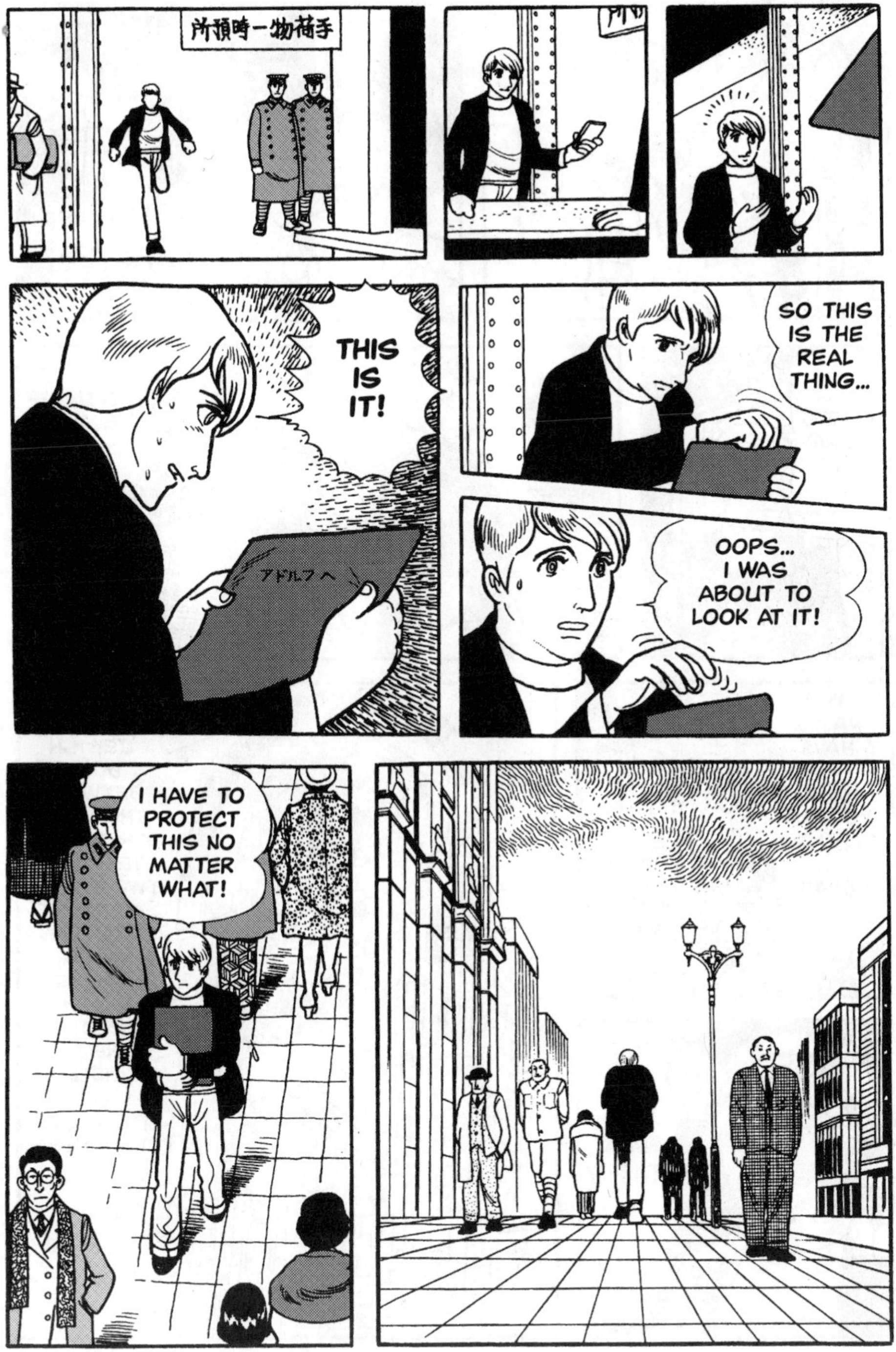
手荷物一時預所
THIS IS IT!
アドルフへ
SO THIS IS THE REAL THING...
OOPS... I WAS ABOUT TO LOOK AT IT!
I HAVE TO PROTECT THIS NO MATTER WHAT!

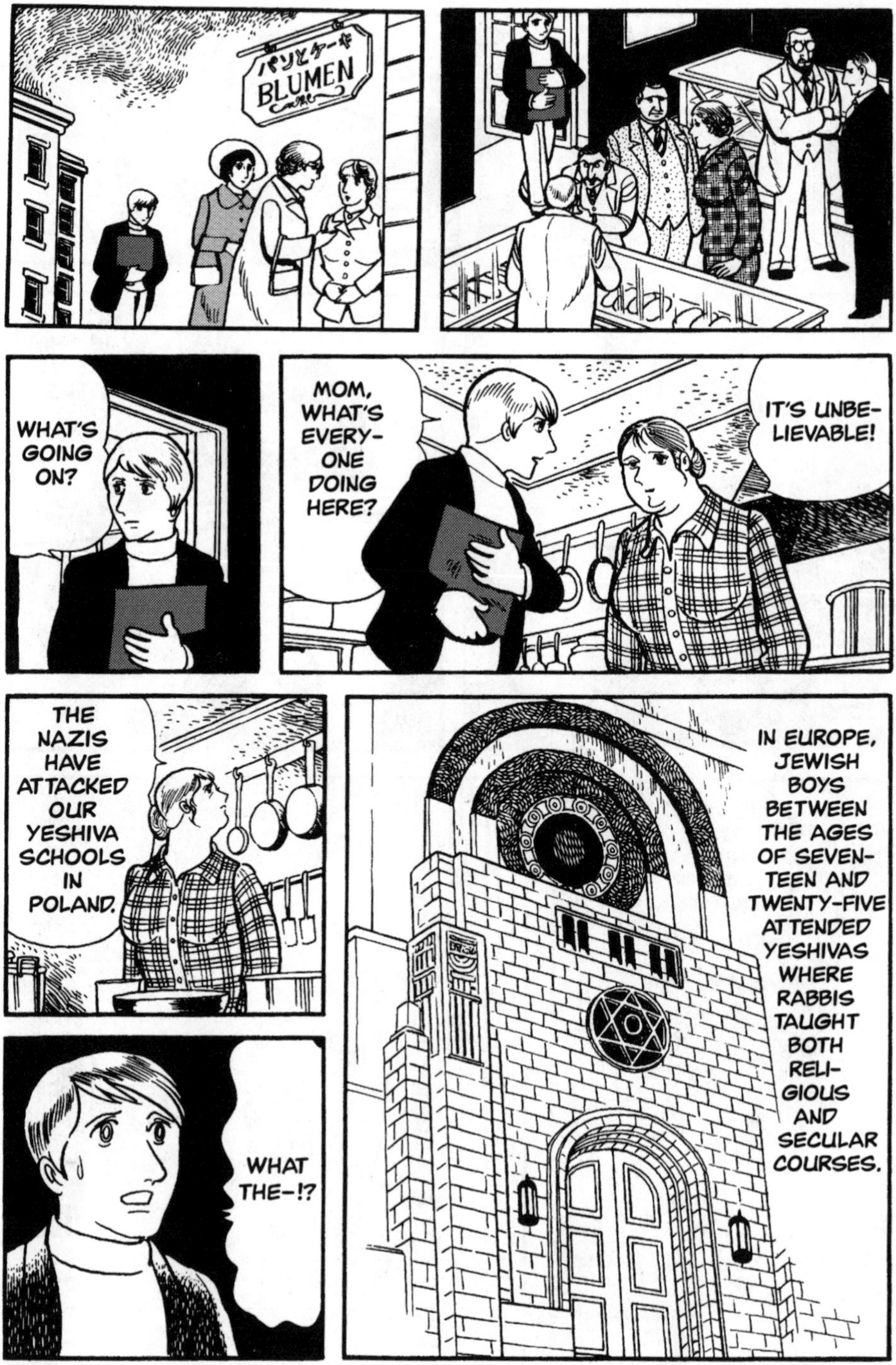
パンとケーキ
BLUMEN
WHAT'S GOING ON?
MOM, WHAT'S EVERY-ONE DOING HERE?
IT'S UNBE-LIEVABLE!
THE NAZIS HAVE ATTACKED OUR YESHIVA SCHOOLS IN POLAND.
WHAT THE-!?
IN EUROPE, JEWISH BOYS BETWEEN THE AGES OF SEVEN-TEEN AND TWENTY-FIVE ATTENDED YESHIVAS WHERE RABBIS TAUGHT BOTH RELI-GIOUS AND SECULAR COURSES.

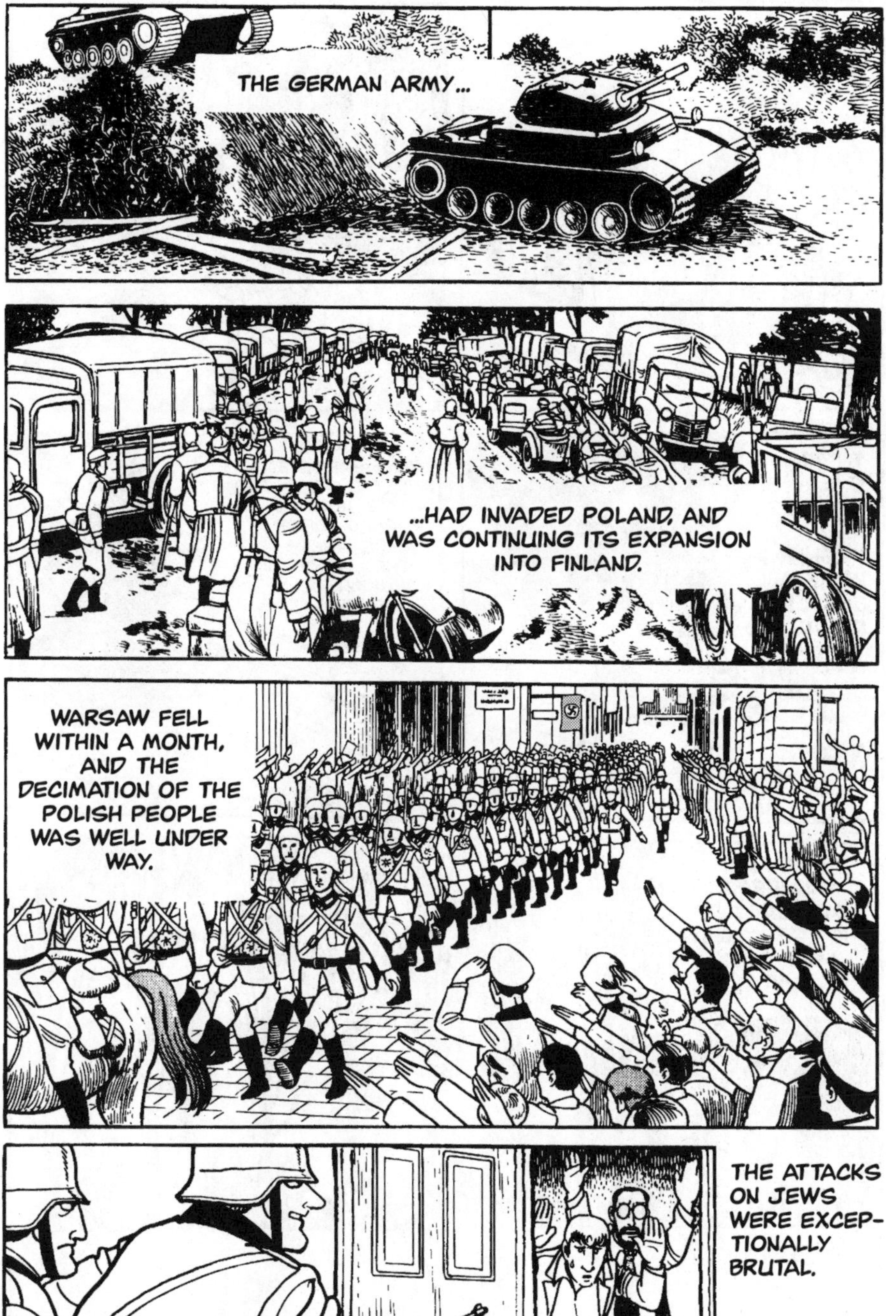
THE GERMAN ARMY...
...HAD INVADED POLAND, AND WAS CONTINUING ITS EXPANSION INTO FINLAND.
WARSAW FELL WITHIN A MONTH, AND THE DECIMATION OF THE POLISH PEOPLE WAS WELL UNDER WAY.
THE ATTACKS ON JEWS WERE EXCEPTIONALLY BRUTAL.

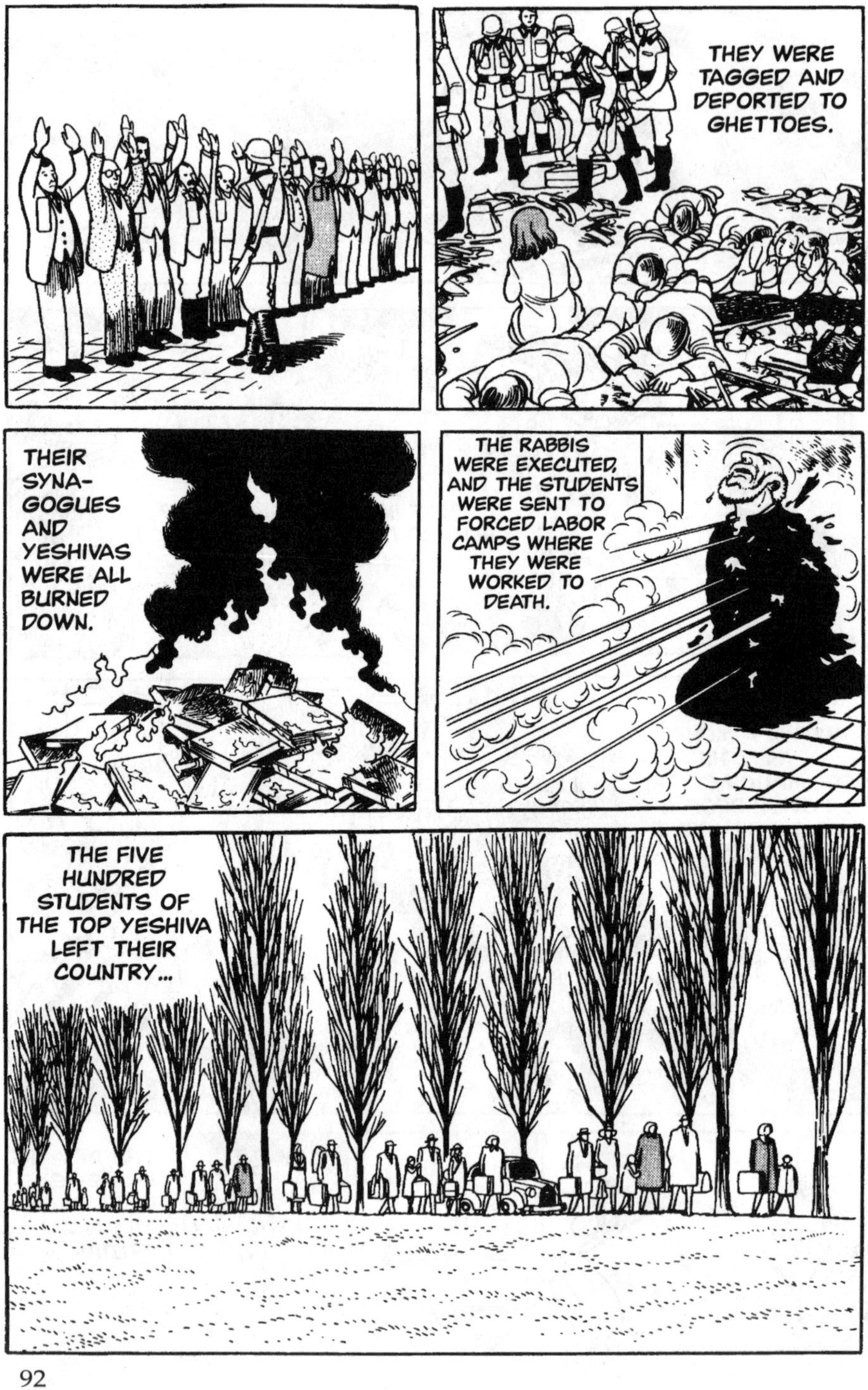
THEY WERE TAGGED AND DEPORTED TO GHETTOES.
THEIR SYNA-GOGUES AND YESHIVAS WERE ALL BURNED DOWN.
THE RABBIS WERE EXECUTED, AND THE STUDENTS WERE SENT TO FORCED LABOR CAMPS WHERE THEY WERE WORKED TO DEATH.
THE FIVE HUNDRED STUDENTS OF THE TOP YESHIVA LEFT THEIR COUNTRY...

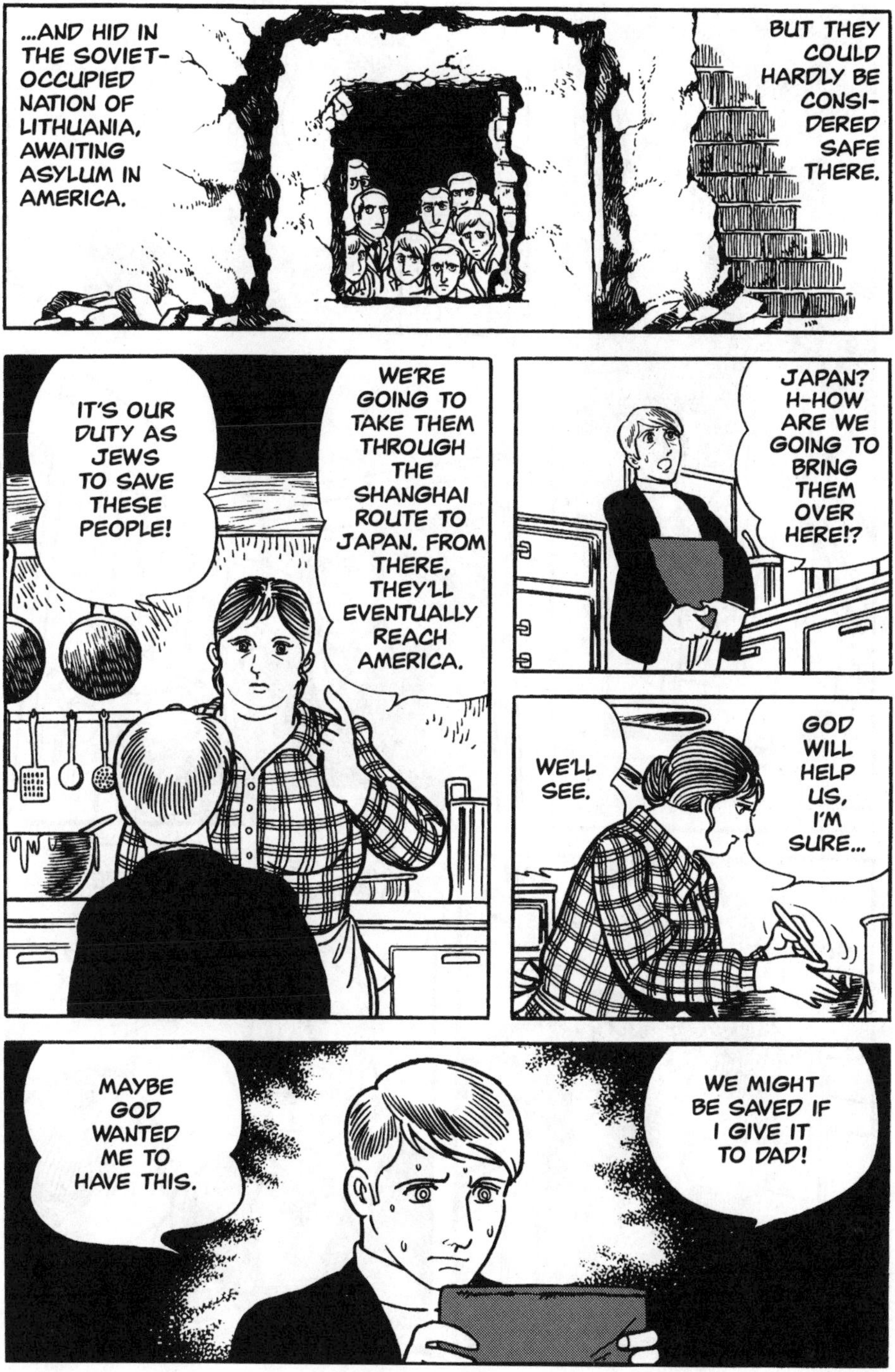
...AND HID IN THE SOVIET-OCCUPIED NATION OF LITHUANIA, AWAITING ASYLUM IN AMERICA.
BUT THEY COULD HARDLY BE CONSIDERED SAFE THERE.
IT'S OUR DUTY AS JEWS TO SAVE THESE PEOPLE!
WE'RE GOING TO TAKE THEM THROUGH THE SHANGHAI ROUTE TO JAPAN. FROM THERE, THEY'LL EVENTUALLY REACH AMERICA.
JAPAN? H-HOW ARE WE GOING TO BRING THEM OVER HERE!?
GOD WILL HELP US, I'M SURE...
WE'LL SEE.
MAYBE GOD WANTED ME TO HAVE THIS.
WE MIGHT BE SAVED IF I GIVE IT TO DAD!

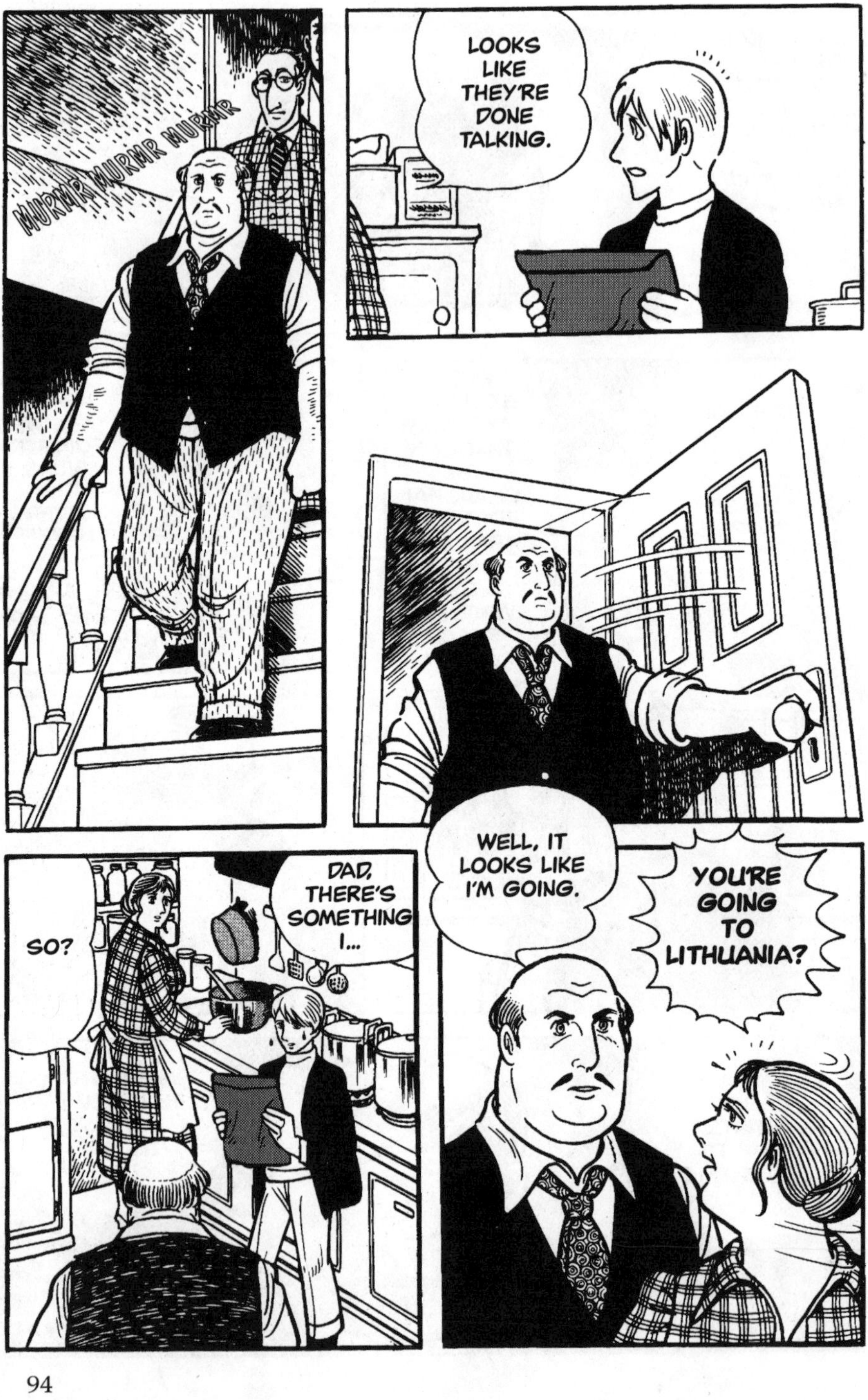
MURMR MURMR MURMR
LOOKS LIKE THEY'RE DONE TALKING.
DAD, THERE'S SOMETHING I...
SO?
WELL, IT LOOKS LIKE I'M GOING.
YOU'RE GOING TO LITHUANIA?

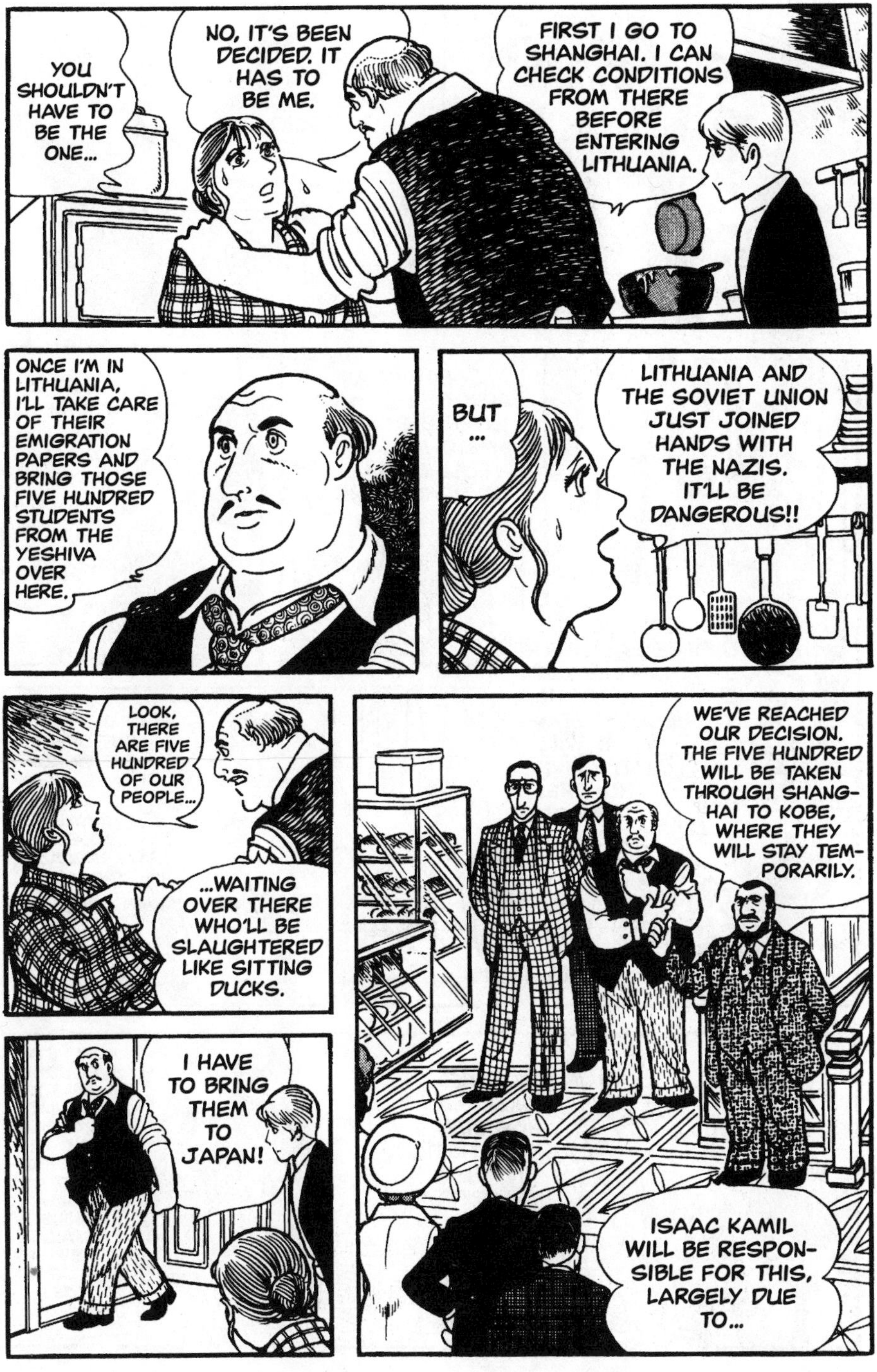
YOU SHOULDN'T HAVE TO BE THE ONE...
NO, IT'S BEEN DECIDED. IT HAS TO BE ME.
FIRST I GO TO SHANGHAI. I CAN CHECK CONDITIONS FROM THERE BEFORE ENTERING LITHUANIA.
ONCE I'M IN LITHUANIA, I'LL TAKE CARE OF THEIR EMIGRATION PAPERS AND BRING THOSE FIVE HUNDRED STUDENTS FROM THE YESHIVA OVER HERE.
BUT ...
LITHUANIA AND THE SOVIET UNION JUST JOINED HANDS WITH THE NAZIS. IT'LL BE DANGEROUS!!
LOOK, THERE ARE FIVE HUNDRED OF OUR PEOPLE...
...WAITING OVER THERE WHO'LL BE SLAUGHTERED LIKE SITTING DUCKS.
WE'VE REACHED OUR DECISION. THE FIVE HUNDRED WILL BE TAKEN THROUGH SHANG-HAI TO KOBE, WHERE THEY WILL STAY TEM-PORARILY.
I HAVE TO BRING THEM TO JAPAN!
ISAAC KAMIL WILL BE RESPON-SIBLE FOR THIS, LARGELY DUE TO...

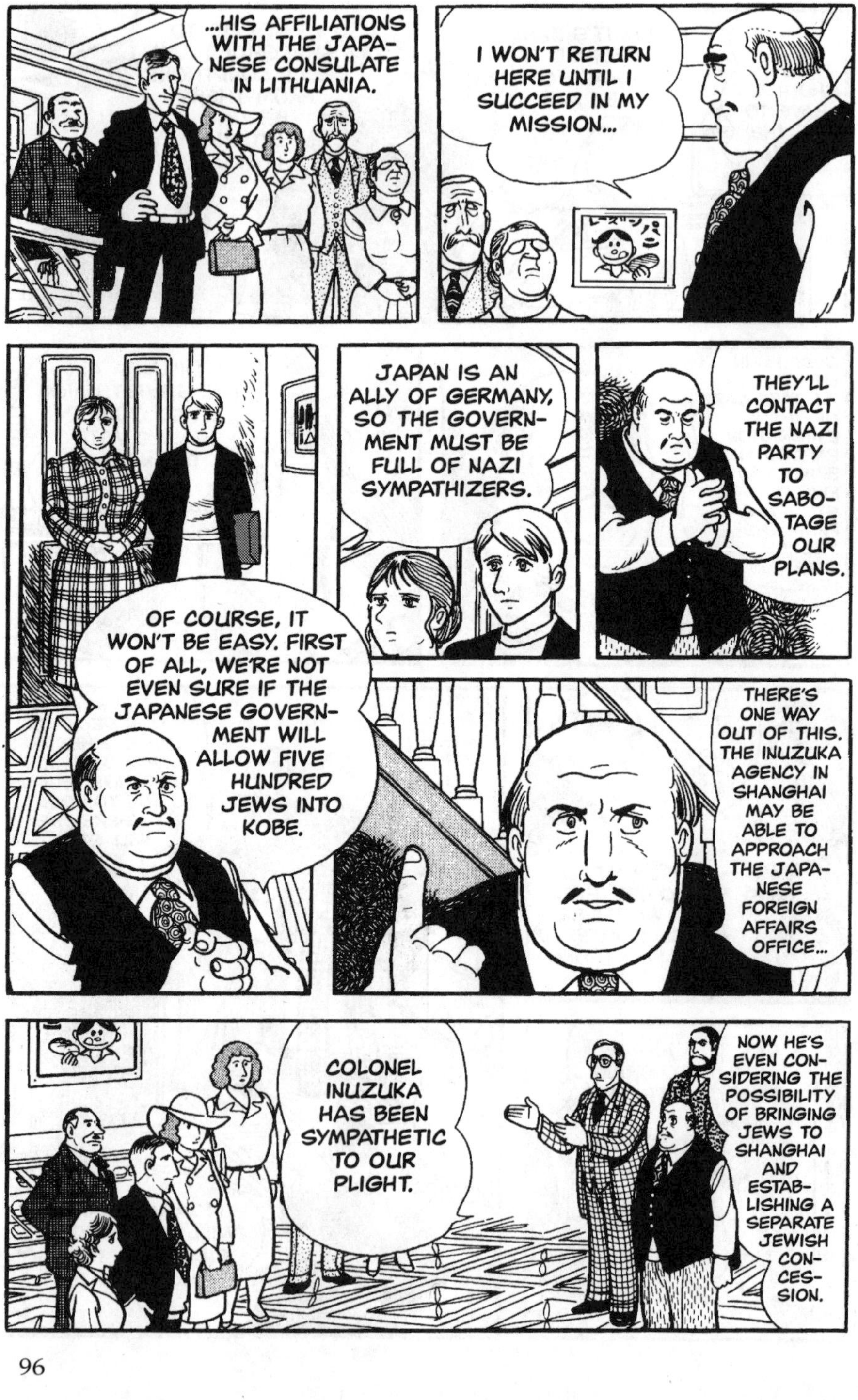
...HIS AFFILIATIONS WITH THE JAPANESE CONSULATE IN LITHUANIA.
I WON'T RETURN HERE UNTIL I SUCCEED IN MY MISSION...
OF COURSE, IT WON'T BE EASY. FIRST OF ALL, WE'RE NOT EVEN SURE IF THE JAPANESE GOVERNMENT WILL ALLOW FIVE HUNDRED JEWS INTO KOBE.
JAPAN IS AN ALLY OF GERMANY, SO THE GOVERNMENT MUST BE FULL OF NAZI SYMPATHIZERS.
THEY'LL CONTACT THE NAZI PARTY TO SABOTAGE OUR PLANS.
THERE'S ONE WAY OUT OF THIS. THE INUZUKA AGENCY IN SHANGHAI MAY BE ABLE TO APPROACH THE JAPANESE FOREIGN AFFAIRS OFFICE...
COLONEL INUZUKA HAS BEEN SYMPATHETIC TO OUR PLIGHT.
NOW HE'S EVEN CONSIDERING THE POSSIBILITY OF BRINGING JEWS TO SHANGHAI AND ESTABLISHING A SEPARATE JEWISH CONCESSION.

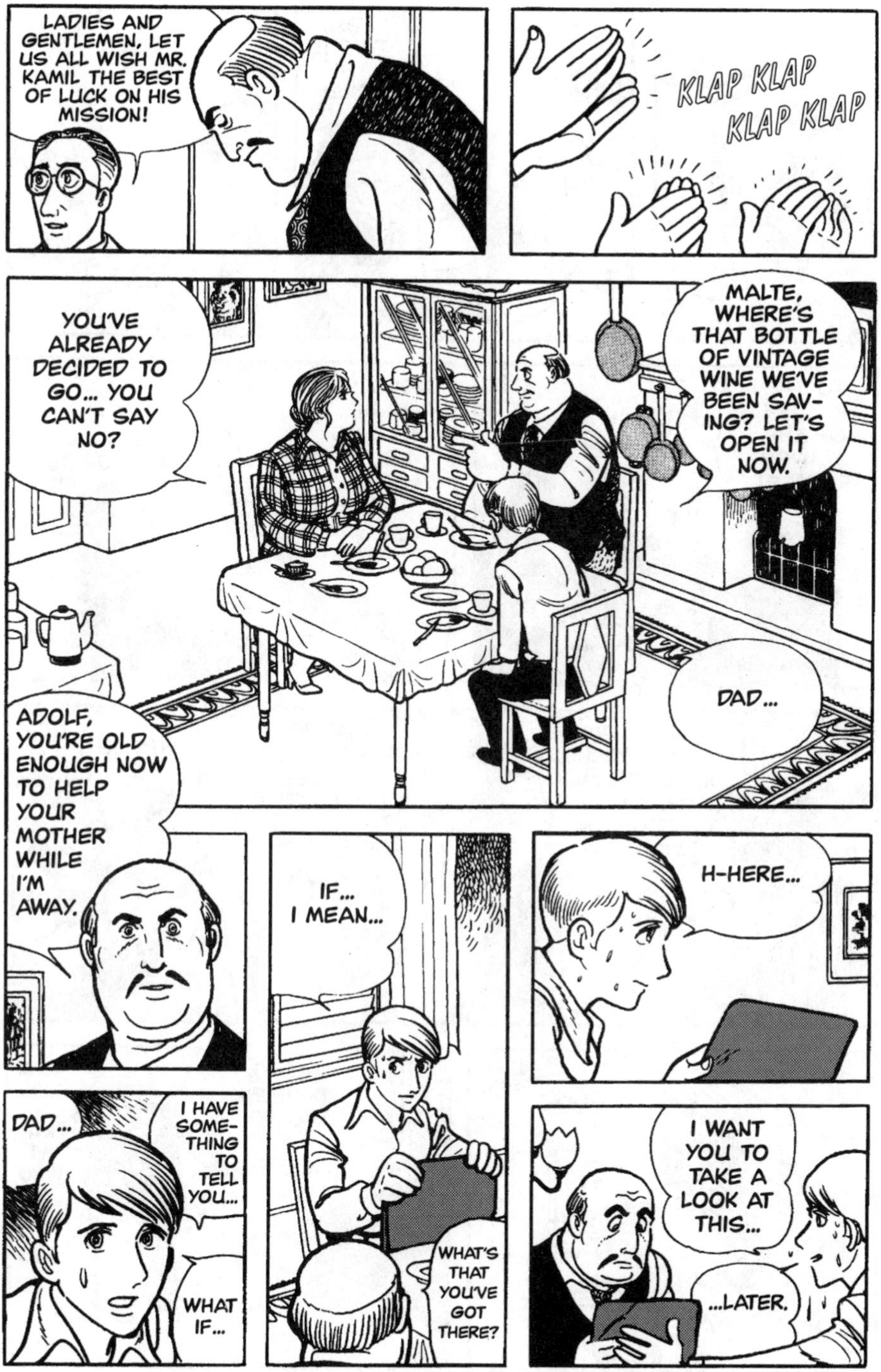
LADIES AND GENTLEMEN, LET US ALL WISH MR. KAMIL THE BEST OF LUCK ON HIS MISSION!
KLAP KLAP
KLAP KLAP
YOU'VE ALREADY DECIDED TO GO... YOU CAN'T SAY NO?
MALTE, WHERE'S THAT BOTTLE OF VINTAGE WINE WE'VE BEEN SAV-ING? LET'S OPEN IT NOW.
DAD...
ADOLF, YOU'RE OLD ENOUGH NOW TO HELP YOUR MOTHER WHILE I'M AWAY.
DAD...
I HAVE SOME-THING TO TELL YOU...
WHAT IF...
IF... I MEAN...
WHAT'S THAT YOU'VE GOT THERE?
H-HERE...
I WANT YOU TO TAKE A LOOK AT THIS...
...LATER.

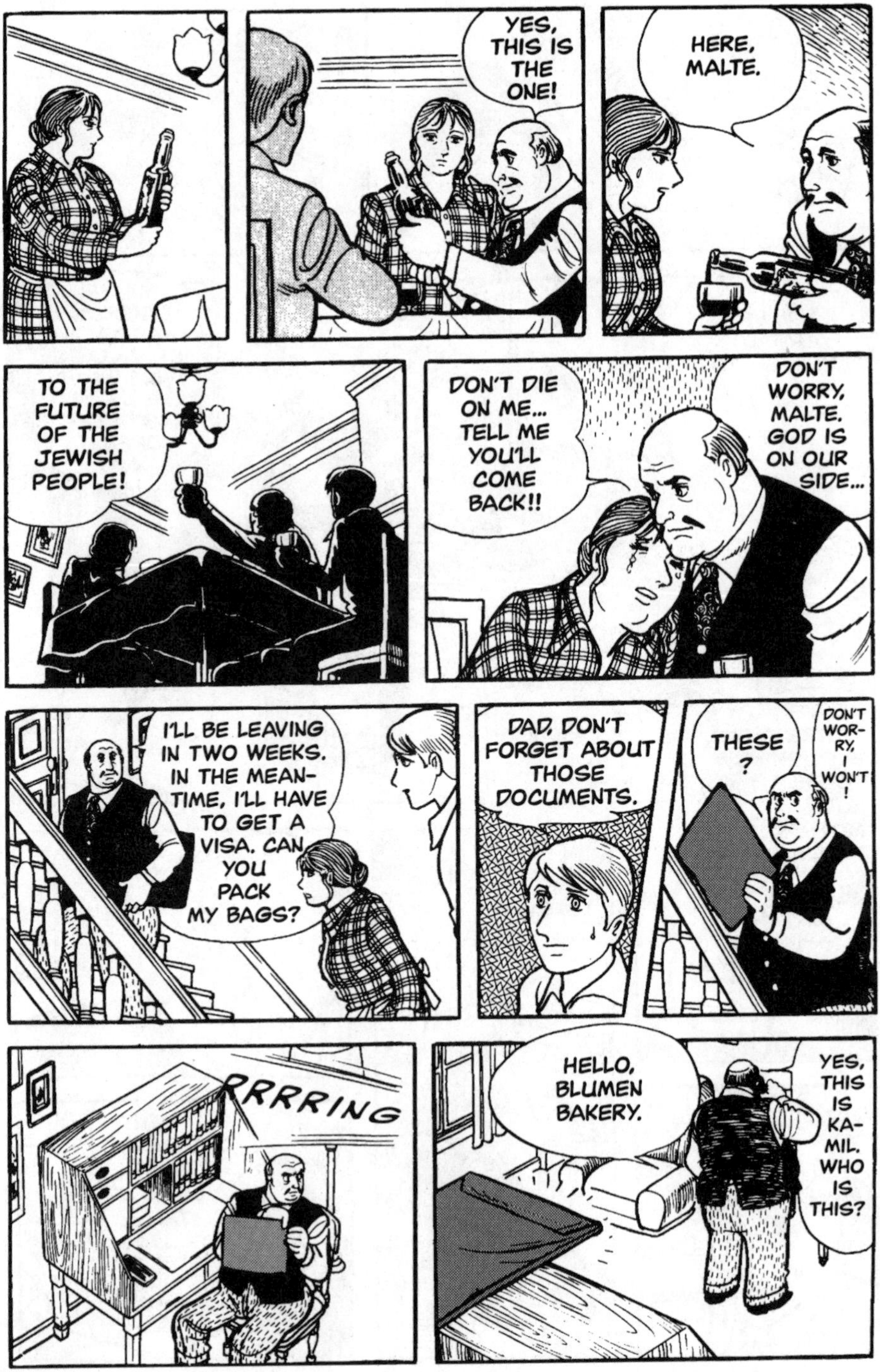
YES, THIS IS THE ONE!
HERE, MALTE.
TO THE FUTURE OF THE JEWISH PEOPLE!
DON'T DIE ON ME... TELL ME YOU'LL COME BACK!!
DON'T WORRY, MALTE. GOD IS ON OUR SIDE...
I'LL BE LEAVING IN TWO WEEKS. IN THE MEAN-TIME, I'LL HAVE TO GET A VISA. CAN YOU PACK MY BAGS?
DAD, DON'T FORGET ABOUT THOSE DOCUMENTS.
THESE?
DON'T WOR-RY, I WON'T!
RRRRING
HELLO, BLUMEN BAKERY.
YES, THIS IS KA-MIL. WHO IS THIS?

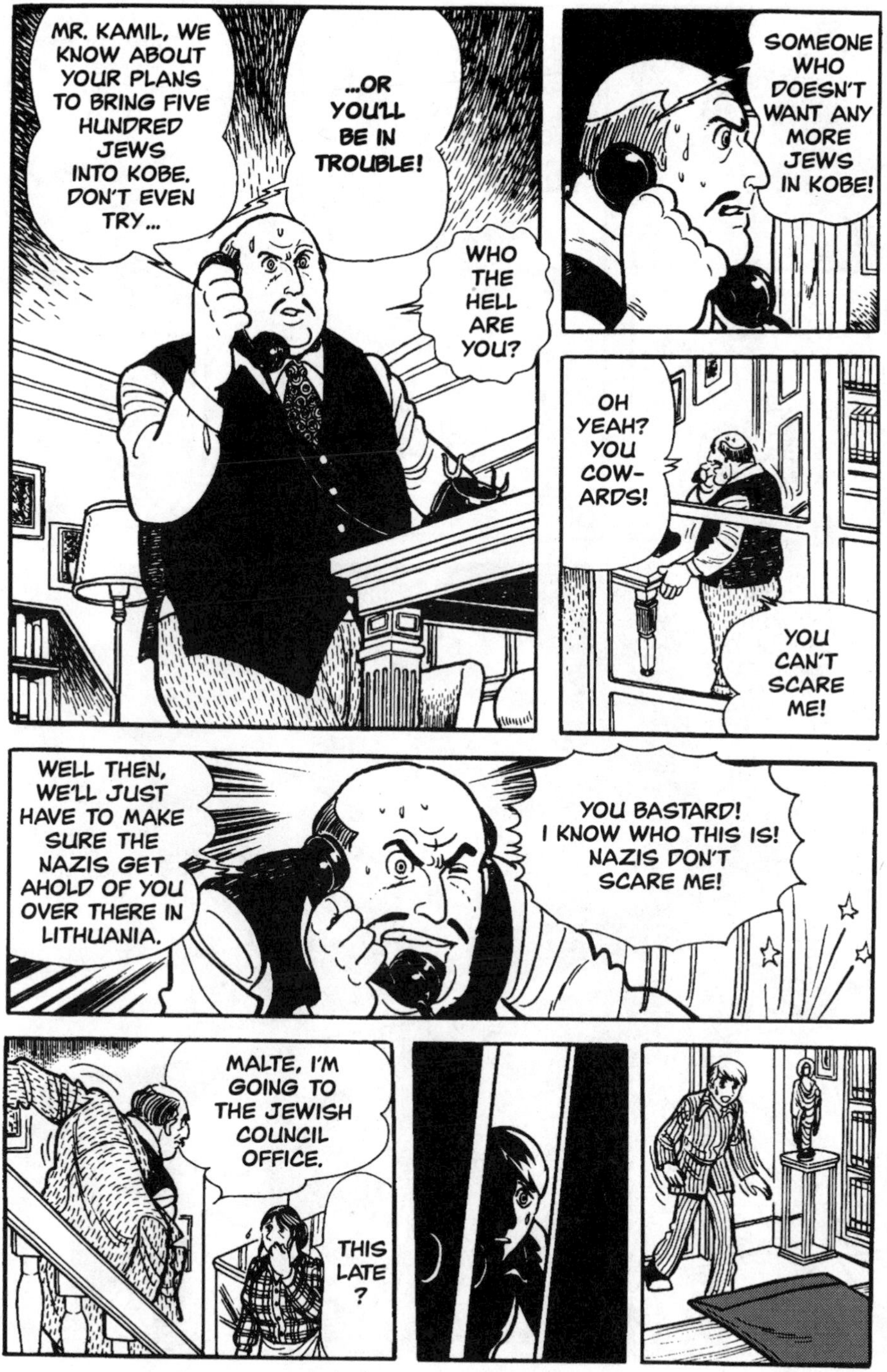
MR. KAMIL, WE KNOW ABOUT YOUR PLANS TO BRING FIVE HUNDRED JEWS INTO KOBE. DON'T EVEN TRY...
...OR YOU'LL BE IN TROUBLE!
WHO THE HELL ARE YOU?
SOMEONE WHO DOESN'T WANT ANY MORE JEWS IN KOBE!
OH YEAH? YOU COW-ARDS!
YOU CAN'T SCARE ME!
WELL THEN, WE'LL JUST HAVE TO MAKE SURE THE NAZIS GET AHOLD OF YOU OVER THERE IN LITHUANIA.
YOU BASTARD! I KNOW WHO THIS IS! NAZIS DON'T SCARE ME!
MALTE, I'M GOING TO THE JEWISH COUNCIL OFFICE.
THIS LATE ?

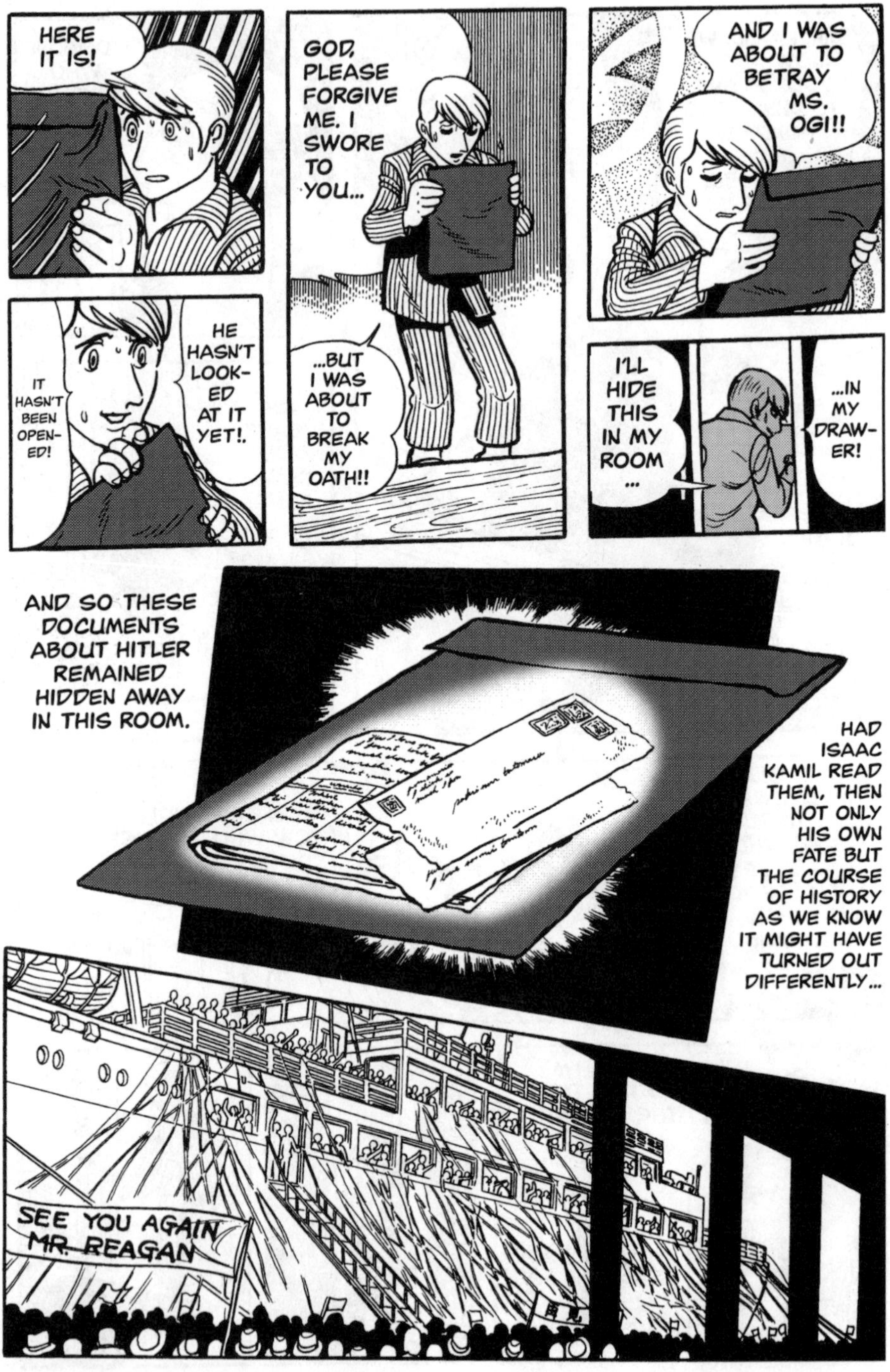
HERE IT IS!
GOD, PLEASE FORGIVE ME. I SWORE TO YOU...
...BUT I WAS ABOUT TO BREAK MY OATH!!
AND I WAS ABOUT TO BETRAY MS. OGI!!
IT HASN'T BEEN OPEN-ED!
HE HASN'T LOOK-ED AT IT YET!.
I'LL HIDE THIS IN MY ROOM ...
...IN MY DRAW-ER!
AND SO THESE DOCUMENTS ABOUT HITLER REMAINED HIDDEN AWAY IN THIS ROOM.
HAD ISAAC KAMIL READ THEM, THEN NOT ONLY HIS OWN FATE BUT THE COURSE OF HISTORY AS WE KNOW IT MIGHT HAVE TURNED OUT DIFFERENTLY...
SEE YOU AGAIN MR. REAGAN

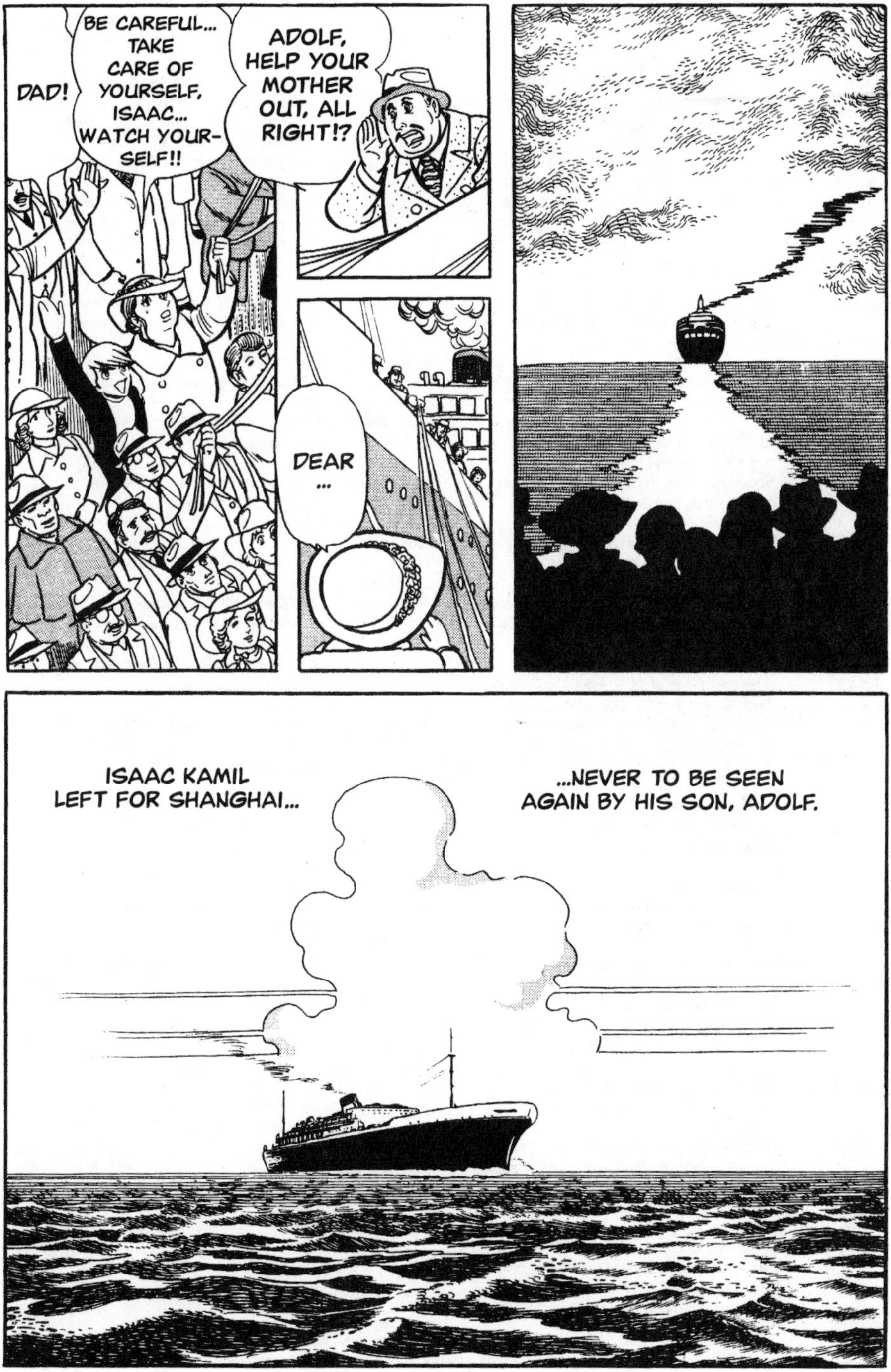
DAD!
BE CAREFUL... TAKE CARE OF YOURSELF, ISAAC... WATCH YOUR-SELF!!
ADOLF, HELP YOUR MOTHER OUT, ALL RIGHT!?
DEAR ...
ISAAC KAMIL LEFT FOR SHANGHAI...
...NEVER TO BE SEEN AGAIN BY HIS SON, ADOLF.

1940 TIMELINE

January 26	The United States permits its 1911 commercial treaty with Japan to lapse.
March 30	A pro-Japanese government for all of China is proclaimed in Nanking. The U.S. refuses to recognize this puppet government.
April 9	Germany invades Denmark and Norway, claiming it possesses "documented proof that England and France have jointly decided, if necessary, to carry out their action through the territory of the Northern States against the will of the latter."
April 27	Himmler orders the construction of a concentration camp, a central "extermination" facility, at Auschwitz, Poland.
May 1	Jews are prohibited from leaving the Lodz ghetto.
May 10	Germany invades the Low Countries, claiming the British and French are preparing to attack Germany through Belgium, the Netherlands, and Luxembourg.
	Winston Churchill becomes Britain's prime minister.
May 16	Roosevelt requests $1.2 billion for military spending and modernization of the United States Army and Navy.
May 26	The evacuation of Allied troops at Dunkirk begins. In one of the most dramatic withdrawals in military history, over the course of a week, a hastily assembled fleet of 861 ships and boats evacuates 224,585 British and 112,546 French and Belgians. The British leave behind 11,000 machine guns, 1,200 artillery guns, 6,400 antitank rifles, and 75,000 vehicles.
June 10	Italian forces invade France and declare war on France and Britain. Canada, in turn, declares war on Italy.
June 14	German troops march into Paris.
June 18	General de Gaulle, broadcasting from London, calls on the French to join him in the resistance against Germany.
June 21	France surrenders to Germany, and the collaborative Vichy government is established.
July 4	Roosevelt begins a limited embargo against Japan by banning the shipment of strategic minerals, chemicals, aircraft parts and engines.
July 16	After Minister of War General Shunroku Hata steps down and demands sweeping governmental changes, the Japanese cabinet resigns and Prince Konoye again becomes prime minister.
July 27	Japanese secret police begin arresting foreign nationals for alleged spying activities.
August 1	Foreign Minister Matsuoka defines Tokyo's policy for "Greater East Asia": "...the immediate aim of our foreign policy at present is to establish a great East Asian chain of common prosperity with the Japan-Manchukuo-China group as one of the links. We shall thus be able to demonstrate the imperial way in the most effective manner and pave the way towards the establishment of world peace."
August 15	German planes launch a massive offensive to cripple the British Royal Air Force.
August 21	Leon Trotsky, Stalin's one-time rival, is assassinated. Moscow denies any responsibility.
September 7	In Germany's initial blitz on Britain, a force of 625 bombers is directed against London.
September 25	U.S. intelligence cracks Tokyo's top-secret Purple diplomatic code.
September 27	Germany, Italy, and Japan enter into a 10-year military and economic agreement.
October 3-4	The French Vichy government bars Jews from public office and most areas of economic life, and authorizes the internment of foreign Jews. Similar anti-Jewish legislation is enacted in Romania.
October 5	Prime Minister Konoye claims a war between Japan and the U.S. is inevitable if the U.S. views the Axis alliance as "hostile."
October 22	Jews are deported from Alsace-Lorraine and the Rhineland.
October 28	Italy invades Greece.
November 15	Jews are prohibited from leaving the Warsaw ghetto.
November 23-25	Romania and Slovakia sign the Tripartite Pact, thereby joining the Axis, but Bulgaria refuses.
November 30	The U.S. grants another $100 million in loans and credits to China.
December 4	Japan and Thailand conclude a treaty of friendship.
December 29	The British civilian air raid casualty toll for the month is 3,793 killed, 5,244 injured.

CHAPTER THREE

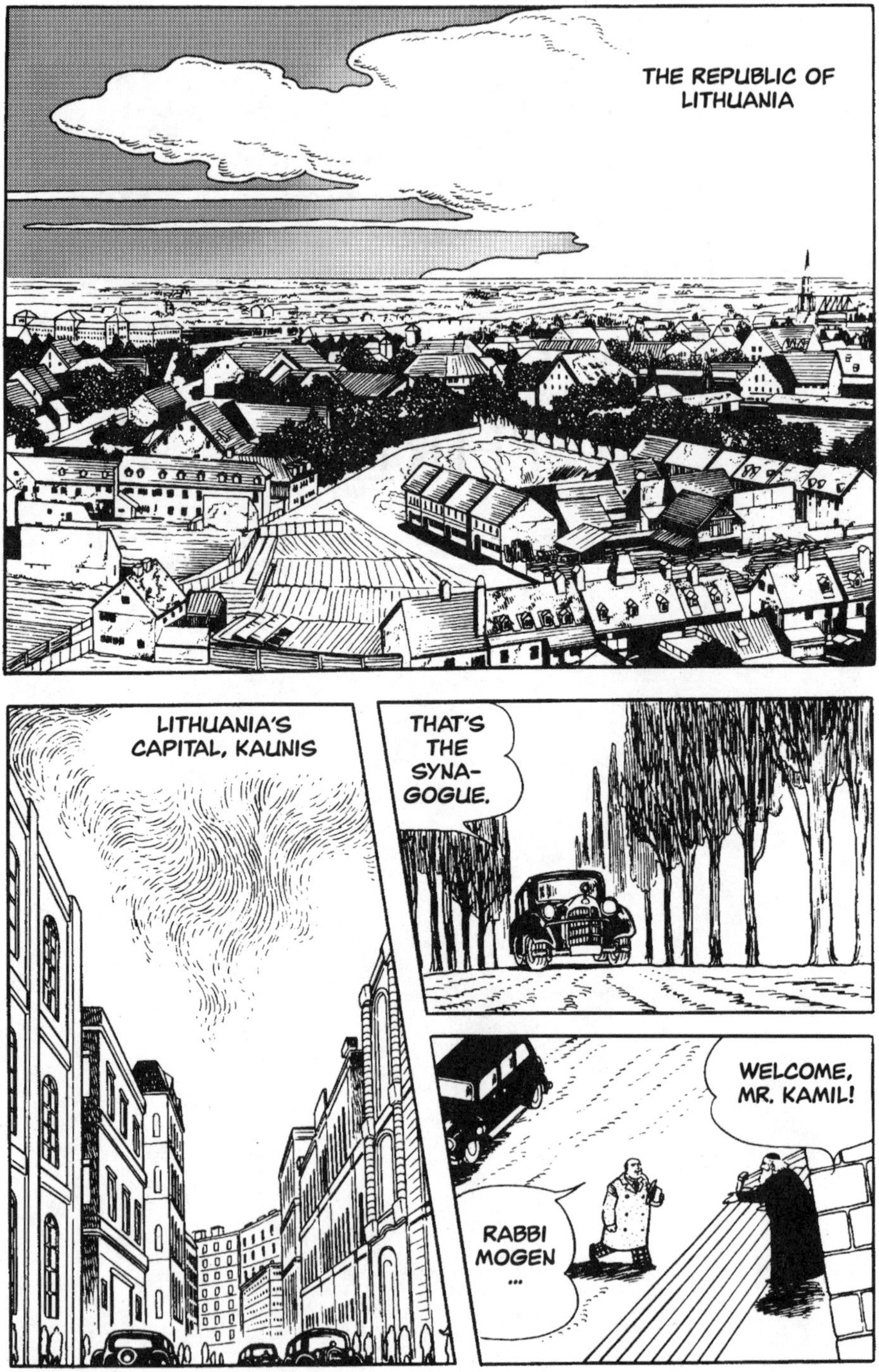
THE REPUBLIC OF LITHUANIA
LITHUANIA'S CAPITAL, KAUNIS
THAT'S THE SYNA-GOGUE.
WELCOME, MR. KAMIL!
RABBI MOGEN ...

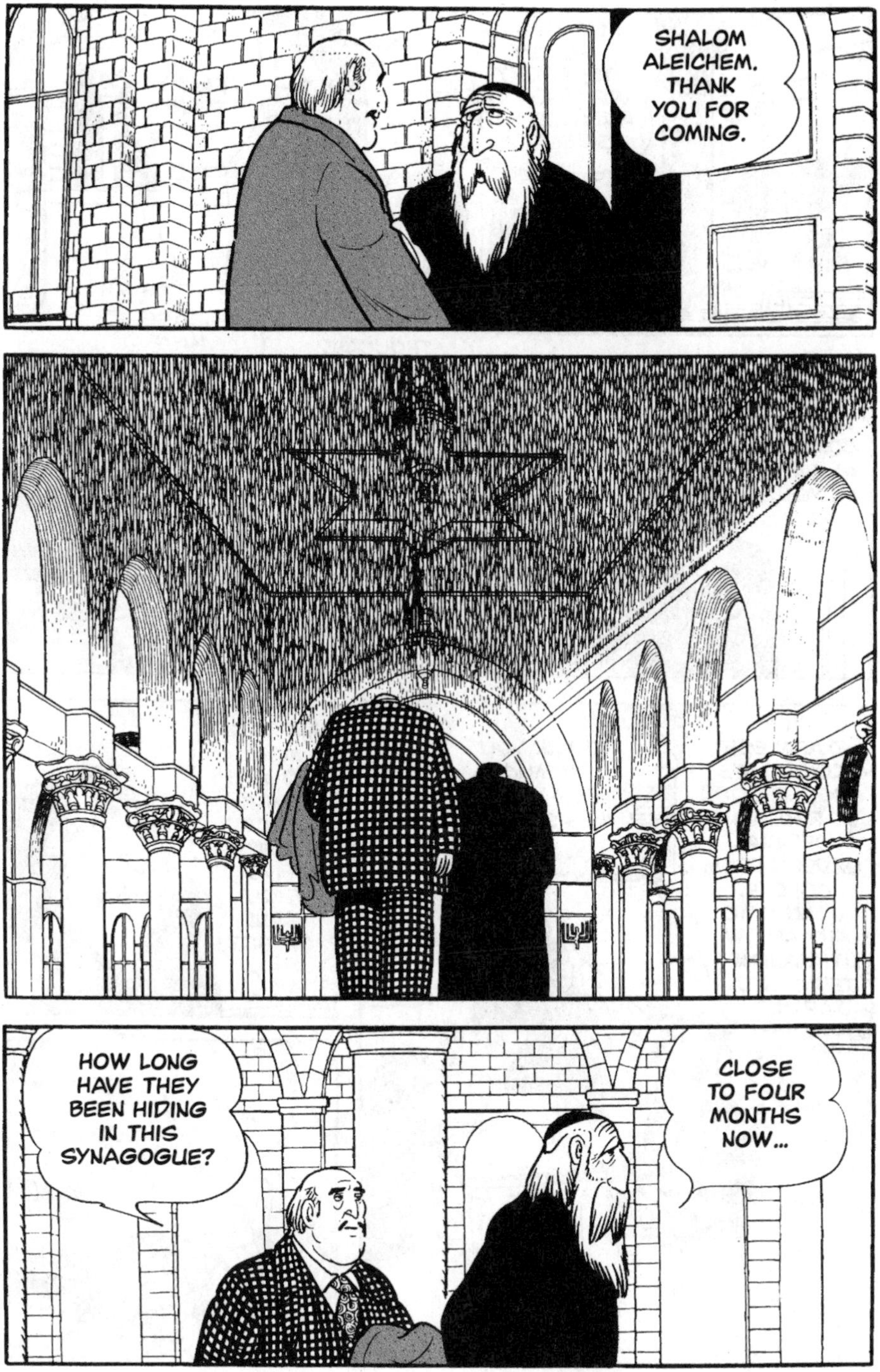
SHALOM ALEICHEM. THANK YOU FOR COMING.
HOW LONG HAVE THEY BEEN HIDING IN THIS SYNAGOGUE?
CLOSE TO FOUR MONTHS NOW...

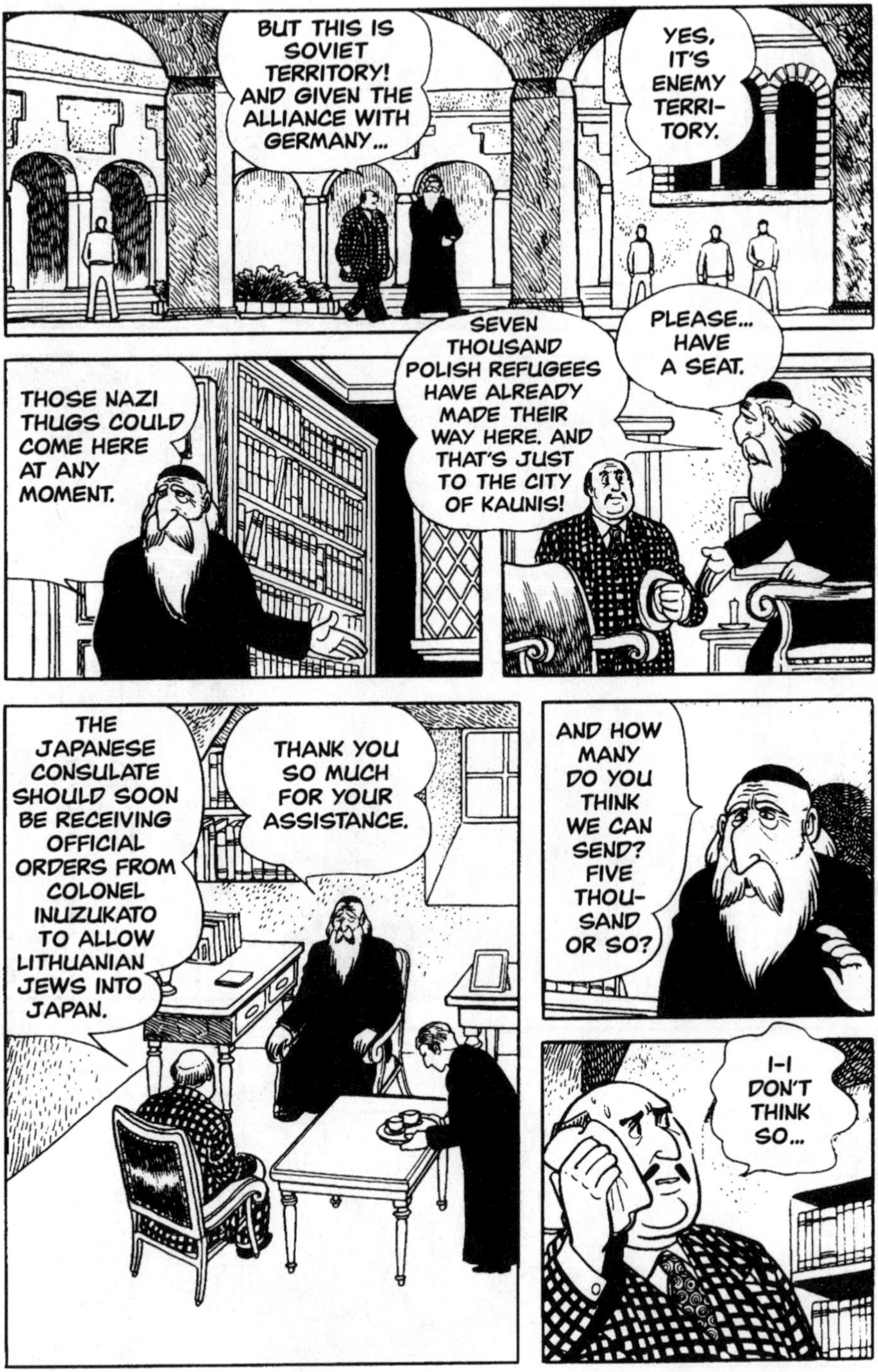
BUT THIS IS SOVIET TERRITORY! AND GIVEN THE ALLIANCE WITH GERMANY...
YES, IT'S ENEMY TERRI-TORY.
THOSE NAZI THUGS COULD COME HERE AT ANY MOMENT.
SEVEN THOUSAND POLISH REFUGEES HAVE ALREADY MADE THEIR WAY HERE. AND THAT'S JUST TO THE CITY OF KAUNIS!
PLEASE... HAVE A SEAT.
THE JAPANESE CONSULATE SHOULD SOON BE RECEIVING OFFICIAL ORDERS FROM COLONEL INUZUKATO TO ALLOW LITHUANIAN JEWS INTO JAPAN.
THANK YOU SO MUCH FOR YOUR ASSISTANCE.
AND HOW MANY DO YOU THINK WE CAN SEND? FIVE THOU-SAND OR SO?
I-I DON'T THINK SO...

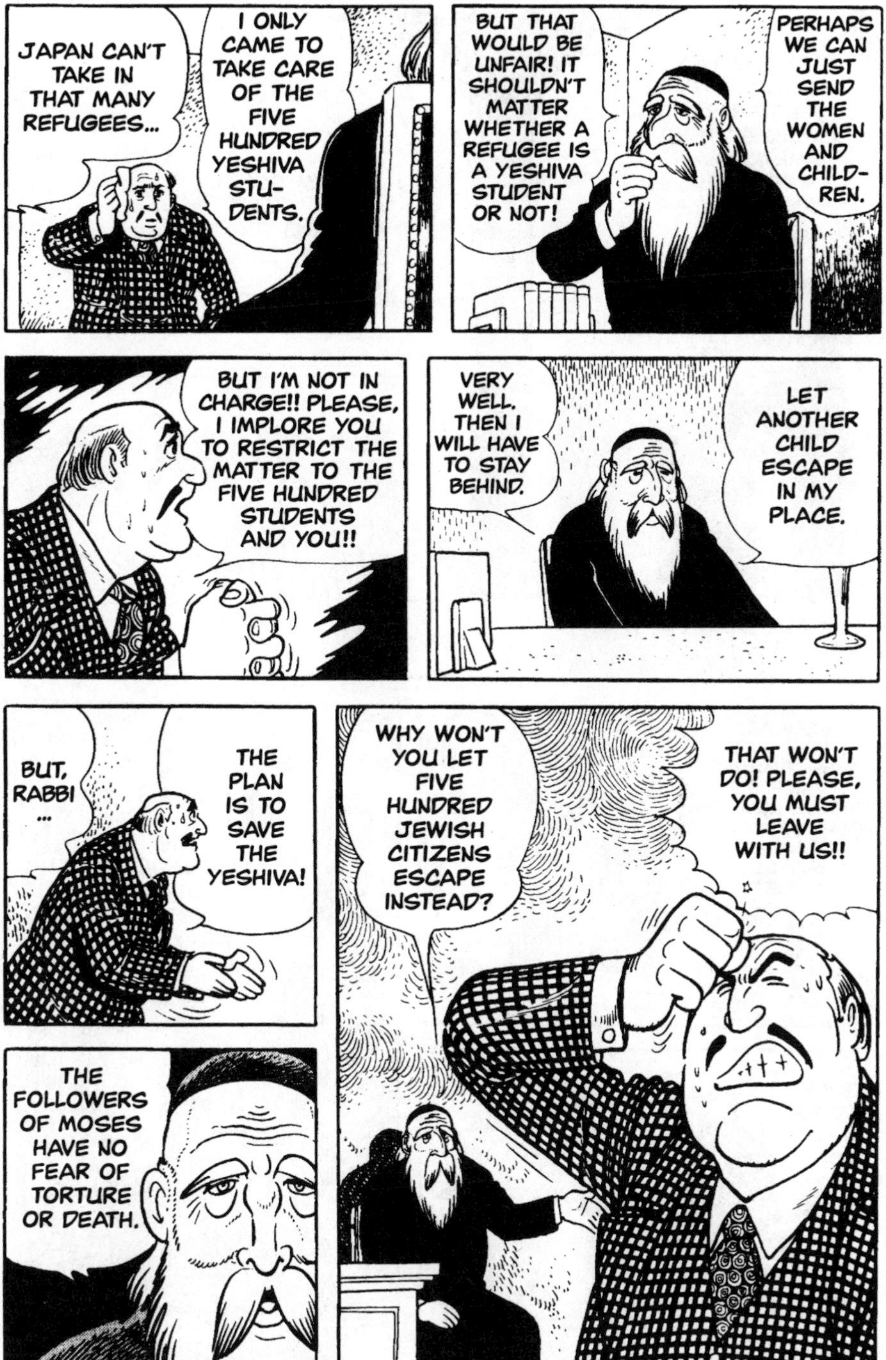
JAPAN CAN'T TAKE IN THAT MANY REFUGEES...
I ONLY CAME TO TAKE CARE OF THE FIVE HUNDRED YESHIVA STU-DENTS.
BUT THAT WOULD BE UNFAIR! IT SHOULDN'T MATTER WHETHER A REFUGEE IS A YESHIVA STUDENT OR NOT!
PERHAPS WE CAN JUST SEND THE WOMEN AND CHILD-REN.
BUT I'M NOT IN CHARGE!! PLEASE, I IMPLORE YOU TO RESTRICT THE MATTER TO THE FIVE HUNDRED STUDENTS AND YOU!!
VERY WELL. THEN I WILL HAVE TO STAY BEHIND.
LET ANOTHER CHILD ESCAPE IN MY PLACE.
BUT, RABBI ...
THE PLAN IS TO SAVE THE YESHIVA!
WHY WON'T YOU LET FIVE HUNDRED JEWISH CITIZENS ESCAPE INSTEAD?
THAT WON'T DO! PLEASE, YOU MUST LEAVE WITH US!!
THE FOLLOWERS OF MOSES HAVE NO FEAR OF TORTURE OR DEATH.

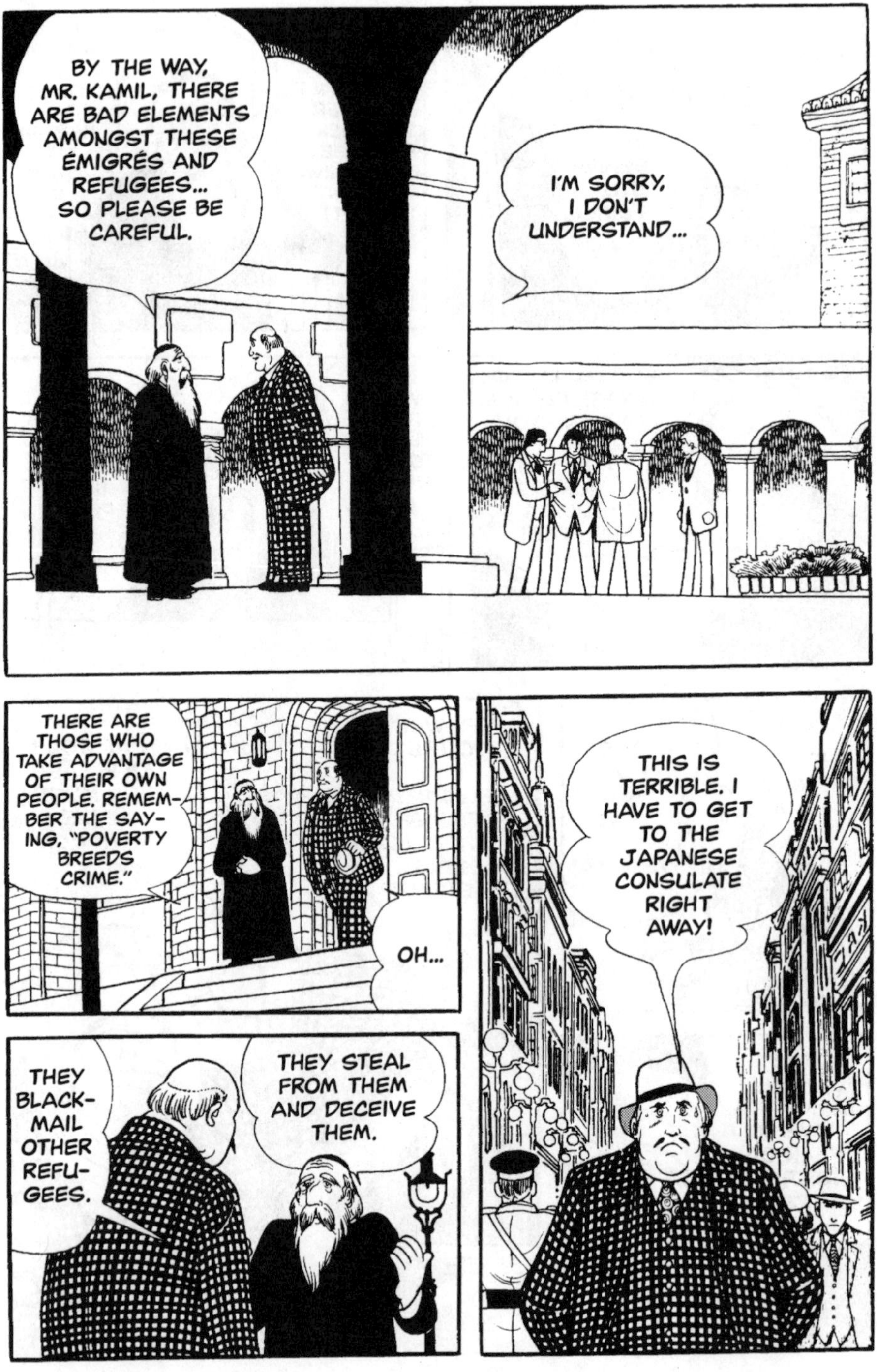
BY THE WAY, MR. KAMIL, THERE ARE BAD ELEMENTS AMONGST THESE ÉMIGRÉS AND REFUGEES... SO PLEASE BE CAREFUL.
I'M SORRY, I DON'T UNDERSTAND...
THERE ARE THOSE WHO TAKE ADVANTAGE OF THEIR OWN PEOPLE. REMEMBER THE SAYING, "POVERTY BREEDS CRIME."
OH...
THEY BLACKMAIL OTHER REFUGEES.
THEY STEAL FROM THEM AND DECEIVE THEM.
THIS IS TERRIBLE. I HAVE TO GET TO THE JAPANESE CONSULATE RIGHT AWAY!

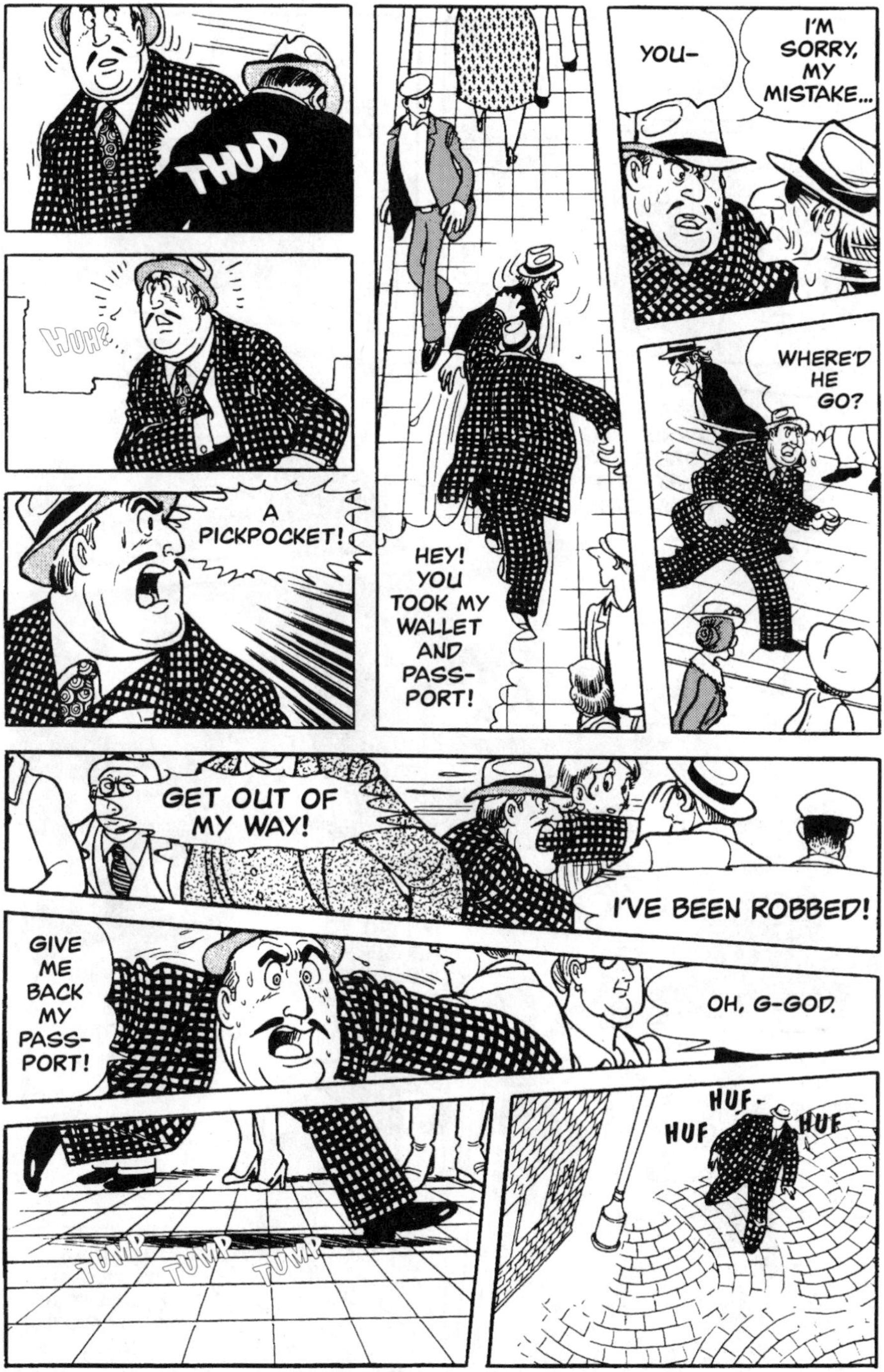
THUD
YOU-
I'M SORRY, MY MISTAKE...
HUH?
A PICKPOCKET!
HEY! YOU TOOK MY WALLET AND PASS-PORT!
WHERE'D HE GO?
GET OUT OF MY WAY!
I'VE BEEN ROBBED!
GIVE ME BACK MY PASS-PORT!
OH, G-GOD.
TUMP TUMP TUMP
HUF HUF HUF

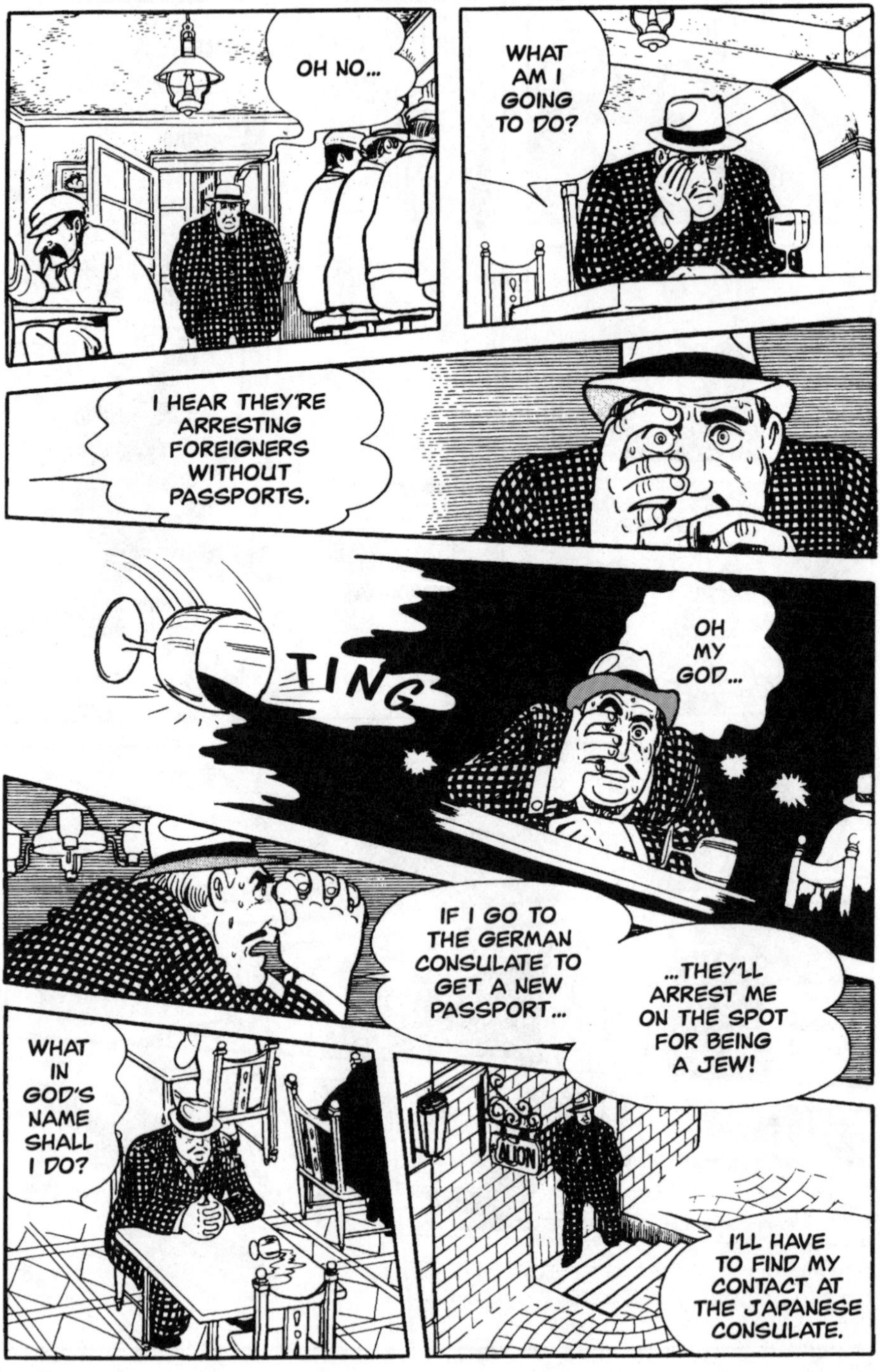
OH NO...
WHAT AM I GOING TO DO?
I HEAR THEY'RE ARRESTING FOREIGNERS WITHOUT PASSPORTS.
TING
OH MY GOD...
IF I GO TO THE GERMAN CONSULATE TO GET A NEW PASSPORT...
...THEY'LL ARREST ME ON THE SPOT FOR BEING A JEW!
WHAT IN GOD'S NAME SHALL I DO?
ALION
I'LL HAVE TO FIND MY CONTACT AT THE JAPANESE CONSULATE.

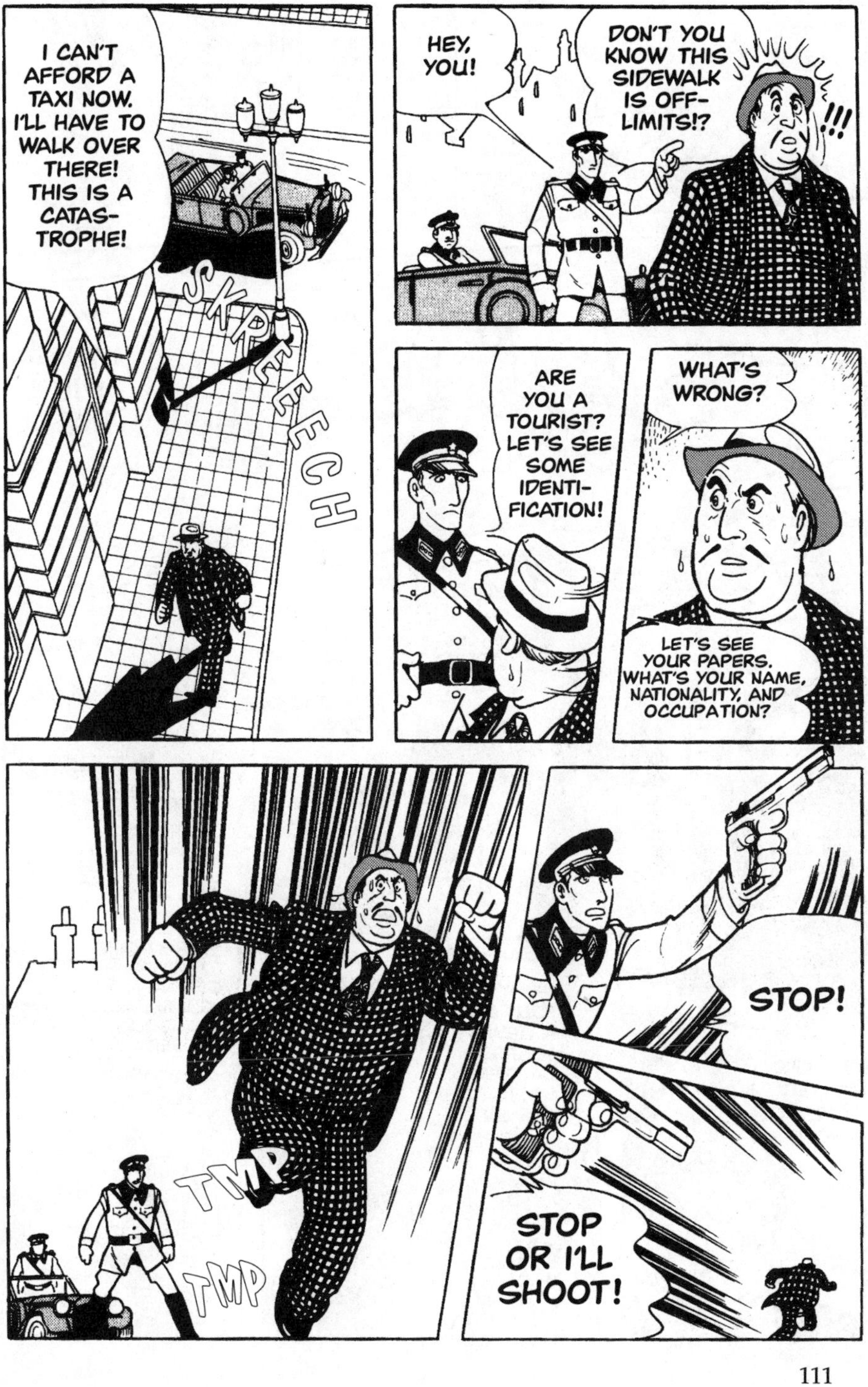
I CAN'T AFFORD A TAXI NOW. I'LL HAVE TO WALK OVER THERE! THIS IS A CATASTROPHE!
SKREEEECH
HEY, YOU!
DON'T YOU KNOW THIS SIDEWALK IS OFF-LIMITS!?
!!!
ARE YOU A TOURIST? LET'S SEE SOME IDENTIFICATION!
WHAT'S WRONG?
LET'S SEE YOUR PAPERS. WHAT'S YOUR NAME, NATIONALITY, AND OCCUPATION?
TMP
TMP
STOP!
STOP OR I'LL SHOOT!

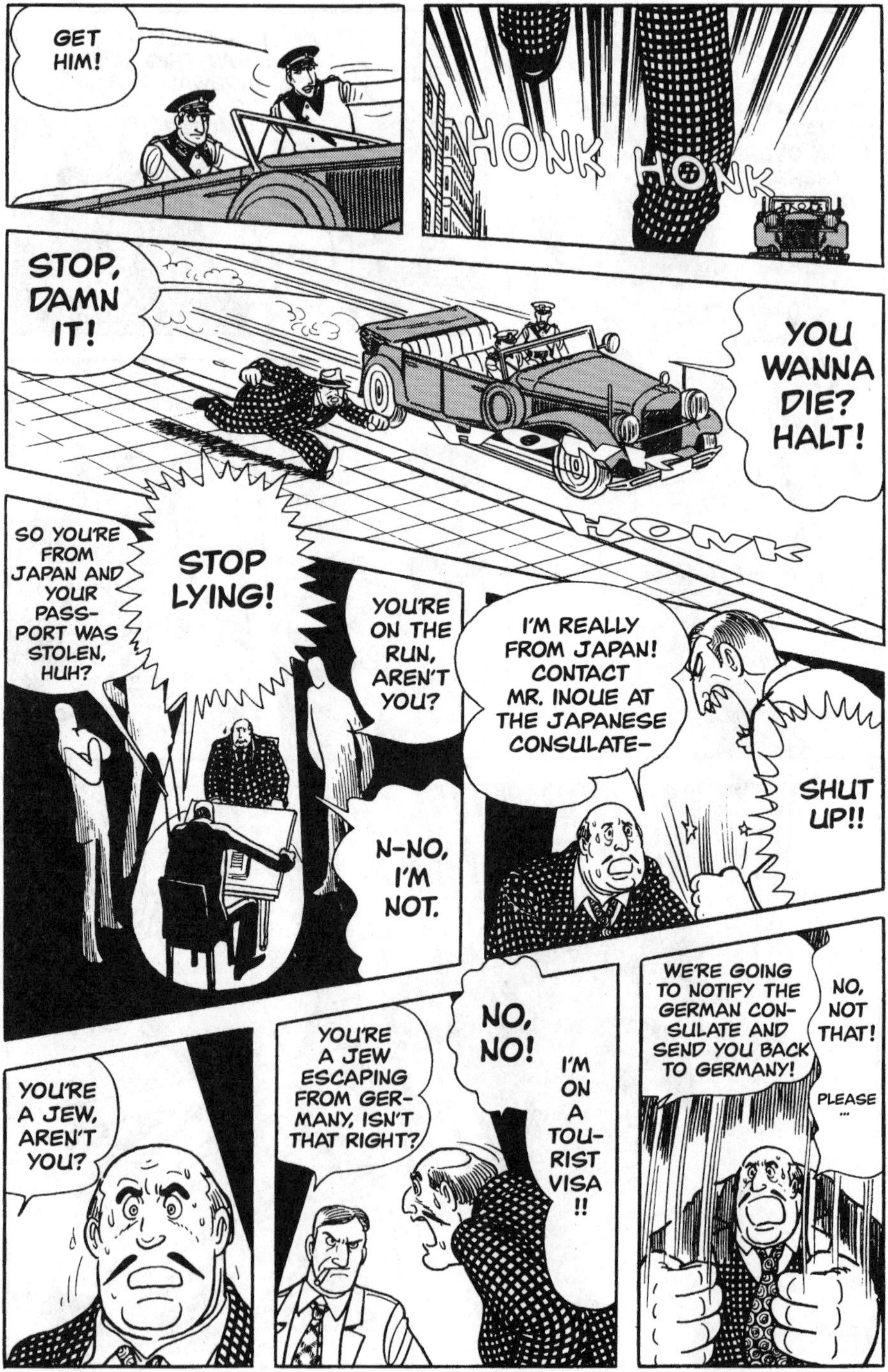
GET HIM!
HONK HONK
STOP, DAMN IT!
YOU WANNA DIE? HALT!
HONK
HONK
SO YOU'RE FROM JAPAN AND YOUR PASS-PORT WAS STOLEN, HUH?
STOP LYING!
YOU'RE ON THE RUN, AREN'T YOU?
N-NO, I'M NOT.
I'M REALLY FROM JAPAN! CONTACT MR. INOUE AT THE JAPANESE CONSULATE-
SHUT UP!!
YOU'RE A JEW, AREN'T YOU?
YOU'RE A JEW ESCAPING FROM GER-MANY, ISN'T THAT RIGHT?
NO, NO!
I'M ON A TOU-RIST VISA!!
WE'RE GOING TO NOTIFY THE GERMAN CON-SULATE AND SEND YOU BACK TO GERMANY!
NO, NOT THAT!
PLEASE...

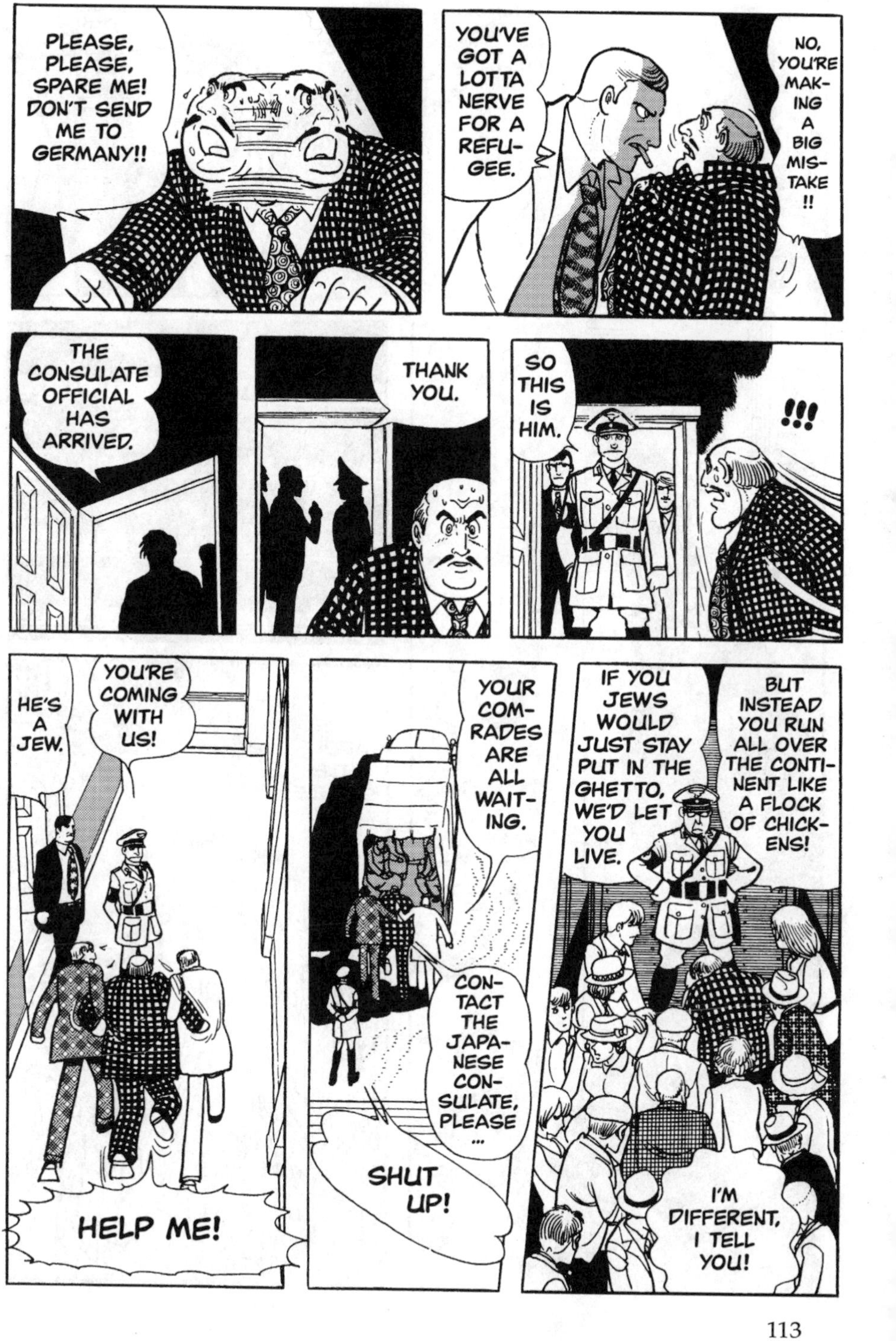
PLEASE, PLEASE, SPARE ME! DON'T SEND ME TO GERMANY!!
YOU'VE GOT A LOTTA NERVE FOR A REFUGEE.
NO, YOU'RE MAKING A BIG MISTAKE !!
THE CONSULATE OFFICIAL HAS ARRIVED.
THANK YOU.
SO THIS IS HIM.
!!!
HE'S A JEW.
YOU'RE COMING WITH US!
HELP ME!
YOUR COMRADES ARE ALL WAITING.
CONTACT THE JAPANESE CONSULATE, PLEASE ...
SHUT UP!
IF YOU JEWS WOULD JUST STAY PUT IN THE GHETTO, WE'D LET YOU LIVE.
BUT INSTEAD YOU RUN ALL OVER THE CONTINENT LIKE A FLOCK OF CHICKENS!
I'M DIFFERENT, I TELL YOU!

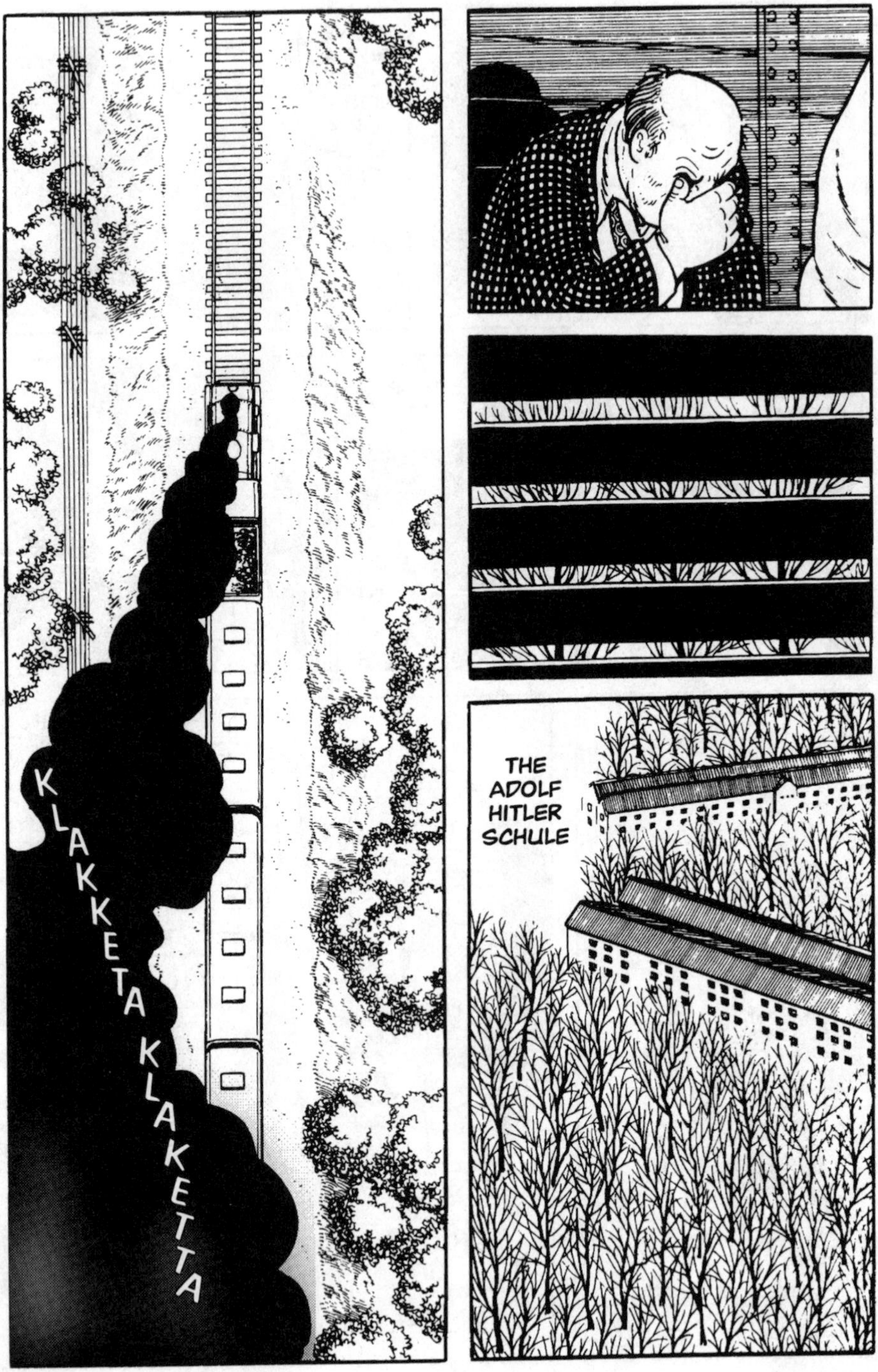
KLAKKETA KLAKETTA
THE ADOLF HITLER SCHULE

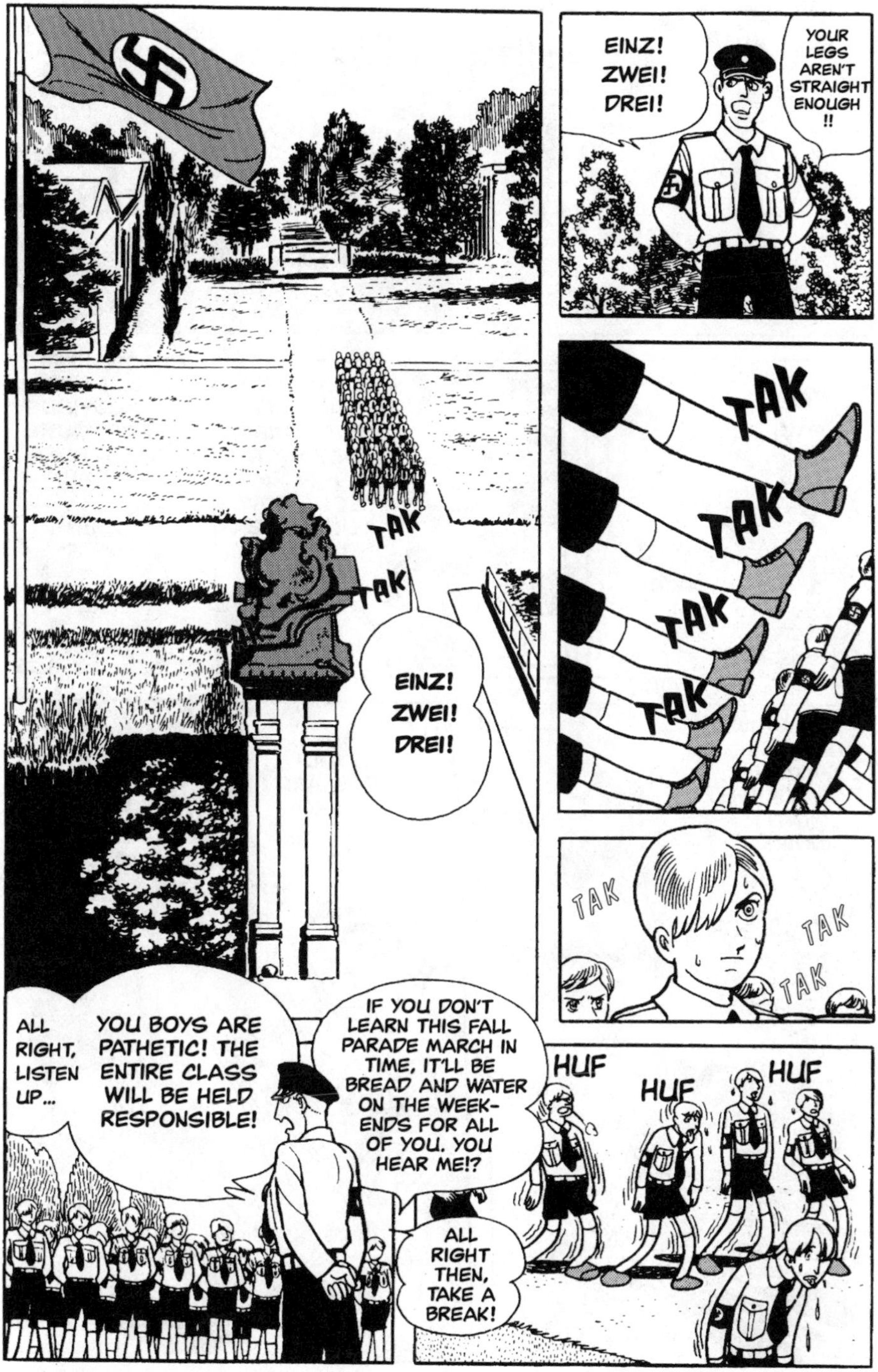
TAK
TAK
EINZ! ZWEI! DREI!
EINZ! ZWEI! DREI!
YOUR LEGS AREN'T STRAIGHT ENOUGH !!
TAK
TAK
TAK
TAK
TAK
TAK
TAK
ALL RIGHT, LISTEN UP...
YOU BOYS ARE PATHETIC! THE ENTIRE CLASS WILL BE HELD RESPONSIBLE!
IF YOU DON'T LEARN THIS FALL PARADE MARCH IN TIME, IT'LL BE BREAD AND WATER ON THE WEEK-ENDS FOR ALL OF YOU. YOU HEAR ME!?
HUF
HUF
HUF
ALL RIGHT THEN, TAKE A BREAK!

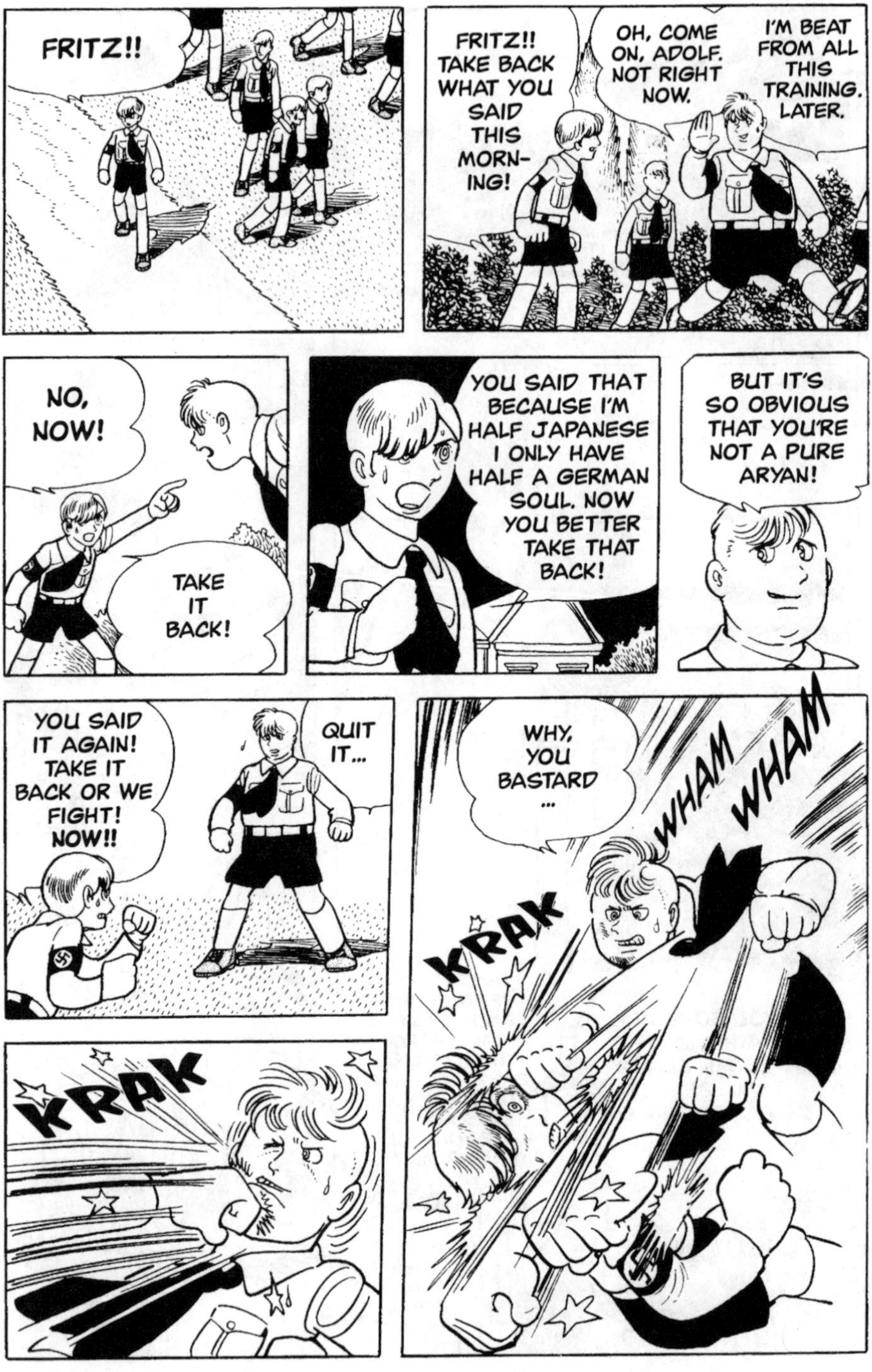
FRITZ!!
FRITZ!! TAKE BACK WHAT YOU SAID THIS MORN-ING!
OH, COME ON, ADOLF. NOT RIGHT NOW.
I'M BEAT FROM ALL THIS TRAINING. LATER.
NO, NOW!
TAKE IT BACK!
YOU SAID THAT BECAUSE I'M HALF JAPANESE I ONLY HAVE HALF A GERMAN SOUL. NOW YOU BETTER TAKE THAT BACK!
BUT IT'S SO OBVIOUS THAT YOU'RE NOT A PURE ARYAN!
YOU SAID IT AGAIN! TAKE IT BACK OR WE FIGHT! NOW!!
QUIT IT...
KRAK
WHY, YOU BASTARD ...
WHAM
WHAM
KRAK

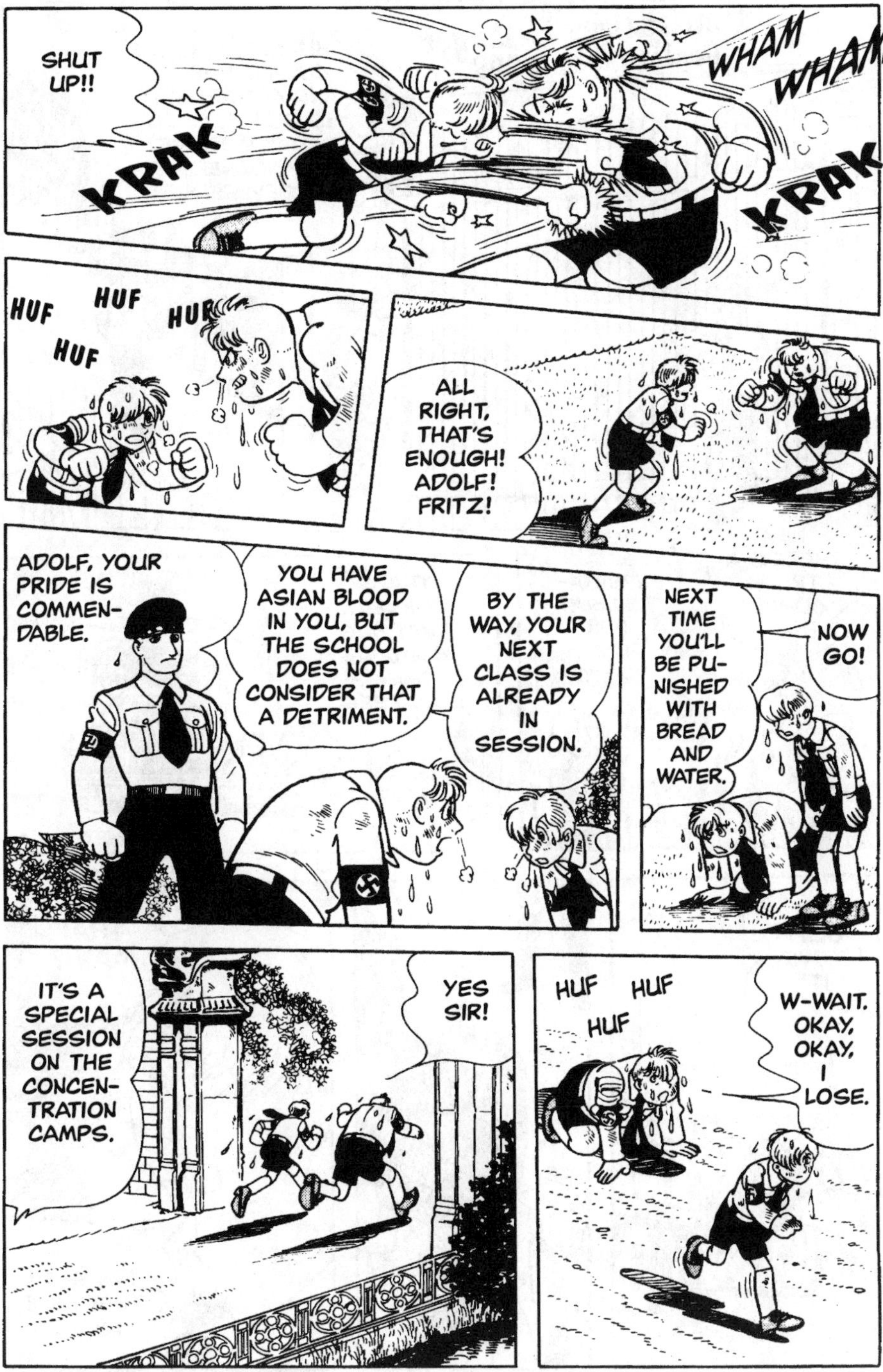
SHUT UP!!
KRAK
WHAM
WHAM
KRAK
HUF
HUF
HUF
HUF
ALL RIGHT, THAT'S ENOUGH! ADOLF! FRITZ!
ADOLF, YOUR PRIDE IS COMMENDABLE.
YOU HAVE ASIAN BLOOD IN YOU, BUT THE SCHOOL DOES NOT CONSIDER THAT A DETRIMENT.
BY THE WAY, YOUR NEXT CLASS IS ALREADY IN SESSION.
NEXT TIME YOU'LL BE PUNISHED WITH BREAD AND WATER.
NOW GO!
IT'S A SPECIAL SESSION ON THE CONCENTRATION CAMPS.
YES SIR!
HUF
HUF
HUF
W-WAIT. OKAY, OKAY, I LOSE.

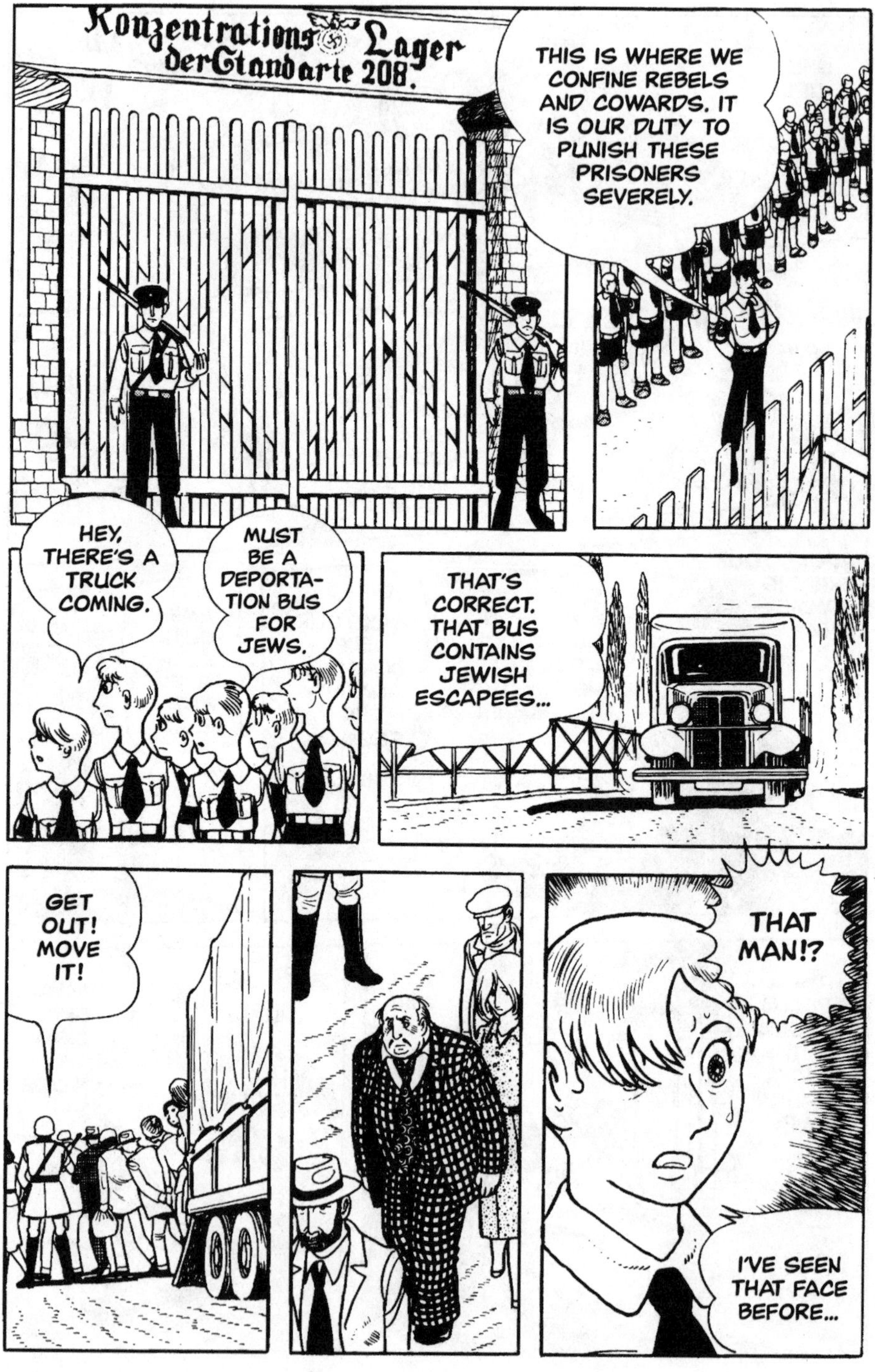
Konzentrations Lager der Standarte 208.
THIS IS WHERE WE CONFINE REBELS AND COWARDS. IT IS OUR DUTY TO PUNISH THESE PRISONERS SEVERELY.
HEY, THERE'S A TRUCK COMING.
MUST BE A DEPORTATION BUS FOR JEWS.
THAT'S CORRECT. THAT BUS CONTAINS JEWISH ESCAPEES...
GET OUT! MOVE IT!
THAT MAN!?
I'VE SEEN THAT FACE BEFORE...

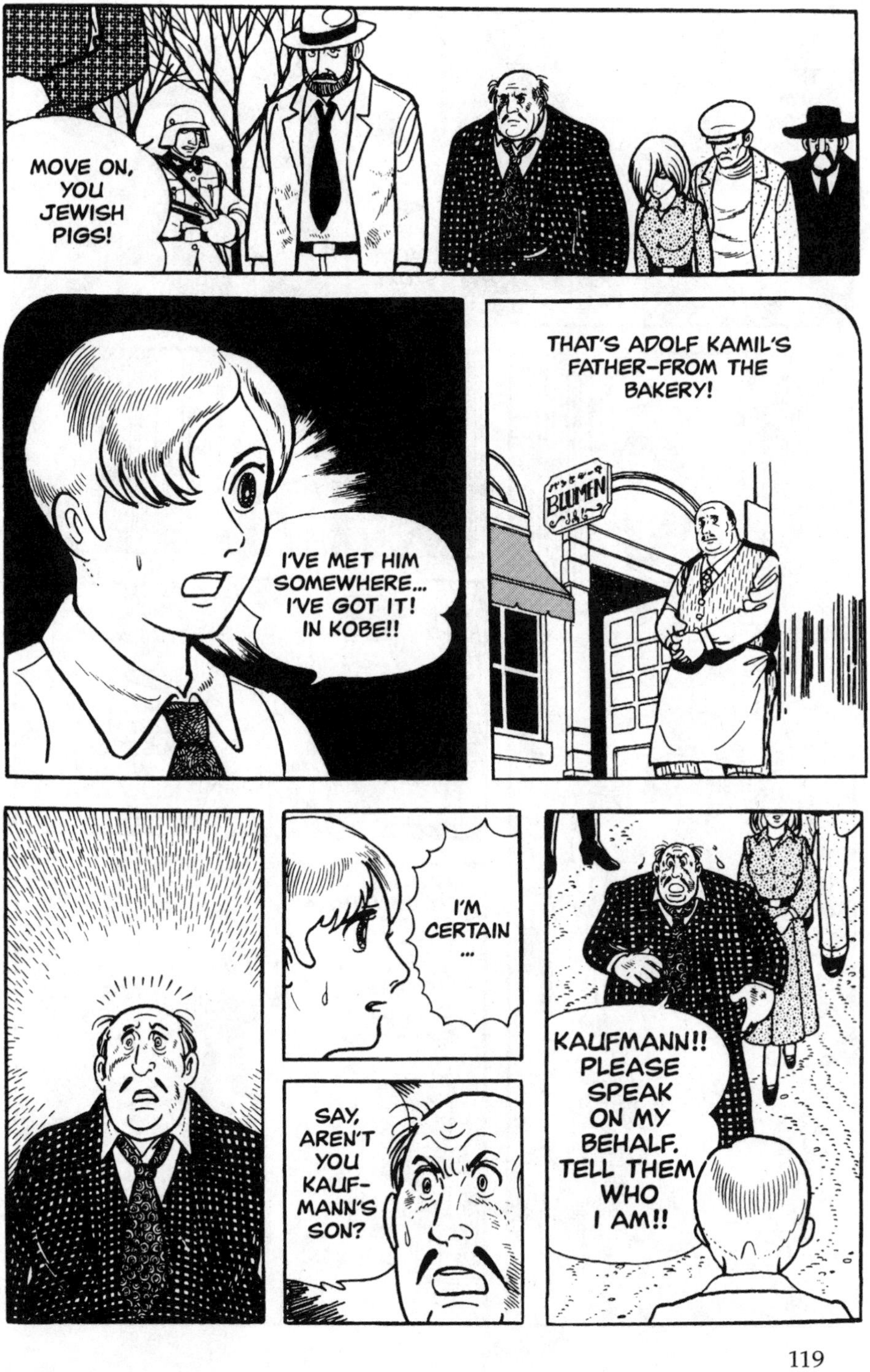
MOVE ON, YOU JEWISH PIGS!
I'VE MET HIM SOMEWHERE... I'VE GOT IT! IN KOBE!!
THAT'S ADOLF KAMIL'S FATHER–FROM THE BAKERY!
BLUMEN
I'M CERTAIN ...
SAY, AREN'T YOU KAUF-MANN'S SON?
KAUFMANN!! PLEASE SPEAK ON MY BEHALF. TELL THEM WHO I AM!!

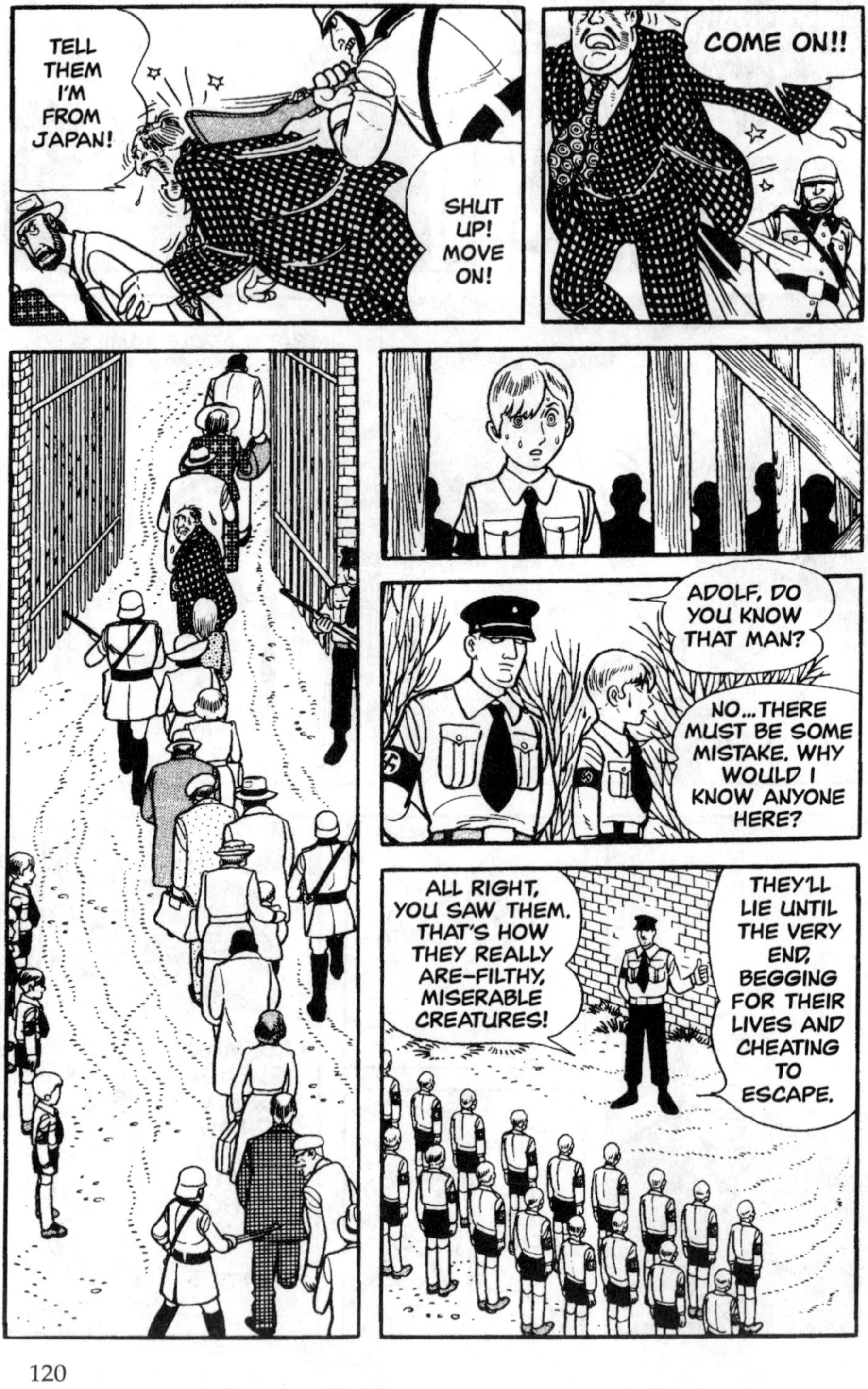
TELL THEM I'M FROM JAPAN!
SHUT UP! MOVE ON!
COME ON!!
ADOLF, DO YOU KNOW THAT MAN?
NO...THERE MUST BE SOME MISTAKE. WHY WOULD I KNOW ANYONE HERE?
ALL RIGHT, YOU SAW THEM. THAT'S HOW THEY REALLY ARE–FILTHY, MISERABLE CREATURES!
THEY'LL LIE UNTIL THE VERY END, BEGGING FOR THEIR LIVES AND CHEATING TO ESCAPE.

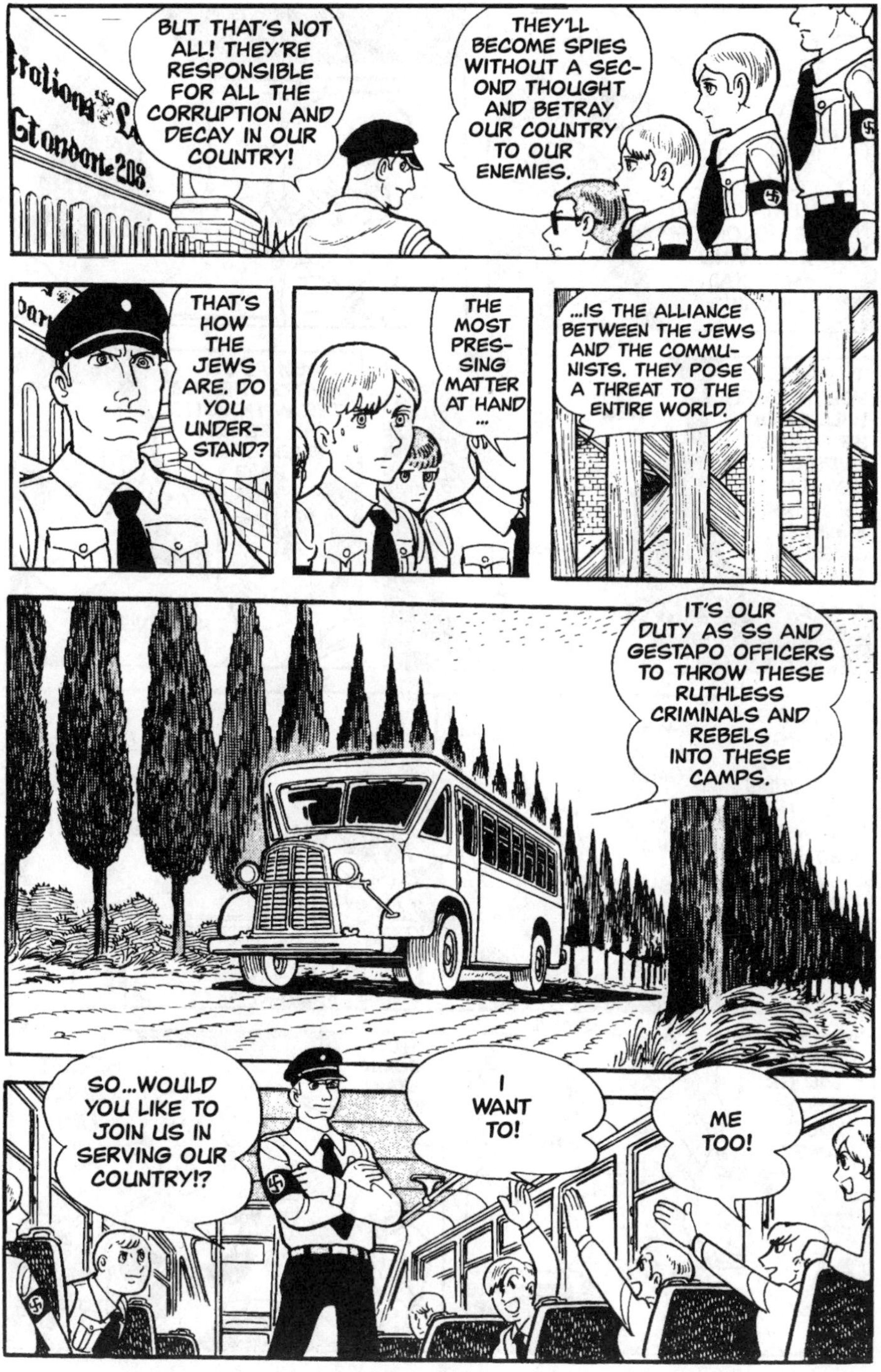
BUT THAT'S NOT ALL! THEY'RE RESPONSIBLE FOR ALL THE CORRUPTION AND DECAY IN OUR COUNTRY!
THEY'LL BECOME SPIES WITHOUT A SEC- OND THOUGHT AND BETRAY OUR COUNTRY TO OUR ENEMIES.
THAT'S HOW THE JEWS ARE. DO YOU UNDER- STAND?
THE MOST PRES- SING MATTER AT HAND ...
...IS THE ALLIANCE BETWEEN THE JEWS AND THE COMMU- NISTS. THEY POSE A THREAT TO THE ENTIRE WORLD.
IT'S OUR DUTY AS SS AND GESTAPO OFFICERS TO THROW THESE RUTHLESS CRIMINALS AND REBELS INTO THESE CAMPS.
SO...WOULD YOU LIKE TO JOIN US IN SERVING OUR COUNTRY!?
I WANT TO!
ME TOO!

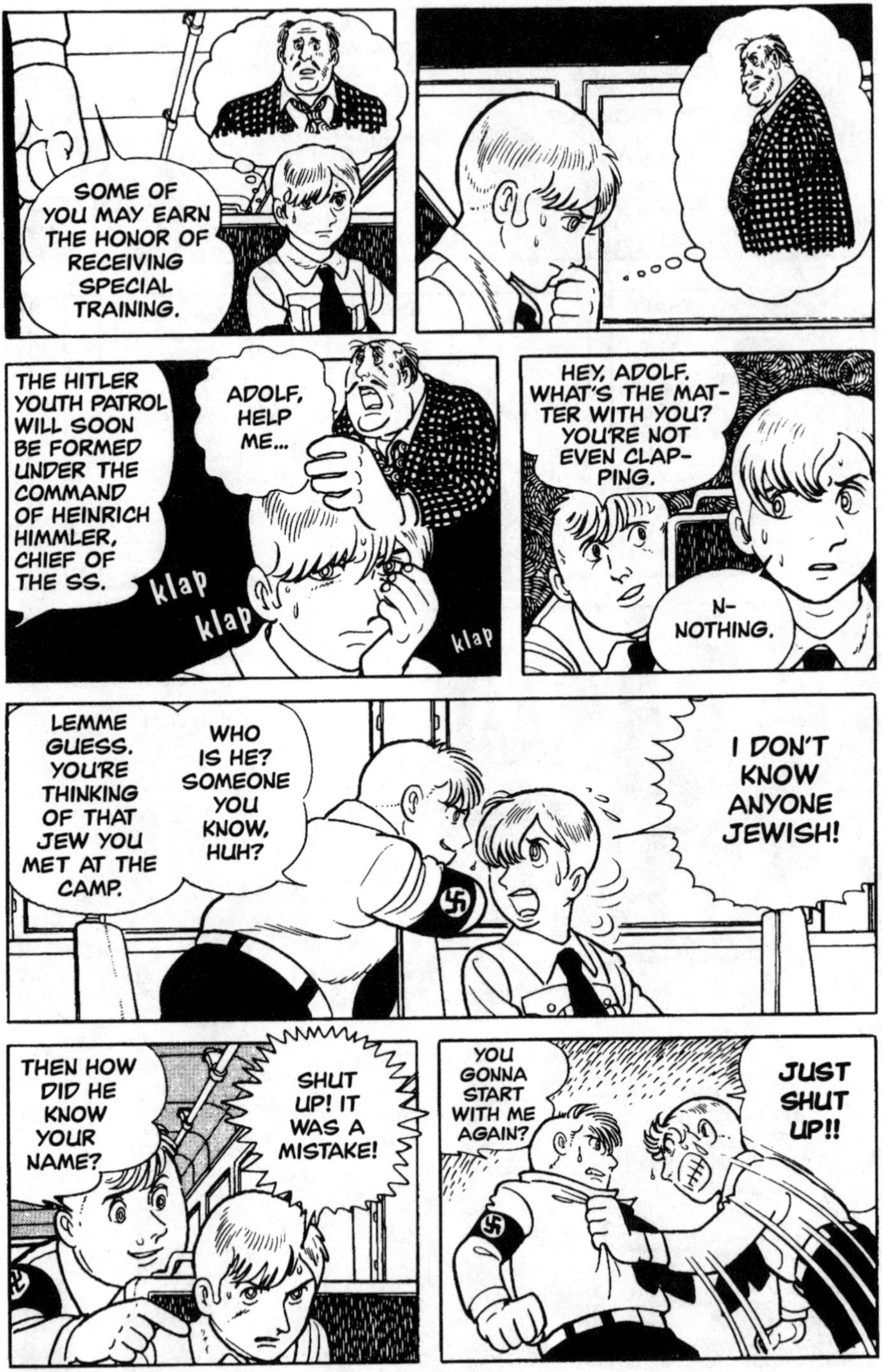
SOME OF YOU MAY EARN THE HONOR OF RECEIVING SPECIAL TRAINING.
THE HITLER YOUTH PATROL WILL SOON BE FORMED UNDER THE COMMAND OF HEINRICH HIMMLER, CHIEF OF THE SS.
ADOLF, HELP ME...
klap
klap
klap
HEY, ADOLF. WHAT'S THE MATTER WITH YOU? YOU'RE NOT EVEN CLAPPING.
N-NOTHING.
LEMME GUESS. YOU'RE THINKING OF THAT JEW YOU MET AT THE CAMP.
WHO IS HE? SOMEONE YOU KNOW, HUH?
I DON'T KNOW ANYONE JEWISH!
THEN HOW DID HE KNOW YOUR NAME?
SHUT UP! IT WAS A MISTAKE!
YOU GONNA START WITH ME AGAIN?
JUST SHUT UP!!

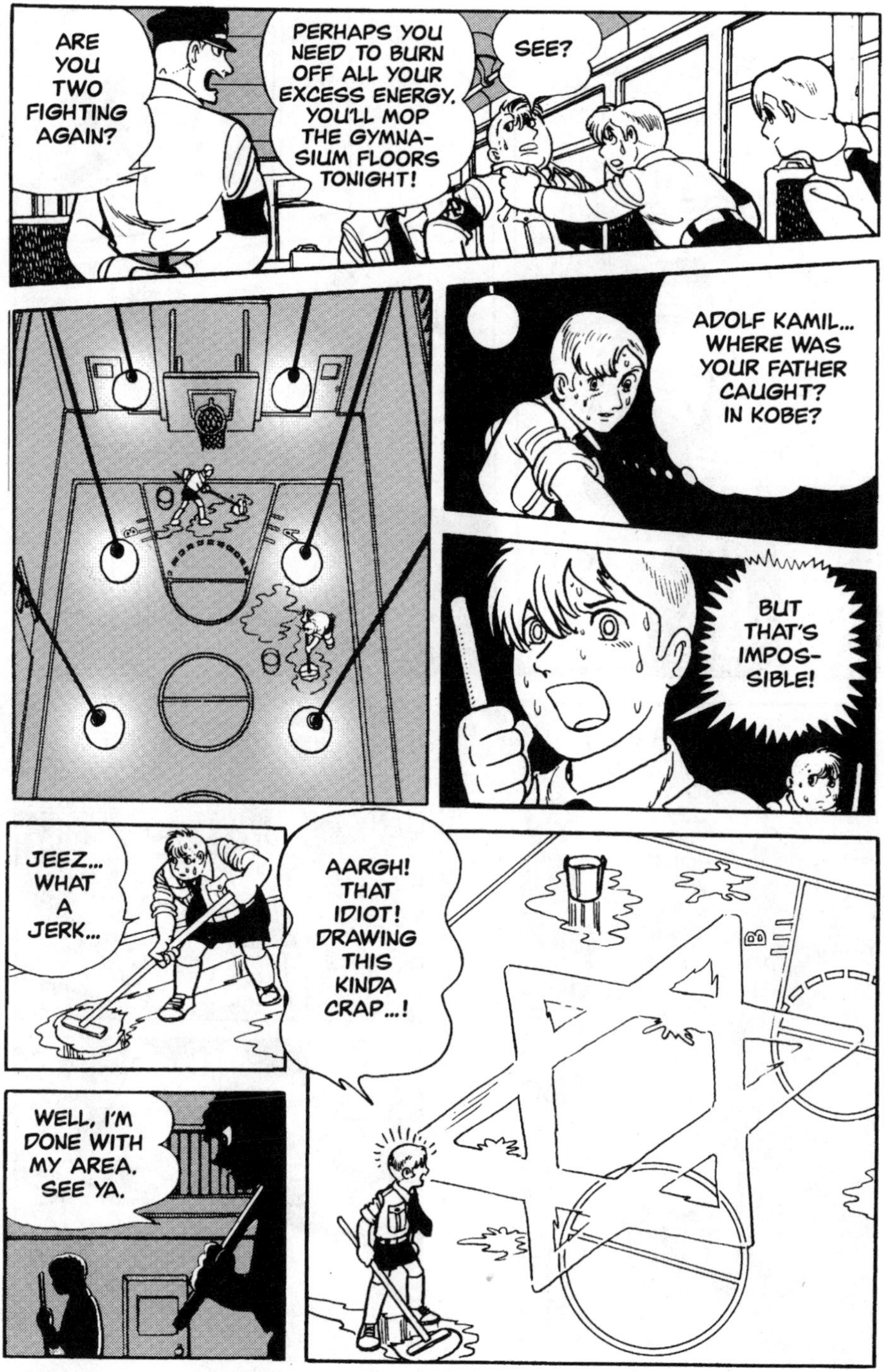
ARE YOU TWO FIGHTING AGAIN?
PERHAPS YOU NEED TO BURN OFF ALL YOUR EXCESS ENERGY. YOU'LL MOP THE GYMNASIUM FLOORS TONIGHT!
SEE?
ADOLF KAMIL... WHERE WAS YOUR FATHER CAUGHT? IN KOBE?
BUT THAT'S IMPOSSIBLE!
JEEZ... WHAT A JERK...
AARGH! THAT IDIOT! DRAWING THIS KINDA CRAP...!
WELL, I'M DONE WITH MY AREA. SEE YA.

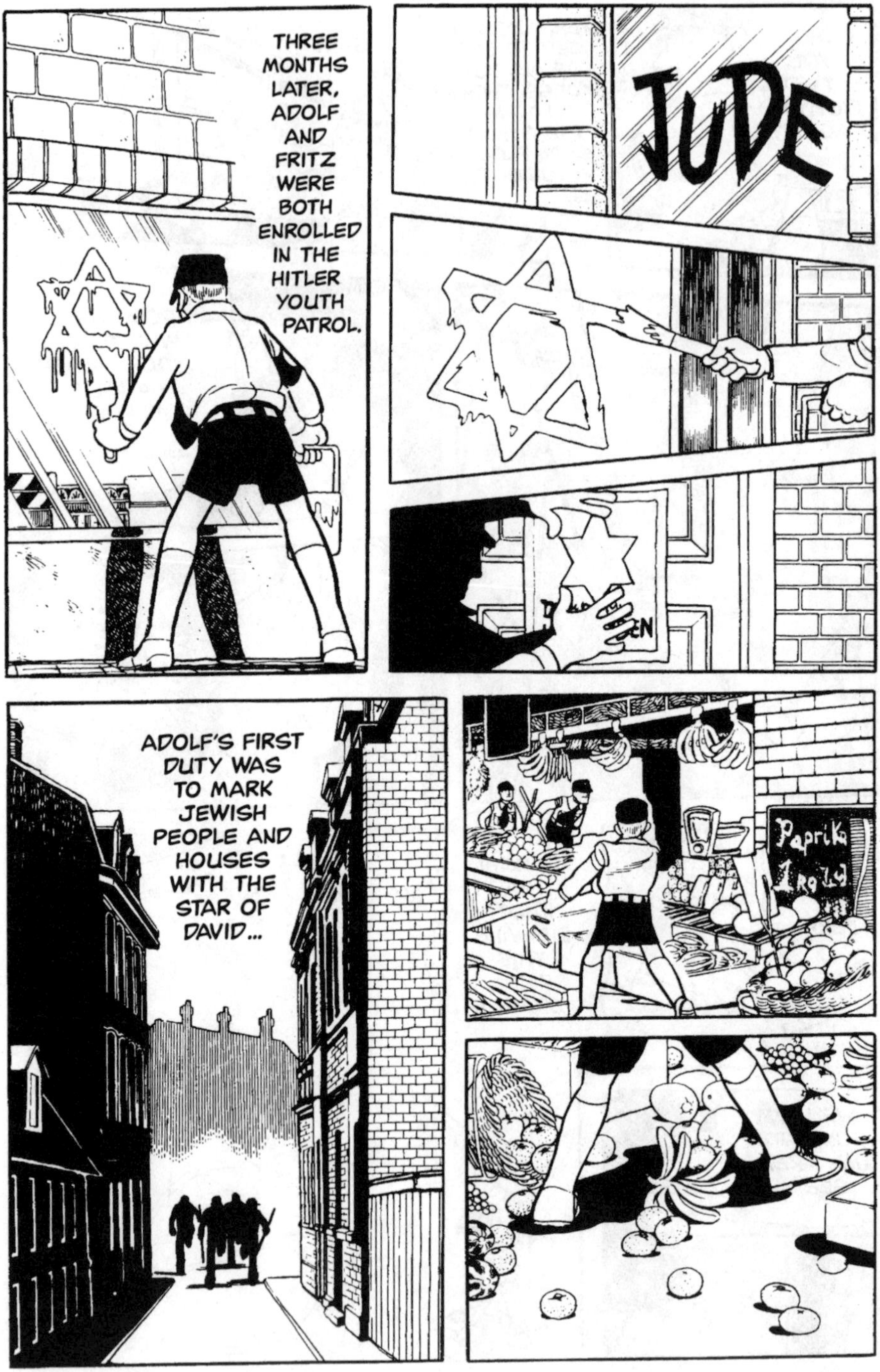
THREE MONTHS LATER, ADOLF AND FRITZ WERE BOTH ENROLLED IN THE HITLER YOUTH PATROL.
JUDE
ADOLF'S FIRST DUTY WAS TO MARK JEWISH PEOPLE AND HOUSES WITH THE STAR OF DAVID...
Paprika

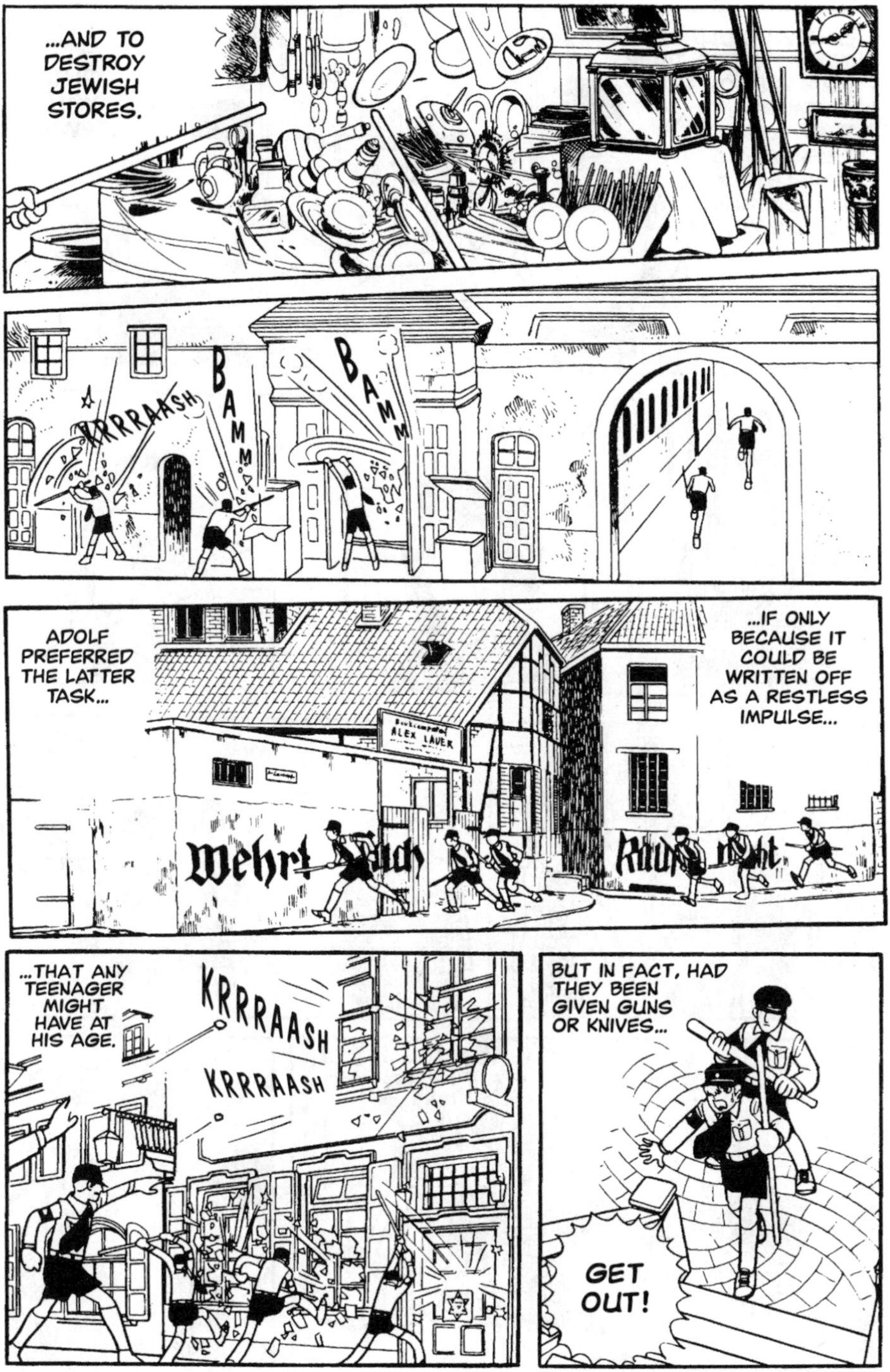
...AND TO DESTROY JEWISH STORES.
KRRRAASH
BAMM
BAMM
ADOLF PREFERRED THE LATTER TASK...
ALEX LAUER
Wehrt
...IF ONLY BECAUSE IT COULD BE WRITTEN OFF AS A RESTLESS IMPULSE...
...THAT ANY TEENAGER MIGHT HAVE AT HIS AGE.
KRRRAASH
KRRRAASH
BUT IN FACT, HAD THEY BEEN GIVEN GUNS OR KNIVES...
GET OUT!

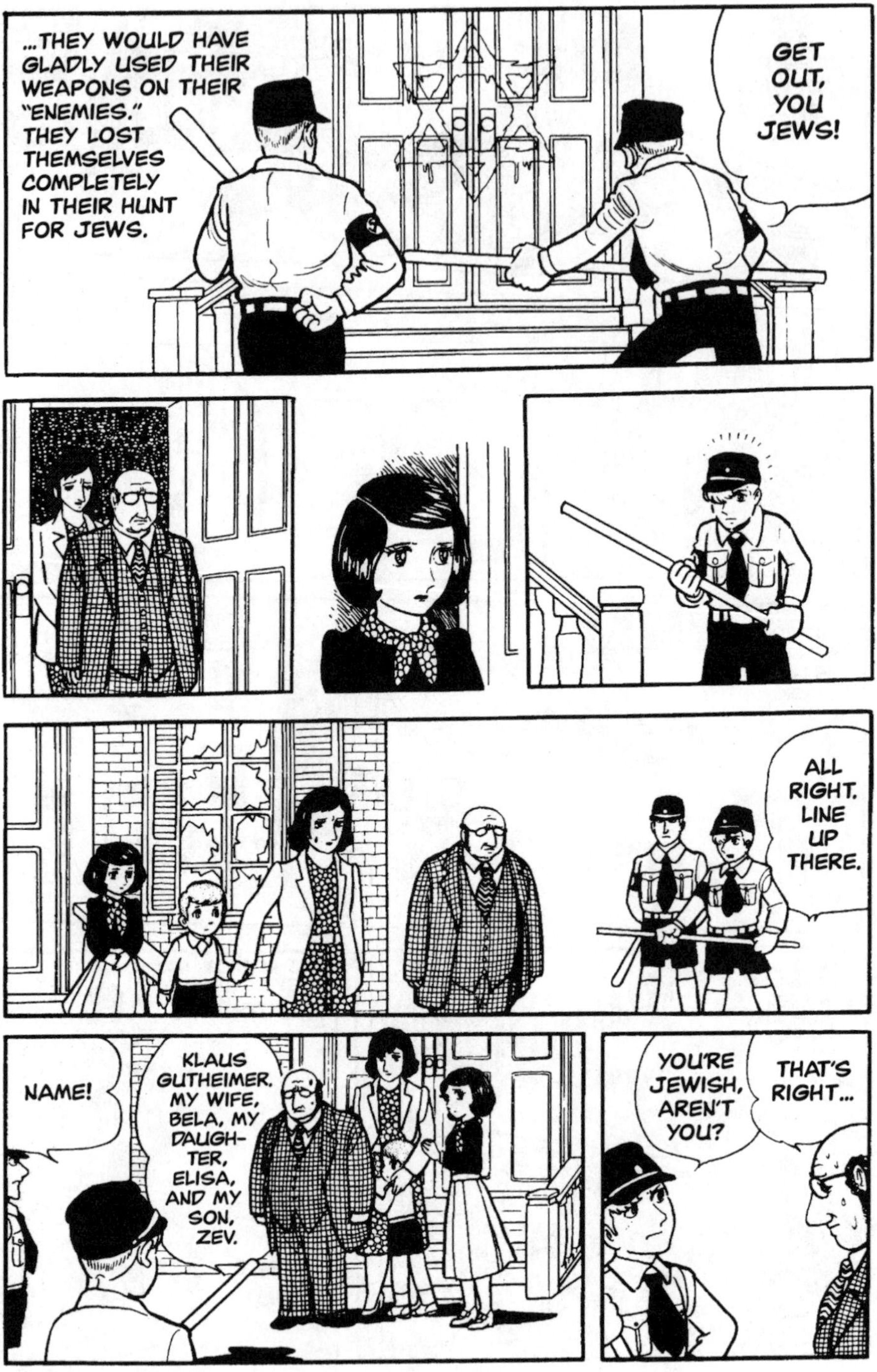
...THEY WOULD HAVE GLADLY USED THEIR WEAPONS ON THEIR "ENEMIES." THEY LOST THEMSELVES COMPLETELY IN THEIR HUNT FOR JEWS.
GET OUT, YOU JEWS!
ALL RIGHT. LINE UP THERE.
NAME!
KLAUS GUTHEIMER. MY WIFE, BELA, MY DAUGH-TER, ELISA, AND MY SON, ZEV.
YOU'RE JEWISH, AREN'T YOU?
THAT'S RIGHT...

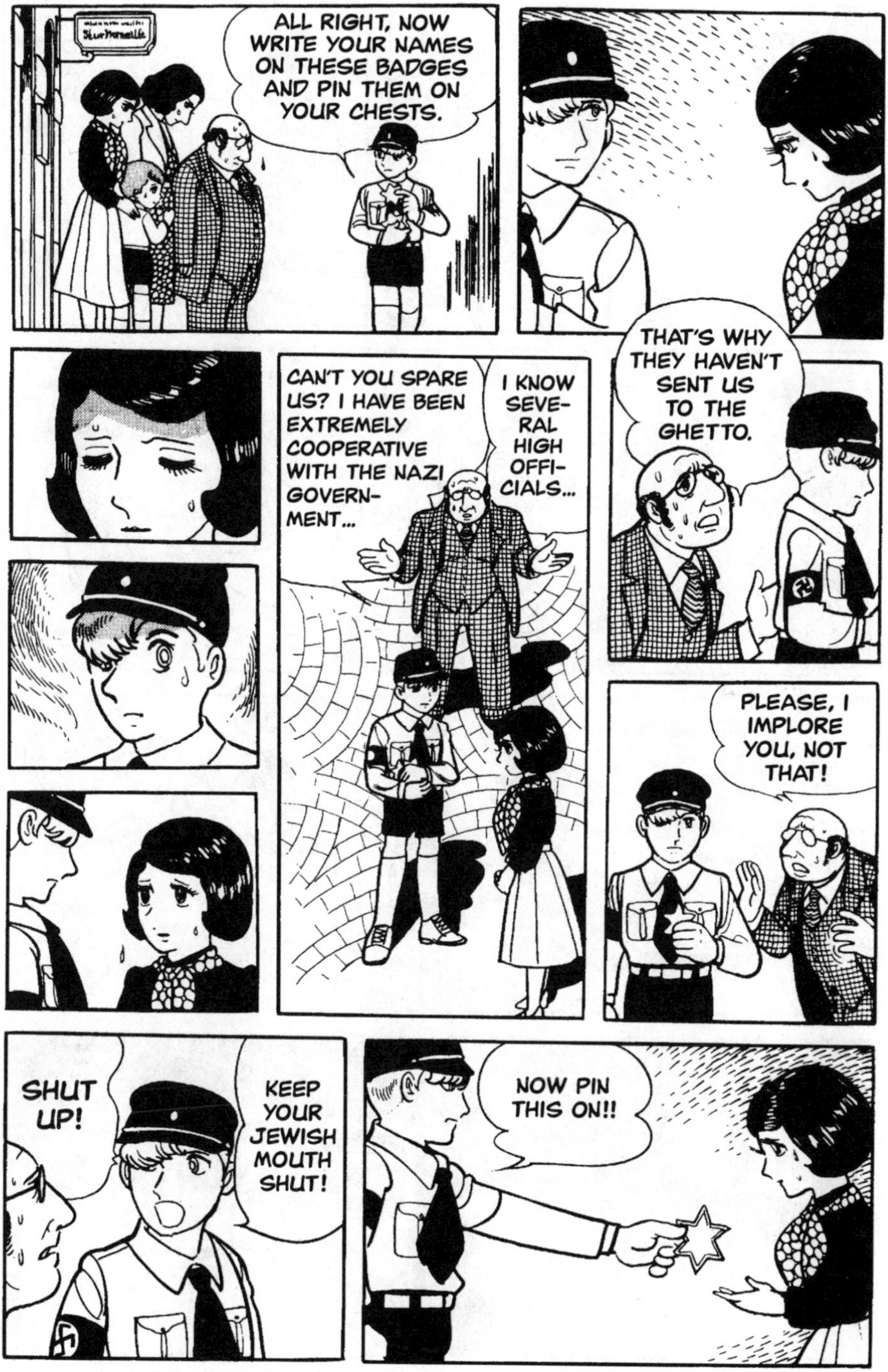
ALL RIGHT, NOW WRITE YOUR NAMES ON THESE BADGES AND PIN THEM ON YOUR CHESTS.
CAN'T YOU SPARE US? I HAVE BEEN EXTREMELY COOPERATIVE WITH THE NAZI GOVERNMENT...
I KNOW SEVERAL HIGH OFFICIALS...
THAT'S WHY THEY HAVEN'T SENT US TO THE GHETTO.
PLEASE, I IMPLORE YOU, NOT THAT!
SHUT UP!
KEEP YOUR JEWISH MOUTH SHUT!
NOW PIN THIS ON!!

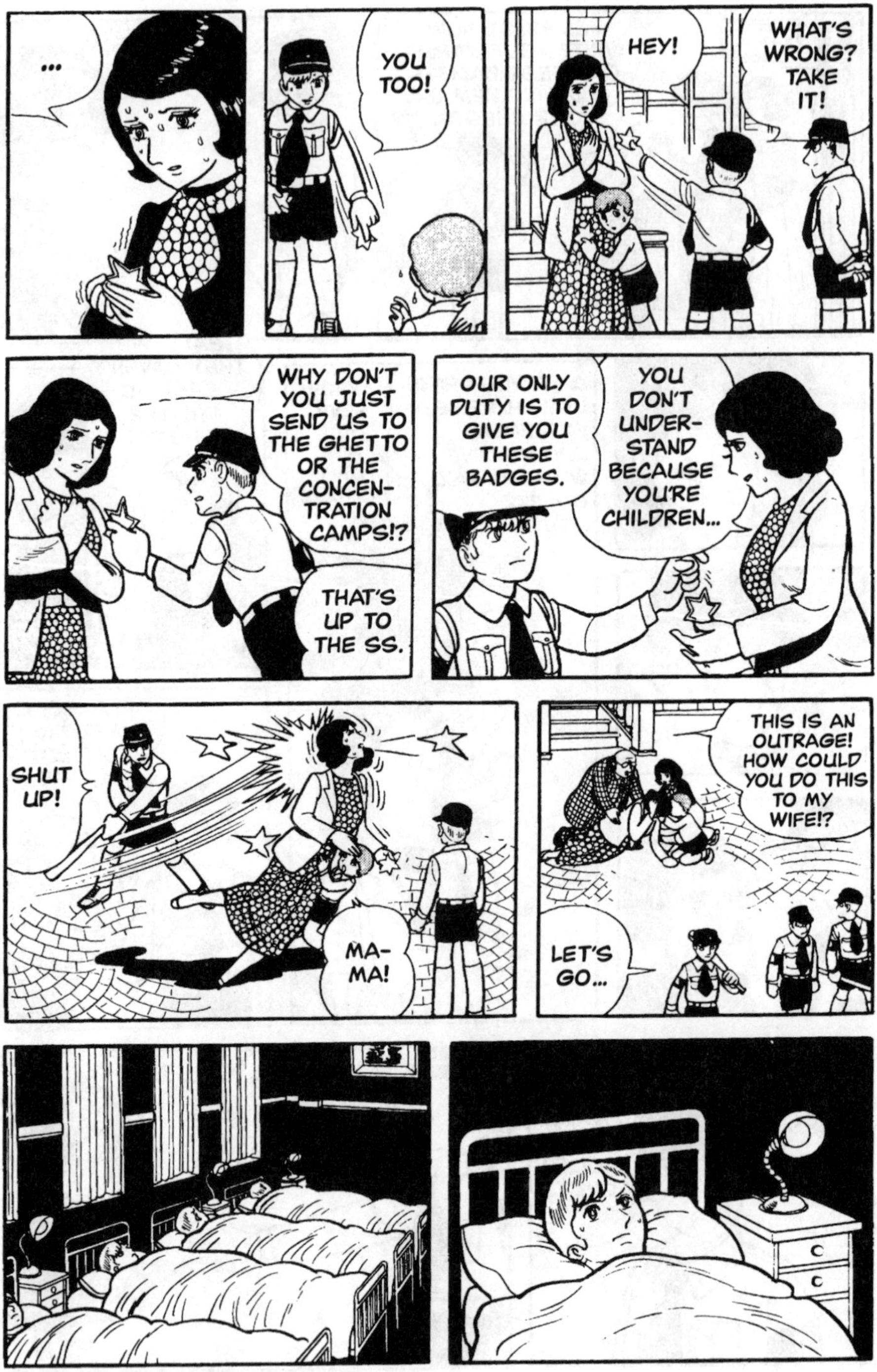
...
YOU TOO!
HEY!
WHAT'S WRONG? TAKE IT!
WHY DON'T YOU JUST SEND US TO THE GHETTO OR THE CONCENTRATION CAMPS!?
THAT'S UP TO THE SS.
OUR ONLY DUTY IS TO GIVE YOU THESE BADGES.
YOU DON'T UNDERSTAND BECAUSE YOU'RE CHILDREN...
SHUT UP!
MA-MA!
THIS IS AN OUTRAGE! HOW COULD YOU DO THIS TO MY WIFE!?
LET'S GO...

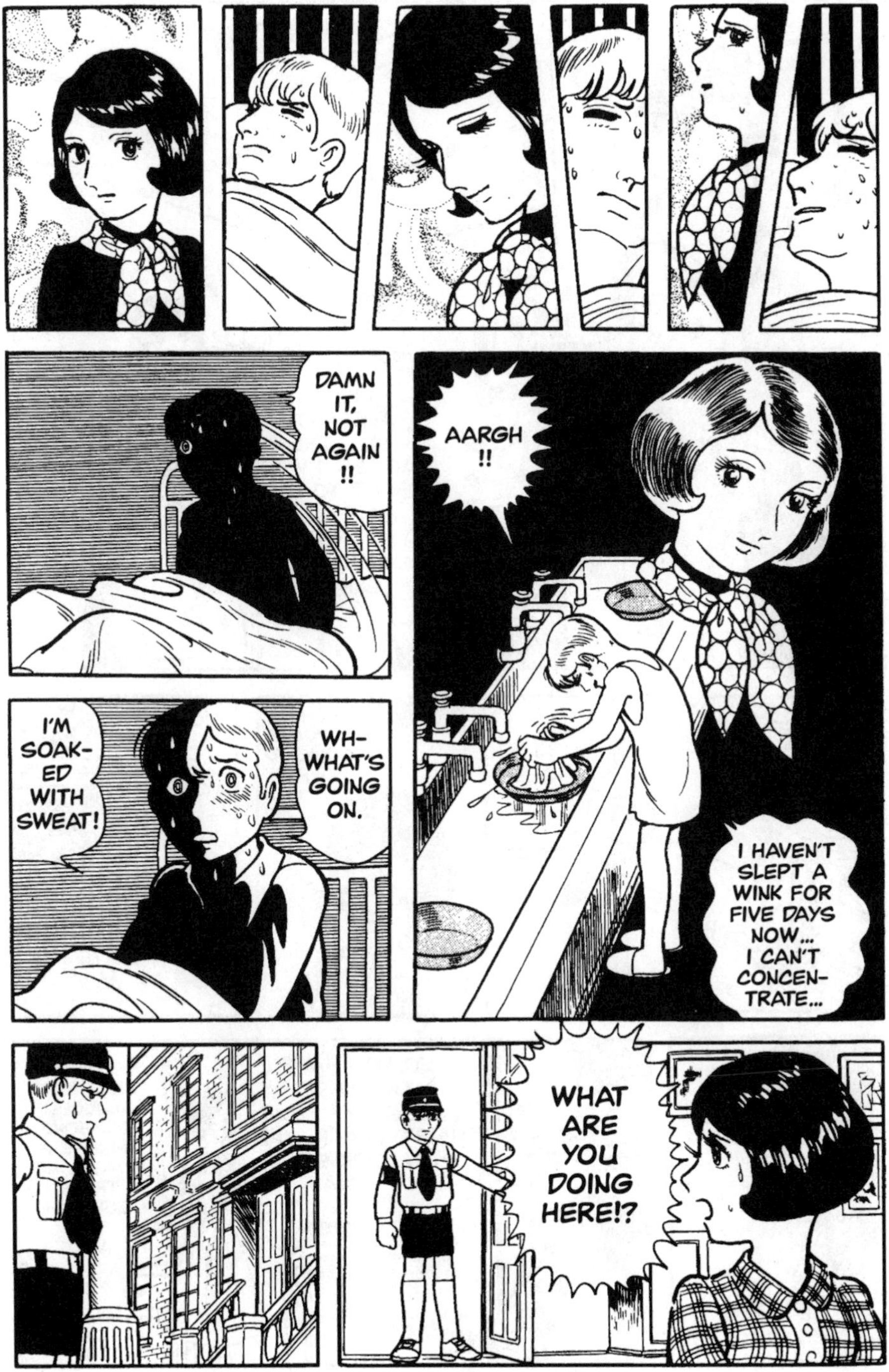
DAMN IT, NOT AGAIN !!
AARGH !!
I'M SOAKED WITH SWEAT!
WH-WHAT'S GOING ON.
I HAVEN'T SLEPT A WINK FOR FIVE DAYS NOW... I CAN'T CONCENTRATE...
WHAT ARE YOU DOING HERE!?

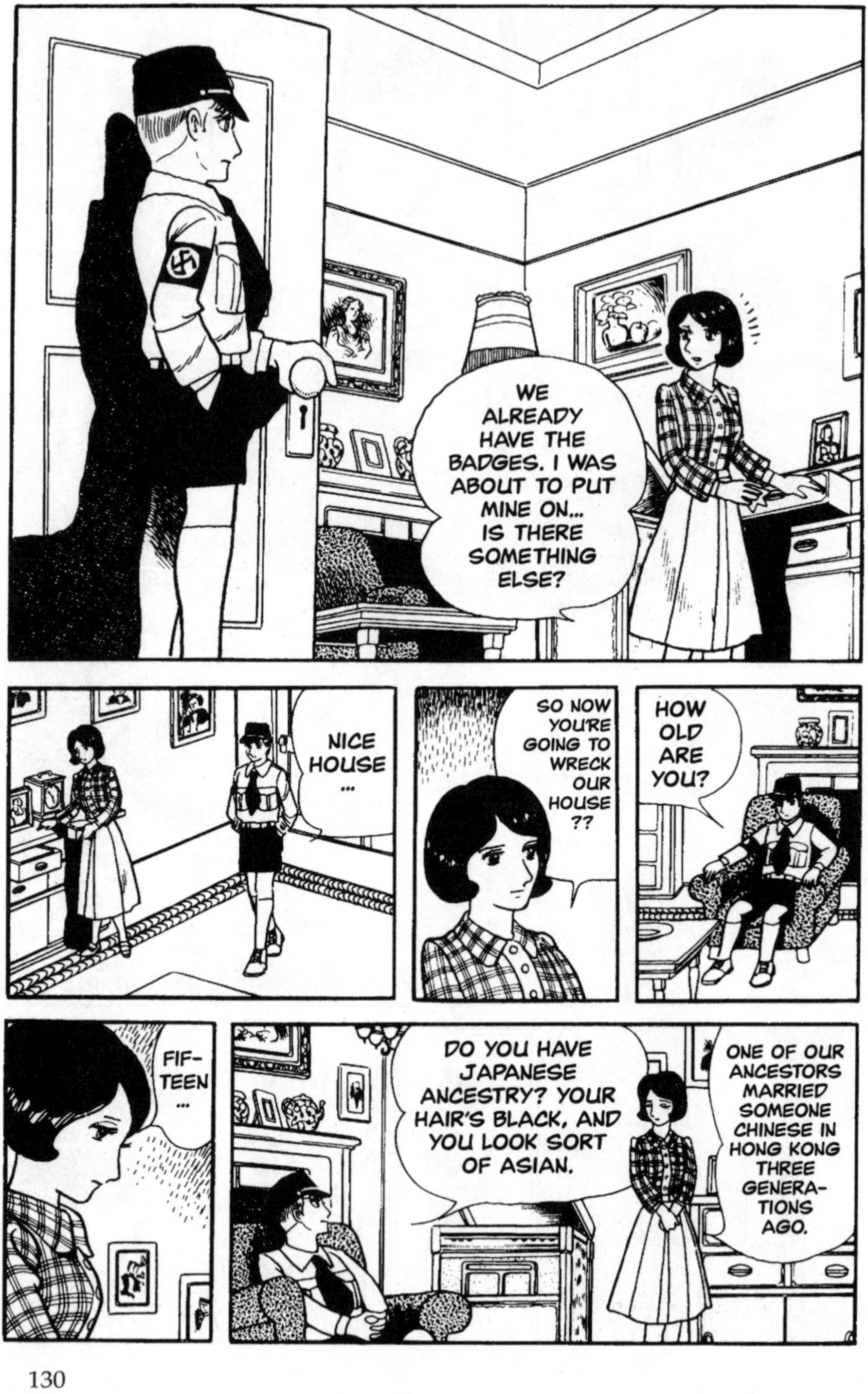
WE ALREADY HAVE THE BADGES. I WAS ABOUT TO PUT MINE ON... IS THERE SOMETHING ELSE?
NICE HOUSE ...
SO NOW YOU'RE GOING TO WRECK OUR HOUSE ??
HOW OLD ARE YOU?
FIF-TEEN ...
DO YOU HAVE JAPANESE ANCESTRY? YOUR HAIR'S BLACK, AND YOU LOOK SORT OF ASIAN.
ONE OF OUR ANCESTORS MARRIED SOMEONE CHINESE IN HONG KONG THREE GENERA-TIONS AGO.

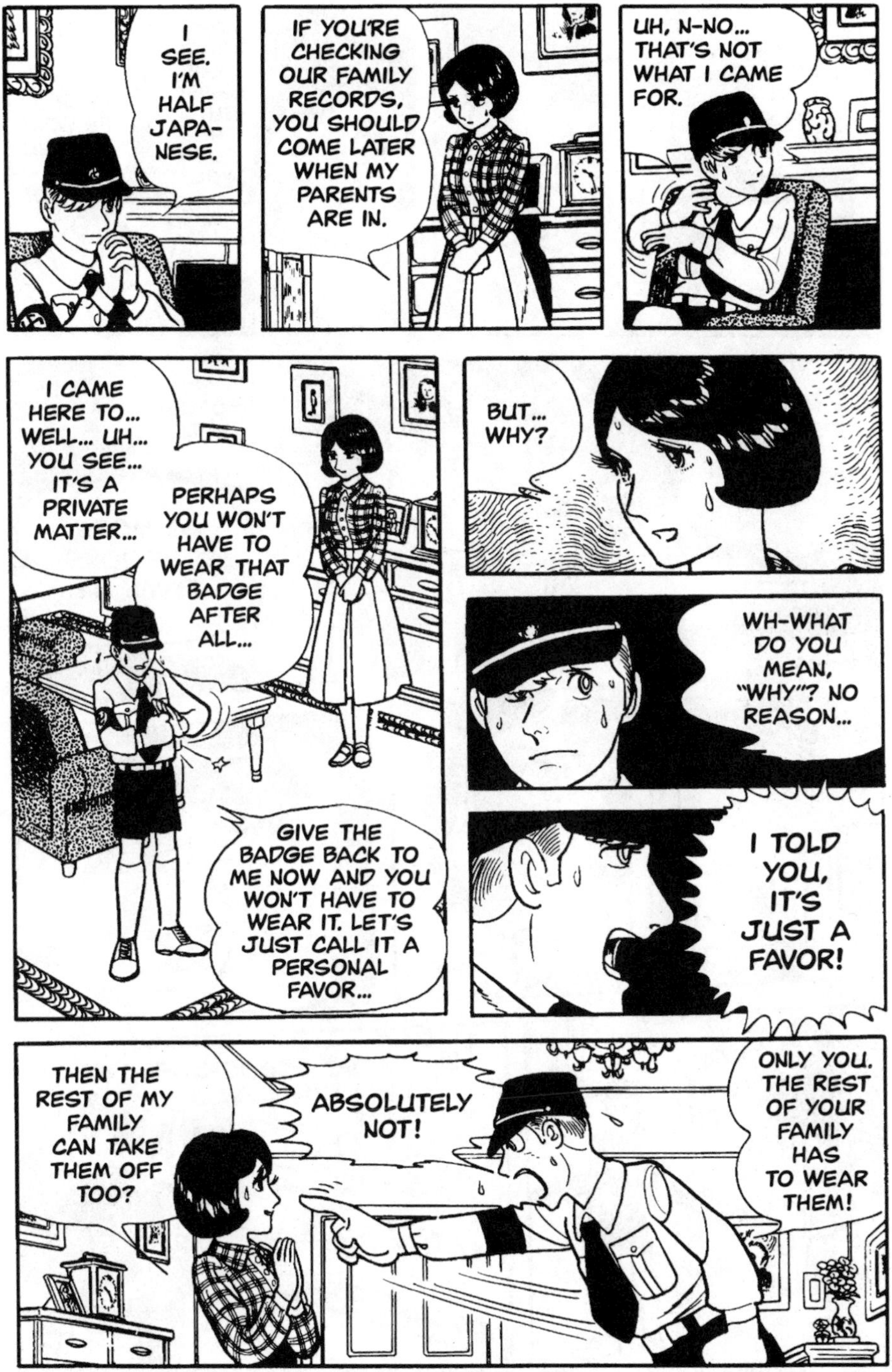
I SEE. I'M HALF JAPANESE.
IF YOU'RE CHECKING OUR FAMILY RECORDS, YOU SHOULD COME LATER WHEN MY PARENTS ARE IN.
UH, N-NO... THAT'S NOT WHAT I CAME FOR.
I CAME HERE TO... WELL... UH... YOU SEE... IT'S A PRIVATE MATTER...
PERHAPS YOU WON'T HAVE TO WEAR THAT BADGE AFTER ALL...
GIVE THE BADGE BACK TO ME NOW AND YOU WON'T HAVE TO WEAR IT. LET'S JUST CALL IT A PERSONAL FAVOR...
BUT... WHY?
WH-WHAT DO YOU MEAN, "WHY"? NO REASON...
I TOLD YOU, IT'S JUST A FAVOR!
THEN THE REST OF MY FAMILY CAN TAKE THEM OFF TOO?
ABSOLUTELY NOT!
ONLY YOU. THE REST OF YOUR FAMILY HAS TO WEAR THEM!

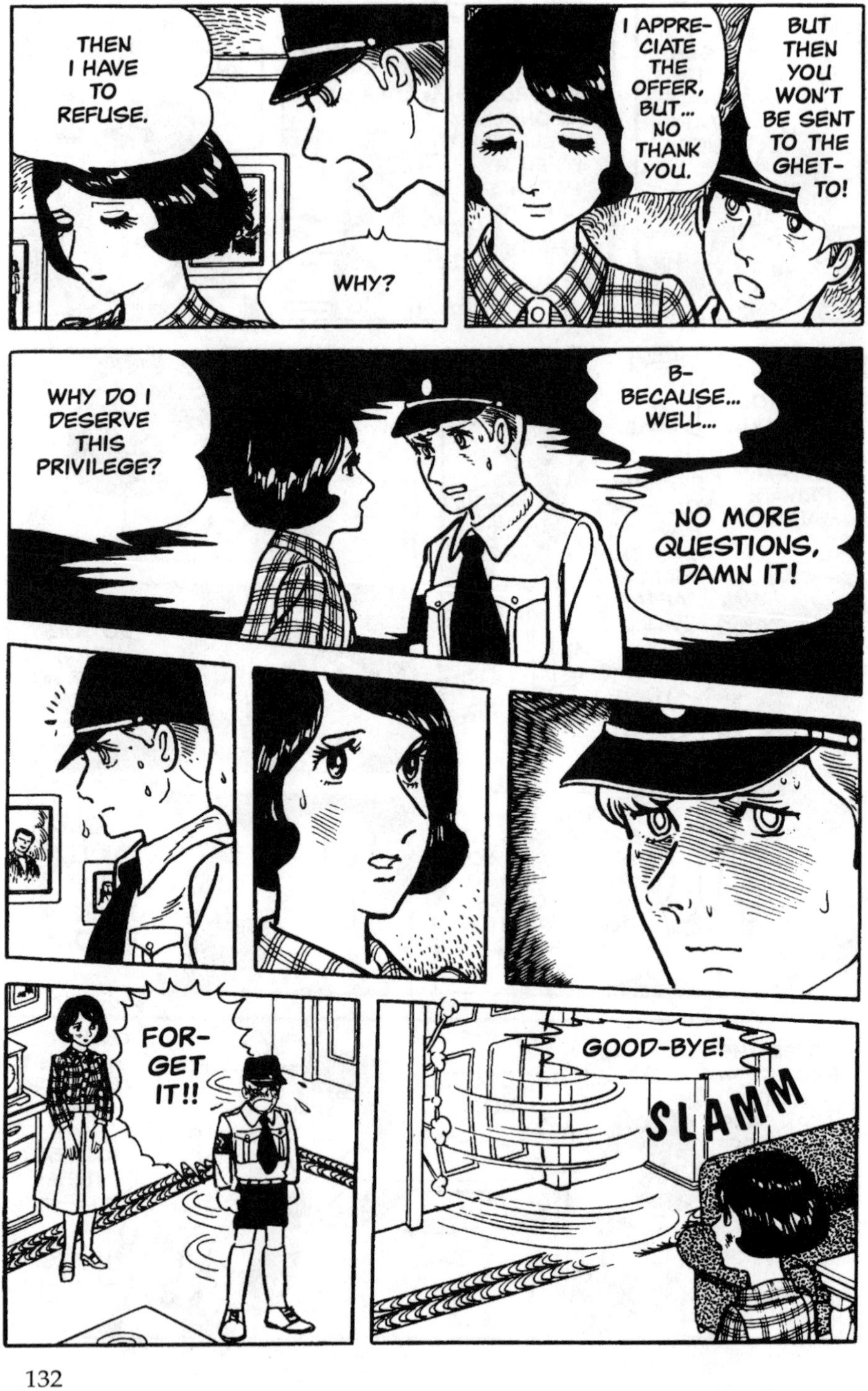
THEN I HAVE TO REFUSE.
WHY?
I APPRECIATE THE OFFER, BUT... NO THANK YOU.
BUT THEN YOU WON'T BE SENT TO THE GHETTO!
WHY DO I DESERVE THIS PRIVILEGE?
B-BECAUSE... WELL...
NO MORE QUESTIONS, DAMN IT!
FORGET IT!!
GOOD-BYE!
SLAMM

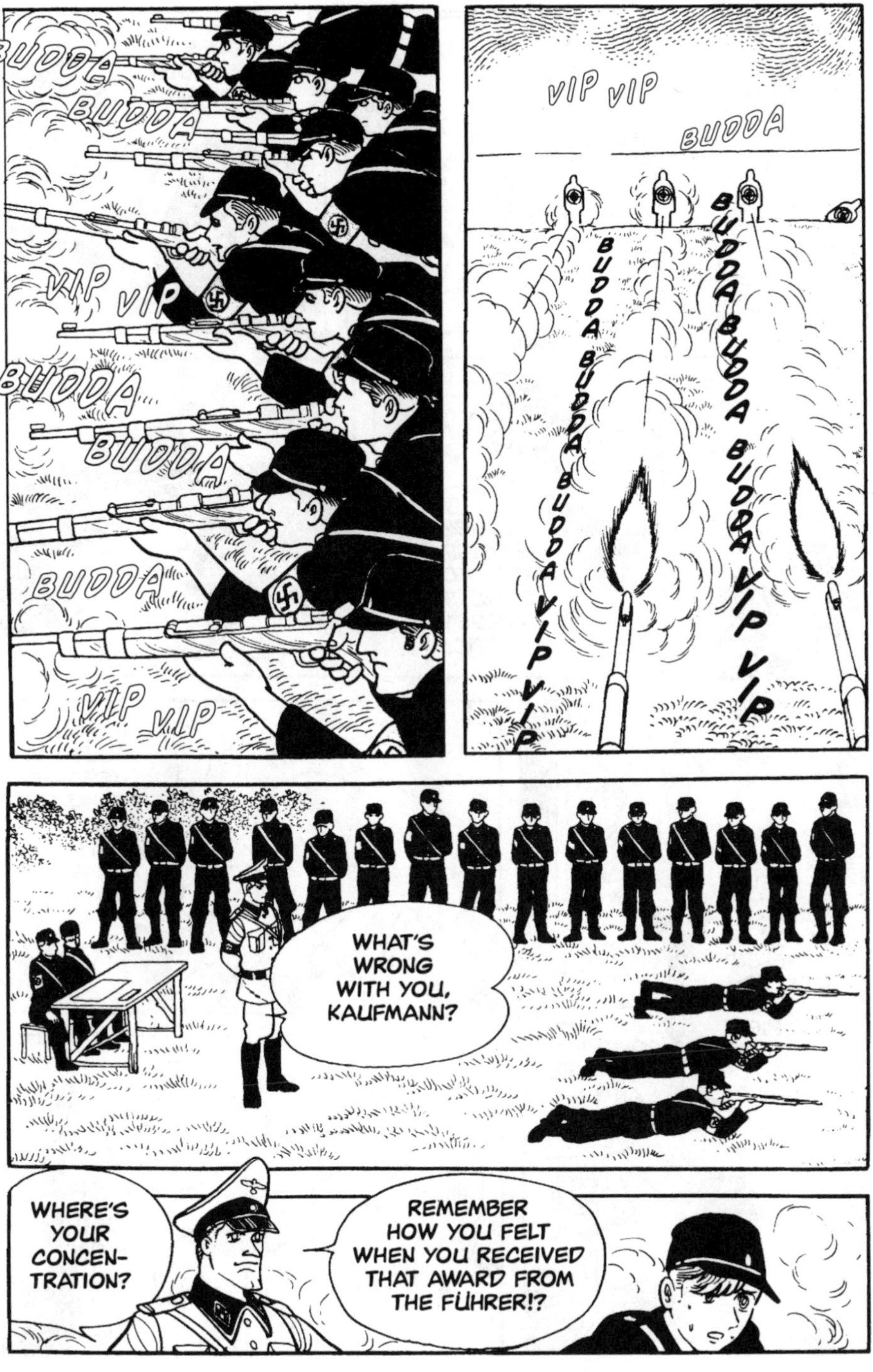
BUDDA
BUDDA
VIP VIP
BUDDA
BUDDA
BUDDA
VIP VIP
VIP VIP
BUDDA
BUDDA BUDDA BUDDA BUDDA VIP VIP
BUDDA BUDDA BUDDA BUDDA VIP VIP
WHAT'S WRONG WITH YOU, KAUFMANN?
WHERE'S YOUR CONCEN-TRATION?
REMEMBER HOW YOU FELT WHEN YOU RECEIVED THAT AWARD FROM THE FÜHRER!?

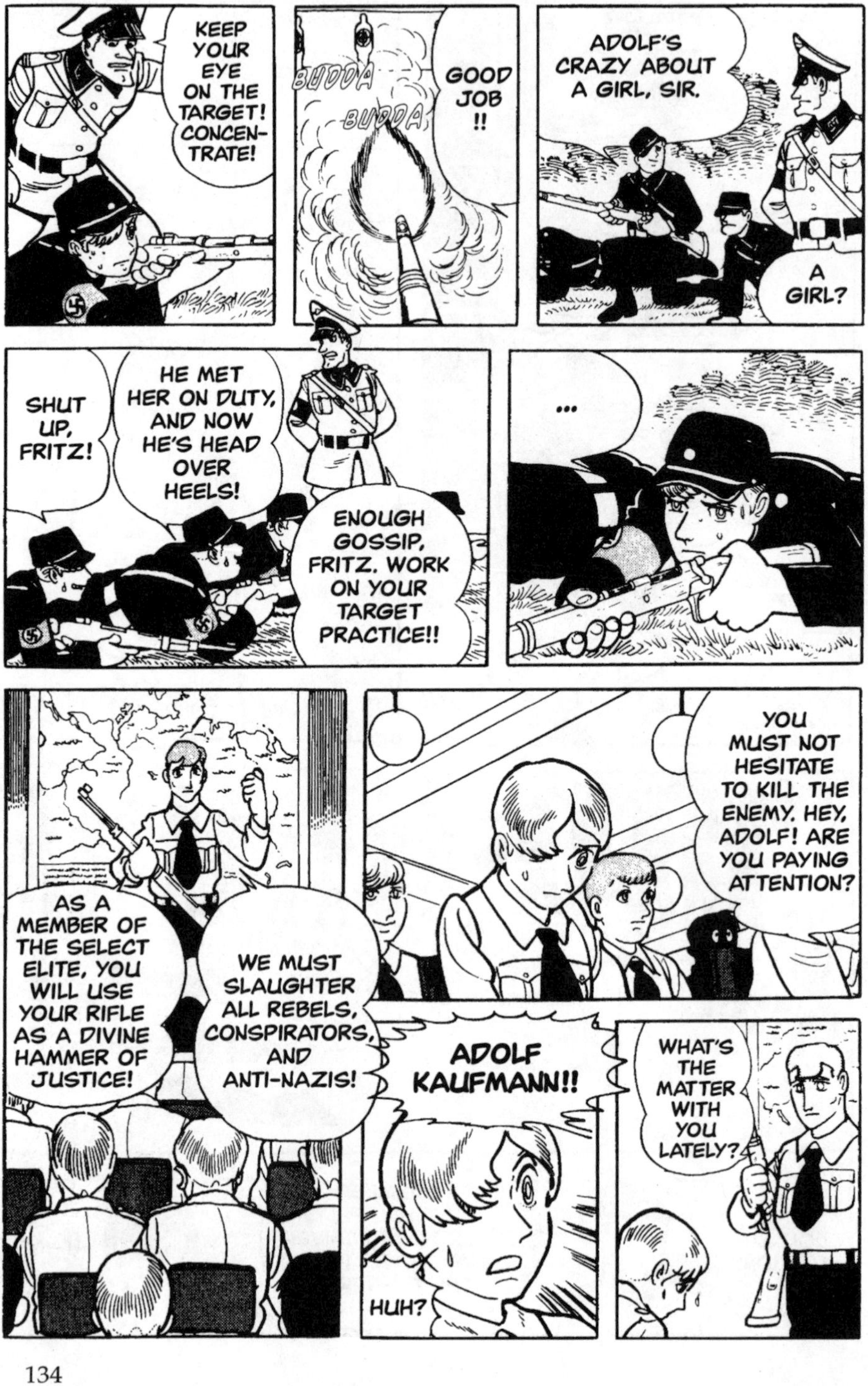
KEEP YOUR EYE ON THE TARGET! CONCENTRATE!
BUDDA
BUDDA
GOOD JOB !!
ADOLF'S CRAZY ABOUT A GIRL, SIR.
A GIRL?
HE MET HER ON DUTY, AND NOW HE'S HEAD OVER HEELS!
SHUT UP, FRITZ!
ENOUGH GOSSIP, FRITZ. WORK ON YOUR TARGET PRACTICE!!
...
AS A MEMBER OF THE SELECT ELITE, YOU WILL USE YOUR RIFLE AS A DIVINE HAMMER OF JUSTICE!
WE MUST SLAUGHTER ALL REBELS, CONSPIRATORS, AND ANTI-NAZIS!
YOU MUST NOT HESITATE TO KILL THE ENEMY. HEY, ADOLF! ARE YOU PAYING ATTENTION?
ADOLF KAUFMANN!!
HUH?
WHAT'S THE MATTER WITH YOU LATELY?

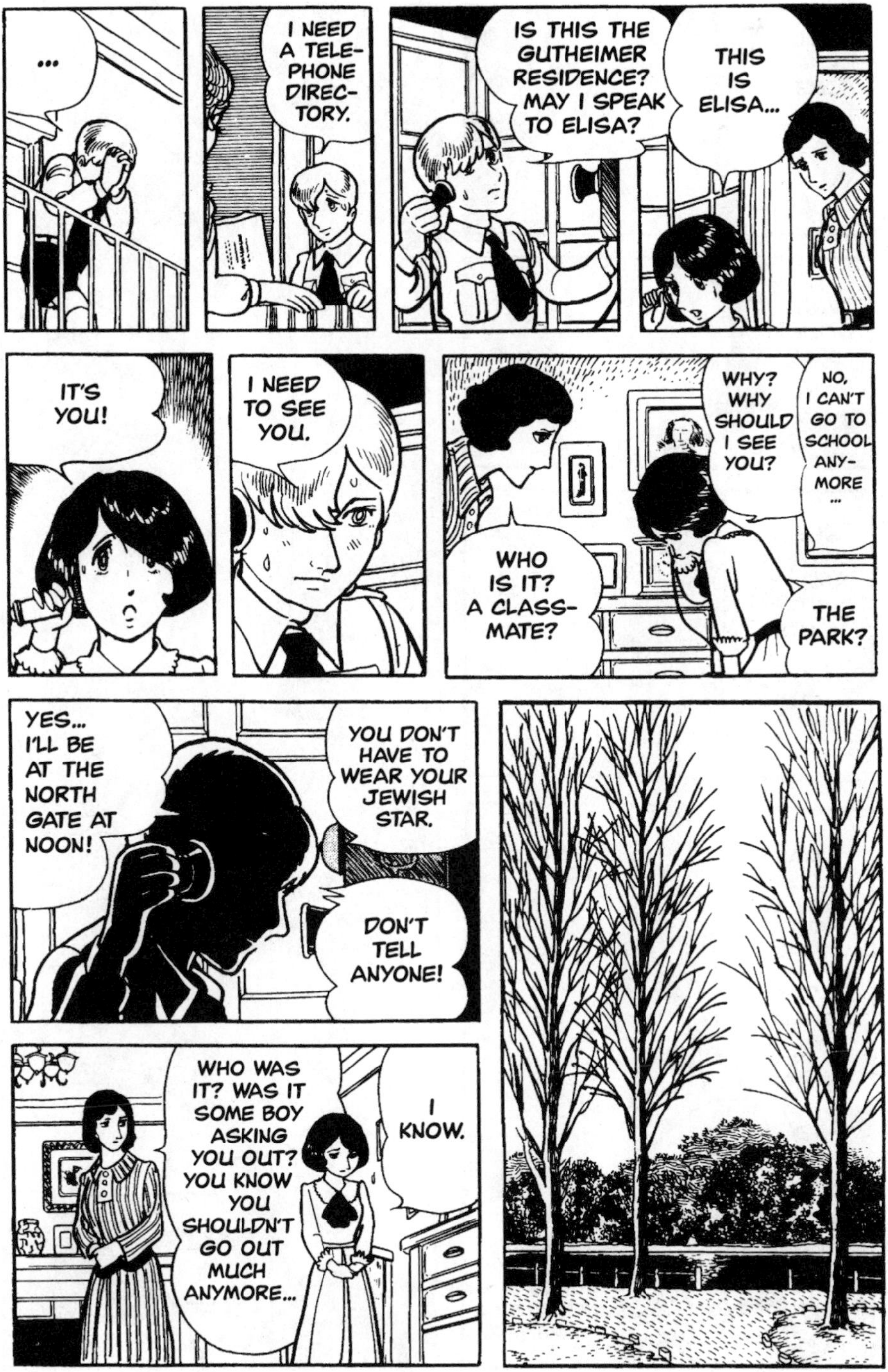
...
I NEED A TELEPHONE DIRECTORY.
IS THIS THE GUTHEIMER RESIDENCE? MAY I SPEAK TO ELISA?
THIS IS ELISA...
IT'S YOU!
I NEED TO SEE YOU.
WHO IS IT? A CLASSMATE?
WHY? WHY SHOULD I SEE YOU?
NO, I CAN'T GO TO SCHOOL ANYMORE ...
THE PARK?
YES... I'LL BE AT THE NORTH GATE AT NOON!
YOU DON'T HAVE TO WEAR YOUR JEWISH STAR.
DON'T TELL ANYONE!
WHO WAS IT? WAS IT SOME BOY ASKING YOU OUT? YOU KNOW YOU SHOULDN'T GO OUT MUCH ANYMORE...
I KNOW.

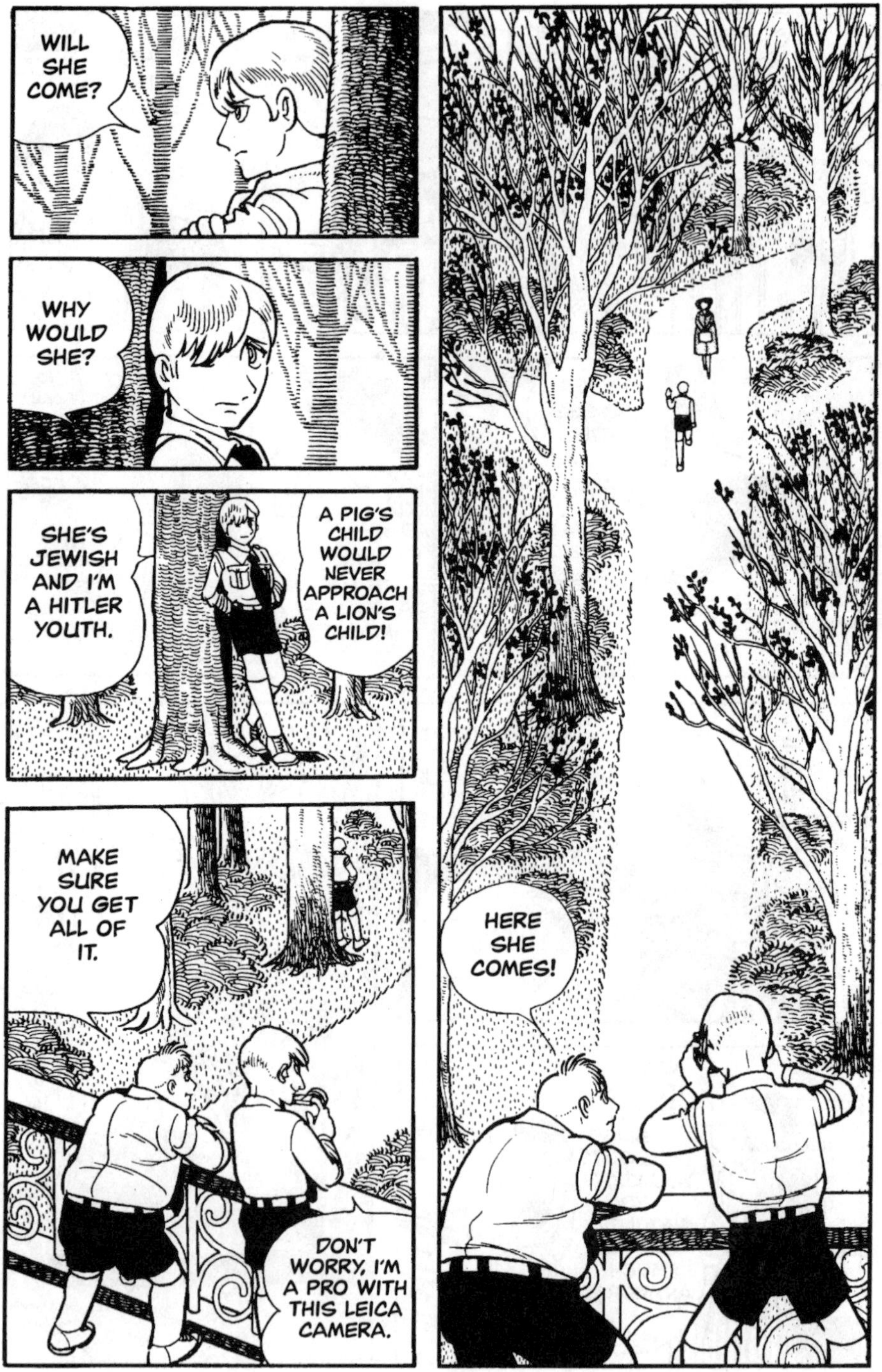
WILL SHE COME?
WHY WOULD SHE?
SHE'S JEWISH AND I'M A HITLER YOUTH.
A PIG'S CHILD WOULD NEVER APPROACH A LION'S CHILD!
MAKE SURE YOU GET ALL OF IT.
DON'T WORRY, I'M A PRO WITH THIS LEICA CAMERA.
HERE SHE COMES!

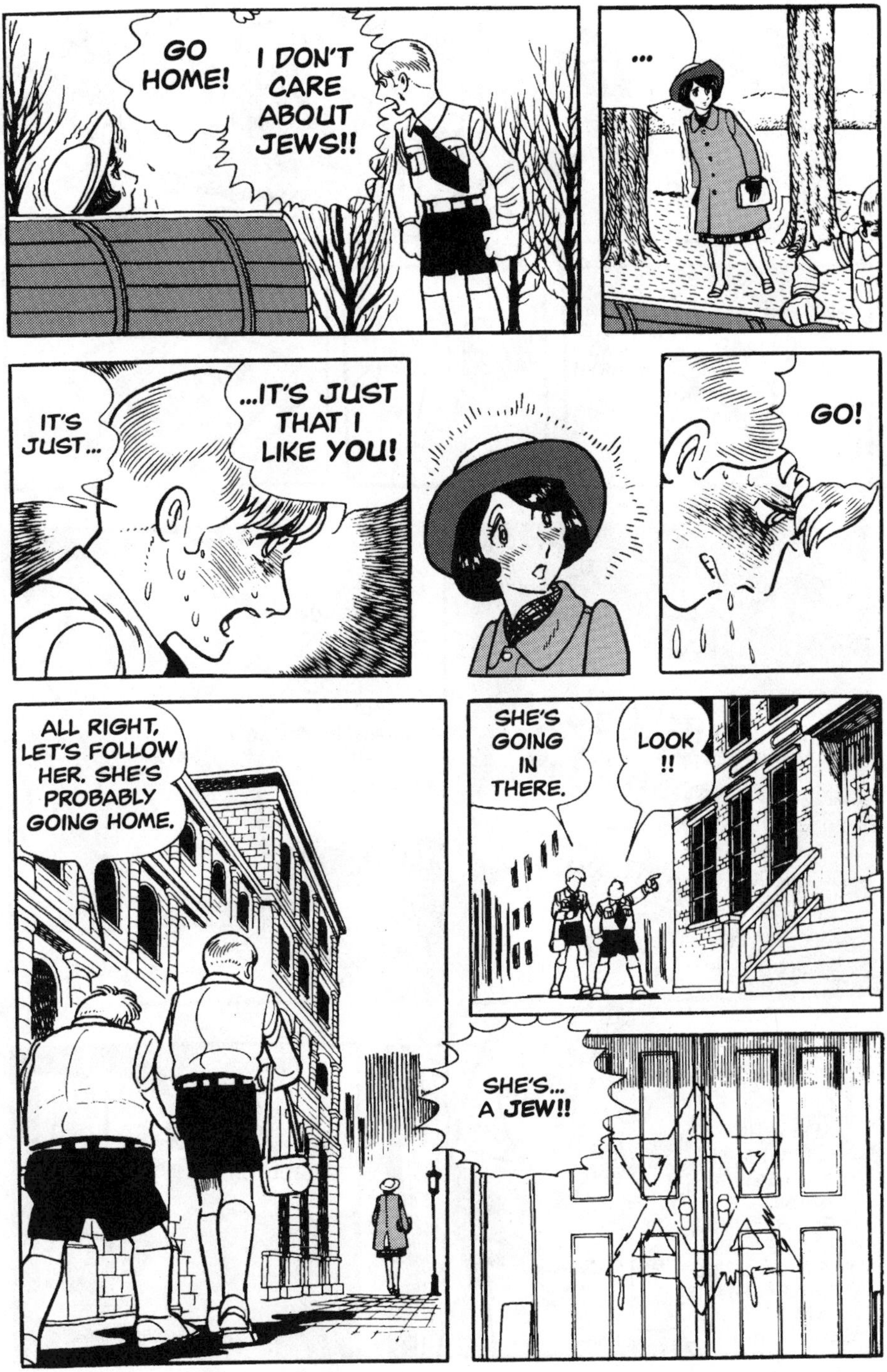
GO HOME!
I DON'T CARE ABOUT JEWS!!
...
IT'S JUST...
...IT'S JUST THAT I LIKE YOU!
GO!
ALL RIGHT, LET'S FOLLOW HER. SHE'S PROBABLY GOING HOME.
SHE'S GOING IN THERE.
LOOK !!
SHE'S... A JEW!!

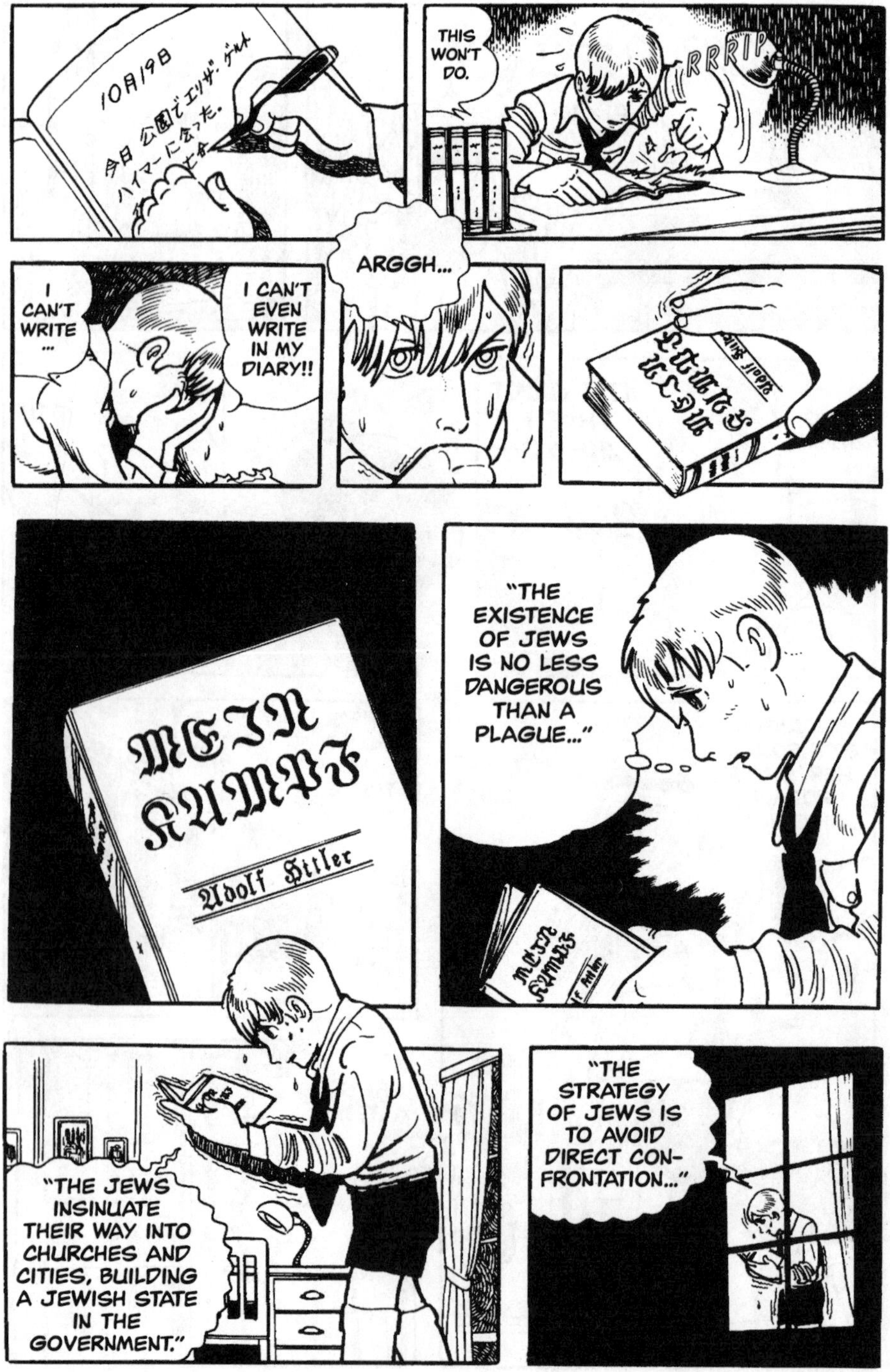
10月19日
今日 公園でエリザ・ゲルト
ハイマーに会った。
THIS WON'T DO.
RRRIP
I CAN'T WRITE...
I CAN'T EVEN WRITE IN MY DIARY!!
ARGGH...
MEIN KAMPF
Adolf Hitler
"THE EXISTENCE OF JEWS IS NO LESS DANGEROUS THAN A PLAGUE..."
"THE JEWS INSINUATE THEIR WAY INTO CHURCHES AND CITIES, BUILDING A JEWISH STATE IN THE GOVERNMENT."
"THE STRATEGY OF JEWS IS TO AVOID DIRECT CON-FRONTATION..."

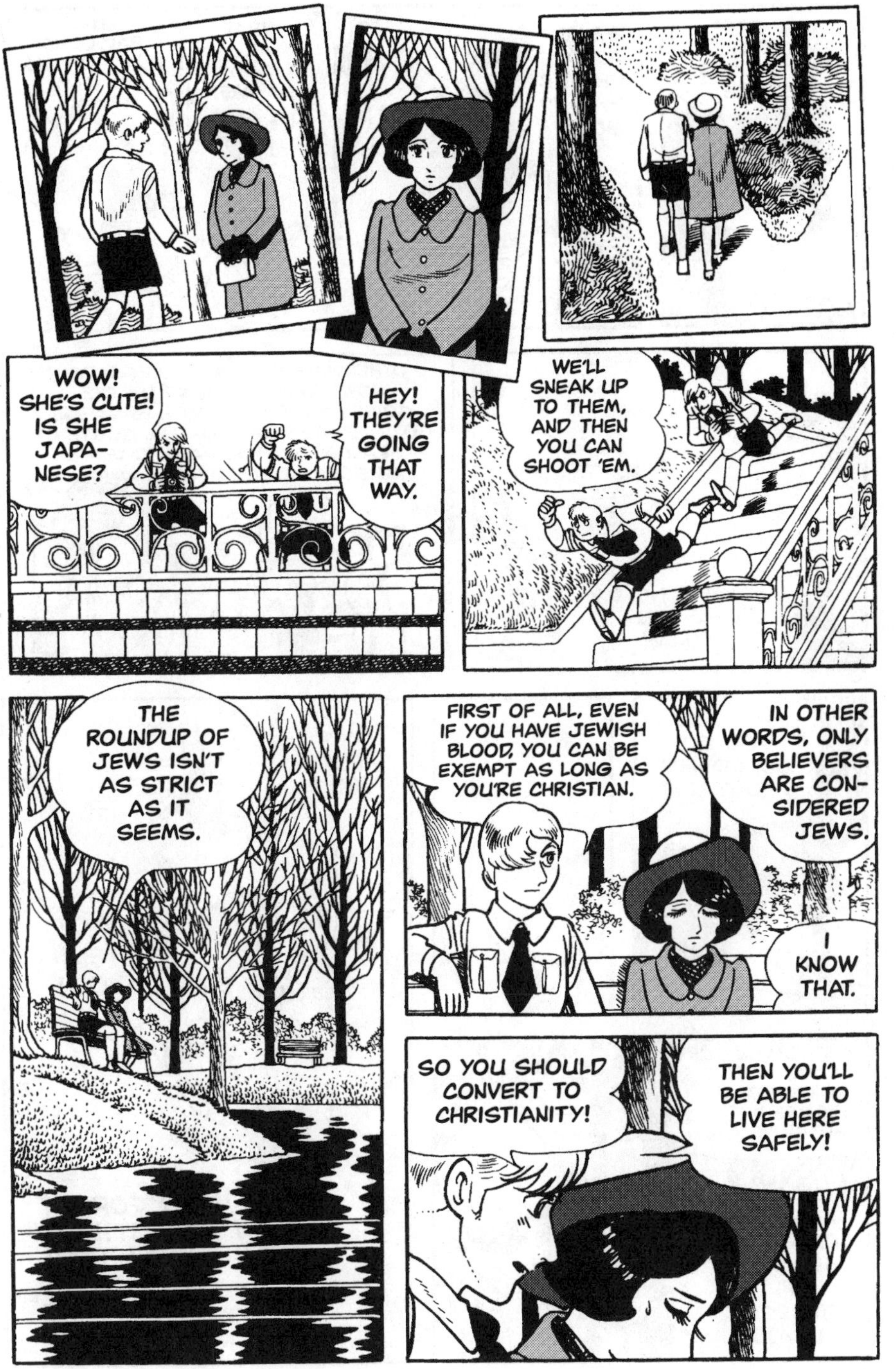
WOW! SHE'S CUTE! IS SHE JAPANESE?
HEY! THEY'RE GOING THAT WAY.
WE'LL SNEAK UP TO THEM, AND THEN YOU CAN SHOOT 'EM.
THE ROUNDUP OF JEWS ISN'T AS STRICT AS IT SEEMS.
FIRST OF ALL, EVEN IF YOU HAVE JEWISH BLOOD, YOU CAN BE EXEMPT AS LONG AS YOU'RE CHRISTIAN.
IN OTHER WORDS, ONLY BELIEVERS ARE CONSIDERED JEWS.
I KNOW THAT.
SO YOU SHOULD CONVERT TO CHRISTIANITY!
THEN YOU'LL BE ABLE TO LIVE HERE SAFELY!

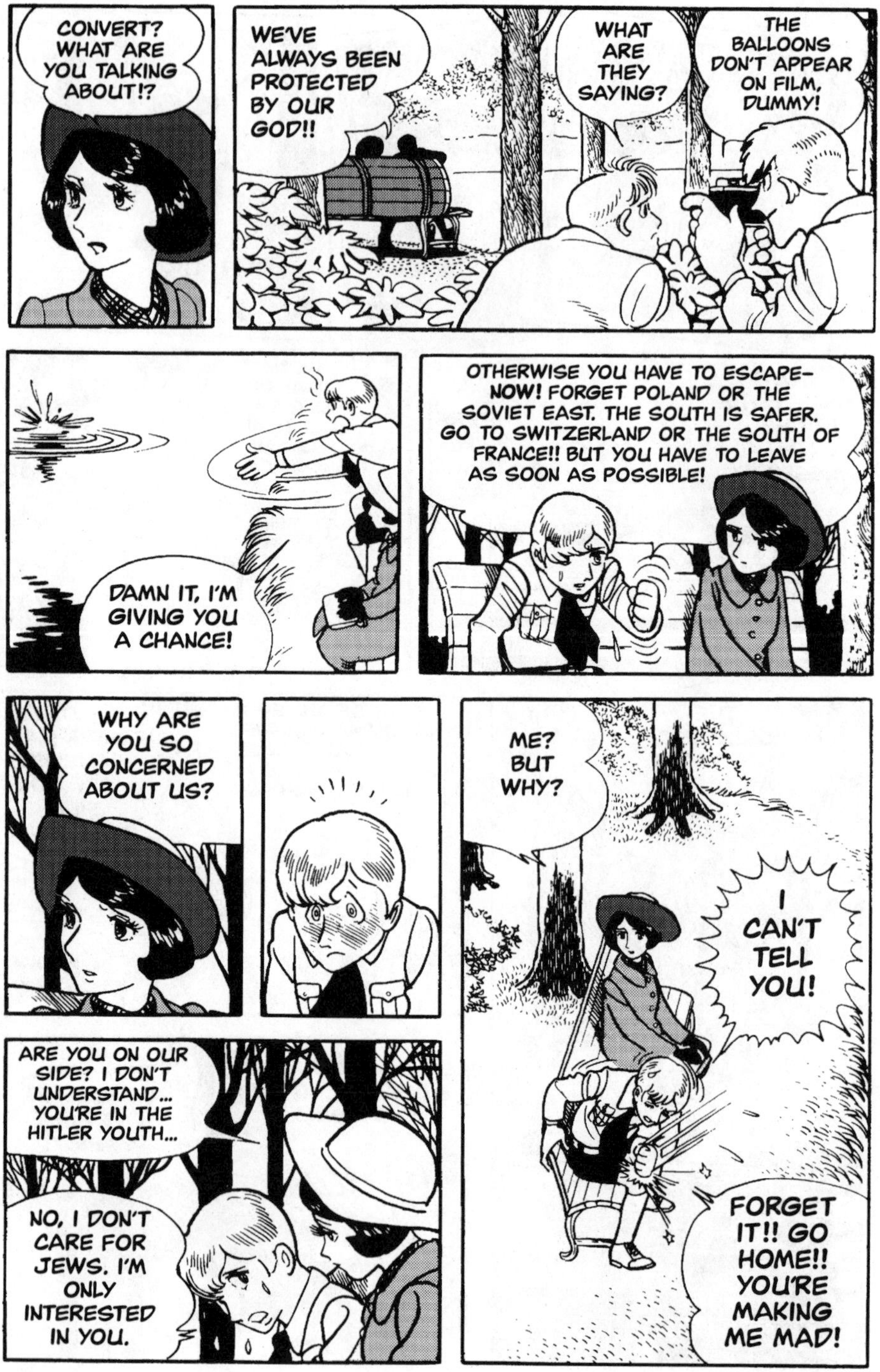
CONVERT? WHAT ARE YOU TALKING ABOUT!?
WE'VE ALWAYS BEEN PROTECTED BY OUR GOD!!
WHAT ARE THEY SAYING?
THE BALLOONS DON'T APPEAR ON FILM, DUMMY!
DAMN IT, I'M GIVING YOU A CHANCE!
OTHERWISE YOU HAVE TO ESCAPE-NOW! FORGET POLAND OR THE SOVIET EAST. THE SOUTH IS SAFER. GO TO SWITZERLAND OR THE SOUTH OF FRANCE!! BUT YOU HAVE TO LEAVE AS SOON AS POSSIBLE!
WHY ARE YOU SO CONCERNED ABOUT US?
ARE YOU ON OUR SIDE? I DON'T UNDERSTAND... YOU'RE IN THE HITLER YOUTH...
NO, I DON'T CARE FOR JEWS. I'M ONLY INTERESTED IN YOU.
ME? BUT WHY?
I CAN'T TELL YOU!
FORGET IT!! GO HOME!! YOU'RE MAKING ME MAD!

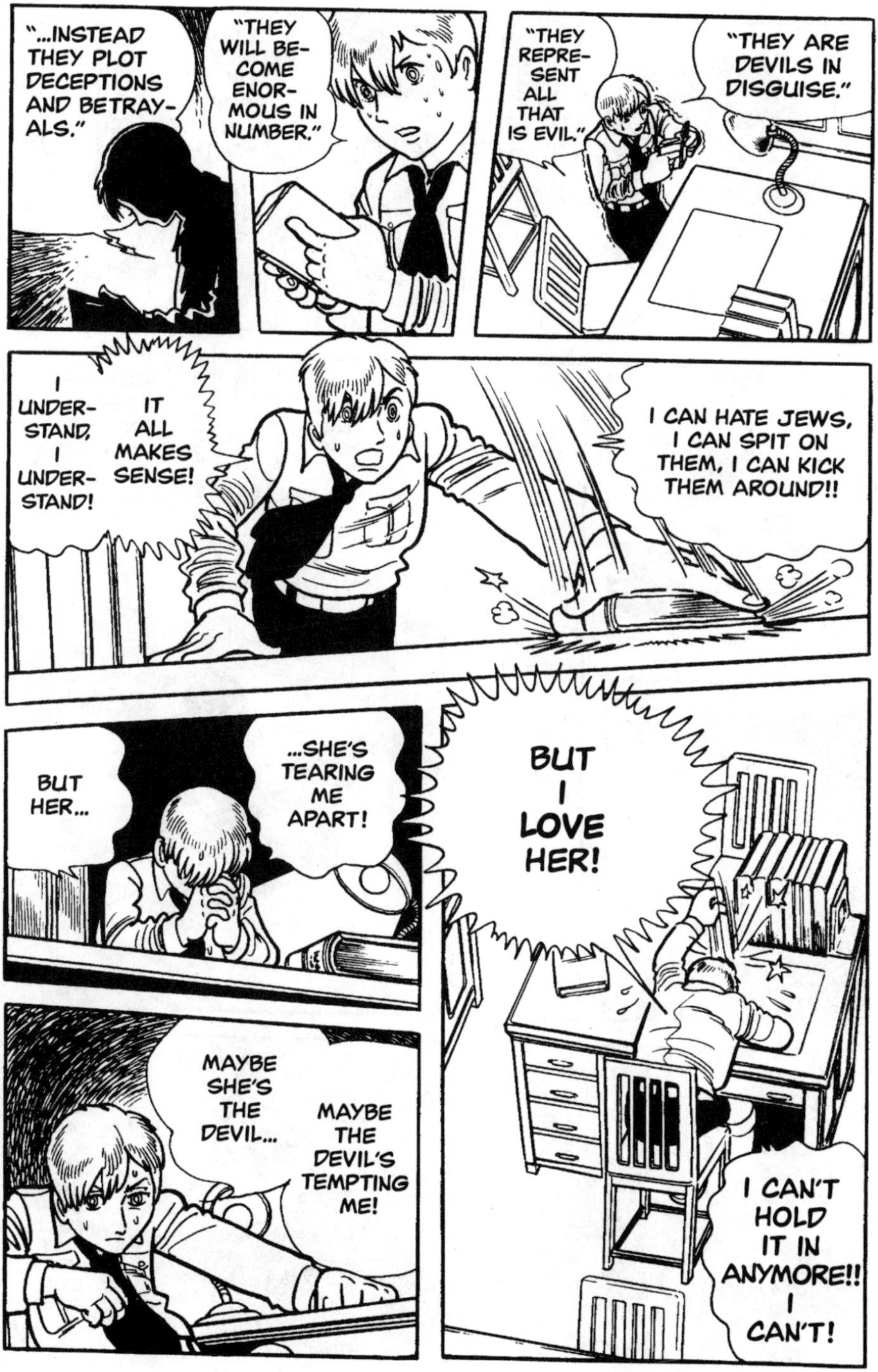
"...INSTEAD THEY PLOT DECEPTIONS AND BETRAYALS."
"THEY WILL BECOME ENORMOUS IN NUMBER."
"THEY REPRESENT ALL THAT IS EVIL."
"THEY ARE DEVILS IN DISGUISE."
I UNDERSTAND, I UNDERSTAND!
IT ALL MAKES SENSE!
I CAN HATE JEWS, I CAN SPIT ON THEM, I CAN KICK THEM AROUND!!
BUT HER...
...SHE'S TEARING ME APART!
MAYBE SHE'S THE DEVIL...
MAYBE THE DEVIL'S TEMPTING ME!
BUT I LOVE HER!
I CAN'T HOLD IT IN ANYMORE!! I CAN'T!

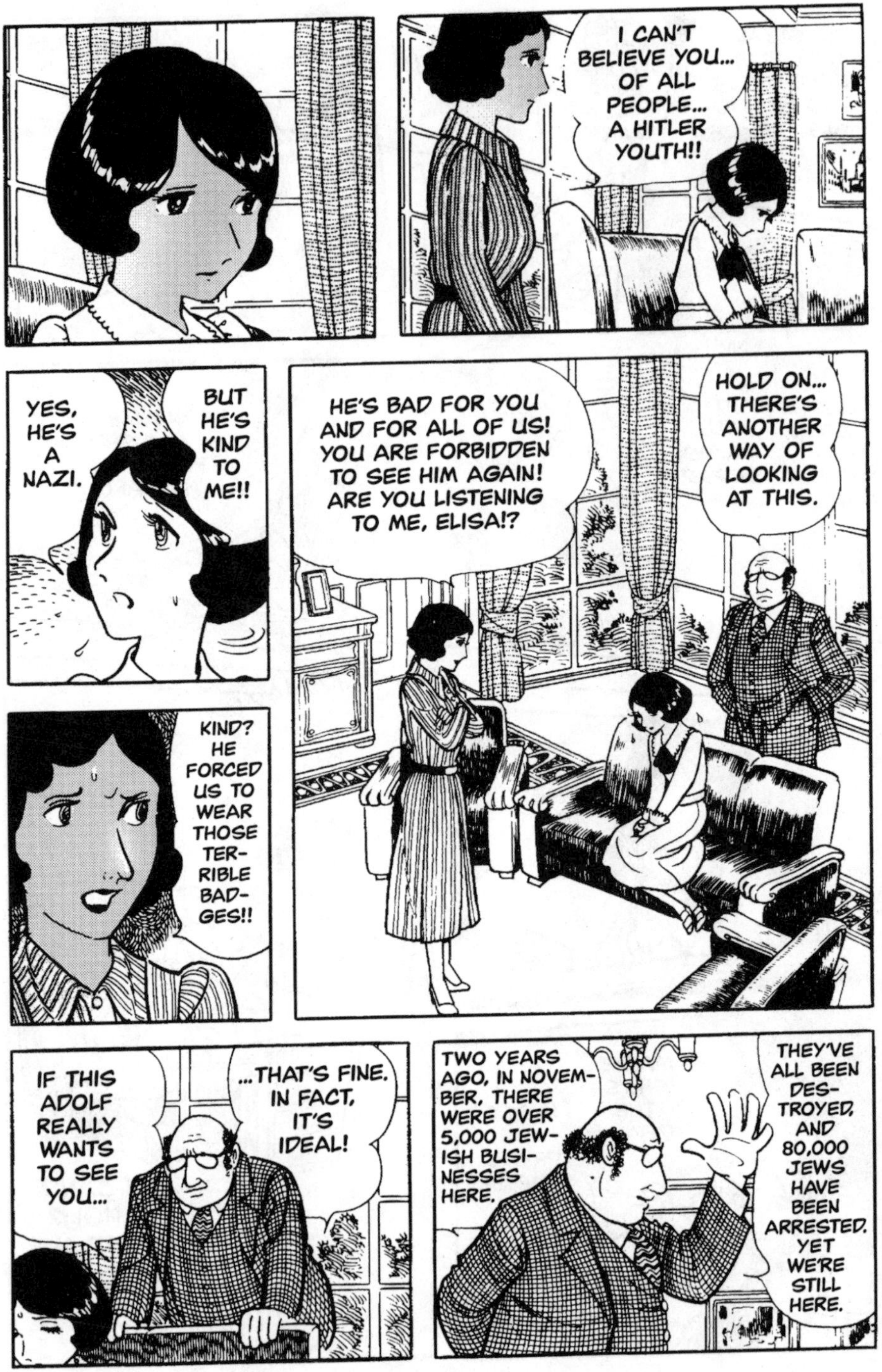
I CAN'T BELIEVE YOU... OF ALL PEOPLE... A HITLER YOUTH!!
YES, HE'S A NAZI.
BUT HE'S KIND TO ME!!
HE'S BAD FOR YOU AND FOR ALL OF US! YOU ARE FORBIDDEN TO SEE HIM AGAIN! ARE YOU LISTENING TO ME, ELISA!?
HOLD ON... THERE'S ANOTHER WAY OF LOOKING AT THIS.
KIND? HE FORCED US TO WEAR THOSE TER-RIBLE BAD-GES!!
IF THIS ADOLF REALLY WANTS TO SEE YOU...
...THAT'S FINE. IN FACT, IT'S IDEAL!
TWO YEARS AGO, IN NOVEM-BER, THERE WERE OVER 5,000 JEW-ISH BUSI-NESSES HERE.
THEY'VE ALL BEEN DES-TROYED, AND 80,000 JEWS HAVE BEEN ARRESTED. YET WE'RE STILL HERE.

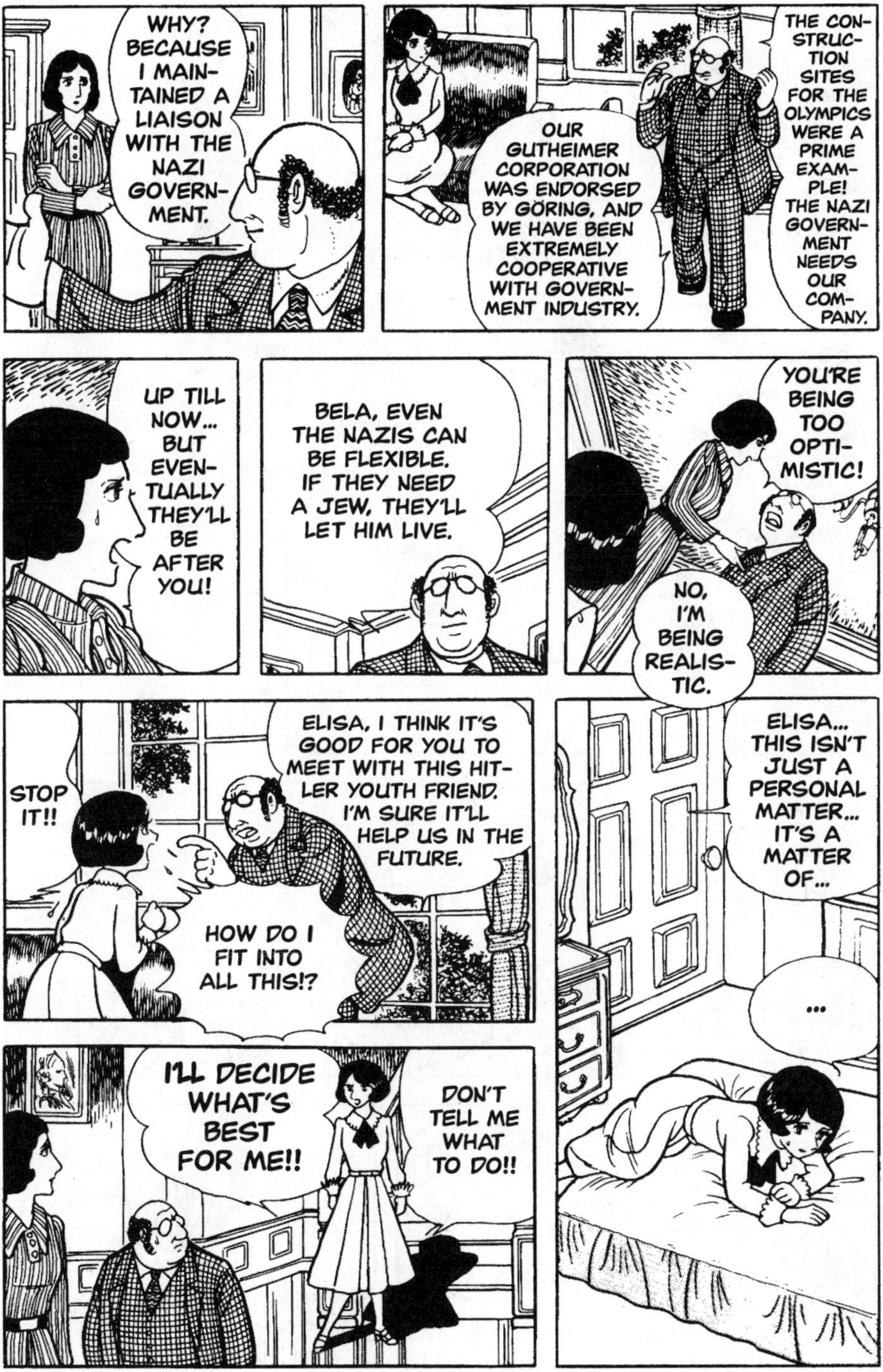
WHY? BECAUSE I MAINTAINED A LIAISON WITH THE NAZI GOVERNMENT.
OUR GUTHEIMER CORPORATION WAS ENDORSED BY GÖRING, AND WE HAVE BEEN EXTREMELY COOPERATIVE WITH GOVERNMENT INDUSTRY.
THE CONSTRUCTION SITES FOR THE OLYMPICS WERE A PRIME EXAMPLE! THE NAZI GOVERNMENT NEEDS OUR COMPANY.
UP TILL NOW... BUT EVENTUALLY THEY'LL BE AFTER YOU!
BELA, EVEN THE NAZIS CAN BE FLEXIBLE. IF THEY NEED A JEW, THEY'LL LET HIM LIVE.
YOU'RE BEING TOO OPTIMISTIC!
NO, I'M BEING REALISTIC.
STOP IT!!
ELISA, I THINK IT'S GOOD FOR YOU TO MEET WITH THIS HITLER YOUTH FRIEND. I'M SURE IT'LL HELP US IN THE FUTURE.
HOW DO I FIT INTO ALL THIS!?
I'LL DECIDE WHAT'S BEST FOR ME!!
DON'T TELL ME WHAT TO DO!!
ELISA... THIS ISN'T JUST A PERSONAL MATTER... IT'S A MATTER OF...
...

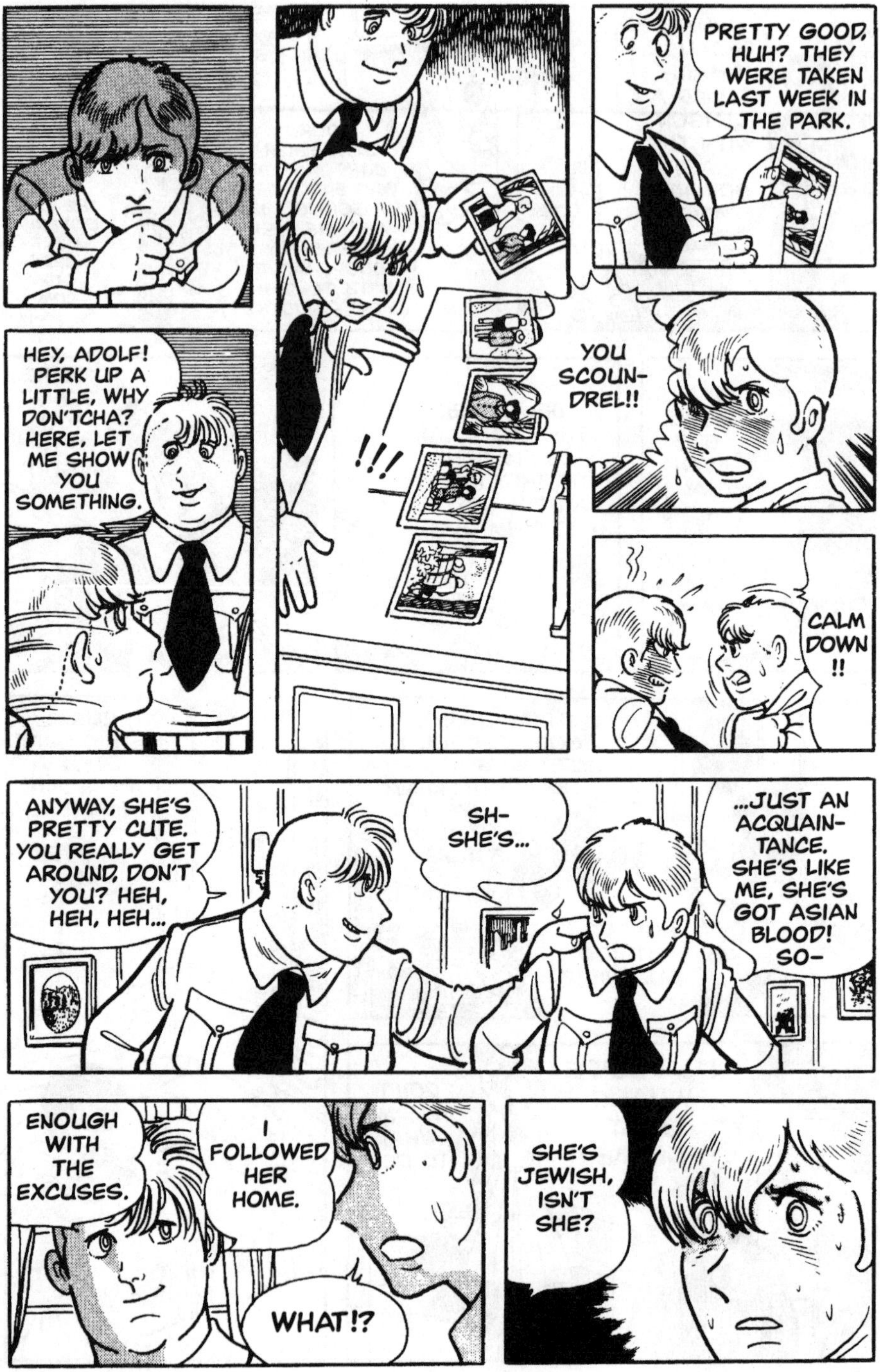
HEY, ADOLF! PERK UP A LITTLE, WHY DON'TCHA? HERE, LET ME SHOW YOU SOMETHING.
!!!
PRETTY GOOD, HUH? THEY WERE TAKEN LAST WEEK IN THE PARK.
YOU SCOUNDREL!!
CALM DOWN !!
ANYWAY, SHE'S PRETTY CUTE. YOU REALLY GET AROUND, DON'T YOU? HEH, HEH, HEH...
SH- SHE'S...
...JUST AN ACQUAINTANCE. SHE'S LIKE ME, SHE'S GOT ASIAN BLOOD! SO-
ENOUGH WITH THE EXCUSES.
I FOLLOWED HER HOME.
WHAT!?
SHE'S JEWISH, ISN'T SHE?

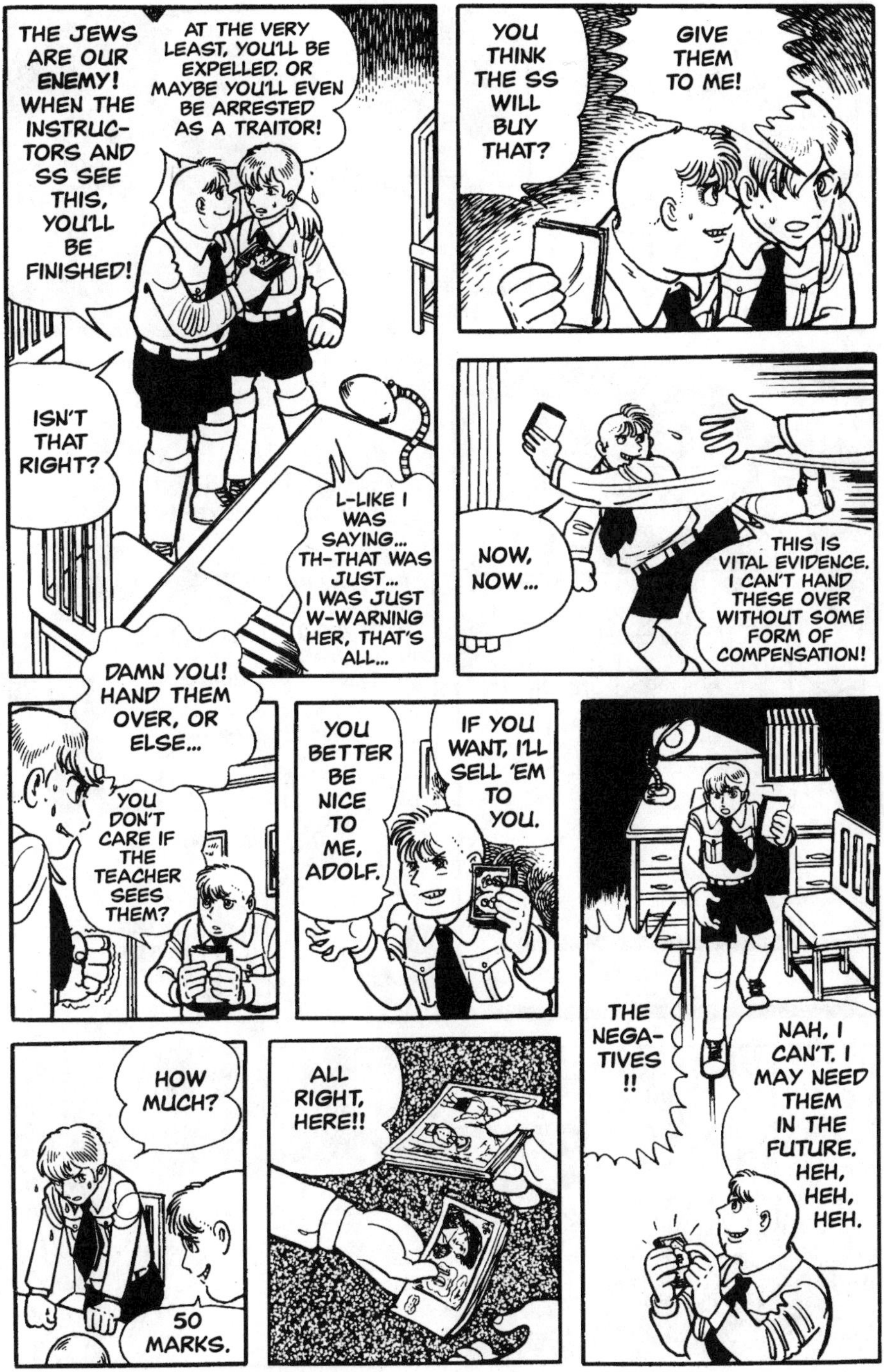
THE JEWS ARE OUR ENEMY! WHEN THE INSTRUCTORS AND SS SEE THIS, YOU'LL BE FINISHED!
AT THE VERY LEAST, YOU'LL BE EXPELLED. OR MAYBE YOU'LL EVEN BE ARRESTED AS A TRAITOR!
ISN'T THAT RIGHT?
L-LIKE I WAS SAYING... TH-THAT WAS JUST... I WAS JUST W-WARNING HER, THAT'S ALL...
YOU THINK THE SS WILL BUY THAT?
GIVE THEM TO ME!
NOW, NOW...
THIS IS VITAL EVIDENCE. I CAN'T HAND THESE OVER WITHOUT SOME FORM OF COMPENSATION!
DAMN YOU! HAND THEM OVER, OR ELSE...
YOU DON'T CARE IF THE TEACHER SEES THEM?
YOU BETTER BE NICE TO ME, ADOLF.
IF YOU WANT, I'LL SELL 'EM TO YOU.
HOW MUCH?
50 MARKS.
ALL RIGHT, HERE!!
THE NEGATIVES!!
NAH, I CAN'T. I MAY NEED THEM IN THE FUTURE. HEH, HEH, HEH.

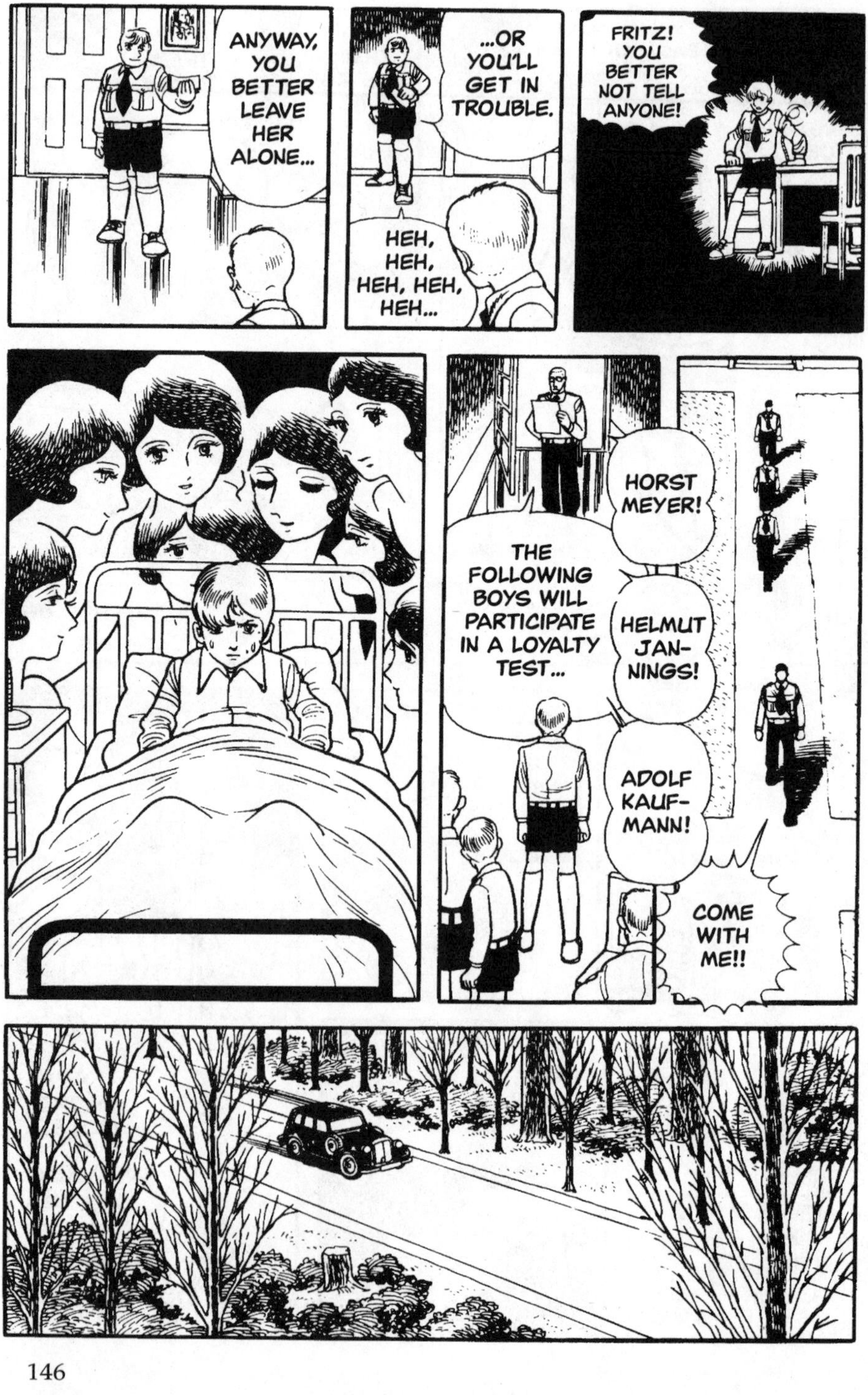
ANYWAY, YOU BETTER LEAVE HER ALONE...
...OR YOU'LL GET IN TROUBLE.
HEH, HEH, HEH, HEH, HEH...
FRITZ! YOU BETTER NOT TELL ANYONE!
THE FOLLOWING BOYS WILL PARTICIPATE IN A LOYALTY TEST...
HORST MEYER!
HELMUT JAN-NINGS!
ADOLF KAUF-MANN!
COME WITH ME!!

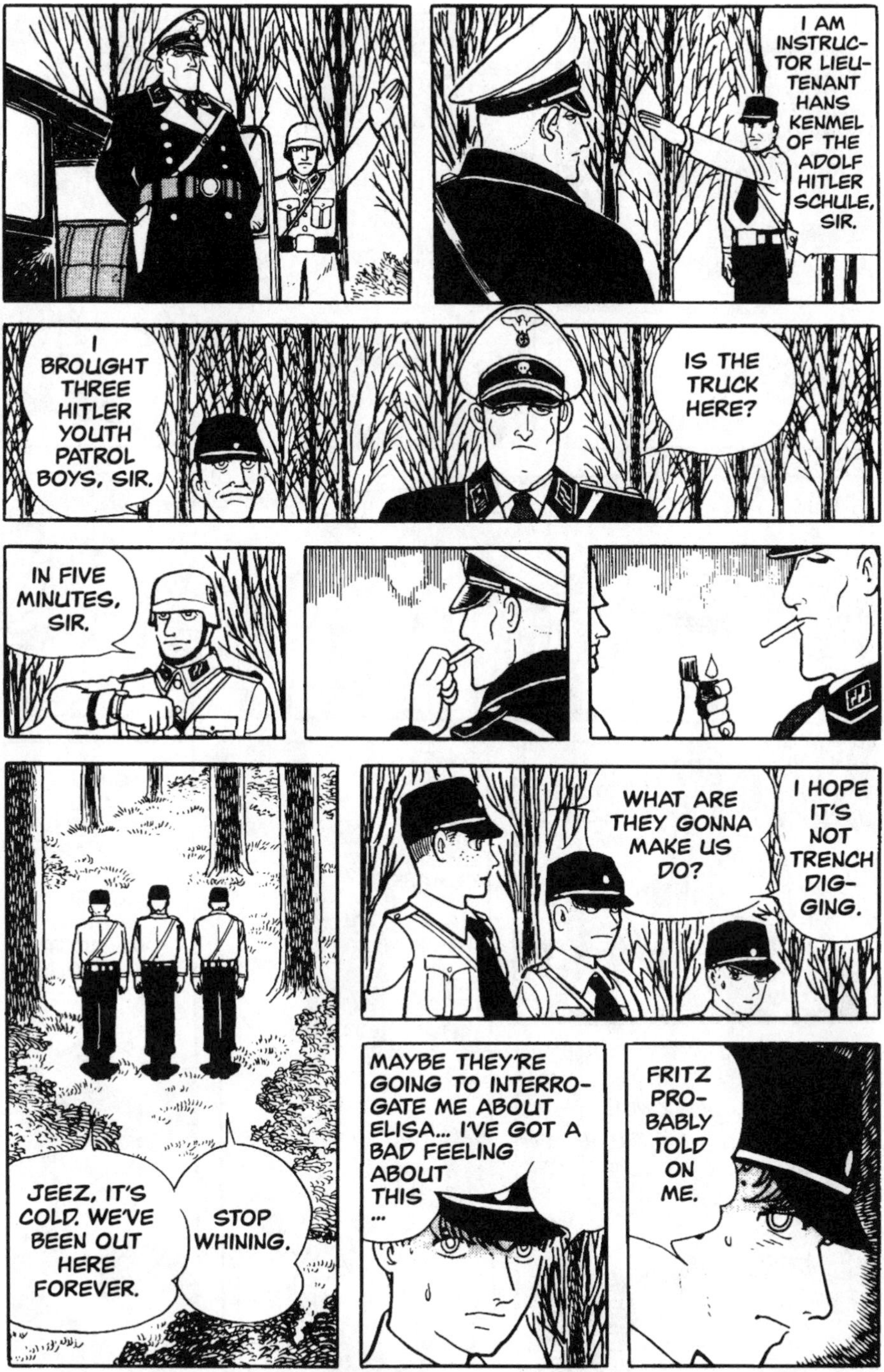
I AM INSTRUCTOR LIEUTENANT HANS KENMEL OF THE ADOLF HITLER SCHULE, SIR.
I BROUGHT THREE HITLER YOUTH PATROL BOYS, SIR.
IS THE TRUCK HERE?
IN FIVE MINUTES, SIR.
JEEZ, IT'S COLD. WE'VE BEEN OUT HERE FOREVER.
STOP WHINING.
WHAT ARE THEY GONNA MAKE US DO?
I HOPE IT'S NOT TRENCH DIGGING.
MAYBE THEY'RE GOING TO INTERROGATE ME ABOUT ELISA... I'VE GOT A BAD FEELING ABOUT THIS ...
FRITZ PROBABLY TOLD ON ME.

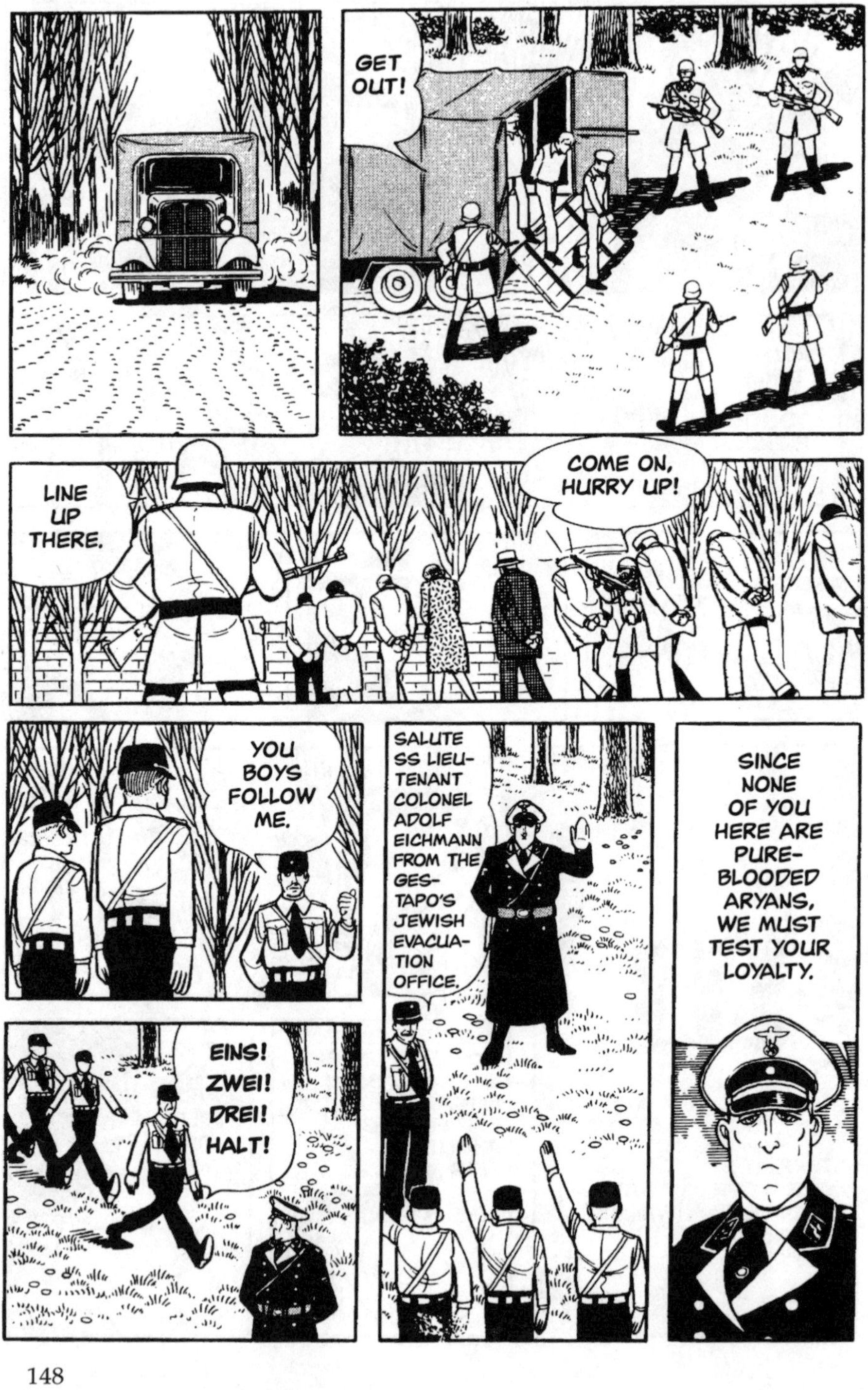
GET OUT!
LINE UP THERE.
COME ON, HURRY UP!
YOU BOYS FOLLOW ME.
EINS! ZWEI! DREI! HALT!
SALUTE SS LIEU-TENANT COLONEL ADOLF EICHMANN FROM THE GES-TAPO'S JEWISH EVACUA-TION OFFICE.
SINCE NONE OF YOU HERE ARE PURE-BLOODED ARYANS, WE MUST TEST YOUR LOYALTY.

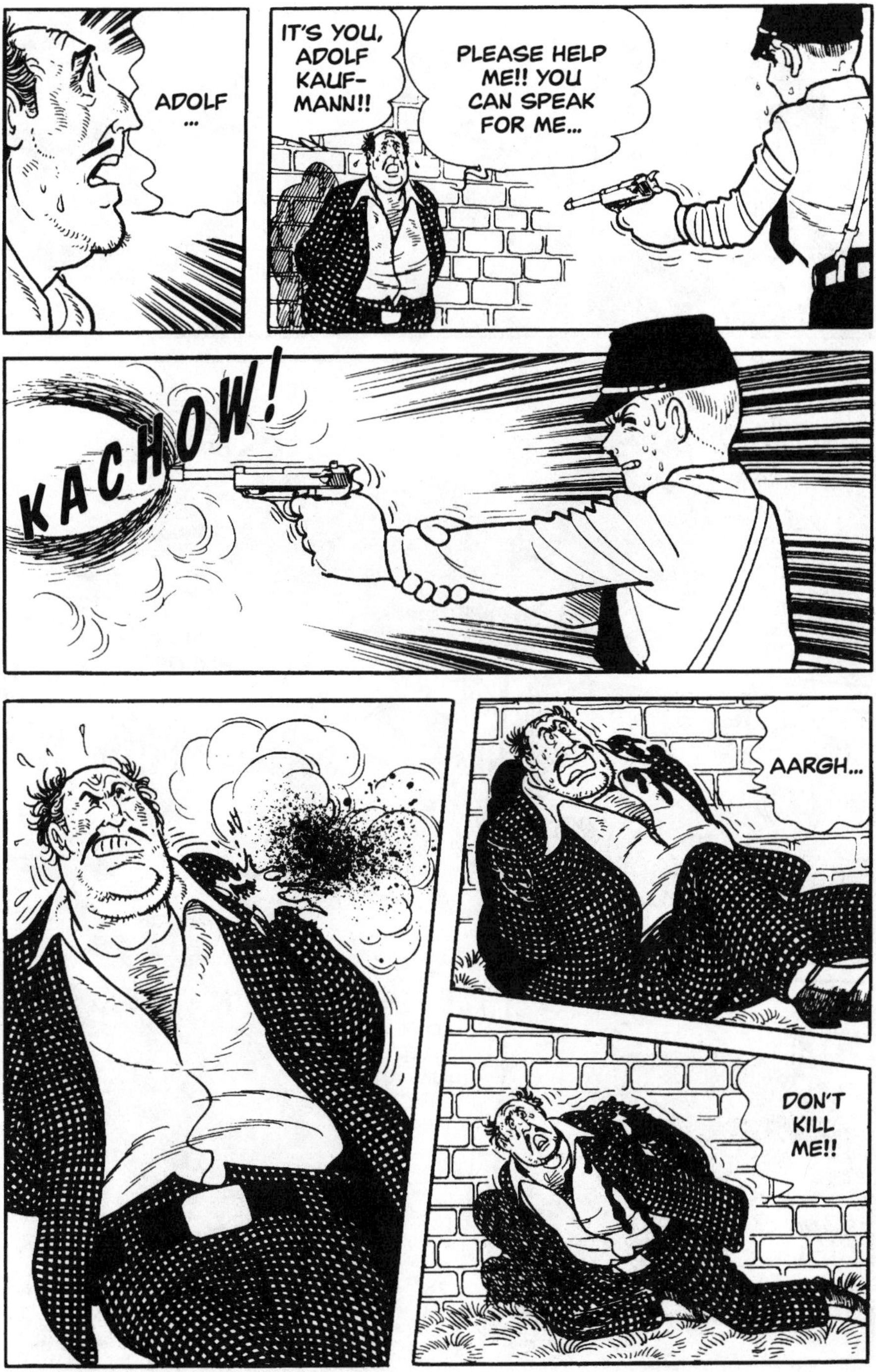
ADOLF ...
IT'S YOU, ADOLF KAUF-MANN!!
PLEASE HELP ME!! YOU CAN SPEAK FOR ME...
KACHOW!
AARGH...
DON'T KILL ME!!

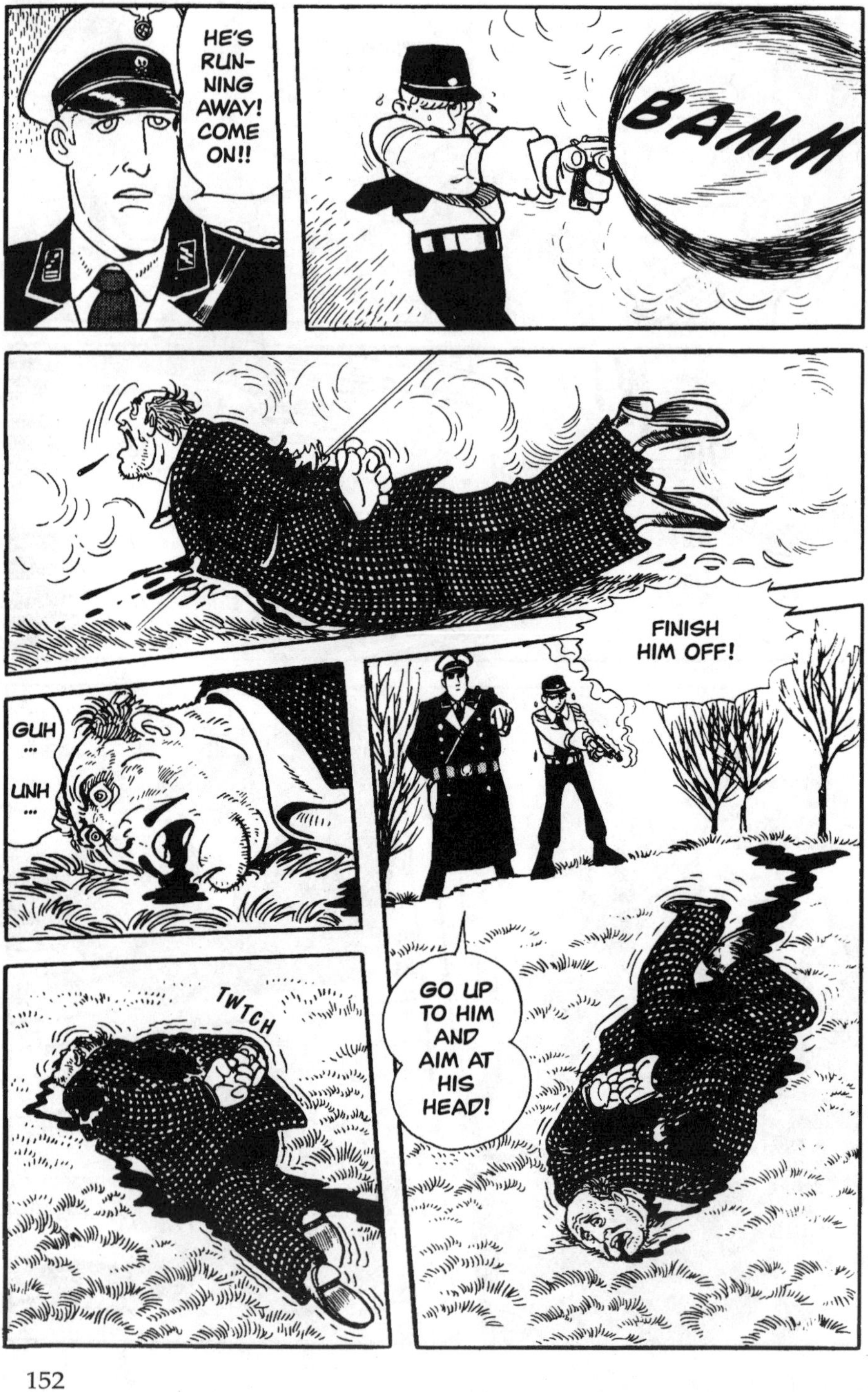
HE'S RUNNING AWAY! COME ON!!
BAMM
GUH ... UNH ...
FINISH HIM OFF!
TWTCH
GO UP TO HIM AND AIM AT HIS HEAD!

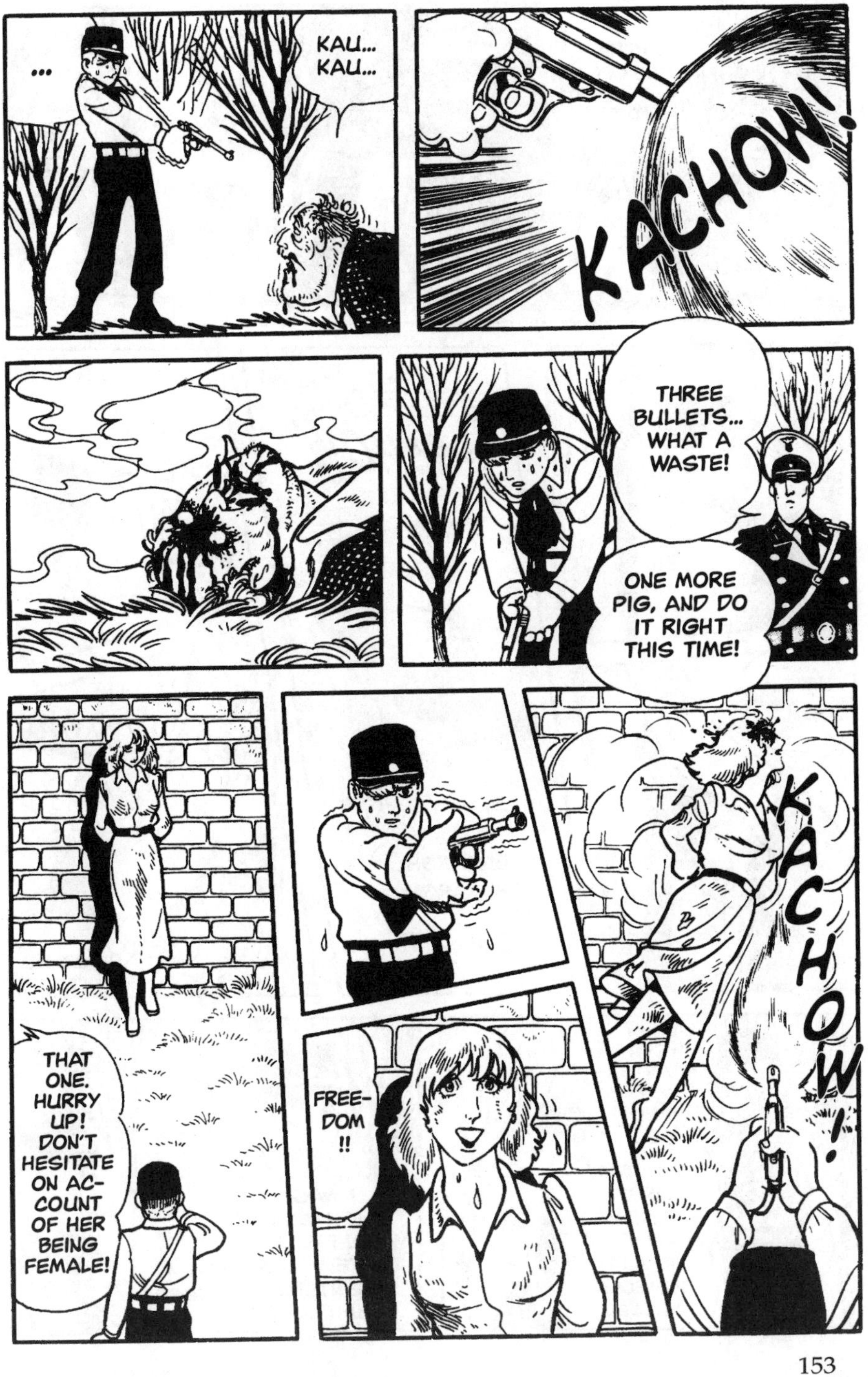
...
KAU... KAU...
KACHOW!
THREE BULLETS... WHAT A WASTE!
ONE MORE PIG, AND DO IT RIGHT THIS TIME!
THAT ONE. HURRY UP! DON'T HESITATE ON AC-COUNT OF HER BEING FEMALE!
KACHOW!
FREE-DOM !!

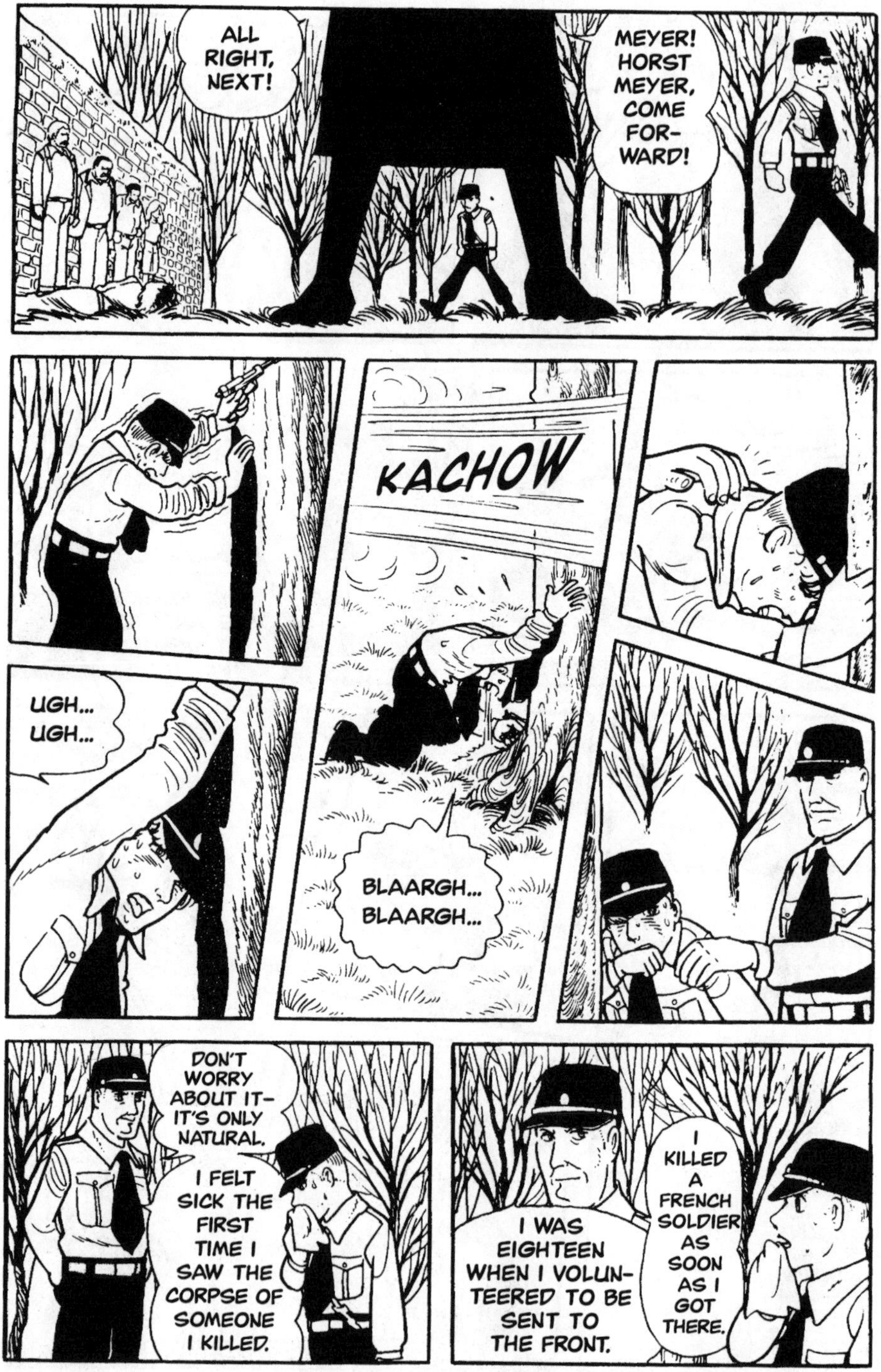
ALL RIGHT, NEXT!
MEYER! HORST MEYER, COME FOR-WARD!
KACHOW
UGH... UGH...
BLAARGH... BLAARGH...
DON'T WORRY ABOUT IT–IT'S ONLY NATURAL.
I FELT SICK THE FIRST TIME I SAW THE CORPSE OF SOMEONE I KILLED.
I WAS EIGHTEEN WHEN I VOLUN-TEERED TO BE SENT TO THE FRONT.
I KILLED A FRENCH SOLDIER AS SOON AS I GOT THERE.

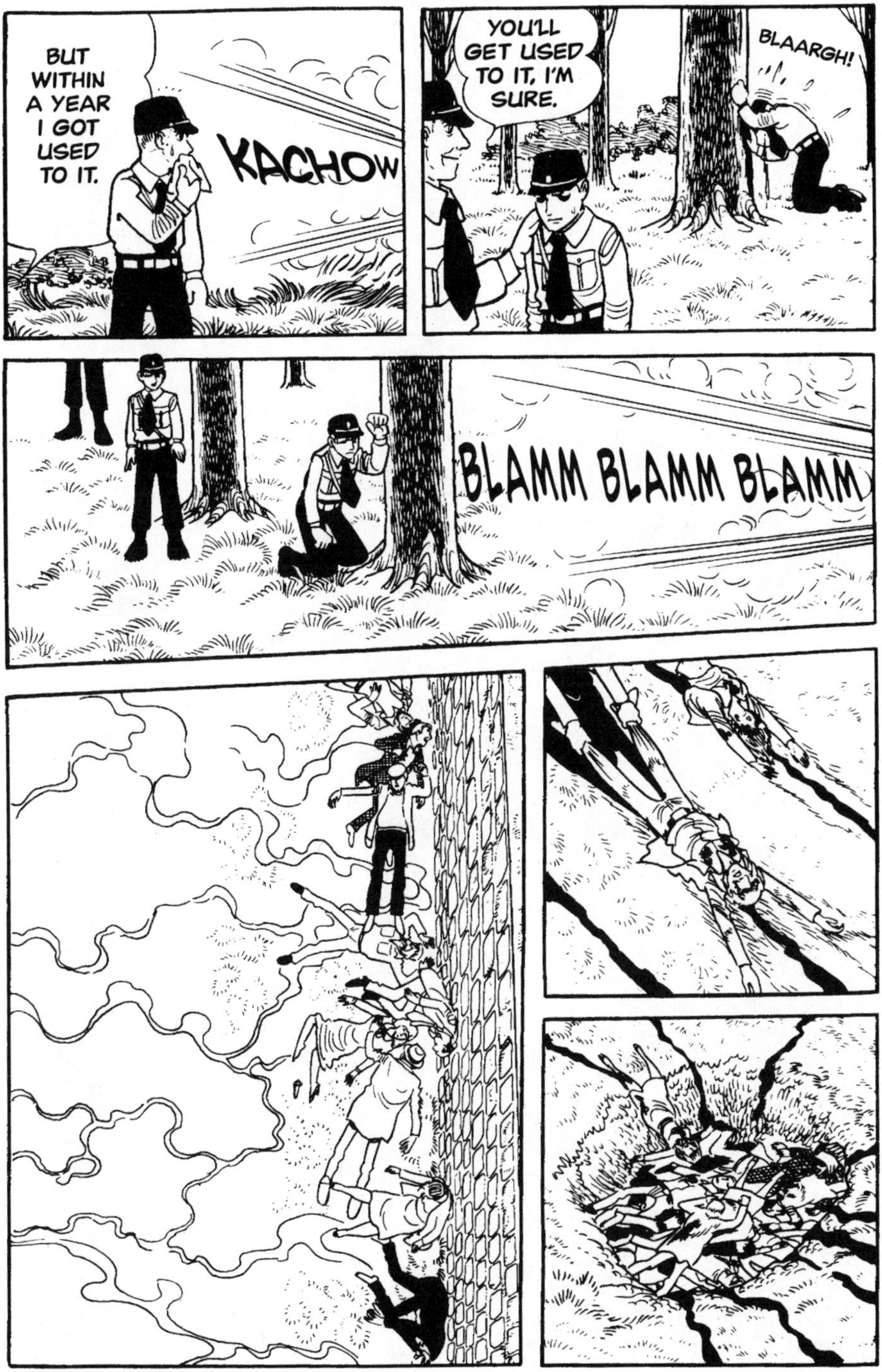
BUT WITHIN A YEAR I GOT USED TO IT.
KACHOW
YOU'LL GET USED TO IT, I'M SURE.
BLAARGH!
BLAMM BLAMM BLAMM

CHAPTER
FOUR

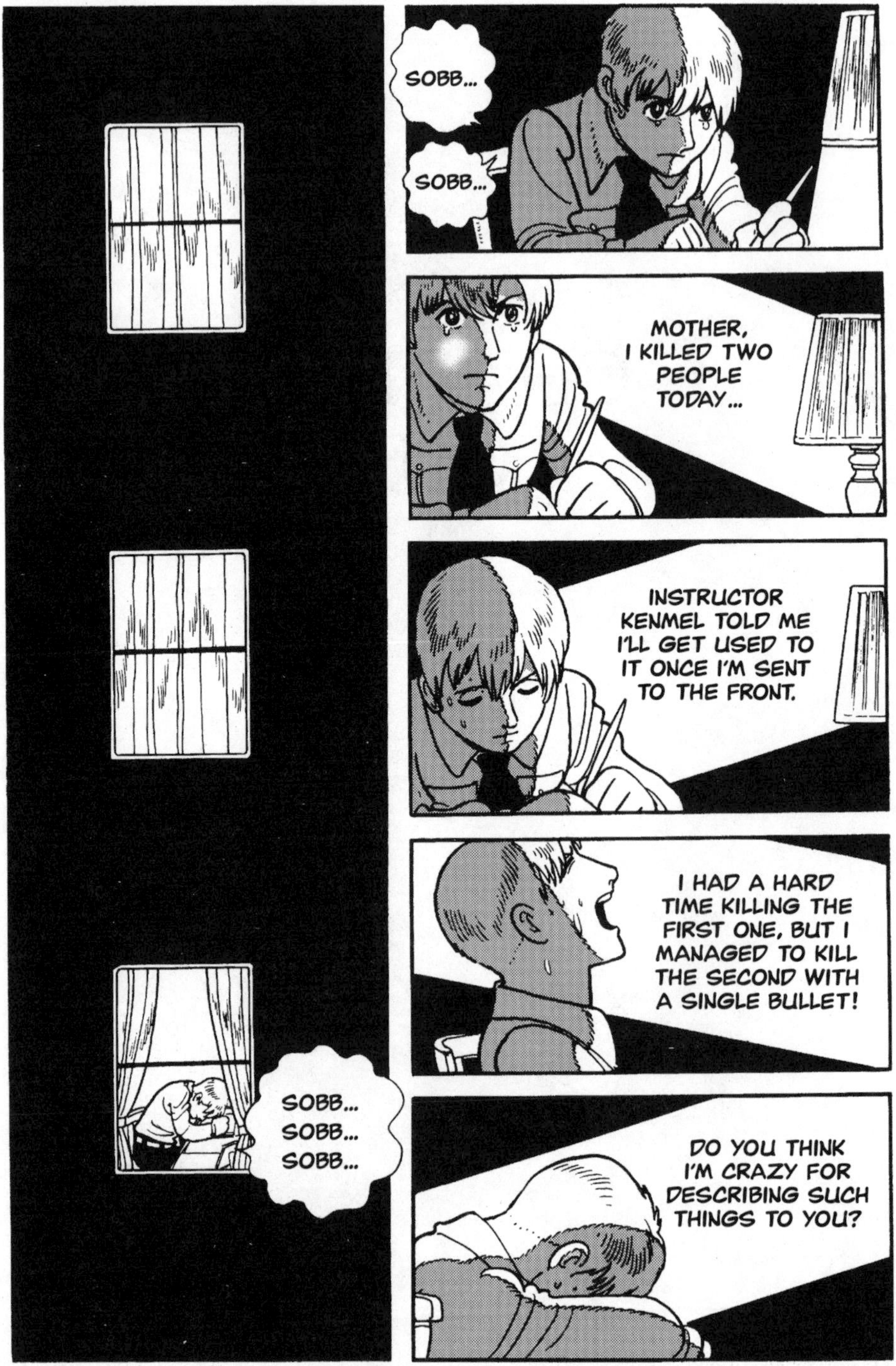
SOBB... SOBB... SOBB...
SOBB...
SOBB...
MOTHER, I KILLED TWO PEOPLE TODAY...
INSTRUCTOR KENMEL TOLD ME I'LL GET USED TO IT ONCE I'M SENT TO THE FRONT.
I HAD A HARD TIME KILLING THE FIRST ONE, BUT I MANAGED TO KILL THE SECOND WITH A SINGLE BULLET!
DO YOU THINK I'M CRAZY FOR DESCRIBING SUCH THINGS TO YOU?

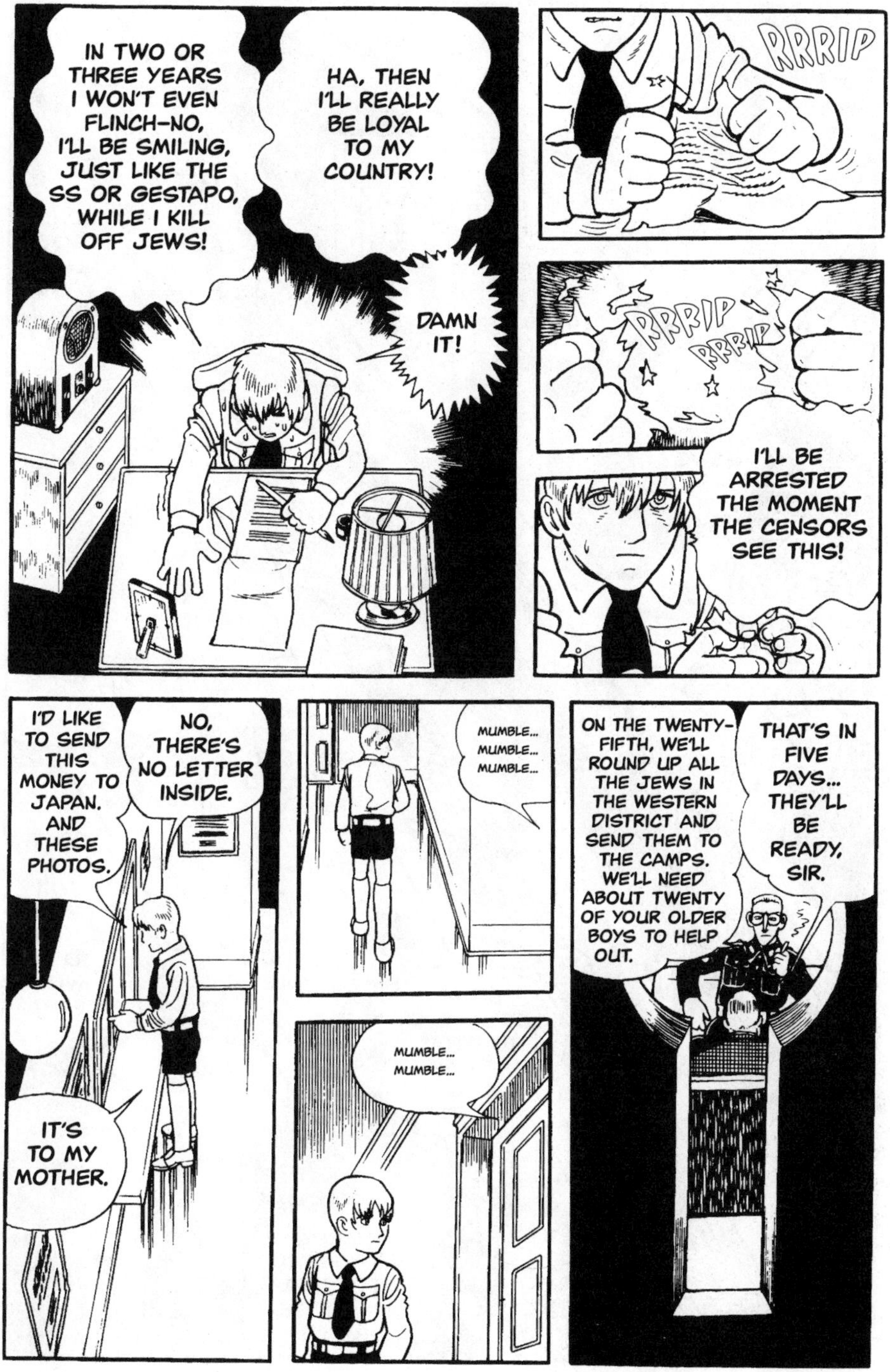
IN TWO OR THREE YEARS I WON'T EVEN FLINCH–NO, I'LL BE SMILING, JUST LIKE THE SS OR GESTAPO, WHILE I KILL OFF JEWS!
HA, THEN I'LL REALLY BE LOYAL TO MY COUNTRY!
DAMN IT!
RRRIP
RRRIP
RRRIP
I'LL BE ARRESTED THE MOMENT THE CENSORS SEE THIS!
I'D LIKE TO SEND THIS MONEY TO JAPAN. AND THESE PHOTOS.
NO, THERE'S NO LETTER INSIDE.
IT'S TO MY MOTHER.
MUMBLE... MUMBLE... MUMBLE...
MUMBLE... MUMBLE...
ON THE TWENTY-FIFTH, WE'LL ROUND UP ALL THE JEWS IN THE WESTERN DISTRICT AND SEND THEM TO THE CAMPS. WE'LL NEED ABOUT TWENTY OF YOUR OLDER BOYS TO HELP OUT.
THAT'S IN FIVE DAYS... THEY'LL BE READY, SIR.

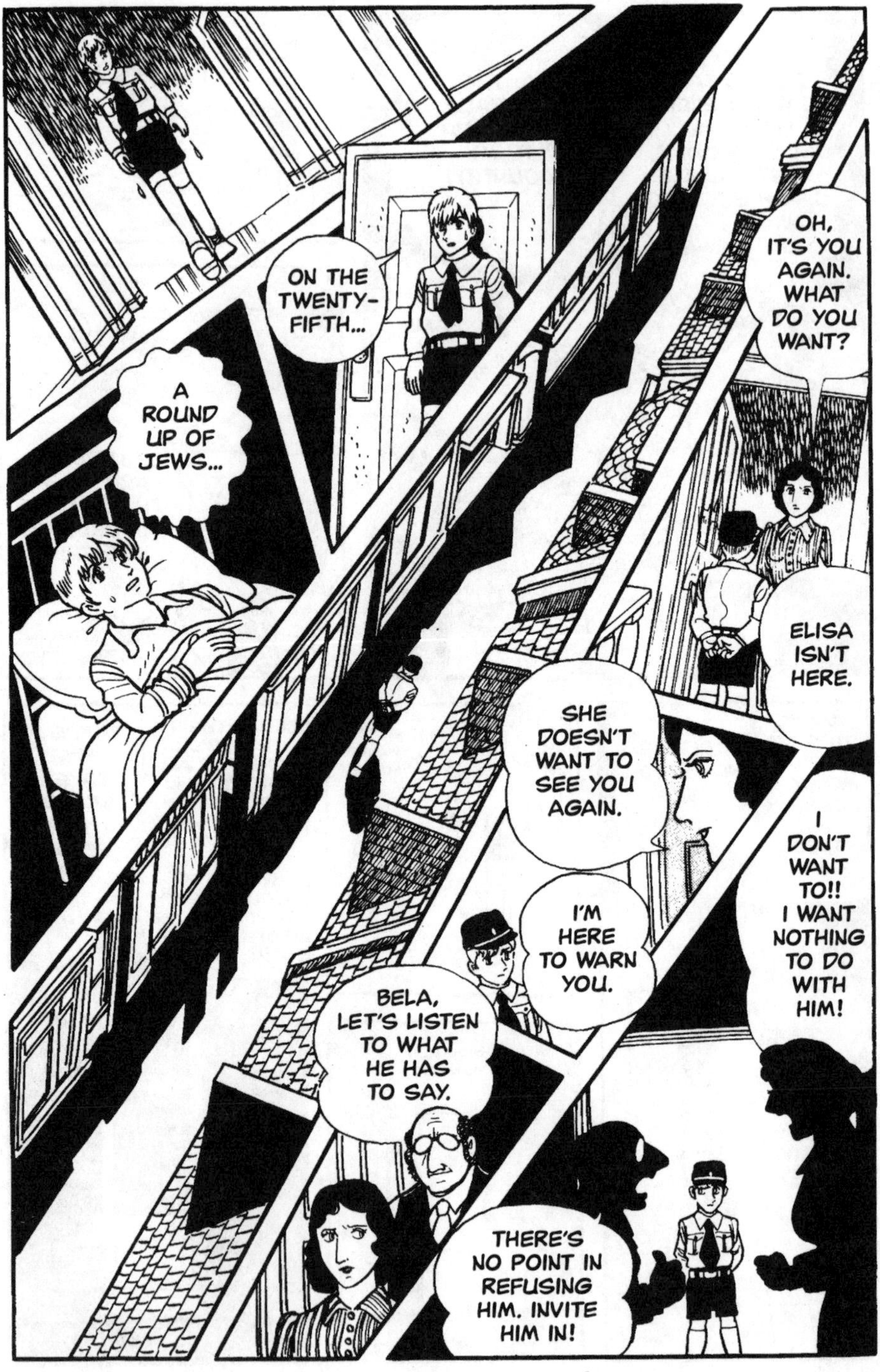
ON THE TWENTY-FIFTH...
A ROUND UP OF JEWS...
OH, IT'S YOU AGAIN. WHAT DO YOU WANT?
ELISA ISN'T HERE.
SHE DOESN'T WANT TO SEE YOU AGAIN.
I'M HERE TO WARN YOU.
I DON'T WANT TO!! I WANT NOTHING TO DO WITH HIM!
BELA, LET'S LISTEN TO WHAT HE HAS TO SAY.
THERE'S NO POINT IN REFUSING HIM. INVITE HIM IN!

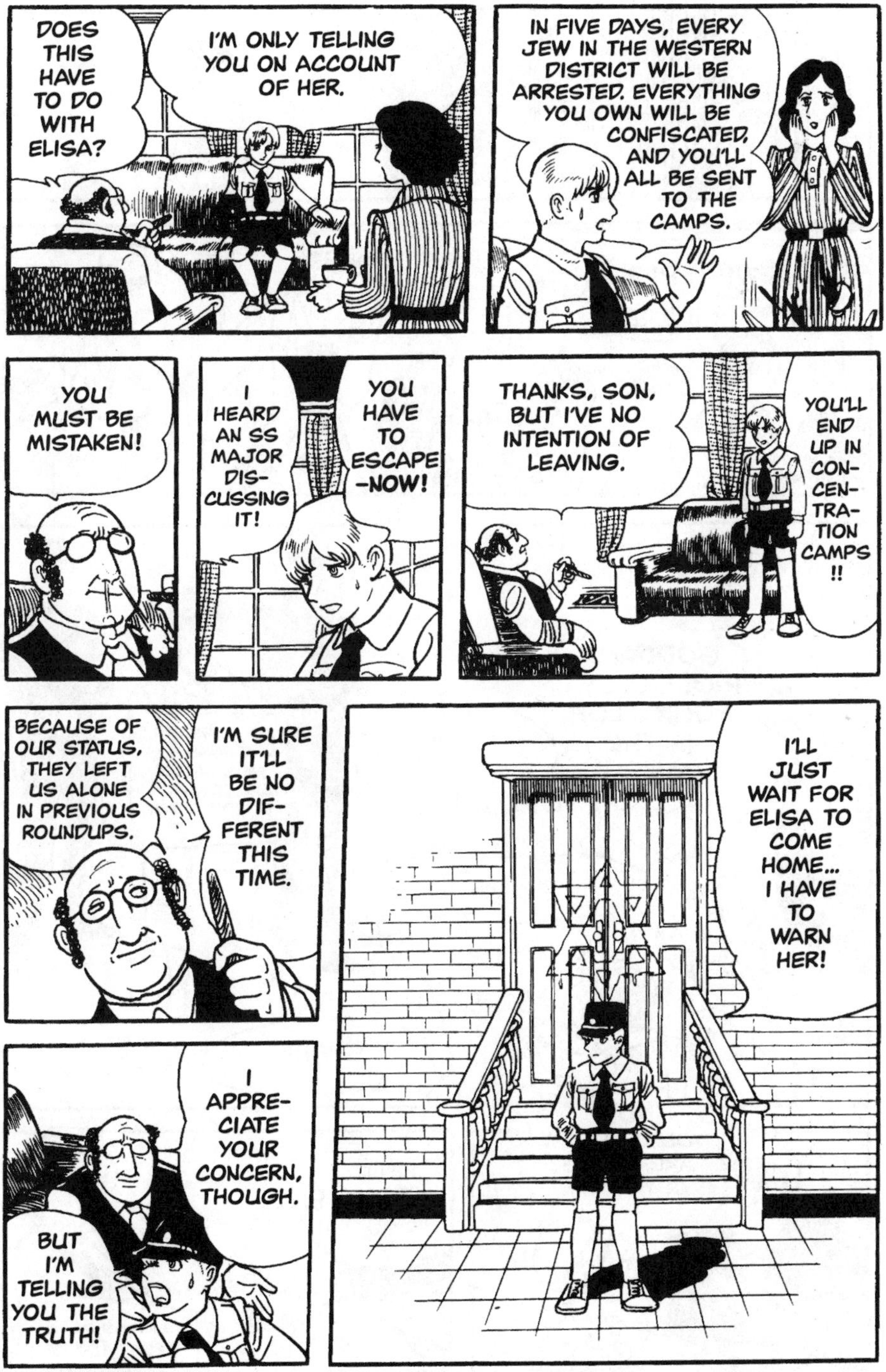
DOES THIS HAVE TO DO WITH ELISA?
I'M ONLY TELLING YOU ON ACCOUNT OF HER.
IN FIVE DAYS, EVERY JEW IN THE WESTERN DISTRICT WILL BE ARRESTED. EVERYTHING YOU OWN WILL BE CONFISCATED, AND YOU'LL ALL BE SENT TO THE CAMPS.
YOU MUST BE MISTAKEN!
I HEARD AN SS MAJOR DISCUSSING IT!
YOU HAVE TO ESCAPE —NOW!
THANKS, SON, BUT I'VE NO INTENTION OF LEAVING.
YOU'LL END UP IN CONCENTRATION CAMPS !!
BECAUSE OF OUR STATUS, THEY LEFT US ALONE IN PREVIOUS ROUNDUPS.
I'M SURE IT'LL BE NO DIFFERENT THIS TIME.
I APPRECIATE YOUR CONCERN, THOUGH.
BUT I'M TELLING YOU THE TRUTH!
I'LL JUST WAIT FOR ELISA TO COME HOME... I HAVE TO WARN HER!

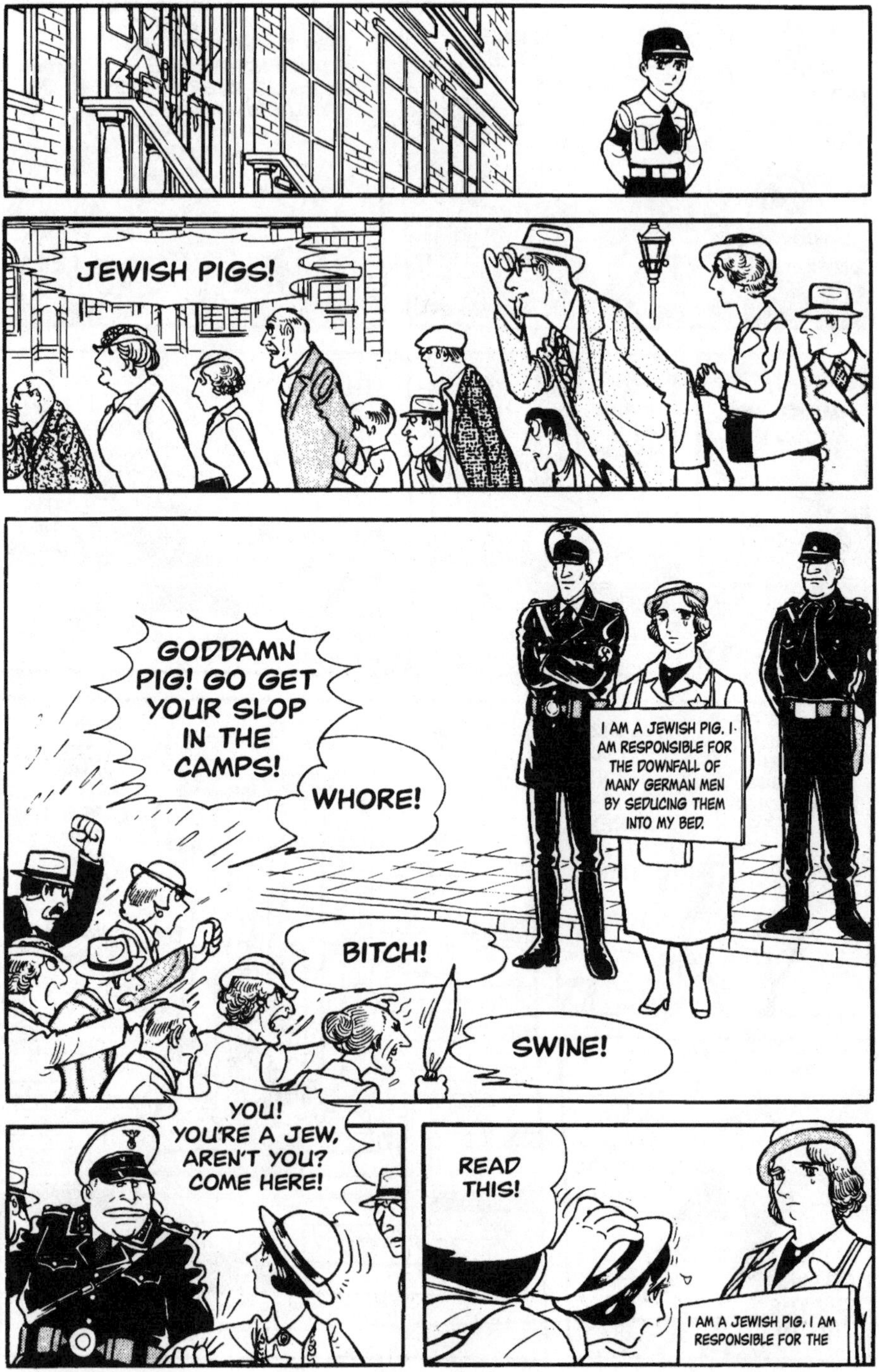
JEWISH PIGS!
GODDAMN PIG! GO GET YOUR SLOP IN THE CAMPS!
WHORE!
I AM A JEWISH PIG. I AM RESPONSIBLE FOR THE DOWNFALL OF MANY GERMAN MEN BY SEDUCING THEM INTO MY BED.
BITCH!
SWINE!
YOU! YOU'RE A JEW, AREN'T YOU? COME HERE!
READ THIS!
I AM A JEWISH PIG. I AM RESPONSIBLE FOR THE

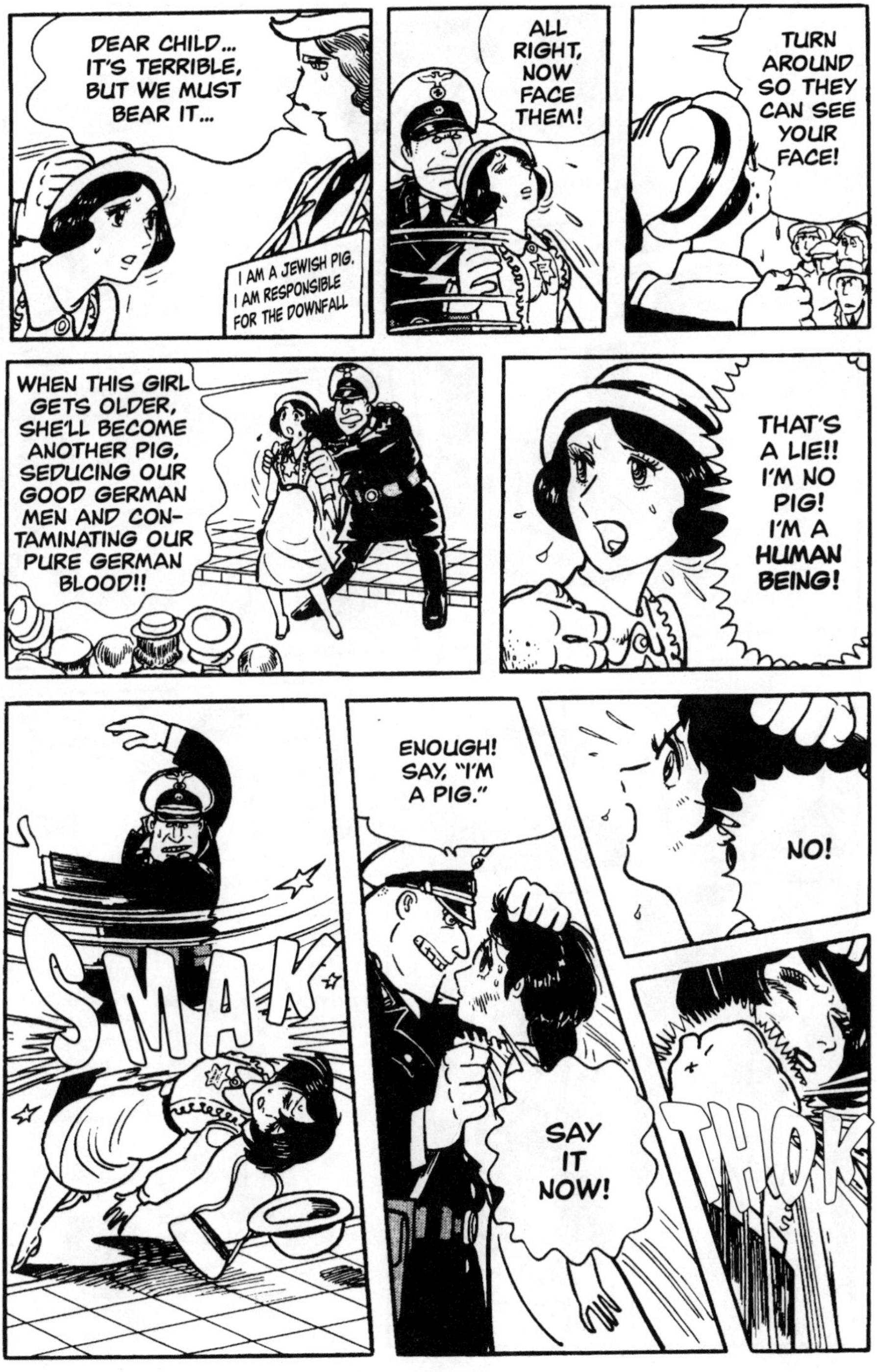
DEAR CHILD... IT'S TERRIBLE, BUT WE MUST BEAR IT...
I AM A JEWISH PIG. I AM RESPONSIBLE FOR THE DOWNFALL
ALL RIGHT, NOW FACE THEM!
TURN AROUND SO THEY CAN SEE YOUR FACE!
WHEN THIS GIRL GETS OLDER, SHE'LL BECOME ANOTHER PIG, SEDUCING OUR GOOD GERMAN MEN AND CON-TAMINATING OUR PURE GERMAN BLOOD!!
THAT'S A LIE!! I'M NO PIG! I'M A HUMAN BEING!
SMAK
ENOUGH! SAY, "I'M A PIG."
SAY IT NOW!
NO!
THOK

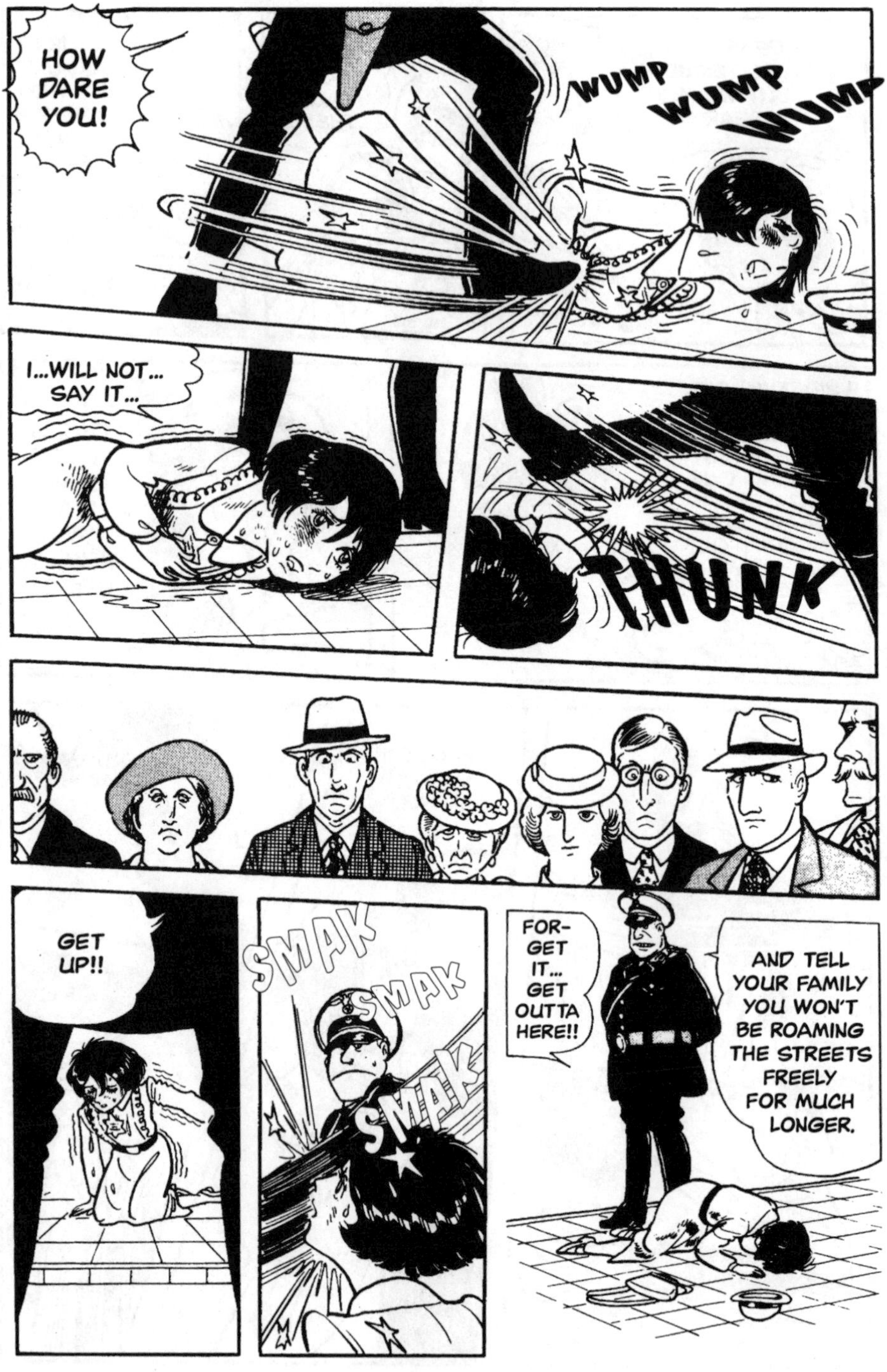
HOW DARE YOU!
WUMP
WUMP
WUMP
I...WILL NOT... SAY IT...
THUNK
GET UP!!
SMAK
SMAK
SMAK
FOR-GET IT... GET OUTTA HERE!!
AND TELL YOUR FAMILY YOU WON'T BE ROAMING THE STREETS FREELY FOR MUCH LONGER.

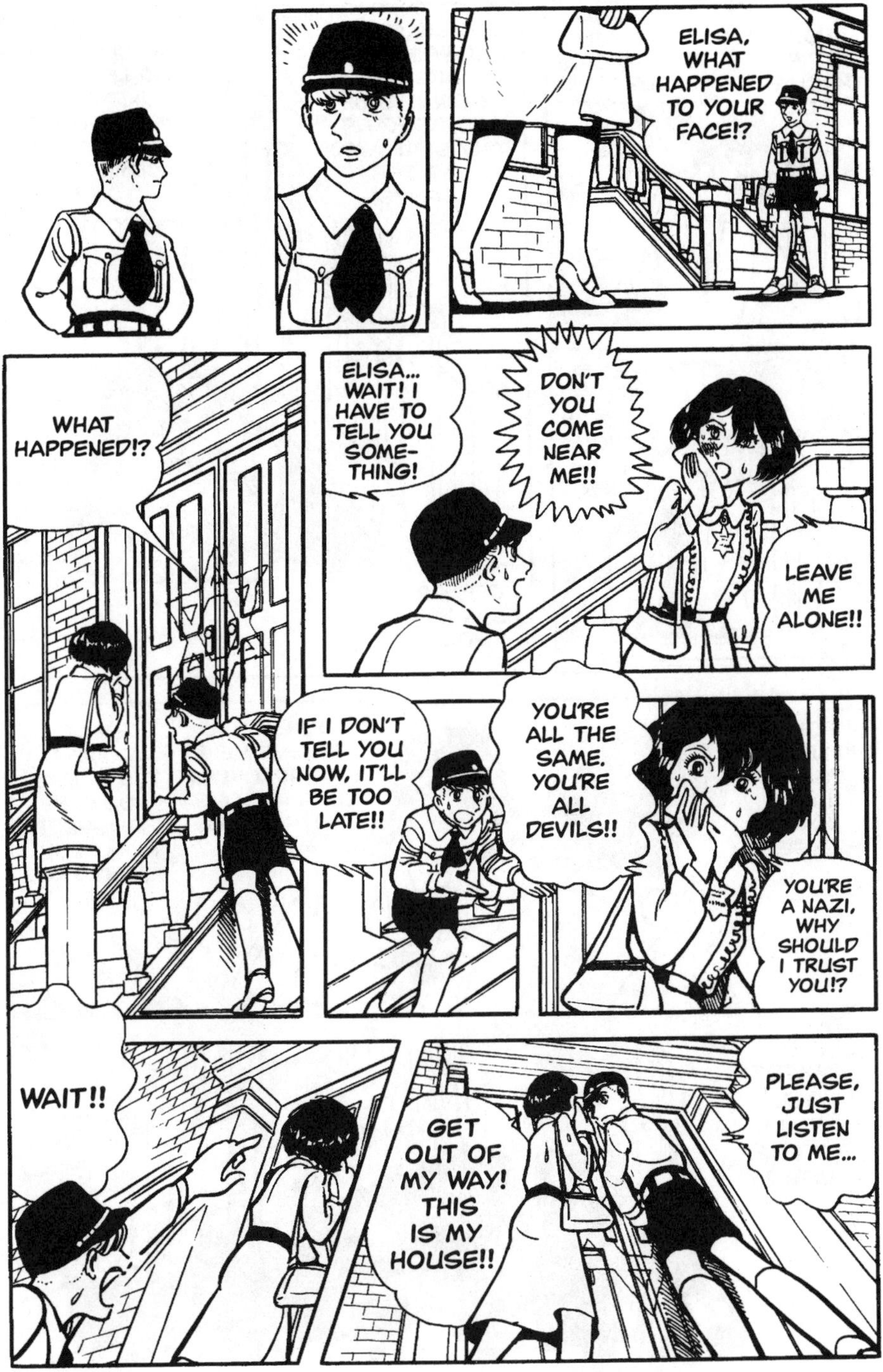
ELISA, WHAT HAPPENED TO YOUR FACE!?
WHAT HAPPENED!?
ELISA... WAIT! I HAVE TO TELL YOU SOME-THING!
DON'T YOU COME NEAR ME!!
LEAVE ME ALONE!!
IF I DON'T TELL YOU NOW, IT'LL BE TOO LATE!!
YOU'RE ALL THE SAME. YOU'RE ALL DEVILS!!
YOU'RE A NAZI, WHY SHOULD I TRUST YOU!?
WAIT!!
GET OUT OF MY WAY! THIS IS MY HOUSE!!
PLEASE, JUST LISTEN TO ME...

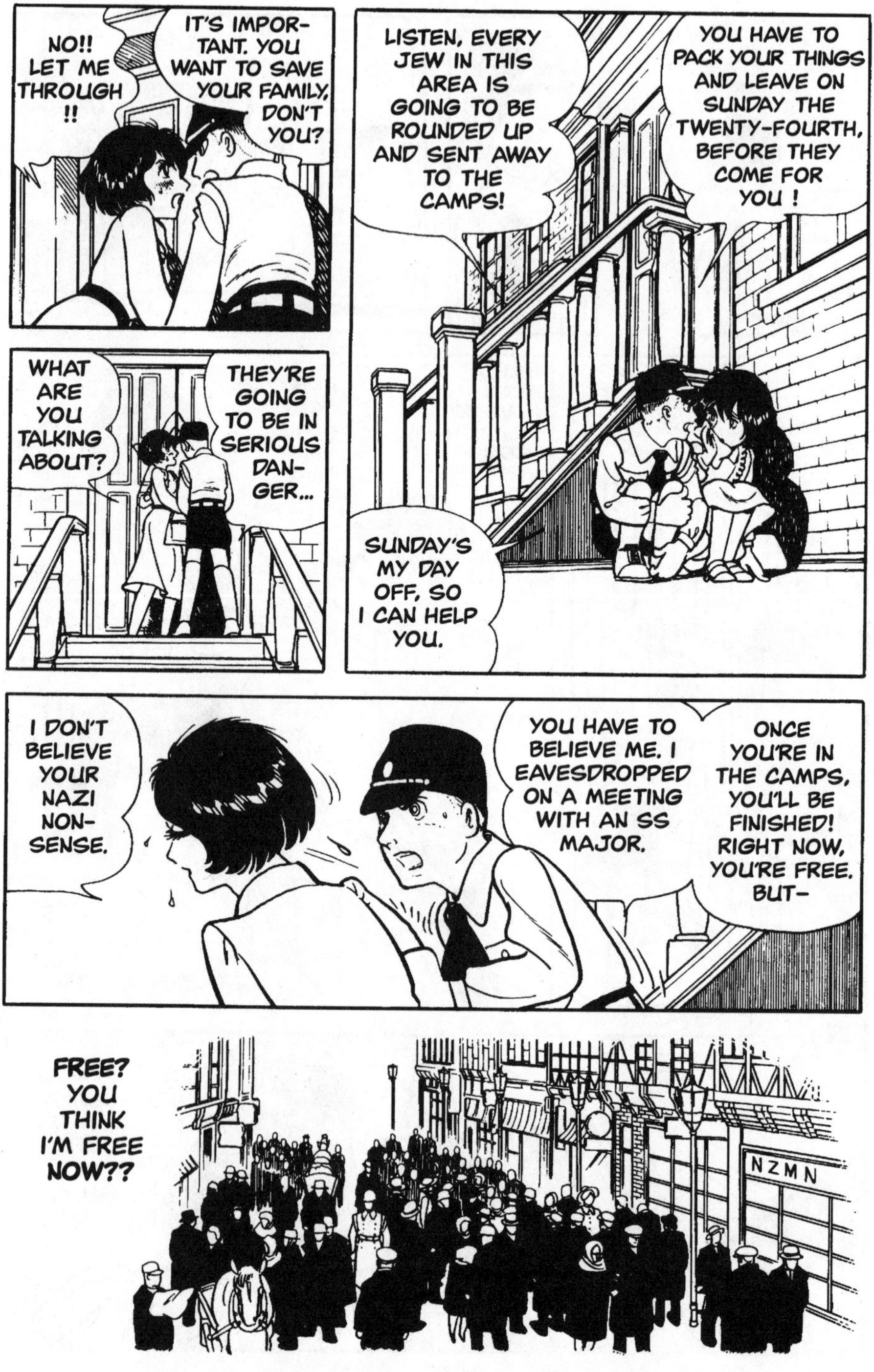
NO!! LET ME THROUGH !!
IT'S IMPORTANT. YOU WANT TO SAVE YOUR FAMILY, DON'T YOU?
WHAT ARE YOU TALKING ABOUT?
THEY'RE GOING TO BE IN SERIOUS DANGER...
LISTEN, EVERY JEW IN THIS AREA IS GOING TO BE ROUNDED UP AND SENT AWAY TO THE CAMPS!
YOU HAVE TO PACK YOUR THINGS AND LEAVE ON SUNDAY THE TWENTY-FOURTH, BEFORE THEY COME FOR YOU !
SUNDAY'S MY DAY OFF, SO I CAN HELP YOU.
I DON'T BELIEVE YOUR NAZI NONSENSE.
YOU HAVE TO BELIEVE ME. I EAVESDROPPED ON A MEETING WITH AN SS MAJOR.
ONCE YOU'RE IN THE CAMPS, YOU'LL BE FINISHED! RIGHT NOW, YOU'RE FREE. BUT–
FREE? YOU THINK I'M FREE NOW??
NZMN

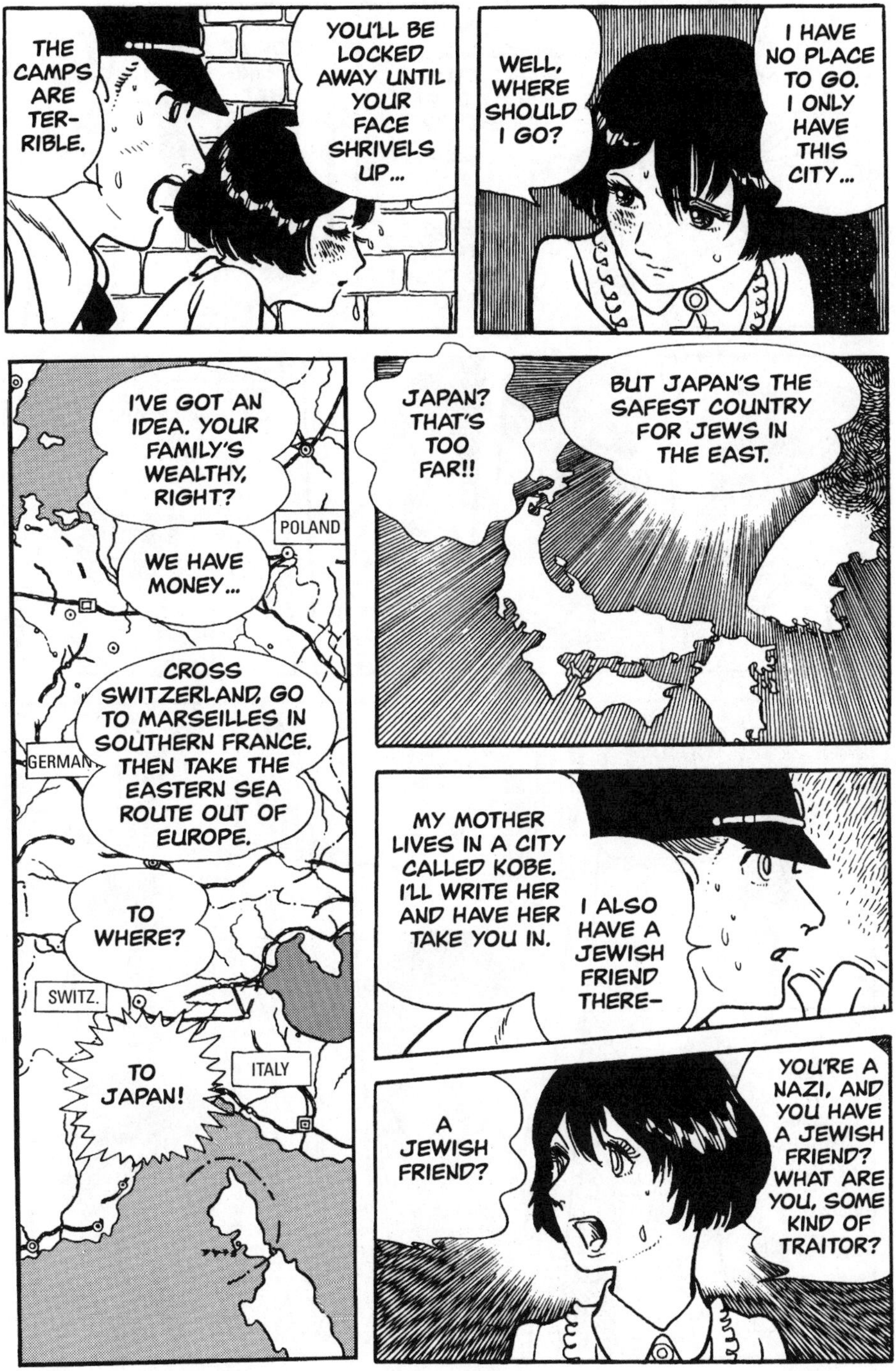
THE CAMPS ARE TERRIBLE.
YOU'LL BE LOCKED AWAY UNTIL YOUR FACE SHRIVELS UP...
WELL, WHERE SHOULD I GO?
I HAVE NO PLACE TO GO. I ONLY HAVE THIS CITY...
I'VE GOT AN IDEA. YOUR FAMILY'S WEALTHY, RIGHT?
POLAND
WE HAVE MONEY...
CROSS SWITZERLAND, GO TO MARSEILLES IN SOUTHERN FRANCE. THEN TAKE THE EASTERN SEA ROUTE OUT OF EUROPE.
GERMAN
TO WHERE?
SWITZ.
TO JAPAN!
ITALY
JAPAN? THAT'S TOO FAR!!
BUT JAPAN'S THE SAFEST COUNTRY FOR JEWS IN THE EAST.
MY MOTHER LIVES IN A CITY CALLED KOBE. I'LL WRITE HER AND HAVE HER TAKE YOU IN.
I ALSO HAVE A JEWISH FRIEND THERE–
A JEWISH FRIEND?
YOU'RE A NAZI, AND YOU HAVE A JEWISH FRIEND? WHAT ARE YOU, SOME KIND OF TRAITOR?

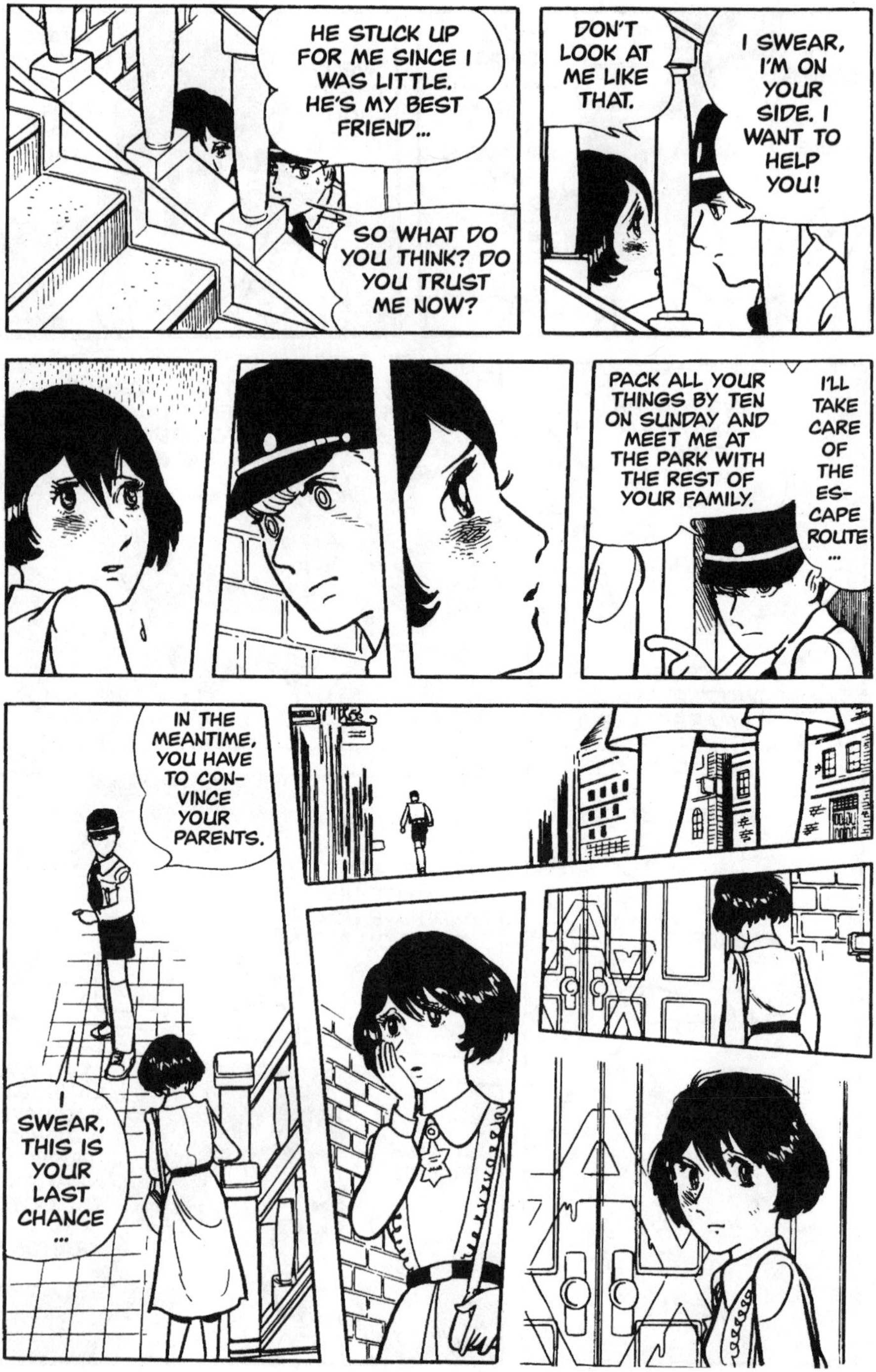
HE STUCK UP FOR ME SINCE I WAS LITTLE. HE'S MY BEST FRIEND...
SO WHAT DO YOU THINK? DO YOU TRUST ME NOW?
DON'T LOOK AT ME LIKE THAT.
I SWEAR, I'M ON YOUR SIDE. I WANT TO HELP YOU!
PACK ALL YOUR THINGS BY TEN ON SUNDAY AND MEET ME AT THE PARK WITH THE REST OF YOUR FAMILY.
I'LL TAKE CARE OF THE ES-CAPE ROUTE...
IN THE MEANTIME, YOU HAVE TO CON-VINCE YOUR PARENTS.
I SWEAR, THIS IS YOUR LAST CHANCE...

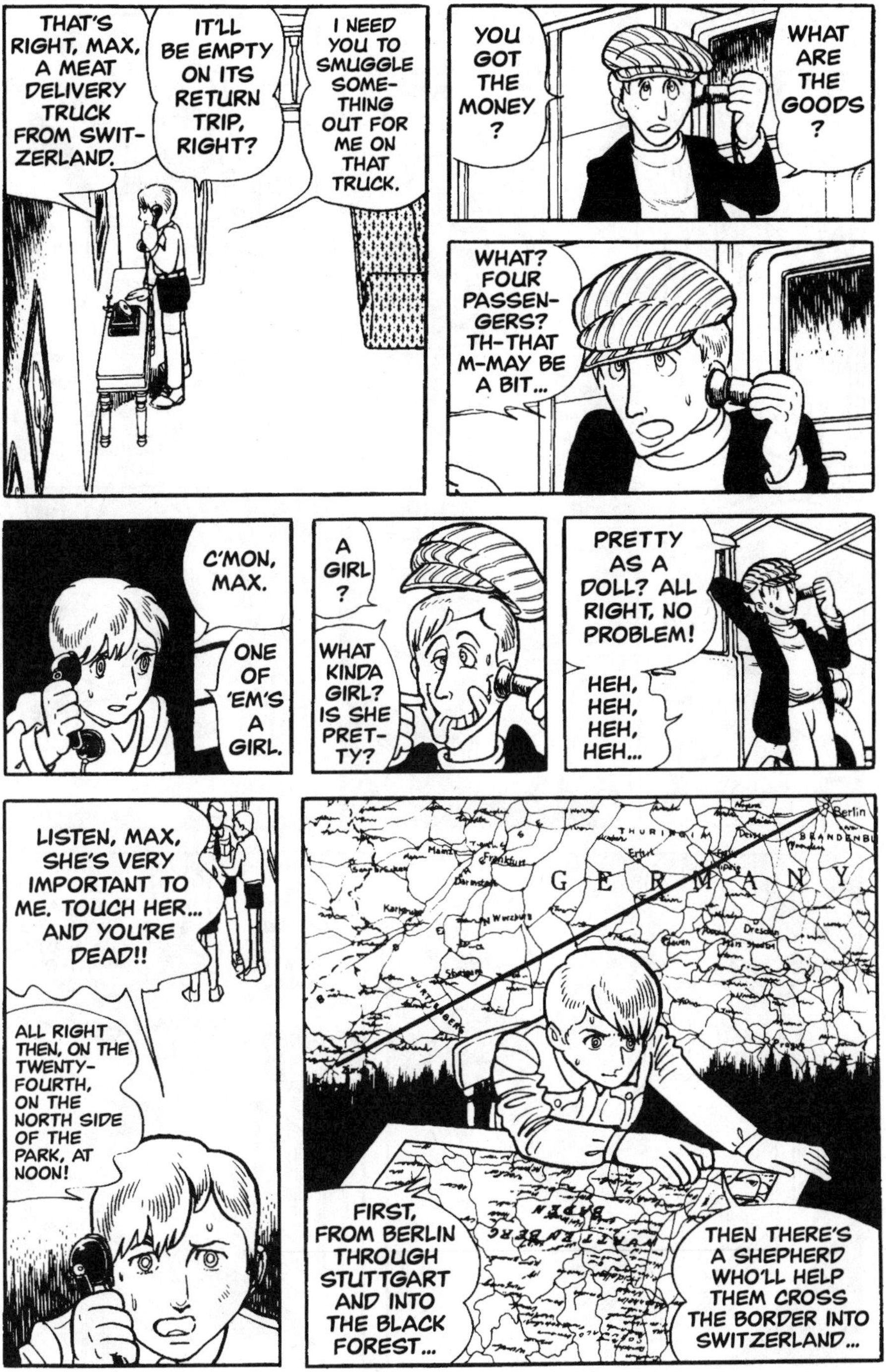
THAT'S RIGHT, MAX, A MEAT DELIVERY TRUCK FROM SWITZERLAND.
IT'LL BE EMPTY ON ITS RETURN TRIP, RIGHT?
I NEED YOU TO SMUGGLE SOMETHING OUT FOR ME ON THAT TRUCK.
YOU GOT THE MONEY?
WHAT ARE THE GOODS?
WHAT? FOUR PASSENGERS? TH-THAT M-MAY BE A BIT...
C'MON, MAX.
ONE OF 'EM'S A GIRL.
A GIRL?
WHAT KINDA GIRL? IS SHE PRETTY?
PRETTY AS A DOLL? ALL RIGHT, NO PROBLEM!
HEH, HEH, HEH, HEH...
LISTEN, MAX, SHE'S VERY IMPORTANT TO ME. TOUCH HER... AND YOU'RE DEAD!!
ALL RIGHT THEN, ON THE TWENTY-FOURTH, ON THE NORTH SIDE OF THE PARK, AT NOON!
Berlin
Frankfurt
Dresden
G E R M A N Y
FIRST, FROM BERLIN THROUGH STUTTGART AND INTO THE BLACK FOREST...
THEN THERE'S A SHEPHERD WHO'LL HELP THEM CROSS THE BORDER INTO SWITZERLAND...

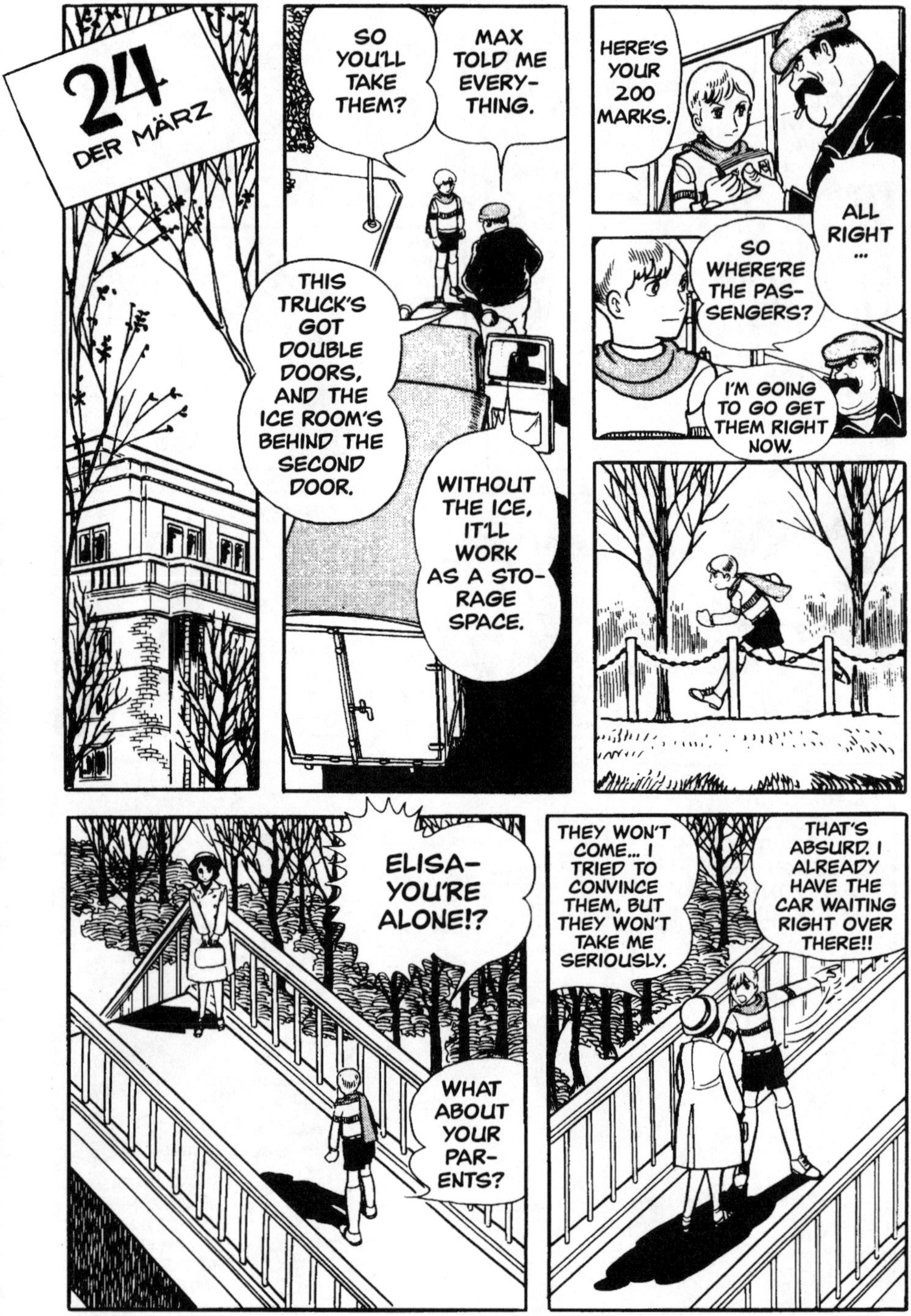
24
DER MÄRZ
SO YOU'LL TAKE THEM?
MAX TOLD ME EVERY-THING.
THIS TRUCK'S GOT DOUBLE DOORS, AND THE ICE ROOM'S BEHIND THE SECOND DOOR.
WITHOUT THE ICE, IT'LL WORK AS A STO-RAGE SPACE.
HERE'S YOUR 200 MARKS.
ALL RIGHT ...
SO WHERE'RE THE PAS-SENGERS?
I'M GOING TO GO GET THEM RIGHT NOW.
ELISA-YOU'RE ALONE!?
WHAT ABOUT YOUR PAR-ENTS?
THEY WON'T COME... I TRIED TO CONVINCE THEM, BUT THEY WON'T TAKE ME SERIOUSLY.
THAT'S ABSURD. I ALREADY HAVE THE CAR WAITING RIGHT OVER THERE!!

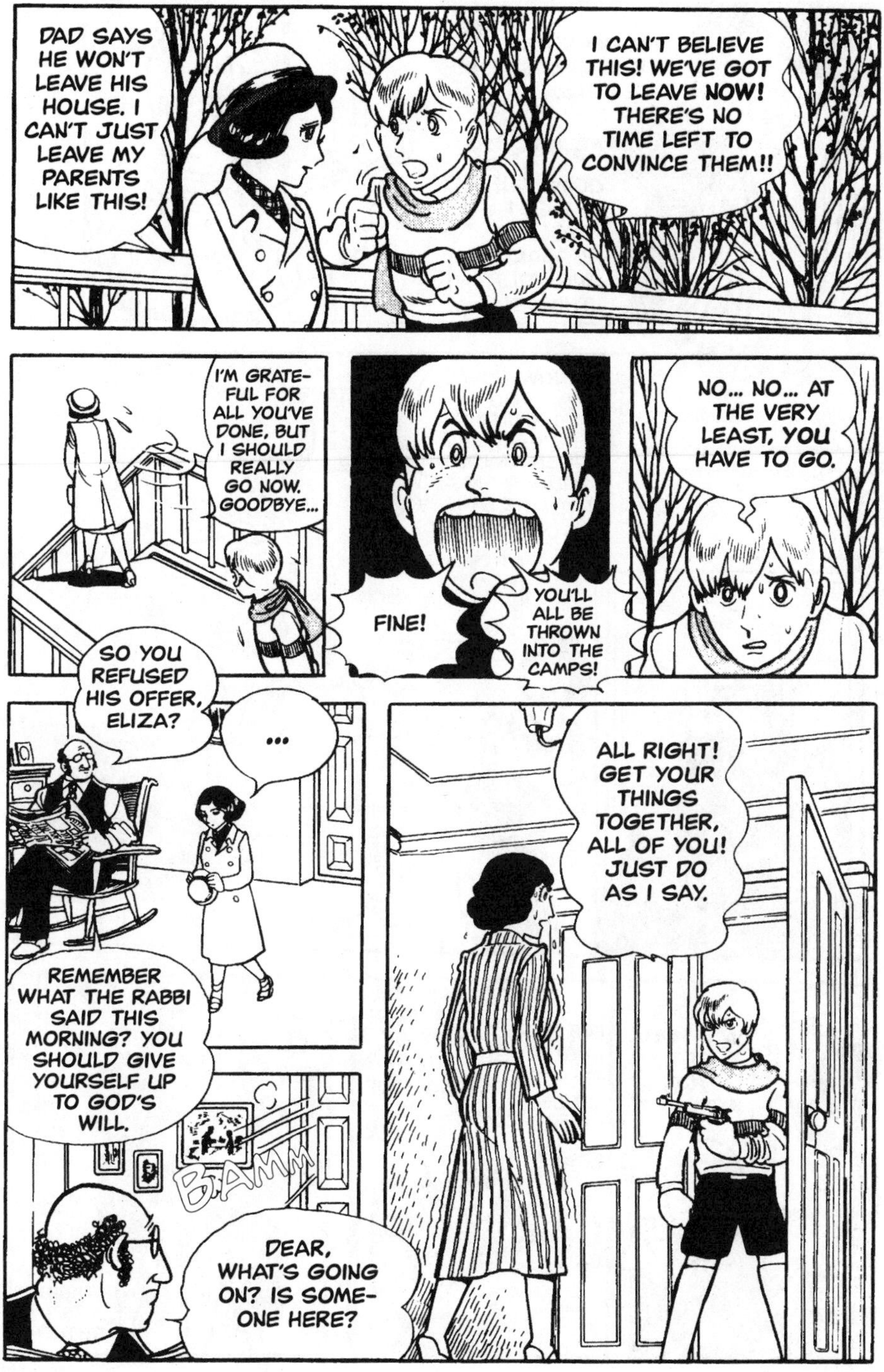
DAD SAYS HE WON'T LEAVE HIS HOUSE. I CAN'T JUST LEAVE MY PARENTS LIKE THIS!
I CAN'T BELIEVE THIS! WE'VE GOT TO LEAVE NOW! THERE'S NO TIME LEFT TO CONVINCE THEM!!
I'M GRATEFUL FOR ALL YOU'VE DONE, BUT I SHOULD REALLY GO NOW. GOODBYE...
FINE!
YOU'LL ALL BE THROWN INTO THE CAMPS!
NO... NO... AT THE VERY LEAST, YOU HAVE TO GO.
SO YOU REFUSED HIS OFFER, ELIZA?
...
REMEMBER WHAT THE RABBI SAID THIS MORNING? YOU SHOULD GIVE YOURSELF UP TO GOD'S WILL.
BAMM
DEAR, WHAT'S GOING ON? IS SOMEONE HERE?
ALL RIGHT! GET YOUR THINGS TOGETHER, ALL OF YOU! JUST DO AS I SAY.

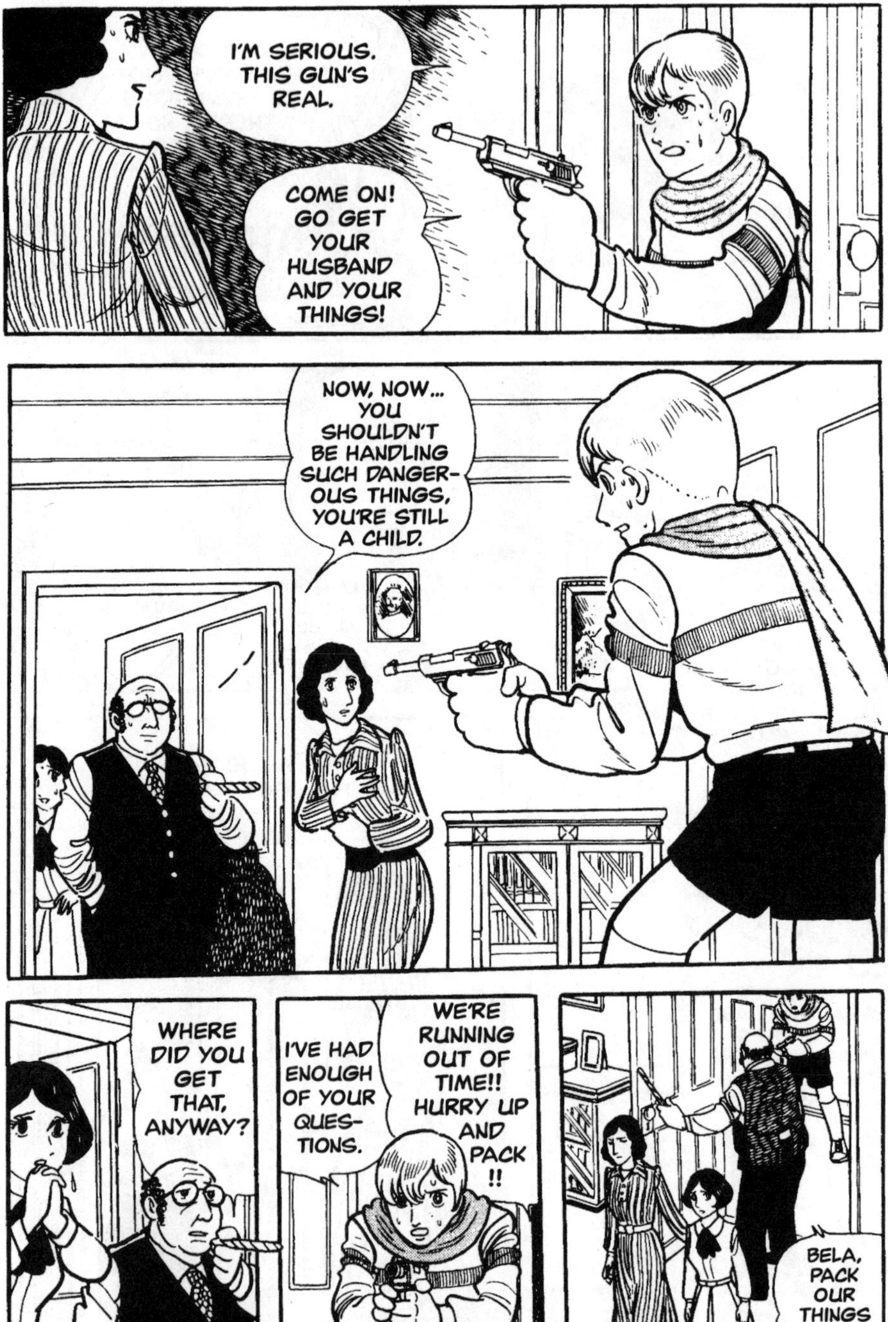
I'M SERIOUS. THIS GUN'S REAL.
COME ON! GO GET YOUR HUSBAND AND YOUR THINGS!
NOW, NOW... YOU SHOULDN'T BE HANDLING SUCH DANGER-OUS THINGS, YOU'RE STILL A CHILD.
WHERE DID YOU GET THAT, ANYWAY?
I'VE HAD ENOUGH OF YOUR QUES-TIONS.
WE'RE RUNNING OUT OF TIME!! HURRY UP AND PACK !!
BELA, PACK OUR THINGS TO-GETHER...

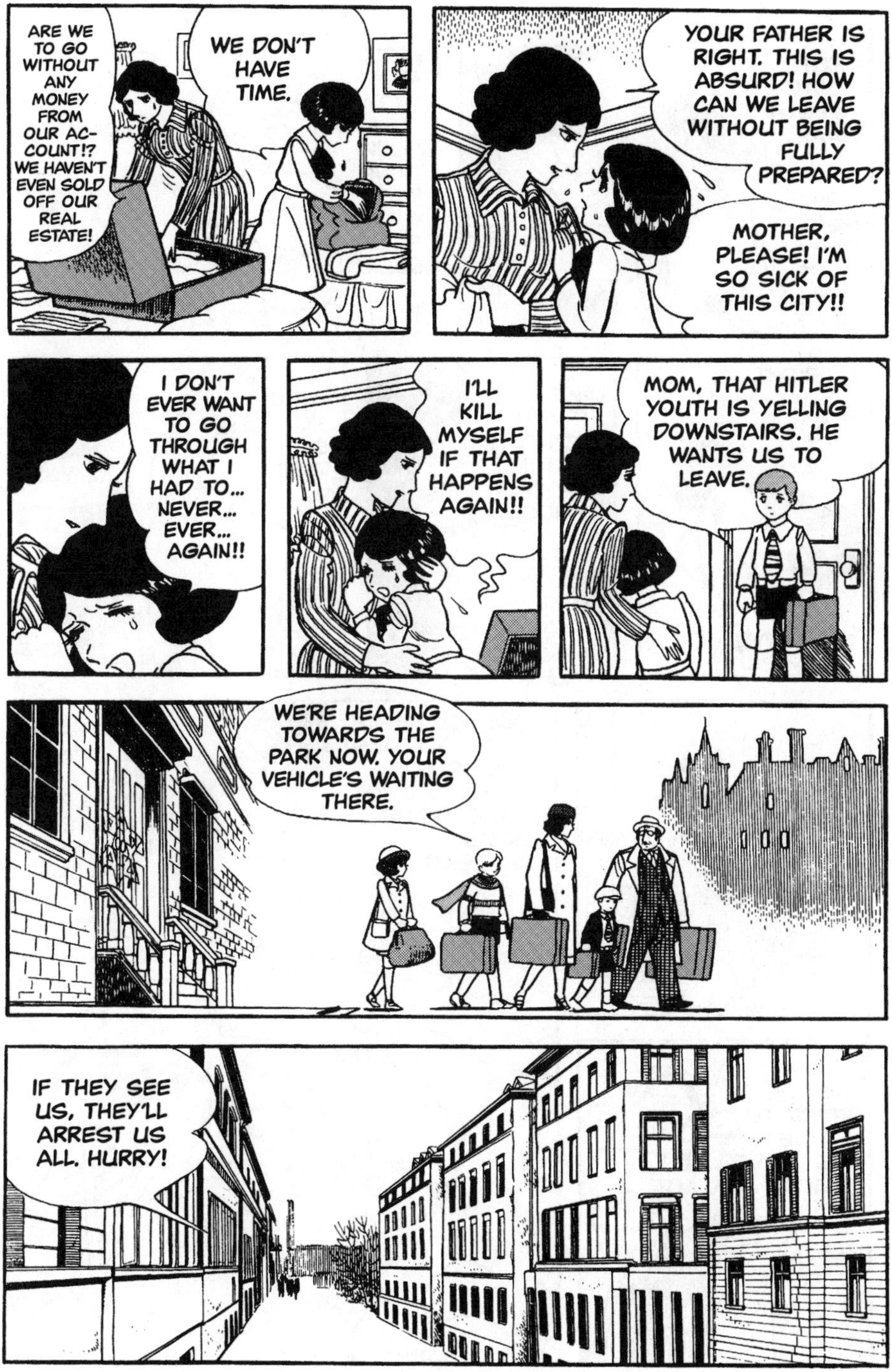
ARE WE TO GO WITHOUT ANY MONEY FROM OUR AC-COUNT!? WE HAVEN'T EVEN SOLD OFF OUR REAL ESTATE!
WE DON'T HAVE TIME.
YOUR FATHER IS RIGHT. THIS IS ABSURD! HOW CAN WE LEAVE WITHOUT BEING FULLY PREPARED?
MOTHER, PLEASE! I'M SO SICK OF THIS CITY!!
I DON'T EVER WANT TO GO THROUGH WHAT I HAD TO... NEVER... EVER... AGAIN!!
I'LL KILL MYSELF IF THAT HAPPENS AGAIN!!
MOM, THAT HITLER YOUTH IS YELLING DOWNSTAIRS. HE WANTS US TO LEAVE.
WE'RE HEADING TOWARDS THE PARK NOW. YOUR VEHICLE'S WAITING THERE.
IF THEY SEE US, THEY'LL ARREST US ALL. HURRY!

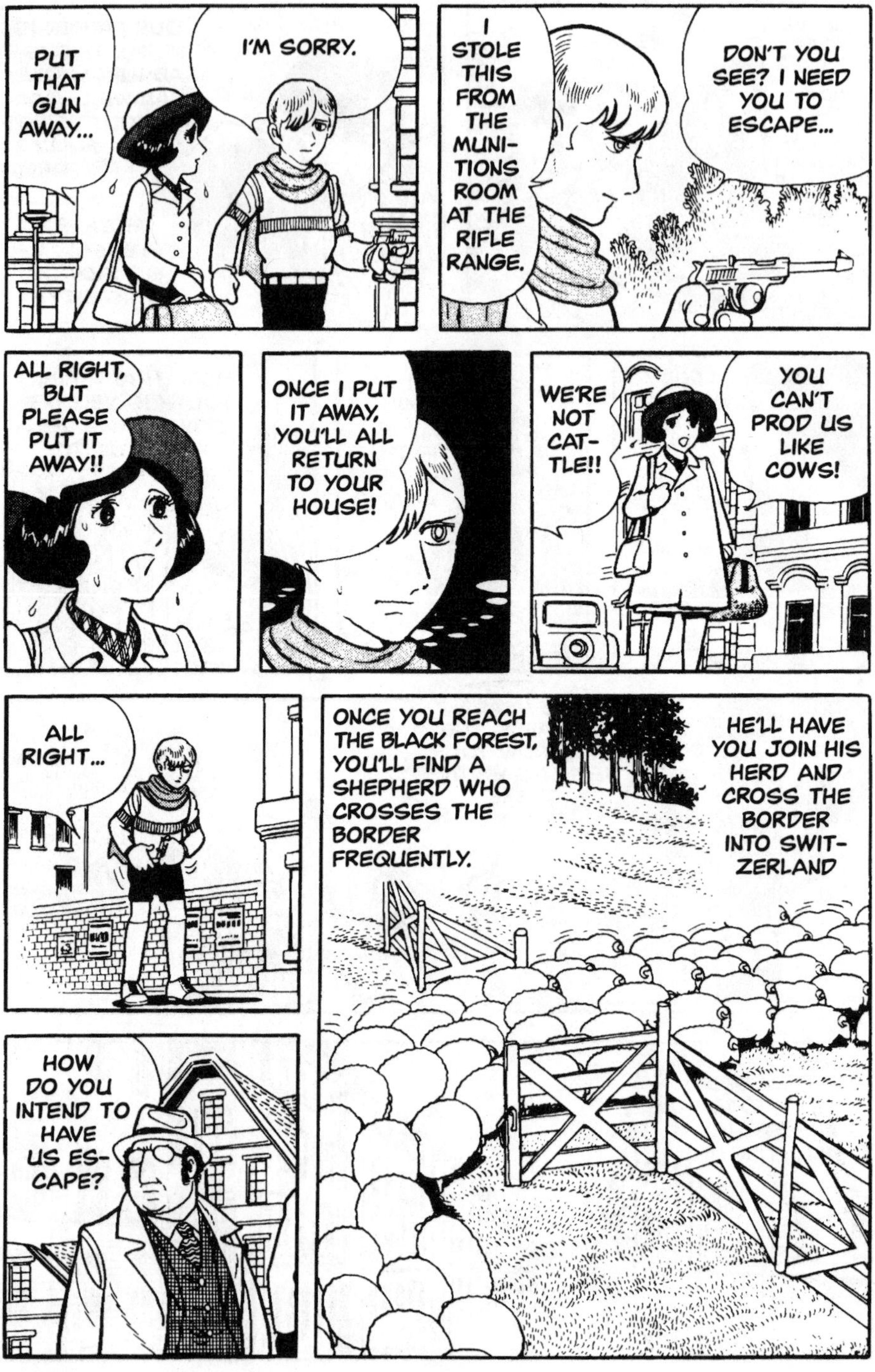
PUT THAT GUN AWAY...
I'M SORRY.
I STOLE THIS FROM THE MUNITIONS ROOM AT THE RIFLE RANGE.
DON'T YOU SEE? I NEED YOU TO ESCAPE...
ALL RIGHT, BUT PLEASE PUT IT AWAY!!
ONCE I PUT IT AWAY, YOU'LL ALL RETURN TO YOUR HOUSE!
WE'RE NOT CATTLE!!
YOU CAN'T PROD US LIKE COWS!
ALL RIGHT...
HOW DO YOU INTEND TO HAVE US ESCAPE?
ONCE YOU REACH THE BLACK FOREST, YOU'LL FIND A SHEPHERD WHO CROSSES THE BORDER FREQUENTLY.
HE'LL HAVE YOU JOIN HIS HERD AND CROSS THE BORDER INTO SWITZERLAND

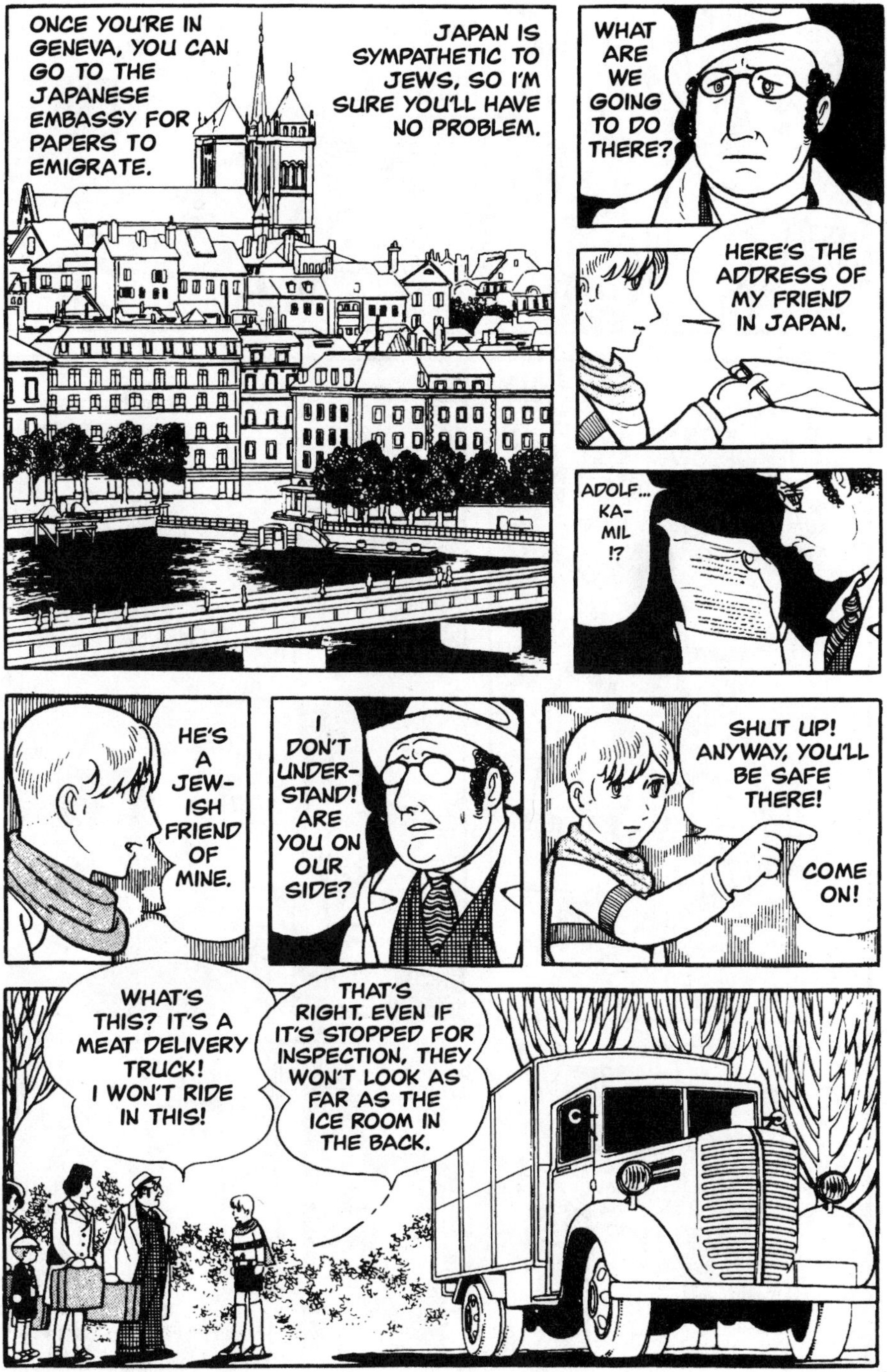
ONCE YOU'RE IN GENEVA, YOU CAN GO TO THE JAPANESE EMBASSY FOR PAPERS TO EMIGRATE.
JAPAN IS SYMPATHETIC TO JEWS, SO I'M SURE YOU'LL HAVE NO PROBLEM.
WHAT ARE WE GOING TO DO THERE?
HERE'S THE ADDRESS OF MY FRIEND IN JAPAN.
ADOLF... KA-MIL !?
HE'S A JEW-ISH FRIEND OF MINE.
I DON'T UNDER-STAND! ARE YOU ON OUR SIDE?
SHUT UP! ANYWAY, YOU'LL BE SAFE THERE!
COME ON!
WHAT'S THIS? IT'S A MEAT DELIVERY TRUCK! I WON'T RIDE IN THIS!
THAT'S RIGHT. EVEN IF IT'S STOPPED FOR INSPECTION, THEY WON'T LOOK AS FAR AS THE ICE ROOM IN THE BACK.

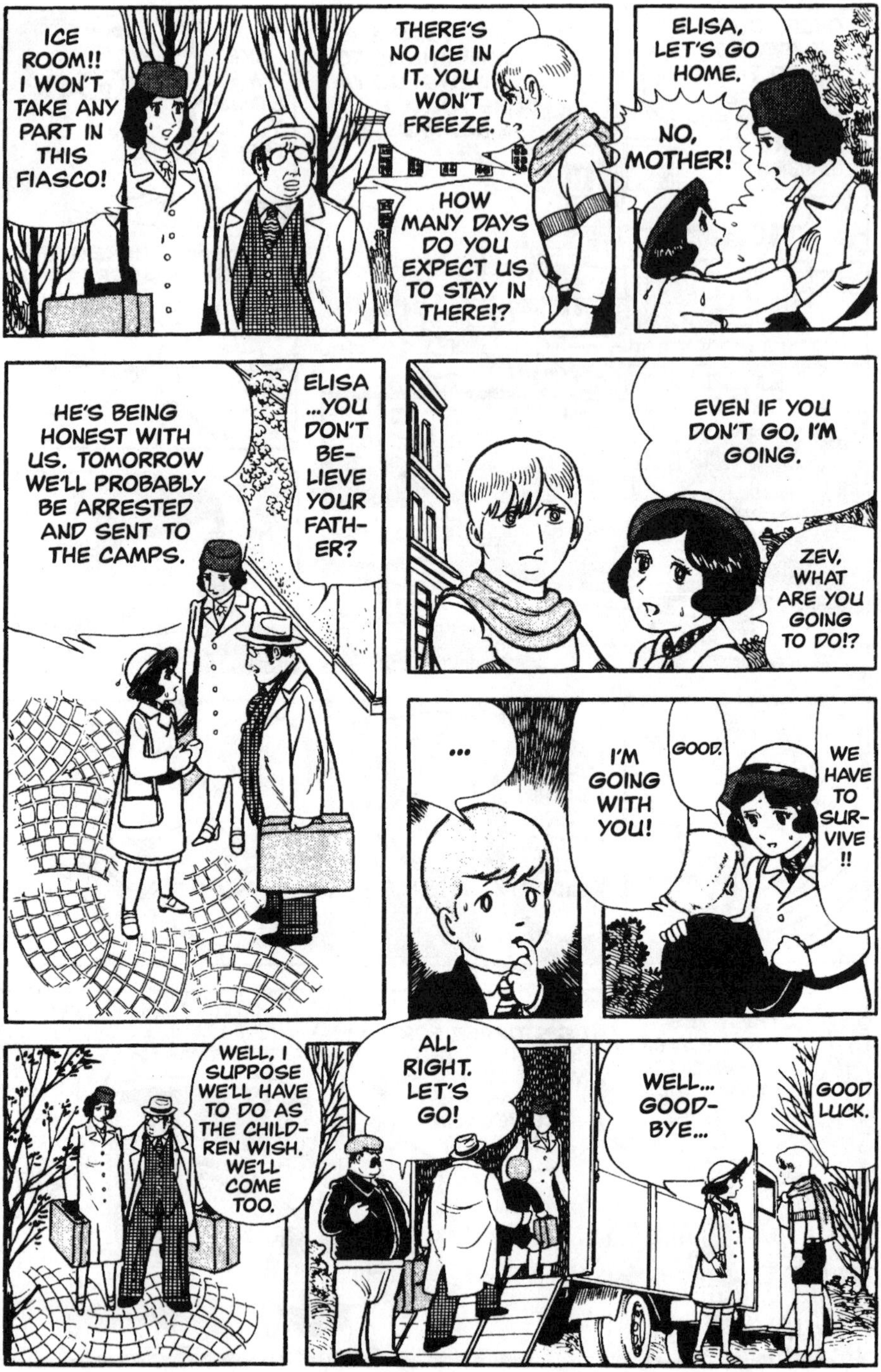
ICE ROOM!! I WON'T TAKE ANY PART IN THIS FIASCO!
THERE'S NO ICE IN IT. YOU WON'T FREEZE.
HOW MANY DAYS DO YOU EXPECT US TO STAY IN THERE!?
ELISA, LET'S GO HOME.
NO, MOTHER!
HE'S BEING HONEST WITH US. TOMORROW WE'LL PROBABLY BE ARRESTED AND SENT TO THE CAMPS.
ELISA ...YOU DON'T BELIEVE YOUR FATHER?
EVEN IF YOU DON'T GO, I'M GOING.
ZEV, WHAT ARE YOU GOING TO DO!?
...
I'M GOING WITH YOU!
GOOD.
WE HAVE TO SURVIVE!!
WELL, I SUPPOSE WE'LL HAVE TO DO AS THE CHILDREN WISH. WE'LL COME TOO.
ALL RIGHT. LET'S GO!
WELL... GOODBYE...
GOOD LUCK.

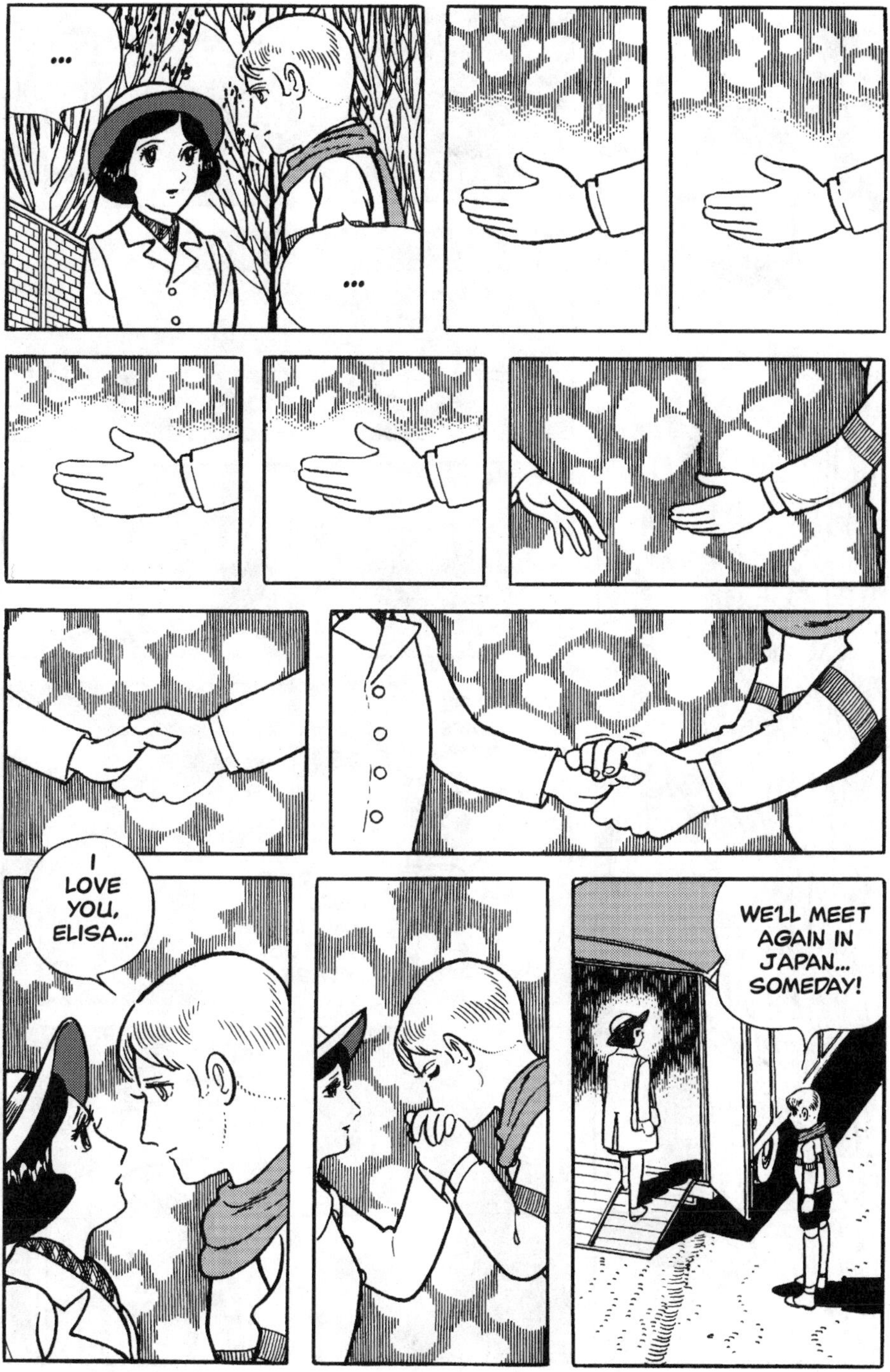
...
...
I LOVE YOU, ELISA...
WE'LL MEET AGAIN IN JAPAN... SOMEDAY!

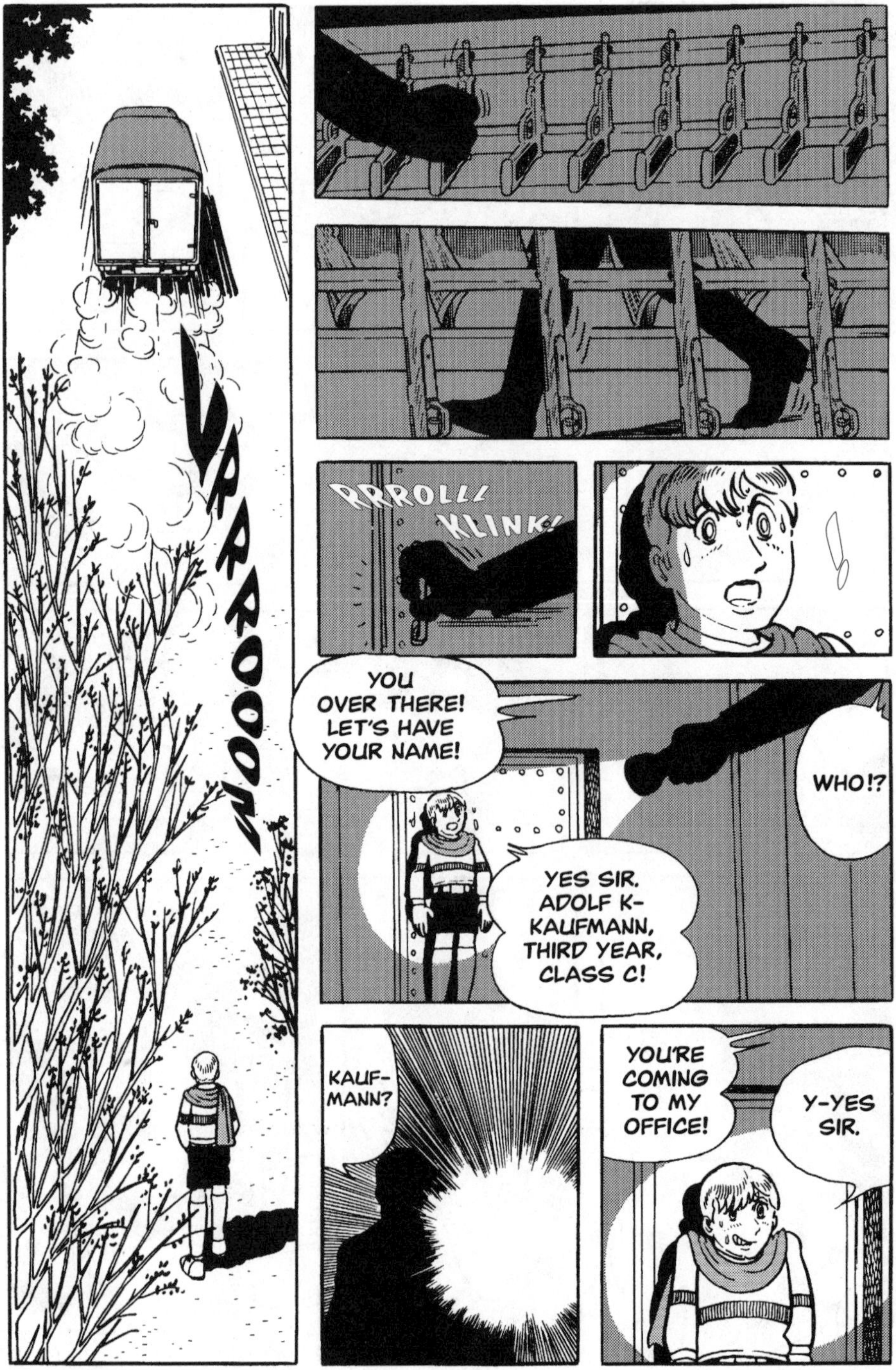
VRRROOOM
RRROLLL
KLINK!
!
YOU OVER THERE! LET'S HAVE YOUR NAME!
WHO!?
YES SIR. ADOLF K-KAUFMANN, THIRD YEAR, CLASS C!
KAUF-MANN?
YOU'RE COMING TO MY OFFICE!
Y-YES SIR.

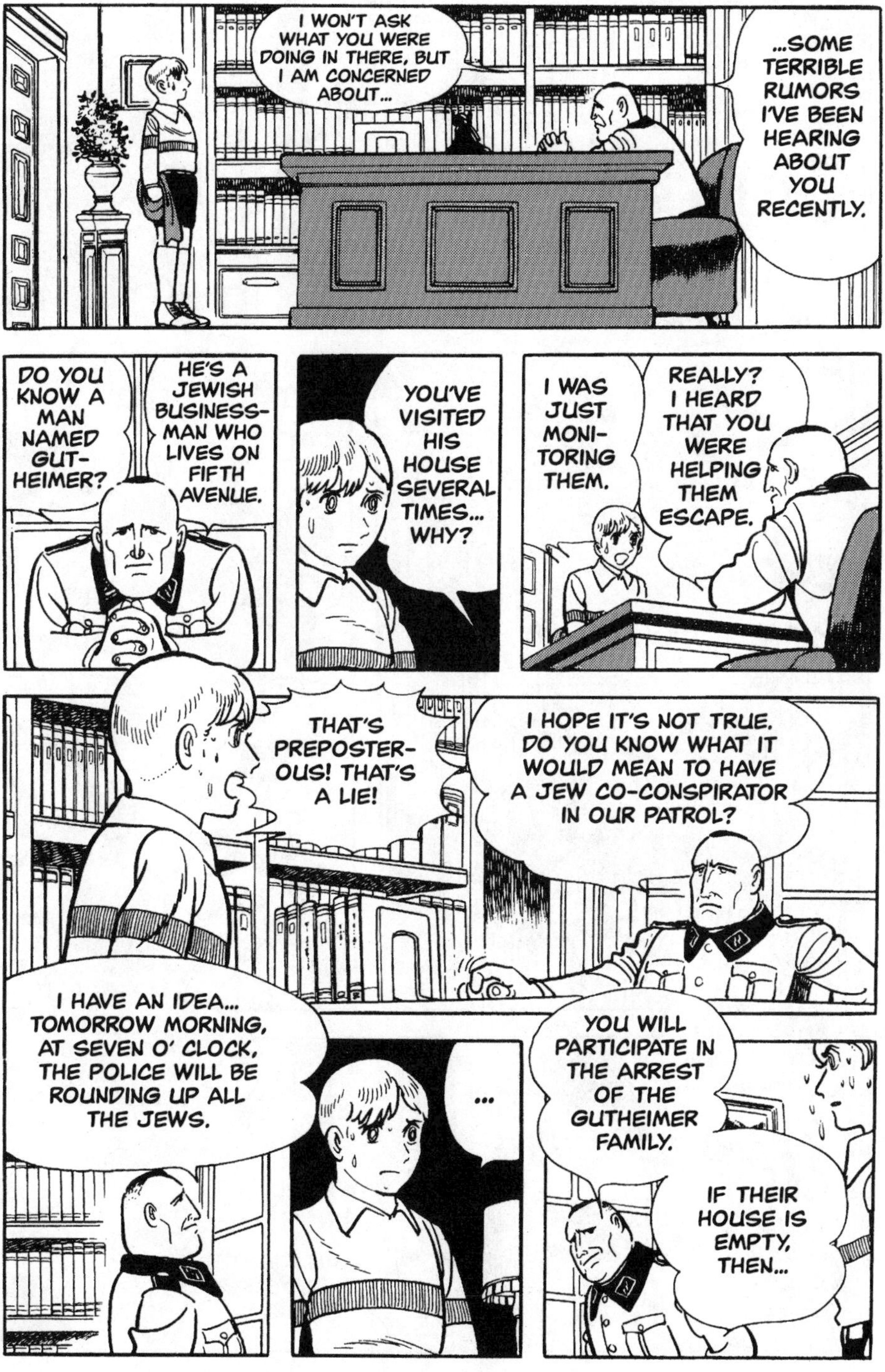
I WON'T ASK WHAT YOU WERE DOING IN THERE, BUT I AM CONCERNED ABOUT...
...SOME TERRIBLE RUMORS I'VE BEEN HEARING ABOUT YOU RECENTLY.
DO YOU KNOW A MAN NAMED GUT-HEIMER?
HE'S A JEWISH BUSINESS-MAN WHO LIVES ON FIFTH AVENUE.
YOU'VE VISITED HIS HOUSE SEVERAL TIMES... WHY?
I WAS JUST MONI-TORING THEM.
REALLY? I HEARD THAT YOU WERE HELPING THEM ESCAPE.
THAT'S PREPOSTER-OUS! THAT'S A LIE!
I HOPE IT'S NOT TRUE. DO YOU KNOW WHAT IT WOULD MEAN TO HAVE A JEW CO-CONSPIRATOR IN OUR PATROL?
I HAVE AN IDEA... TOMORROW MORNING, AT SEVEN O' CLOCK, THE POLICE WILL BE ROUNDING UP ALL THE JEWS.
...
YOU WILL PARTICIPATE IN THE ARREST OF THE GUTHEIMER FAMILY.
IF THEIR HOUSE IS EMPTY, THEN...

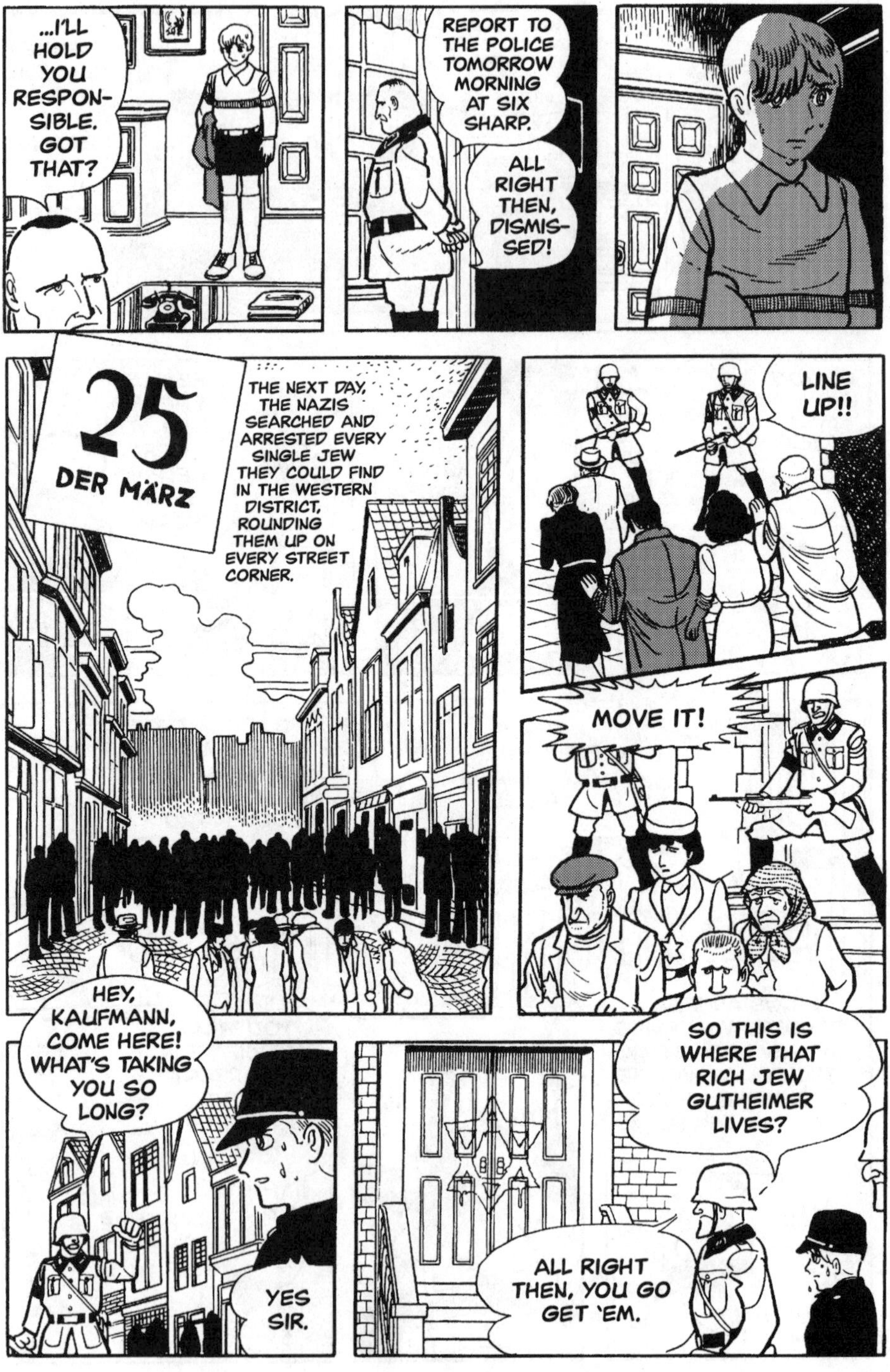
...I'LL HOLD YOU RESPONSIBLE. GOT THAT?
REPORT TO THE POLICE TOMORROW MORNING AT SIX SHARP.
ALL RIGHT THEN, DISMISSED!
25
DER MÄRZ
THE NEXT DAY, THE NAZIS SEARCHED AND ARRESTED EVERY SINGLE JEW THEY COULD FIND IN THE WESTERN DISTRICT, ROUNDING THEM UP ON EVERY STREET CORNER.
LINE UP!!
MOVE IT!
HEY, KAUFMANN, COME HERE! WHAT'S TAKING YOU SO LONG?
YES SIR.
SO THIS IS WHERE THAT RICH JEW GUTHEIMER LIVES?
ALL RIGHT THEN, YOU GO GET 'EM.

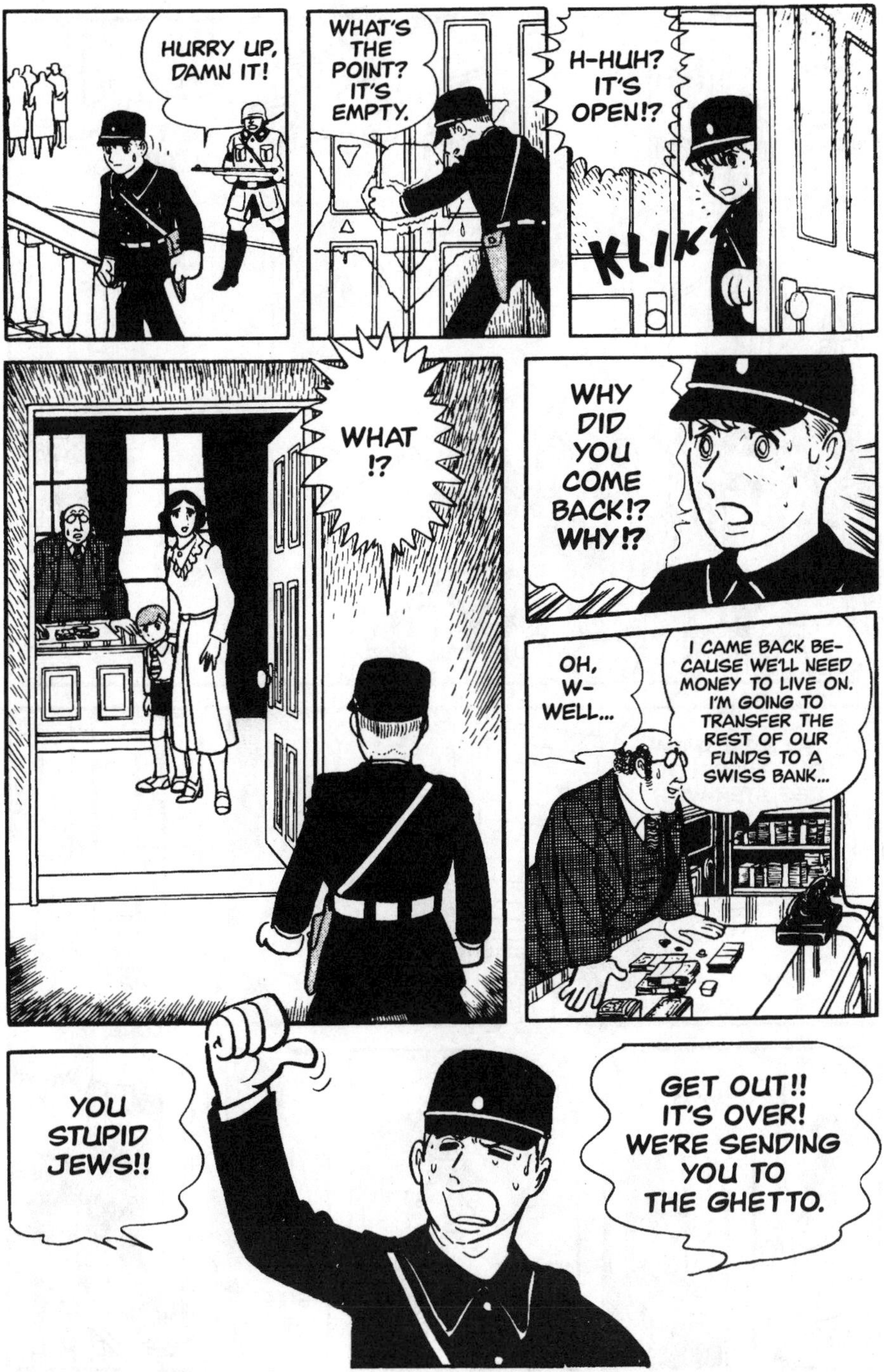
HURRY UP, DAMN IT!
WHAT'S THE POINT? IT'S EMPTY.
H-HUH? IT'S OPEN!?
KLIK
WHAT !?
WHY DID YOU COME BACK!? WHY!?
OH, W-WELL...
I CAME BACK BE-CAUSE WE'LL NEED MONEY TO LIVE ON. I'M GOING TO TRANSFER THE REST OF OUR FUNDS TO A SWISS BANK...
YOU STUPID JEWS!!
GET OUT!! IT'S OVER! WE'RE SENDING YOU TO THE GHETTO.

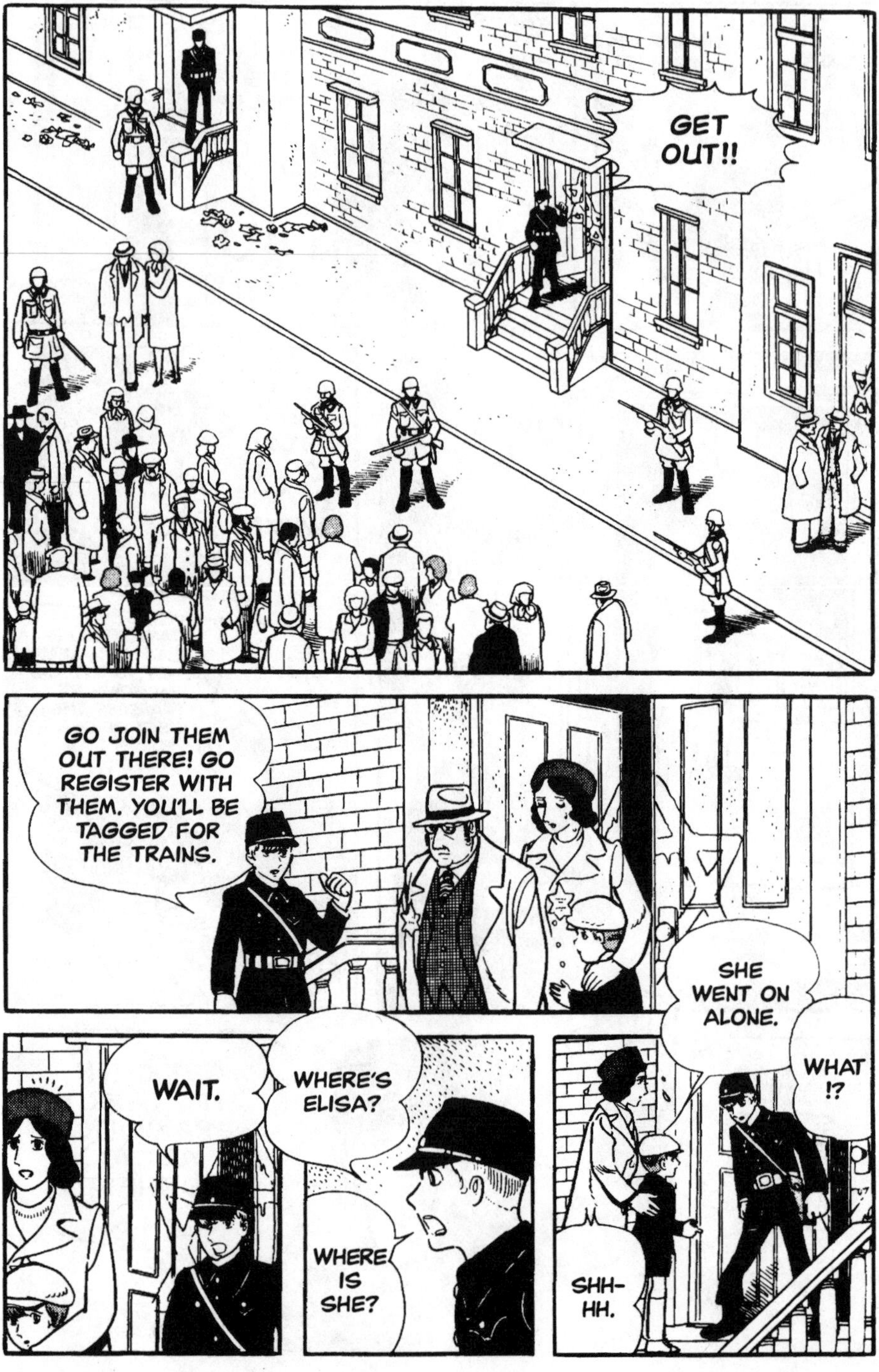
GET OUT!!
GO JOIN THEM OUT THERE! GO REGISTER WITH THEM. YOU'LL BE TAGGED FOR THE TRAINS.
WAIT.
WHERE'S ELISA?
WHERE IS SHE?
SHE WENT ON ALONE.
WHAT !?
SHH-HH.

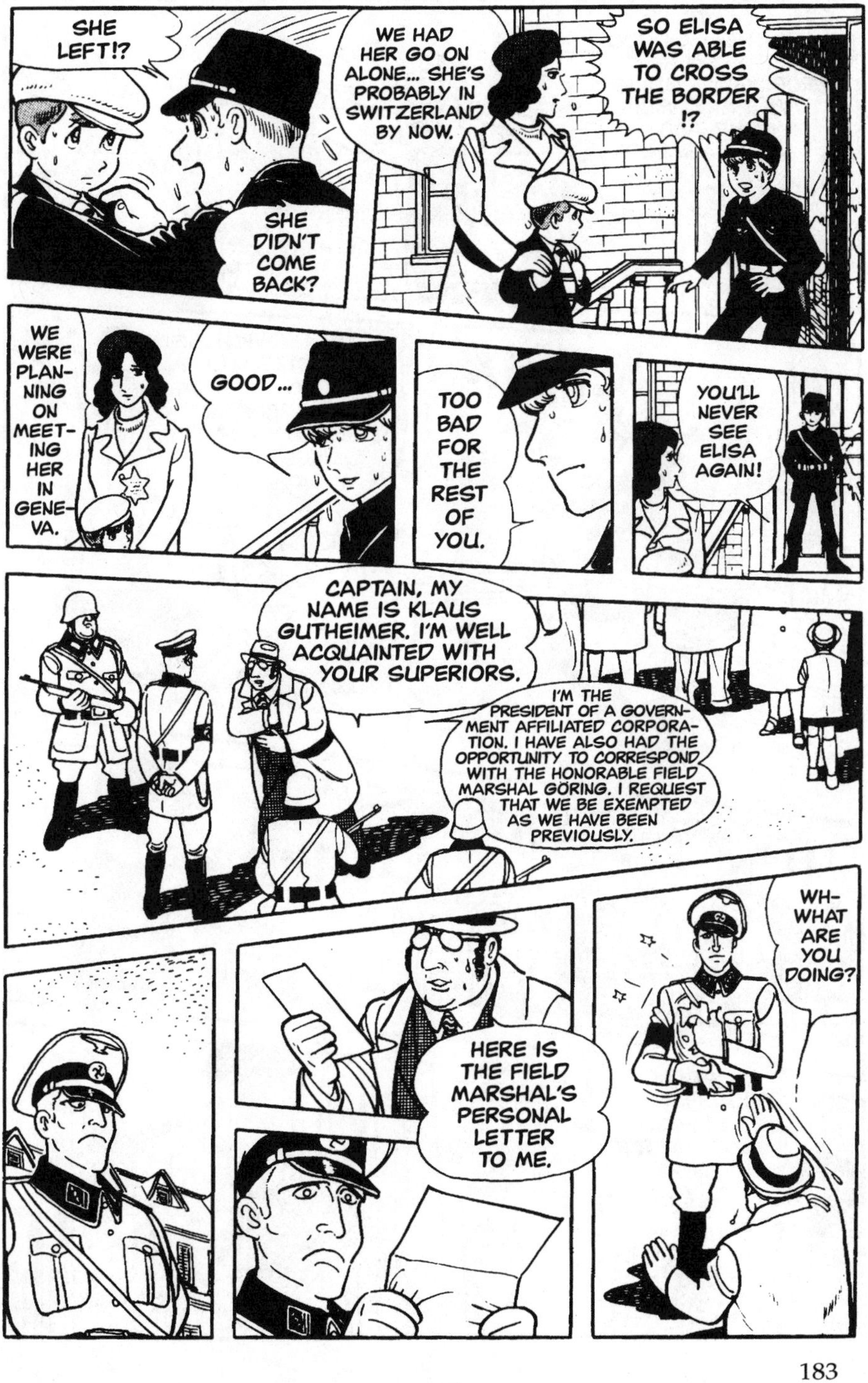
SHE LEFT!?
SHE DIDN'T COME BACK?
WE HAD HER GO ON ALONE... SHE'S PROBABLY IN SWITZERLAND BY NOW.
SO ELISA WAS ABLE TO CROSS THE BORDER !?
WE WERE PLANNING ON MEETING HER IN GENEVA.
GOOD...
TOO BAD FOR THE REST OF YOU.
YOU'LL NEVER SEE ELISA AGAIN!
CAPTAIN, MY NAME IS KLAUS GUTHEIMER. I'M WELL ACQUAINTED WITH YOUR SUPERIORS.
I'M THE PRESIDENT OF A GOVERNMENT AFFILIATED CORPORATION. I HAVE ALSO HAD THE OPPORTUNITY TO CORRESPOND WITH THE HONORABLE FIELD MARSHAL GÖRING. I REQUEST THAT WE BE EXEMPTED AS WE HAVE BEEN PREVIOUSLY.
HERE IS THE FIELD MARSHAL'S PERSONAL LETTER TO ME.
WH-WHAT ARE YOU DOING?

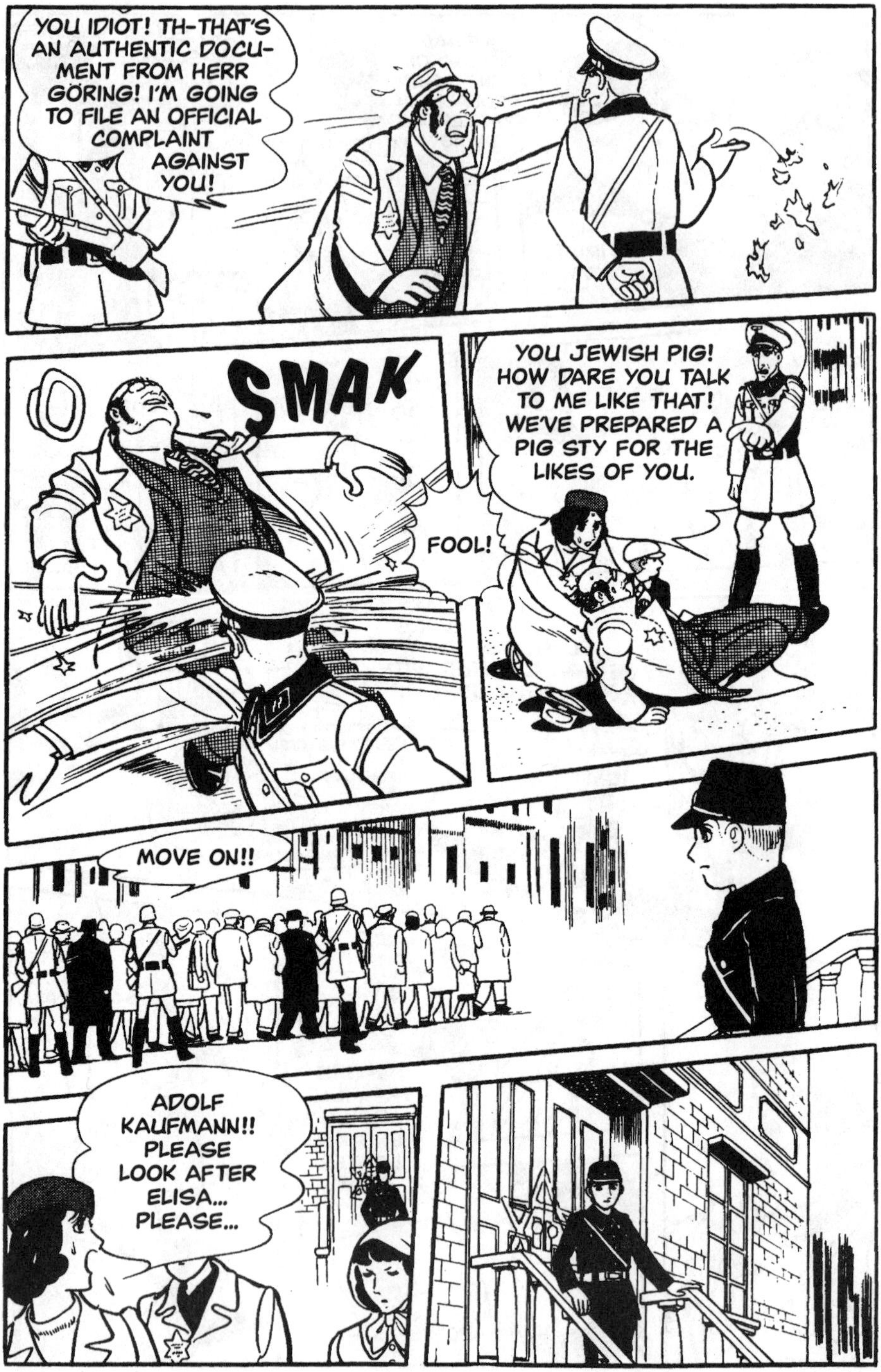
YOU IDIOT! TH-THAT'S AN AUTHENTIC DOCUMENT FROM HERR GÖRING! I'M GOING TO FILE AN OFFICIAL COMPLAINT AGAINST YOU!
SMAK
FOOL!
YOU JEWISH PIG! HOW DARE YOU TALK TO ME LIKE THAT! WE'VE PREPARED A PIG STY FOR THE LIKES OF YOU.
MOVE ON!!
ADOLF KAUFMANN!! PLEASE LOOK AFTER ELISA... PLEASE...

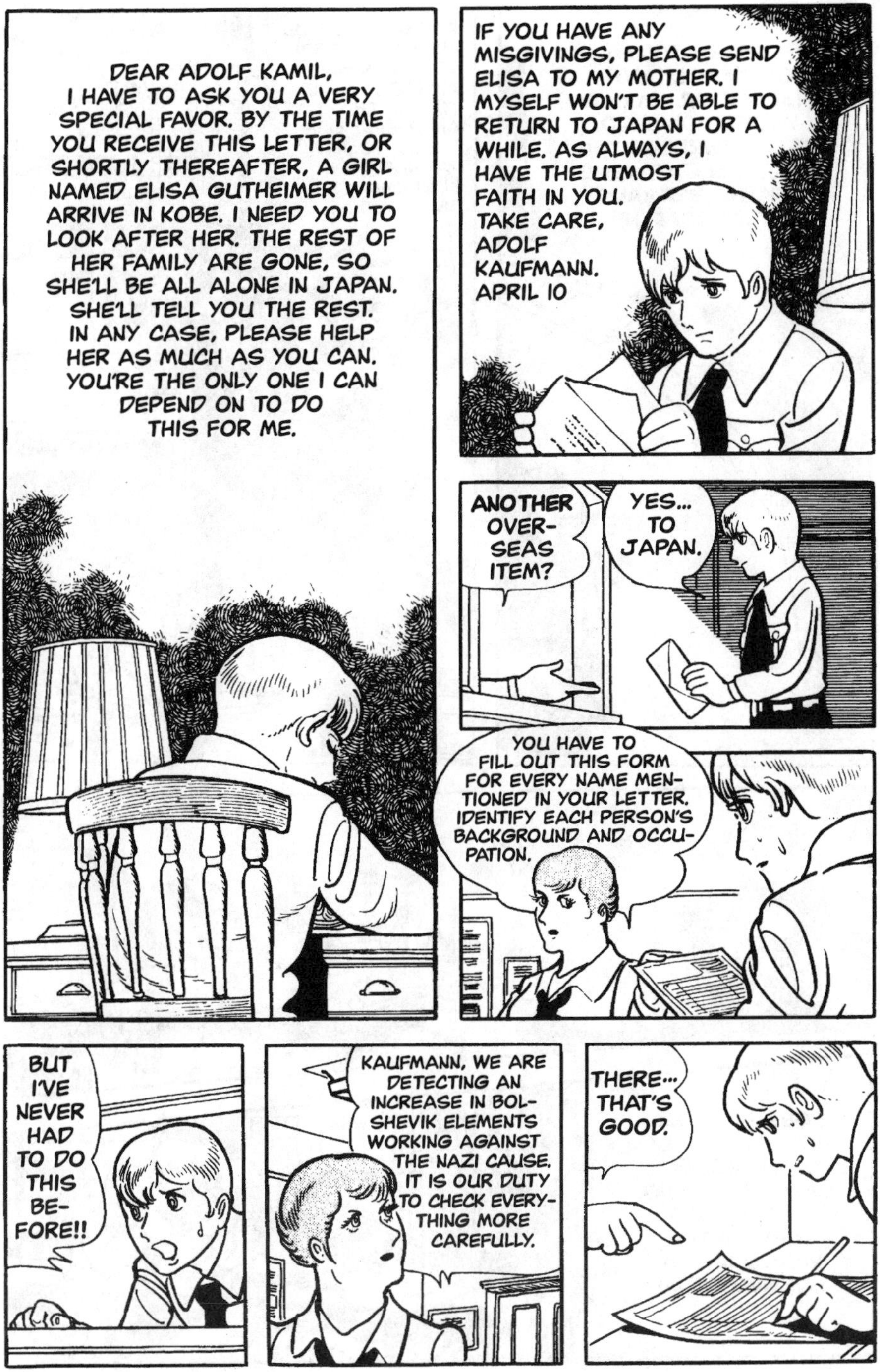
DEAR ADOLF KAMIL,
I HAVE TO ASK YOU A VERY SPECIAL FAVOR. BY THE TIME YOU RECEIVE THIS LETTER, OR SHORTLY THEREAFTER, A GIRL NAMED ELISA GUTHEIMER WILL ARRIVE IN KOBE. I NEED YOU TO LOOK AFTER HER. THE REST OF HER FAMILY ARE GONE, SO SHE'LL BE ALL ALONE IN JAPAN. SHE'LL TELL YOU THE REST. IN ANY CASE, PLEASE HELP HER AS MUCH AS YOU CAN. YOU'RE THE ONLY ONE I CAN DEPEND ON TO DO THIS FOR ME.
IF YOU HAVE ANY MISGIVINGS, PLEASE SEND ELISA TO MY MOTHER. I MYSELF WON'T BE ABLE TO RETURN TO JAPAN FOR A WHILE. AS ALWAYS, I HAVE THE UTMOST FAITH IN YOU.
TAKE CARE,
ADOLF KAUFMANN.
APRIL 10
ANOTHER OVERSEAS ITEM?
YES... TO JAPAN.
YOU HAVE TO FILL OUT THIS FORM FOR EVERY NAME MENTIONED IN YOUR LETTER. IDENTIFY EACH PERSON'S BACKGROUND AND OCCUPATION.
BUT I'VE NEVER HAD TO DO THIS BEFORE!!
KAUFMANN, WE ARE DETECTING AN INCREASE IN BOLSHEVIK ELEMENTS WORKING AGAINST THE NAZI CAUSE. IT IS OUR DUTY TO CHECK EVERYTHING MORE CAREFULLY.
THERE... THAT'S GOOD.

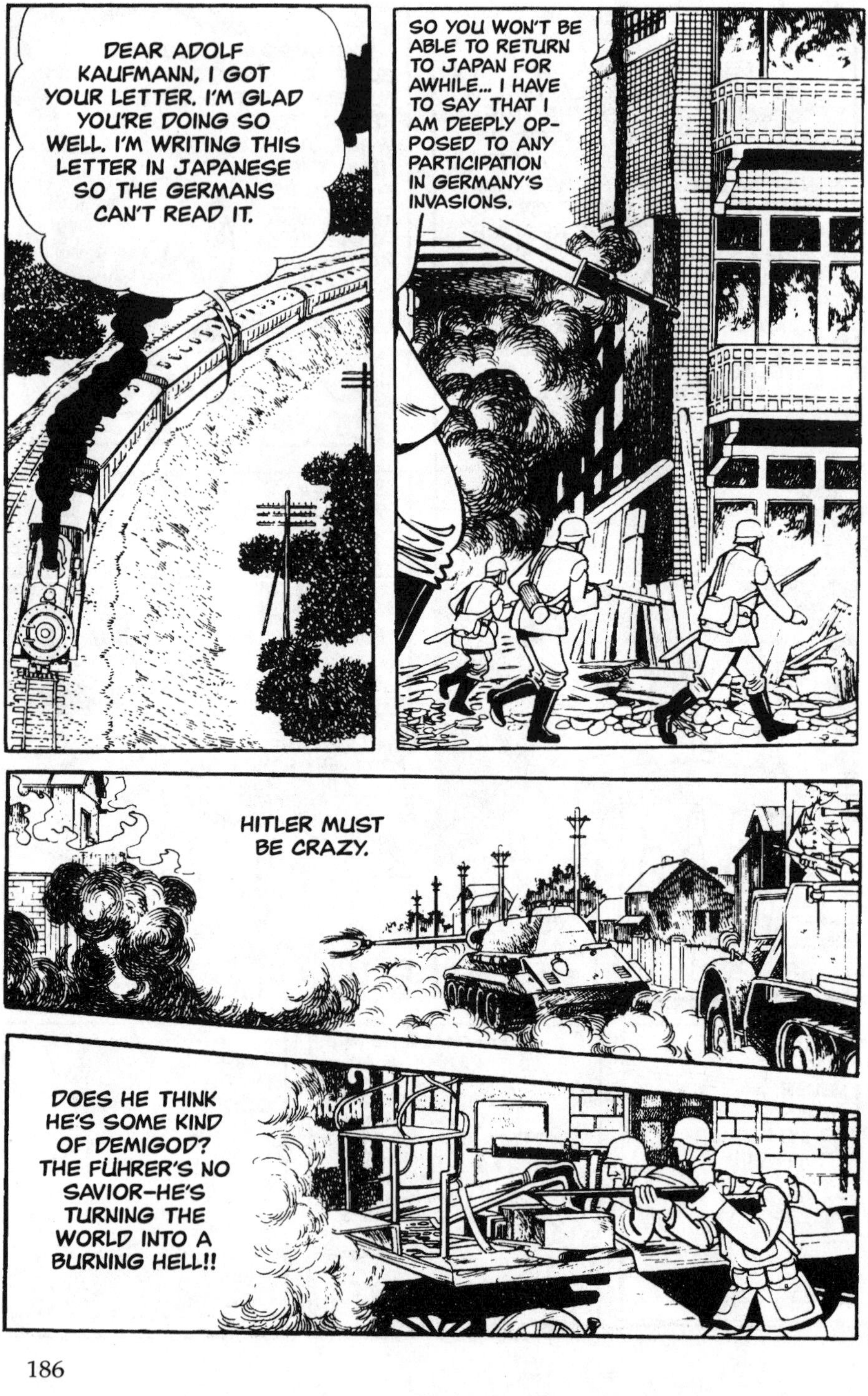
DEAR ADOLF KAUFMANN, I GOT YOUR LETTER. I'M GLAD YOU'RE DOING SO WELL. I'M WRITING THIS LETTER IN JAPANESE SO THE GERMANS CAN'T READ IT.
SO YOU WON'T BE ABLE TO RETURN TO JAPAN FOR AWHILE... I HAVE TO SAY THAT I AM DEEPLY OP-POSED TO ANY PARTICIPATION IN GERMANY'S INVASIONS.
HITLER MUST BE CRAZY.
DOES HE THINK HE'S SOME KIND OF DEMIGOD? THE FÜHRER'S NO SAVIOR—HE'S TURNING THE WORLD INTO A BURNING HELL!!

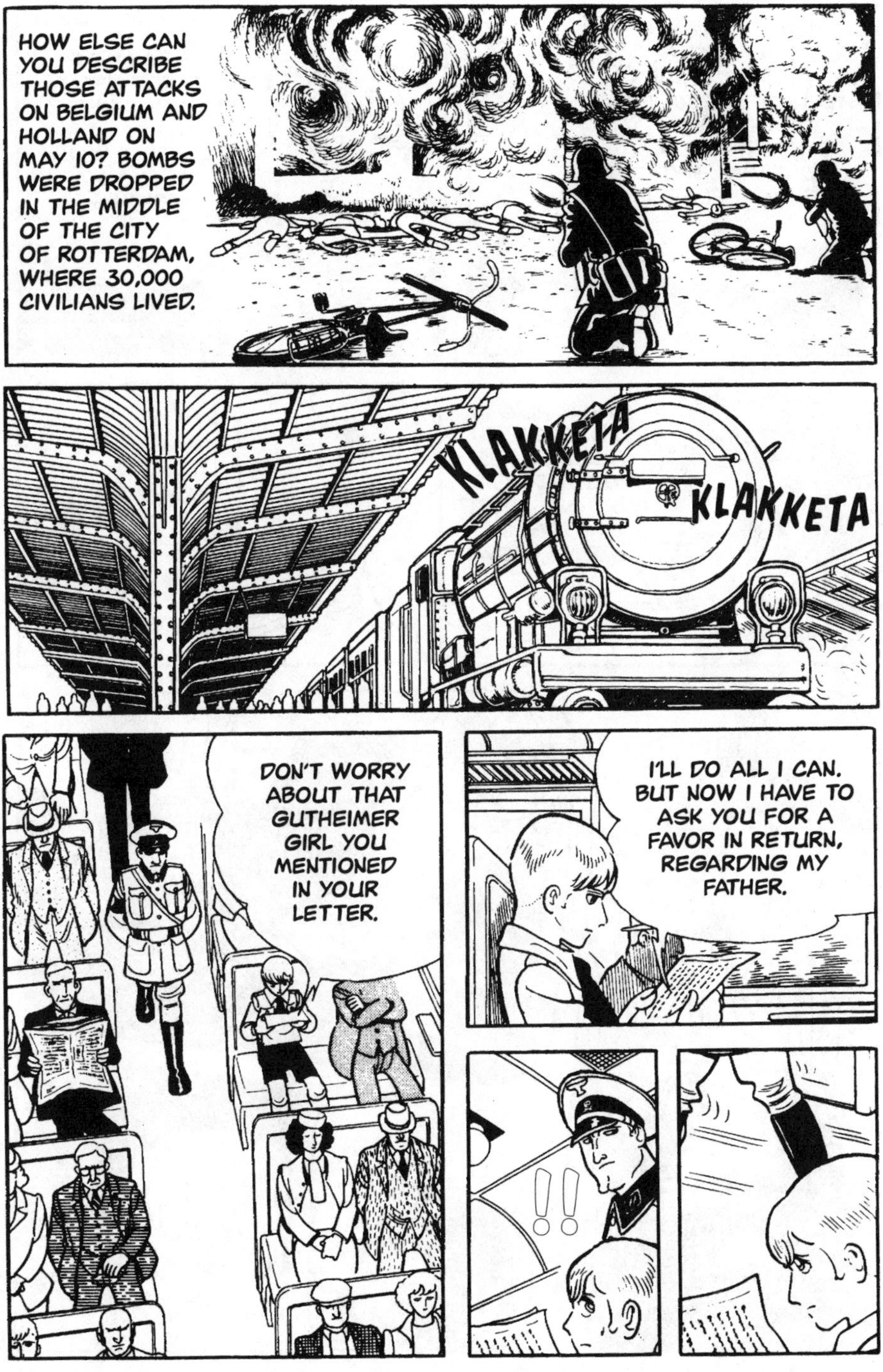
HOW ELSE CAN YOU DESCRIBE THOSE ATTACKS ON BELGIUM AND HOLLAND ON MAY 10? BOMBS WERE DROPPED IN THE MIDDLE OF THE CITY OF ROTTERDAM, WHERE 30,000 CIVILIANS LIVED.
KLAKKETA
KLAKKETA
DON'T WORRY ABOUT THAT GUTHEIMER GIRL YOU MENTIONED IN YOUR LETTER.
I'LL DO ALL I CAN. BUT NOW I HAVE TO ASK YOU FOR A FAVOR IN RETURN, REGARDING MY FATHER.
!!

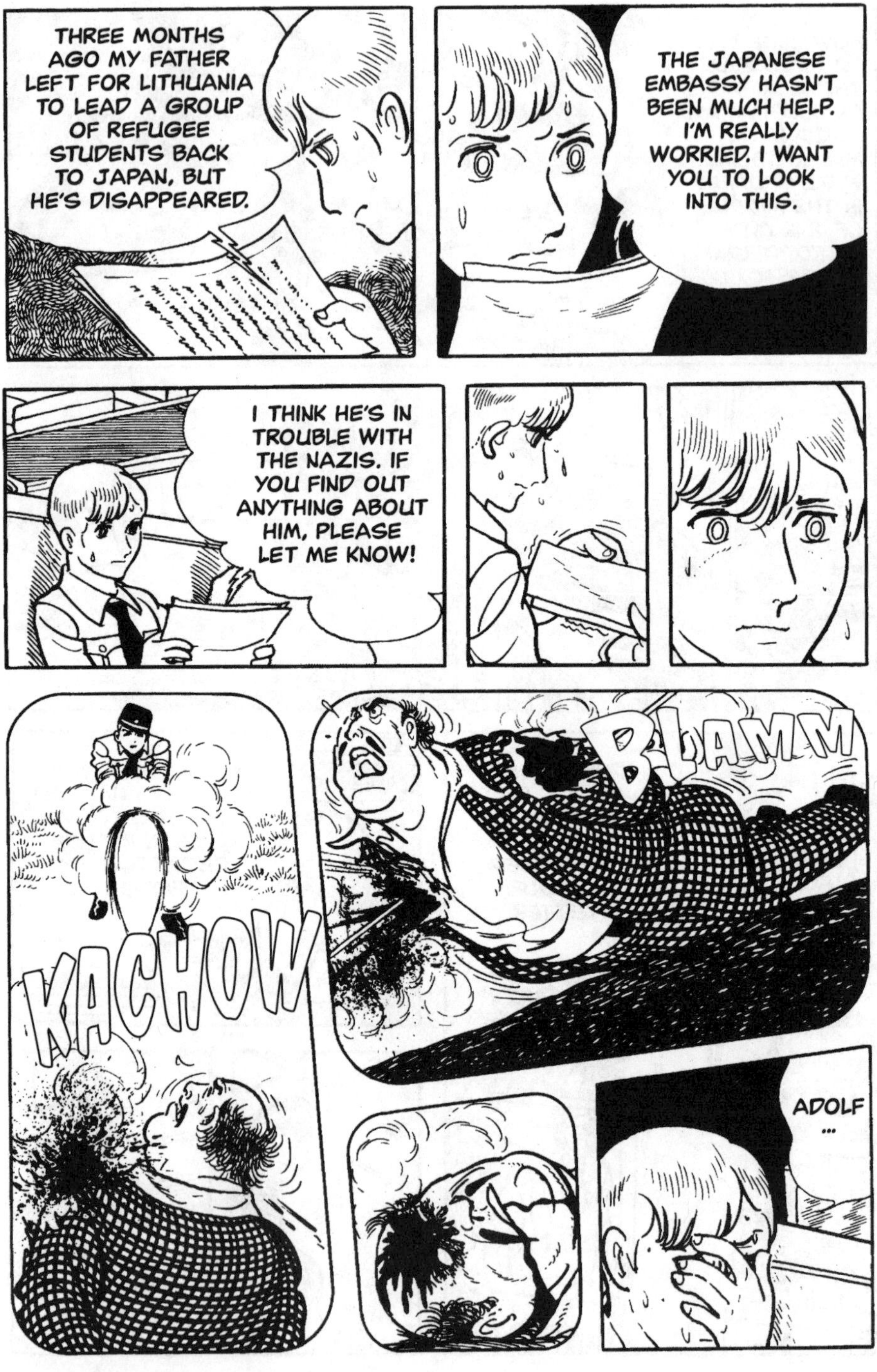
THREE MONTHS AGO MY FATHER LEFT FOR LITHUANIA TO LEAD A GROUP OF REFUGEE STUDENTS BACK TO JAPAN, BUT HE'S DISAPPEARED.
THE JAPANESE EMBASSY HASN'T BEEN MUCH HELP. I'M REALLY WORRIED. I WANT YOU TO LOOK INTO THIS.
I THINK HE'S IN TROUBLE WITH THE NAZIS. IF YOU FIND OUT ANYTHING ABOUT HIM, PLEASE LET ME KNOW!
KACHOW
BLAMM
ADOLF ...

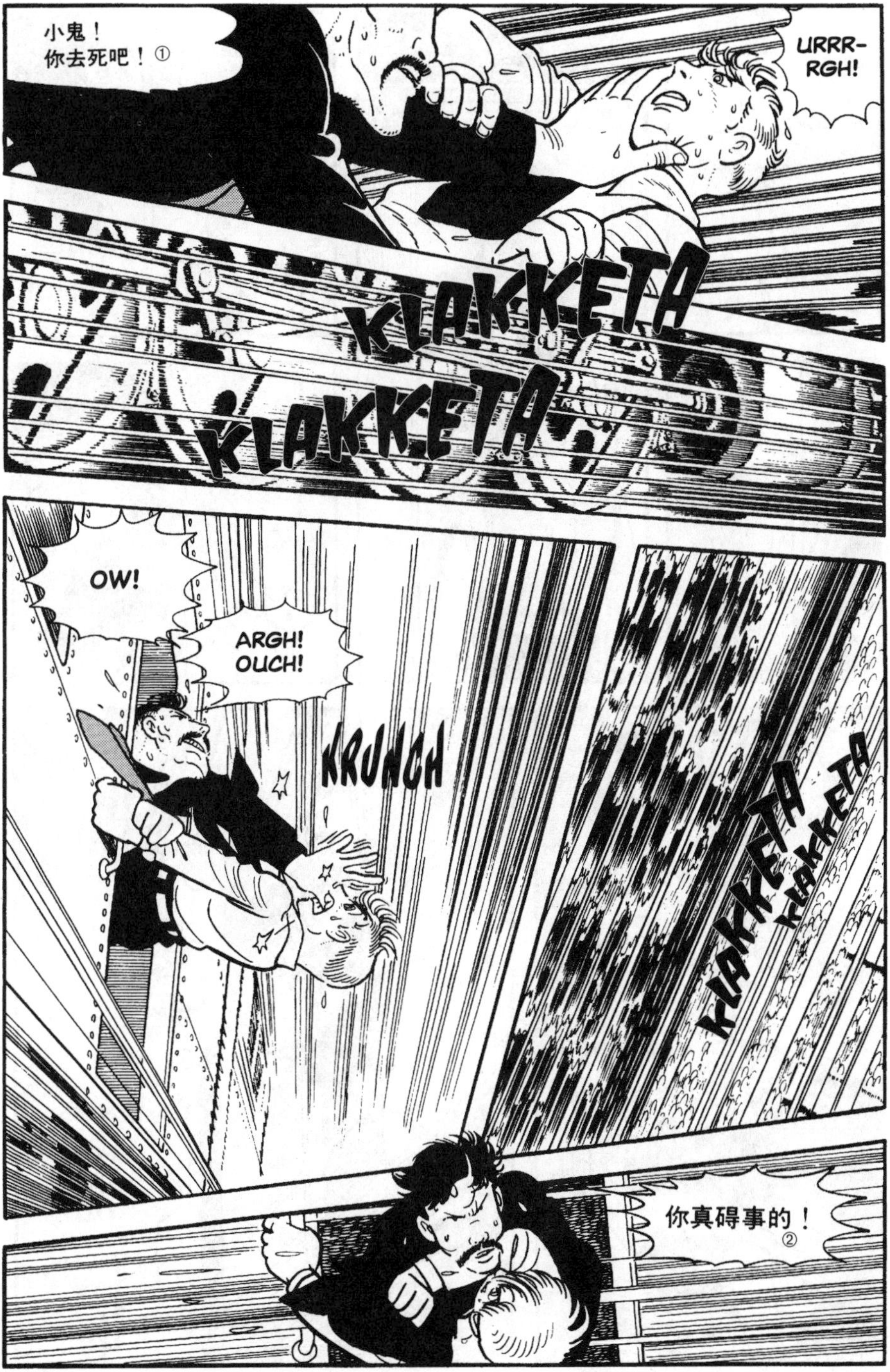
小鬼！
你去死吧！①
URRR-
RGH!
KLAKKETA
KLAKKETA
OW!
ARGH!
OUCH!
KRUNCH
KLAKKETA
KLAKKETA
你真碍事的！
②

① You're dead, kid! ② You're in my way!

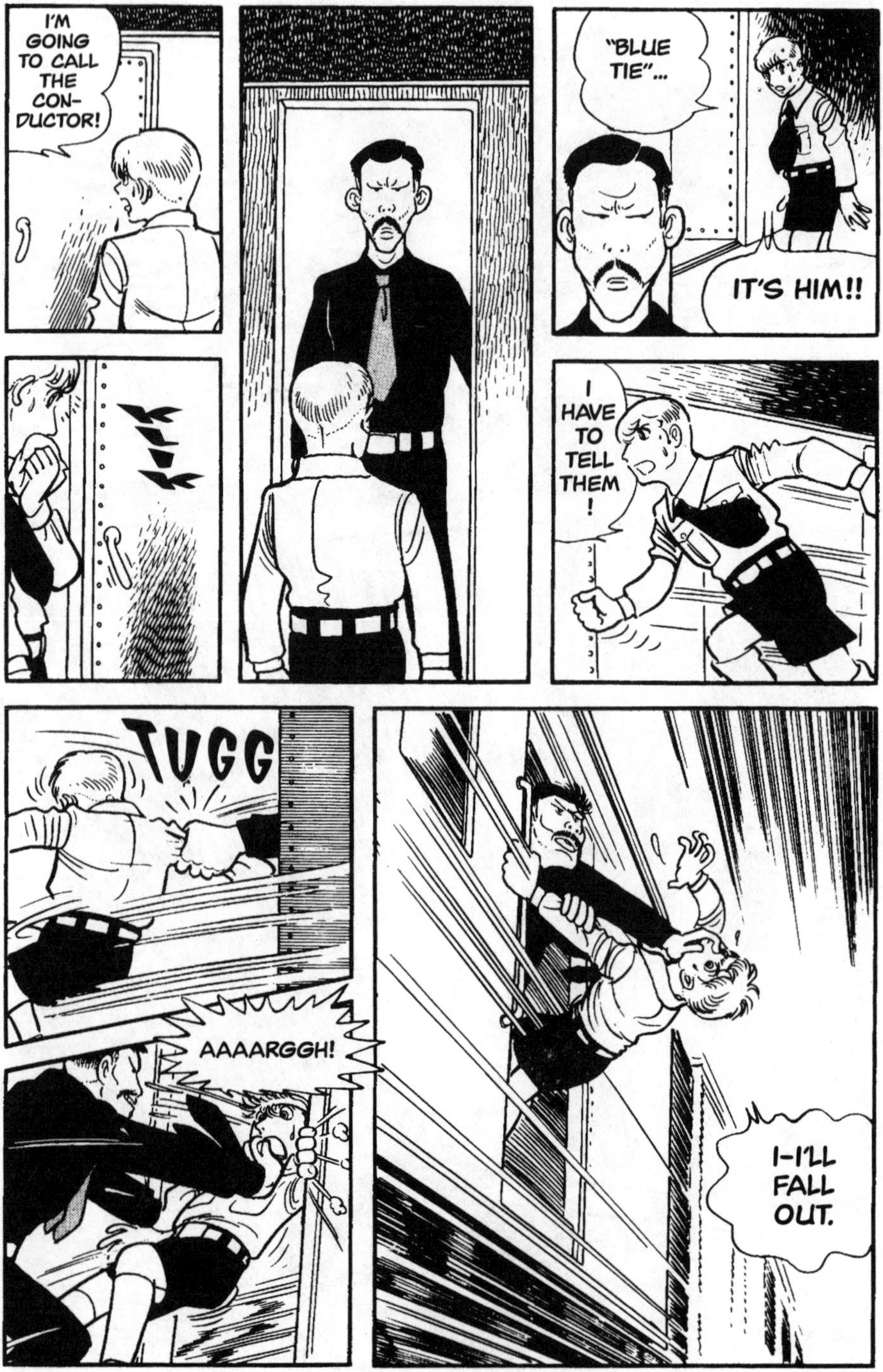
I'M GOING TO CALL THE CON-DUCTOR!
"BLUE TIE"...
IT'S HIM!!
I HAVE TO TELL THEM!
TUGG
AAAARGGH!
I-I'LL FALL OUT.

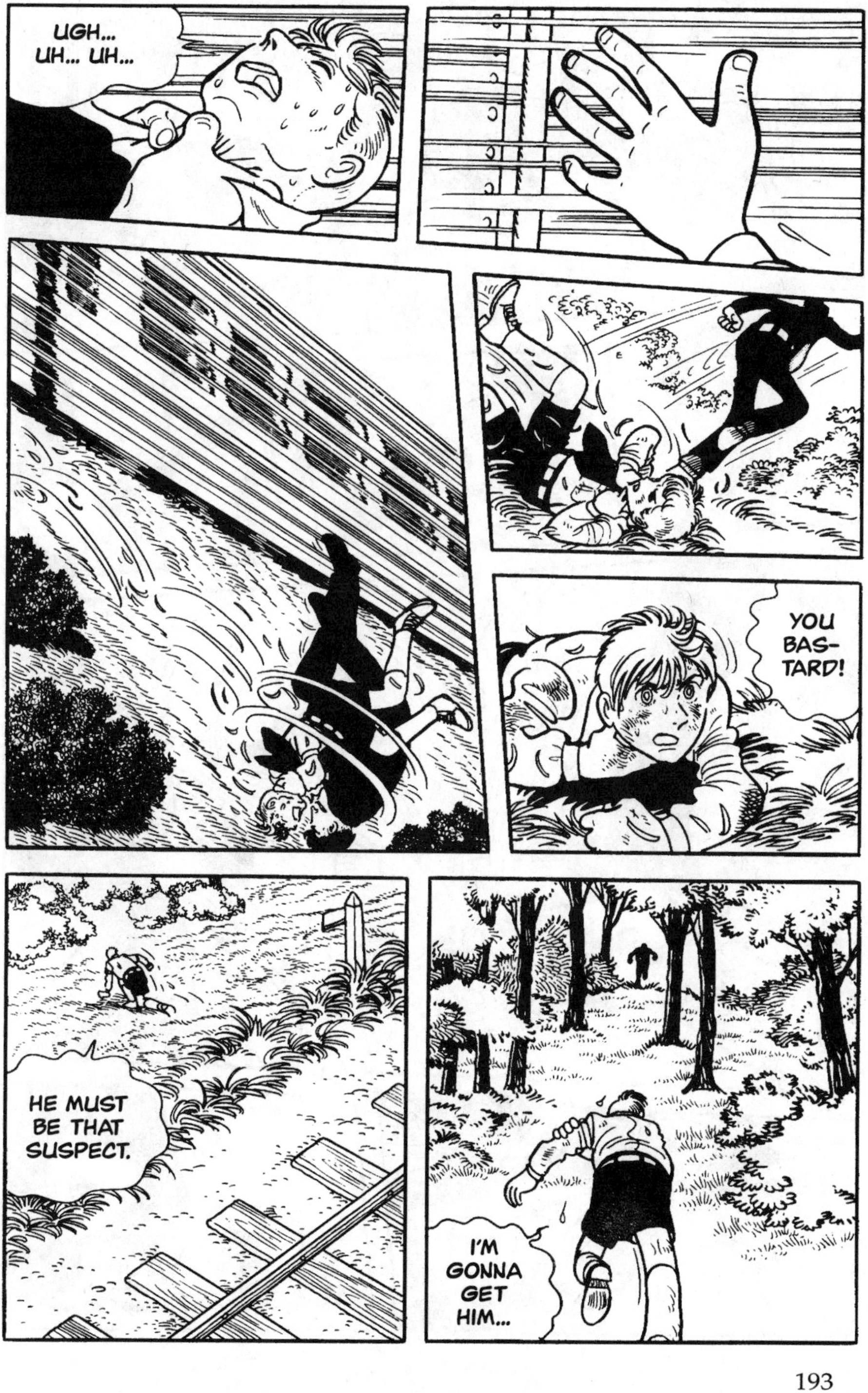
UGH... UH... UH...
YOU BAS-TARD!
HE MUST BE THAT SUSPECT.
I'M GONNA GET HIM...

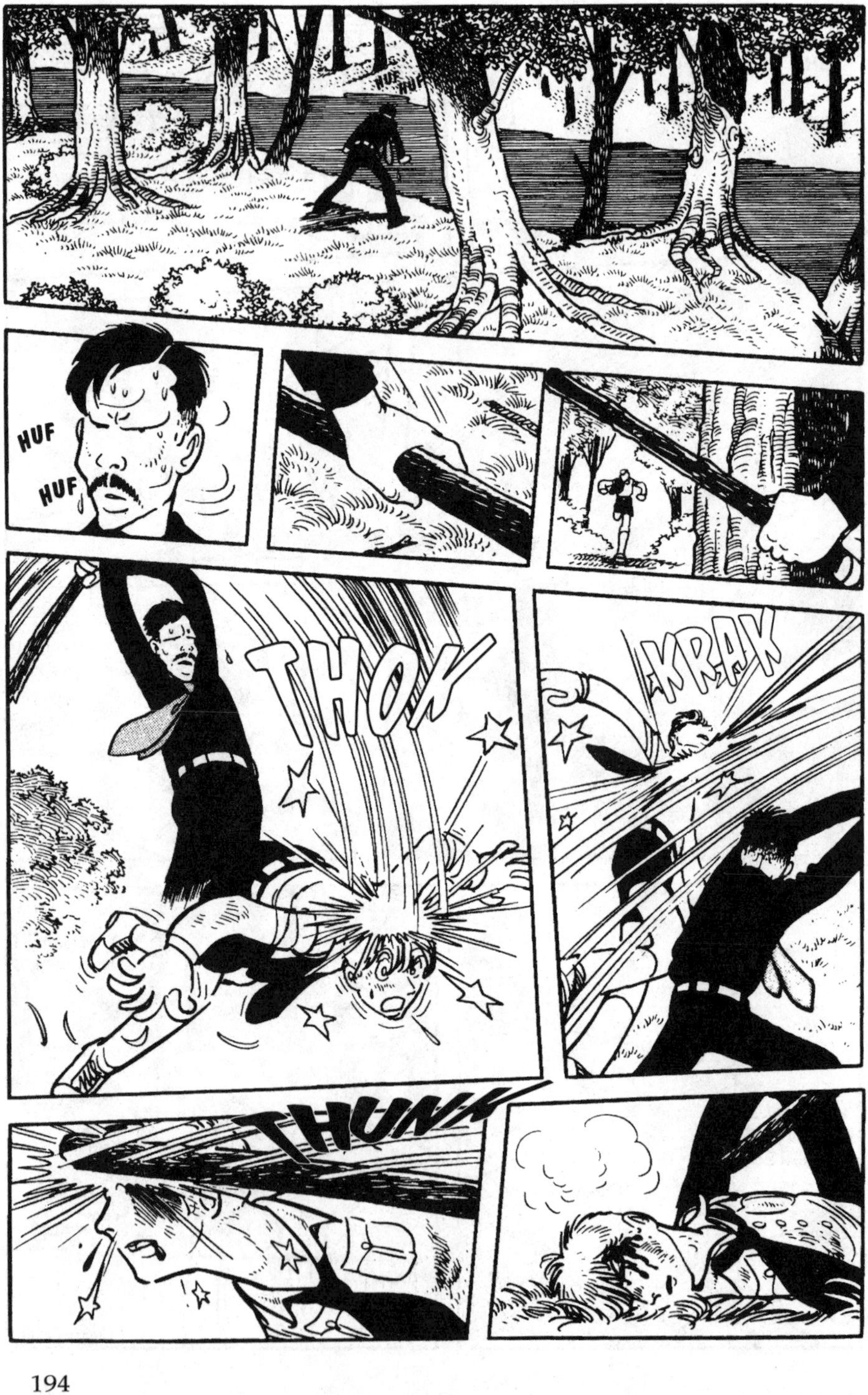
HUF
HUF
HUF
HUF
THOK
KRAK
THUNK

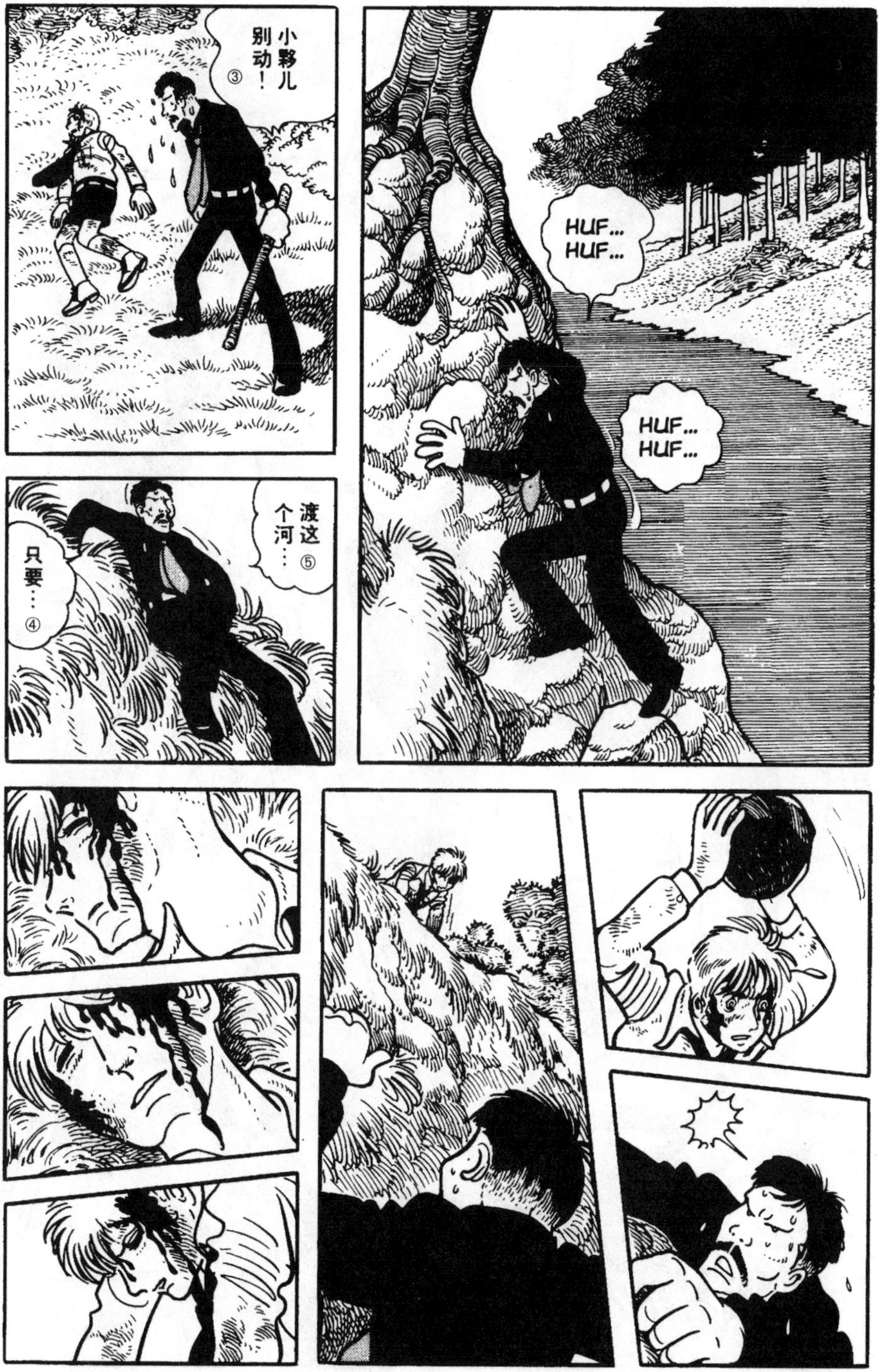
小夥儿别动！③
只要…④
渡这个河…⑤
HUF… HUF…
HUF… HUF…

③ Sweet dreams, kid! ④ Now… ⑤ If I can just cross this river!

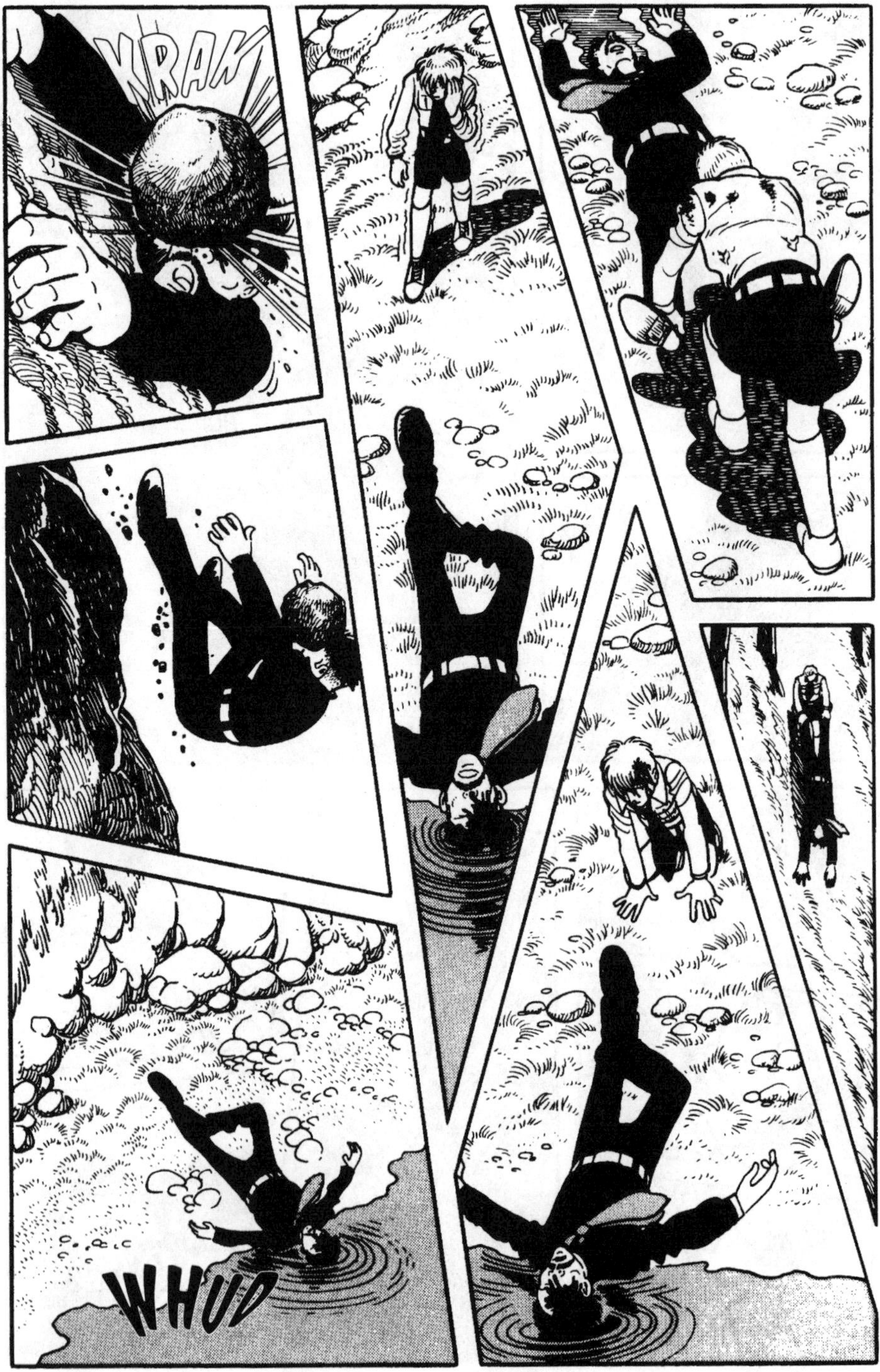
KRAK
WHUD

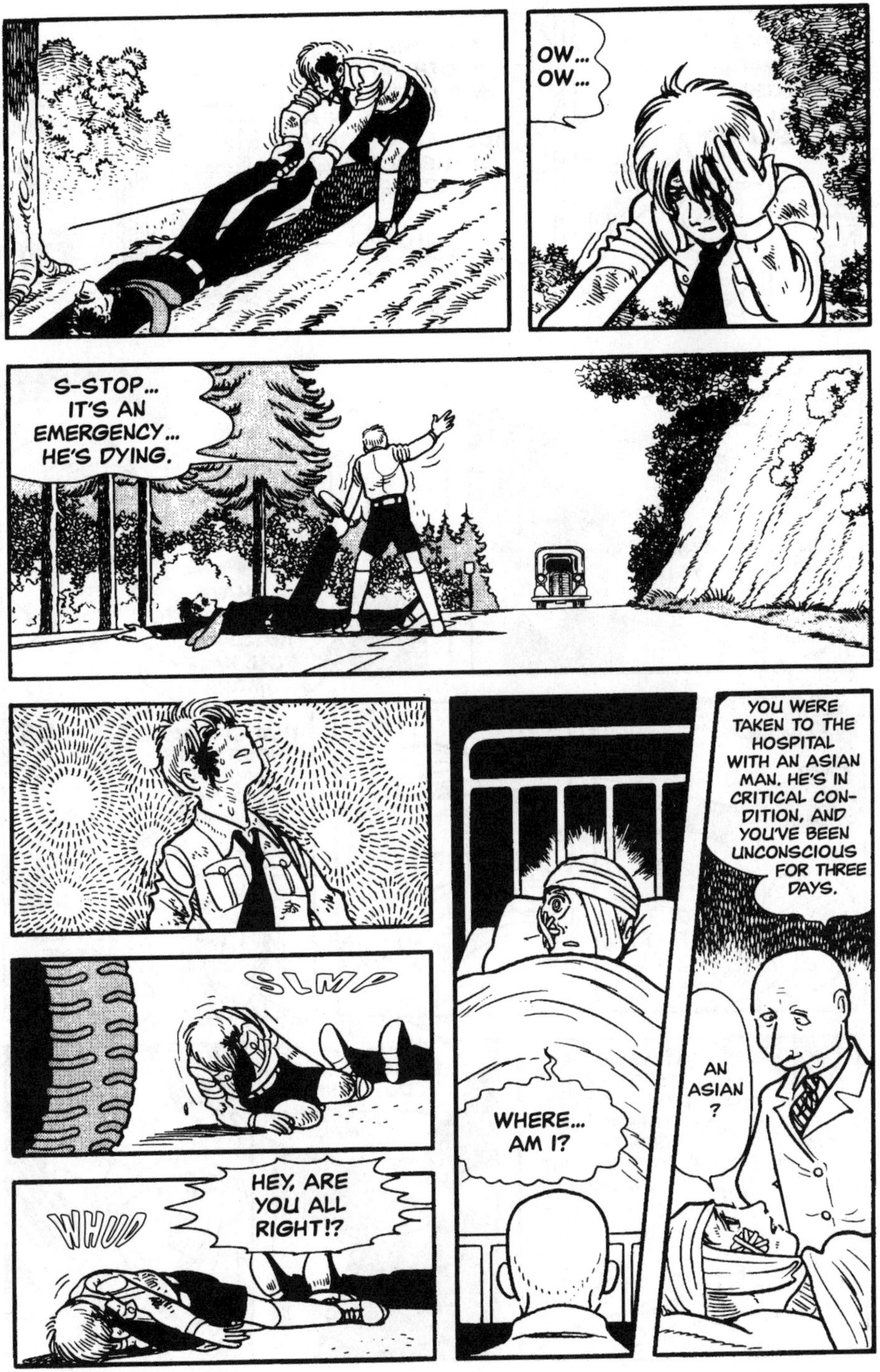
OW... OW...
S-STOP... IT'S AN EMERGENCY... HE'S DYING.
SLMP
HEY, ARE YOU ALL RIGHT!?
WHUD
WHERE... AM I?
YOU WERE TAKEN TO THE HOSPITAL WITH AN ASIAN MAN. HE'S IN CRITICAL CONDITION, AND YOU'VE BEEN UNCONSCIOUS FOR THREE DAYS.
AN ASIAN ?

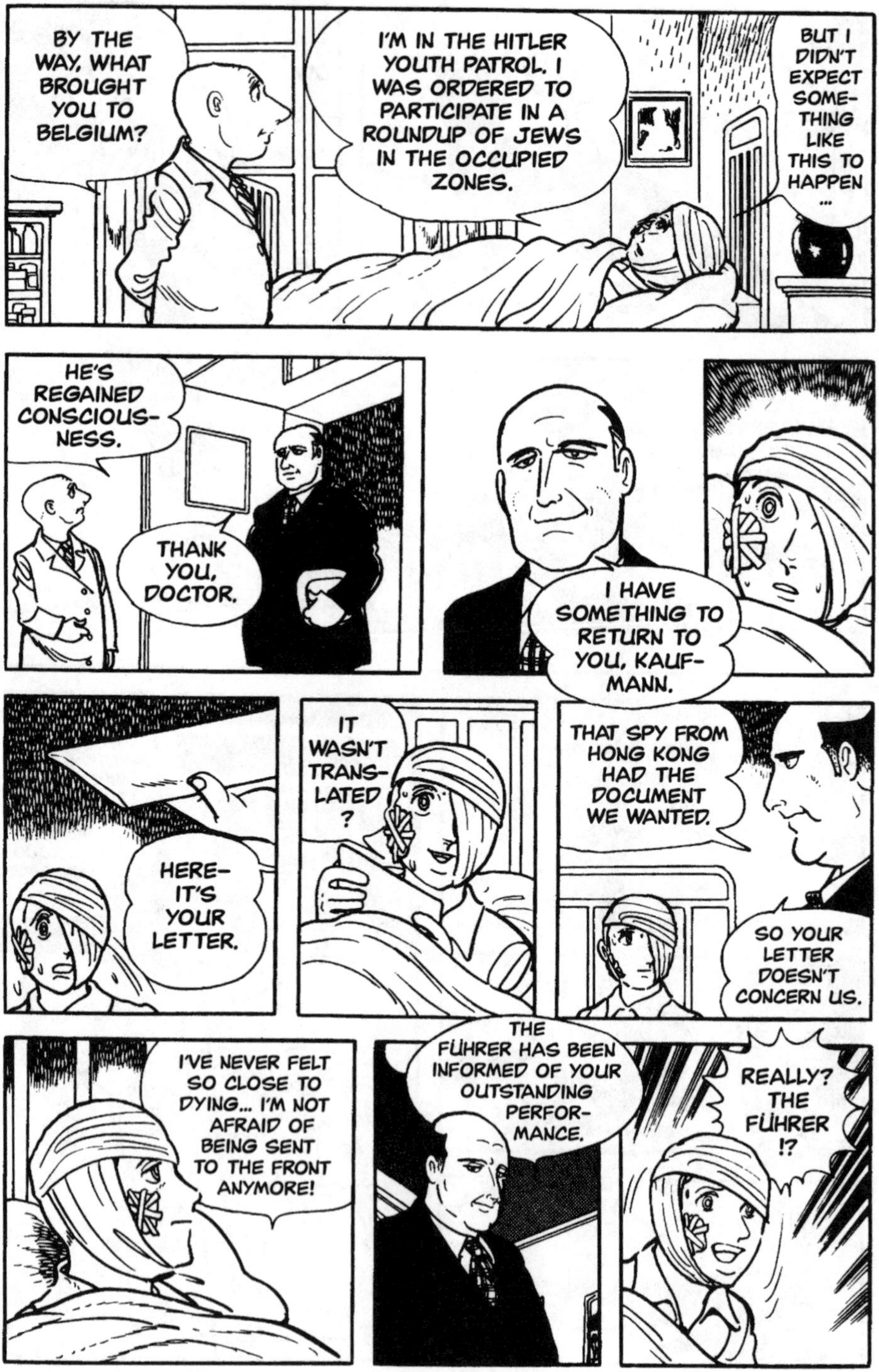
BY THE WAY, WHAT BROUGHT YOU TO BELGIUM?
I'M IN THE HITLER YOUTH PATROL. I WAS ORDERED TO PARTICIPATE IN A ROUNDUP OF JEWS IN THE OCCUPIED ZONES.
BUT I DIDN'T EXPECT SOME-THING LIKE THIS TO HAPPEN ...
HE'S REGAINED CONSCIOUS-NESS.
THANK YOU, DOCTOR.
I HAVE SOMETHING TO RETURN TO YOU, KAUF-MANN.
HERE-IT'S YOUR LETTER.
IT WASN'T TRANS-LATED ?
THAT SPY FROM HONG KONG HAD THE DOCUMENT WE WANTED.
SO YOUR LETTER DOESN'T CONCERN US.
I'VE NEVER FELT SO CLOSE TO DYING... I'M NOT AFRAID OF BEING SENT TO THE FRONT ANYMORE!
THE FÜHRER HAS BEEN INFORMED OF YOUR OUTSTANDING PERFOR-MANCE.
REALLY? THE FÜHRER !?

CHAPTER
FIVE

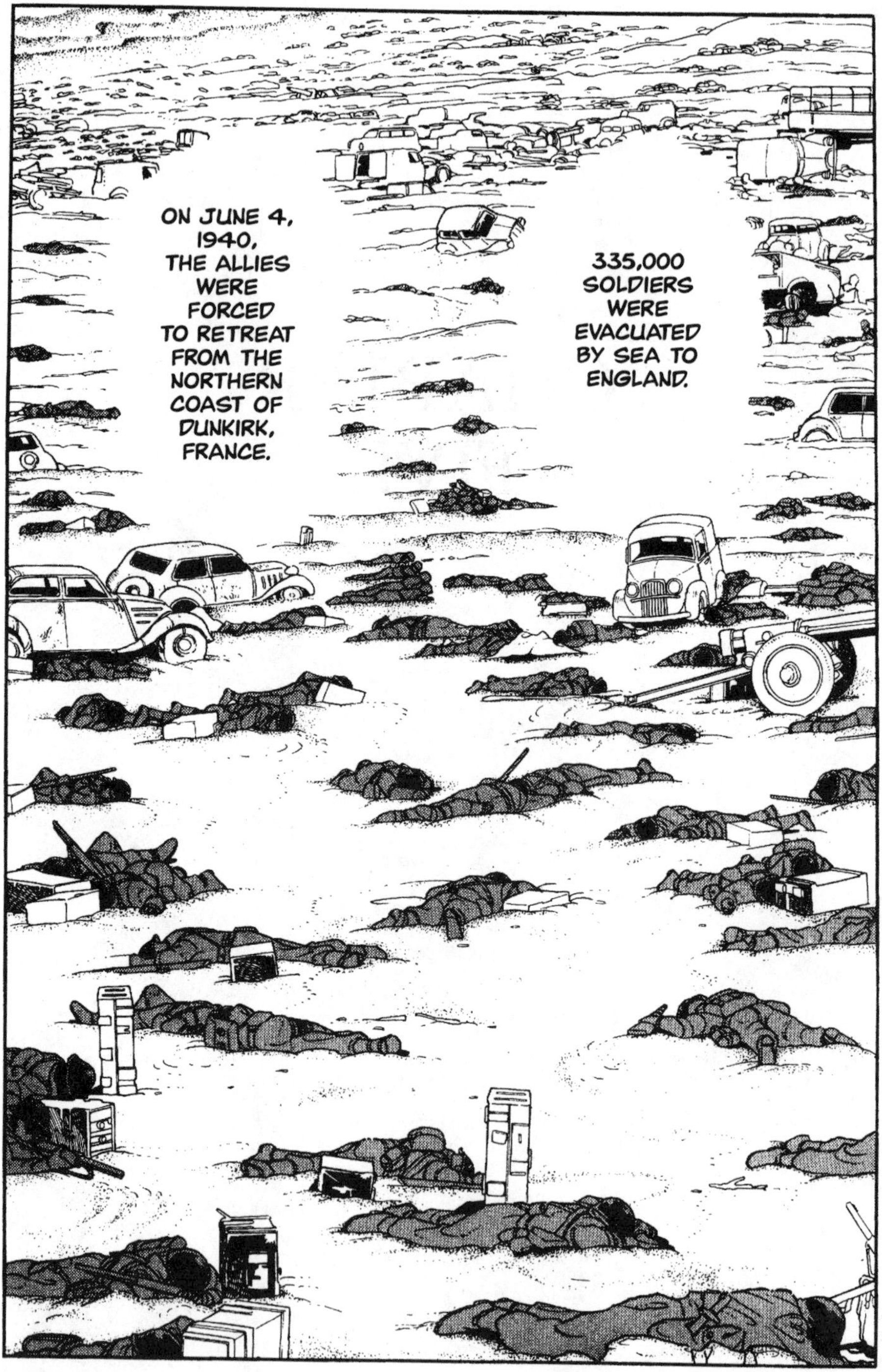
ON JUNE 4, 1940, THE ALLIES WERE FORCED TO RETREAT FROM THE NORTHERN COAST OF DUNKIRK, FRANCE.
335,000 SOLDIERS WERE EVACUATED BY SEA TO ENGLAND.

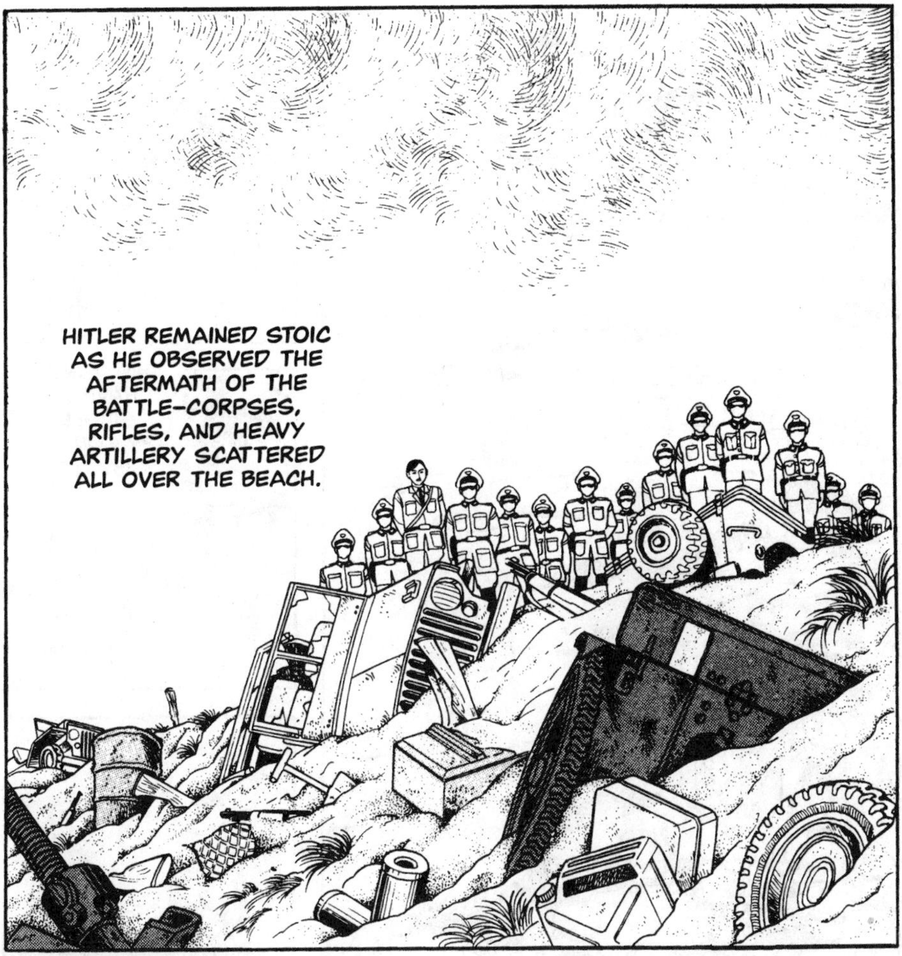
HITLER REMAINED STOIC AS HE OBSERVED THE AFTERMATH OF THE BATTLE-CORPSES, RIFLES, AND HEAVY ARTILLERY SCATTERED ALL OVER THE BEACH.

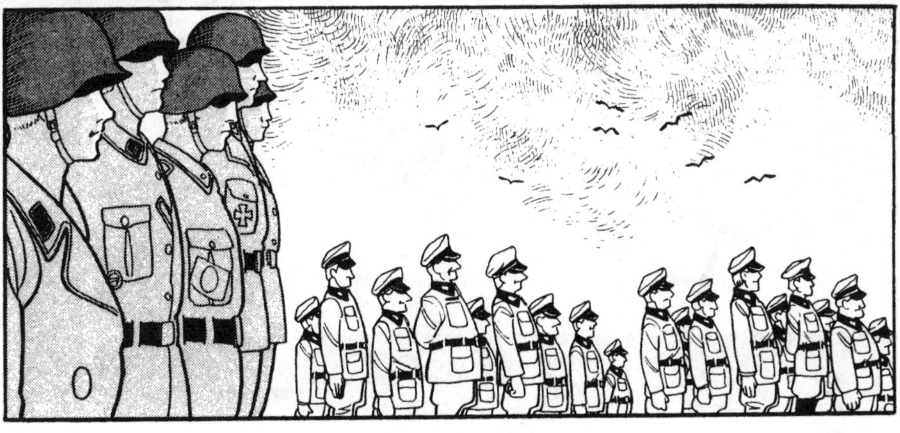

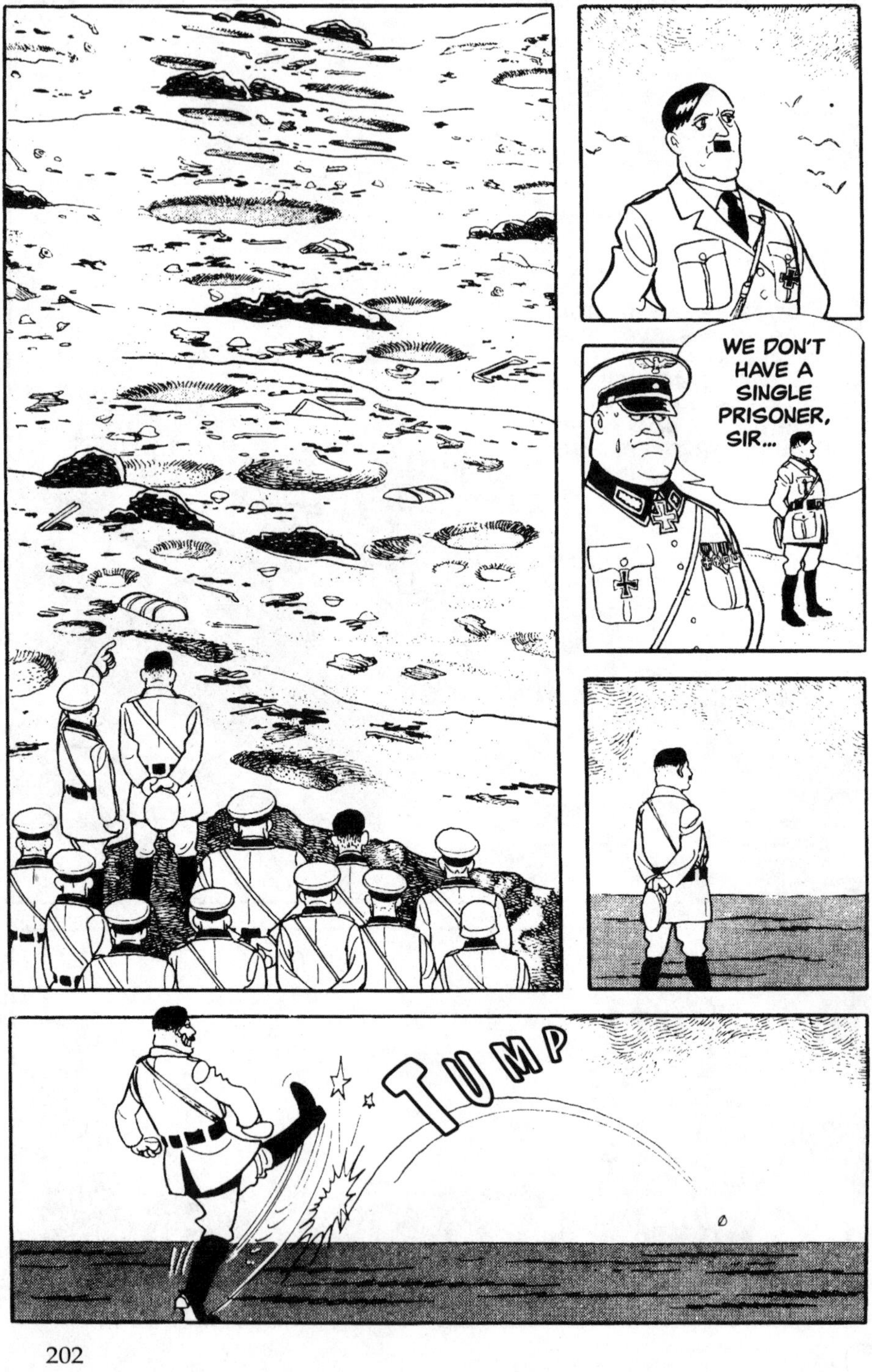
WE DON'T HAVE A SINGLE PRISONER, SIR...
TUMP

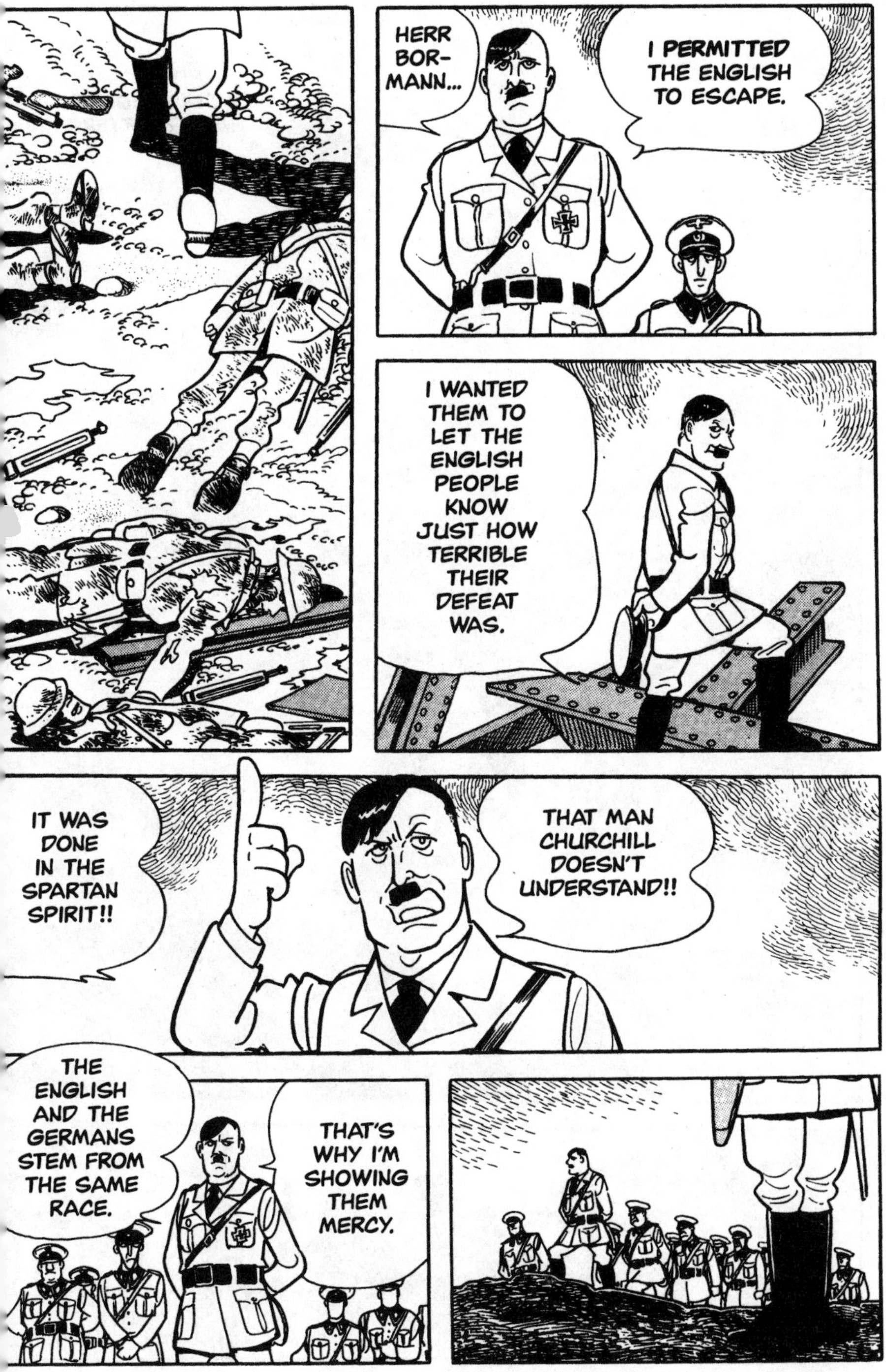
HERR BOR-MANN...
I PERMITTED THE ENGLISH TO ESCAPE.
I WANTED THEM TO LET THE ENGLISH PEOPLE KNOW JUST HOW TERRIBLE THEIR DEFEAT WAS.
IT WAS DONE IN THE SPARTAN SPIRIT!!
THAT MAN CHURCHILL DOESN'T UNDERSTAND!!
THE ENGLISH AND THE GERMANS STEM FROM THE SAME RACE.
THAT'S WHY I'M SHOWING THEM MERCY.

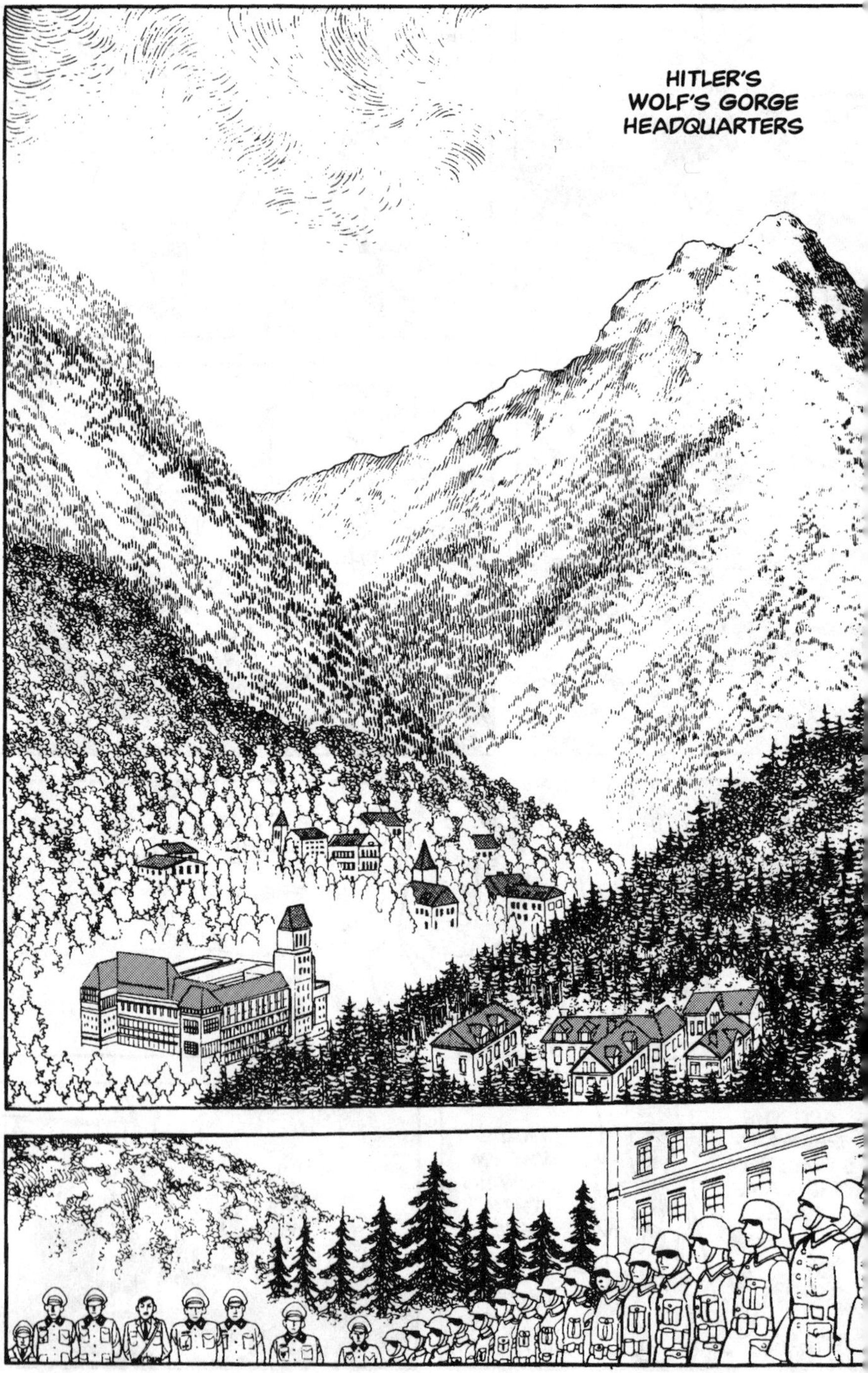
HITLER'S
WOLF'S GORGE
HEADQUARTERS

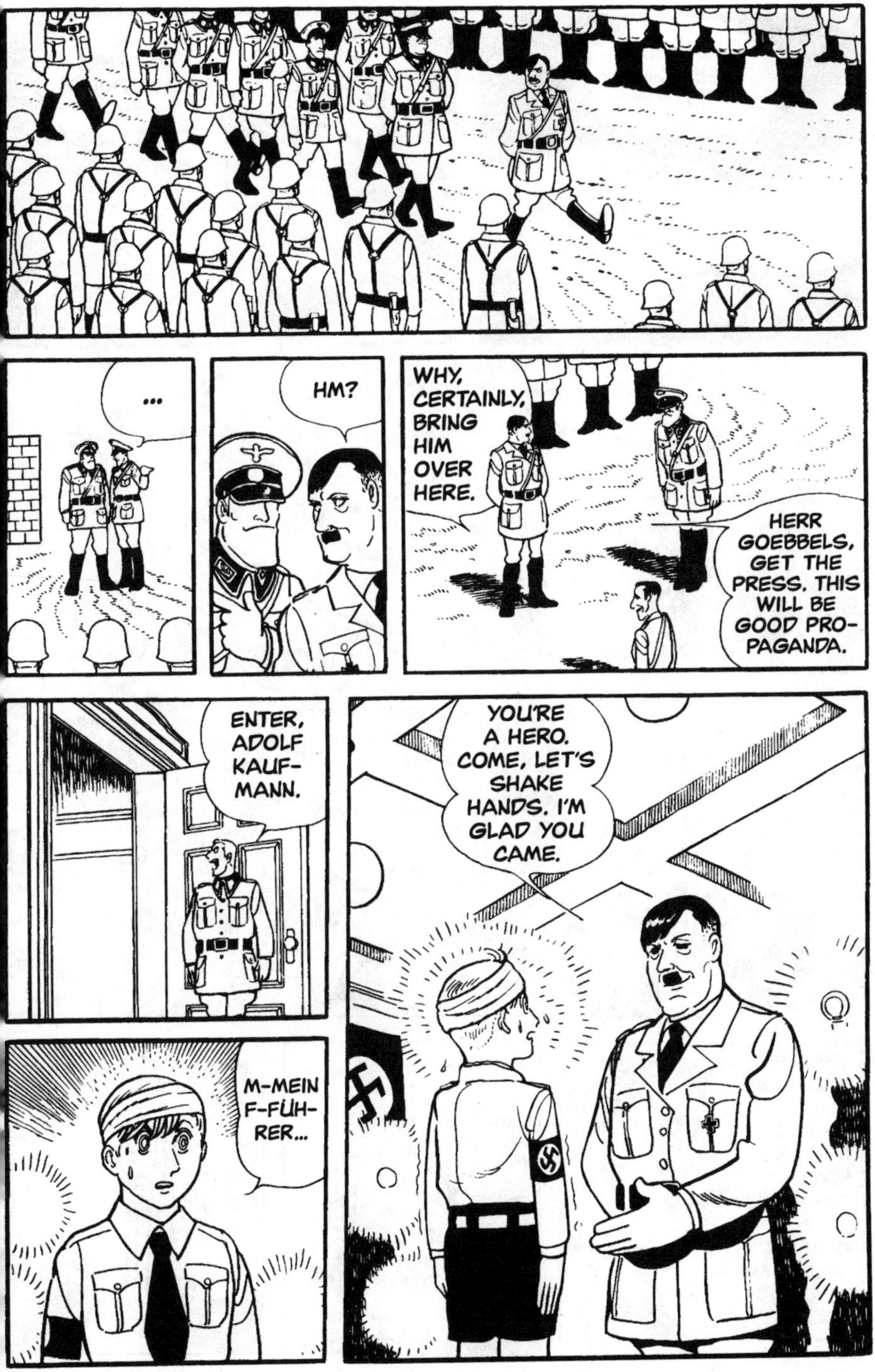
...
HM?
WHY, CERTAINLY, BRING HIM OVER HERE.
HERR GOEBBELS, GET THE PRESS. THIS WILL BE GOOD PRO-PAGANDA.
ENTER, ADOLF KAUF-MANN.
M-MEIN F-FÜH-RER...
YOU'RE A HERO. COME, LET'S SHAKE HANDS. I'M GLAD YOU CAME.

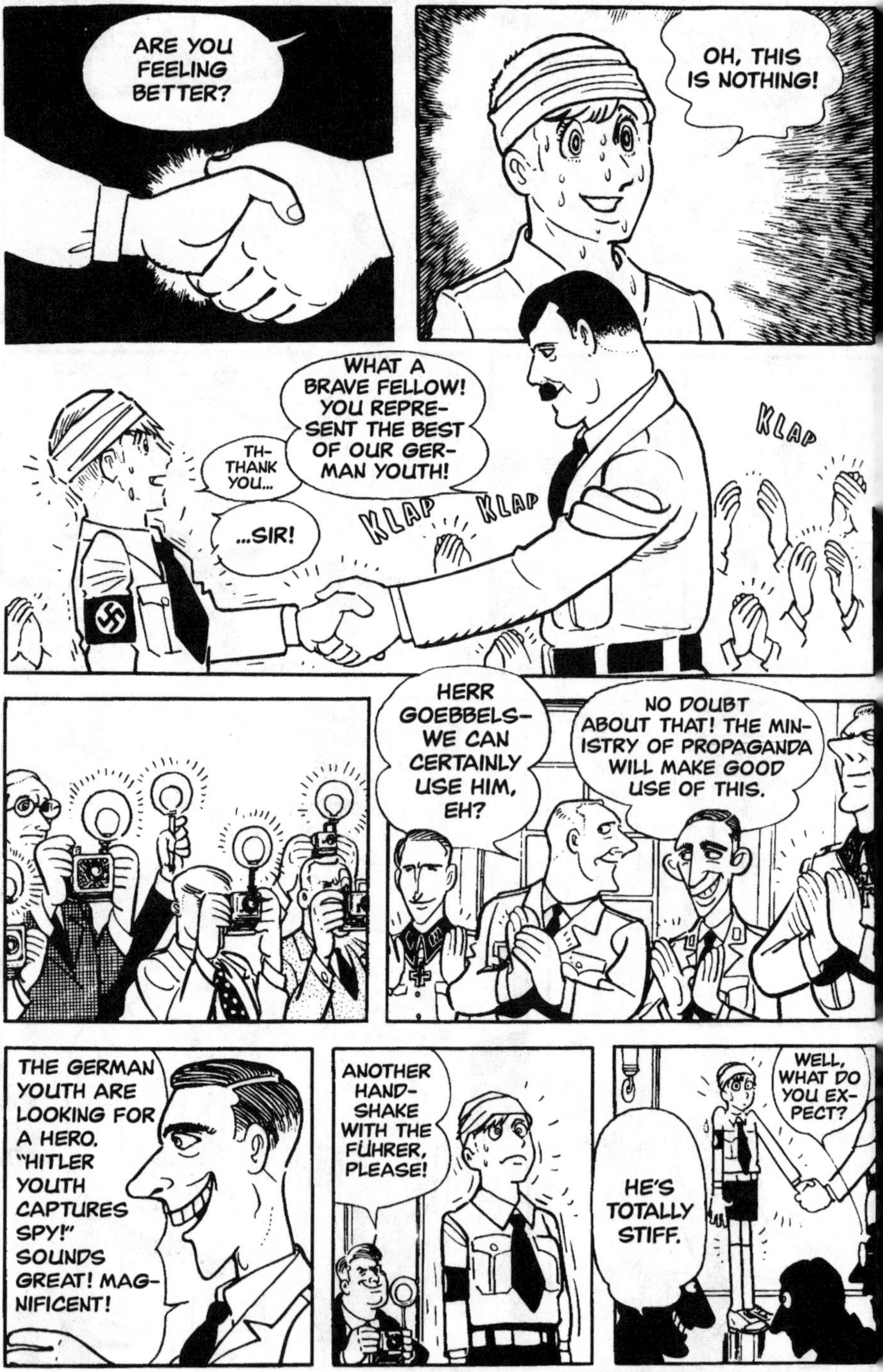
ARE YOU FEELING BETTER?
OH, THIS IS NOTHING!
TH- THANK YOU...
WHAT A BRAVE FELLOW! YOU REPRESENT THE BEST OF OUR GERMAN YOUTH!
...SIR!
KLAP
KLAP
KLAP
HERR GOEBBELS- WE CAN CERTAINLY USE HIM, EH?
NO DOUBT ABOUT THAT! THE MINISTRY OF PROPAGANDA WILL MAKE GOOD USE OF THIS.
THE GERMAN YOUTH ARE LOOKING FOR A HERO. "HITLER YOUTH CAPTURES SPY!" SOUNDS GREAT! MAGNIFICENT!
ANOTHER HANDSHAKE WITH THE FÜHRER, PLEASE!
HE'S TOTALLY STIFF.
WELL, WHAT DO YOU EXPECT?

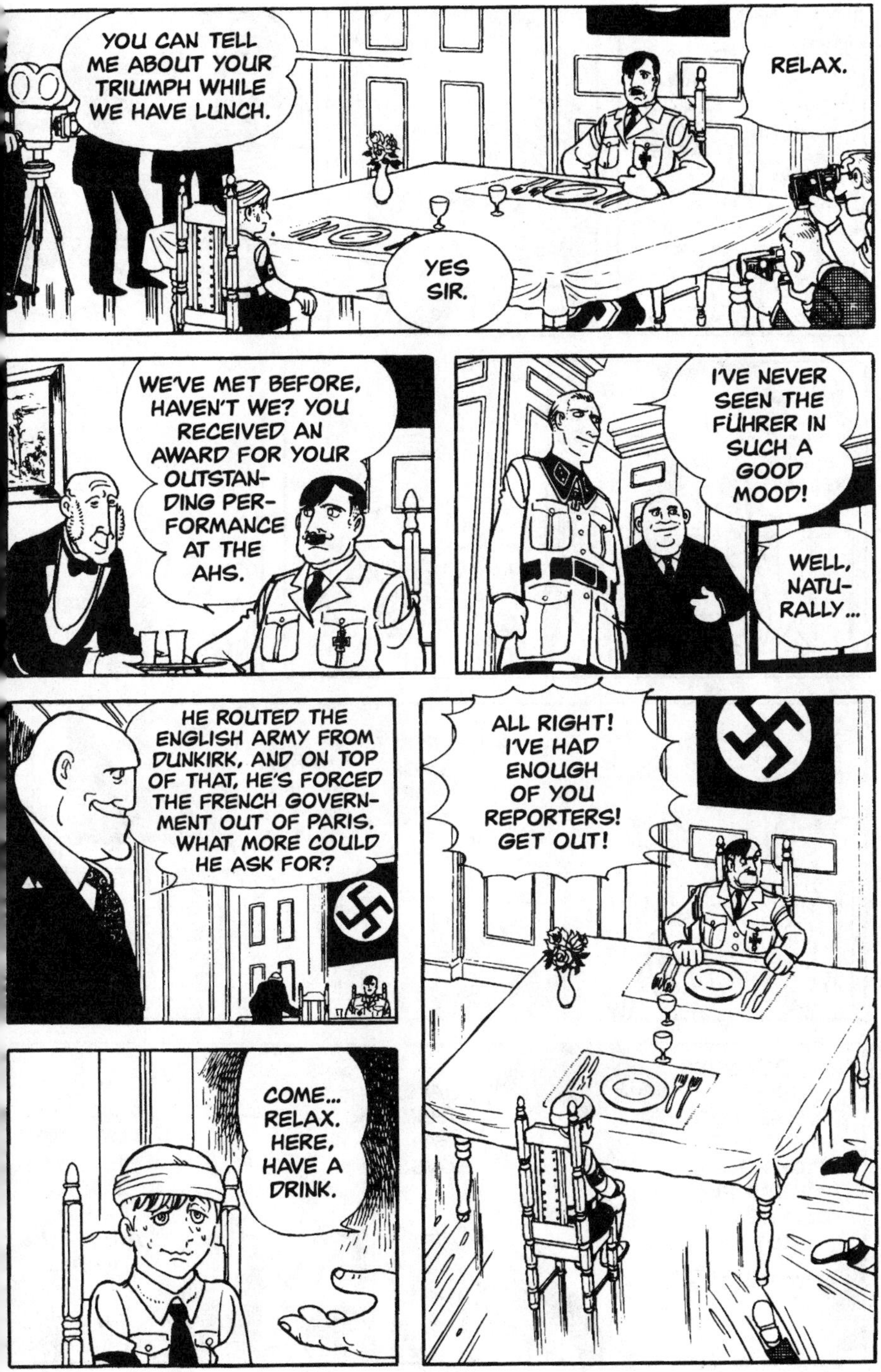
YOU CAN TELL ME ABOUT YOUR TRIUMPH WHILE WE HAVE LUNCH.
RELAX.
YES SIR.
WE'VE MET BEFORE, HAVEN'T WE? YOU RECEIVED AN AWARD FOR YOUR OUTSTAND-ING PER-FORMANCE AT THE AHS.
I'VE NEVER SEEN THE FÜHRER IN SUCH A GOOD MOOD!
WELL, NATU-RALLY...
HE ROUTED THE ENGLISH ARMY FROM DUNKIRK, AND ON TOP OF THAT, HE'S FORCED THE FRENCH GOVERN-MENT OUT OF PARIS. WHAT MORE COULD HE ASK FOR?
ALL RIGHT! I'VE HAD ENOUGH OF YOU REPORTERS! GET OUT!
COME... RELAX. HERE, HAVE A DRINK.

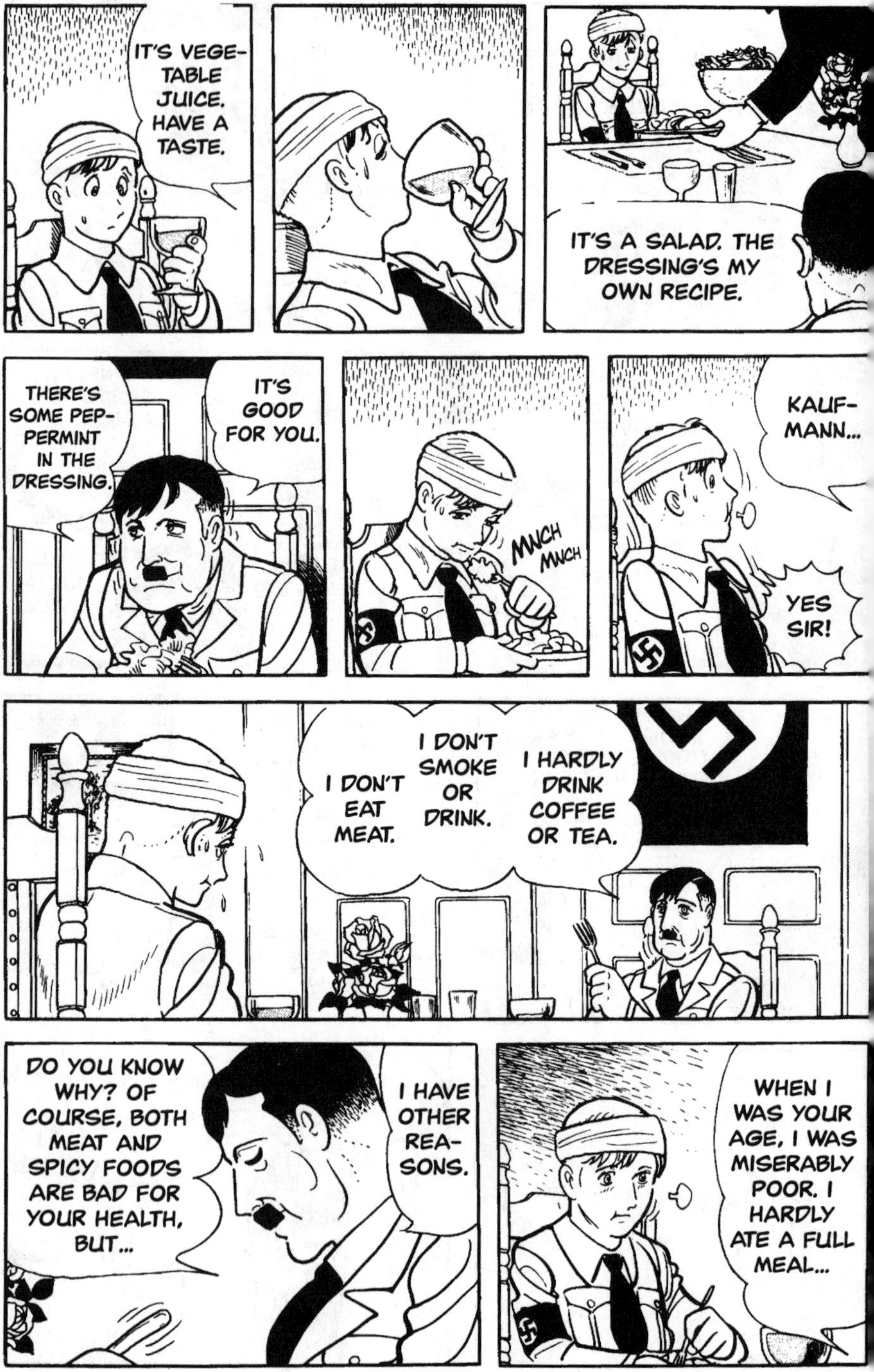
IT'S VEGE-TABLE JUICE. HAVE A TASTE.
IT'S A SALAD. THE DRESSING'S MY OWN RECIPE.
THERE'S SOME PEP-PERMINT IN THE DRESSING.
IT'S GOOD FOR YOU.
MNCH MNCH
KAUF-MANN...
YES SIR!
I DON'T EAT MEAT.
I DON'T SMOKE OR DRINK.
I HARDLY DRINK COFFEE OR TEA.
DO YOU KNOW WHY? OF COURSE, BOTH MEAT AND SPICY FOODS ARE BAD FOR YOUR HEALTH, BUT...
I HAVE OTHER REA-SONS.
WHEN I WAS YOUR AGE, I WAS MISERABLY POOR. I HARDLY ATE A FULL MEAL...

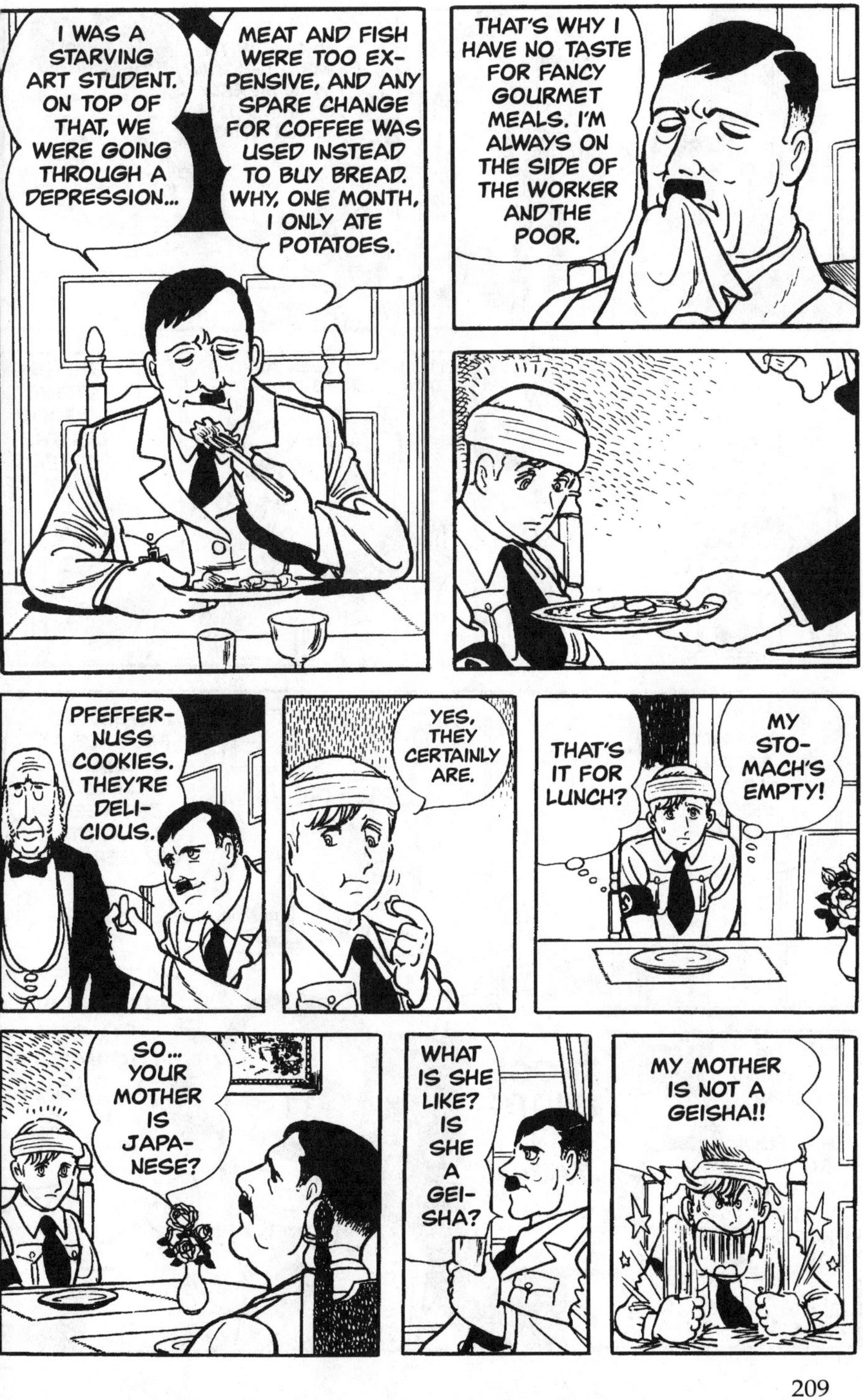
I WAS A STARVING ART STUDENT. ON TOP OF THAT, WE WERE GOING THROUGH A DEPRESSION...
MEAT AND FISH WERE TOO EX-PENSIVE, AND ANY SPARE CHANGE FOR COFFEE WAS USED INSTEAD TO BUY BREAD. WHY, ONE MONTH, I ONLY ATE POTATOES.
THAT'S WHY I HAVE NO TASTE FOR FANCY GOURMET MEALS. I'M ALWAYS ON THE SIDE OF THE WORKER AND THE POOR.
PFEFFER-NUSS COOKIES. THEY'RE DELI-CIOUS.
YES, THEY CERTAINLY ARE.
THAT'S IT FOR LUNCH?
MY STO-MACH'S EMPTY!
SO... YOUR MOTHER IS JAPA-NESE?
WHAT IS SHE LIKE? IS SHE A GEI-SHA?
MY MOTHER IS NOT A GEISHA!!

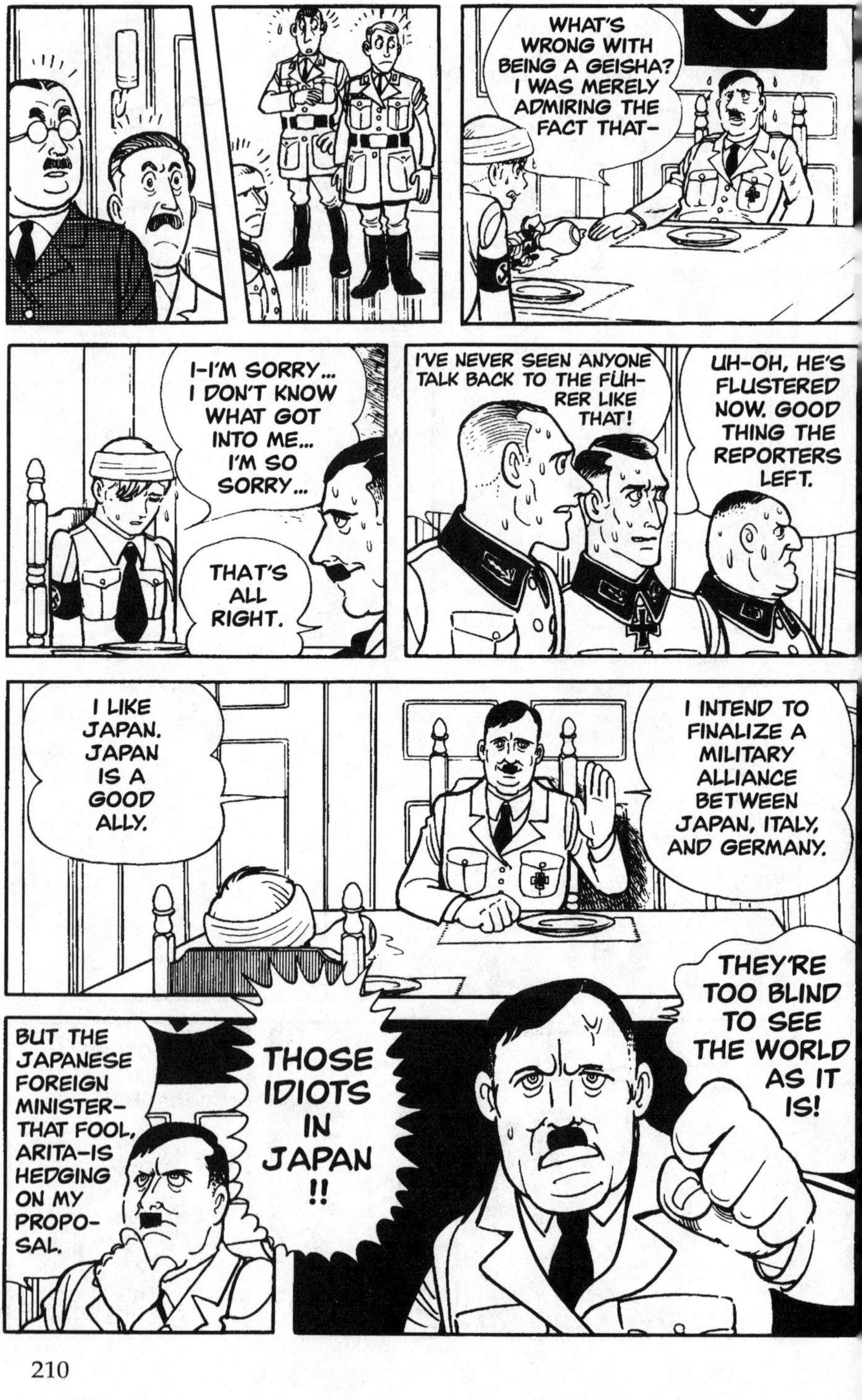
WHAT'S WRONG WITH BEING A GEISHA? I WAS MERELY ADMIRING THE FACT THAT-
I-I'M SORRY... I DON'T KNOW WHAT GOT INTO ME... I'M SO SORRY...
THAT'S ALL RIGHT.
I'VE NEVER SEEN ANYONE TALK BACK TO THE FÜHRER LIKE THAT!
UH-OH, HE'S FLUSTERED NOW. GOOD THING THE REPORTERS LEFT.
I LIKE JAPAN. JAPAN IS A GOOD ALLY.
I INTEND TO FINALIZE A MILITARY ALLIANCE BETWEEN JAPAN, ITALY, AND GERMANY.
BUT THE JAPANESE FOREIGN MINISTER- THAT FOOL, ARITA-IS HEDGING ON MY PROPOSAL.
THOSE IDIOTS IN JAPAN !!
THEY'RE TOO BLIND TO SEE THE WORLD AS IT IS!

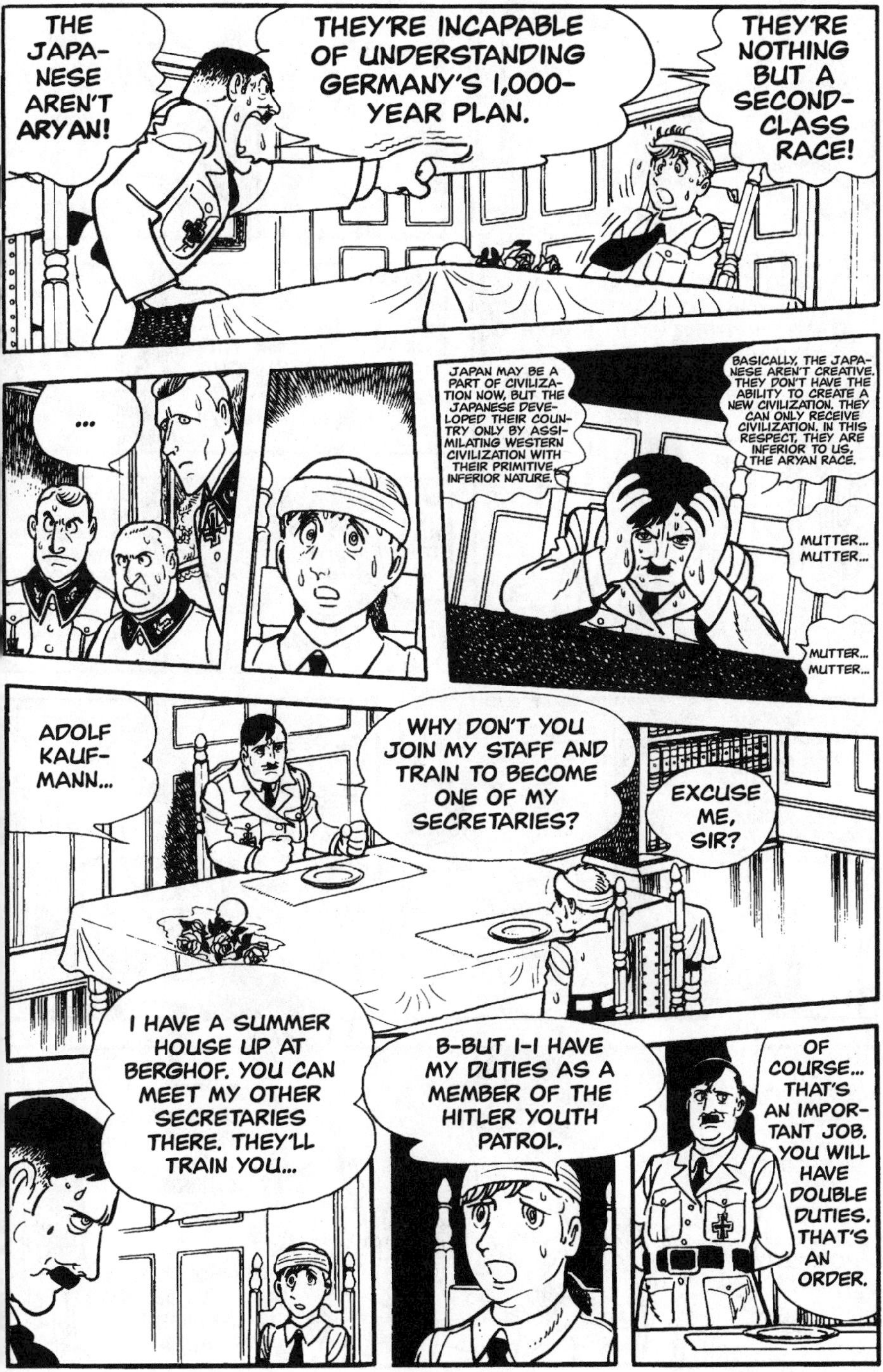
THE JAPANESE AREN'T ARYAN!
THEY'RE INCAPABLE OF UNDERSTANDING GERMANY'S 1,000-YEAR PLAN.
THEY'RE NOTHING BUT A SECOND-CLASS RACE!
...
JAPAN MAY BE A PART OF CIVILIZATION NOW, BUT THE JAPANESE DEVELOPED THEIR COUNTRY ONLY BY ASSIMILATING WESTERN CIVILIZATION WITH THEIR PRIMITIVE INFERIOR NATURE.
BASICALLY, THE JAPANESE AREN'T CREATIVE. THEY DON'T HAVE THE ABILITY TO CREATE A NEW CIVILIZATION. THEY CAN ONLY RECEIVE CIVILIZATION. IN THIS RESPECT, THEY ARE INFERIOR TO US, THE ARYAN RACE.
MUTTER... MUTTER...
MUTTER... MUTTER...
ADOLF KAUFMANN...
WHY DON'T YOU JOIN MY STAFF AND TRAIN TO BECOME ONE OF MY SECRETARIES?
EXCUSE ME, SIR?
I HAVE A SUMMER HOUSE UP AT BERGHOF. YOU CAN MEET MY OTHER SECRETARIES THERE. THEY'LL TRAIN YOU...
B-BUT I-I HAVE MY DUTIES AS A MEMBER OF THE HITLER YOUTH PATROL.
OF COURSE... THAT'S AN IMPORTANT JOB. YOU WILL HAVE DOUBLE DUTIES. THAT'S AN ORDER.

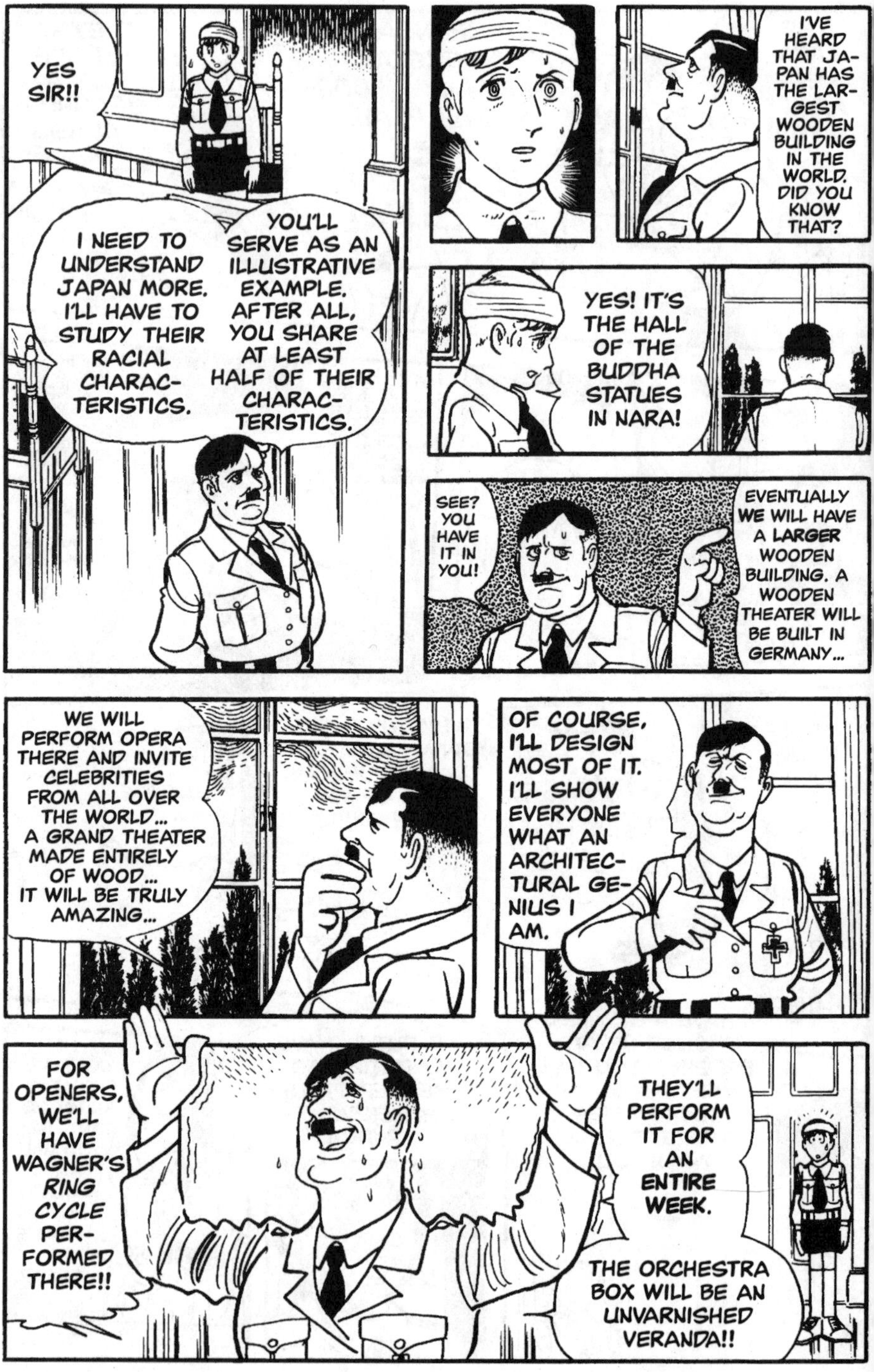

YES SIR!!
I NEED TO UNDERSTAND JAPAN MORE. I'LL HAVE TO STUDY THEIR RACIAL CHARAC-TERISTICS.
YOU'LL SERVE AS AN ILLUSTRATIVE EXAMPLE. AFTER ALL, YOU SHARE AT LEAST HALF OF THEIR CHARAC-TERISTICS.
I'VE HEARD THAT JA-PAN HAS THE LAR-GEST WOODEN BUILDING IN THE WORLD. DID YOU KNOW THAT?
YES! IT'S THE HALL OF THE BUDDHA STATUES IN NARA!
SEE? YOU HAVE IT IN YOU!
EVENTUALLY WE WILL HAVE A LARGER WOODEN BUILDING. A WOODEN THEATER WILL BE BUILT IN GERMANY...
WE WILL PERFORM OPERA THERE AND INVITE CELEBRITIES FROM ALL OVER THE WORLD... A GRAND THEATER MADE ENTIRELY OF WOOD... IT WILL BE TRULY AMAZING...
OF COURSE, I'LL DESIGN MOST OF IT. I'LL SHOW EVERYONE WHAT AN ARCHITEC-TURAL GE-NIUS I AM.
FOR OPENERS, WE'LL HAVE WAGNER'S RING CYCLE PER-FORMED THERE!!
THEY'LL PERFORM IT FOR AN ENTIRE WEEK.
THE ORCHESTRA BOX WILL BE AN UNVARNISHED VERANDA!!

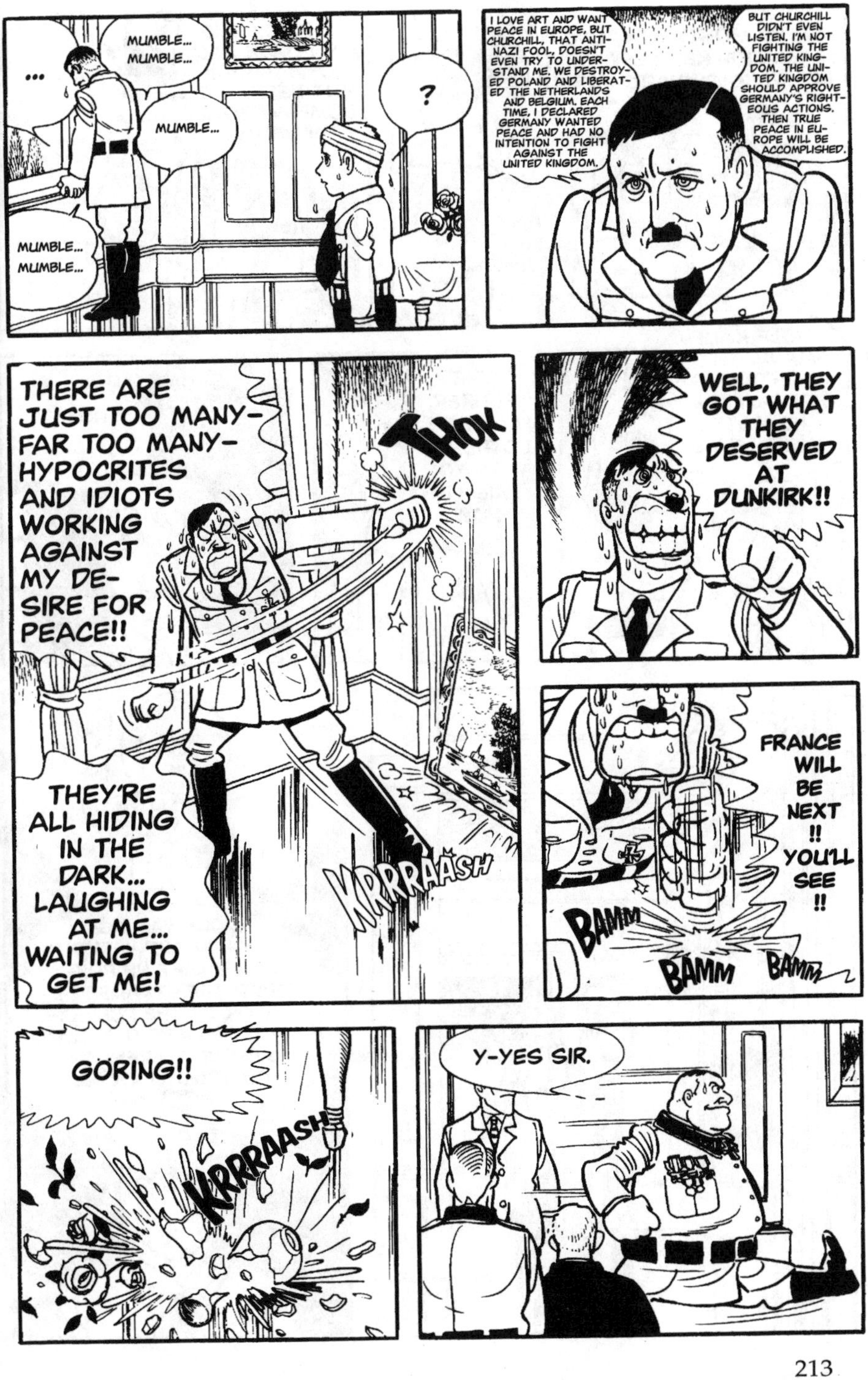
...
MUMBLE... MUMBLE...
MUMBLE...
MUMBLE... MUMBLE...
?
I LOVE ART AND WANT PEACE IN EUROPE, BUT CHURCHILL, THAT ANTI-NAZI FOOL, DOESN'T EVEN TRY TO UNDERSTAND ME. WE DESTROYED POLAND AND LIBERATED THE NETHERLANDS AND BELGIUM. EACH TIME, I DECLARED GERMANY WANTED PEACE AND HAD NO INTENTION TO FIGHT AGAINST THE UNITED KINGDOM.
BUT CHURCHILL DIDN'T EVEN LISTEN. I'M NOT FIGHTING THE UNITED KINGDOM. THE UNITED KINGDOM SHOULD APPROVE GERMANY'S RIGHTEOUS ACTIONS. THEN TRUE PEACE IN EUROPE WILL BE ACCOMPLISHED.
THERE ARE JUST TOO MANY-FAR TOO MANY-HYPOCRITES AND IDIOTS WORKING AGAINST MY DESIRE FOR PEACE!!
THOK
THEY'RE ALL HIDING IN THE DARK... LAUGHING AT ME... WAITING TO GET ME!
KRRRAASH
WELL, THEY GOT WHAT THEY DESERVED AT DUNKIRK!!
FRANCE WILL BE NEXT!! YOU'LL SEE!!
BAMM
BAMM
BAMM
GÖRING!!
KRRRAASH
Y-YES SIR.

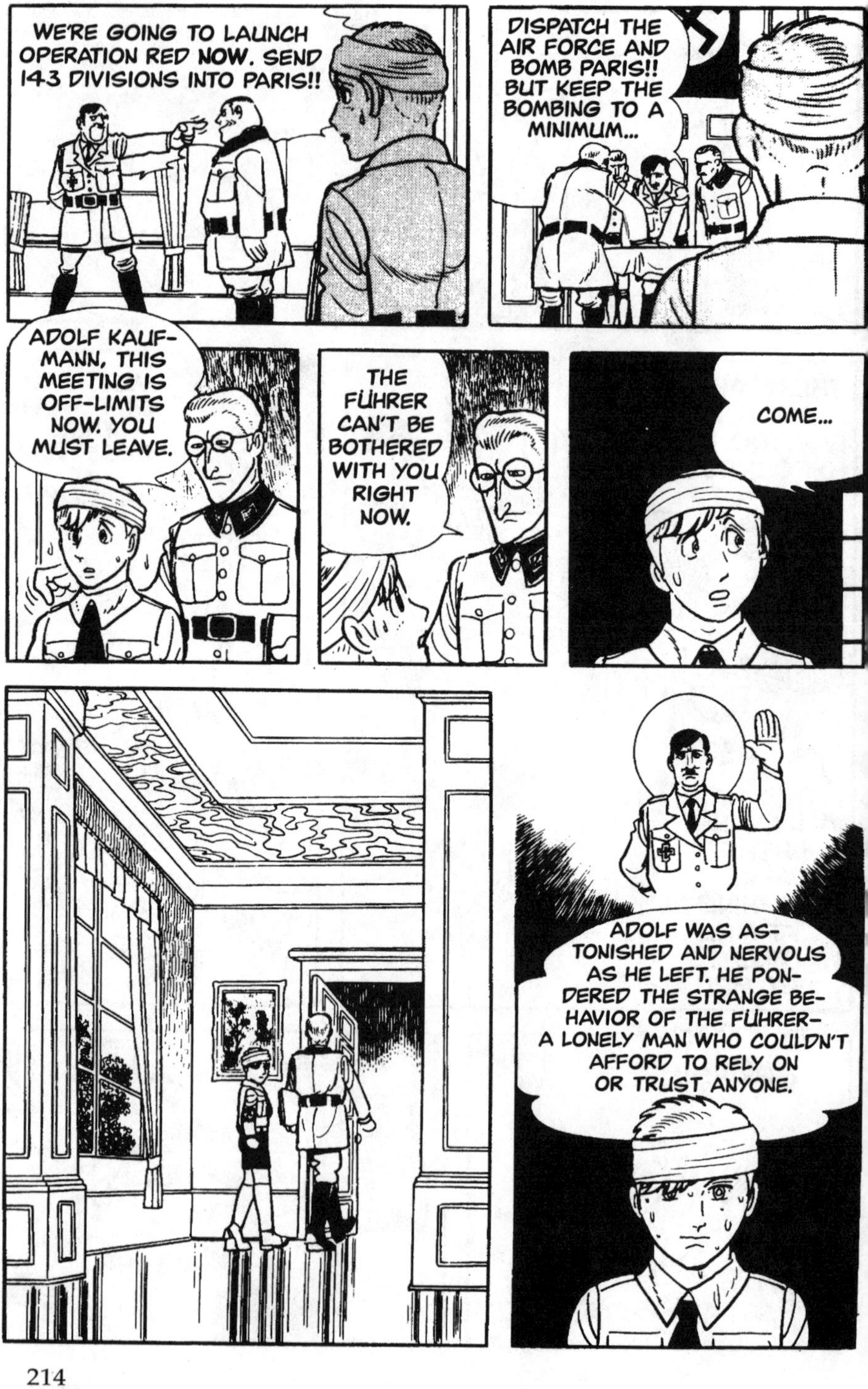
WE'RE GOING TO LAUNCH OPERATION RED NOW. SEND 143 DIVISIONS INTO PARIS!!
DISPATCH THE AIR FORCE AND BOMB PARIS!! BUT KEEP THE BOMBING TO A MINIMUM...
ADOLF KAUFMANN, THIS MEETING IS OFF-LIMITS NOW. YOU MUST LEAVE.
THE FÜHRER CAN'T BE BOTHERED WITH YOU RIGHT NOW.
COME...
ADOLF WAS ASTONISHED AND NERVOUS AS HE LEFT. HE PONDERED THE STRANGE BEHAVIOR OF THE FÜHRER–A LONELY MAN WHO COULDN'T AFFORD TO RELY ON OR TRUST ANYONE.

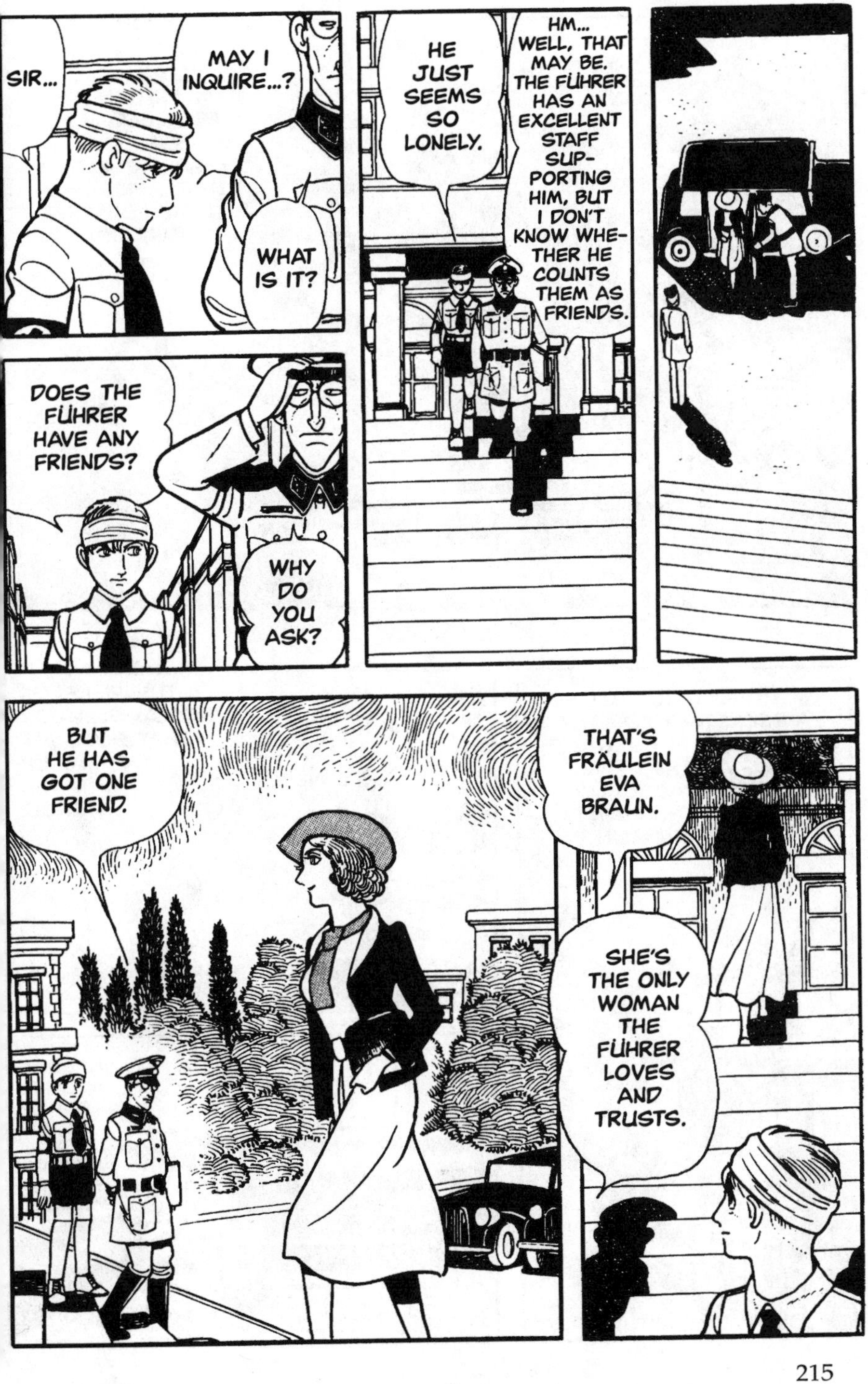
SIR...
MAY I INQUIRE...?
WHAT IS IT?
DOES THE FÜHRER HAVE ANY FRIENDS?
WHY DO YOU ASK?
HE JUST SEEMS SO LONELY.
HM... WELL, THAT MAY BE. THE FÜHRER HAS AN EXCELLENT STAFF SUP-PORTING HIM, BUT I DON'T KNOW WHE-THER HE COUNTS THEM AS FRIENDS.
BUT HE HAS GOT ONE FRIEND.
THAT'S FRÄULEIN EVA BRAUN.
SHE'S THE ONLY WOMAN THE FÜHRER LOVES AND TRUSTS.

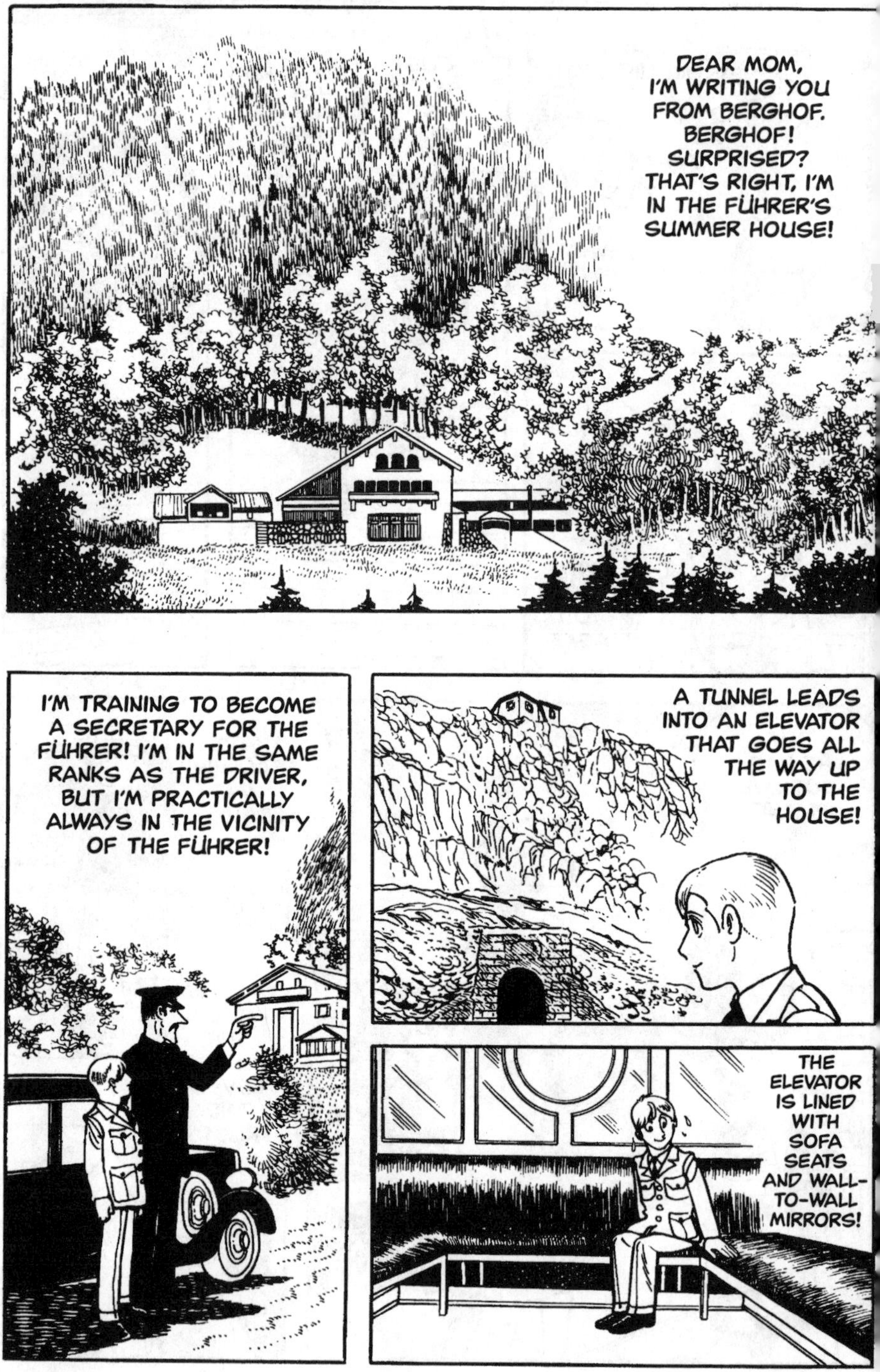
DEAR MOM, I'M WRITING YOU FROM BERGHOF. BERGHOF! SURPRISED? THAT'S RIGHT, I'M IN THE FÜHRER'S SUMMER HOUSE!
I'M TRAINING TO BECOME A SECRETARY FOR THE FÜHRER! I'M IN THE SAME RANKS AS THE DRIVER, BUT I'M PRACTICALLY ALWAYS IN THE VICINITY OF THE FÜHRER!
A TUNNEL LEADS INTO AN ELEVATOR THAT GOES ALL THE WAY UP TO THE HOUSE!
THE ELEVATOR IS LINED WITH SOFA SEATS AND WALL-TO-WALL MIRRORS!

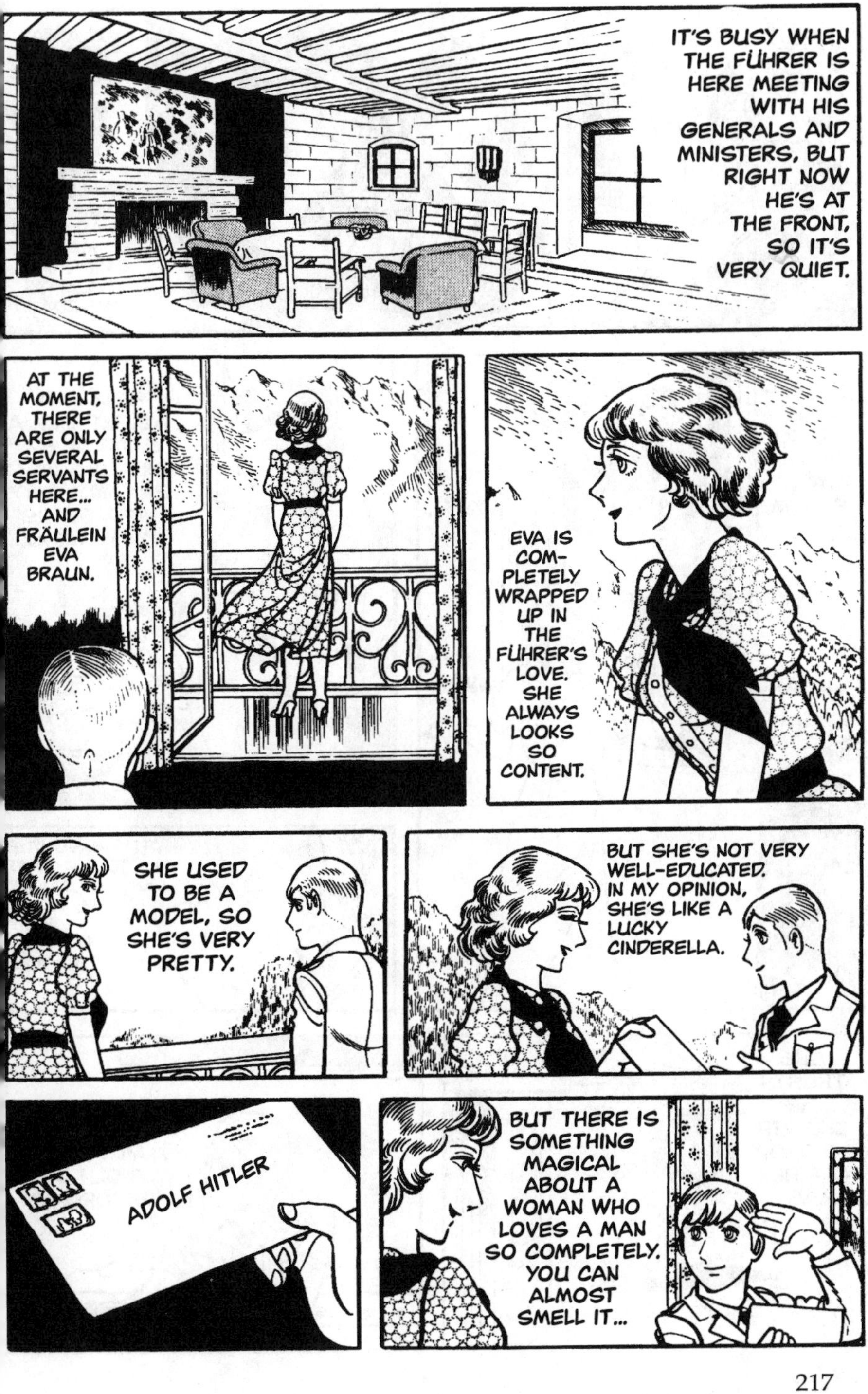
IT'S BUSY WHEN THE FÜHRER IS HERE MEETING WITH HIS GENERALS AND MINISTERS, BUT RIGHT NOW HE'S AT THE FRONT, SO IT'S VERY QUIET.
AT THE MOMENT, THERE ARE ONLY SEVERAL SERVANTS HERE... AND FRÄULEIN EVA BRAUN.
EVA IS COMPLETELY WRAPPED UP IN THE FÜHRER'S LOVE. SHE ALWAYS LOOKS SO CONTENT.
SHE USED TO BE A MODEL, SO SHE'S VERY PRETTY.
BUT SHE'S NOT VERY WELL-EDUCATED. IN MY OPINION, SHE'S LIKE A LUCKY CINDERELLA.
ADOLF HITLER
BUT THERE IS SOMETHING MAGICAL ABOUT A WOMAN WHO LOVES A MAN SO COMPLETELY. YOU CAN ALMOST SMELL IT...

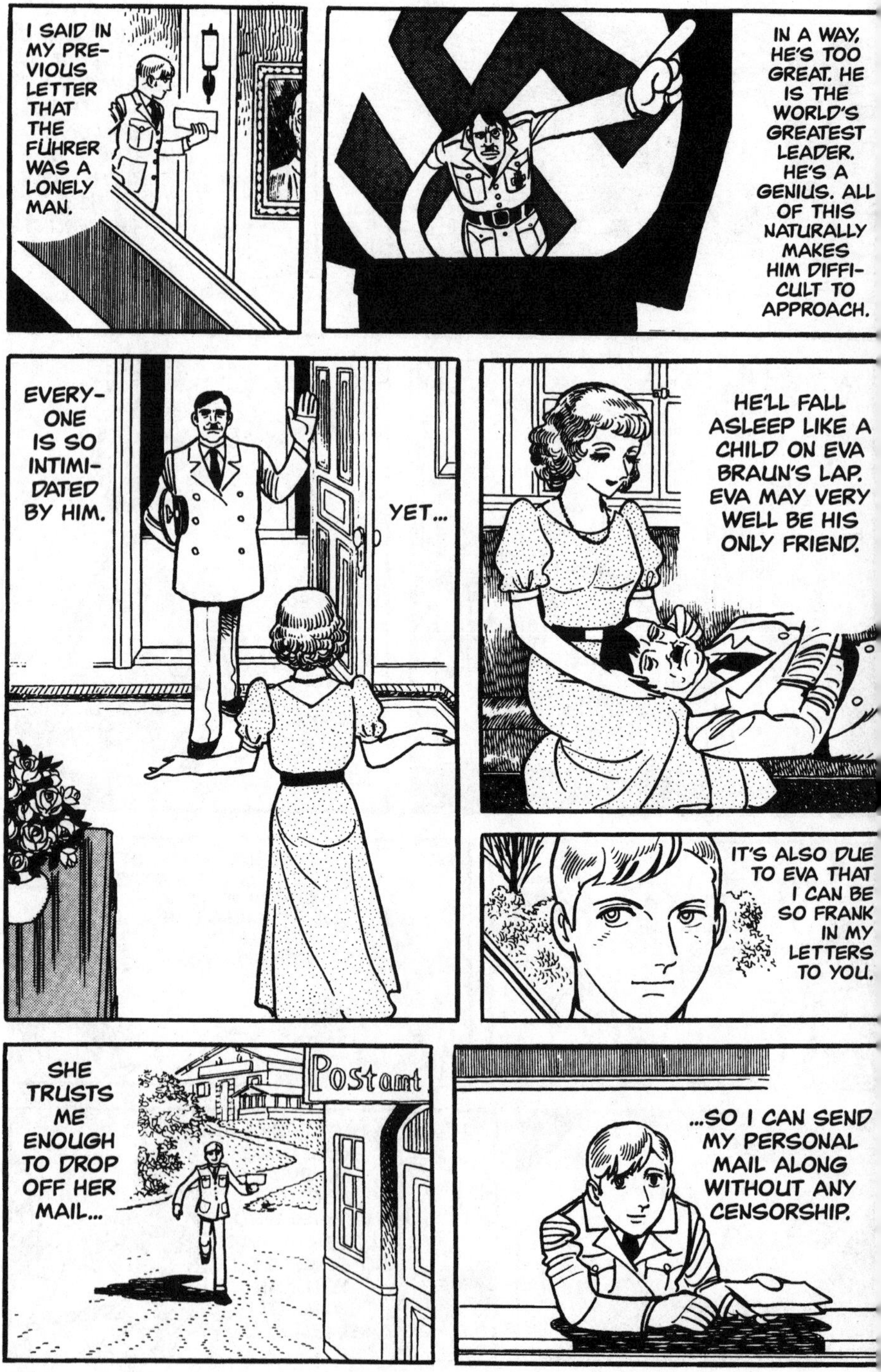
I SAID IN MY PREVIOUS LETTER THAT THE FÜHRER WAS A LONELY MAN.
IN A WAY, HE'S TOO GREAT. HE IS THE WORLD'S GREATEST LEADER. HE'S A GENIUS. ALL OF THIS NATURALLY MAKES HIM DIFFICULT TO APPROACH.
EVERYONE IS SO INTIMIDATED BY HIM.
YET...
HE'LL FALL ASLEEP LIKE A CHILD ON EVA BRAUN'S LAP. EVA MAY VERY WELL BE HIS ONLY FRIEND.
IT'S ALSO DUE TO EVA THAT I CAN BE SO FRANK IN MY LETTERS TO YOU.
SHE TRUSTS ME ENOUGH TO DROP OFF HER MAIL...
Postamt
...SO I CAN SEND MY PERSONAL MAIL ALONG WITHOUT ANY CENSORSHIP.

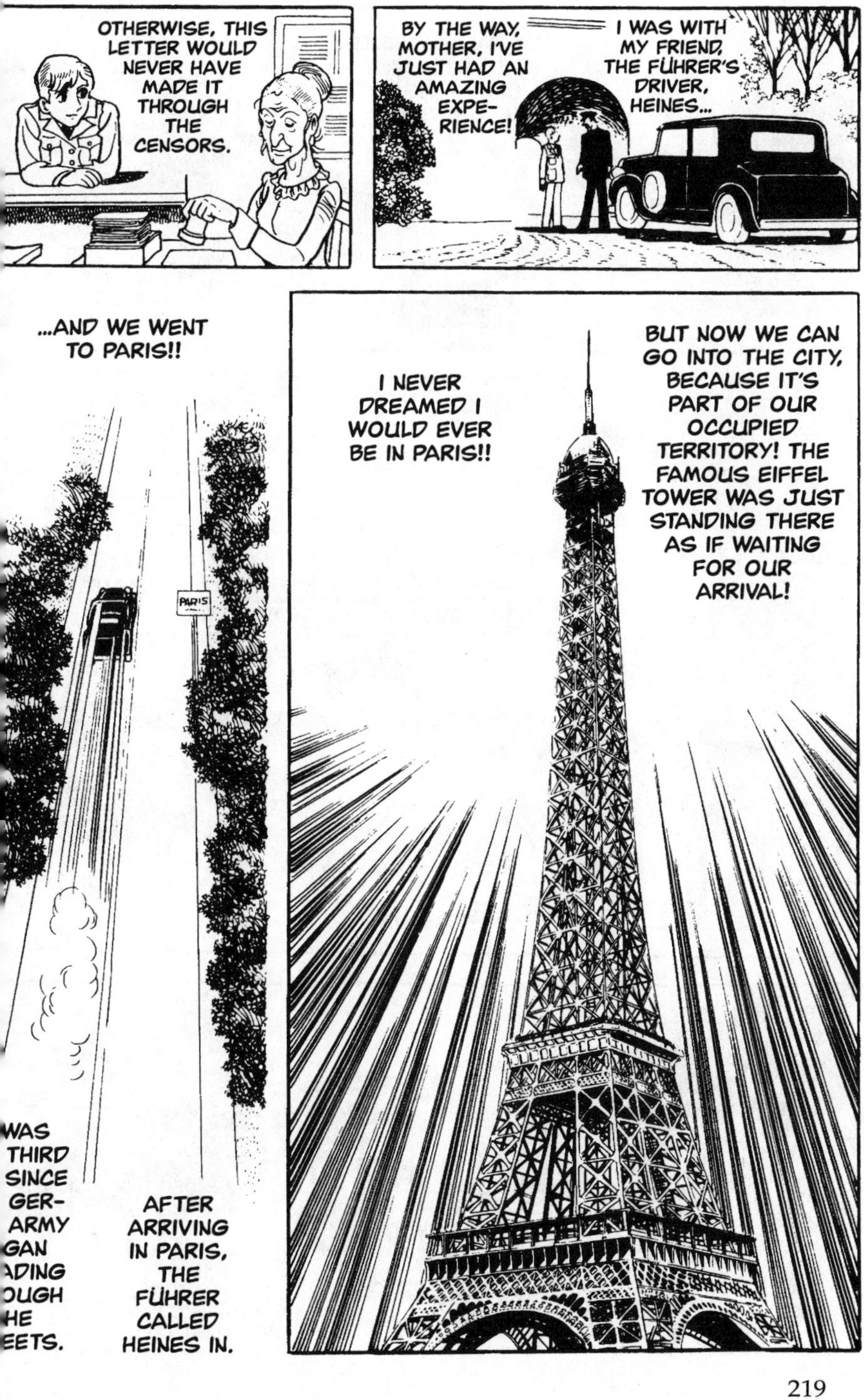
OTHERWISE, THIS LETTER WOULD NEVER HAVE MADE IT THROUGH THE CENSORS.
BY THE WAY, MOTHER, I'VE JUST HAD AN AMAZING EXPE- RIENCE!
I WAS WITH MY FRIEND, THE FÜHRER'S DRIVER, HEINES...
...AND WE WENT TO PARIS!!
PARIS
WAS THIRD SINCE GER- ARMY GAN DING OUGH HE EETS.
AFTER ARRIVING IN PARIS, THE FÜHRER CALLED HEINES IN.
I NEVER DREAMED I WOULD EVER BE IN PARIS!!
BUT NOW WE CAN GO INTO THE CITY, BECAUSE IT'S PART OF OUR OCCUPIED TERRITORY! THE FAMOUS EIFFEL TOWER WAS JUST STANDING THERE AS IF WAITING FOR OUR ARRIVAL!

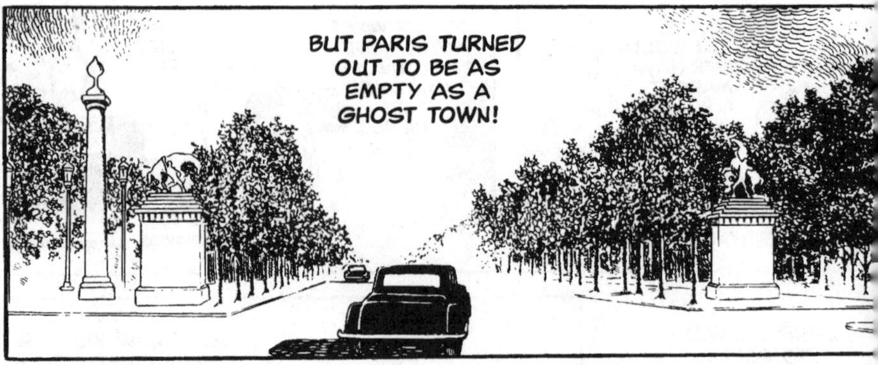
BUT PARIS TURNED OUT TO BE AS EMPTY AS A GHOST TOWN!

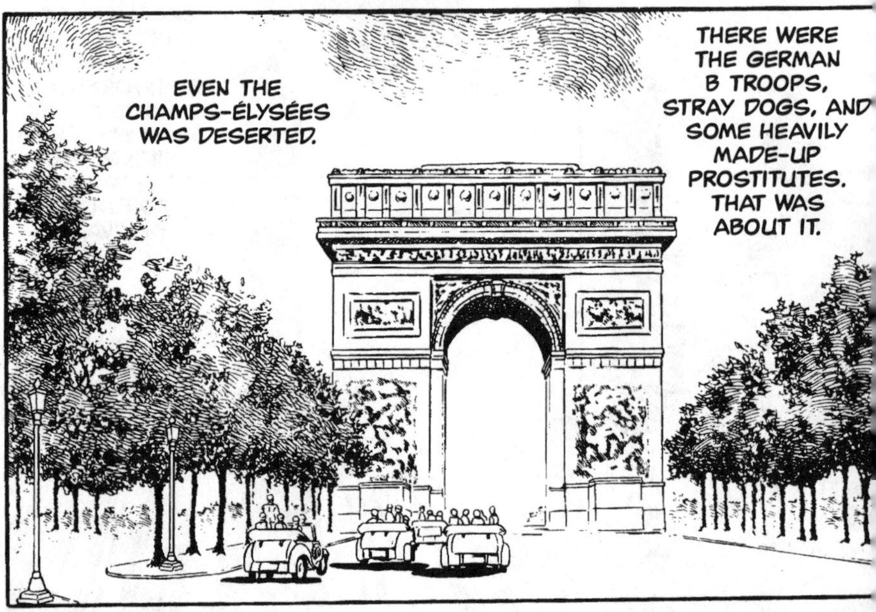
EVEN THE CHAMPS-ÉLYSÉES WAS DESERTED.
THERE WERE THE GERMAN B TROOPS, STRAY DOGS, AND SOME HEAVILY MADE-UP PROSTITUTES. THAT WAS ABOUT IT.

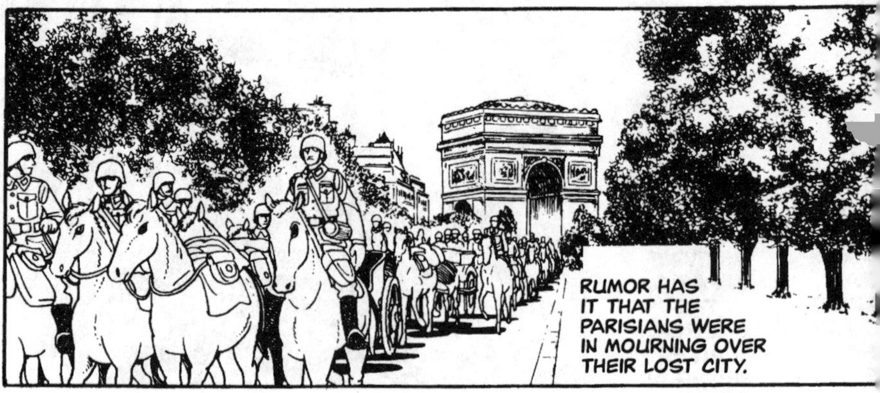
RUMOR HAS IT THAT THE PARISIANS WERE IN MOURNING OVER THEIR LOST CITY.

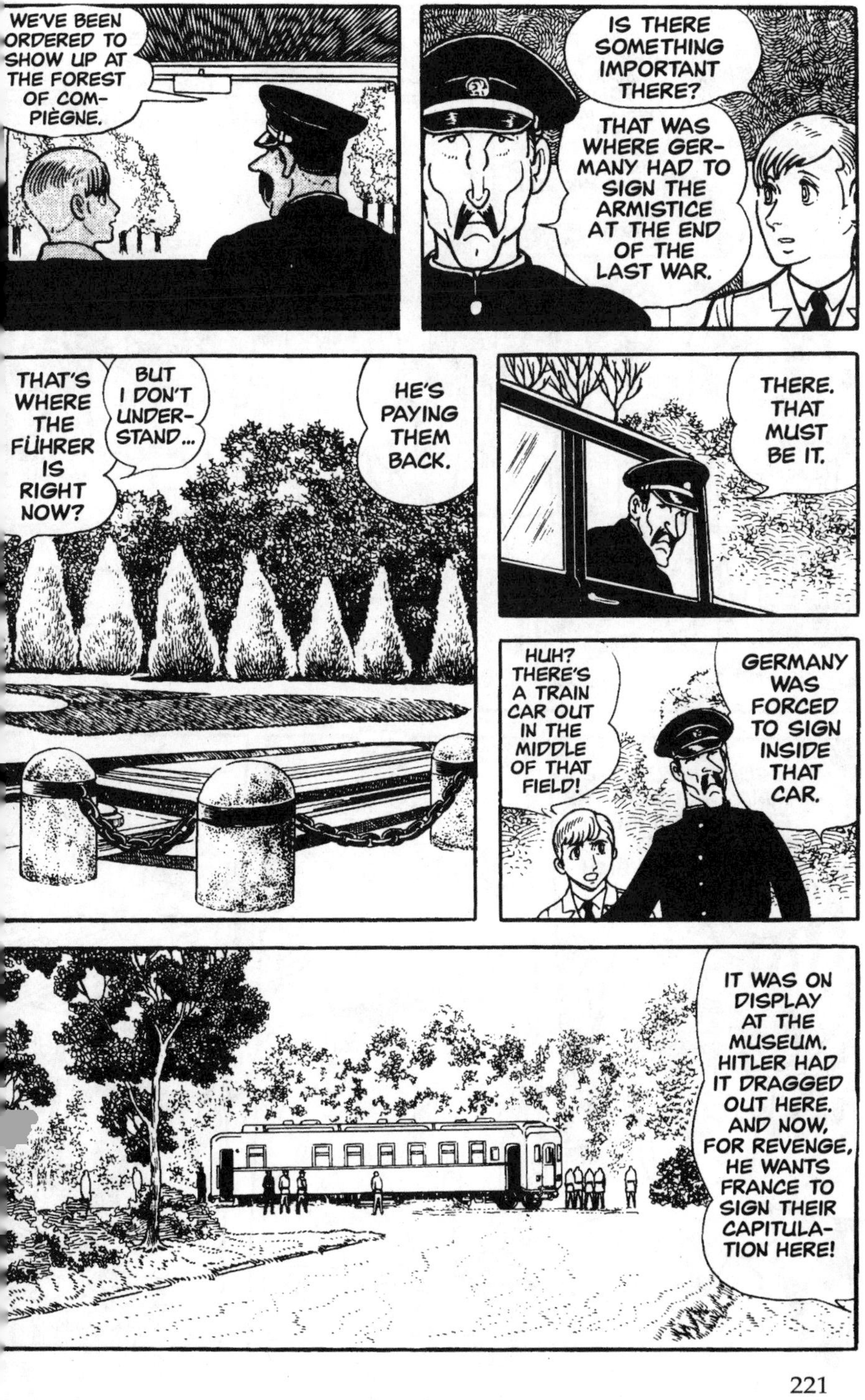
WE'VE BEEN ORDERED TO SHOW UP AT THE FOREST OF COMPIÈGNE.
IS THERE SOMETHING IMPORTANT THERE?
THAT WAS WHERE GERMANY HAD TO SIGN THE ARMISTICE AT THE END OF THE LAST WAR.
THAT'S WHERE THE FÜHRER IS RIGHT NOW?
BUT I DON'T UNDERSTAND...
HE'S PAYING THEM BACK.
THERE. THAT MUST BE IT.
HUH? THERE'S A TRAIN CAR OUT IN THE MIDDLE OF THAT FIELD!
GERMANY WAS FORCED TO SIGN INSIDE THAT CAR.
IT WAS ON DISPLAY AT THE MUSEUM. HITLER HAD IT DRAGGED OUT HERE. AND NOW, FOR REVENGE, HE WANTS FRANCE TO SIGN THEIR CAPITULATION HERE!

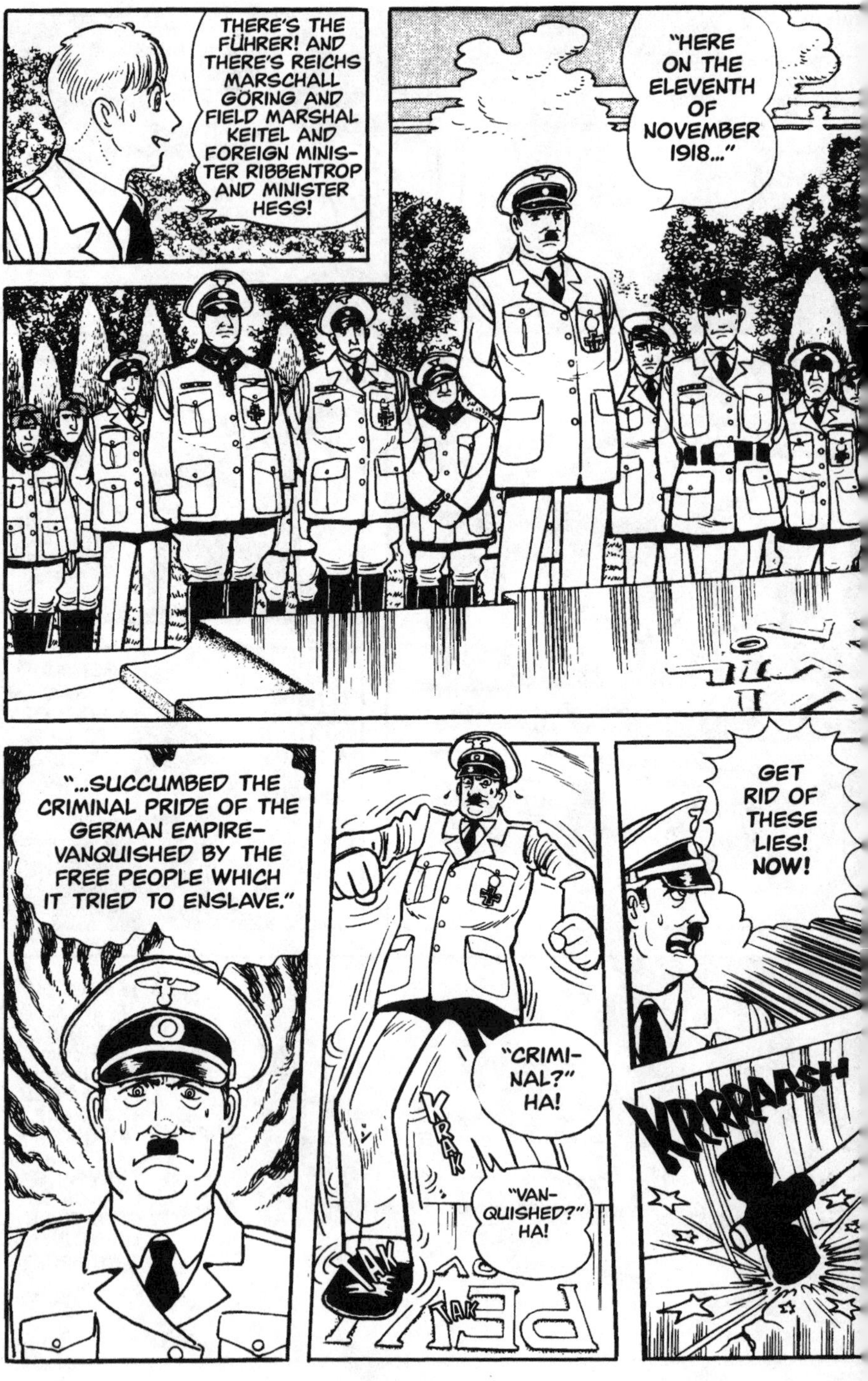
THERE'S THE FÜHRER! AND THERE'S REICHS MARSCHALL GÖRING AND FIELD MARSHAL KEITEL AND FOREIGN MINISTER RIBBENTROP AND MINISTER HESS!
"HERE ON THE ELEVENTH OF NOVEMBER 1918..."
"...SUCCUMBED THE CRIMINAL PRIDE OF THE GERMAN EMPIRE– VANQUISHED BY THE FREE PEOPLE WHICH IT TRIED TO ENSLAVE."
"CRIMINAL?" HA!
KRAK
"VANQUISHED?" HA!
TAK
TAK
GET RID OF THESE LIES! NOW!
KRRRAASH

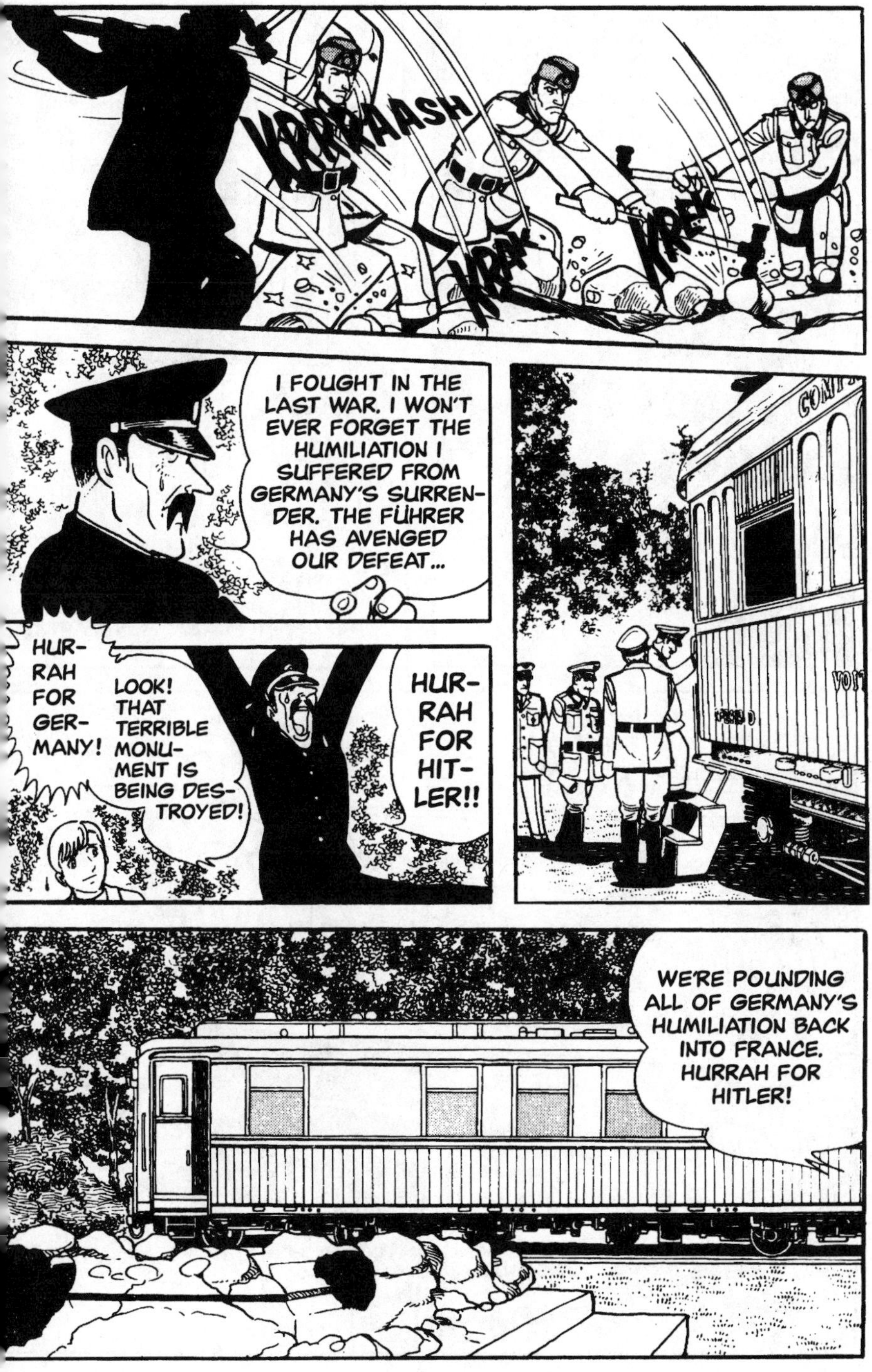
KRRRAASH
KRAK
KREK
I FOUGHT IN THE LAST WAR. I WON'T EVER FORGET THE HUMILIATION I SUFFERED FROM GERMANY'S SURRENDER. THE FÜHRER HAS AVENGED OUR DEFEAT...
HURRAH FOR GERMANY!
LOOK! THAT TERRIBLE MONUMENT IS BEING DESTROYED!
HURRAH FOR HITLER!!
WE'RE POUNDING ALL OF GERMANY'S HUMILIATION BACK INTO FRANCE. HURRAH FOR HITLER!

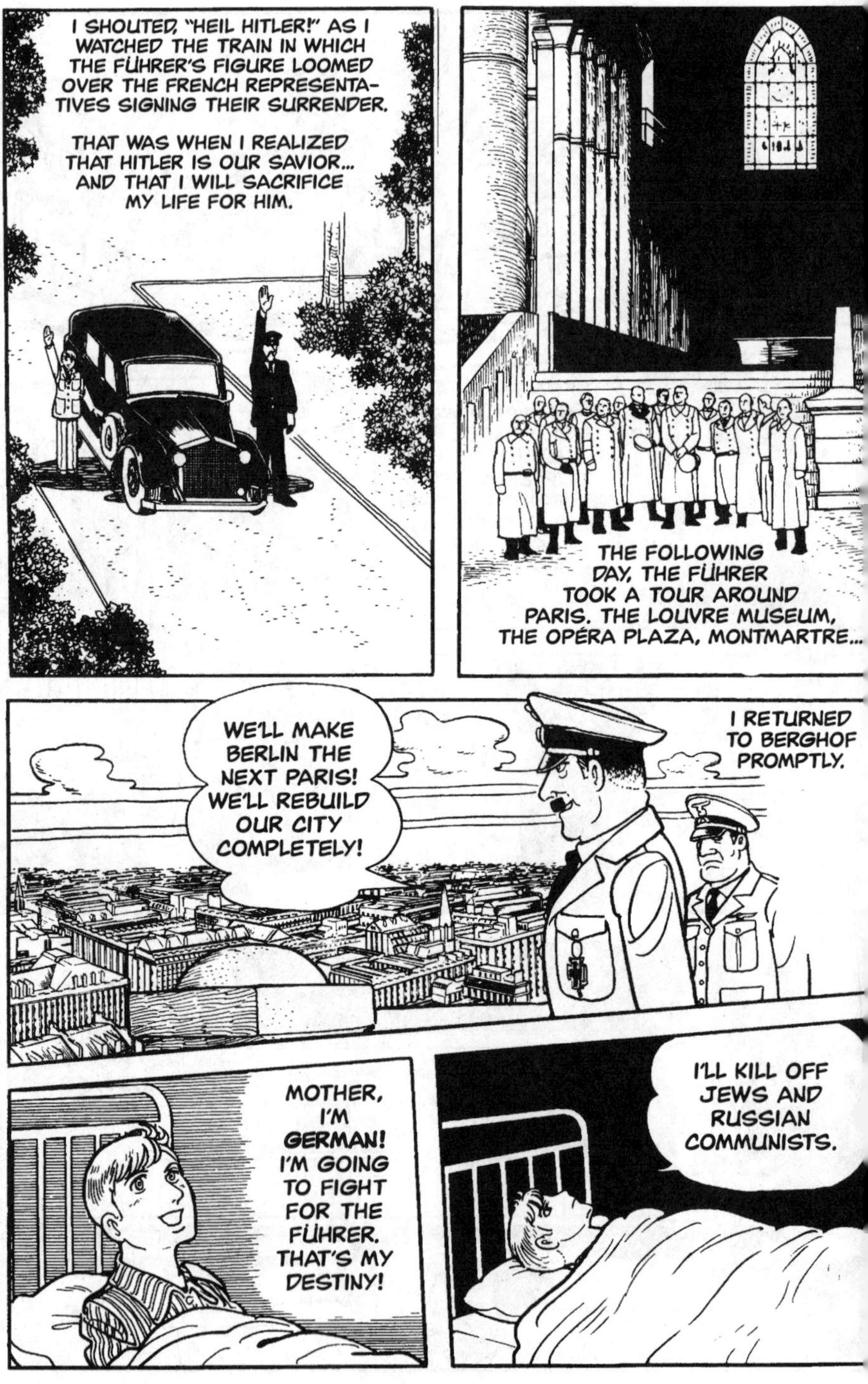
I SHOUTED, "HEIL HITLER!" AS I WATCHED THE TRAIN IN WHICH THE FÜHRER'S FIGURE LOOMED OVER THE FRENCH REPRESENTATIVES SIGNING THEIR SURRENDER.
THAT WAS WHEN I REALIZED THAT HITLER IS OUR SAVIOR... AND THAT I WILL SACRIFICE MY LIFE FOR HIM.
THE FOLLOWING DAY, THE FÜHRER TOOK A TOUR AROUND PARIS. THE LOUVRE MUSEUM, THE OPÉRA PLAZA, MONTMARTRE...
WE'LL MAKE BERLIN THE NEXT PARIS! WE'LL REBUILD OUR CITY COMPLETELY!
I RETURNED TO BERGHOF PROMPTLY.
MOTHER, I'M GERMAN! I'M GOING TO FIGHT FOR THE FÜHRER. THAT'S MY DESTINY!
I'LL KILL OFF JEWS AND RUSSIAN COMMUNISTS.

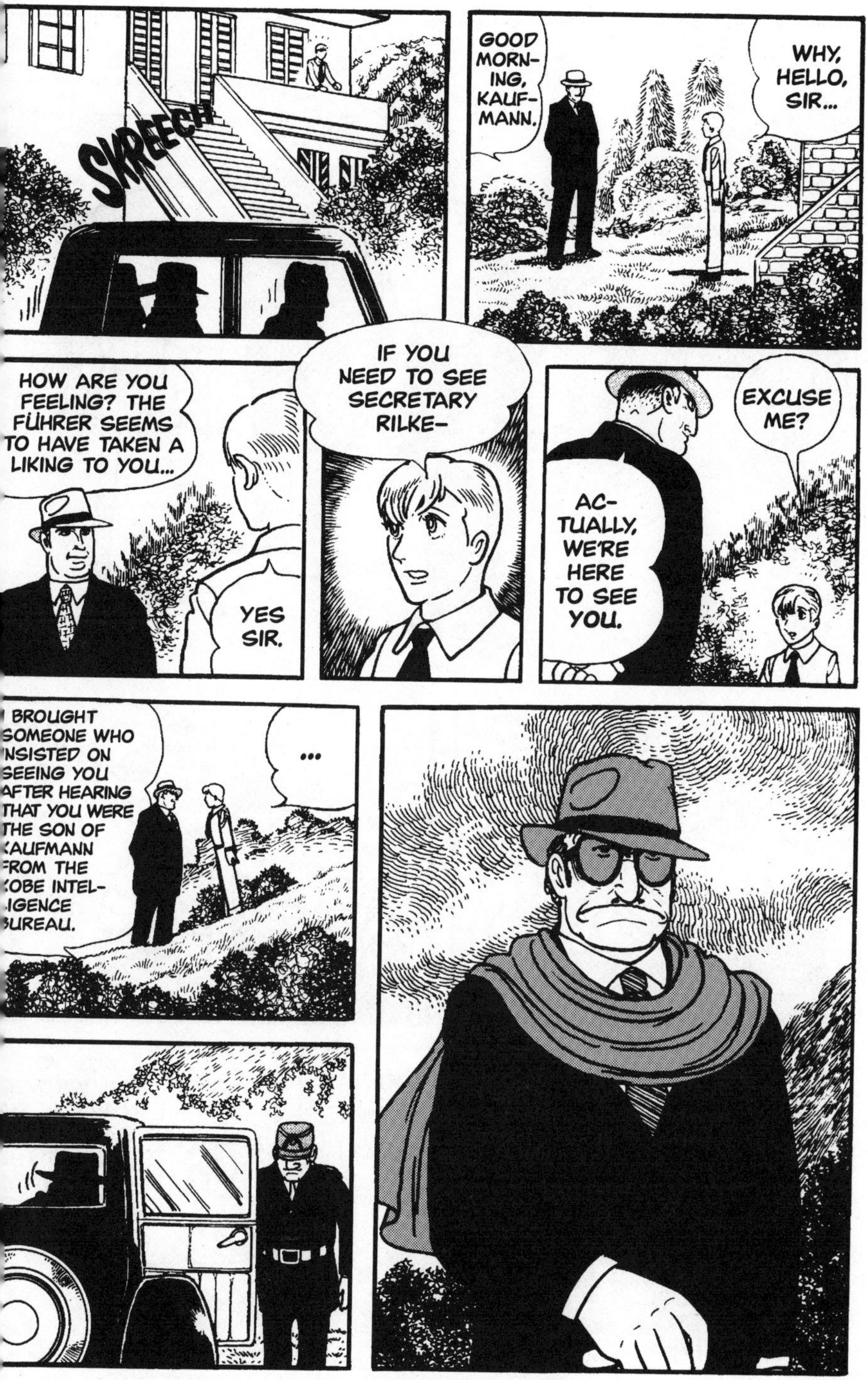
SKREECH
GOOD MORNING, KAUFMANN.
WHY, HELLO, SIR...
HOW ARE YOU FEELING? THE FÜHRER SEEMS TO HAVE TAKEN A LIKING TO YOU...
YES SIR.
IF YOU NEED TO SEE SECRETARY RILKE-
ACTUALLY, WE'RE HERE TO SEE YOU.
EXCUSE ME?
I BROUGHT SOMEONE WHO INSISTED ON SEEING YOU AFTER HEARING THAT YOU WERE THE SON OF KAUFMANN FROM THE KOBE INTELLIGENCE BUREAU.
...

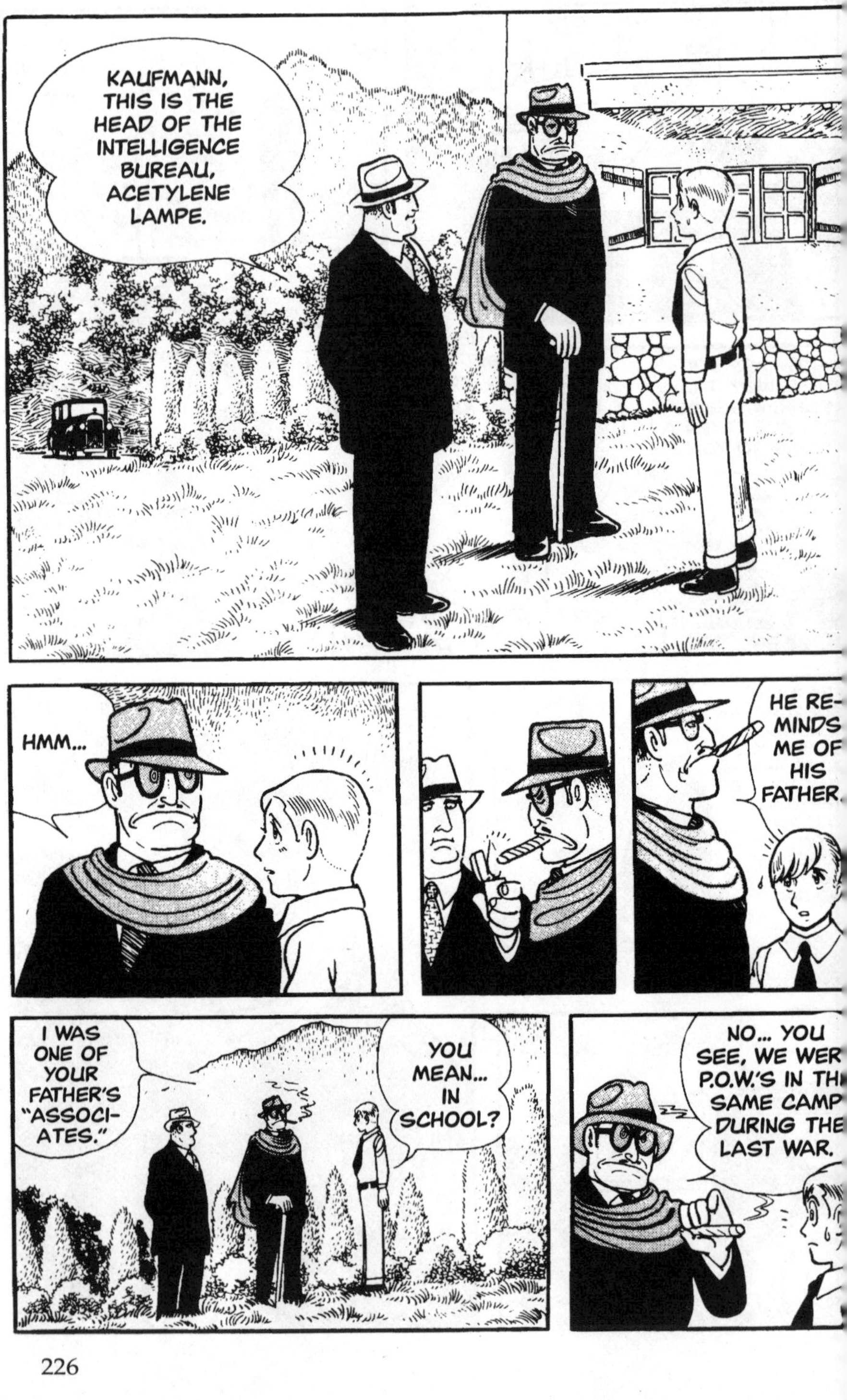
KAUFMANN, THIS IS THE HEAD OF THE INTELLIGENCE BUREAU, ACETYLENE LAMPE.
HMM...
HE RE-MINDS ME OF HIS FATHER.
I WAS ONE OF YOUR FATHER'S "ASSOCI-ATES."
YOU MEAN... IN SCHOOL?
NO... YOU SEE, WE WER P.O.W.'S IN TH SAME CAMP DURING THE LAST WAR.

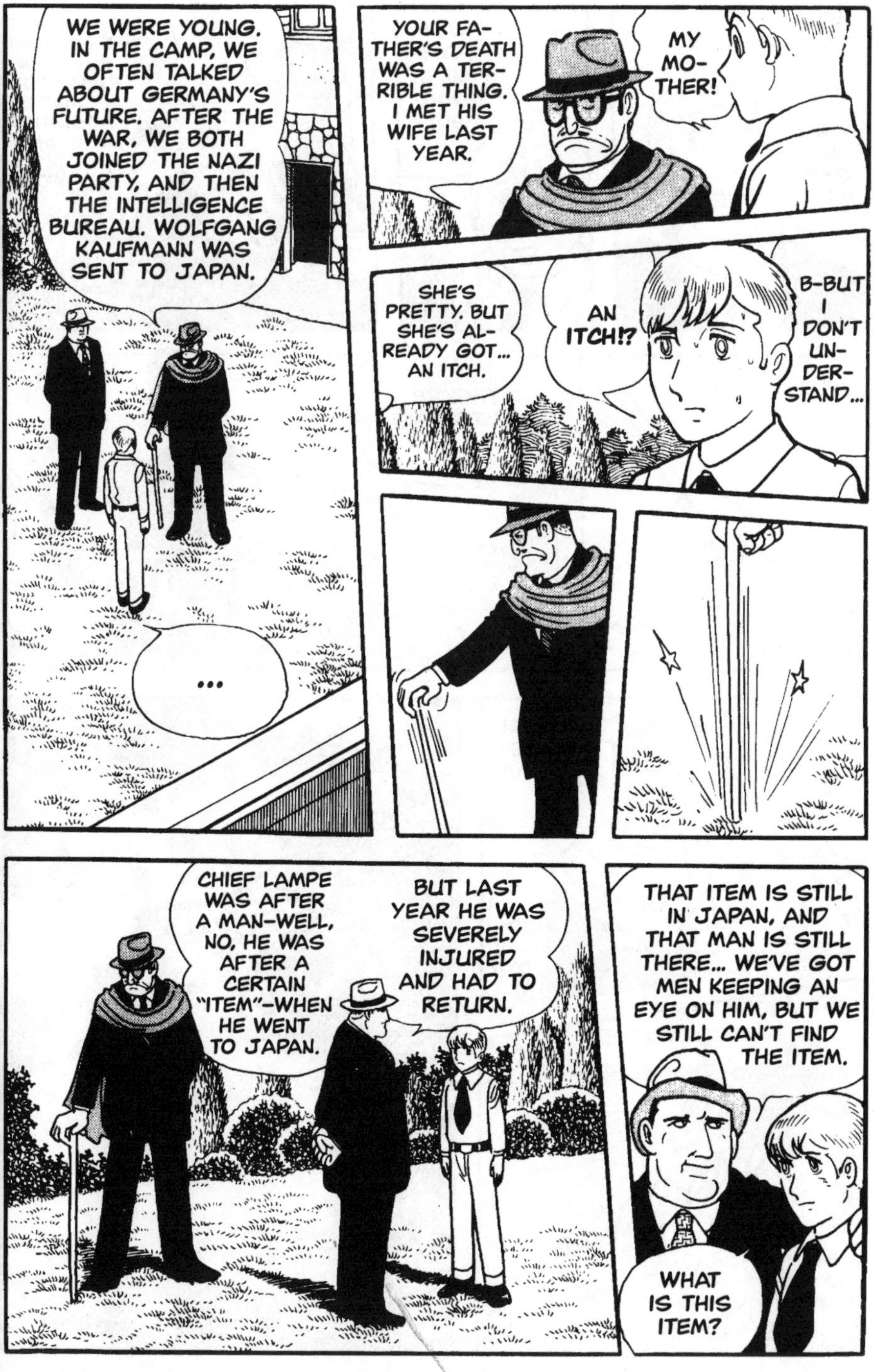
WE WERE YOUNG. IN THE CAMP, WE OFTEN TALKED ABOUT GERMANY'S FUTURE. AFTER THE WAR, WE BOTH JOINED THE NAZI PARTY, AND THEN THE INTELLIGENCE BUREAU. WOLFGANG KAUFMANN WAS SENT TO JAPAN.
...
YOUR FATHER'S DEATH WAS A TERRIBLE THING. I MET HIS WIFE LAST YEAR.
MY MOTHER!
SHE'S PRETTY. BUT SHE'S ALREADY GOT... AN ITCH.
AN ITCH!?
B-BUT I DON'T UNDERSTAND...
CHIEF LAMPE WAS AFTER A MAN—WELL, NO, HE WAS AFTER A CERTAIN "ITEM"—WHEN HE WENT TO JAPAN.
BUT LAST YEAR HE WAS SEVERELY INJURED AND HAD TO RETURN.
THAT ITEM IS STILL IN JAPAN, AND THAT MAN IS STILL THERE... WE'VE GOT MEN KEEPING AN EYE ON HIM, BUT WE STILL CAN'T FIND THE ITEM.
WHAT IS THIS ITEM?

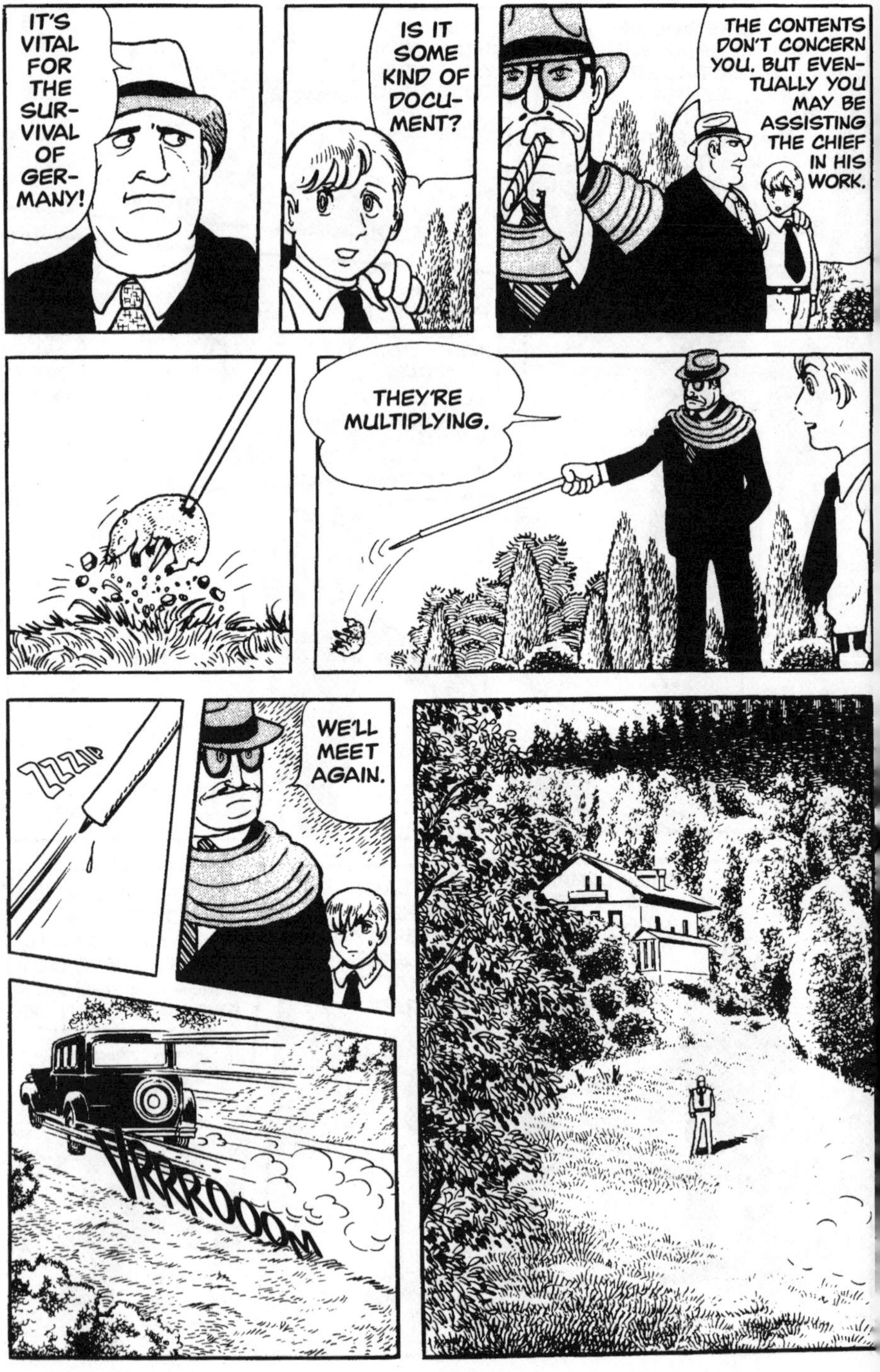
IT'S VITAL FOR THE SURVIVAL OF GERMANY!
IS IT SOME KIND OF DOCUMENT?
THE CONTENTS DON'T CONCERN YOU. BUT EVENTUALLY YOU MAY BE ASSISTING THE CHIEF IN HIS WORK.
THEY'RE MULTIPLYING.
ZZZIP
WE'LL MEET AGAIN.
VRRROOOM

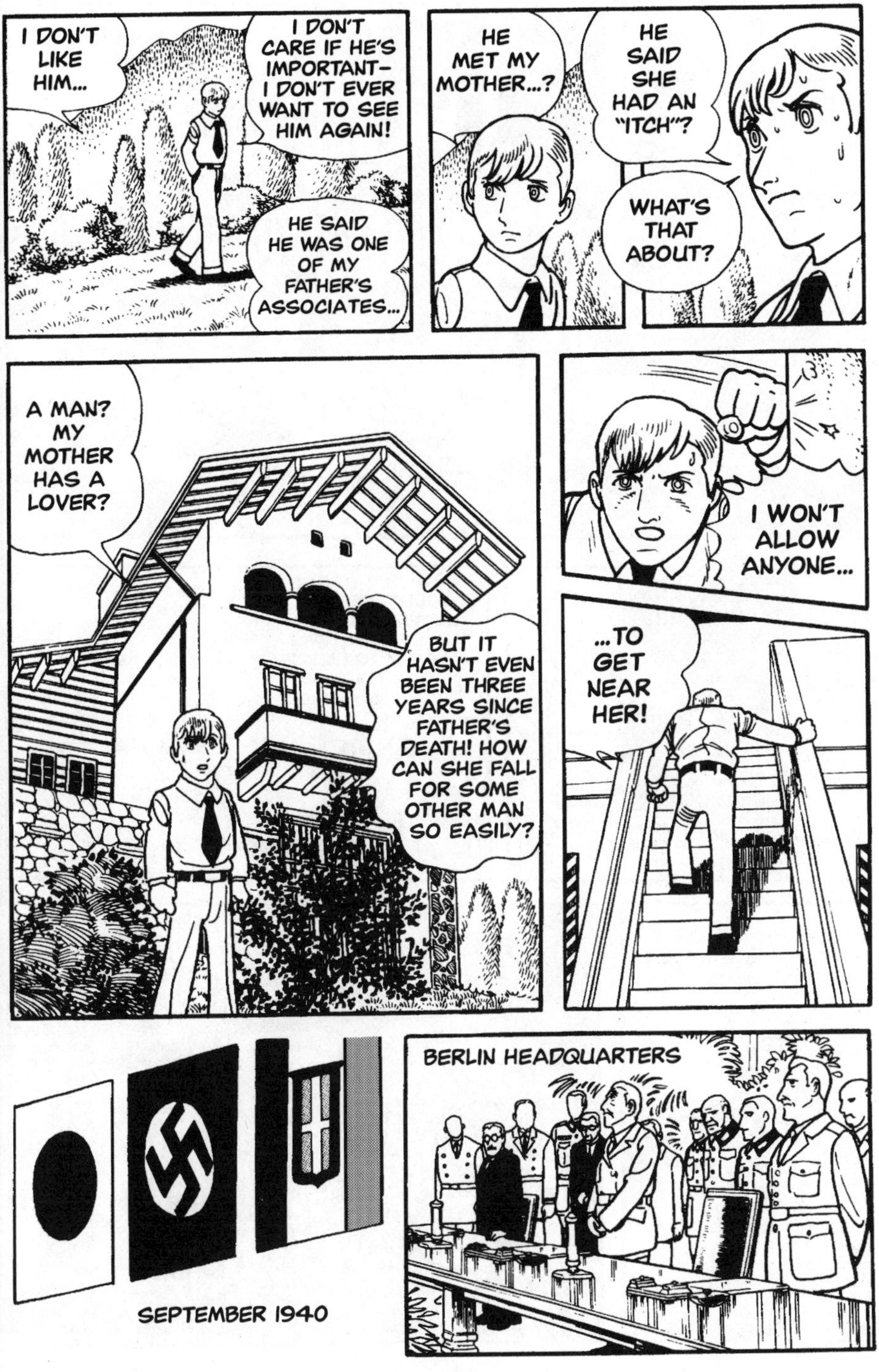
I DON'T LIKE HIM...
I DON'T CARE IF HE'S IMPORTANT— I DON'T EVER WANT TO SEE HIM AGAIN!
HE SAID HE WAS ONE OF MY FATHER'S ASSOCIATES...
HE MET MY MOTHER...?
HE SAID SHE HAD AN "ITCH"?
WHAT'S THAT ABOUT?
A MAN? MY MOTHER HAS A LOVER?
BUT IT HASN'T EVEN BEEN THREE YEARS SINCE FATHER'S DEATH! HOW CAN SHE FALL FOR SOME OTHER MAN SO EASILY?
I WON'T ALLOW ANYONE...
...TO GET NEAR HER!
SEPTEMBER 1940
BERLIN HEADQUARTERS

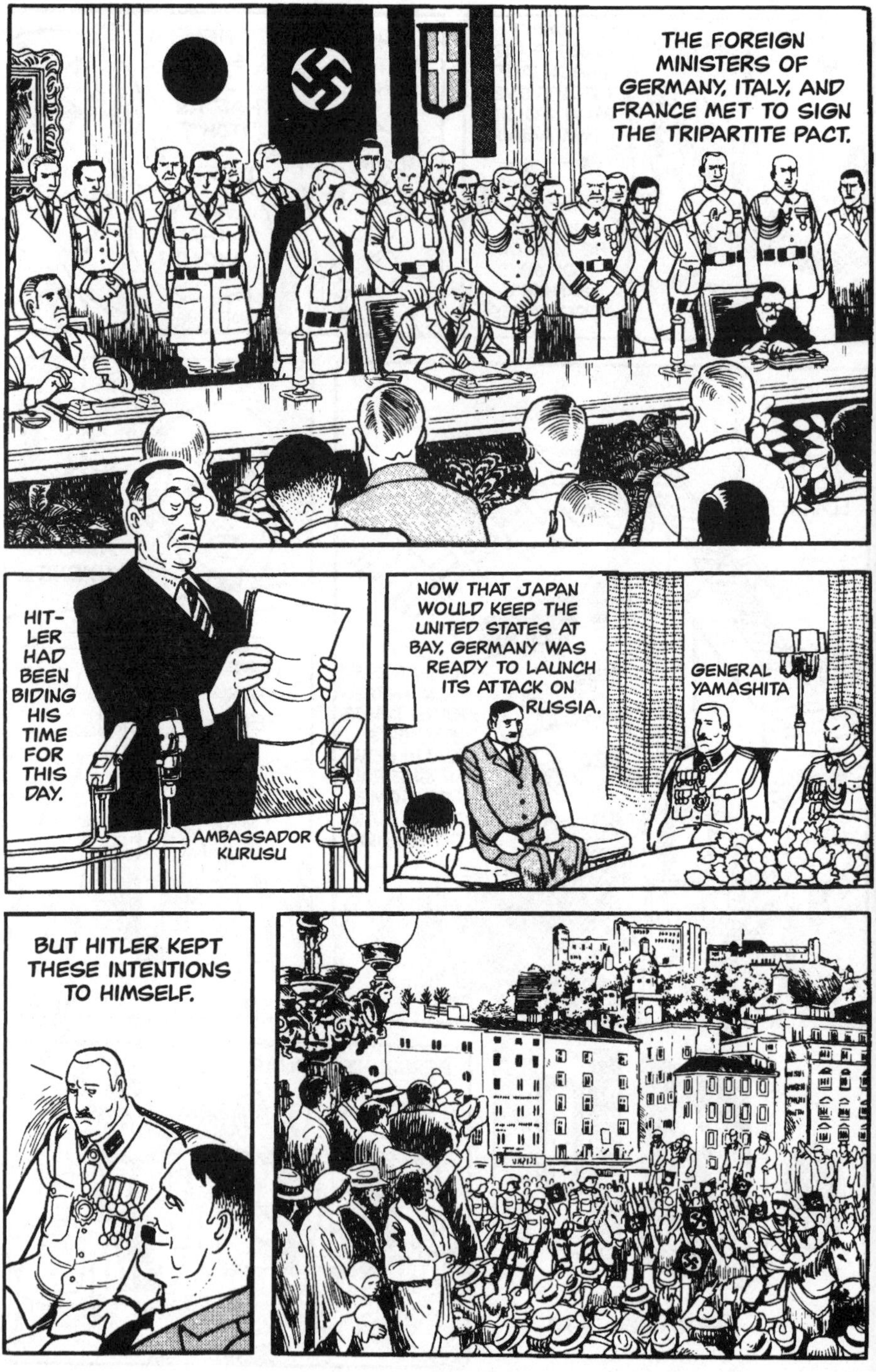
THE FOREIGN MINISTERS OF GERMANY, ITALY, AND FRANCE MET TO SIGN THE TRIPARTITE PACT.
HIT-LER HAD BEEN BIDING HIS TIME FOR THIS DAY.
AMBASSADOR KURUSU
NOW THAT JAPAN WOULD KEEP THE UNITED STATES AT BAY, GERMANY WAS READY TO LAUNCH ITS ATTACK ON RUSSIA.
GENERAL YAMASHITA
BUT HITLER KEPT THESE INTENTIONS TO HIMSELF.

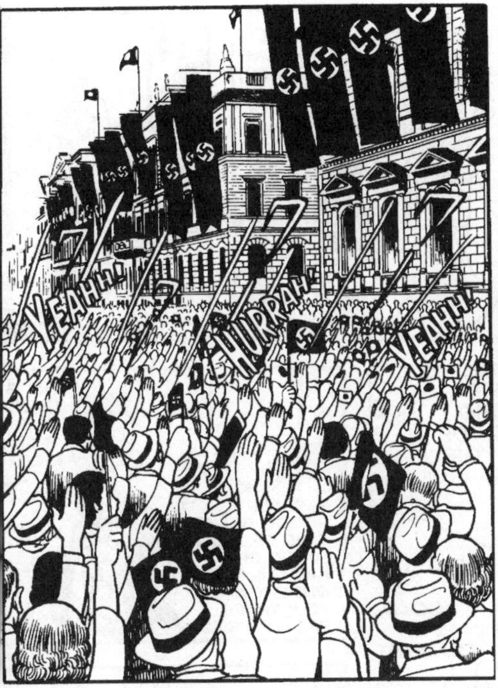
YEAHH!
HURRAH!
YEAHH!

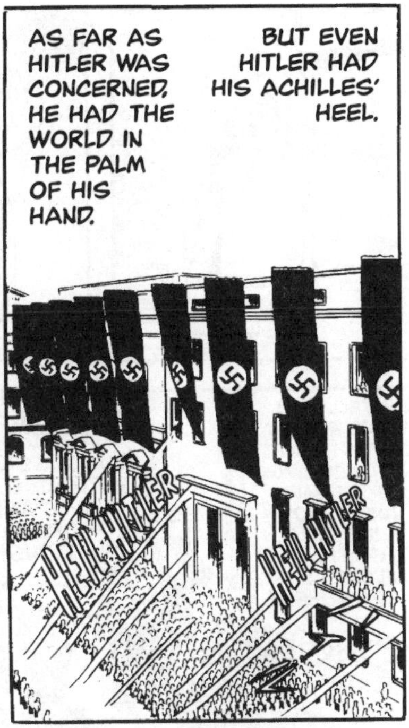
AS FAR AS HITLER WAS CONCERNED, HE HAD THE WORLD IN THE PALM OF HIS HAND.
BUT EVEN HITLER HAD HIS ACHILLES' HEEL.
HEIL HITLER
HEIL HITLER

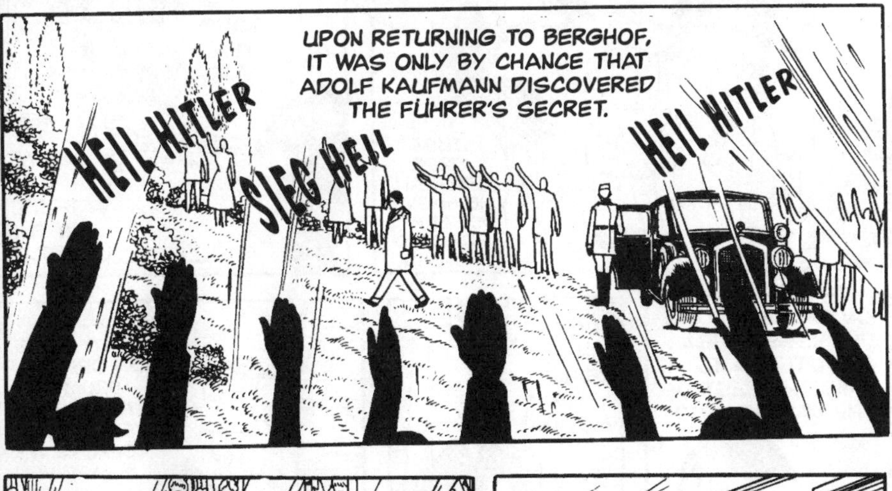
UPON RETURNING TO BERGHOF, IT WAS ONLY BY CHANCE THAT ADOLF KAUFMANN DISCOVERED THE FÜHRER'S SECRET.
HEIL HITLER
SIEG HEIL
HEIL HITLER

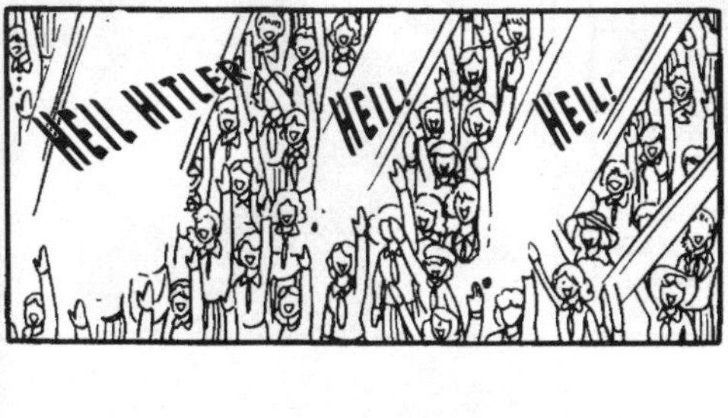
HEIL HITLER
HEIL!
HEIL!

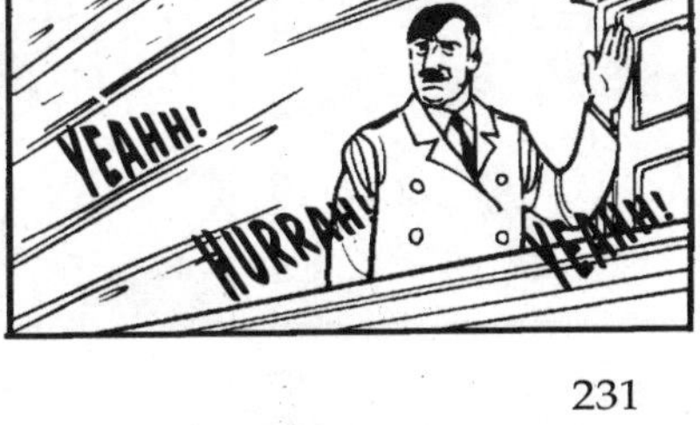
YEAHH!
HURRAH!
YEAHH!

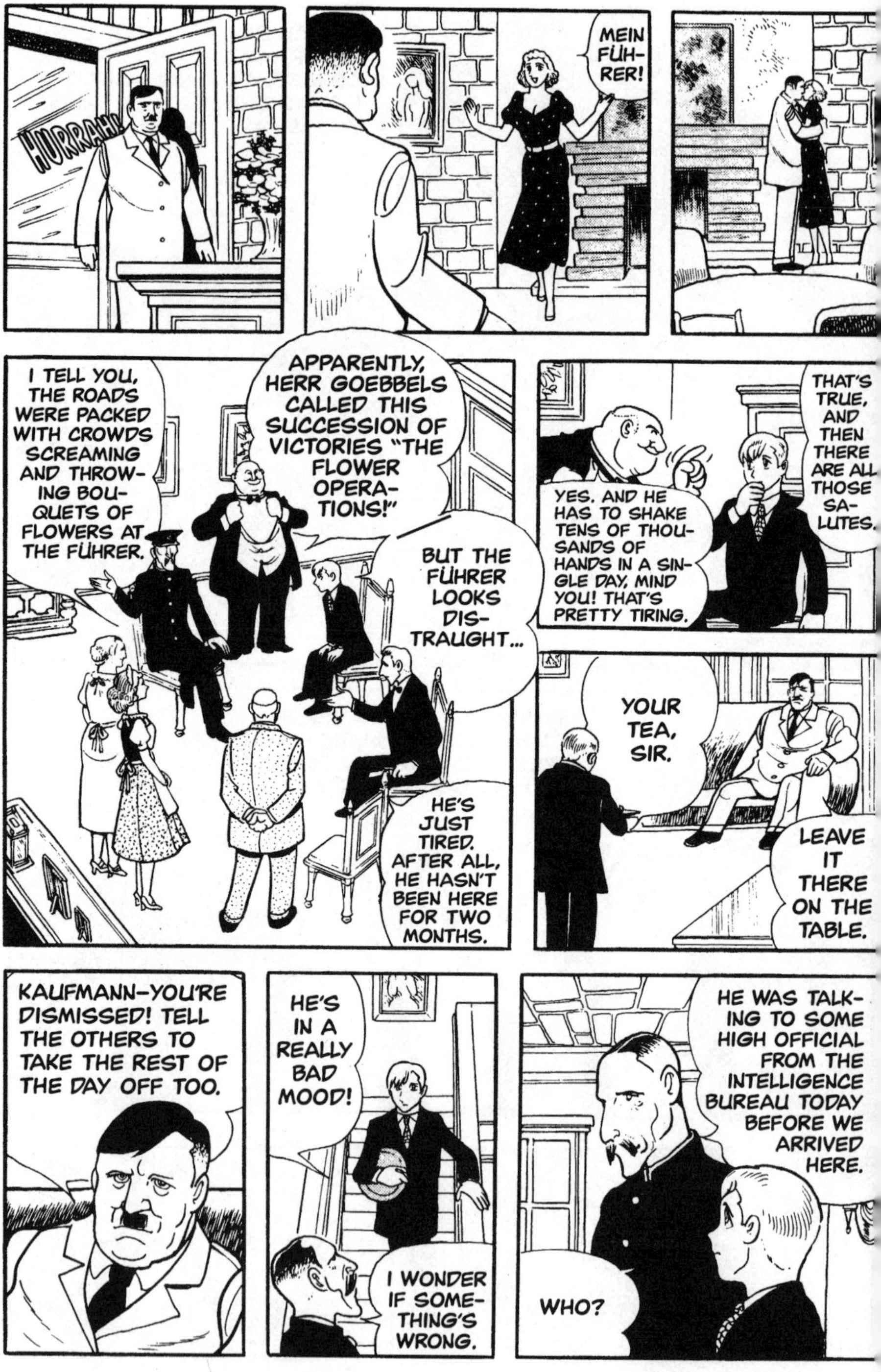
HURRAH!
MEIN FÜHRER!
I TELL YOU, THE ROADS WERE PACKED WITH CROWDS SCREAMING AND THROWING BOUQUETS OF FLOWERS AT THE FÜHRER.
APPARENTLY, HERR GOEBBELS CALLED THIS SUCCESSION OF VICTORIES "THE FLOWER OPERATIONS!"
BUT THE FÜHRER LOOKS DISTRAUGHT...
HE'S JUST TIRED. AFTER ALL, HE HASN'T BEEN HERE FOR TWO MONTHS.
YES. AND HE HAS TO SHAKE TENS OF THOUSANDS OF HANDS IN A SINGLE DAY, MIND YOU! THAT'S PRETTY TIRING.
THAT'S TRUE, AND THEN THERE ARE ALL THOSE SALUTES.
YOUR TEA, SIR.
LEAVE IT THERE ON THE TABLE.
KAUFMANN—YOU'RE DISMISSED! TELL THE OTHERS TO TAKE THE REST OF THE DAY OFF TOO.
HE'S IN A REALLY BAD MOOD!
I WONDER IF SOMETHING'S WRONG.
HE WAS TALKING TO SOME HIGH OFFICIAL FROM THE INTELLIGENCE BUREAU TODAY BEFORE WE ARRIVED HERE.
WHO?

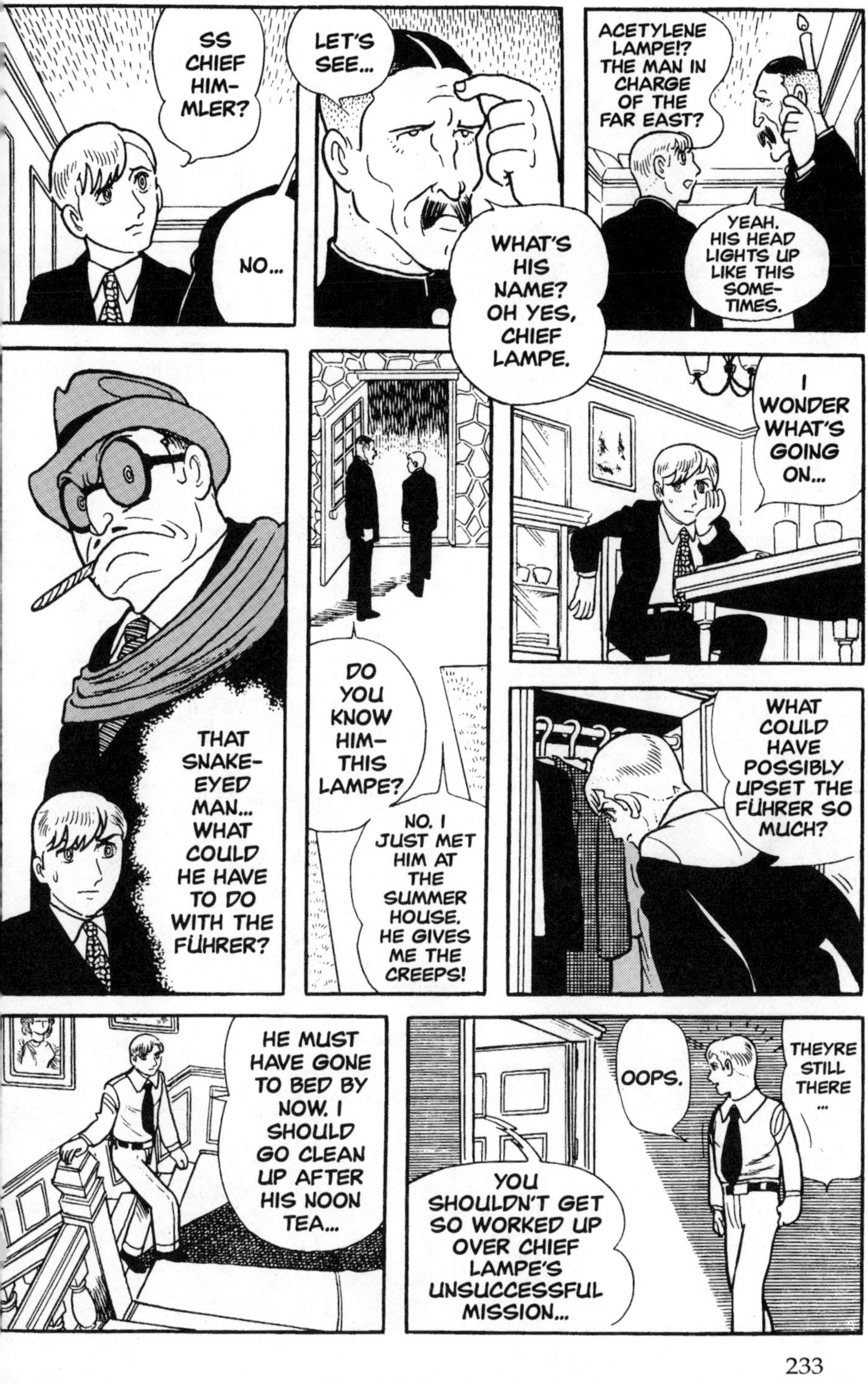
SS CHIEF HIMMLER?
NO...
LET'S SEE...
WHAT'S HIS NAME? OH YES, CHIEF LAMPE.
ACETYLENE LAMPE!? THE MAN IN CHARGE OF THE FAR EAST?
YEAH. HIS HEAD LIGHTS UP LIKE THIS SOMETIMES.
THAT SNAKE-EYED MAN... WHAT COULD HE HAVE TO DO WITH THE FÜHRER?
DO YOU KNOW HIM—THIS LAMPE?
NO. I JUST MET HIM AT THE SUMMER HOUSE. HE GIVES ME THE CREEPS!
I WONDER WHAT'S GOING ON...
WHAT COULD HAVE POSSIBLY UPSET THE FÜHRER SO MUCH?
HE MUST HAVE GONE TO BED BY NOW. I SHOULD GO CLEAN UP AFTER HIS NOON TEA...
OOPS.
THEYRE STILL THERE ...
YOU SHOULDN'T GET SO WORKED UP OVER CHIEF LAMPE'S UNSUCCESSFUL MISSION...

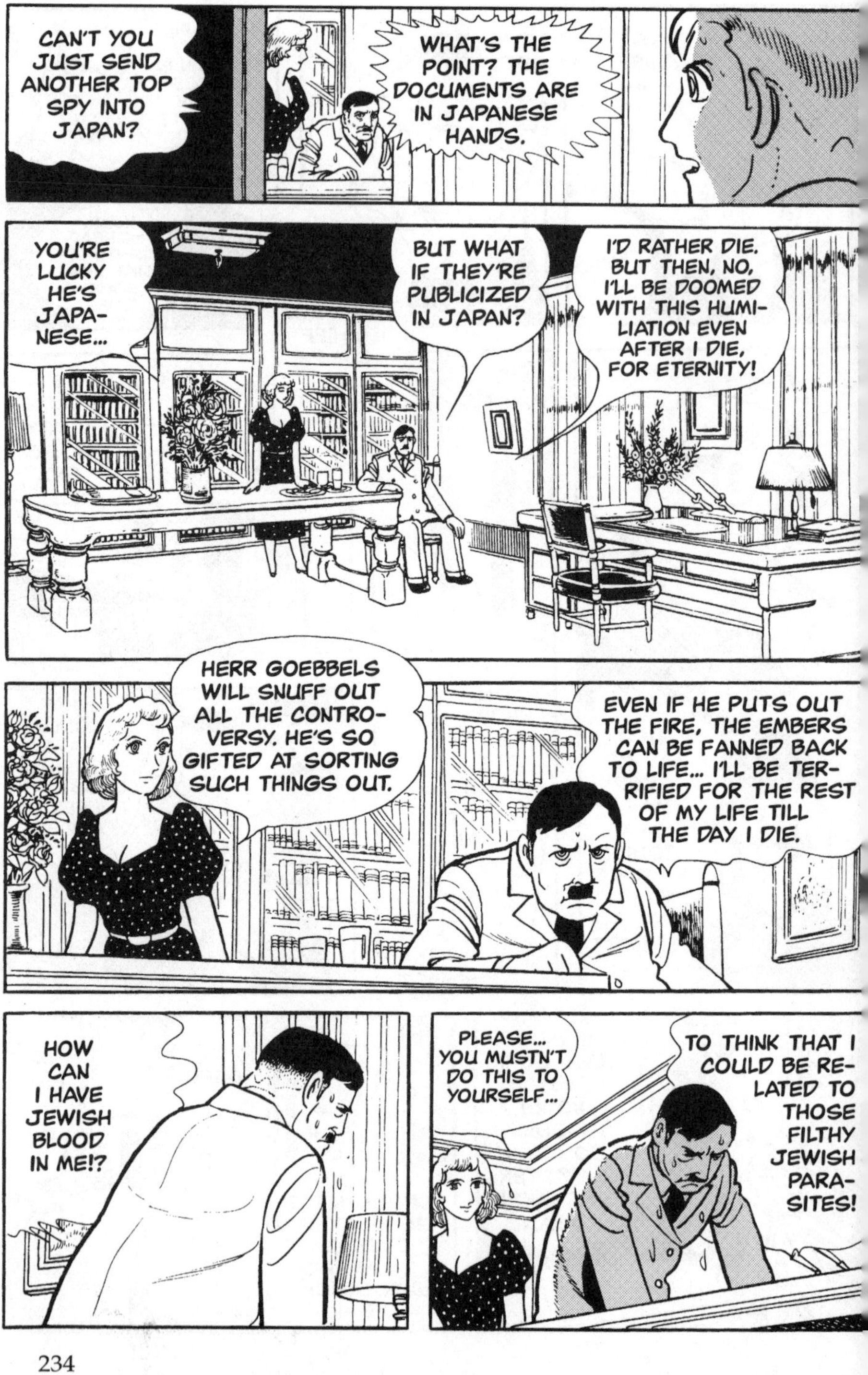
CAN'T YOU JUST SEND ANOTHER TOP SPY INTO JAPAN?
WHAT'S THE POINT? THE DOCUMENTS ARE IN JAPANESE HANDS.
YOU'RE LUCKY HE'S JAPANESE...
BUT WHAT IF THEY'RE PUBLICIZED IN JAPAN?
I'D RATHER DIE. BUT THEN, NO, I'LL BE DOOMED WITH THIS HUMILIATION EVEN AFTER I DIE, FOR ETERNITY!
HERR GOEBBELS WILL SNUFF OUT ALL THE CONTROVERSY. HE'S SO GIFTED AT SORTING SUCH THINGS OUT.
EVEN IF HE PUTS OUT THE FIRE, THE EMBERS CAN BE FANNED BACK TO LIFE... I'LL BE TERRIFIED FOR THE REST OF MY LIFE TILL THE DAY I DIE.
HOW CAN I HAVE JEWISH BLOOD IN ME!?
PLEASE... YOU MUSTN'T DO THIS TO YOURSELF...
TO THINK THAT I COULD BE RELATED TO THOSE FILTHY JEWISH PARASITES!

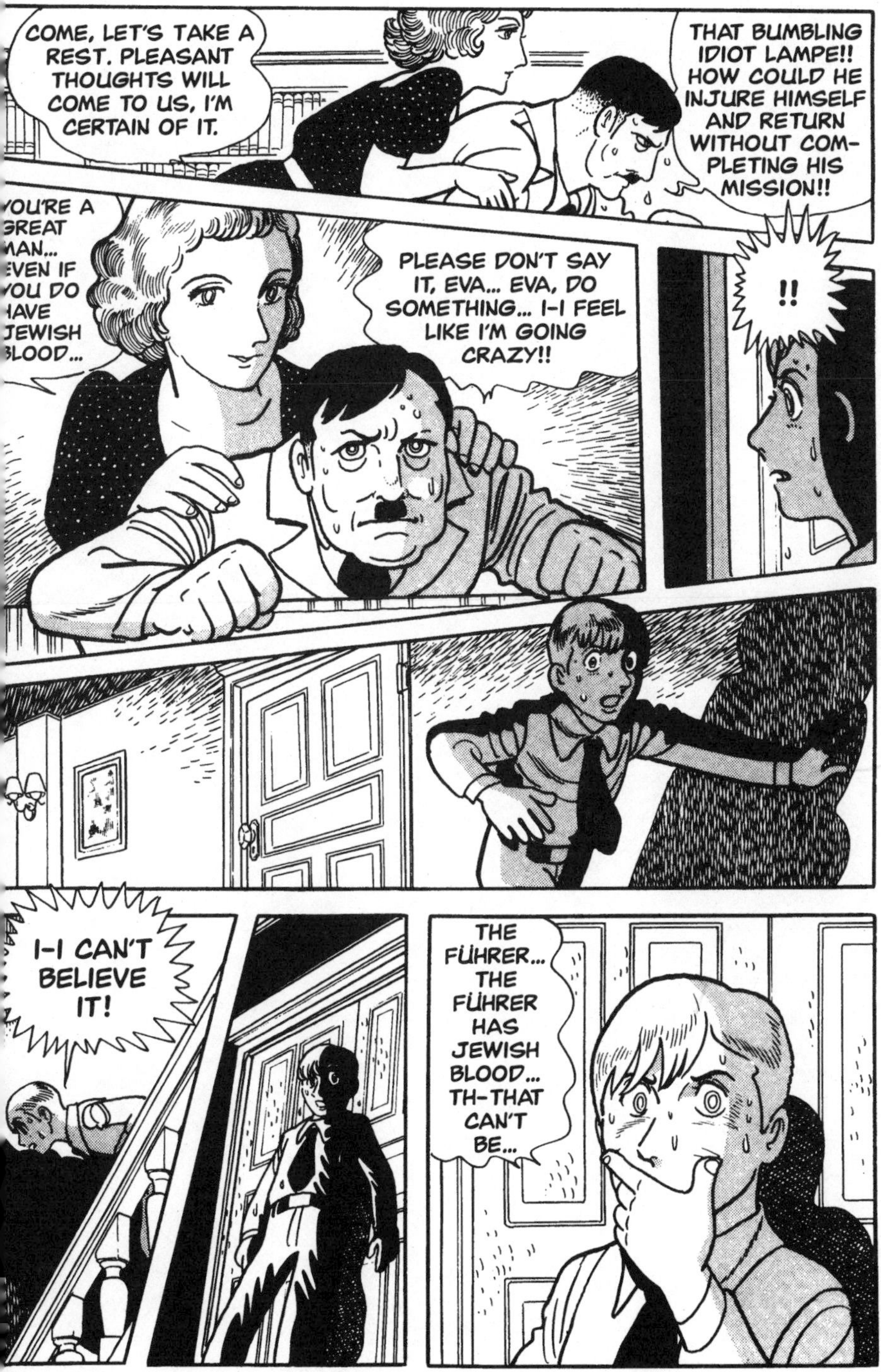
COME, LET'S TAKE A REST. PLEASANT THOUGHTS WILL COME TO US, I'M CERTAIN OF IT.
THAT BUMBLING IDIOT LAMPE!! HOW COULD HE INJURE HIMSELF AND RETURN WITHOUT COMPLETING HIS MISSION!!
YOU'RE A GREAT MAN... EVEN IF YOU DO HAVE JEWISH BLOOD...
PLEASE DON'T SAY IT, EVA... EVA, DO SOMETHING... I-I FEEL LIKE I'M GOING CRAZY!!
!!
I-I CAN'T BELIEVE IT!
THE FÜHRER... THE FÜHRER HAS JEWISH BLOOD... TH-THAT CAN'T BE...

CHAPTER
SIX

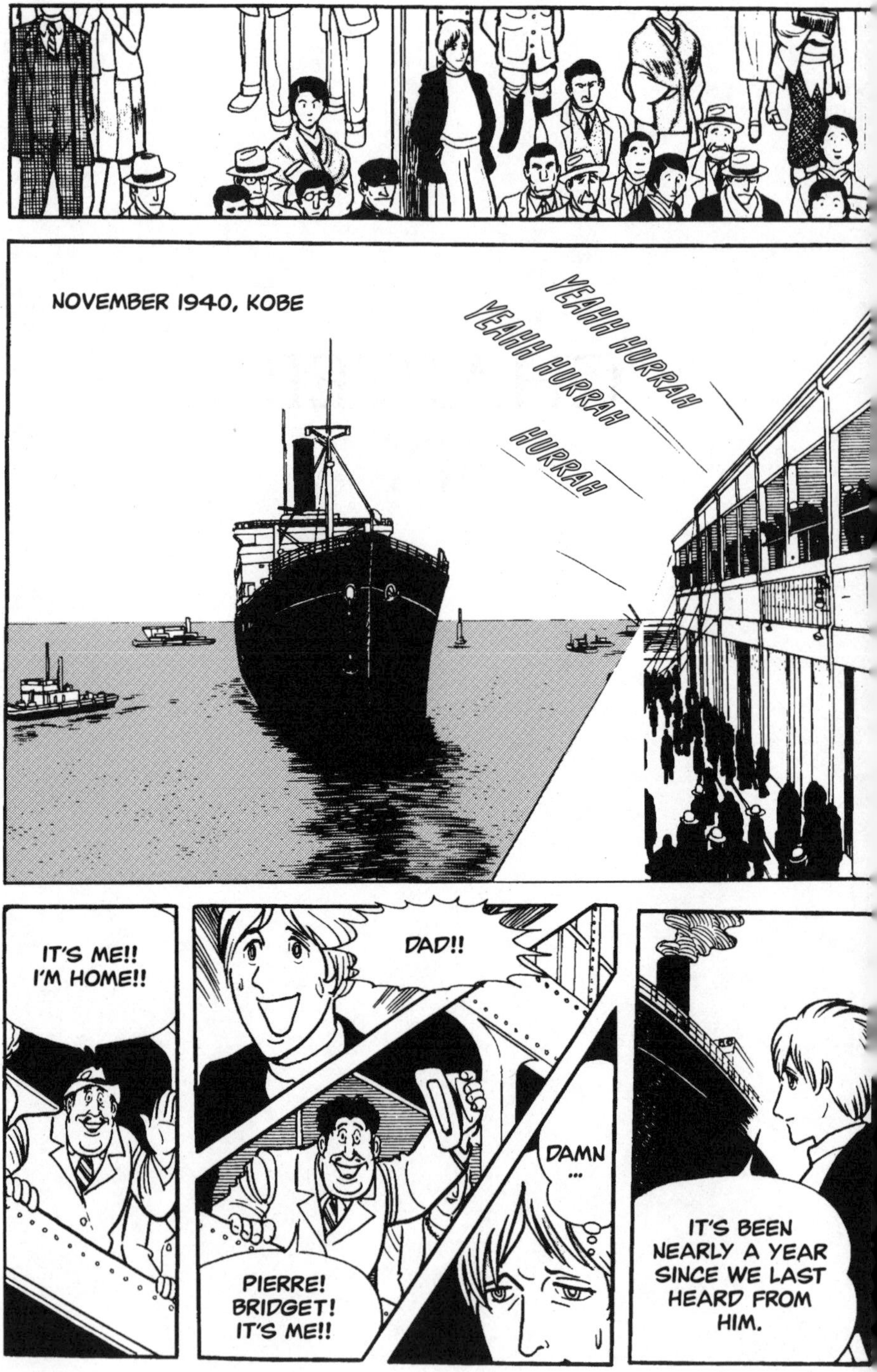
NOVEMBER 1940, KOBE
YEAHH HURRAH
YEAHH HURRAH
HURRAH
IT'S ME!! I'M HOME!!
DAD!!
PIERRE! BRIDGET! IT'S ME!!
DAMN ...
IT'S BEEN NEARLY A YEAR SINCE WE LAST HEARD FROM HIM.

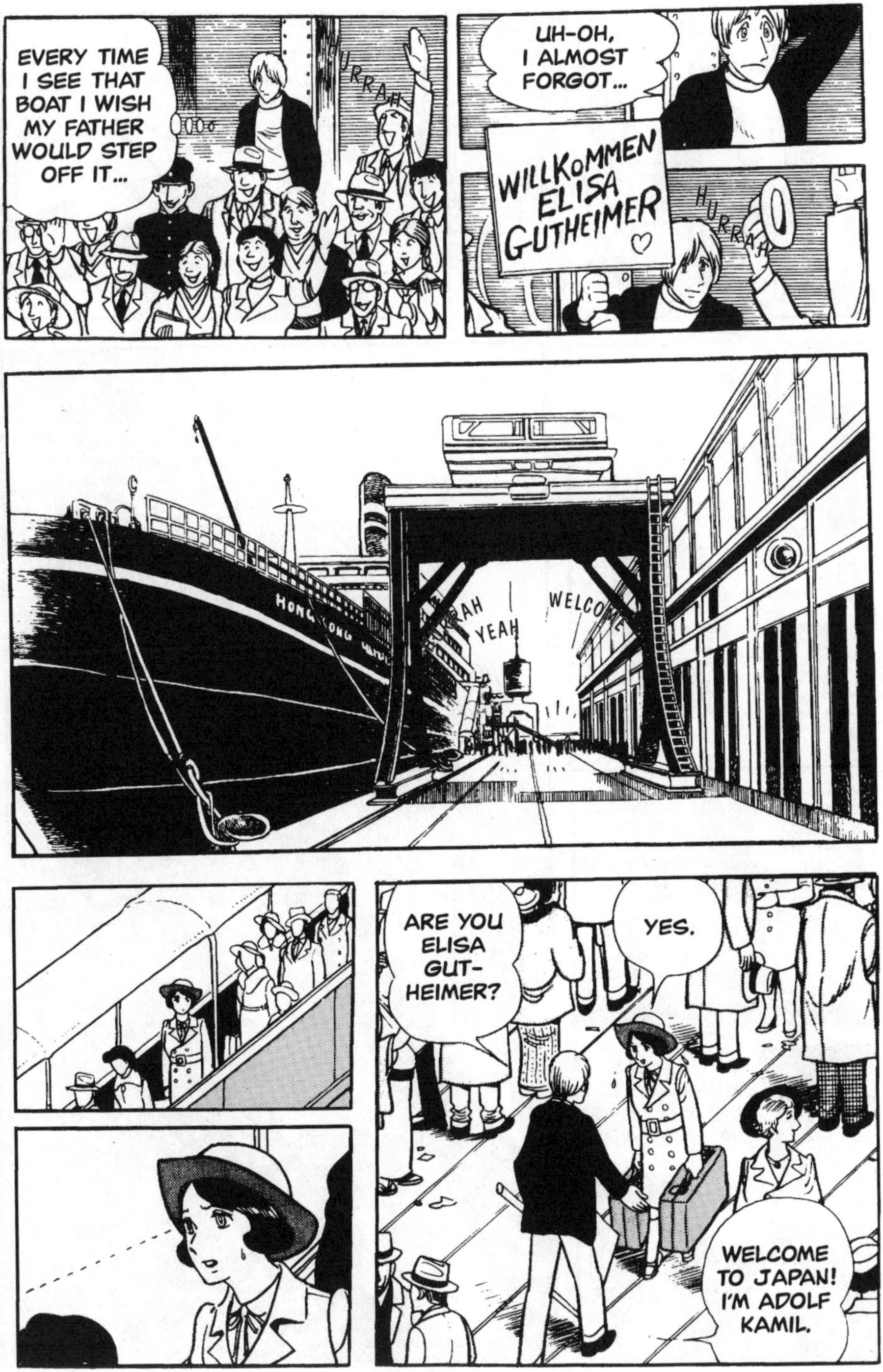
EVERY TIME I SEE THAT BOAT I WISH MY FATHER WOULD STEP OFF IT...
HURRAH
UH-OH, I ALMOST FORGOT...
WILLKOMMEN ELISA GUTHEIMER
HURRAH
HONG KONG
RAH
YEAH
WELCOME
ARE YOU ELISA GUT-HEIMER?
YES.
WELCOME TO JAPAN! I'M ADOLF KAMIL.

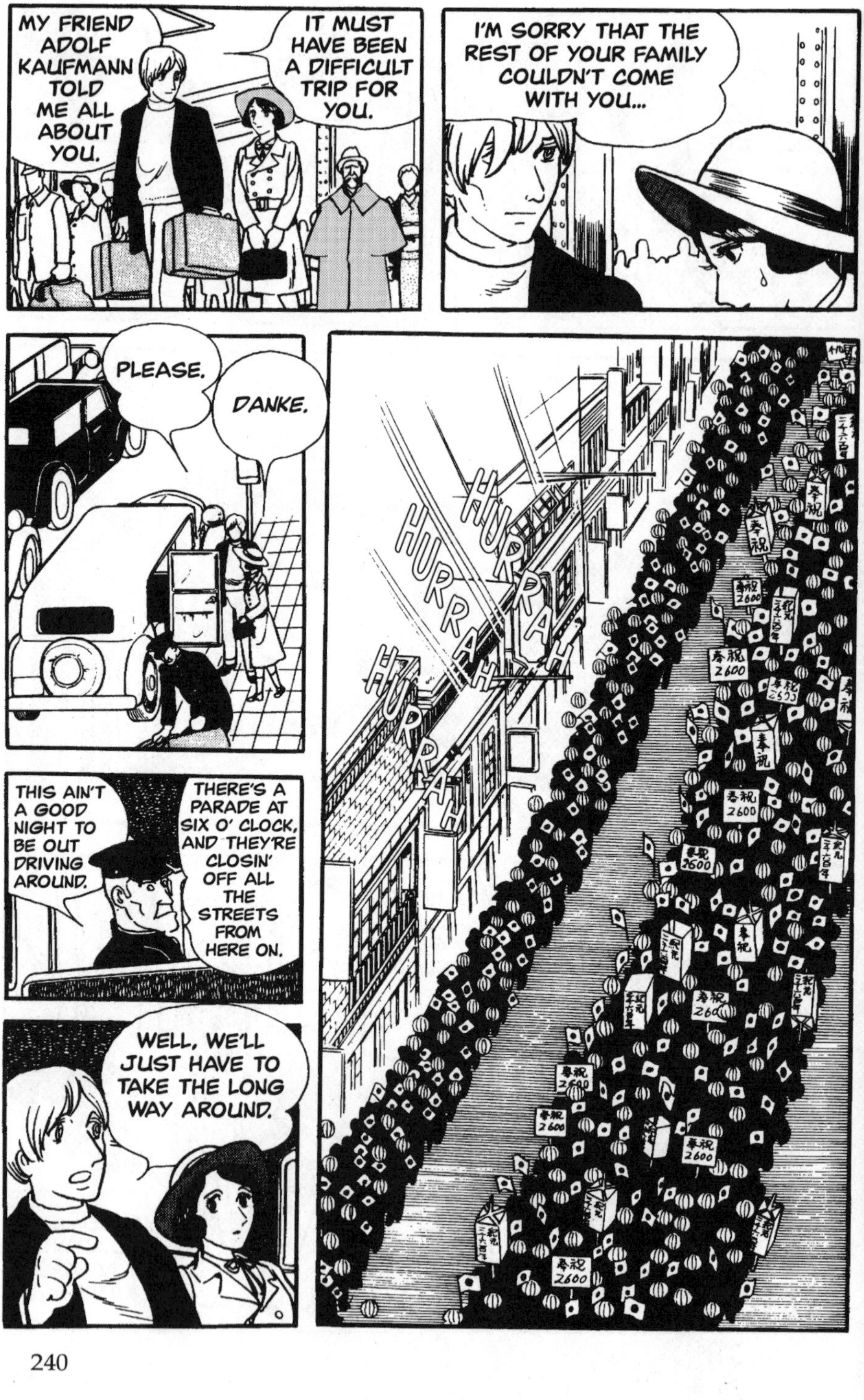
MY FRIEND ADOLF KAUFMANN TOLD ME ALL ABOUT YOU.
IT MUST HAVE BEEN A DIFFICULT TRIP FOR YOU.
I'M SORRY THAT THE REST OF YOUR FAMILY COULDN'T COME WITH YOU...
PLEASE.
DANKE.
THIS AIN'T A GOOD NIGHT TO BE OUT DRIVING AROUND.
THERE'S A PARADE AT SIX O' CLOCK, AND THEY'RE CLOSIN' OFF ALL THE STREETS FROM HERE ON.
WELL, WE'LL JUST HAVE TO TAKE THE LONG WAY AROUND.
HURRAH
HURRAH
HURRAH

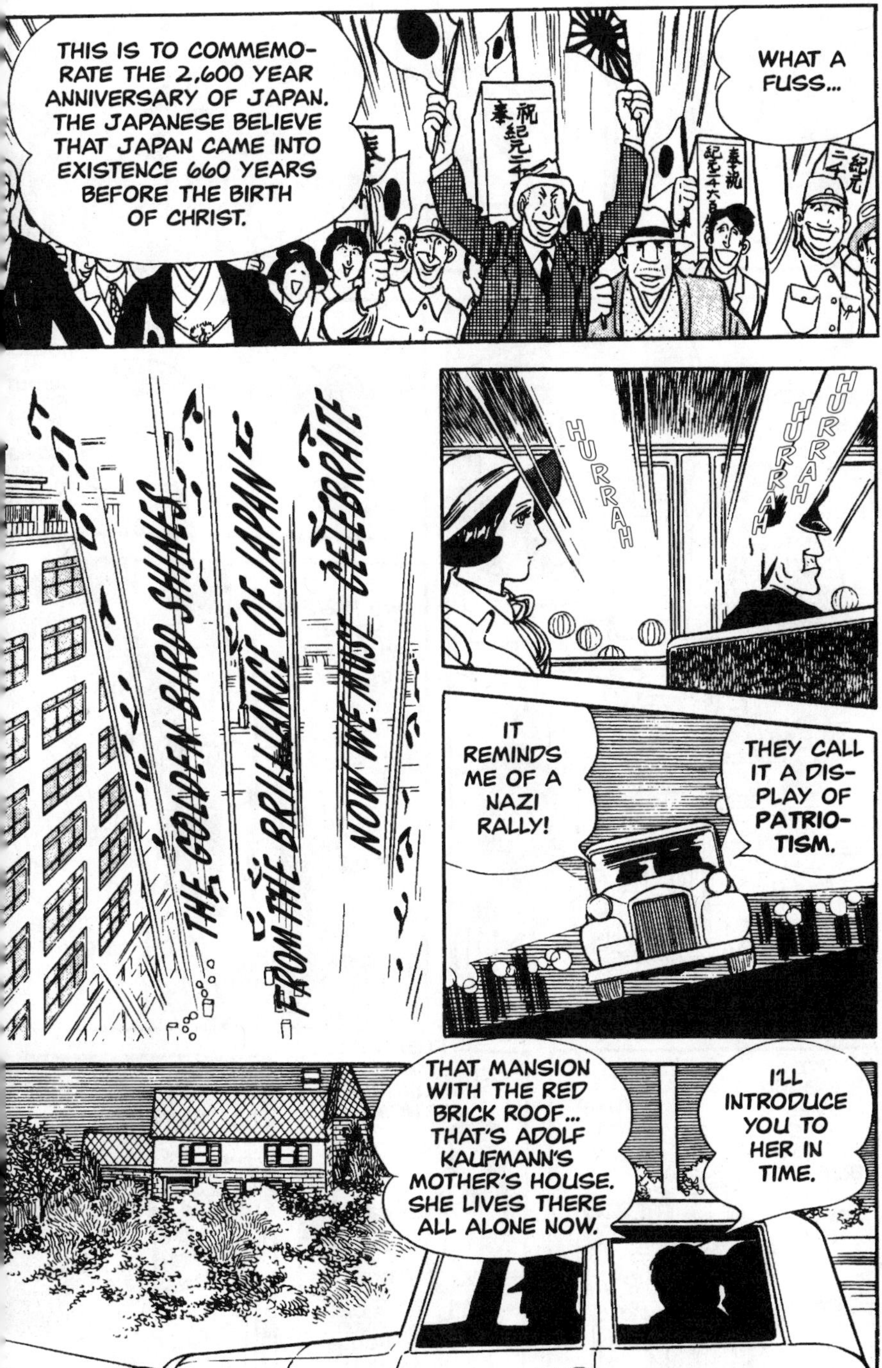
THIS IS TO COMMEMORATE THE 2,600 YEAR ANNIVERSARY OF JAPAN. THE JAPANESE BELIEVE THAT JAPAN CAME INTO EXISTENCE 660 YEARS BEFORE THE BIRTH OF CHRIST.
WHAT A FUSS...
THE GOLDEN BIRD SHINES
FROM THE BRILLIANCE OF JAPAN
NOW WE MUST CELEBRATE
HURRAH
HURRAH
HURRAH
IT REMINDS ME OF A NAZI RALLY!
THEY CALL IT A DISPLAY OF PATRIOTISM.
THAT MANSION WITH THE RED BRICK ROOF... THAT'S ADOLF KAUFMANN'S MOTHER'S HOUSE. SHE LIVES THERE ALL ALONE NOW.
I'LL INTRODUCE YOU TO HER IN TIME.

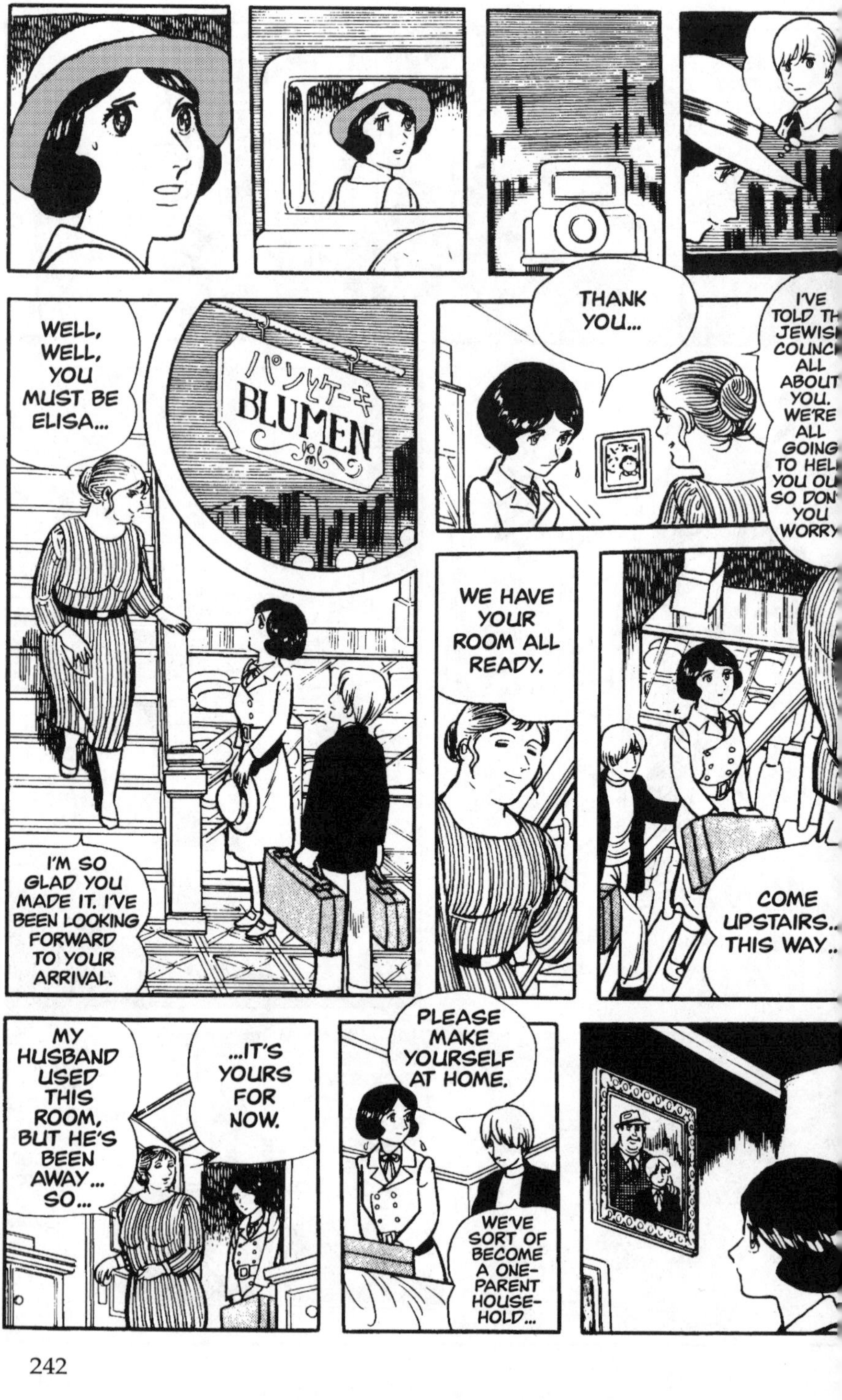
WELL, WELL, YOU MUST BE ELISA...
パンとケーキ
BLUMEN
I'M SO GLAD YOU MADE IT. I'VE BEEN LOOKING FORWARD TO YOUR ARRIVAL.
THANK YOU...
I'VE TOLD TH JEWIS COUNC ALL ABOUT YOU. WE'RE ALL GOING TO HEL YOU OU SO DON YOU WORRY
WE HAVE YOUR ROOM ALL READY.
COME UPSTAIRS... THIS WAY...
MY HUSBAND USED THIS ROOM, BUT HE'S BEEN AWAY... SO...
...IT'S YOURS FOR NOW.
PLEASE MAKE YOURSELF AT HOME.
WE'VE SORT OF BECOME A ONE-PARENT HOUSE-HOLD...

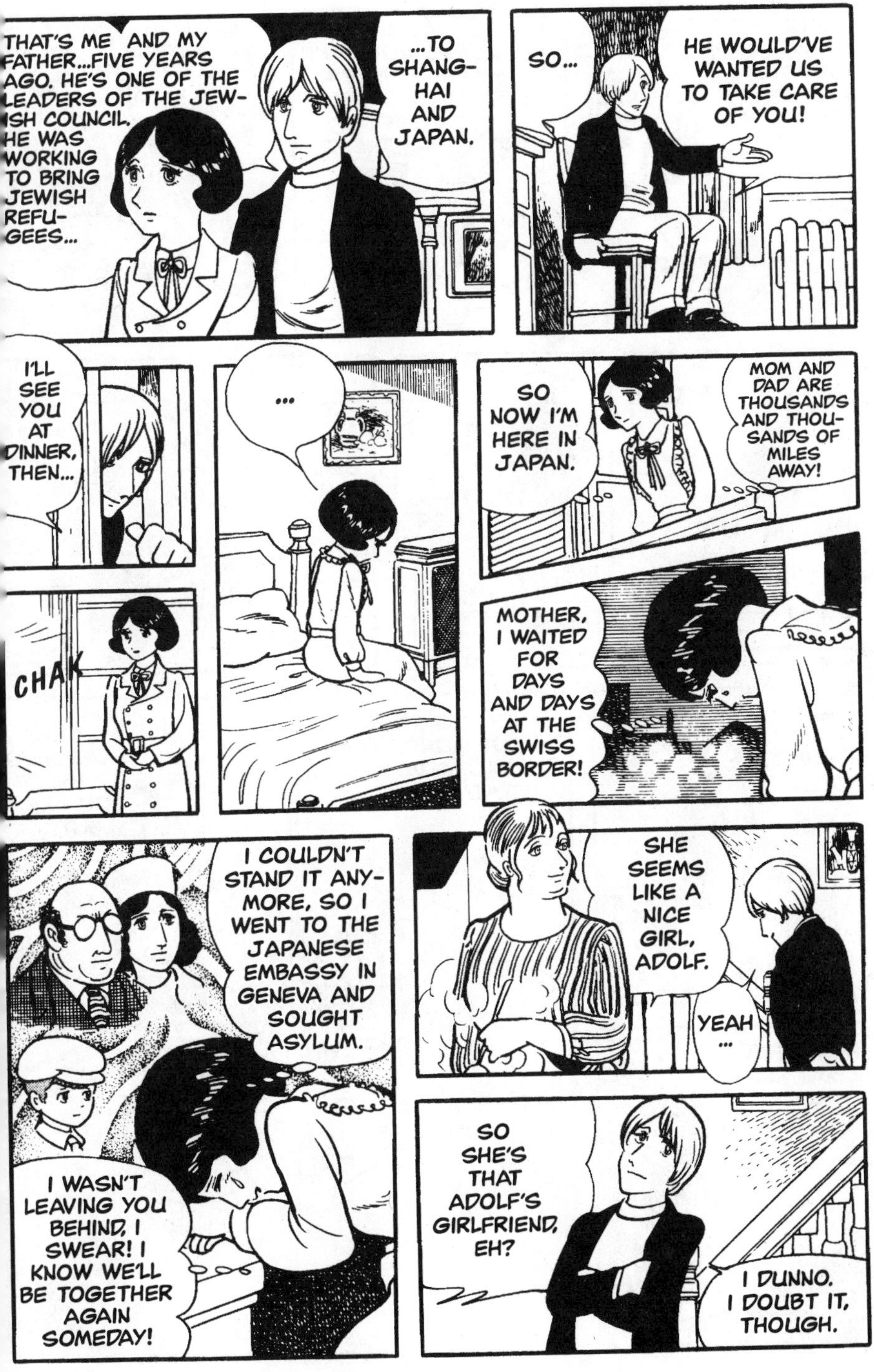
THAT'S ME AND MY FATHER...FIVE YEARS AGO. HE'S ONE OF THE LEADERS OF THE JEWISH COUNCIL. HE WAS WORKING TO BRING JEWISH REFUGEES...
...TO SHANGHAI AND JAPAN.
SO...
HE WOULD'VE WANTED US TO TAKE CARE OF YOU!
I'LL SEE YOU AT DINNER, THEN...
CHAK
...
SO NOW I'M HERE IN JAPAN.
MOM AND DAD ARE THOUSANDS AND THOUSANDS OF MILES AWAY!
MOTHER, I WAITED FOR DAYS AND DAYS AT THE SWISS BORDER!
I COULDN'T STAND IT ANYMORE, SO I WENT TO THE JAPANESE EMBASSY IN GENEVA AND SOUGHT ASYLUM.
I WASN'T LEAVING YOU BEHIND, I SWEAR! I KNOW WE'LL BE TOGETHER AGAIN SOMEDAY!
SHE SEEMS LIKE A NICE GIRL, ADOLF.
YEAH...
SO SHE'S THAT ADOLF'S GIRLFRIEND, EH?
I DUNNO. I DOUBT IT, THOUGH.

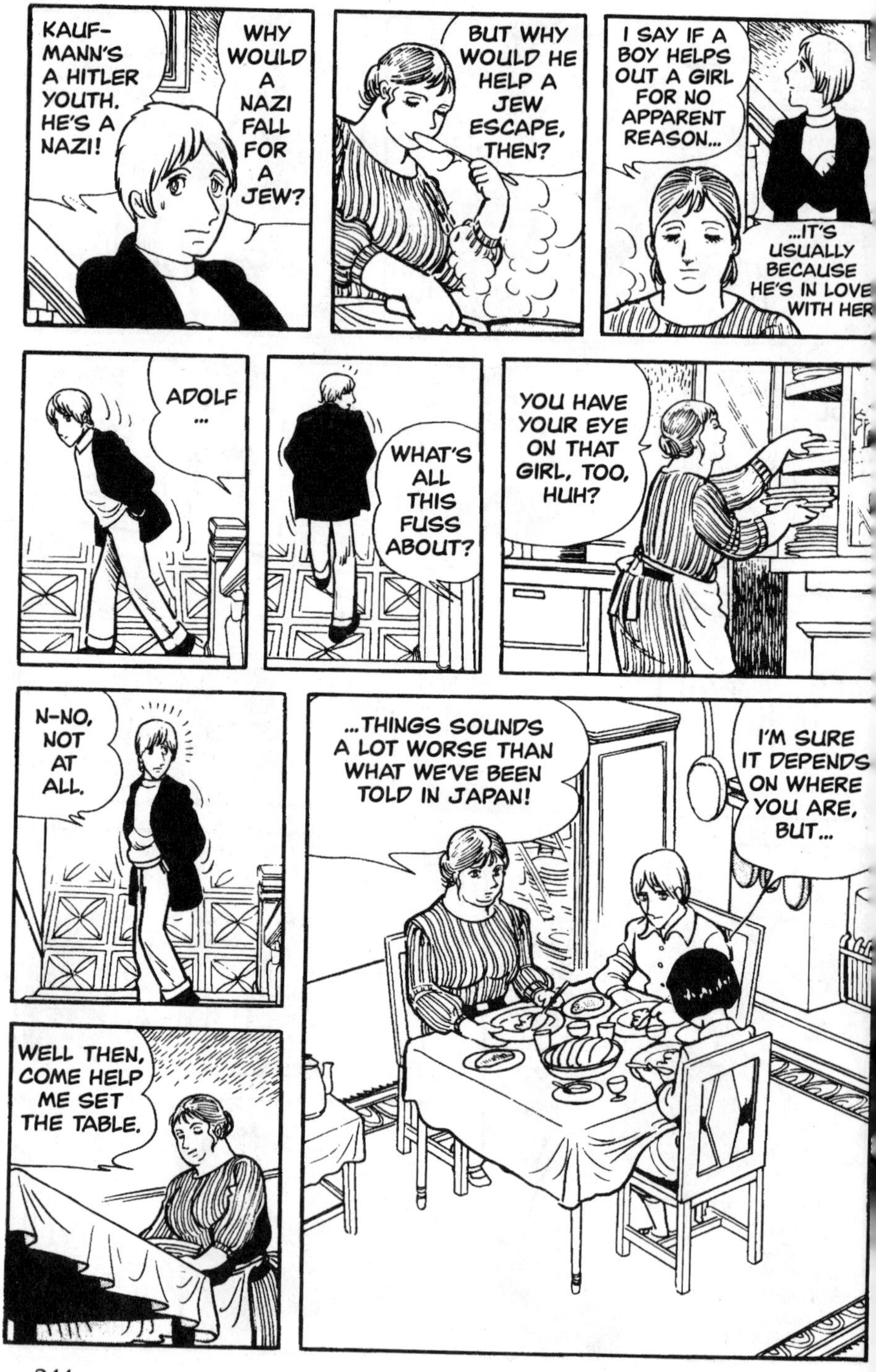
KAUF-MANN'S A HITLER YOUTH. HE'S A NAZI!
WHY WOULD A NAZI FALL FOR A JEW?
BUT WHY WOULD HE HELP A JEW ESCAPE, THEN?
I SAY IF A BOY HELPS OUT A GIRL FOR NO APPARENT REASON...
...IT'S USUALLY BECAUSE HE'S IN LOVE WITH HER
ADOLF ...
WHAT'S ALL THIS FUSS ABOUT?
YOU HAVE YOUR EYE ON THAT GIRL, TOO, HUH?
N-NO, NOT AT ALL.
WELL THEN, COME HELP ME SET THE TABLE.
...THINGS SOUNDS A LOT WORSE THAN WHAT WE'VE BEEN TOLD IN JAPAN!
I'M SURE IT DEPENDS ON WHERE YOU ARE, BUT...

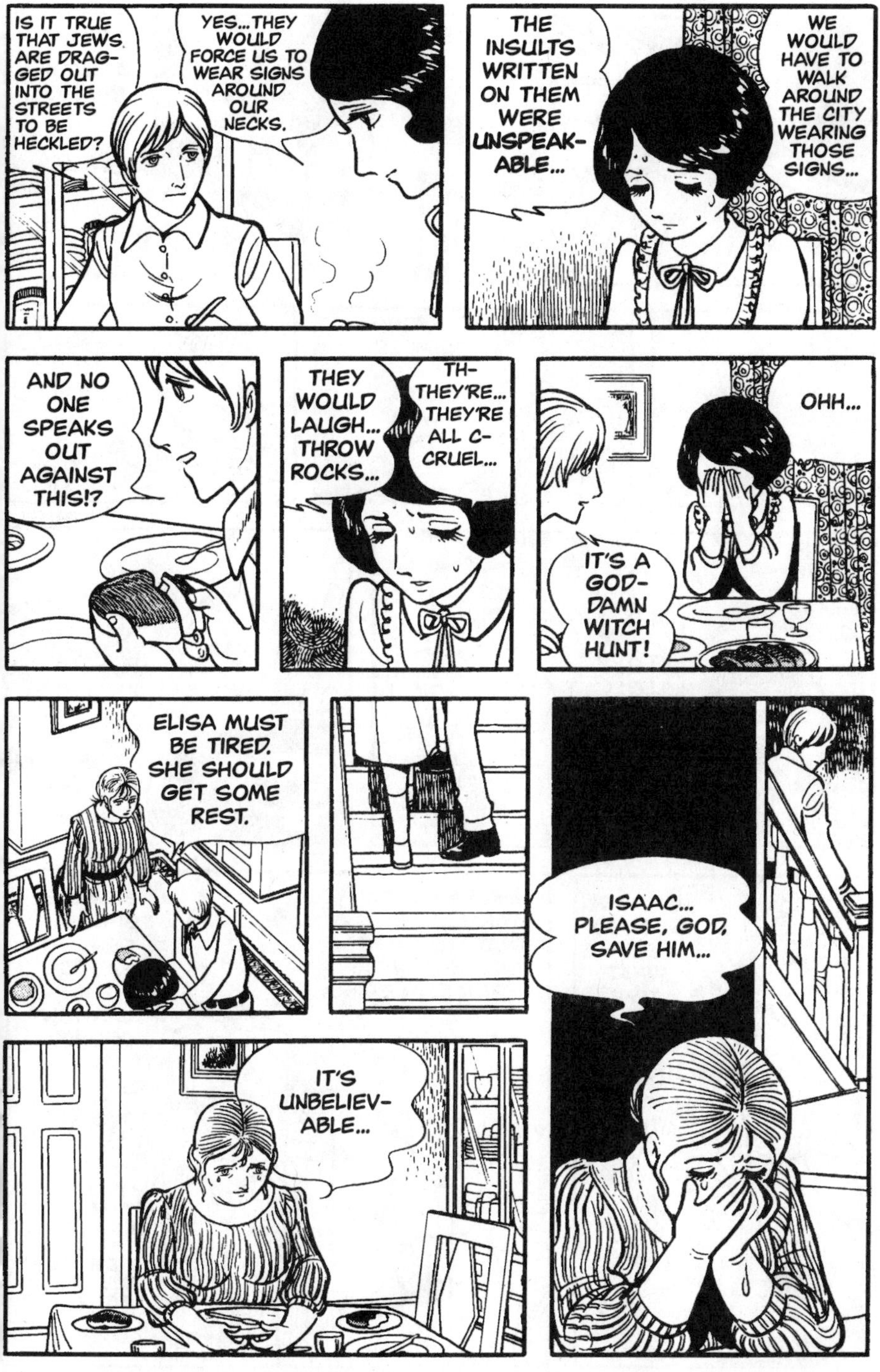
IS IT TRUE THAT JEWS ARE DRAGGED OUT INTO THE STREETS TO BE HECKLED?
YES...THEY WOULD FORCE US TO WEAR SIGNS AROUND OUR NECKS.
THE INSULTS WRITTEN ON THEM WERE UNSPEAKABLE...
WE WOULD HAVE TO WALK AROUND THE CITY WEARING THOSE SIGNS...
AND NO ONE SPEAKS OUT AGAINST THIS!?
THEY WOULD LAUGH... THROW ROCKS...
TH- THEY'RE... THEY'RE ALL C- CRUEL...
OHH...
IT'S A GOD-DAMN WITCH HUNT!
ELISA MUST BE TIRED. SHE SHOULD GET SOME REST.
ISAAC... PLEASE, GOD, SAVE HIM...
IT'S UNBELIEVABLE...

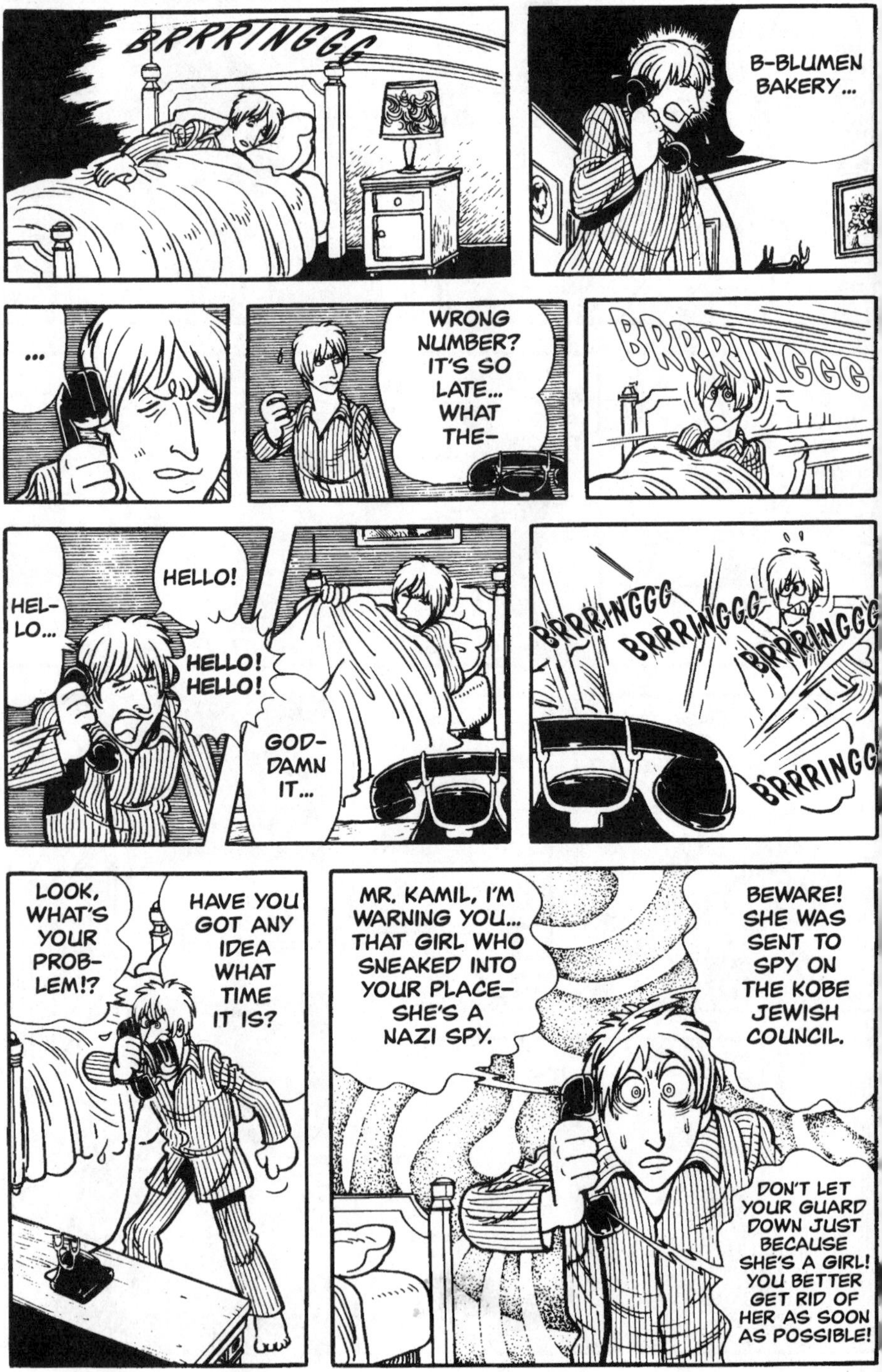
BRRRINGGGG
B-BLUMEN BAKERY...
...
WRONG NUMBER? IT'S SO LATE... WHAT THE-
BRRRINGGG
HEL-LO...
HELLO!
HELLO! HELLO!
GOD-DAMN IT...
BRRRINGGG
BRRRINGGG
BRRRINGGG
BRRRINGG
LOOK, WHAT'S YOUR PROB-LEM!?
HAVE YOU GOT ANY IDEA WHAT TIME IT IS?
MR. KAMIL, I'M WARNING YOU... THAT GIRL WHO SNEAKED INTO YOUR PLACE- SHE'S A NAZI SPY.
BEWARE! SHE WAS SENT TO SPY ON THE KOBE JEWISH COUNCIL.
DON'T LET YOUR GUARD DOWN JUST BECAUSE SHE'S A GIRL! YOU BETTER GET RID OF HER AS SOON AS POSSIBLE!

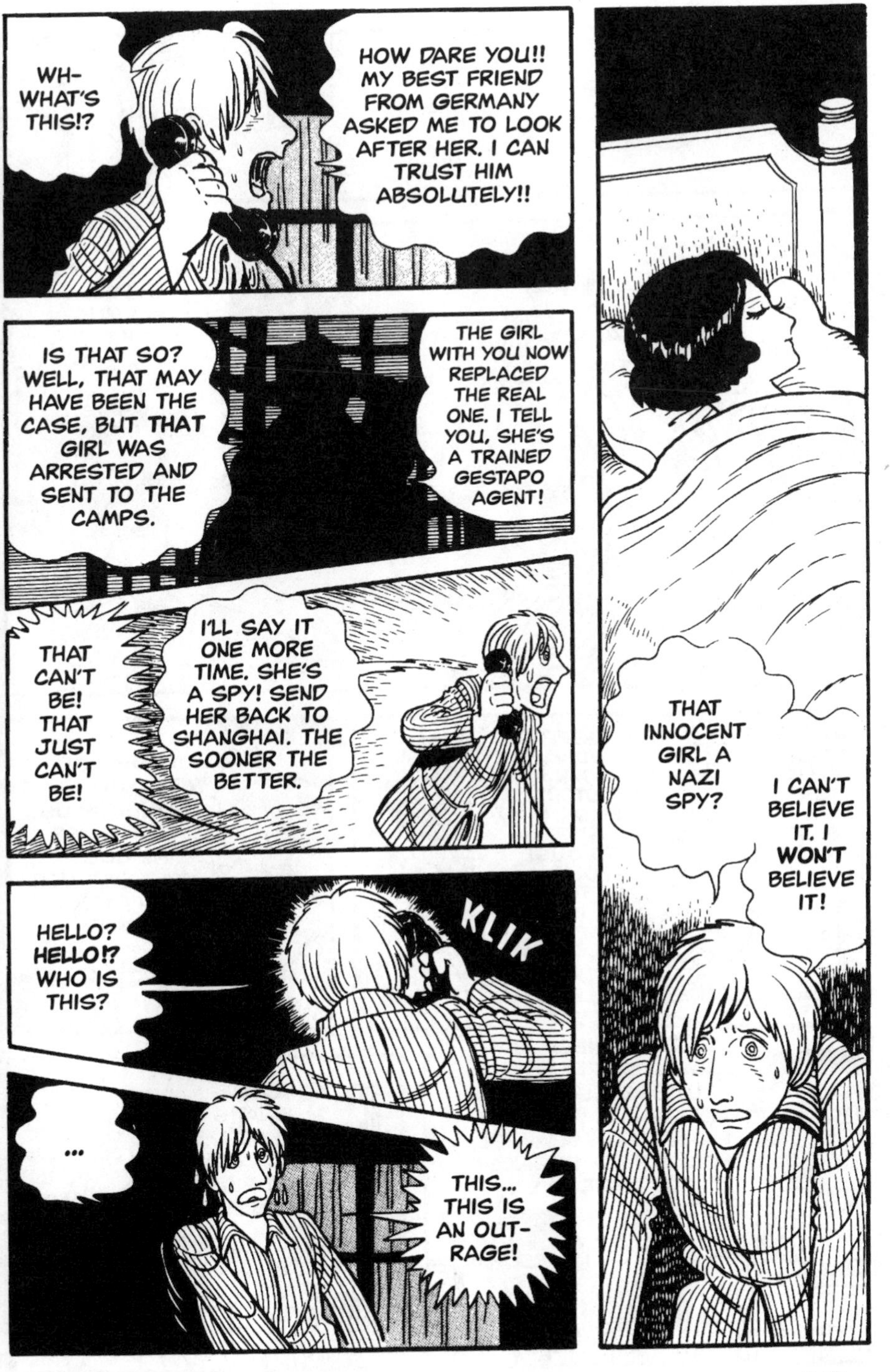
WH- WHAT'S THIS!?
HOW DARE YOU!! MY BEST FRIEND FROM GERMANY ASKED ME TO LOOK AFTER HER. I CAN TRUST HIM ABSOLUTELY!!
IS THAT SO? WELL, THAT MAY HAVE BEEN THE CASE, BUT THAT GIRL WAS ARRESTED AND SENT TO THE CAMPS.
THE GIRL WITH YOU NOW REPLACED THE REAL ONE. I TELL YOU, SHE'S A TRAINED GESTAPO AGENT!
THAT CAN'T BE! THAT JUST CAN'T BE!
I'LL SAY IT ONE MORE TIME. SHE'S A SPY! SEND HER BACK TO SHANGHAI. THE SOONER THE BETTER.
HELLO? HELLO!? WHO IS THIS?
KLIK
...
THIS... THIS IS AN OUT-RAGE!
THAT INNOCENT GIRL A NAZI SPY?
I CAN'T BELIEVE IT. I WON'T BELIEVE IT!

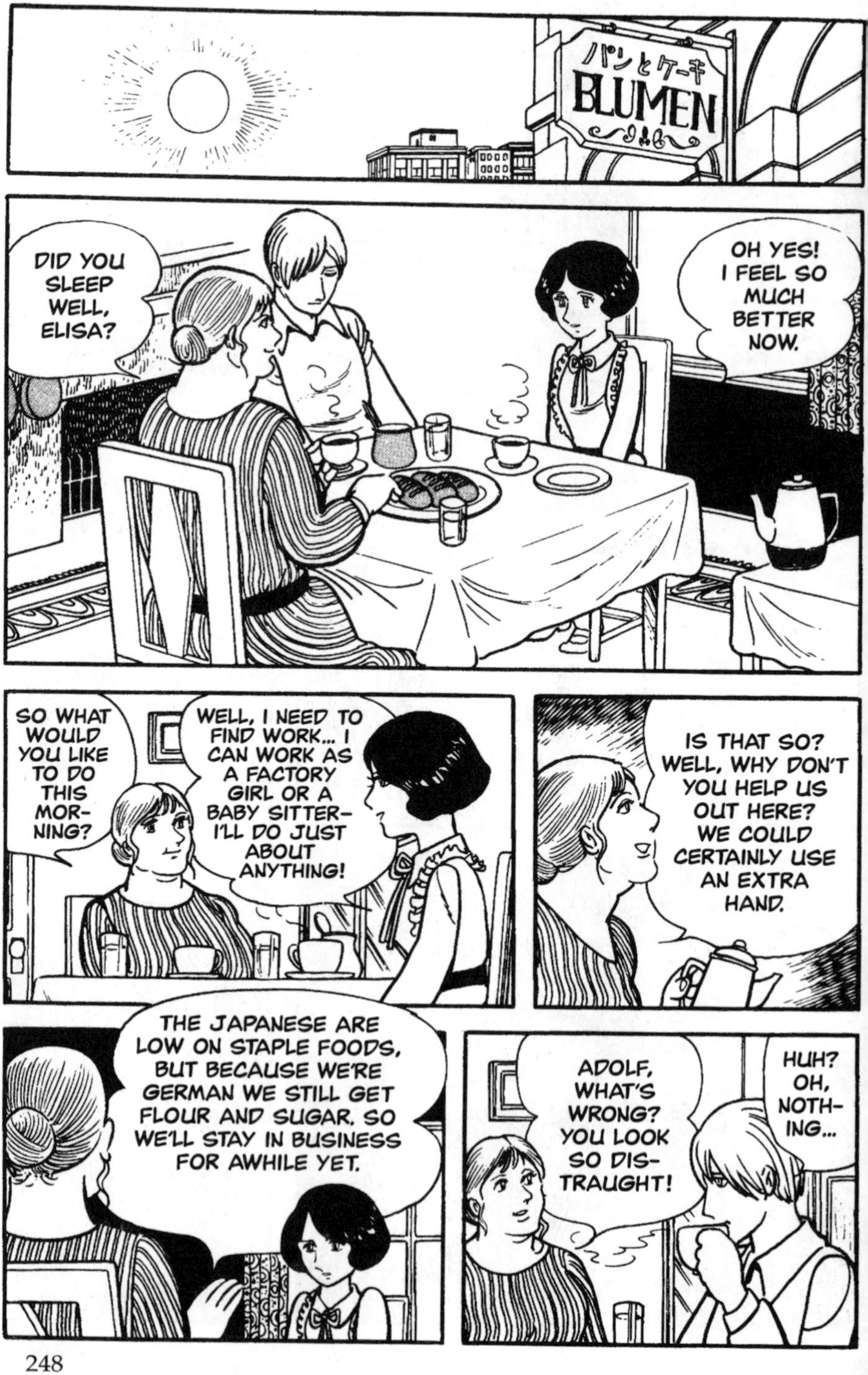
パンとケーキ
BLUMEN
DID YOU SLEEP WELL, ELISA?
OH YES! I FEEL SO MUCH BETTER NOW.
SO WHAT WOULD YOU LIKE TO DO THIS MOR-NING?
WELL, I NEED TO FIND WORK... I CAN WORK AS A FACTORY GIRL OR A BABY SITTER-- I'LL DO JUST ABOUT ANYTHING!
IS THAT SO? WELL, WHY DON'T YOU HELP US OUT HERE? WE COULD CERTAINLY USE AN EXTRA HAND.
THE JAPANESE ARE LOW ON STAPLE FOODS, BUT BECAUSE WE'RE GERMAN WE STILL GET FLOUR AND SUGAR. SO WE'LL STAY IN BUSINESS FOR AWHILE YET.
ADOLF, WHAT'S WRONG? YOU LOOK SO DIS-TRAUGHT!
HUH? OH, NOTH-ING...

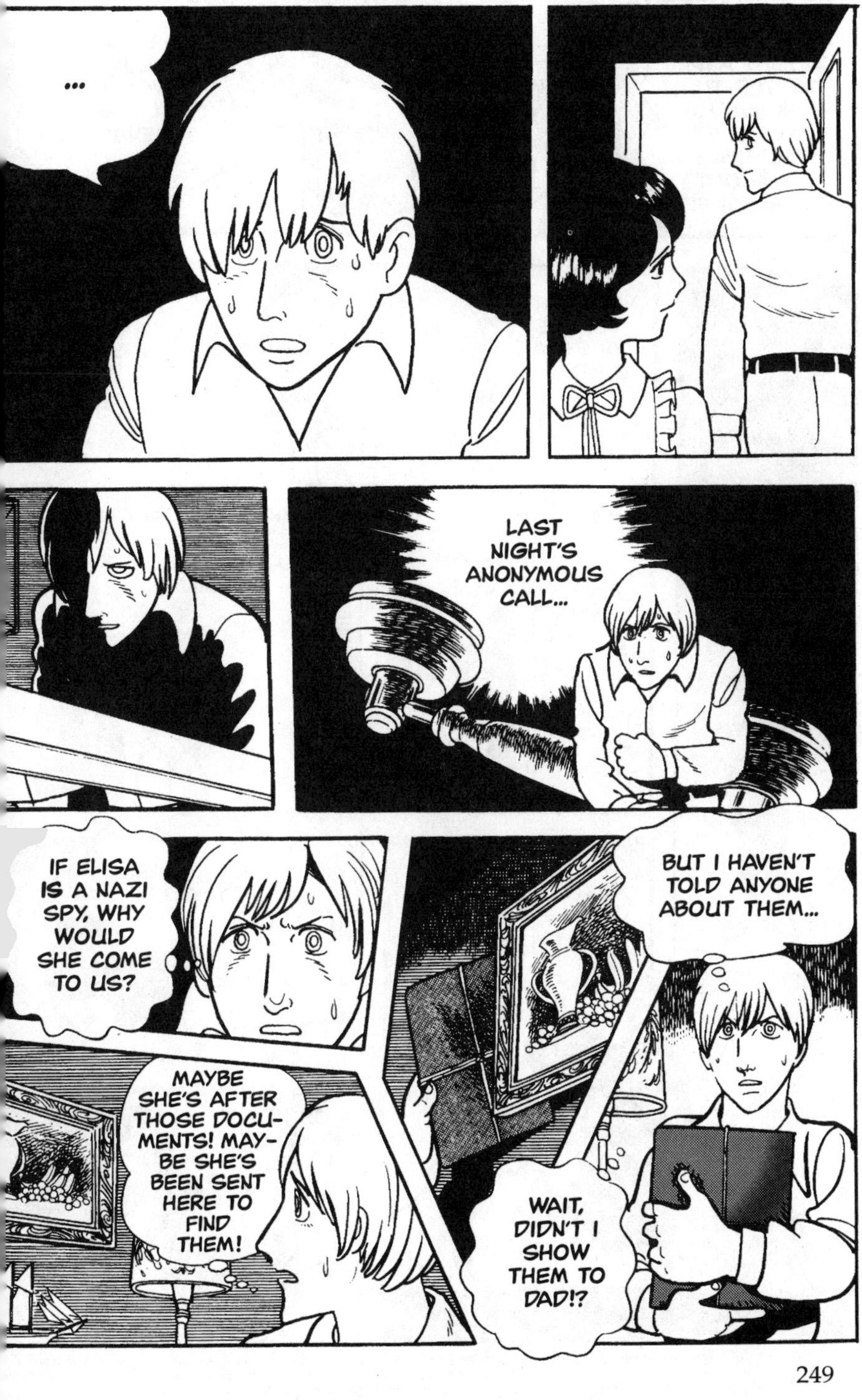
...
LAST NIGHT'S ANONYMOUS CALL...
IF ELISA IS A NAZI SPY, WHY WOULD SHE COME TO US?
BUT I HAVEN'T TOLD ANYONE ABOUT THEM...
MAYBE SHE'S AFTER THOSE DOCU-MENTS! MAY-BE SHE'S BEEN SENT HERE TO FIND THEM!
WAIT, DIDN'T I SHOW THEM TO DAD!?

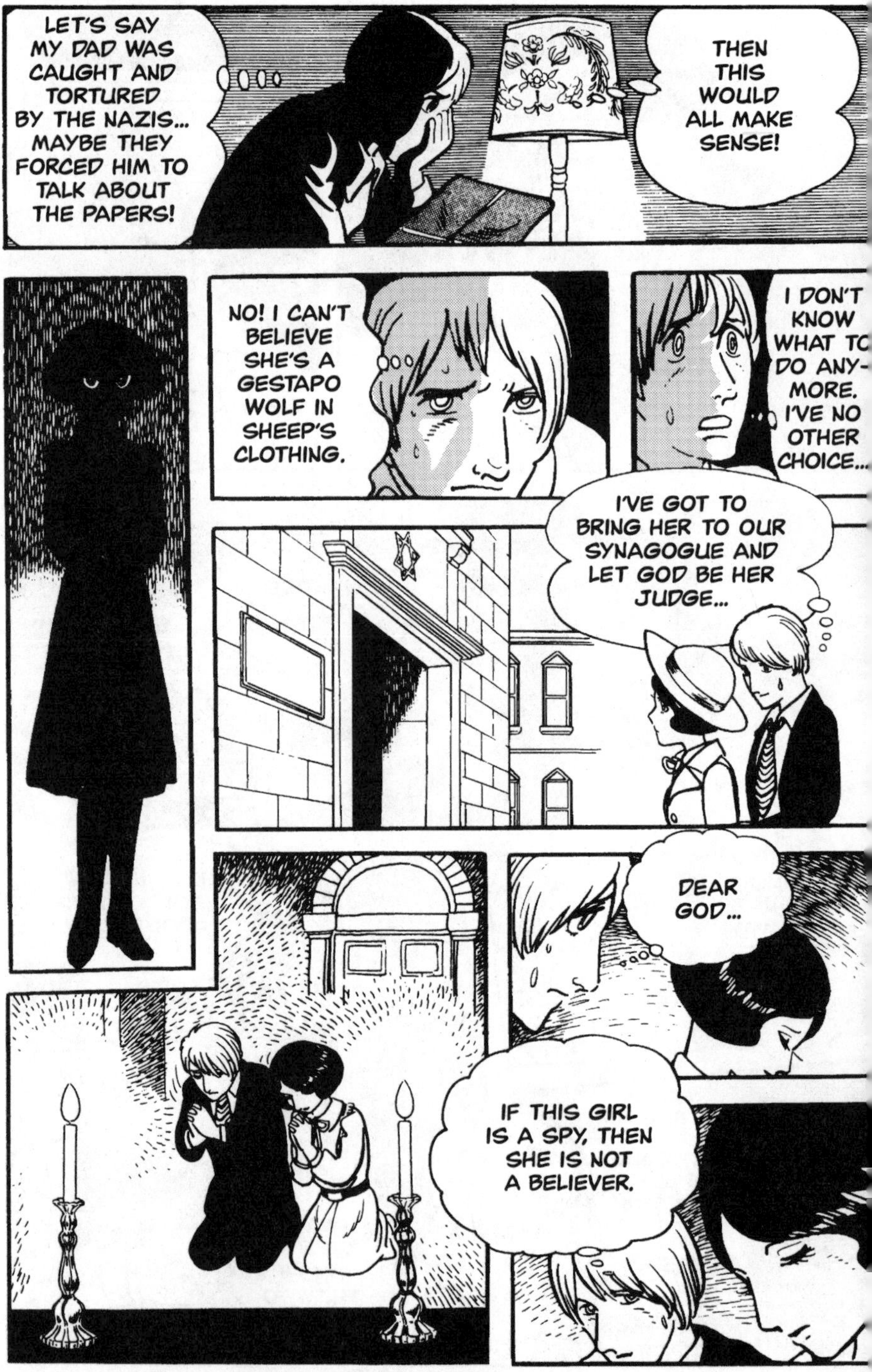
LET'S SAY MY DAD WAS CAUGHT AND TORTURED BY THE NAZIS... MAYBE THEY FORCED HIM TO TALK ABOUT THE PAPERS!
THEN THIS WOULD ALL MAKE SENSE!
NO! I CAN'T BELIEVE SHE'S A GESTAPO WOLF IN SHEEP'S CLOTHING.
I DON'T KNOW WHAT TO DO ANY-MORE. I'VE NO OTHER CHOICE...
I'VE GOT TO BRING HER TO OUR SYNAGOGUE AND LET GOD BE HER JUDGE...
DEAR GOD...
IF THIS GIRL IS A SPY, THEN SHE IS NOT A BELIEVER.

★ As someone raised outside the Judeo-Christian tradition, Osamu Tezuka occasionally erred when depicting the details of Jewish and Christian religious customs. In this case, he shows Adolf Kamil praying in a Christian pose. No offense was, or is, intended. Since Osamu Tezuka is no longer alive, the publishers have chosen to respect the integrity of his original art work.

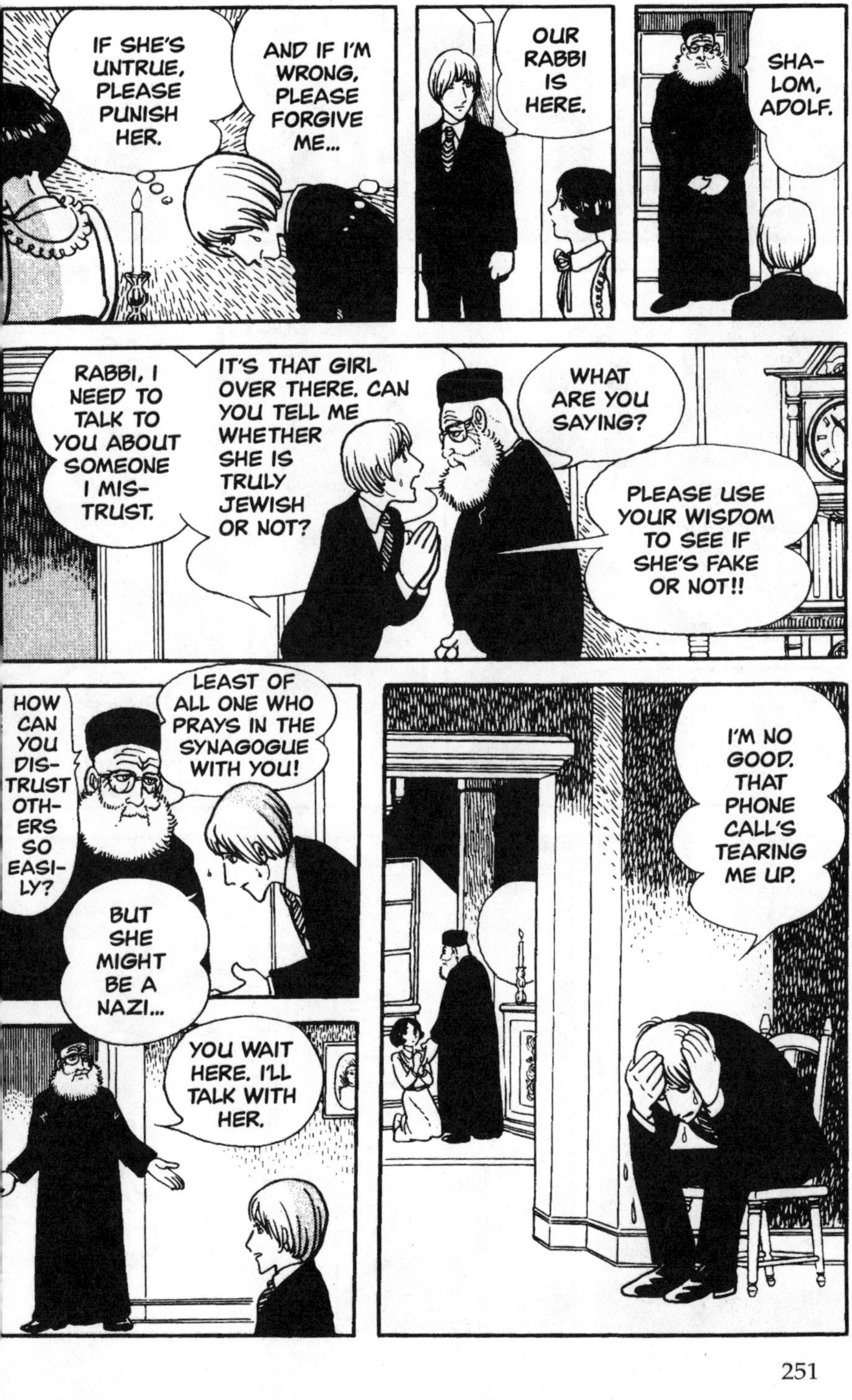
IF SHE'S UNTRUE, PLEASE PUNISH HER.
AND IF I'M WRONG, PLEASE FORGIVE ME...
OUR RABBI IS HERE.
SHA-LOM, ADOLF.
RABBI, I NEED TO TALK TO YOU ABOUT SOMEONE I MIS-TRUST.
IT'S THAT GIRL OVER THERE. CAN YOU TELL ME WHETHER SHE IS TRULY JEWISH OR NOT?
WHAT ARE YOU SAYING?
PLEASE USE YOUR WISDOM TO SEE IF SHE'S FAKE OR NOT!!
HOW CAN YOU DIS-TRUST OTH-ERS SO EASI-LY?
LEAST OF ALL ONE WHO PRAYS IN THE SYNAGOGUE WITH YOU!
BUT SHE MIGHT BE A NAZI...
YOU WAIT HERE. I'LL TALK WITH HER.
I'M NO GOOD. THAT PHONE CALL'S TEARING ME UP.

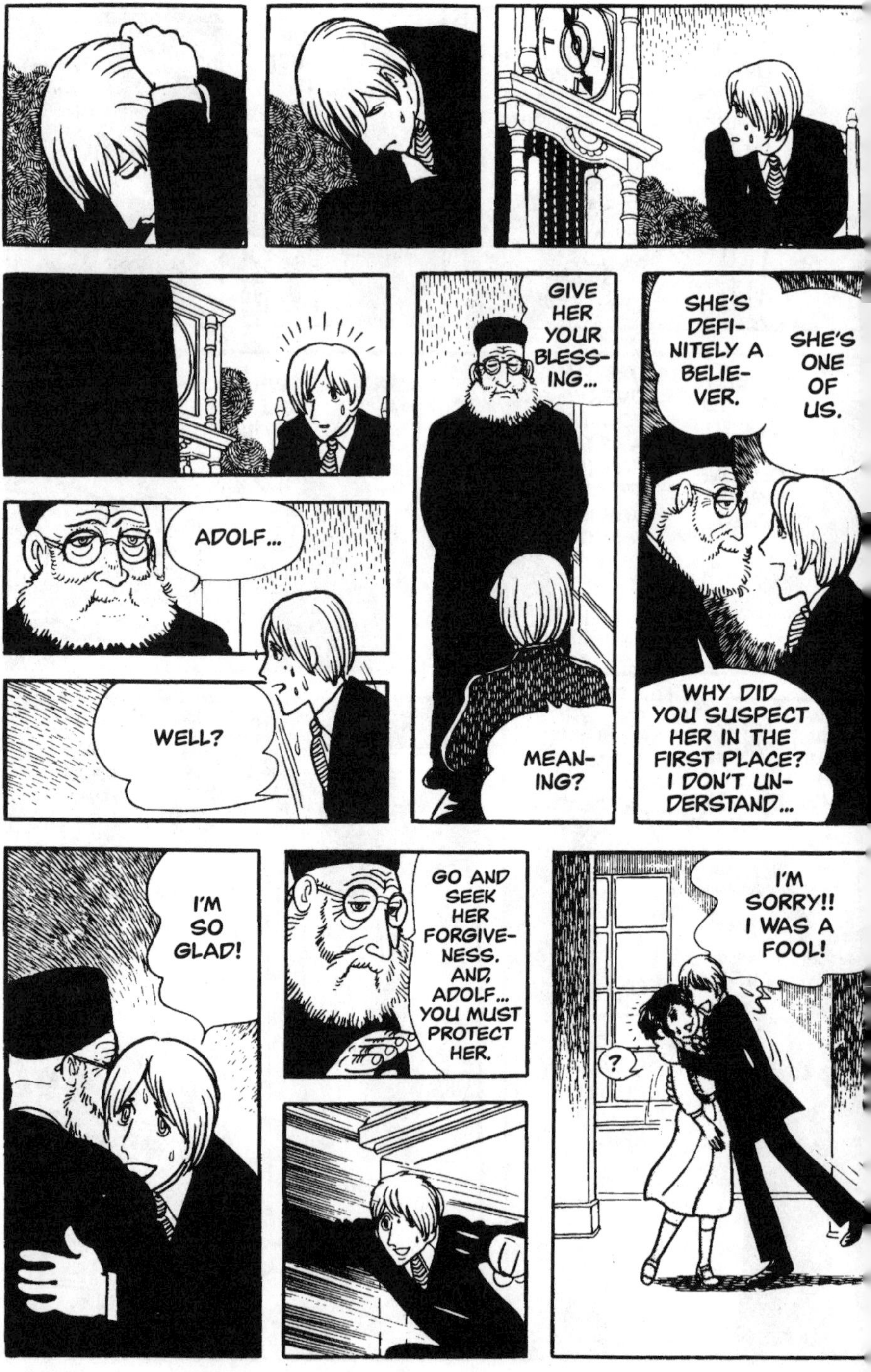
ADOLF...
WELL?
GIVE HER YOUR BLESSING...
MEANING?
SHE'S DEFINITELY A BELIEVER.
SHE'S ONE OF US.
WHY DID YOU SUSPECT HER IN THE FIRST PLACE? I DON'T UNDERSTAND...
I'M SO GLAD!
GO AND SEEK HER FORGIVENESS. AND, ADOLF... YOU MUST PROTECT HER.
?
I'M SORRY!! I WAS A FOOL!

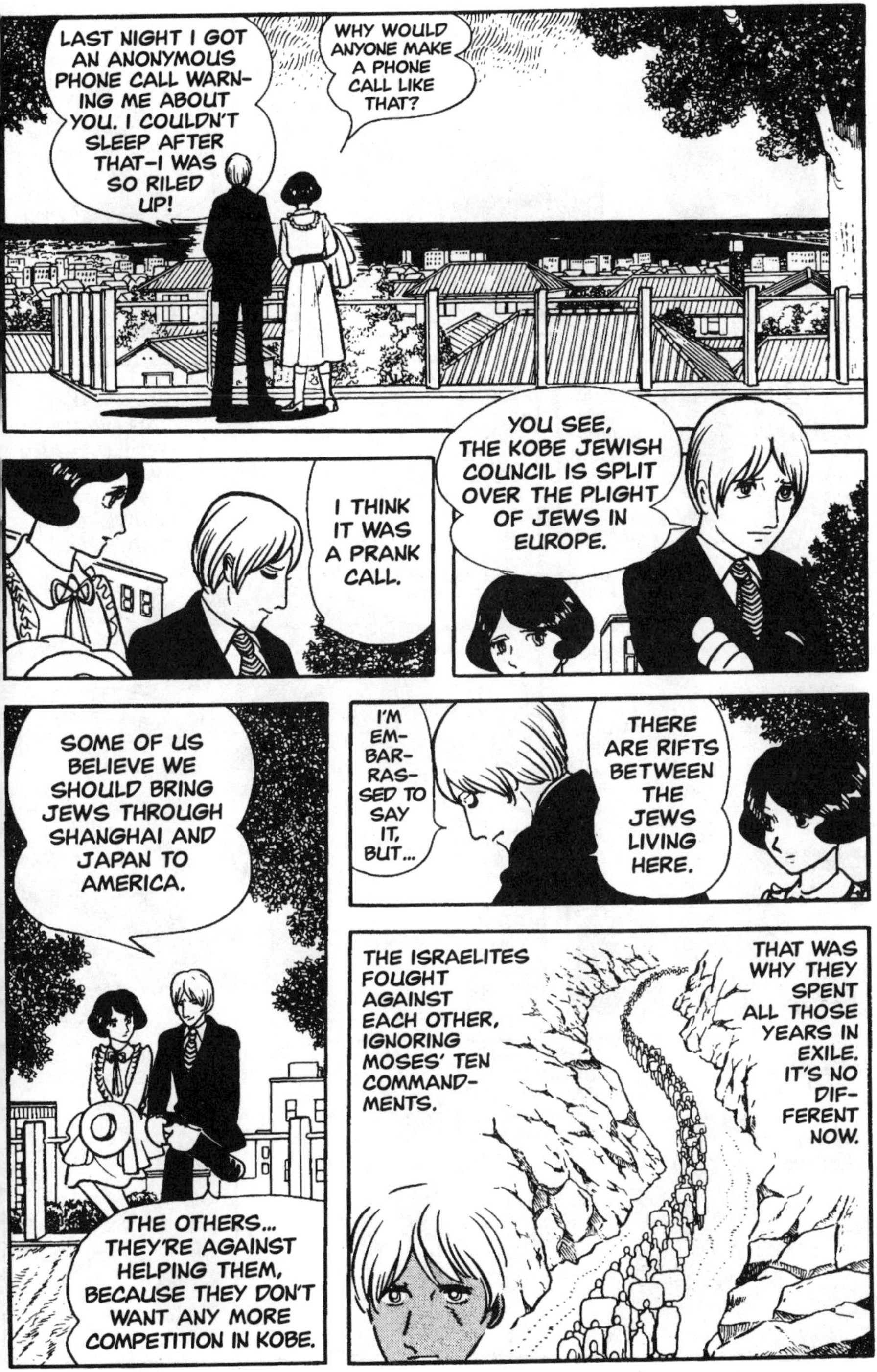
LAST NIGHT I GOT AN ANONYMOUS PHONE CALL WARNING ME ABOUT YOU. I COULDN'T SLEEP AFTER THAT–I WAS SO RILED UP!
WHY WOULD ANYONE MAKE A PHONE CALL LIKE THAT?
I THINK IT WAS A PRANK CALL.
YOU SEE, THE KOBE JEWISH COUNCIL IS SPLIT OVER THE PLIGHT OF JEWS IN EUROPE.
SOME OF US BELIEVE WE SHOULD BRING JEWS THROUGH SHANGHAI AND JAPAN TO AMERICA.
THE OTHERS... THEY'RE AGAINST HELPING THEM, BECAUSE THEY DON'T WANT ANY MORE COMPETITION IN KOBE.
I'M EMBARRASSED TO SAY IT, BUT...
THERE ARE RIFTS BETWEEN THE JEWS LIVING HERE.
THE ISRAELITES FOUGHT AGAINST EACH OTHER, IGNORING MOSES' TEN COMMANDMENTS.
THAT WAS WHY THEY SPENT ALL THOSE YEARS IN EXILE. IT'S NO DIFFERENT NOW.

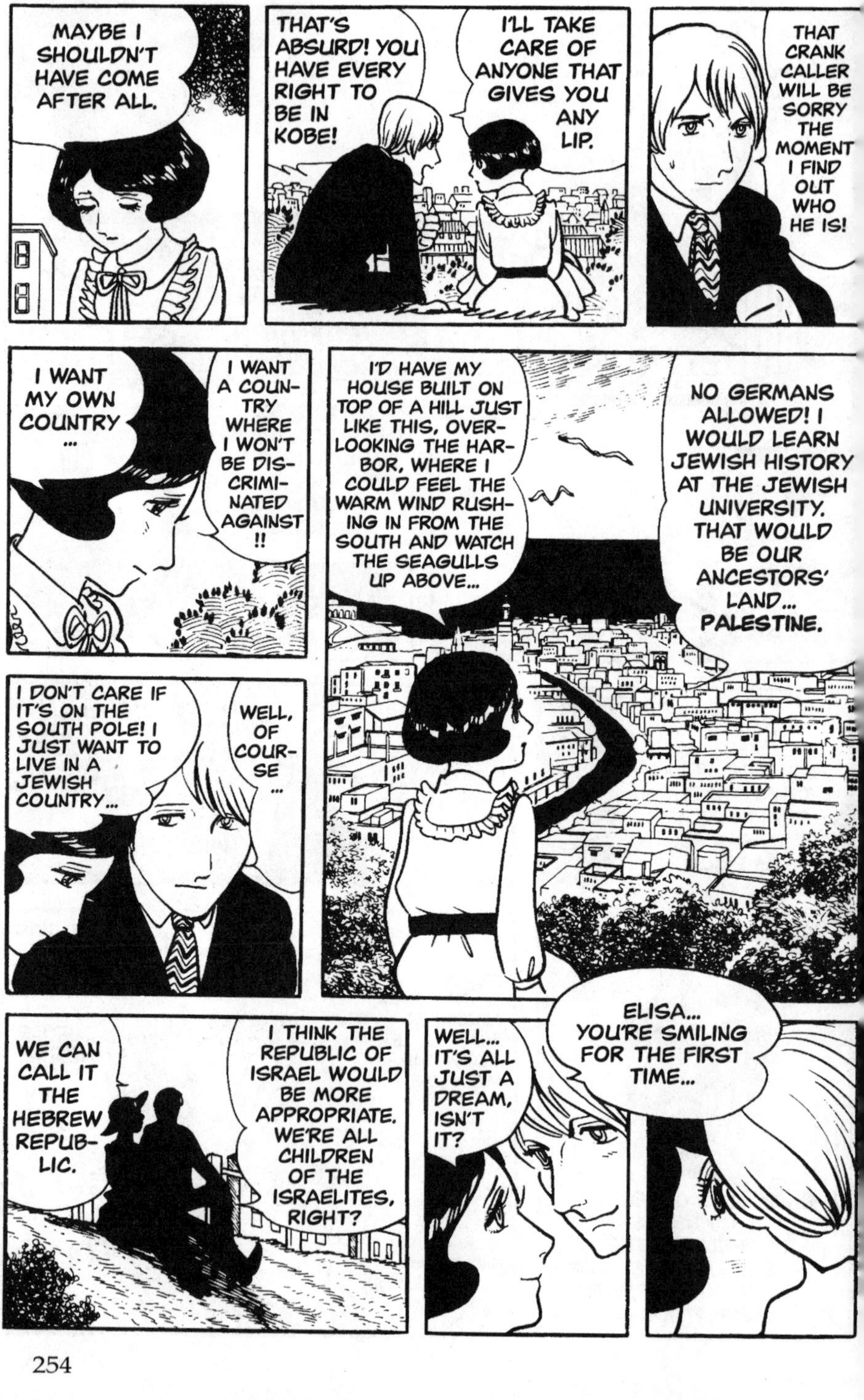
MAYBE I SHOULDN'T HAVE COME AFTER ALL.
THAT'S ABSURD! YOU HAVE EVERY RIGHT TO BE IN KOBE!
I'LL TAKE CARE OF ANYONE THAT GIVES YOU ANY LIP.
THAT CRANK CALLER WILL BE SORRY THE MOMENT I FIND OUT WHO HE IS!
I WANT MY OWN COUNTRY ...
I WANT A COUNTRY WHERE I WON'T BE DISCRIMINATED AGAINST !!
I'D HAVE MY HOUSE BUILT ON TOP OF A HILL JUST LIKE THIS, OVERLOOKING THE HARBOR, WHERE I COULD FEEL THE WARM WIND RUSHING IN FROM THE SOUTH AND WATCH THE SEAGULLS UP ABOVE...
NO GERMANS ALLOWED! I WOULD LEARN JEWISH HISTORY AT THE JEWISH UNIVERSITY. THAT WOULD BE OUR ANCESTORS' LAND... PALESTINE.
I DON'T CARE IF IT'S ON THE SOUTH POLE! I JUST WANT TO LIVE IN A JEWISH COUNTRY...
WELL, OF COURSE ...
WE CAN CALL IT THE HEBREW REPUBLIC.
I THINK THE REPUBLIC OF ISRAEL WOULD BE MORE APPROPRIATE. WE'RE ALL CHILDREN OF THE ISRAELITES, RIGHT?
WELL... IT'S ALL JUST A DREAM, ISN'T IT?
ELISA... YOU'RE SMILING FOR THE FIRST TIME...

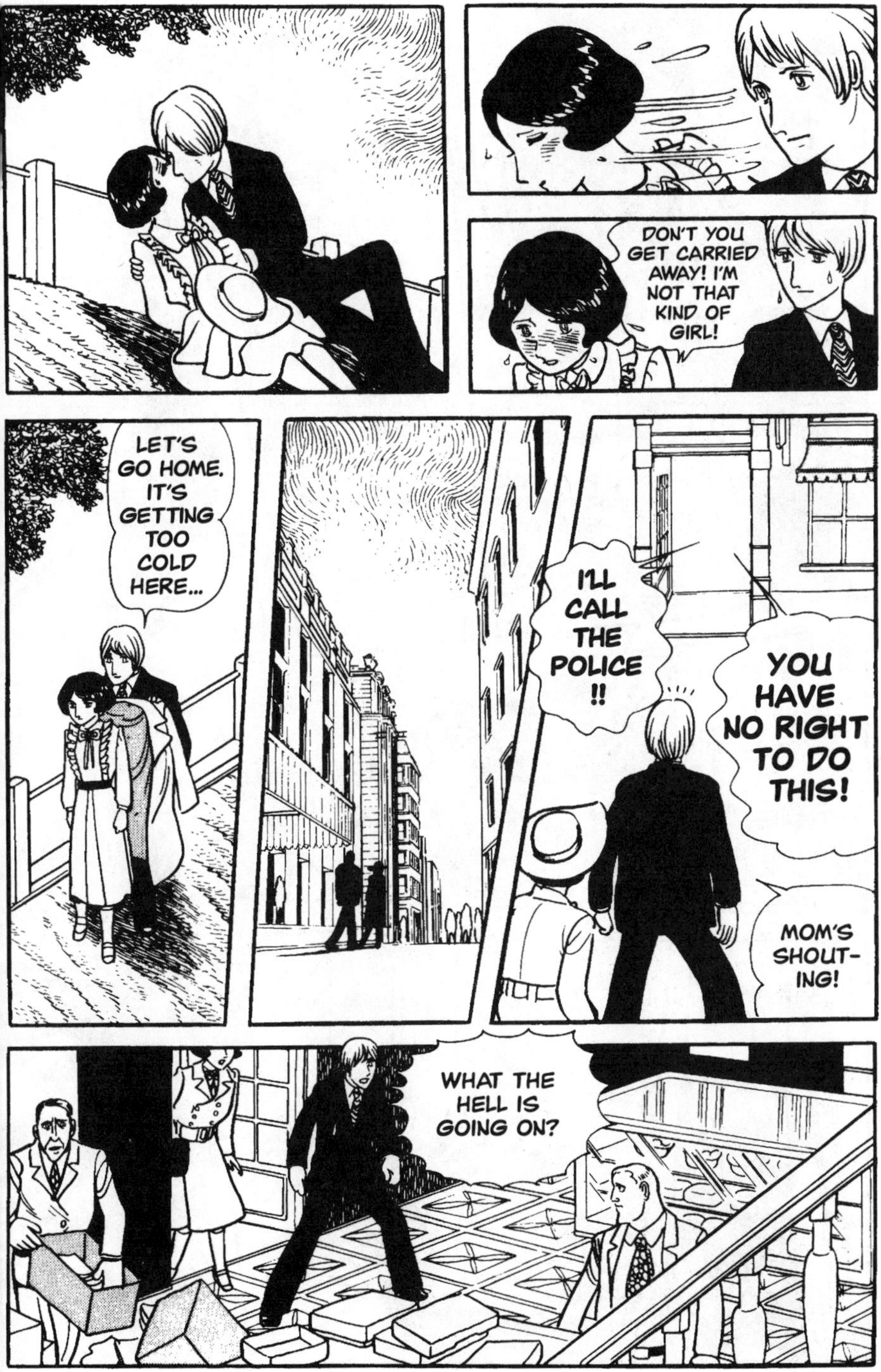
DON'T YOU GET CARRIED AWAY! I'M NOT THAT KIND OF GIRL!
LET'S GO HOME. IT'S GETTING TOO COLD HERE...
I'LL CALL THE POLICE !!
YOU HAVE NO RIGHT TO DO THIS!
MOM'S SHOUT-ING!
WHAT THE HELL IS GOING ON?

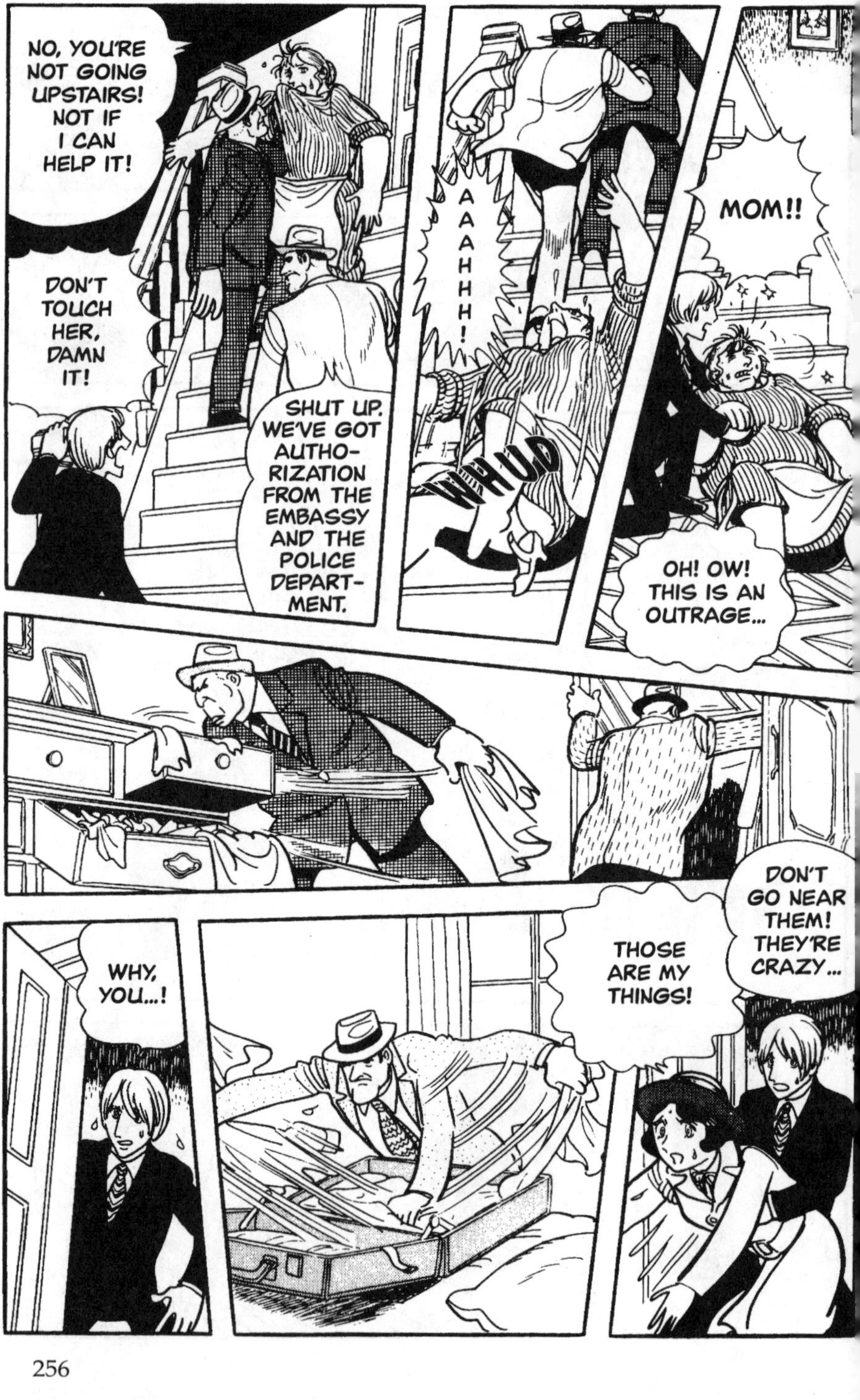
NO, YOU'RE NOT GOING UPSTAIRS! NOT IF I CAN HELP IT!
DON'T TOUCH HER, DAMN IT!
SHUT UP. WE'VE GOT AUTHORIZATION FROM THE EMBASSY AND THE POLICE DEPARTMENT.
AAAHHH!
WHUD
MOM!!
OH! OW! THIS IS AN OUTRAGE...
WHY, YOU...!
THOSE ARE MY THINGS!
DON'T GO NEAR THEM! THEY'RE CRAZY...

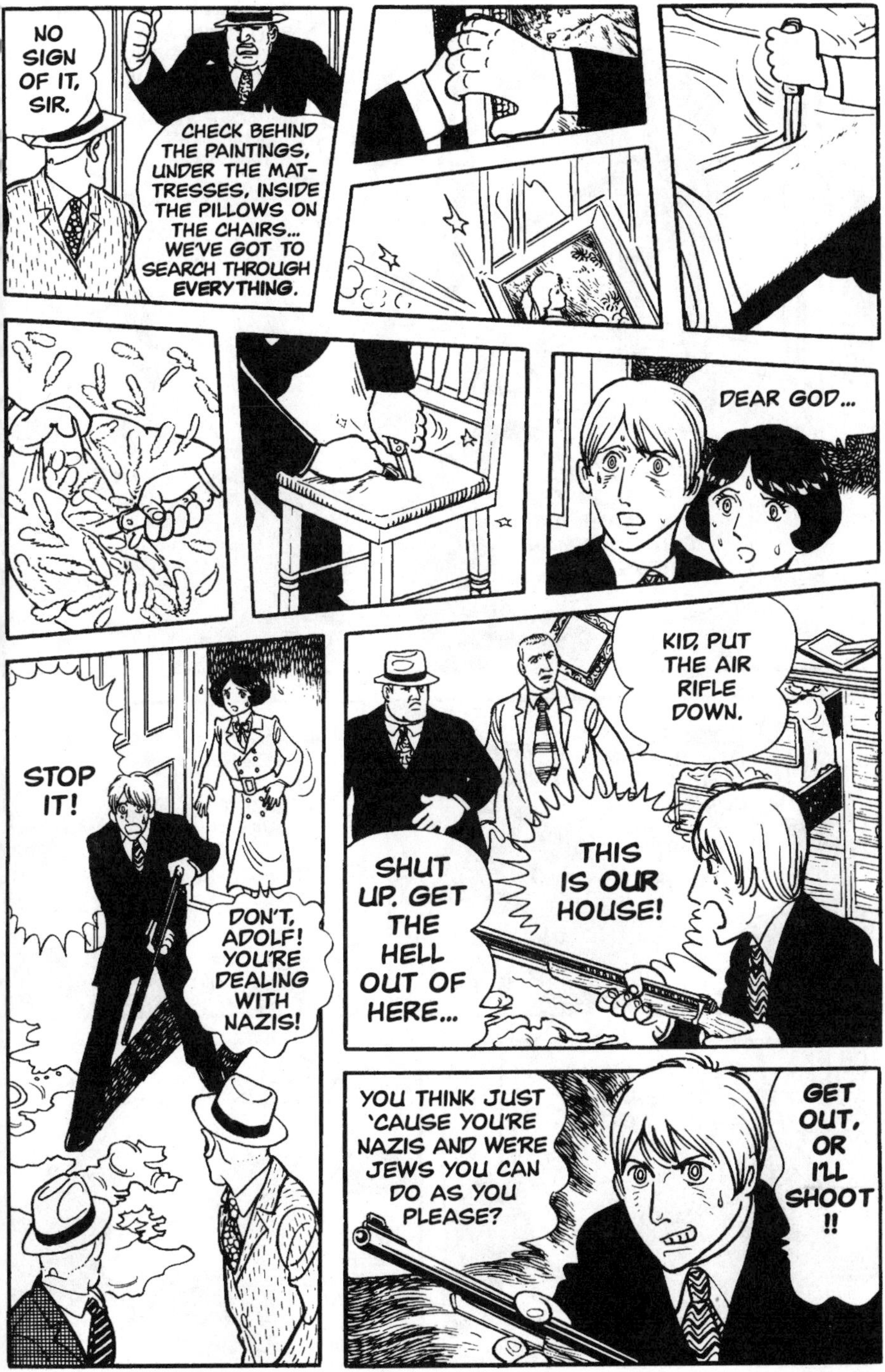
NO SIGN OF IT, SIR.
CHECK BEHIND THE PAINTINGS, UNDER THE MATTRESSES, INSIDE THE PILLOWS ON THE CHAIRS... WE'VE GOT TO SEARCH THROUGH EVERYTHING.
DEAR GOD...
STOP IT!
DON'T, ADOLF! YOU'RE DEALING WITH NAZIS!
KID, PUT THE AIR RIFLE DOWN.
THIS IS OUR HOUSE!
SHUT UP. GET THE HELL OUT OF HERE...
YOU THINK JUST 'CAUSE YOU'RE NAZIS AND WE'RE JEWS YOU CAN DO AS YOU PLEASE?
GET OUT, OR I'LL SHOOT!!

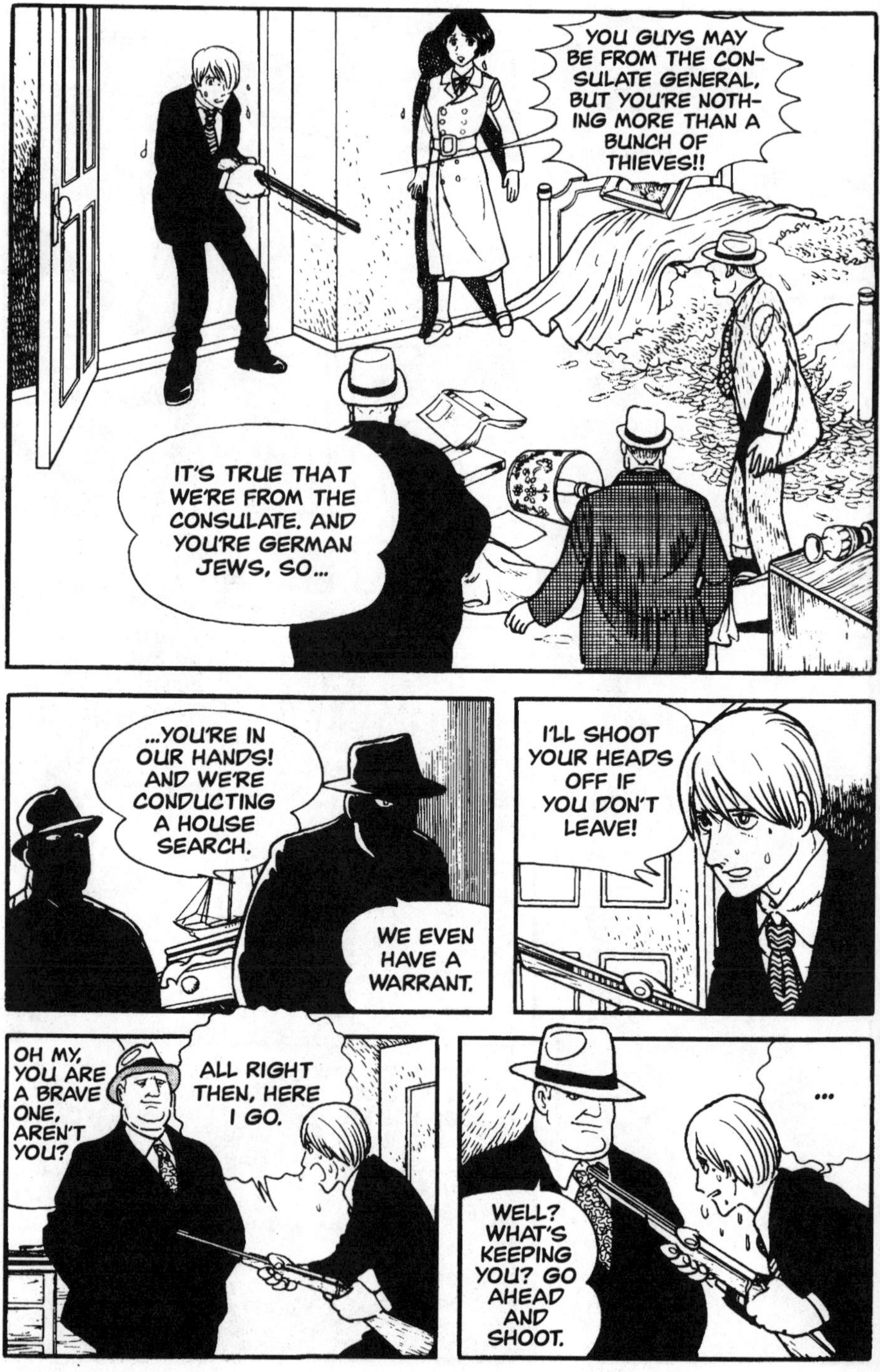
YOU GUYS MAY BE FROM THE CON-SULATE GENERAL, BUT YOU'RE NOTH-ING MORE THAN A BUNCH OF THIEVES!!
IT'S TRUE THAT WE'RE FROM THE CONSULATE. AND YOU'RE GERMAN JEWS, SO...
...YOU'RE IN OUR HANDS! AND WE'RE CONDUCTING A HOUSE SEARCH.
WE EVEN HAVE A WARRANT.
I'LL SHOOT YOUR HEADS OFF IF YOU DON'T LEAVE!
OH MY, YOU ARE A BRAVE ONE, AREN'T YOU?
ALL RIGHT THEN, HERE I GO.
...
WELL? WHAT'S KEEPING YOU? GO AHEAD AND SHOOT.

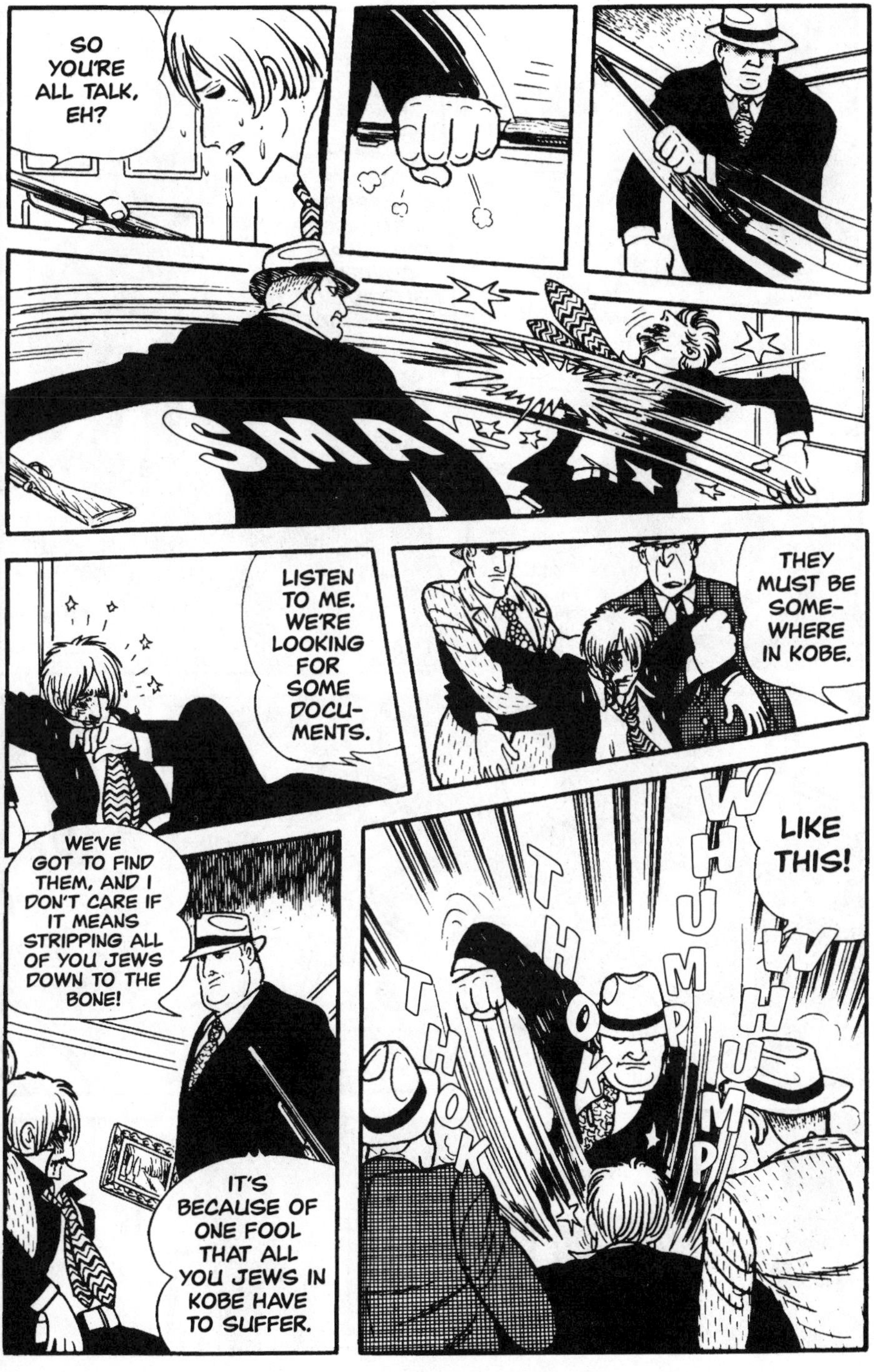
SO YOU'RE ALL TALK, EH?
SMA
LISTEN TO ME. WE'RE LOOKING FOR SOME DOCU-MENTS.
THEY MUST BE SOME-WHERE IN KOBE.
WE'VE GOT TO FIND THEM, AND I DON'T CARE IF IT MEANS STRIPPING ALL OF YOU JEWS DOWN TO THE BONE!
IT'S BECAUSE OF ONE FOOL THAT ALL YOU JEWS IN KOBE HAVE TO SUFFER.
WHUMP
LIKE THIS!
THOK
WHUMP
THOK
WHUMP
THOK

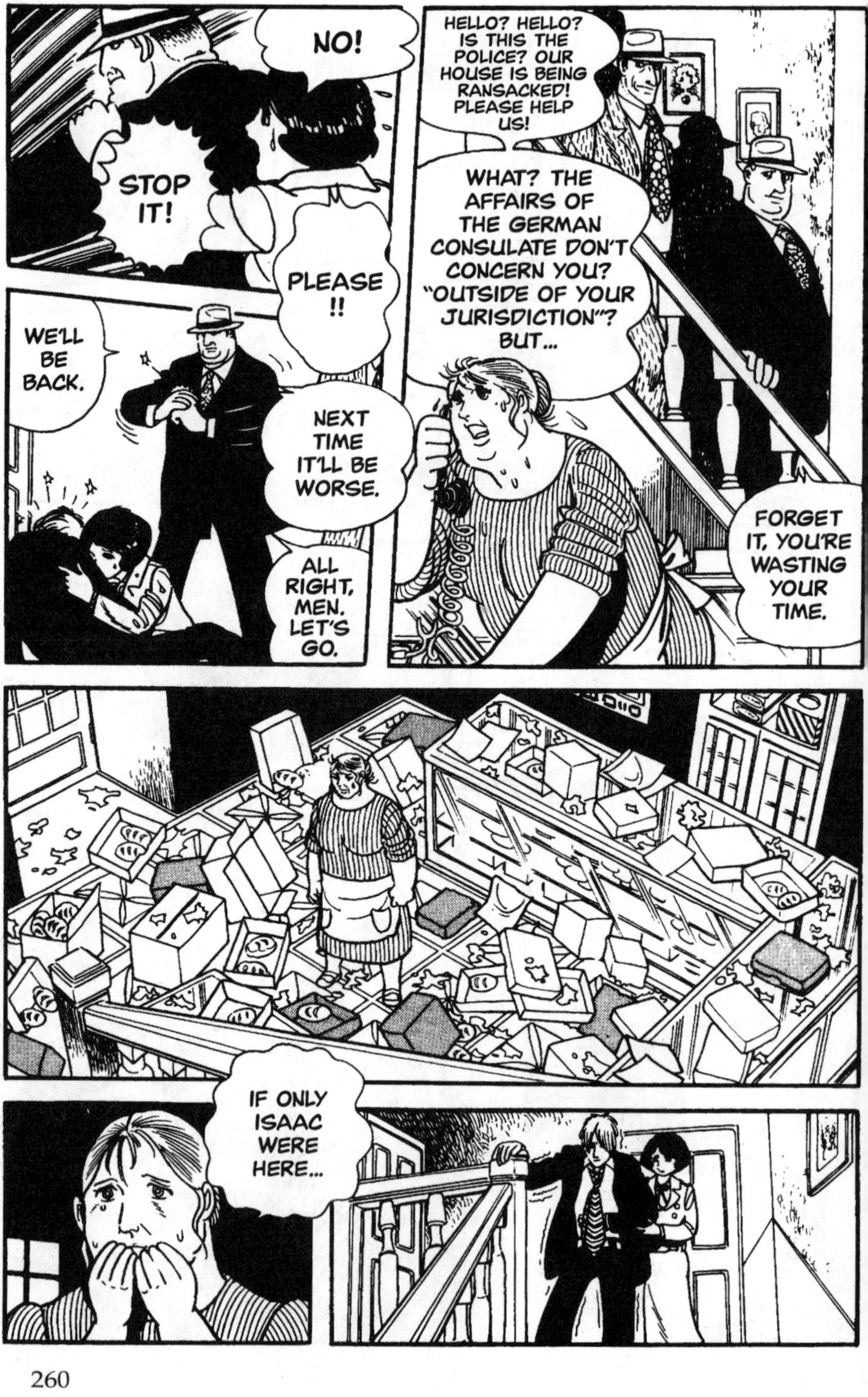
NO!
STOP IT!
PLEASE !!
WE'LL BE BACK.
NEXT TIME IT'LL BE WORSE.
ALL RIGHT, MEN. LET'S GO.
HELLO? HELLO? IS THIS THE POLICE? OUR HOUSE IS BEING RANSACKED! PLEASE HELP US!
WHAT? THE AFFAIRS OF THE GERMAN CONSULATE DON'T CONCERN YOU? "OUTSIDE OF YOUR JURISDICTION"? BUT...
FORGET IT, YOU'RE WASTING YOUR TIME.
IF ONLY ISAAC WERE HERE...

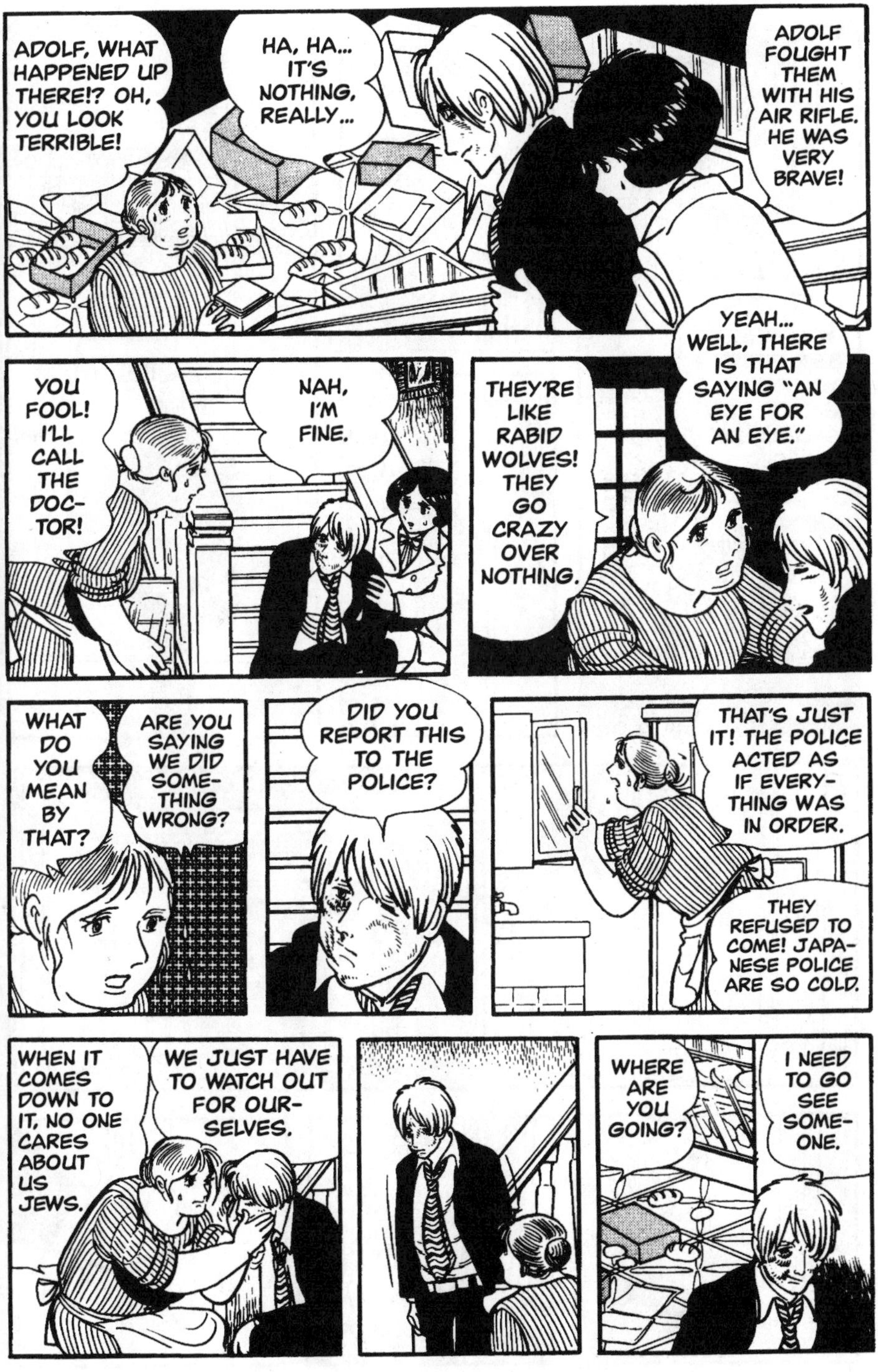
ADOLF, WHAT HAPPENED UP THERE!? OH, YOU LOOK TERRIBLE!
HA, HA... IT'S NOTHING, REALLY...
ADOLF FOUGHT THEM WITH HIS AIR RIFLE. HE WAS VERY BRAVE!
YOU FOOL! I'LL CALL THE DOCTOR!
NAH, I'M FINE.
THEY'RE LIKE RABID WOLVES! THEY GO CRAZY OVER NOTHING.
YEAH... WELL, THERE IS THAT SAYING "AN EYE FOR AN EYE."
WHAT DO YOU MEAN BY THAT?
ARE YOU SAYING WE DID SOMETHING WRONG?
DID YOU REPORT THIS TO THE POLICE?
THAT'S JUST IT! THE POLICE ACTED AS IF EVERYTHING WAS IN ORDER.
THEY REFUSED TO COME! JAPANESE POLICE ARE SO COLD.
WHEN IT COMES DOWN TO IT, NO ONE CARES ABOUT US JEWS.
WE JUST HAVE TO WATCH OUT FOR OURSELVES.
WHERE ARE YOU GOING?
I NEED TO GO SEE SOMEONE.

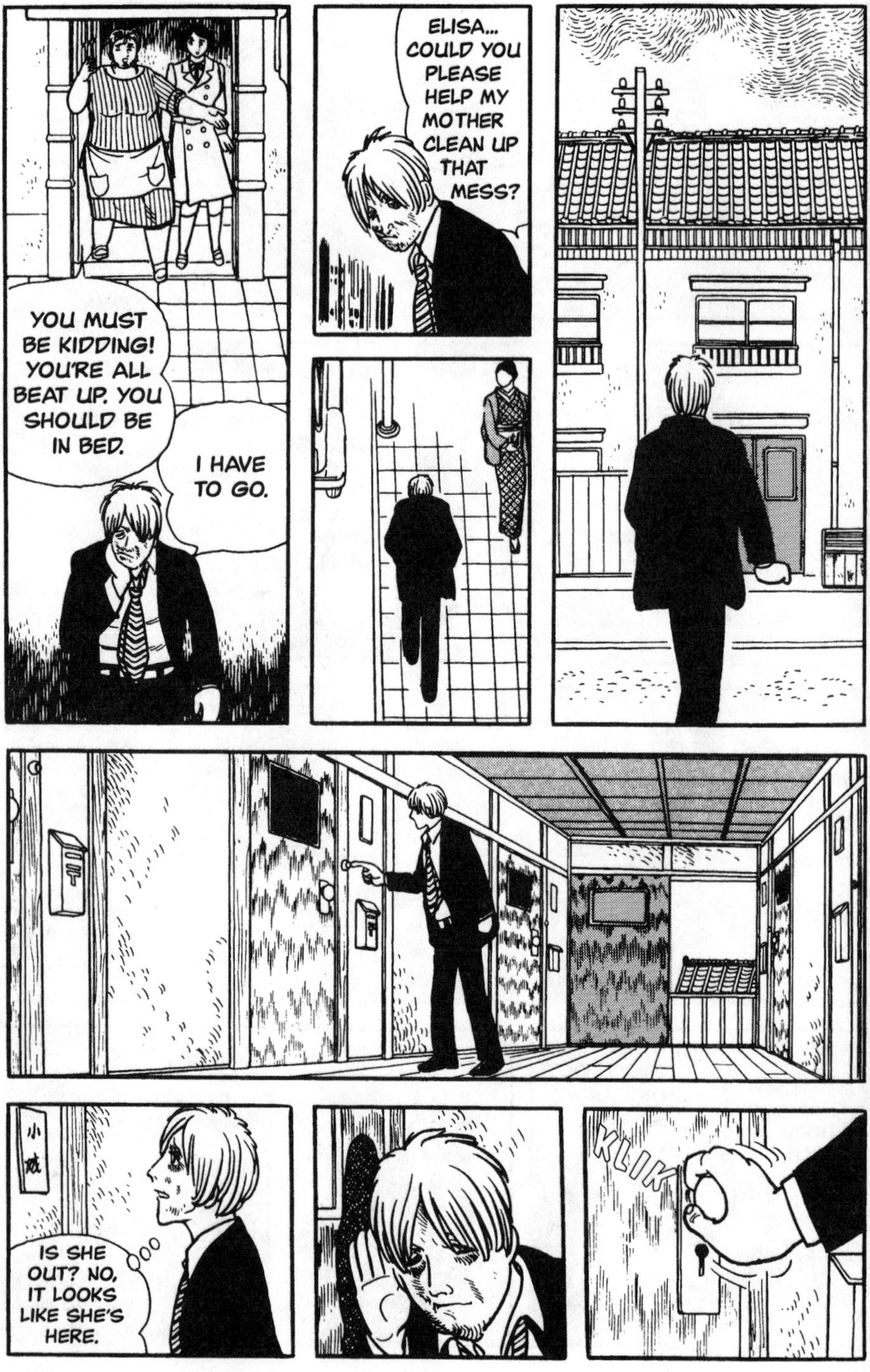
YOU MUST BE KIDDING! YOU'RE ALL BEAT UP. YOU SHOULD BE IN BED.
I HAVE TO GO.
ELISA... COULD YOU PLEASE HELP MY MOTHER CLEAN UP THAT MESS?
IS SHE OUT? NO, IT LOOKS LIKE SHE'S HERE.
KLIK

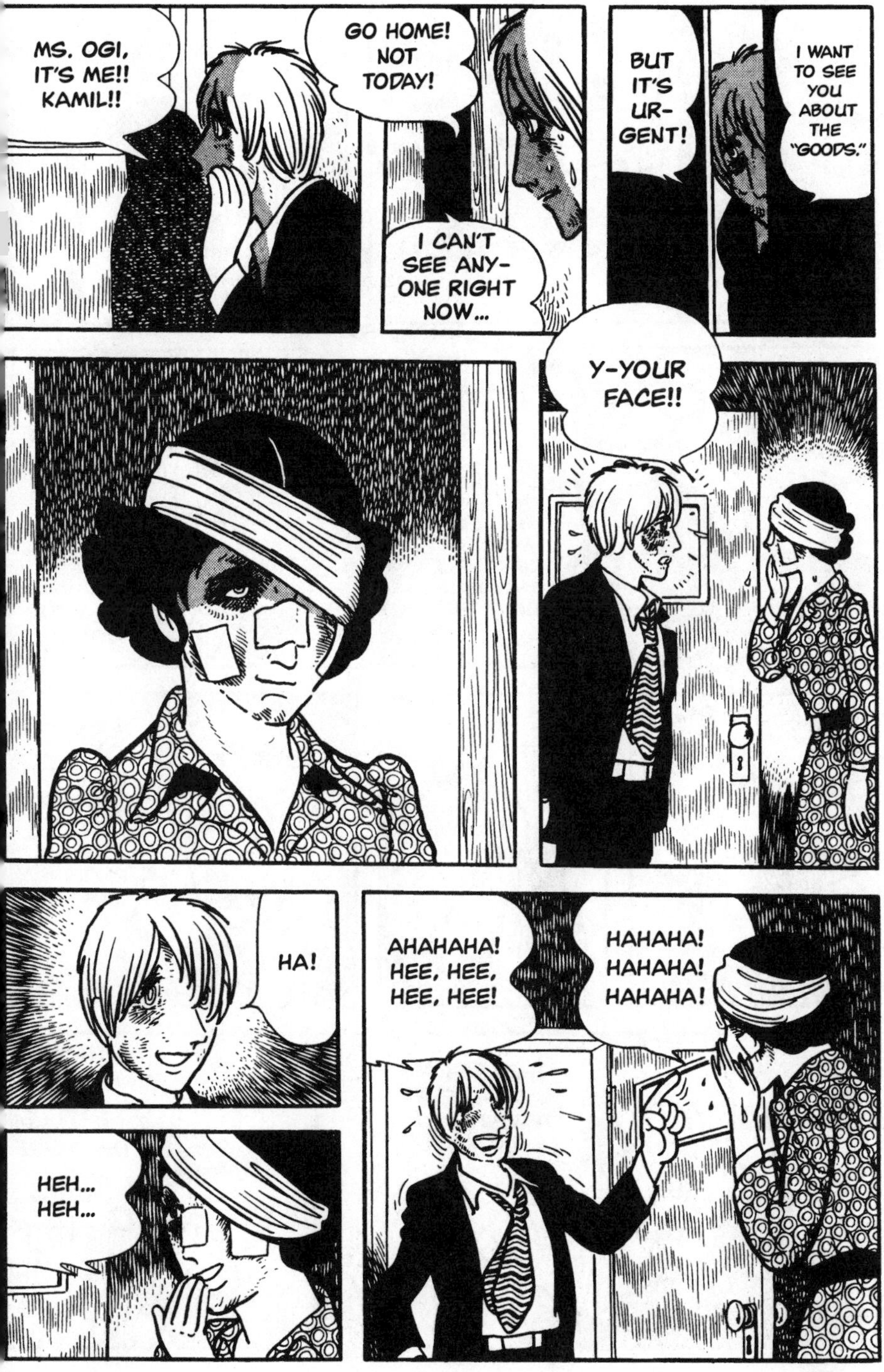
MS. OGI, IT'S ME!! KAMIL!!
GO HOME! NOT TODAY!
I CAN'T SEE ANY-ONE RIGHT NOW...
BUT IT'S UR-GENT!
I WANT TO SEE YOU ABOUT THE "GOODS."
Y-YOUR FACE!!
HA!
HEH... HEH...
AHAHAHA! HEE, HEE, HEE, HEE!
HAHAHA! HAHAHA! HAHAHA!

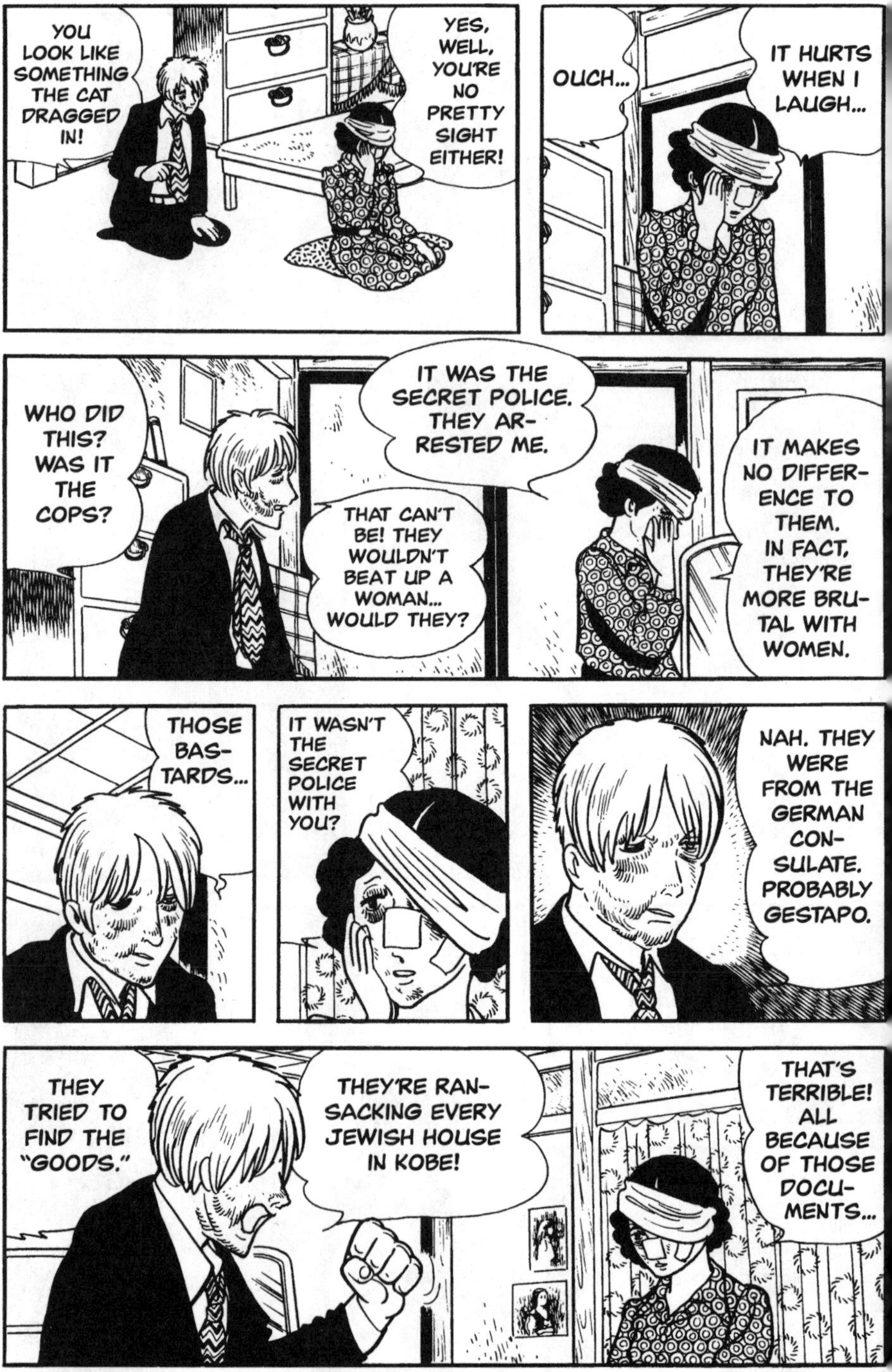
YOU LOOK LIKE SOMETHING THE CAT DRAGGED IN!
YES, WELL, YOU'RE NO PRETTY SIGHT EITHER!
OUCH...
IT HURTS WHEN I LAUGH...
WHO DID THIS? WAS IT THE COPS?
IT WAS THE SECRET POLICE. THEY ARRESTED ME.
THAT CAN'T BE! THEY WOULDN'T BEAT UP A WOMAN... WOULD THEY?
IT MAKES NO DIFFERENCE TO THEM. IN FACT, THEY'RE MORE BRUTAL WITH WOMEN.
THOSE BASTARDS...
IT WASN'T THE SECRET POLICE WITH YOU?
NAH. THEY WERE FROM THE GERMAN CONSULATE. PROBABLY GESTAPO.
THEY TRIED TO FIND THE "GOODS."
THEY'RE RANSACKING EVERY JEWISH HOUSE IN KOBE!
THAT'S TERRIBLE! ALL BECAUSE OF THOSE DOCUMENTS...

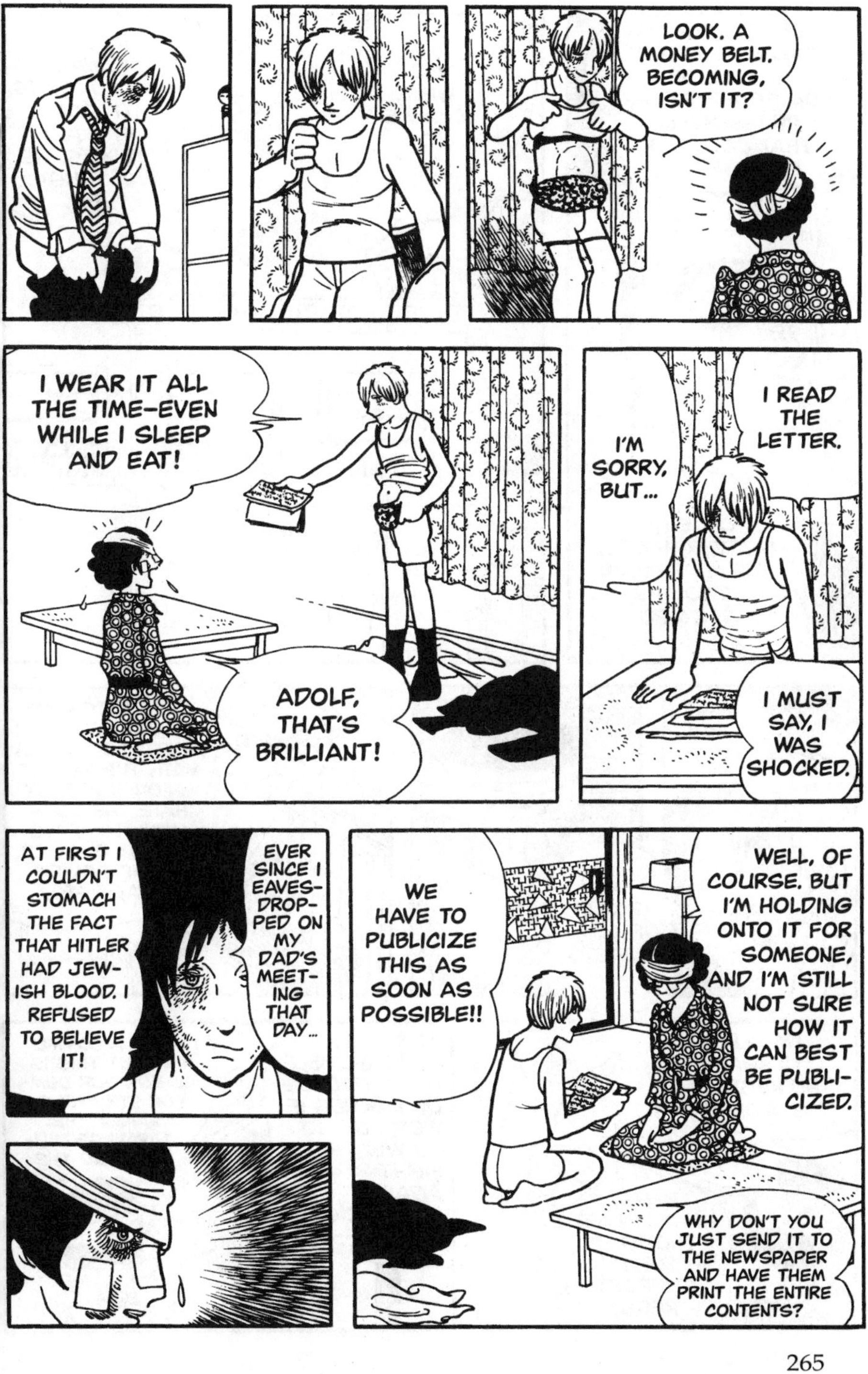
LOOK. A MONEY BELT. BECOMING, ISN'T IT?
I WEAR IT ALL THE TIME–EVEN WHILE I SLEEP AND EAT!
ADOLF, THAT'S BRILLIANT!
I'M SORRY, BUT...
I READ THE LETTER.
I MUST SAY, I WAS SHOCKED.
AT FIRST I COULDN'T STOMACH THE FACT THAT HITLER HAD JEWISH BLOOD. I REFUSED TO BELIEVE IT!
EVER SINCE I EAVES-DROPPED ON MY DAD'S MEETING THAT DAY...
WE HAVE TO PUBLICIZE THIS AS SOON AS POSSIBLE!!
WELL, OF COURSE. BUT I'M HOLDING ONTO IT FOR SOMEONE, AND I'M STILL NOT SURE HOW IT CAN BEST BE PUBLICIZED.
WHY DON'T YOU JUST SEND IT TO THE NEWSPAPER AND HAVE THEM PRINT THE ENTIRE CONTENTS?

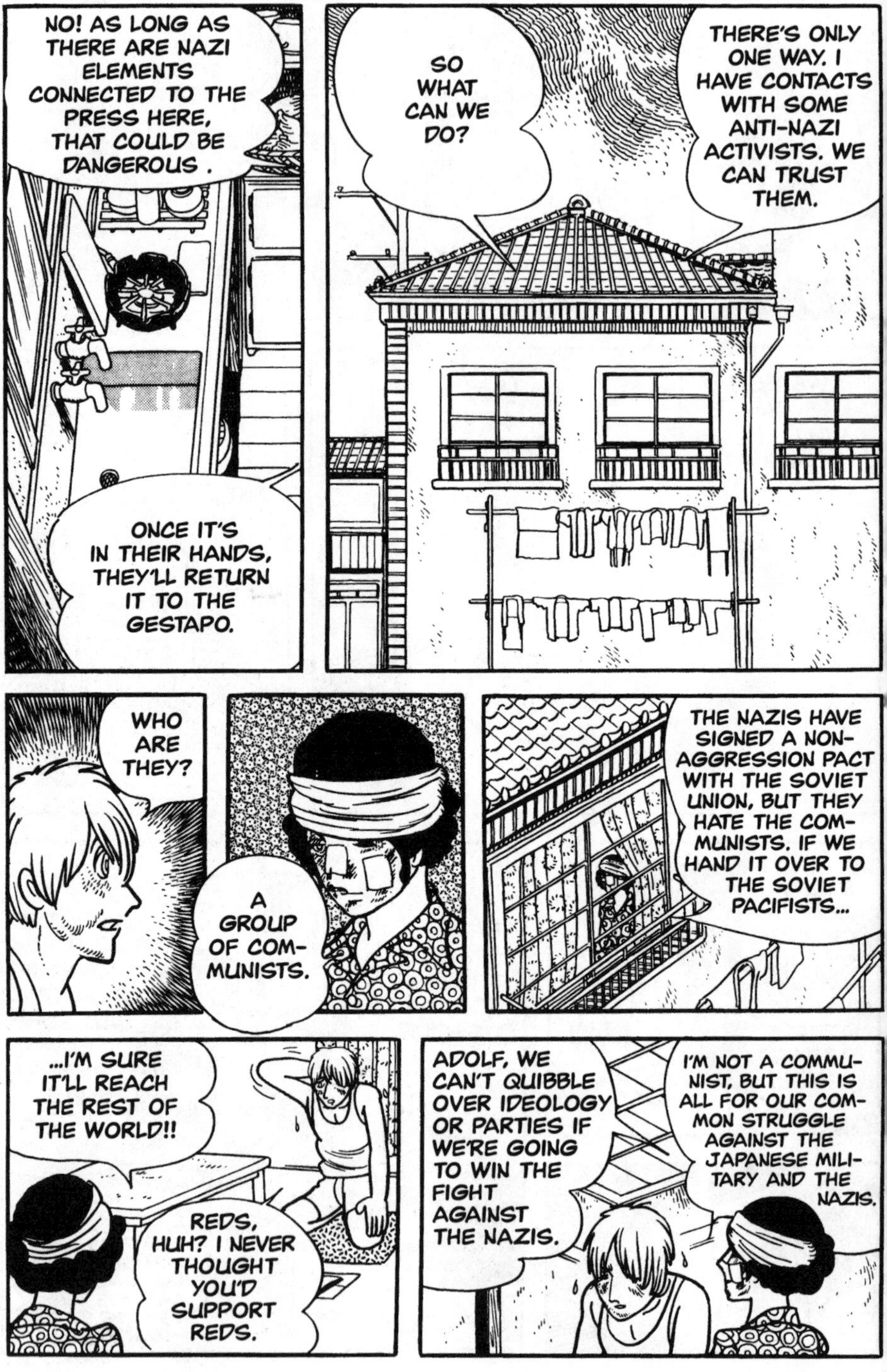
NO! AS LONG AS THERE ARE NAZI ELEMENTS CONNECTED TO THE PRESS HERE, THAT COULD BE DANGEROUS .
ONCE IT'S IN THEIR HANDS, THEY'LL RETURN IT TO THE GESTAPO.
SO WHAT CAN WE DO?
THERE'S ONLY ONE WAY. I HAVE CONTACTS WITH SOME ANTI-NAZI ACTIVISTS. WE CAN TRUST THEM.
WHO ARE THEY?
A GROUP OF COM-MUNISTS.
THE NAZIS HAVE SIGNED A NON-AGGRESSION PACT WITH THE SOVIET UNION, BUT THEY HATE THE COM-MUNISTS. IF WE HAND IT OVER TO THE SOVIET PACIFISTS...
...I'M SURE IT'LL REACH THE REST OF THE WORLD!!
REDS, HUH? I NEVER THOUGHT YOU'D SUPPORT REDS.
ADOLF, WE CAN'T QUIBBLE OVER IDEOLOGY OR PARTIES IF WE'RE GOING TO WIN THE FIGHT AGAINST THE NAZIS.
I'M NOT A COMMU-NIST, BUT THIS IS ALL FOR OUR COM-MON STRUGGLE AGAINST THE JAPANESE MILI-TARY AND THE NAZIS.

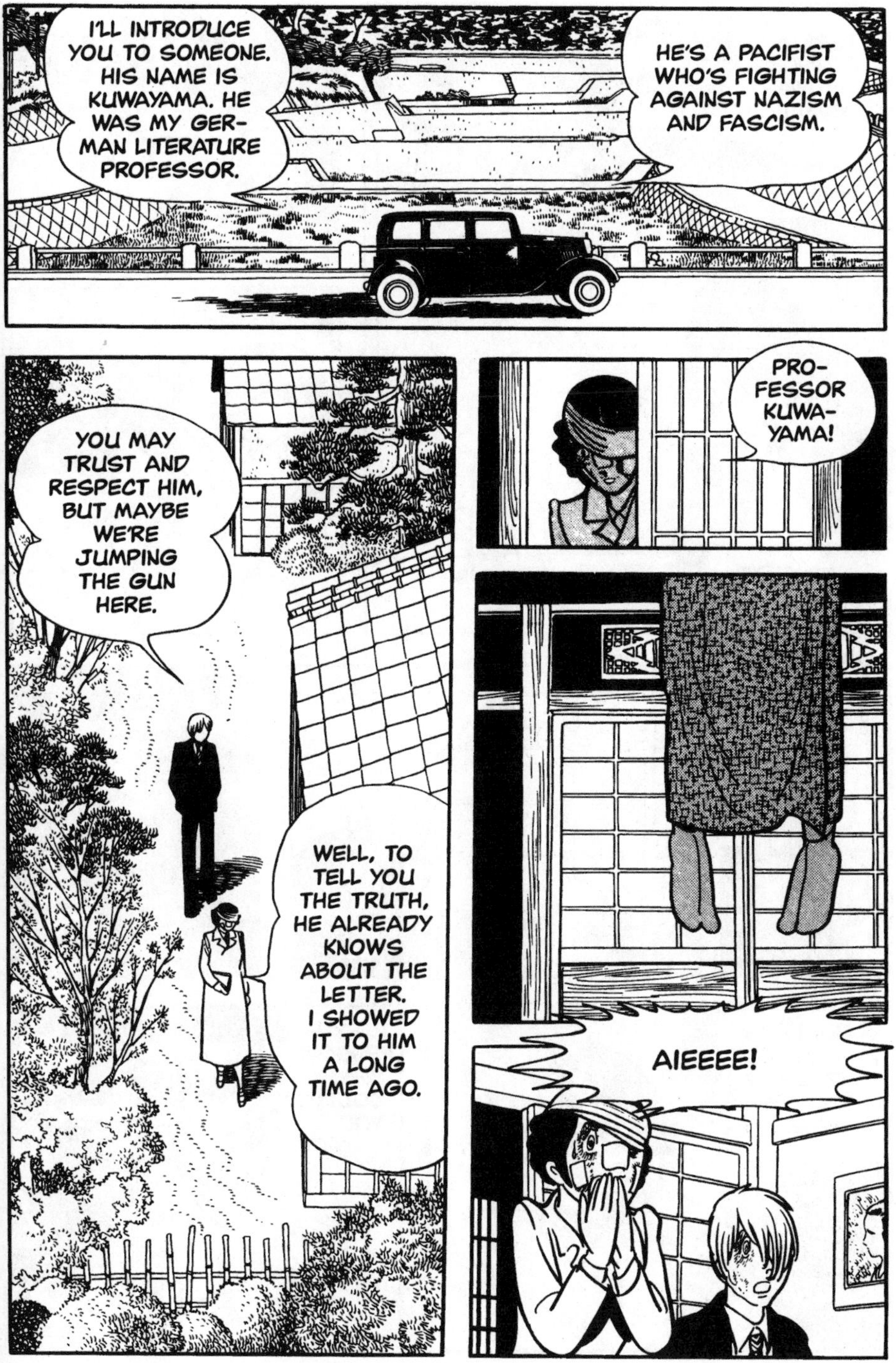
I'LL INTRODUCE YOU TO SOMEONE. HIS NAME IS KUWAYAMA. HE WAS MY GER-MAN LITERATURE PROFESSOR.
HE'S A PACIFIST WHO'S FIGHTING AGAINST NAZISM AND FASCISM.
YOU MAY TRUST AND RESPECT HIM, BUT MAYBE WE'RE JUMPING THE GUN HERE.
WELL, TO TELL YOU THE TRUTH, HE ALREADY KNOWS ABOUT THE LETTER. I SHOWED IT TO HIM A LONG TIME AGO.
PRO-FESSOR KUWA-YAMA!
AIEEEE!

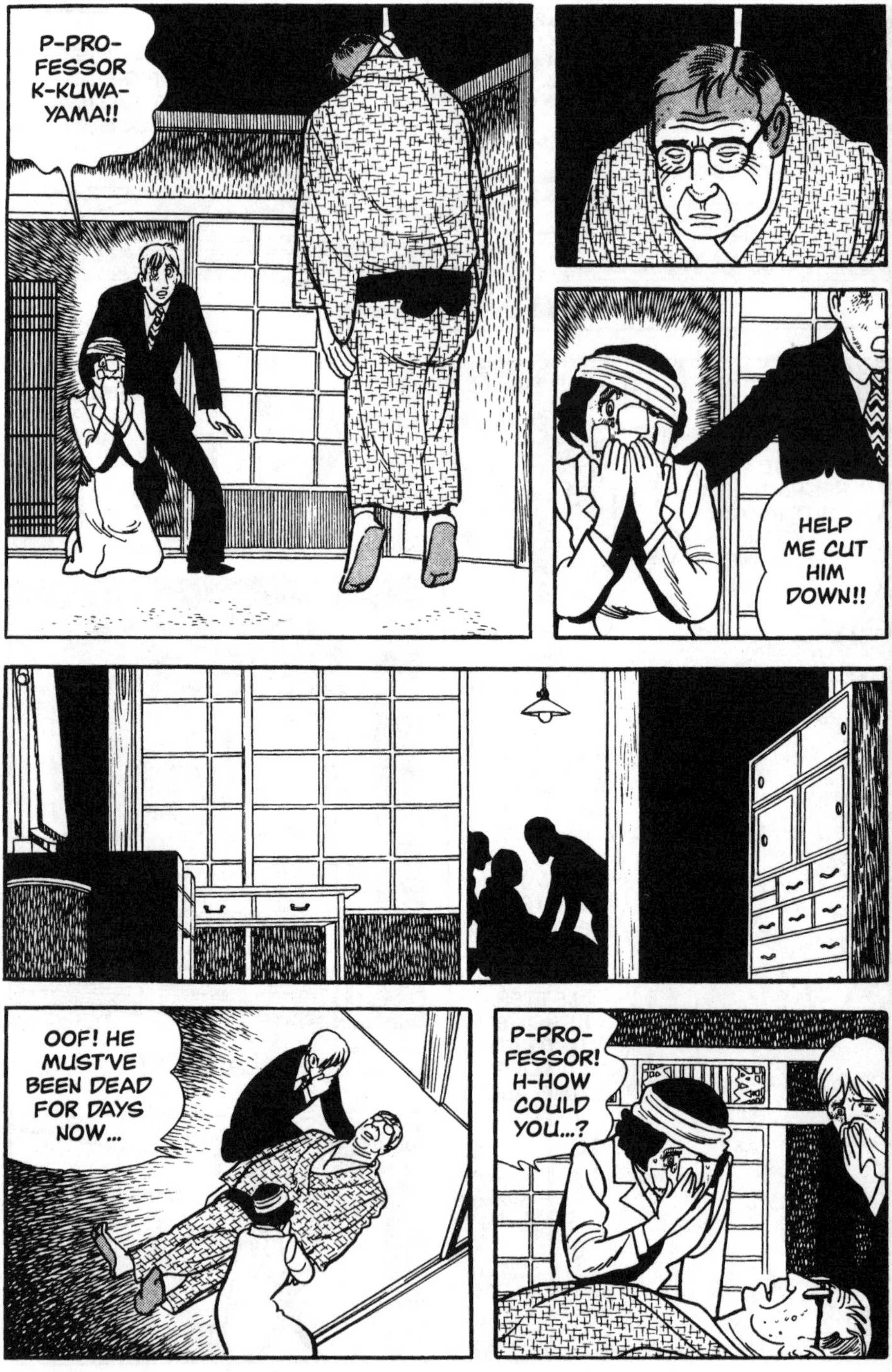
P-PRO-FESSOR K-KUWA-YAMA!!
HELP ME CUT HIM DOWN!!
OOF! HE MUST'VE BEEN DEAD FOR DAYS NOW...
P-PRO-FESSOR! H-HOW COULD YOU...?

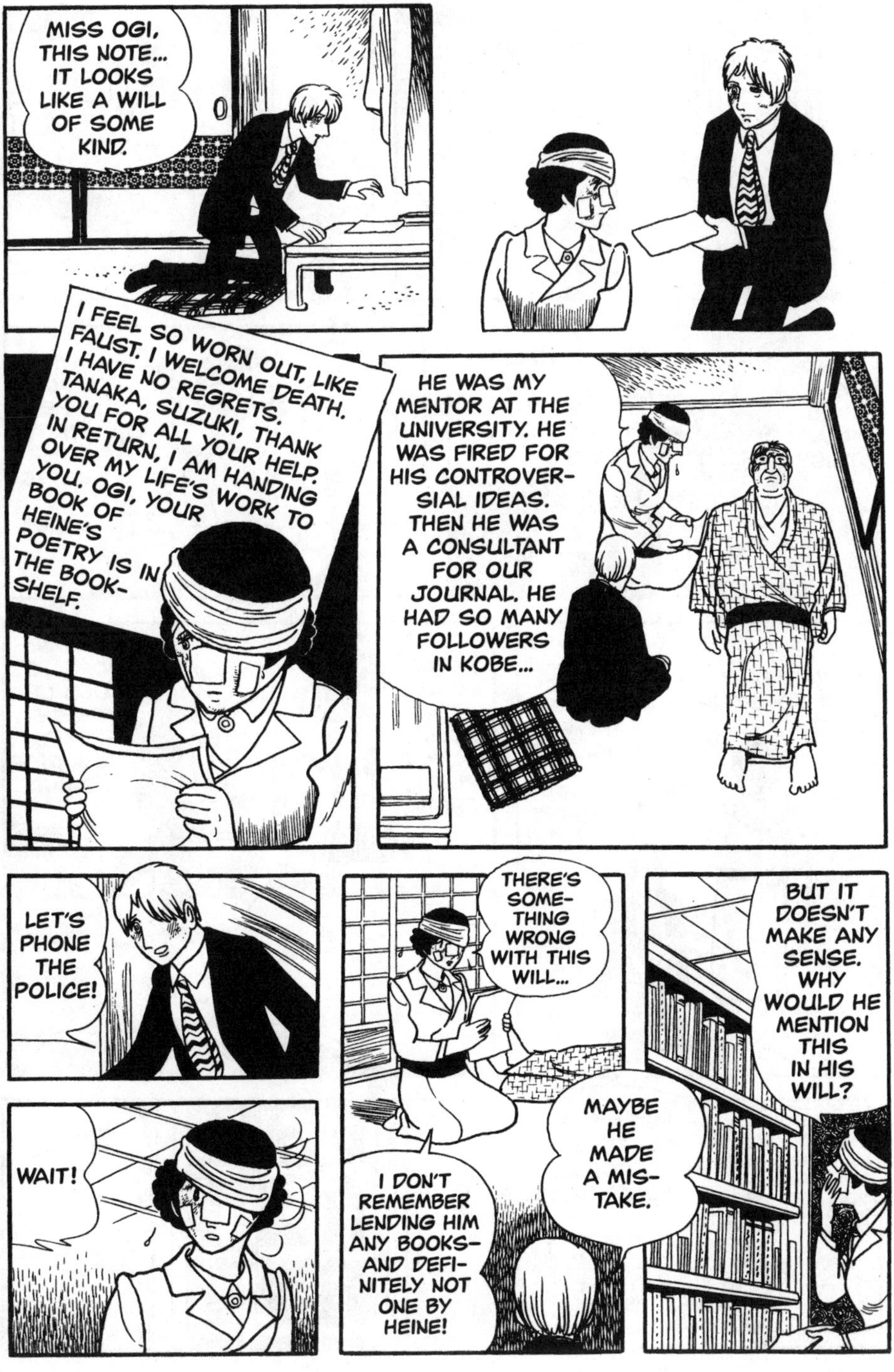
MISS OGI, THIS NOTE... IT LOOKS LIKE A WILL OF SOME KIND.
I FEEL SO WORN OUT, LIKE FAUST. I WELCOME DEATH. I HAVE NO REGRETS. TANAKA, SUZUKI, THANK YOU FOR ALL YOUR HELP. IN RETURN, I AM HANDING OVER MY LIFE'S WORK TO YOU. OGI, YOUR BOOK OF HEINE'S POETRY IS IN THE BOOK-SHELF.
HE WAS MY MENTOR AT THE UNIVERSITY. HE WAS FIRED FOR HIS CONTROVER-SIAL IDEAS. THEN HE WAS A CONSULTANT FOR OUR JOURNAL. HE HAD SO MANY FOLLOWERS IN KOBE...
LET'S PHONE THE POLICE!
WAIT!
THERE'S SOME-THING WRONG WITH THIS WILL...
I DON'T REMEMBER LENDING HIM ANY BOOKS-AND DEFI-NITELY NOT ONE BY HEINE!
MAYBE HE MADE A MIS-TAKE.
BUT IT DOESN'T MAKE ANY SENSE. WHY WOULD HE MENTION THIS IN HIS WILL?

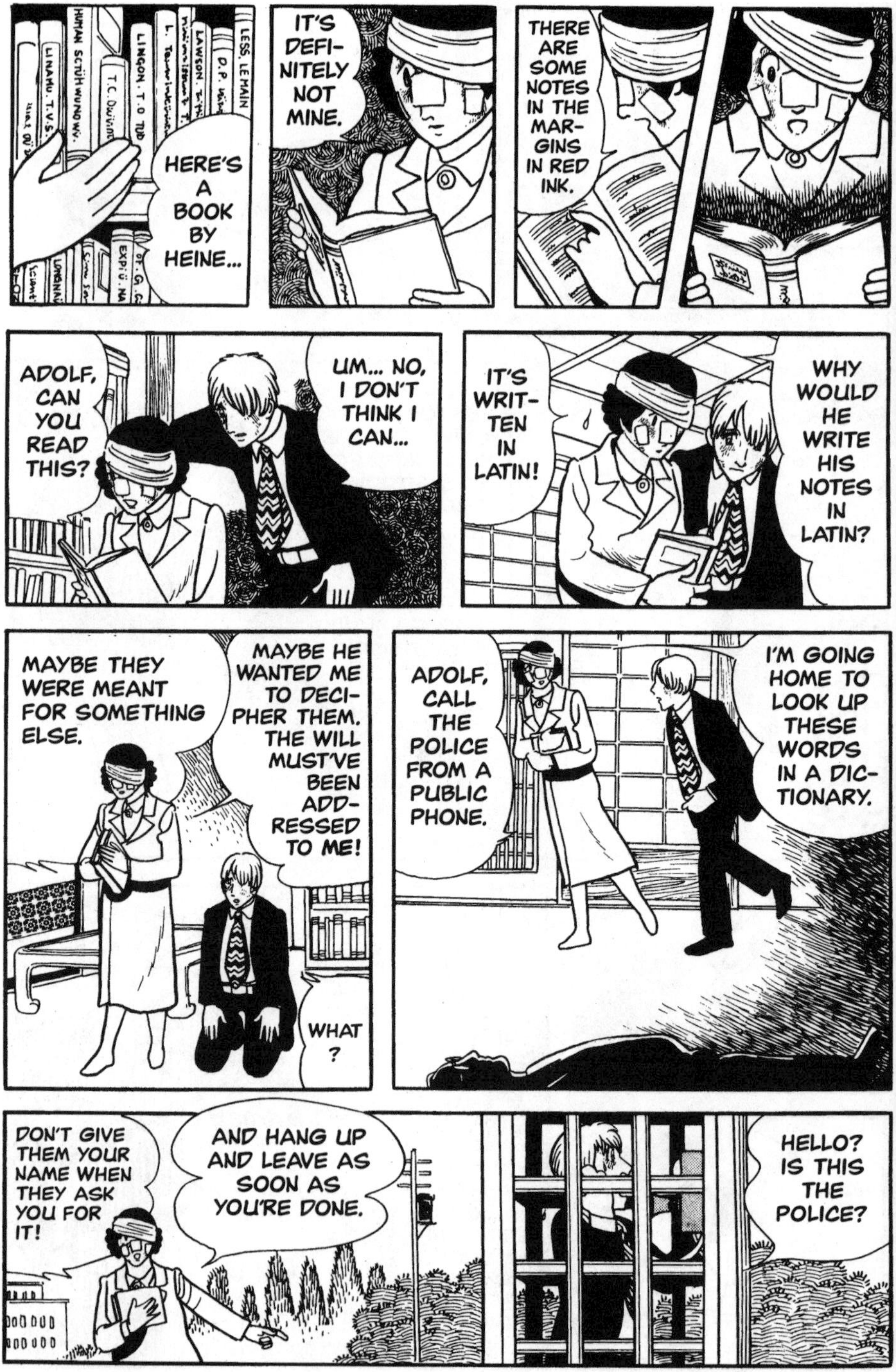
HERE'S A BOOK BY HEINE...
IT'S DEFINITELY NOT MINE.
THERE ARE SOME NOTES IN THE MARGINS IN RED INK.
ADOLF, CAN YOU READ THIS?
UM... NO, I DON'T THINK I CAN...
IT'S WRITTEN IN LATIN!
WHY WOULD HE WRITE HIS NOTES IN LATIN?
MAYBE THEY WERE MEANT FOR SOMETHING ELSE.
MAYBE HE WANTED ME TO DECIPHER THEM. THE WILL MUST'VE BEEN ADDRESSED TO ME!
WHAT?
ADOLF, CALL THE POLICE FROM A PUBLIC PHONE.
I'M GOING HOME TO LOOK UP THESE WORDS IN A DICTIONARY.
DON'T GIVE THEM YOUR NAME WHEN THEY ASK YOU FOR IT!
AND HANG UP AND LEAVE AS SOON AS YOU'RE DONE.
HELLO? IS THIS THE POLICE?

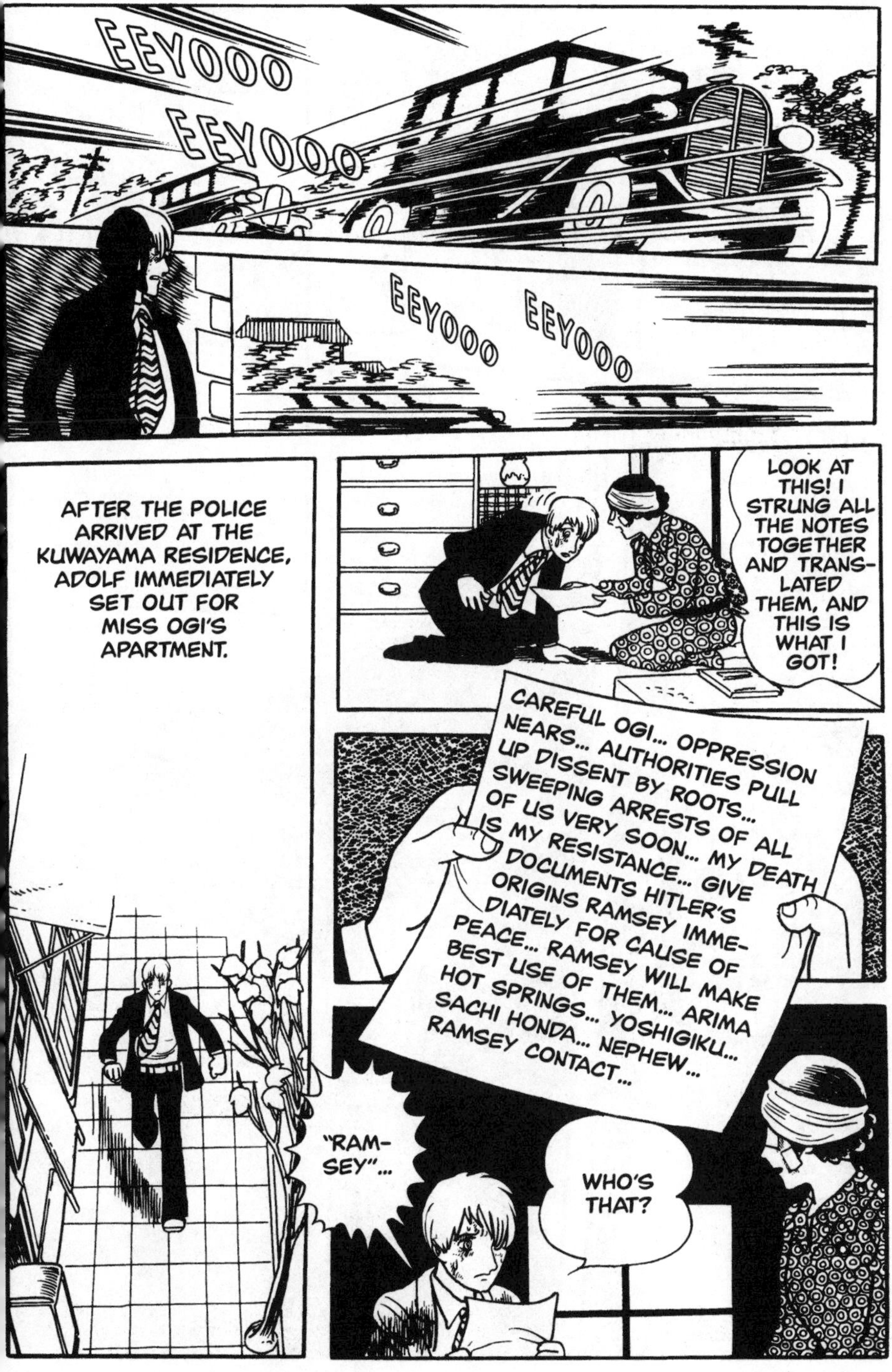
EEYOOO
EEYOOO
EEYOOO
EEYOOO
AFTER THE POLICE ARRIVED AT THE KUWAYAMA RESIDENCE, ADOLF IMMEDIATELY SET OUT FOR MISS OGI'S APARTMENT.
LOOK AT THIS! I STRUNG ALL THE NOTES TOGETHER AND TRANSLATED THEM, AND THIS IS WHAT I GOT!
CAREFUL OGI... OPPRESSION NEARS... AUTHORITIES PULL UP DISSENT BY ROOTS... SWEEPING ARRESTS OF ALL OF US VERY SOON... MY DEATH IS MY RESISTANCE... GIVE DOCUMENTS HITLER'S ORIGINS RAMSEY IMMEDIATELY FOR CAUSE OF PEACE... RAMSEY WILL MAKE BEST USE OF THEM... ARIMA HOT SPRINGS... YOSHIGIKU... SACHI HONDA... NEPHEW... RAMSEY CONTACT...
"RAMSEY"...
WHO'S THAT?

Adolf

SO PROFESSOR KUWAYAMA KILLED HIMSELF TO PROTEST POLICE BRUTALITY... THEY WANT TO BLACKLIST HIS FOLLOWERS.

HE MUST HAVE CHOSEN SUICIDE TO PREVENT HIMSELF FROM GIVING THEIR NAMES WHILE BEING TORTURED. HE DID IT TO PROTECT THEM FROM BEING ARRESTED.

HE WAS CONCERNED ABOUT THOSE DOCUMENTS, TOO.

SO YOU THINK WE CAN TRUST PROFESSOR KUWAYAMA'S WILL?

ABSOLUTELY.

ARIMA HOT SPRINGS TAKARAZUKA BUS STOP

有馬温泉
スバ行塚宝

BUT I WONDER WHO THIS RAMSEY IS...

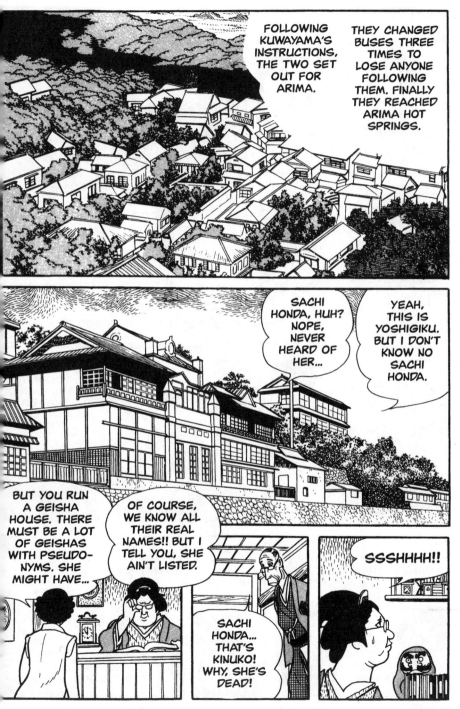

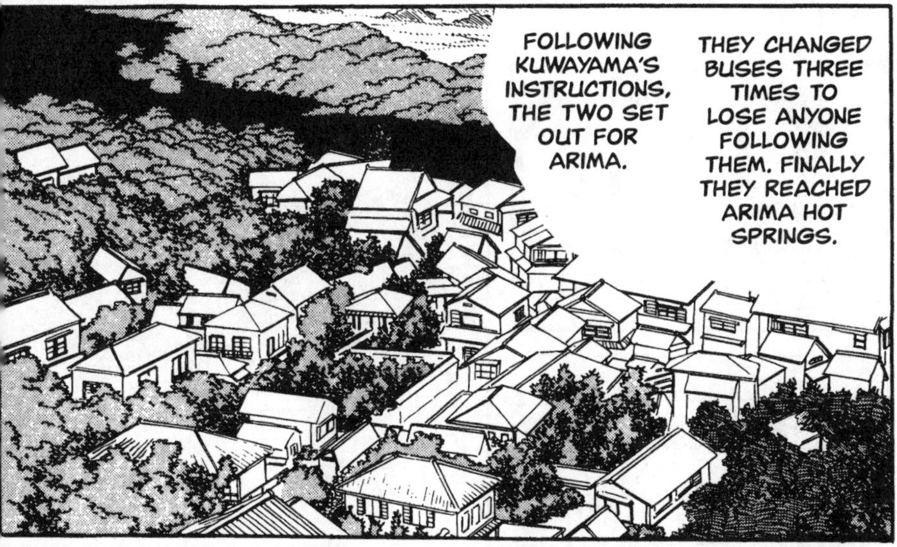
FOLLOWING KUWAYAMA'S INSTRUCTIONS, THE TWO SET OUT FOR ARIMA.
THEY CHANGED BUSES THREE TIMES TO LOSE ANYONE FOLLOWING THEM. FINALLY THEY REACHED ARIMA HOT SPRINGS.

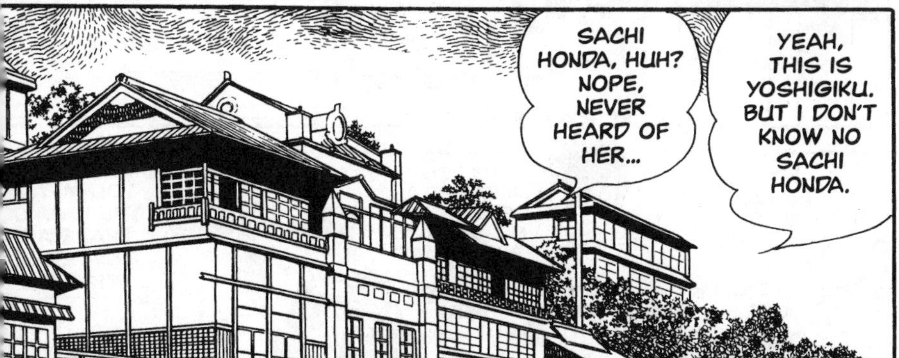
SACHI HONDA, HUH? NOPE, NEVER HEARD OF HER...
YEAH, THIS IS YOSHIGIKU. BUT I DON'T KNOW NO SACHI HONDA.

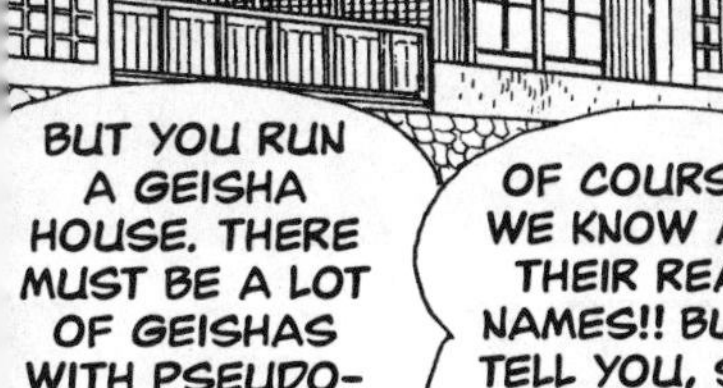
BUT YOU RUN A GEISHA HOUSE. THERE MUST BE A LOT OF GEISHAS WITH PSEUDO-NYMS. SHE MIGHT HAVE...
OF COURSE, WE KNOW ALL THEIR REAL NAMES!! BUT I TELL YOU, SHE AIN'T LISTED.

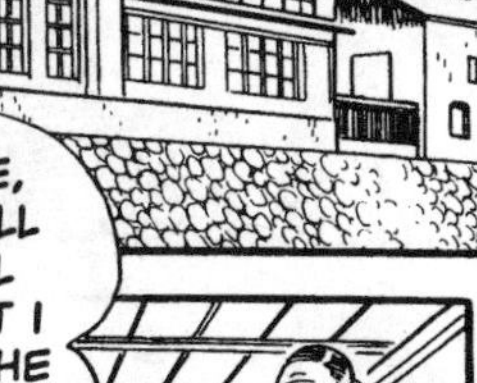
SACHI HONDA... THAT'S KINUKO! WHY, SHE'S DEAD!

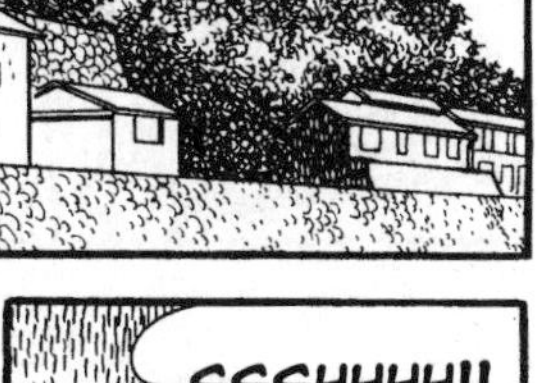
SSSHHHH!!

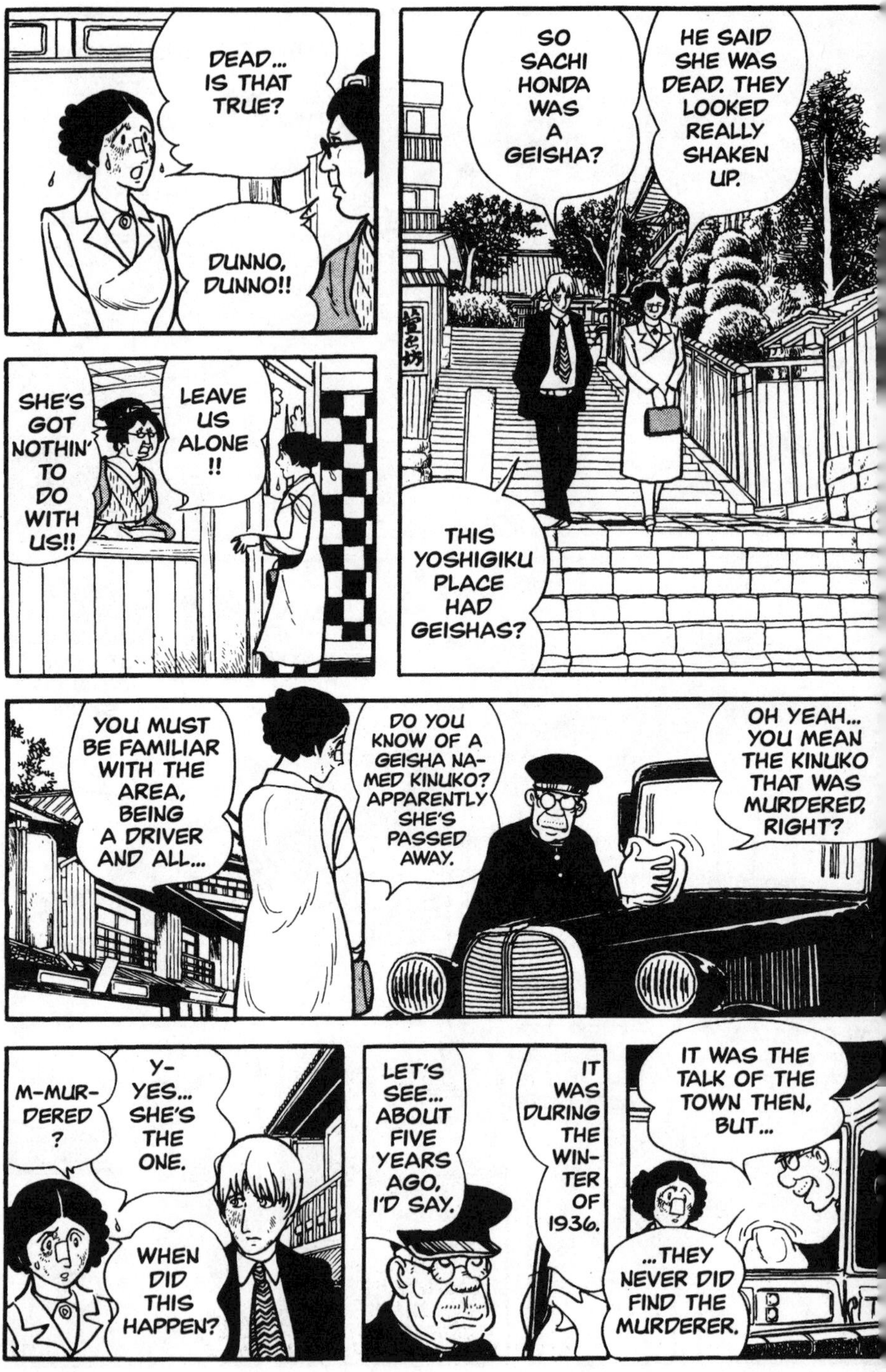
DEAD... IS THAT TRUE?
DUNNO, DUNNO!!
SO SACHI HONDA WAS A GEISHA?
HE SAID SHE WAS DEAD. THEY LOOKED REALLY SHAKEN UP.
SHE'S GOT NOTHIN' TO DO WITH US!!
LEAVE US ALONE !!
THIS YOSHIGIKU PLACE HAD GEISHAS?
YOU MUST BE FAMILIAR WITH THE AREA, BEING A DRIVER AND ALL...
DO YOU KNOW OF A GEISHA NAMED KINUKO? APPARENTLY SHE'S PASSED AWAY.
OH YEAH... YOU MEAN THE KINUKO THAT WAS MURDERED, RIGHT?
M-MURDERED ?
Y- YES... SHE'S THE ONE.
WHEN DID THIS HAPPEN?
LET'S SEE... ABOUT FIVE YEARS AGO, I'D SAY.
IT WAS DURING THE WINTER OF 1936.
IT WAS THE TALK OF THE TOWN THEN, BUT...
...THEY NEVER DID FIND THE MURDERER.

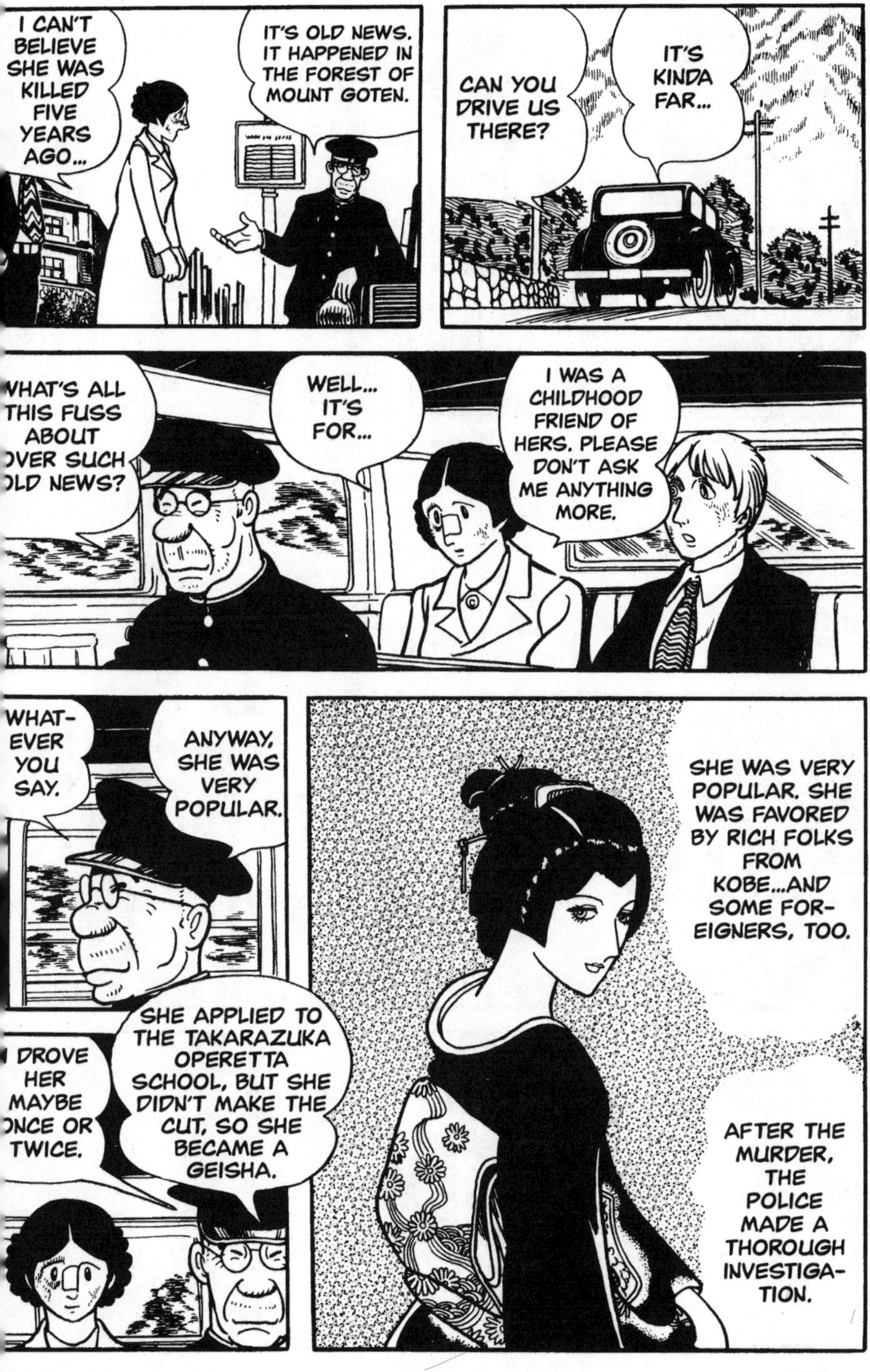
I CAN'T BELIEVE SHE WAS KILLED FIVE YEARS AGO...
IT'S OLD NEWS. IT HAPPENED IN THE FOREST OF MOUNT GOTEN.
CAN YOU DRIVE US THERE?
IT'S KINDA FAR...
WHAT'S ALL THIS FUSS ABOUT OVER SUCH OLD NEWS?
WELL... IT'S FOR...
I WAS A CHILDHOOD FRIEND OF HERS. PLEASE DON'T ASK ME ANYTHING MORE.
WHAT-EVER YOU SAY.
ANYWAY, SHE WAS VERY POPULAR.
I DROVE HER MAYBE ONCE OR TWICE.
SHE APPLIED TO THE TAKARAZUKA OPERETTA SCHOOL, BUT SHE DIDN'T MAKE THE CUT, SO SHE BECAME A GEISHA.
SHE WAS VERY POPULAR. SHE WAS FAVORED BY RICH FOLKS FROM KOBE...AND SOME FOR-EIGNERS, TOO.
AFTER THE MURDER, THE POLICE MADE A THOROUGH INVESTIGA-TION.

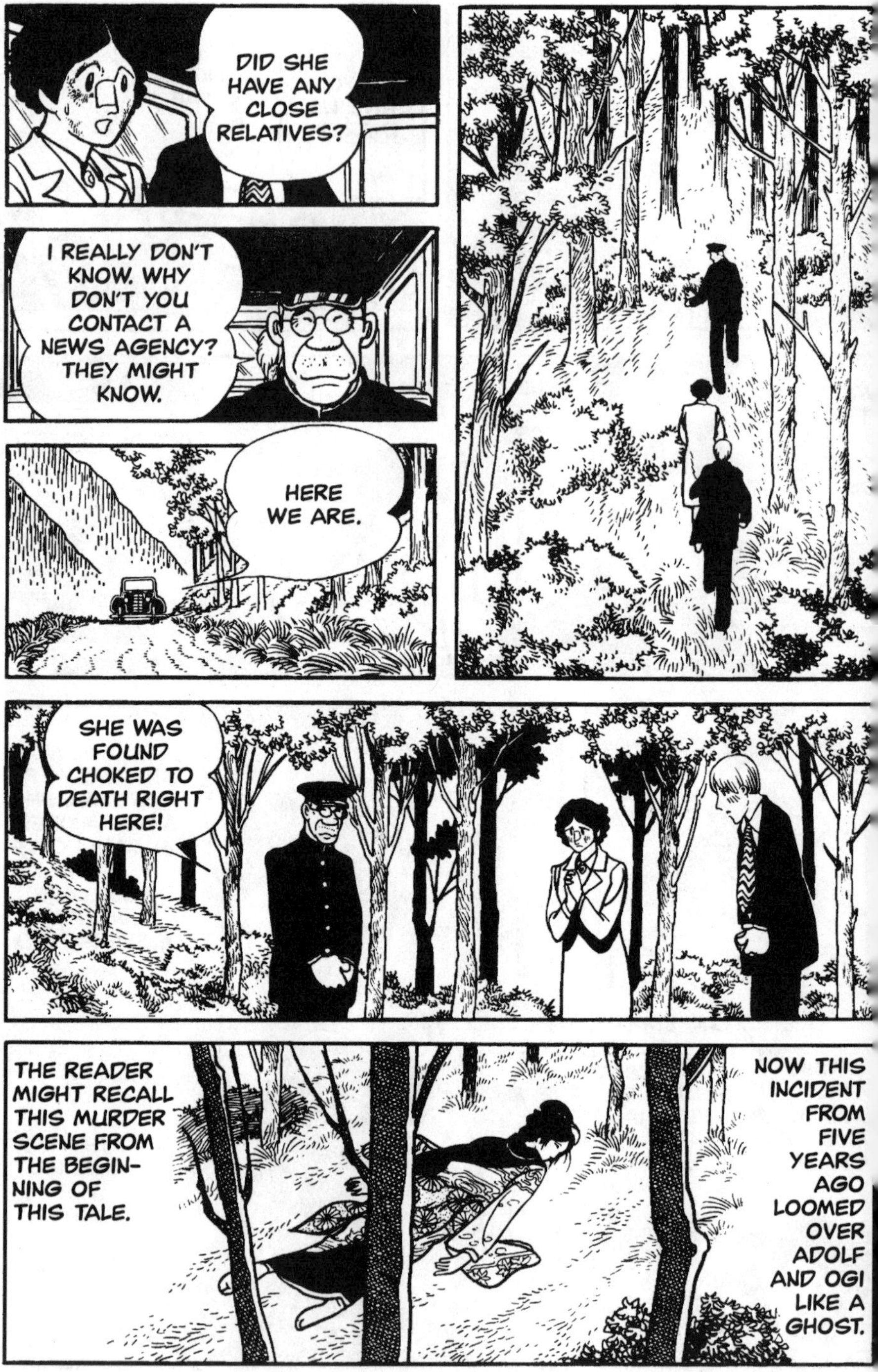
DID SHE HAVE ANY CLOSE RELATIVES?
I REALLY DON'T KNOW. WHY DON'T YOU CONTACT A NEWS AGENCY? THEY MIGHT KNOW.
HERE WE ARE.
SHE WAS FOUND CHOKED TO DEATH RIGHT HERE!
THE READER MIGHT RECALL THIS MURDER SCENE FROM THE BEGIN-NING OF THIS TALE.
NOW THIS INCIDENT FROM FIVE YEARS AGO LOOMED OVER ADOLF AND OGI LIKE A GHOST.

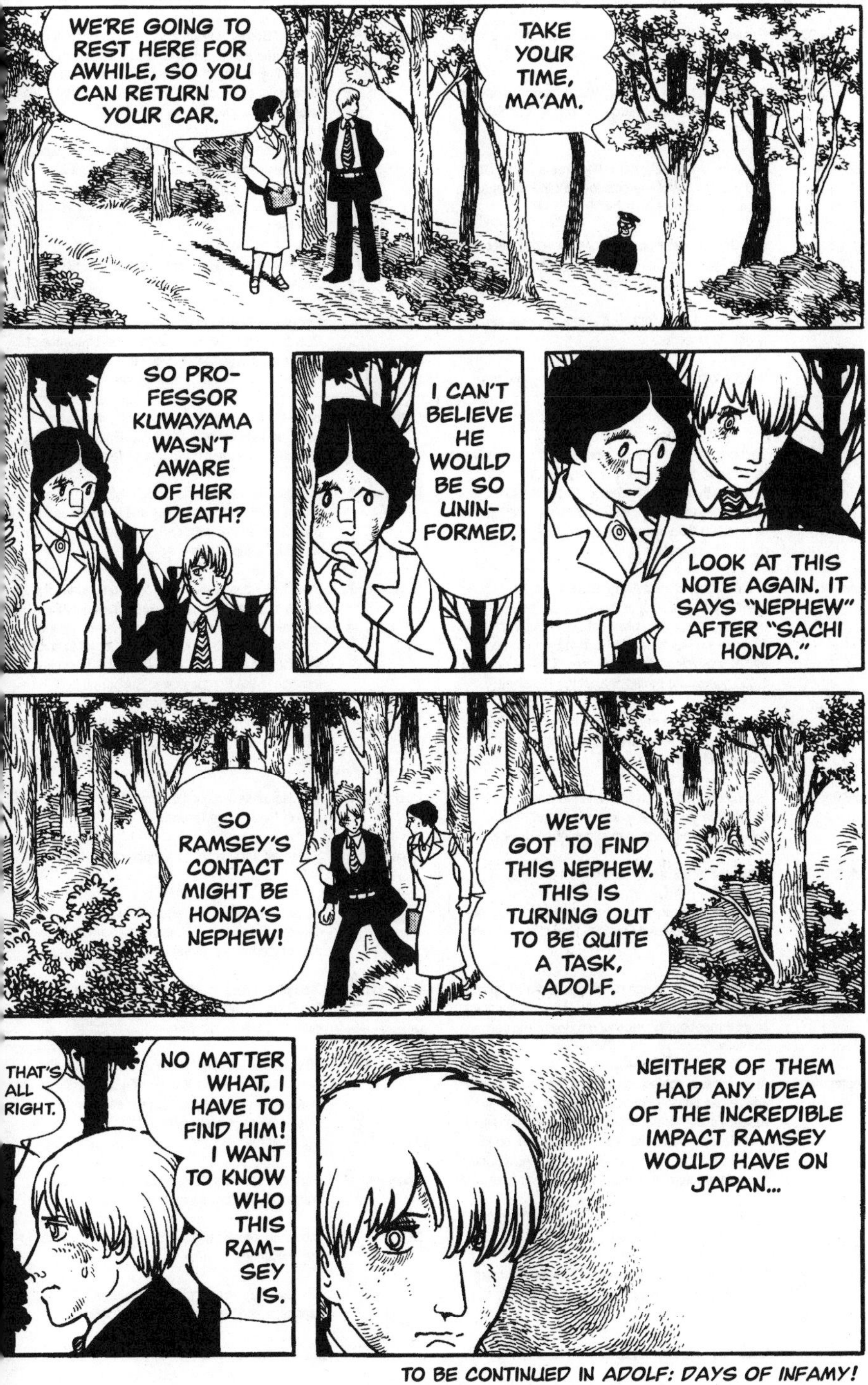
WE'RE GOING TO REST HERE FOR AWHILE, SO YOU CAN RETURN TO YOUR CAR.
TAKE YOUR TIME, MA'AM.
SO PROFESSOR KUWAYAMA WASN'T AWARE OF HER DEATH?
I CAN'T BELIEVE HE WOULD BE SO UNINFORMED.
LOOK AT THIS NOTE AGAIN. IT SAYS "NEPHEW" AFTER "SACHI HONDA."
SO RAMSEY'S CONTACT MIGHT BE HONDA'S NEPHEW!
WE'VE GOT TO FIND THIS NEPHEW. THIS IS TURNING OUT TO BE QUITE A TASK, ADOLF.
THAT'S ALL RIGHT.
NO MATTER WHAT, I HAVE TO FIND HIM! I WANT TO KNOW WHO THIS RAMSEY IS.
NEITHER OF THEM HAD ANY IDEA OF THE INCREDIBLE IMPACT RAMSEY WOULD HAVE ON JAPAN...

TO BE CONTINUED IN ADOLF: DAYS OF INFAMY!

1941 TIMELINE

January 20 — Roosevelt becomes the only president of the United States to be inaugurated for a third term.

January 27 — Ambassador Grew advises Washington of Japanese plans to attack Pearl Harbor in case of "trouble" with the U.S.

February 23 — German Foreign Minister Ribbentrop advises Japan that it is in its best interests to enter the war against Britain "as soon as possible."

April 6 — The German invasion of Yugoslavia and Greece triggers pogroms against Jews and Serbs, carried out by pro-Nazi militia in Croatia.

April 13 — Japan and the Soviet Union sign a five-year neutrality pact in Moscow.

April 23 — Greece formally surrenders to Germany and Italy.

May 7 — Stalin becomes premier of the Soviet Union.

May 20 — Soviet spy Richard Sorge, operating in Tokyo, advises Moscow that Germany is preparing to invade Russia with a force of between 170 and 190 divisions amassed in Poland. Sorge anticipates the invasion will take place on June 20 (missing the actual date by two days).

June 22 — In the largest-scale military attack in history, Germany and its Axis partners invade the Soviet Union along a 1,800-mile front stretching from the Arctic to the Black Sea. More than 3 million troops, 600,000 vehicles, 750,000 horses, 3,580 tanks, and 1,830 planes are hurled against the Russians.

June 27 — Japanese leaders decide not to attack the Soviet Union because they cannot spare forces from the Pacific and China.

July 2 — Having decided to advance into Indochina and Siam, despite the risk of war with the U.S. and Britain, Japan drafts a million men into military service.

July 28 — Japanese troops begin landing in Indochina.

July 31 — Göring carries out Hitler's orders to begin preparations for the "intended Final Solution of the Jewish Question."

August 26 — SS units and Ukrainian militia massacre Hungarian Jewish refugees in the Ukraine. Mass executions of Jews throughout Nazi-occupied Soviet regions intensify.

September 6 — At an imperial conference, Japan's foremost military and civilian leaders conclude that, "Although America's total defeat is judged utterly impossible, it is not inconceivable that a shift in American public opinion due to our victories in southeast Asia or due to England's surrender might bring the war to an end."

September 28-29 — SS troops massacre nearly 34,000 Jews from the Kiev area in the nearby Babi Yar Ravine.

October 14 — Mass deportations of Jews from Greater Germany to the east begin. Thousands are shot on arrival.

October 16 — Richard Sorge, working as a correspondent for the *Frankfurter Zeitung*, is arrested by the Japanese as a Soviet spy, ending the career of perhaps the most successful espionage agent of the war. (Three years later he is hanged.)

Prince Konoye resigns as prime minister of Japan. A completely military-dominated government is inevitable since the Konoye cabinet represented the final civilian effort to resolve the country's impasse with the U.S.

October 17 — General Hideki Tojo becomes prime minister of Japan.

October 19 — Moscow rushes its troops from Siberia and the Far East to the front with Germany, in part because of Soviet spy Sorge's intelligence that Japan will remain neutral in the German-Russian war.

October 23 — Jews are prohibited from emigrating from Germany and German-occupied territories. Romanian troops perpetrate a horrific massacre of Jews in Odessa.

November 3 — Ambassador Grew cables Washington that Japan "might resort with dangerous and dramatic suddenness to measures which might make inevitable war with the United States."

November 20 — President Roosevelt drafts a plan to resume oil shipments to Japan and to participate in negotiations between Japan and China. Japan, in return, is to send no more troops overseas and is not to comply with the Tripartite Pact, even if the U.S. becomes involved in the European war. Supported by Churchill, China opposes these proposals, and they are withdrawn. The U.S. substitutes more severe proposals that are viewed as a counterultimatum to Japan.

December 4 — The Japanese Twenty-fifth Army departs for the invasion of Malaya and Thailand.

December 6 — Roosevelt asks Japan to withdraw its troops from Indochina.

Russian forces under General Zhukov launch their counteroffensive from Moscow, marking the beginning of Germany's retreat and eventual defeat.

December 7 — Japanese forces attack Pearl Harbor and other U.S. and British territories and possessions in the Pacific, launching the Pacific War.

Hitler issues the Night and Fog Decree, directing German authorities in Western Europe to dispose of individuals "endangering German security" in a discreet manner by making them "disappear into the night and fog."

December 11 — Germany and Italy declare war on the U.S. and Washington in turn declares war on them.

December 13 — Japanese aircraft attack U.S. naval and air bases in the Philippines.

The U.S. Department of Justice interns 595 Japanese and 187 German alien residents.